LETTERS OF DANIEL WEBSTER

Daniel Webster

THE LETTERS

OF

DANIEL WEBSTER

FROM DOCUMENTS OWNED PRINCIPALLY
BY THE NEW HAMPSHIRE
HISTORICAL SOCIETY

EDITED BY

C. H. VAN TYNE, Ph.D.

SENIOR FELLOW IN AMERICAN HISTORY
UNIVERSITY OF PENNSYLVANIA

McCLURE, PHILLIPS & CO.
NEW YORK
1902

Republished, 1970
Scholarly Press, 22929 Industrial Drive East
St. Clair Shores, Michigan 48080

Published October, 1902, N

Library of Congress Catalog Card Number: 79-108553
Standard Book Number 403-00261-3

This edition is printed on a high-quality,
acid-free paper that meets specification
requirements for fine book paper referred
to as "300-year" paper

PREFACE

AT the time of Daniel Webster's death in October of 1852, his papers were for the most part at Marshfield, though some had been left in the State Department and in his rooms in Washington. An attempt was evidently made within a month to issue a volume of the letters, for Edward Everett wrote to Webster's son, Fletcher, on November 3, urging him to enjoin the Harpers not to print his father's letters. A postscript added that Mr. Lanman, who had been Webster's private secretary, should be dissuaded from any publication. A few days later Mr. Everett, writing from Washington, informed Fletcher Webster that the letters, papers and pamphlets in the State Department belonging to Webster would be boxed at once and forwarded to Marshfield. He requested that HIS letters to Webster, if found among the papers, should be returned to him. After these letters were sent North, Mr. Abbott, who had been Webster's amanuensis, received permission from President Fillmore to make copies of the semi-official correspondence between himself and his ex-Secretary of State. This manuscript was also added to the mass of the Webster papers.

By the will of the deceased, four literary executors had been appointed: Edward Everett, George Ticknor, C. C. Felton and George T. Curtis were to receive Webster's papers and determine their disposition. Within sixty days they began energetic efforts to get the letters of which no draft or copy had been kept. Cards were sent to a large number of persons known to have had correspondence with Webster. Many responded with copies of the desired letters, or sent the originals to be copied. Thus far the work of preserving the memory of the great statesman was well and efficiently done.

The will had provided for the literary remains in the following manner: "And I direct my son, Fletcher Webster, to seal up all my letters, manuscripts, and papers, & at a proper time to select those relating to my personal history & my professional and public life, which, in his judgment, should be placed at their *(the executors) disposal, & to transfer the same to them, to be used by them in such manner as they may think fit." With a view to effecting this wish, Edward Everett, for the executors, wrote Fletcher Webster in June of 1854, as follows: "Since the choice out of so great a mass of materials of those adapted for the press can only be made to advantage on a collective view of the whole, we shall be gratified to receive from you, as soon as convenient, such of the papers as you shall judge proper to be placed at our disposal, and we will then, as soon as possible, select from them & the collection made by ourselves those which it may be expedient to publish, at the present time, and these we will place in your hands for that purpose, agreeably to your request.*

"What further use may be made of the papers as materials for a comprehensive history of your father's life, will be a question for further consideration; and on this, and every other part of our duty, we shall at all times be desirous to learn your views, and most happy to have it in our power to comply with your wishes."

From the time of this letter the whole matter seems to have rested for over a year, when Everett, having been importuned by Fletcher Webster for an opinion, writes, September 10, 1855, that "he has no hesitation in stating his confident belief that the correspondence & other papers of your late honored father now in your possession & in that of his literary executors containample material for several volumes not less interesting and valuable than those already published;—perhaps for the general reader still more interesting.

"It may be proper to add that at their meeting on the 11th. June, 1854, it was resolved by the Literary Executors, that such portions of your father's correspondence & papers as it might be deemed expedient to publish, should be placed in your hands for that purpose."

Then, late in October, we find Edward Everett writing of bags and trunks of papers laid before the trustees a week previously. He had been directed to address an official letter to Fletcher Webster concerning the papers. He makes some suggestions about speeches to be preserved—which never were—and the form to be given any publication of the letters. He then reveals to us that Fletcher Webster had only put into the literary executors' possession the letters which he "proposed to publish," and Mr. Everett urges the propriety of placing all in their hands—"who will make a business of examining, classing, probably binding, & otherwise carefully preparing for permanent preservation & fu-

ture use, such as are adapted for it.—Your father's will, I think, evidently contemplates the performance of this office by us. His reference to Mr. Abbott implies it. Great value will hereafter attach to these papers, scarcely inferior to those of Washington. It is desirable for your Father's reputation as a statesman & jurist, that they should be put into the most convenient form for consultation. Washington's papers were as good (or as bad) as burn'd, till Mr. Sparks took them in hand, 25 years after his death, arranged, bound, & indexed them.

"The performance of this great work—for such it is—will not delay the contemplated publication of two additional volumes of correspondence, speeches, & writings;—though I fear you over rate the impression, that it is to be the affair of three or four months."

A week later Mr. Everett sent Fletcher Webster the mass of correspondence, with some advice as to the proprieties in editing them. He did not think it proper to publish the letters to and from Webster's first and second wife; just a few "specimens to illustrate his domestic relations." He urged the omission of the parts of letters relating to money matters. He thought it not expedient to publish the letters relating to the Randolph duel.

Fletcher Webster then made a formal request of the executors for the copies of letters which surviving friends of Webster had placed in their hands. He had, he asserted, promised to have the volumes of correspondence ready for the press in January, 1856, and had not time to recur to the sources of these letters. He offered to submit his selection to the executors.

Thus far the editor has the story from original manuscripts; the rest is partly derived from conversation with persons who are in a position to know the truth. He has also the story told in Fletcher Webster's preface and that of Curtis in his "Life of Webster." Finally, he has the results of observations made while examining the several collections of Webster manuscripts.

Fletcher Webster's "Private Correspondence of Daniel Webster" appeared in 1856. After its publication he returned the borrowed copies to the literary executors, but in a confused condition. The papers left by his father were not turned over to the executors in any logical way. The three principal collections now existing seem to be a hodge-podge. The letters might have been laid upon the floor and shoveled into three heaps. There is no division on the basis of intimacy, date, or subject.

The letters kept by Fletcher Webster were finally given to

Professor Sanborn, who had aided him in the editing, and the greater part to Peter Harvey, who had been Daniel Webster's, closest friend toward the close of his life.   Mr. Harvey evidently added to his collection, and June 14, 1876, personally presented them to the New Hampshire Historical Society.   Here for the first time they were unfolded, fastened in volumes made for such purposes, and carefully preserved.   It is this great collection of over 3,500 letters which furnishes the mass of correspondence herein published.   The society, with a generous desire to place Webster's correspondence before the public, has given every facility to the editor for getting correct copies of the unpublished letters and papers.

But the fate of the rest of the letters is not to be forgotten. After Mr. Everett and Mr. Felton left the work undone, Mr. Ticknor had been regarded as the fit biographer of Webster; but he never performed the service, and it fell to George T. Curtis. With the letters collected by the executors, the volumes of the "Private Correspondence" and a few papers borrowed from Peter Harvey and Professor Sanborn, Mr. Curtis wrote his work. There is evidence in plenty that Mr. Harvey did not know what was among his papers, or that he did not choose to allow them to be used.   Mr. Curtis reports as lost a number of documents which are now published from the letters once in Peter Harvey's possession.   After making this use of the executors' collection, Mr. Curtis kept the mass of papers in a supposed fireproof warehouse, and it is to the discriminating selection by Mr. C. P. Greenough of the majority of the valuable letters in this aggregation that we owe their preservation.   He obtained permission to examine and take those which he selected for his own collection.   After he had examined about two-thirds of the mass of papers, the warehouse was burned, and the remaining papers with it.

Now, of these three preserved collections of Mr. Webster's papers, the editor has had free use of two, that of the New Hampshire Historical Society and that of Mr. Edwin W. Sanborn, of New York City.   From the latter's collection there are about 30 letters incorporated in this book.   The failure to get the use of all of the letters in Mr. Greenough's collection* has greatly altered the plan of the editor, who hoped to make this

---

* Mr. Greenough has very kindly permitted me to use ten of the letters which I regarded as the most important in his fine collection.   It ought to be explained also that the great majority of the letters in Mr. Greenough's collection are letters *to* Webster and not *from* him.

collection complete. That ideal is impossible without the nearly 400 DESIRABLE *letters contained in Mr. Greenough's collection.*

Solely with a desire to aid accurate study of Webster, the editor wishes to state the results of a critical comparison of some of the original letters with those published in Fletcher Webster's edition of his father's correspondence. Of greatest importance is the fact that omissions in the text, often for very poor reasons, are not indicated. Where the parts omitted are of value, they have been incorporated in their proper place in this work. Over forty unindicated omissions have been discovered in the process of comparing only a small per cent. of the whole number there published. Again, there are many evidences of careless work— names are confused, dates are wrong, words and phrases are incorrect, and initials are used where the original has the full name. There is a systematic omission of unpleasant things that Webster had to say concerning Abolitionists. It must be remembered, however, that the book was published before the war and while the anti-slavery agitation was at its height. The editorial sin in most cases is not in the omission, but in not indicating the omission. Another exhibition of editorial frailty is in the correction of spelling. The rough farmers, John Taylor and Porter Wright, are made to write like cultured scholars. The real charm of their letters to their fellow-farmer, Daniel Webster, is thus lost.

In carrying out this work a number of facts about the fate of Webster papers have been brought to the notice of the editor. Every effort has been made to trace Webster letters, and possible owners in all parts of the country have been written for that purpose. Nevertheless, letters which surely were written, and, in fact, letters the preservation of which, is positively attested, are not to be found. Even correspondence sent the literary executors and listed in letters to them, which the editor has seen, are missing. Webster's letters to his first wife he must personally have destroyed, though he kept her letters to himself nearly 25 years. Again, many letters written by him to Fletcher Webster, and of which the latter makes especial mention, are not to be found. It is known that Julia Webster deliberately destroyed her father's letters to her. In a list of known English correspondents of Webster, there is but one name which may be found among the published or unpublished letters. The Earl of Derby, Lord Wharncliffe, Sir Charles R. Vaughn, Mr. Kenyon, Robert Walsh, Sir James Graham, Earl Spencer, Miss Edge-

*worth, and the Archbishop of York are known to have been corre-
spondents of Webster. One of the most remarkable* lacunæ *is
the absence of letters to and from Rufus Choate. It seems incredible that these two men could have been such warm friends
for many years and have exchanged only two or three letters.*

*In preparing the papers for publication, the editor has sought
to render to the reader an exact copy* of such letters, to which he
has had access, as reflect the character of the man, show his relations with his family, friends, or the public, and illustrate his
political motives. The mass of petty letters to him which constitute one of the penalties of greatness has hardly a claim for
preservation. Curiosity gets a transitory pleasure upon the discovery that there were hundreds of silly people who wanted a lock
of Webster's hair, or poets who hoped that he would "grant to
the bard the boon" of permitting a poem to be dedicated to himself, "the wondrous man." One came "all the way from the far
Hesperus to the Athens of America" to see his hero. If Webster was in trouble, there came a flood of anonymous condolences
full of absurd sentiment. If he was ill, every anonymous granny
sent her sovereign remedy, and even his corns did not escape the
solicitude of admirers. When he rendered his country some
great service, and, in consequence, was more than usually bur-
dened, every little debating society over the broad land* HONORED
*him by choosing him to deliver an oration at their next meeting.
Boats about to be launched were named for him, and he had only
to deliver the oration at the launching-festival. Anonymous
words of warning apprised him of secret machinations making
against him, and prophets foretold his election to the Presidency
at an early date. Hundreds of nobodies sent him their valuable
advice in great historical crises. As a matter of course, all such
ephemeral literature has been discarded. But there are letters
of another sort, homely, quiet letters from the wife or children,
containing much that is trivial and commonplace, mingled with a
few sentences that reveal the home life or the characters of the
family. These the editor has taken the liberty to mutilate and
to print only such portions as can be a source of information.
With Webster's letters to others no such liberty has been taken.
It may be added that in no case has any letter been anatomized
for the purpose of concealing unpleasant facts or characteristics.*

---

* All errors in the manuscript are reproduced in the printed copies, whether
of spelling, punctuation, or grammar.

The same may be said of the letters themselves which have been examined by the editor. He has had no reason for discarding except that of economizing space by ignoring the relatively unimportant. In using his editorial judgment for this purpose, he has not forgotten that persons will come to these letters for widely different purposes. He has tried to keep in mind the wants of all, from the economist to the theologian. In the letters about the farm even the botanist and zoologist have not been forgotten, and the mathematician can ply his mysterious trade in untangling Webster's financial affairs. The editor ought to mention in this connection that in the New Hampshire Historical Society vault (Section B, Shelf I, No. 16) there are a large number of notes about routine work that passed between Webster and Fillmore, the contents of which have no possible value now, but in the mass indicate the volume of business that passed between them. There are also (Section B, Shelf I, No. 18) many packages of legal papers pertaining to Webster's law practice, but not in any way illuminating his own business methods.

Finally, as to the arrangement of material in this volume, it has seemed to the editor unwise to place every letter in its chronological order, regardless of its nature. Many letters make no mention whatever of the statesman's public life, and deal only with the farm, home affairs, abstract questions of morals not connected with the events of the day, and matters having no effect upon political motives. The editor will grant that his judgment may err in this, and to meet that possibility a chronological list of all the letters has been made.

The arrangement adopted presents the different aspects of the great character of Webster. Sydney Smith said that "the meaning of an extraordinary man is that he is EIGHT men, not one man; that he has as much wit as if he had no sense, and as much sense as if he had no wit; that his conduct is as judicious as if he were the dullest of men, and his imagination as brilliant as though he were irretrievably ruined." It is to illustrate the eight men that this division serves. If it were possible, it would be desirable to set apart Webster as the orator, the statesman, the jurist, and the diplomat; but those phases are so woven in the woof of the letters that only the mind is subtle enough to extricate them; the hand cannot divide them one from another. Therefore, the fragments which throw a little light upon his early life, the more related letters which narrate his career as politician with local interests, and the volume of correspondence

*which tells with fair completeness the story of his life as a great
national statesman have been selected for those purposes. Then
the unrelated residue has been used to portray the man.*

*In the matter of annotation the editor has attempted only to
account for letters, when preceding or following letters do not
do it, and to give a few brief statistics about those persons writing or written to whose reputation was local rather than national.
Such explanations are only made upon the first mention of the
persons in question. The sources of the letters are also indicated, except the great number printed from the New Hampshire
Historical Society collection. The assumption may be made that
the original is there, if not otherwise indicated. As to the accuracy of the copies, the editor has with very few exceptions personally compared the originals with the copies, which were made
by experienced and trustworthy typewriters.*

*It is with real pleasure that the editor takes up the subject of
his obligations. To have experienced the kindness that he has
everywhere met in the prosecution of this work is in itself a rich
reward. It seemed as if every one's enthusiasm and love for the
great character of Webster went out to the humble compiler of
his correspondence. In several instances the persons to whom a
letter of inquiry had been sent—persons wholly unknown to the
editor—wrote an urgent invitation to come, stay under their own
roof, and examine their letters at leisure. If the invitation was
accepted, the host received and treated the guest as royally as if
he were the great "Expounder" himself. Then there has been
the kindly counsel and the earnest enthusiasm for the success of
the work. To Professor John Bach McMaster, of the University
of Pennsylvania, I am especially indebted in that particular.
From the librarian of the New Hampshire Historical Society,
Rev. N. F. Carter, I have received such kind consideration, assistance and warm approval of my work that mere acknowledgment here seems trivial. Nor is the library committee of that
society, Amos Hadley, Rev. C. L. Tappan, Mrs. Frances C.
Stevens, to be forgotten in the expression of my gratitude. Their
broad views of the demands of such a publication have given
me a latitude in the execution of this work which greatly adds to
its value. For friendly aid in the matter of tracing letters, I am
indebted to Mr. Albert S. Batchellor, of Littleton, N. H., who
also lent his warm approbation and earnest argument in favor
of permitting me to use the N. H. Historical Society collection,
as did Mr. L. D. Stevens and Rev. C. L. Tappan, of that society.*

*Mr. Otis G. Hammond, of the New Hampshire State Library,
placed every facility of that library at my disposal and manifested great personal interest in the execution of the work. Mr.
Fred L. Paxson, of Philadelphia, lent me the earnest aid of a
friend in the work of research. In the labor of editing I have been
greatly aided by the privileges granted me at the Harvard
Library and in the Pennsylvania Historical Society Library.
Mr. John W. Jordan, of the latter institution, has shown especial
interest in this work, and gave valuable suggestions as to the
sources of letters, as well as personally soliciting the owners of
letters. Mr. C. E. Bliss, of Bangor, Me., who owns one of the
finest collections of Websteriana in existence, personally aided my
work with his material, and gave many valuable suggestions.
My obligation to the Honorable George F. Hoar is unique. Besides placing his collection of Webster letters at my disposal, he
gave kindly and judicious counsel and imparted an enthusiasm
to my work which nothing but his strong sympathy with Webster
could give. Charles Francis Adams unreservedly furnished the
Webster letters found in the Adams archives. Judge Charles R.
Corning, of Concord, N. H., manifested throughout a lively interest in the work and kindly lent the letters in his hands for
copying. The others to whom the reader and editor are indebted
for letters loaned or copies sent are Mr. Charles Roberts, of
Philadelphia; Mr. A. F. Lewis, Fryeburg, Me.; Isabel D. Bronson, Summit, N. J.; Mr. J. B. Foster, of Bangor, Me.; Mr.
Horatio Gates Cilley, of Manchester, N. H.; Mr. M. D. Bisbee,
librarian of Dartmouth College; Mrs. E. H. Gilman, Miss
Frances E. Moulton and Mrs. Mary E. Bell, of Exeter, N. H.;
Mr. Arthur G. Stevens, of Concord, N. H.; Miss Emma E. Webb,
of Bangor, Me., and the Boston Athenæum. The editor has
also selected a few letters of Webster's which had been published
in books either very rare or to which one would not naturally
refer. Such sources are indicated in the annotations. Books
which contain letters which have not been here incorporated are:
"Memoir of R. C. Winthrop," Massachusetts Historical Society
Proceedings, Vol. V., p. 278, and also the last volume issued,
"Life and Writings of Jared Sparks," "Chancellor Kent's Memoirs," "Private Correspondence of Henry Clay" (13 letters),
"Life and Correspondence of Rufus King," "Dickinson's Life,
Letters, and Speeches," "Memoir and Correspondence of Jere-
miah Mason, Cambridge, 1873"; "Scribner's Magazine," Vol.
XXVI. (in the articles by Senator Hoar). These are in addi-*

xvi PREFACE

tion to the well-known sources, such as Curtis' "Life of Daniel Webster," Lanman, Harvey and Lyman's lives of Webster; the "Private Correspondence," the "Works of D. Webster," and the official letters found in the government documents and the volume of "Diplomatic Letters of D. Webster." There are unpublished letters in the American Antiquarian Society and in the Massachusetts Historical Society libraries.

With these dry bits of information the editor takes leave of the work of collecting Webster's unpublished letters and papers. He has learned that there is much of the commonplace in the work even of a truly great man. There is abundant evidence that the massive mind of Webster needed, if it was to manifest its greatest power, the spur of a great national crisis. Webster had to feel that the fate of a nation hung upon his words, if he was to render the best that was in him. It must not be forgotten that even his great formal orations were delivered upon stirring patriotic occasions. His mind had little subtlety, and his letters have none of that ingenuity in the phrasing of trivial matters which is characteristic of the typical literary man. He was always planning some monumental work in the field of literature, but never wrought it out. He seems to have been ever absorbing and thinking, and then, when the hour came for tremendous action, his unwilling mind got under way and we get a glimpse of him hammering out a great speech in a few days or a few hours, only to relax again when the bolt is spent, and to go on in a commonplace way until he is again aroused. The chief charm of his letters is the weight which his judgments carry with them. It is terrible to be denounced by that overwhelming mind, and good to be pleasing in the sight of Jove. Sometimes he was irritable, rarely petty, but usually wholesome, magnanimous, and with a lofty dignity. It is for Webster, the man, that one comes to the letters; the statesman, the jurist, and the orator are in the volumes which we call his works.

CONTENTS

WEBSTER'S FAMILY RELATIONS

WEBSTER'S RELATIONS WITH HIS FRIENDS AND NEIGHBORS

DANIEL WEBSTER, THE FARMER OF MARSHFIELD

WEBSTER'S INTELLECTUAL INTERESTS

WEBSTER, THE SPORTSMAN

WEBSTER'S PERSONAL FINANCES

WEBSTER'S RELIGIOUS AND MORAL CHARACTER

LETTERS OF DANIEL WEBSTER

fragments Concerning Webster's Early Life

PREVIOUS to *Webster's entering the House of Representatives in 1813 his life presents that dull monotony through which genius struggles up to the bright upper air of fame.* In *Curtis' "Life of Webster," and in the private correspondence, we have been given much material from which to construct the story of that formative period.* This division of the book merely pretends to contribute some interesting fragments, which will add to that information.

A bit of genealogy gives a hint as to his ancestry. The oration and reviews show the state of his mental development for the first years after leaving college. Incidentally, we learn something of the rude life from which he sprang. The letters of his sisters and father betray the poor advantages that had fallen to their lot. Several letters from friends reveal their character and the political and economic environment in which Webster began his struggle upward. Most of the letters of this period which the editor has found in the collections examined were mere petty business letters, unrelieved by a line which revealed the character of the writer. Many of the letters which passed between Daniel and his brother, Ezekiel, might have been written by any pettyfogging New England lawyer. They concern John Smith's fifty-dollar note that has been protested, or the hundred-dollar mortgage on Jones' property. Not a word is inserted about the eager ambition for the greater field of action toward which he was doubtless consciously struggling.

(From Nathaniel Sawyer.[1])

CINCINNATI, Feb. 24th, 1851.

My Dear Sir:

As I have before suggested to you, I think I have gotten a very correct history of the family of our Mothers, (Fitts

---

[1] This letter was found among Webster s papers, and he evidently cared to

[3]

or Fitz) in the U. S. But I have been very desirous of tracing it into our Father land, but know not what point across the water to start from. I have accordingly been, for a long time, looking out for some trace of the name there. Last fall I put my eye on one of the name of Fitz—Sir John Fitz at Fitz Ford, in Devonshire, in the reign of Queen Elizabeth. On the 28th of Dec. last, I dropped a letter to the Post Master of that place;—stating our object to get information of our Mothers family, before their emigration to America;— and particularly of *Robert* Fitz, who was our ancestor. And if he, the Post Master, could not give the information, would he be so kind, as to put it into the hands of some one, who would gratify us?— And I took the liberty of saying, that *your* Mother was one of the descendants, & that you was likewise anxious to get the information.— To this letter, I have just recd a reply, covering two sheets of paper.— The letter went into Devonshire but there now being no town of that name, it went the whole length and breadth of the county, after being opened by a proper Government officer, & it was put into the hands of Robert H. Aberdein, Coroner for Devon, Honiton, Devonshire.— Mr. Aberdein seems to be a man of science, and has gone through an examination of the different histories of the county, since the commencement of the reign of Eliza.— Sir John Fitz, (our great ancestor, as there is now a probability, so far as the investigation has proceeded), resided near the passage across the River Tavy, at the period when the River was forded,—the crossing being near his seat, it took the name of Fitz Ford, and is so represented in the book through the reigns of Eliza. 1st Jas.—1st Chs.—

The first word of the family is given by Sir W. Pole, who lived in the reigns of Eliza.—Jas. 1 & Chs. 1, and died in the year 1635— He says that Sir John Fitz had issue 3 sons,—John, Walter, and Roger,—John died without issue,—Walter his brother married Mary Samson, and had issue John and *Robert*.— John married Agnes Grenville of Honer, and had issue John, Edward & George &c. Nothing is said of what became of *Robert*.— Sir W. Pole does not give dates, but from others afterwards, it would seem that *Robert* would have been about the right age to have emigrated, say 12 or 15 years after the first settlement at Plymouth.— From all I can gather, I am confident,

preserve it. Of the value of the information the editor can say nothing. It is included as possibly containing information of Webster's ancestors.

Robert our ancestor, was a very strict puritan, & a pious man. This idea I suggested in my letter;—and Mr. Aberdein (who is a dissenter) observed that, if that Robert were our ancestor, & had been a Puritan,—the family were so *high* Church, that they undoubtedly would have disowned him.— From all I gather from the historians, the family appears to have held a high standing, and many of them Knighted.— Several Barristers of Lincoln's Inn. I send you a copy of the Coat of Arms, which Mr. A. has enclosed me. Do you know there the Fitz coat of Arms can be gotten in the United States?— There was John Fitz who was for many years Town Clerk of Newburyport, & a few years since died in New York, I think had them.— But I now think of no one there, who was acquainted with him.— Mr. A. tells me that there is a bookseller in the City of Exeter by the name of Fitz, whom he should see in a few days, & thinks probably a good deal of information can be obtained from him. Likewise he will show my letter to Mrs. Brage, the daughter of the lady of that name, who wrote the novel called Fitz Ford founded upon the incidents in the life, & the death of a Sir John Fitz who was the last of the legal male line.— Mrs. B. is the wife of the Rector in a church in the same county, & has the papers of her Mother.— Thinks she can throw light upon the subject.— I hope to get a good deal more, & your fame will assist me *much.*— I will now give you two extracts from Mr. A.'s letter,—which will discover his feeling upon the subject.—

"Before I begin, however, allow me to say, how much pleasure, I have derived from the desire you & Mr. Webster have to trace out, & authenticate your Anglo-Saxon origin, and how gratified, I am should my exertions & enquiries at all assist you;—and whilst you look back with pride to your ancestors, as being English, we English look with equal satisfaction & pride on our transatlantic Brethren; and feel sure that the more the English & Americans know of each other, the more closely will their hearts be knit together, as having one common descent." * * *

I am very glad Providence has placed you in the situation, which you now occupy. You have had a stormy sea to encounter, but you have done right, & the clouds will all pass off.—

Your affectionate cousin, & friend truly,

NATH. SAWYER.

(To Samuel Bradley.[1])

FRYEBURG, March 3, 1802.

My Friend:—

This is one of those happy mornings when " Spring looks from the lucid chambers of the south." Though we have snow in abundance, yet the air is charmingly serene, and Pequawket puts on more pleasantness than I have before seen it clad in. If I had an engagement of love, I should certainly arrange my thoughts of this morning for a romantic epistle. How fine it would be to point out a resemblance between the clear lustre of the sun and a pair of bright eyes! The snow, too, instead of embarrassing, would much assist me. What fitter emblem of virgin purity? A pair of pigeons that enjoy the morning on the ridge of the barn might be easily transformed into turtle-doves breathing reciprocal vows. How shall I resist this temptation to be a little romantic and poetical? " Loves " and " doves " this moment chime in my fancy, in spite of me. " Sparkling eyes " and " mournful sighs," " constancy of soul," " like needle to the pole," and a whole retinue of poetic and languishing expressions are now ready to pour from my pen. What a pity that all this inspiration should be lost for want of an object! But so it is. Nobody will hear my pretty ditties, unless, forsooth, I should turn gravely about and declaim them to the maid who is setting the table for breakfast; but what an indelicate idea; a *maid* to be the subject of a ballad? 'twere blasphemy. Apollo would never forgive me. Well, then, I will turn about, and drink down all my poetry with my coffee. " Yes, ma'am, I will come to breakfast."

I wish, my good friend, I could think of some good thing to tell you, but Pigwacket does not abound in extraordinary occurrences. The topic of this day's conversation is an intended ride this afternoon to Conway. I think the misses enjoy it finely in prospect, and no doubt the retrospect will be equally pleasant. To me, however, *(ut ad me revertor)* such things are most charming while future, and it is my object, therefore, to keep them future as much as possible.

Mr. Fessenden's mother is dead. She departed to the bourn whence " no traveller returns," about a week ago. With bright prospects of future felicity, she attended the summons without

---

[1] Webster's lifelong friend. This letter is printed in the Fryeburg Webster Memorial, a rare volume in the possession of C. E. Bliss, of Bangor, Me.

a murmur, and, full of years, sunk to repose on the bosom of her Maker. Mr. Fessenden's family have been extremely ill, and his lady continues so yet. He has not yet returned from his attendance of the Legislature.

Our friends Dana and McGaw are gone to Haverhill court, and I have quite a lonely week. 'Twould be a pleasure to call at Harry's house and take a cup of coffee with my friend Samuel, but he is not there; yet this shall tell him that he is remembered with much tenderness and esteem by his

DANIEL WEBSTER

(To James H. Bingham.[1])

HOPKINTON, May 5, 1802.

* * *

N. B. I forgot to tell you, that in June next, I contemplate to set my bachelor friends a laudable example.

* * *

[Dan'l Webster]

(An Oration.[2])

July 5, 1802.

It is at that season when nature is dressed in her pleasantest apparel, when the earth beneath the hand of Industry has become one vast green altar of incense, that the citizens of our Country [assemble in their several temples to commemorate the birth-day of their freedom]. America first in national happiness, is first also in gratitude. On this day she pays her homage to God for his goodness, and renders praises to those heroes who accomplished her revolution as distinguished as their deeds. While compassion weeps over the miseries of three quarters of the globe; while the barbaric ignorance of Africa, the pageant slavery of Asia, and the kingly robberies and despoilings of Europe call from humanity a tear, America exults in her own felicity. She beholds herself possessed of every natural and political blessing. Her rights are founded on the ample charter of Providence, and

---

[1] D. W. to J. H. B. Private corres. of D. W., vol. i., p. 231.
[2] The brackets indicate phrases which are exact duplicates of the Fryeburg 4th of July Oration, 1802, which has been printed. Many of the thoughts in the two productions are alike, but differently phrased.

secured by the valor of her arms. The extent of her territory embraces the most salubrious climes; the richness of her fields and the splendor of her cities rival the boasted gardens and capitals of Europe; her commerce floats in every gale and mingles with each quarter of the globe, while the increase of her population and wealth outrun calculation and almost mock arithmetic. Such, my Countrymen, are the joyful circumstances under which we convene for social festivity; such, ye venerable patriots, are the rich rewards of your toils, your hardships and your dangers. Such the consequences of that fortitude, which on the Fourth of July, 1776, induced you to pledge yourselves before God and the world to be free. That scene was doubtless one of the most solemn and august which mankind has ever witnessed. The inhabitants of a few infant colonies braving the mightiest monarchy on earth! Wherever they turned their eyes, they saw monuments of the power of Britain. France and Spain, deeply wounded by her recent victories had retired from before her in sullen silence. Her flag waved in triumph over every ocean and the extent of her conquests bade a bold challenge to the empires of antiquity. With her right hand she had seized on a portion of this western world larger than the whole of Europe; while she reached her left across the Eastern continent and imposed the shackles of commercial dependency on twenty millions of people on the remote shores of Asia. Gloomy, indeed, were the prospects of America. Oppressed and persecuted, she had no hopes but in her own resources. On the one hand she beheld the frowns of Britain, dark, vindictive, and dreadful. She saw that nation which had lately chastised the world, springing upon her disobedient colonies and crushing them to atoms. On the other, she beheld the horrors of perpetual slavery. Painted in imagination, she saw the frightful form of Despotism, clad in iron robes, reclined on a heap of ruins; in his left hand taxation,—his right grasped the thunders. She saw posterity rise up and imprecate curses on their ancestors for the tameness of their spirit. Here our Country made a pause, but it was not the pause of submission nor despondency; it was neither the cold stupefaction of guilt, nor the trepidation of cowardice. But it was the solemn hesitation which great minds feel when about to enter on "the scenes of untried being—" America deliberately "counted the contest, and saw nothing so dreadful as voluntary slavery." Appealing therefore to Heaven for the rectitude of her motives, she resolutely dared the unequal conflict. Cool and dispassionate, she stood collected in her own strength. Like the morning sun, she was calm, serene, majestic; [her course, like his, brightened as she rose,] and victory was matured by her meridian beam.

The events which immediately preceded and followed the declaration of Independence, irresistibly hurry back our minds to that period. The Fourth of July can never be celebrated without recurring to the scenes of the revolutionary war. The labors, the sufferings, the bloody battles can never be forgotten. They will long be remembered by those veterans who felt the fury of war; who saw cities in flames or trod among their ashes; who heard the deep groan of death, and with a true soldier's spirit wiped the silent tear from the cheek of the houseless orphan; they will long be remembered by their offspring who are proud in the patriotism and renown of their ancestors. The lapse of years does not efface the impression of ancient times. At this distant period, who can hear the story of Bunker's hill without emotion? Who, without feeling all the youthful hero in his bosom, can be pointed to the rising mound, where Warren fell the first martyr to his country?— Contemplate for a moment the forlorn situation of our affairs in the autumn which followed the declaration of Independence, view the shattered remains of our army retreating through the Jersies; pressed by a conquering foe—marched this way today, countermarched tomorrow— without provisions, without clothing—chilled by the northern blast, their marches traced in blood; without shelter from the storms of heaven; without shelter from the more dreadful storms of the enemy— Can the man be found to review these scenes, and not shed a tear over the past sufferings of his country— Yet—a ray of hope breaks in on the darkness of despondency. There is a point of depression, beyond which human affairs are not allowed to proceed. WASHINGTON at once converts this defeated command into a conquering legion— His genius arrests the awards of fortune, and woos back victory to his standard. In despite of the elements, in despite of the united conflicts of winds, waters and enemies, he crosses the Delaware, falls upon Trenton and subdues beneath his arm the hirelings of Germany.

From these scenes our imaginations are carried over those of less importance to behold the boastful champion of the North. Raging like the wind, Burgoyne issues from Canada with an army of soldiers and half an army of titles; as if the might of omnipotence were his, he already beholds America humbled at his feet in dust and ashes. Champlain receives him, and he thinks almost bends beneath the load of his offices and his greatness. His proclamation, swelled with a long list of honors, & puffed with the bug bears of terror, threatened nothing less than destruction, immediate and inevitable. Yet the plains of Saratoga convinced the mighty hero that splendid epithets and lordly titles were poor implements of war; and that all the stars and garters in his master's gift were sorry defences against the cold thrust of a rusted New England bayonet. The victory at Bennington which was the prelude to that at Saratoga, excited and deserved the admiration of the world. That a handful of farmers just collected from their cornfields, uninstructed in the arts of human butchery, without a single cannon to annoy the enemy, with no bulwarks but their bosoms, should march serenely up to the lines of a veteran army, attack, defeat, slaughter and disperse it, will scarcely be credited by posterity. These events were the commencement of a series of successes, which finally terminated in the happy scene of Yorktown. America then saw an end to her disasters; the peace descending as from heaven, and rapturously hailed the bright harbinger of her happiness. The roar of cannon now dies away oñ the ear; the voice of the enemy is heard no more; cities rise fairer from their ashes; commerce displays her whitened sheets, & joy lights up the countenance lately clouded by the gloomy horrors of war.

Having thus rapidly dilated on the prosperity resulting from Independence, and counted its cost, it becomes us, my fellow citizens, on this day ever hallowed to Liberty, to survey the ground of our national standing; to inquire if the privileges we possess are worth preserving, & to reflect on the means requisite for their perpetuation. Americans are possessed of a Constitution free in its principles and successful in experiment, uniting in itself the wisdom & experience of all ages and all nations. It is a Constitution of their own choice, and wisely adapted to the circumstances of the Country. [Not dictated to them by an imperious Chief Consul like those of Holland and Italy], not springing from the deformity of the Feudal system like those of Sweden, Denmark and Russia—not encumbered with a lazy load of aristocracy like that of England, nor *based* in the blood of two millions of people like the military despotism of *Republican* France; but adopted by a whole community, calmly deliberating on the best means for their happiness. This Instrument is the bond of our union and the charter of our rights. To its operation we are indebted for our national prosperity, happiness and honor. It raised us from a state of anarchy and misrule; reconciled the jarring interests of individual states, and matured the fair fruits of Independence. To the preservation of this Constitution every system of policy should ultimately tend. It should be considered as the sacred and inviolable palladium, ready to wither that hand which would lay hold on it with violence. Whatever variety of opinion may exist on other subjects, on this there must be but one— Whoever does not wish to perpetuate our present form of Government in its purity, is either weak or wicked; he cannot be the friend of his Country. Whether he wishes to behold America prostrate before a throne, or set afloat on the stormy ocean of democracy, his principles are equally dangerous and destructive. The first pillar in the temples of Republicanism is correct and *stabile* morality. All Republics are predicated upon this principle; without it they cannot exist. Without virtue honesty and tolerance in rulers, & obedience and respect in people, [Constitutions are waste paper and laws a mockery.] When ambition, wild and lawless seizes on the citizen entrusted with the government; when licentiousness diffuses itself thro' the community and corrupts the sources of power, that Republic is doomed to destruction. Mounds of paper and parchment cannot arrest its progress; the voice of reason will be drowned and Liberty expire. Over men void of principle laws have no force, when they can be transgressed with impunity. If you can stay the current of the ocean by a *bullrush*, then may you impede the course of an aspiring, triumphing demagogue by throwing in his way the laws of his Country. A power of restraining the tumultuous passions of the human heart, is found only in the dictates of solid morality; this therefore is as necessary to Republican Governments as blood to the Constitution of man. [Morality rests on religion; they cannot be separated; if you pull away the foundation, the superstructure must fall.] However plausible may be a theory of moral and rational philosophy, in practice it proves itself a chimera. Our magnanimous sister Republic on the other side of the water will therefore pardon us if we do not follow her sagacious example in voting that God does not exist. She will allow us to be so puritanical, old-fashioned, & superstitious; such dull scholars in the schools of Deism and improvement as to believe the time will come when men must stand or fall by their actions, and to add the force of this belief as an incentive to good conduct— Next to correct morals a watchful guardianship over the Constitution is the proper means for its support. No human advantage is indefeasible. The fairest productions of man have in themselves or receive from accident a tendency to decay. Unless the constitution be constantly fostered on the principles which created it, its excellency will fade; and it will feel, even in its infancy, the weakness and decrepitude of age. Our form of government is superior to all others, in as much, as it provides, in a fair and honorable manner for its own amendment. But it requires no gift of prophecy to foresee that this privilege may be seized on by demagogues, to introduce wild and destructive innovations. Under the gentle name of amendments changes may be proposed which, if unresisted, will undermine the national compact, mar its fairest features and reduce it finally to a dead letter. It abates nothing of the danger to say that alterations may be trifling and inconsiderable. If the Constitution be picked away by piecemeal, it is gone—and gone as effectually as if some military despot had grasped it at once, trampled it beneath his feet, and scattered its loose leaves in the wild winds. It is not intended that our Constitution is incapable of all amendment, or that it bears the stamp divine perfection; It is indeed the work of man, & like the rest of his works is liable to error. Yet essential errors it cannot possess; the unexampled prosperity of the Country forbids the idea, and if it have inconsiderable errors they had better even be reverenced than its worth not duly appreciated. To alter that Instrument which ties together five millions of people, on which rests the happiness of ourselves and posterity, is an important and serious business; not to be undertaken without obvious necessity nor conducted without caution, deliberation and diffidence. The politician who undertakes to make changes in a government with as much indifference as a farmer sets about mending his plough, is no master of his trade. However easy it may be to hack away one provision and one institution after another, he will find it impossible to supply their place, and what came to his hands a fair and lovely charter will go from them a miserable piece of patchwork.

Gratitude to approved public officers is the duty of a good citizen and becoming the dignity of a freeman. Yet it is not generally among the virtues of Republics. Aristides and Camillus and a host of others ancient and modern are proof of the remark. But shall America imitate the faults and the vices of other nations? Shall the vast volume of experience be to her an unprofitable lesson? will she suffer her worthiest children to be traduced and maligned? Shall calumny enter the shades of Quincy and blast the character of that man to whose eloquence in Congress we owe the celebration of this day? Shall the name of Adams be united to Tyrany, Oppression, and Aristocracy, and handed down with them to the damnation of posterity? Forbid it honor! forbid it decency! forbid it gratitude! Let the man have no punishment but his conscience who can wish to cloud the evening of that life uniformly devoted to the good of his Country. Americans, high-spirited and manly, will despise such baseness; they will cultivate a grateful and affectionate regard for their public agents, & submit abuse and calumny to the stones and dirt. They will remember, that on the event of their government is pendent the fate of other ages, and other nations. It is considered as the grand experiment which is to [determine] the practibility or impractability of free Constitutions.— If it should go on from prospering to prosper, if it should continue to ride on the high wave of honor and happiness, the monarchies of the East will gradually tumble away. The diffusion of Literature and Liberty will sap their foundation, and mankind will at *length* respire from the persecution of kings— But if the American Government is destined to tread in the tracks of its predecessors; if it shall be found too feeble to resist the thunderbolt of "Despotism and the more terrible earthquake of democratic commotion," then Farewell to the prospect, the bright, the charming, the fascinating prospect of Liberty and Republicanism!

Ye tyrants, then enjoy in safety your bloody triumphs over humanity! Ye wretched victims of despotism, bound and fettered, lie down and lick your chains in despair!

But let us hope the event will be propitious; that our government will long continue a renowned and matchless instance of human wisdom and Republican virtue; and as its morn in '76 was dark and gloomy, that its noon will be bright and illustrious; and when the angel announces that time is no more, may it go down in cloudless majesty, like the mild radiance of the setting sun![1]—

---

[1] In later life Webster said of such early productions: "While in college I delivered two or three occasional addresses which were published, I trust they are forgotten; they were in very bad taste. I had not then learned that all true power in writing is in the idea, not in the style, an error into which the art rhetoric, as it is usually taught, may easily lead stronger heads than mine." —Autobiography in Private Corres., vol. i, p. 11.

(From Mehitable Webster.¹ (?))

Dear Brothers   SALISBURY [N. H.] October 6 1804

I wish you to write every opportunity you have by private conveys I can not request you to write every week by the mail but I feel anxious to hear from you often, Nabby is failing fast she is but just able to walk her room I suppose her to be in a weak consumtive state if she has not help soon I think she can not continue Long   Mr· Benjm· Huntoons Wife died about a week before her Brother Benjm Page Both of the dysentary,

uncle Wm folks are well as usal.   Isaac Sears was passing there house on monday evening his horse threw him fell on him Broke his Leg in two places Bruised him verry much other ways he was carried in to there house & will be Likely to remain there some time if he Lives, Sally has been up there this week, we have had a Letter from David his house was Burnt while he was down, Last winter, his Grain and Clothing destroyed his family verry narrowly escaped the devouring flames   he writes a verry distressing Letter earnestly requesting Daniel to send him some support but it is in vain for him to expect help from us for we can but just Live our selves   HITTY WEBSTER

your horse arrived Safe is now in Nath Websters care   uncle thinks it not best to keep him for Nat makes an idol of him Brother Eben he worships him he Loves him now better than he does our Ben he Loves Daniel Better than he does me or his Mother, now he is gone he idolises his horse, it is no Matter for my old Mare Justitatus must have all the oats it wont do Brother Eben [says] Nat will be undone soul & Body if that horse ant taken out of his sight it is all he worships

---

(To James H. Bingham.¹)

Dear James,   HANOVER, Septr. 28th, 1803.

Once more I address you from this old place, verily as I believe for the last time—

---

¹ Webster's sister.   Ebenezer Webster's children by the first marriage were Olle, Ebenezer, Susannah, David and Joseph; by his second marriage were Mehitable, Abigail, Ezekiel, Daniel and Sarah.   See Curtis' Life of Webster, vol. i, p. 5.   Letter is addressed to Ez. Webster, Boston.

² A lifelong friend of Webster; classmate at Exeter Academy and Dart-

Jo, & I have spent a day here in a fine way—among the delightful girls— But Jo & I are not Bingham & *Herbert*—This said Herbert seems to be highest in the estimation of the Misses, particularly. M. W. & Jo, & I, & twenty others might woo in vain— And, therefore, since all pains would be lost, they better not be applied.—

I have rec'd yours requesting some account of my wanderings, which I shall answer, in less haste than I write this, when I get home to Salisbury.[1]

I have only [to] add that I want, desire, wish, & long to see your face.

In all sorts of weather, your Most Noble Friend

D W

W. W's Office—Mary in the house—lovely as Heaven—but harder to obtain—

(From Jacob McGaw.[2])

FRYEBURG, July 12, 1804.

My Friend.

When very young I was taught to repeat and fully believe the catechism—and with equal religious reverence I learned and believed whatever was told me as "old sayings"— Among others I believed, and hitherto have continued to believe that "it is an ill wind that blows nobody good"— What good has happened to any mortal by reason of the wind which blew me from Fryeburg a fortnight since? None, I verily believe—and from this moment I damn the proverb, and object to its future appearance in all genuine Almanacks. * * *

How the D——l you could escape so great a marsy as not to stop and read Robert Burns a little while with me, I can not divine. It is better than Allan Ramsay and that you know afforded us many a hearty laugh and hearty feast.

We have Mr. Ramsay with us. He is a man of reputedly great talents—id. est. "quoad" his heels. Anglice, a good dancing master. By means of all which, & by Mr. Cook's aid, the scholars at the academy are making great improvement in their

---

mouth College; later a State Senator and State Representative of New Hampshire. * * * See the Bench and Bar of N. H., by C. H. Bell, p. 208.
[1] See, for promised letter, Private Corres. of D. W., vol. i, p. 144.
[2] This letter is owned by Edwin W. Sanborn, of New York.

heads, heels and souls. If you have ought of sense, or nonsense, on hand, you will oblige me by communicating it "more or less" to me as soon as indolence (by which you and I are, like Sensibleness, "led"). * * *

Yours till death.
Jacob McGaw.

(To Moses Davis.[1])

Dear Sir,   Boston October 20 1804.

It was not until after the departure of Mr. Gilbert from this town that I had the pleasure of receiving yours of the 10th inst. Had it arrived in season I should have answered it by him. I had not the pleasure of seeing Mr. Woodward & do not know when he left, but I believe he was gone before the receipt of yours.— Your requests I attend to very cheerfully—have called on some of the engravers, & the plates will be probably ready by the first conveyance— I am not a little concerned that you have left the *devices* to my taste for in truth my taste in these things does not weigh down a grain of mustard seed— Of necessity I must leave the affair pretty much to the engraver— but if I think they wont do, I will make him alter— I have ordered him to prepare some drawings of which I shall make a choice, though I will not promise you but it may be a very silly one.

I am pleased to hear that the Gazette[2] is coming out in a " new & fanciful appearance " & that it is going " to maintain a dignified rank in the Washington school" [3]—

The newspapers in New Hampshire, generally have appeared more respectable the past summer than they ever did before—& the election of the Federal ticket for Congress is probably the consequence— Having done so much, we stand committed *to do more*— Having chosen Federal Representatives, we *must* (& will) choose Federal Electors— The Federalists throughout the Union expect this of us, because they know *we can do it*—if we do it not, we disgrace the cause—or rather we *disgrace* ourselves —for the cause is too great & noble to be disgraced either by the *calumnies* of its *enemies* or the *sluggishness* of its *friends*—

---

[1] Addressed to " Moses Davis, Printer, Hanover, N. H."
[2] The Dartmouth Gazette, to which Webster contributed.
[3] *i.e.*, Support the Federalists.

I have had the pleasure of seeing Weld here, six or eight days— He was comfortable as a lord, with his *dearly beloved* at his elbow— So we go—& Providence only knows whose turn it may be next!—we ought to take serious warning from these things—those of us I mean who have as yet escaped—and solemnly to reflect, that very soon, you Newspaper Editors may be compelled to introduce *our* names also to your readers, with " married last week, at " &c—!

I am very much obliged to Mrs. Davis for the offer of her " pumpkin pie "—as I could not call at the time I hope she will *keep* it— Ezekiel sends his civilities—the bill you sent him shall be settled in the *plate way* Pray inform me how you wish to have the Plates forwarded—

I am, Dear sir, much your friend,   D. WEBSTER

(From Sally Webster.[1])

SALISBURY, December 21, 1804.

Dear Brother

with pleasure I can now inform you that your friends in this place are all in good health, except Mrs. Hadduck, who is very unwell but we think her some better than when we wrote before. before we received your letters by the mail we heard that you were gone to New York with a gentleman at the moderate price of seven dollars a day for your company, it seems Daniel that your company is very agreeable in Boston as well as in Salisbury, we should all be willing to give as much to see you in this town if we had the change as handy as you have in Boston. I can not think of any news to write to you about at present the people here move on in the same old way as when you were hear here, sometimes we have junkets, sometimes we have freemillers meetings. I had almost forgotten to do my errand to you. a gentleman called here the other day and asked me if my Brother Daniel was then in Boston and if I had heard from him lately and he would have me by all means write to you and send his most profound respects as his regard for you was very great. I asked him to sit down but he could not tarry a moment longer than to do his errand. I have now done mine, and if you can ever find

---

[1] Daniel Webster's sister. The original of this letter is owned by Edwin W. Sanborn, of New York.

him out or tell me what his name is I should be very glad to know as I never saw the man before or anything that looked like him.   before I have done my nonsense I must tell you that our neighbors opposite the door fought a duel the other day, one with the greadiron, the other with a candlestick the female however came of victoriously and he with all speed ran here for some lint and rum to be applied immediately for he was bleeding to death with the wound in his head caused by the greadiron.   I fear you will now say, if Salisbury females fight with such weapons as greadirons it is best for me to stay where I am, and by that means we shall not see you all winter.   I hope Ezekiel will write soon if he is not too much ingaged in his school.   we have no school here now but expect one soon   moses will go all the time. Do write every oppertunity and consider that if my letters are not agreeable to you yours are both pleasing and instructive to me.   Mam sends her love to you both and thanks you for your wishes to send her a present but as she is in no present want of any thing you can git she will not trouble you to git anything now.   I must now end my letter by subscribing myself your friend and often obliged sister,   SALLY WEBSTER.

─────

(From Ebenezer Webster.[1])

Dear Sons: SALISBURY Dec 21. 1804
   Governor Gilman has called on me for money he has a Large payment to make out soon wishes my assistance if you can hire me forty or fifty pounds at Boston and send it on by the next mail I will return it as soon as I can perhaps I can not before March court   I can settle with Wm. Whitehouse without troubling you but I can not make out for the Governor as I should be glad two unless I can hire some money   Nathn. Webster would like to take your horse and sleigh and meet you at Dunstable or go on to Boston if you think it best and will write to us when you wish to Leave Boston.   we received a verry acceptable present from you which makes us verry comfortable this cold weather   As to the place of your Settlement you must determine for your Self   Esqr Bowers, Mr. Greenleaf and others are verry anxious to have you at the center road   Write by the next mail wheth you can obtain the money or not.
                                        EBNR. WEBSTER

[1] This letter accompanied the letter from Sally Webster.

(Review of the First Canto of Terrible Tractoration.[1])

Apr. 1805

A concern for the literary reputation of our country is one of the least suspicious forms, in which true patriotism displays itself. Whoever feels this concern will not take up a poetical volume, the production of his fellow citizen, but with liveliest emotions. Our country has its character to form. We are yet in our literary infancy, just "lisping in numbers", just pressing, with faint and faltering voice, our new and doubtful claim to literature and science. Terrible Tractoration has therefore been read with peculiar interest, and the general sentiment will warrant us in saying, with equal satisfaction. In commending Christopher Caustic, we are only subscribing to the opinions, expressed by the people of another country. To be behind that country in our appreciation of his merits were a stigma; it is very pardonable to go beyond it. National vanity may be a folly; but national ingratitude is a crime, Terrible Tractoration was successful in England on its first appearance, and as yet seems to have lost none of its popularity. It belongs to that class of productions, which have the good fortune to escape what Johnson angrily, but too justly, denominates "the general conspiracy of human nature against contemporary merit". It has already been re-printed a second time; the impression which is read in Boston being a revised and corrected copy of the second London edition. The occasion of the work seems to have been accidental, and its design, originally nothing more than to ridicule the overglowing zeal, with which certain English physicians persecuted the reputation of Perkins' metallick tractors. But the work grew beneath the author's hand. He found that Quackery was not confined to Medicine. He traced it with his eye, and followed it with his scourge, into the regions of Philosophy, Natural History, Politicks, Morality, and Poetry; till, in the end, a scanty newspaper essay grew to be a volume of satire, on various subjects. In the prosecution of his views the author

---

[1] This review by Daniel Webster appeared in the Monthly Anthology, vol. ii, p. 167. A few passages are selected to show the nature of his thought at that period of his life. In D. W's Autobiography, p. 23, vol. i, of "Private Corres.," he says, speaking of 1805–1807: " These were the days of the Boston Anthology, and I had the honor of being a contributor to that publication. There are sundry reviews written by me not worth looking up or remembering." A review of Johnson's "N. Y. Reports " appears in vol. iv, p. 206, of the Monthly Anthology.

has confined himself to legitimate means. While pursuing humorous associations he never grows intemperate, immoral, or indecorous. On this point he is entitled to every commendation. His wit is neither embittered with the malice of Pindar, nor corrupted with the sensuality of Moore.[1] * * *

Dr. Anderson, in the "Recreations in Agriculture and Natural History", has said with great gravity, "that the mathematician can demonstrate with the most decisive certainty, that no fly can alight on this globe which we inhabit without communicating motion to it". This important discovery, and others of the same learned Doctor, are very properly ridiculed.

—— Could tell how far a careless fly
Might chance to turn this globe awry,
If flitting round, in giddy circuit,
With leg or wing, he kick or jerk it.

The follies which disgrace the affected lovers of natural history receive no small share of Caustic's derision. It is indeed time, high time that they were hooted from society, loaded with the reprobation and contempt of every man of sense. Among the crowds of men there is no more despicable, than he who thinks it an object to rear a race of rabbits with one ear; unless it be another, who laments the extinction of a breed of dogs with three legs.

The Whimsies of St. Pierre, the deistical and atheistical speculations of Darwin, that heresiarch in poetry and philosophy, and the fooleries of William Godwin, are assaulted in the canto with much spirit and success. There are two schools in religion and literature, as well as in politicks. It is gratifying to the disciples of the old, that the author of Tractoration displays wit, and sense, and poetry on its side, against the pride and the folly, the ridicule and the ribaldry, the pitiable ignorance and the hateful malignity of philosophists, deists, atheists, and reformers. He believes that the harvest of infidelity and French Philosophism

---

[1] The writer foresees that he shall be charged with Puritanism, for objecting to the delicious verses of the Translator of Anacreon. Be it so. In his opinion the author who cannot please, without endangering the morals of his readers, had better study ethics than write poetry. On the restraints which youth, with infinite pains, imposes on its passions, Mr. M. breathes the effusions of licentious ingenuity, and they dissolve like scorched flax. The association of impure, unhallowed sentiments, with the enchanting power of genius and poetry, is one of the most fatal possible combinations against human happiness.

is sorrow and delusion; that they who sow the wind, shall thereof reap the whirlwind. * * *

If Terrible Tractoration be considered a satire, it is formed rather after the example of Horace, than of Juvenal and Pope. There are exceptions, but as a general rule it may be said to be rather a laugh at the follies, than a censorious reproof of the vices of mankind. To the first canto this observation applies strictly. All is gay, pleasant and playful. There is no angry satire in the poetry, no indignant declamation in the notes. * * *

On opening the book one is reminded of the elegant alliterative metaphor of Sheridan, "a neat rivulet of text murmuring through a meadow of margin". This is certainly matter of questionable propriety, but it is the taste of the times. Modern poets determine to be their own commentators, and to leave nothing to the labours of a future Eustathius, Johnson, or Wharton. It is more easy to account for this practice, than to justify it. Modern poems are occasional performances, deriving their incidents from particular occurrences, and full of allusions to particular characters. The knowledge of such incidents and characters, necessarily confined to a small circle, must be generally circulated, before the poem can be read with general pleasure.

The notes, which constitute the bulk of the volume, partake of the spirit of poetry. In general they are sprightly, appropriate, and occasionally abounding with poignant irony. It is possible they contain some levities of expression, not unexceptionable, even in this sort of composition. To call the moon "miss Luna", or the prophetess "miss Sybil", requires no part of the wit of Christopher Caustic. Such sophomorical associations are made by any body. To speak, too, of a "comet's taking it into its head", is frivolous, if not flat; and so, I imagine, is the imitation of a drunken man, by splitting the words he is made to use. Homer sometimes dozes. On the whole, Terrible Tractoration is a work which does honour to its author, and goes far towards refuting the slanders on American genius.[1]

D. W.

---

[1] Webster also contributed to the Anthology the following: Review of "A Treatise Concerning Political Inquiry and the Liberty of the Press," by Tunis Wartman. New York: Geo. Farman, 1800.—Monthly Anthology, vol. iii, p. 544. Review of Wm. Johnson's N. Y. Reports.—Monthly Anthology, vol. iv, p. 206. Review of Edw. Lewes' "An Elementary Treatise on Pleading and Civil Actions."—Monthly Anthology, vol. v, p. 162. Also, an article on "The French Language," in the Anthology, vol. iv, p. 647.

(From Ezekiel Webster.[1])

BOSTON, May 23d, 1805.
Good Daniel,

In one of my late letters I requested some particular information respecting the probable conditions on which the Clerk's office might be obtained, and likewise the probable emoluments of the office.   I confess. Daniel my acquaintance with the business of teaching a school does not increase my love of it.   If ever I have built any castles I demolish them as readily as ever you saw me demolish a *potatoe* when we travelled over the Sahara of America. It would be the consummation of my wishes to get into some business which would be competent to the support of a small *family*. I hope you will embrace the safe opportunity by Mr. Fifield to write me particularly and give me your advice without the least reserve.   Colo. Sam Thatcher has given me a pretty good offer to go into his office, it would be something more than *pretty* if I contemplated a settlement in that section of the country.

I am glad you do not make money your *Idol*.   If I should ever worship it "twould" be from the same motives that the Indians worship the Devil—to deprecate evil.   As to the politics of the place perhaps I can give you nothing new.   The election comes next week.   The Legislature is to fill the office of Lieutenant Governor.   A majority of the members elect are undoubtedly federal.   As Mr. French does not leave town untill tomorrow I shall send by Mr. Fifield the letter I prepared for him.   I shall write too by Mr. Fifield to Sir.   You have never told me how you came to dine on a white raven of * * *
                    cooking.   He was the last man in my opinion who would have proscribed that dish for your stomach.

Write me very often and believe

                                        Yours

                                              E. WEBSTER.

(To Ezekiel Webster.)

BOSCAWEN, [N. H.] May 25, 1805.
Dear Zeke,

You seem to have treated my request to write weekly, rather scurvily.   Two jaunts to Salisbury P office have procured noth-

---

[1] This letter is owned by Edwin W. Sanborn, of New York.

ing, except a letter from my worthy friend Mr. Thacher, including a note for collection & containing the information, that he has intrusted to you a letter of friendship for me & a "Doct. Caustic" [1]—

Your condemnation shall be double, if, not satisfied, with your own silence, you purloin & delay the letters of my friends.— I expect, however, that some private hand is bringing me a packet by this time.—

My hopes of business are yet alive; but there is no telling how soon fortune may put an extinguisher on them.— Money is scarce as love.—

In all June, I hope to be in Boston, & by fair means or foul, will bring out some Books— I am to have my office in Mr. Dix's[2] house, a room is finishing into which I shall remove in ten or twelve days, he gives me some countenance notwithstanding I made a pretty impertinent push upon him, when I first came, on Mr⁸ G's debt— A confounded breeze was stired by shutting up D͏ͬ Putney—but it has subsided—

The Boston post looks formidable in a Newspaper & hope will prove themselves so to all rascals & jacobins in the Legislature.

Write me if your have a finger in the world—

Yours cordially

D. W.

(From Judson Dana.[3])

ROCHESTER, Jany 18th 1805.

Dear Sir—

Your favor of Decr. 29th ult arrived in my absence and the necessity of my attending Court in this town immediately after its arrival, prevented me from answering the same until this time and now in the bustle of business at Court.

I can not assertain the precise time of your residence at Fryeburg as Preceptor of the Academy, but think you came in Novr or Decr D. 1801 and returned the Sepr following, making a term of about eight months—on your arrival, you informed me that, as you had commenced; you intended to pursue the Study

---

[1] "Doct. Caustic" was the *nom de plume* of the writer of the "Terrible Tractoration," which Webster reviewed in the Anthology.
[2] General John A. Dix. A tablet now marks the site of General Dix's home, and not 50 feet away another marks the site of Webster's office.
[3] This letter is owned by Edwin W. Sanborn, of New York.

of the Law; and asked for the use of my library during said term and you had access to the same—and I expect that you devoted the principal part of your leisure hours; while you were at Fryeburg to the Study of the Law. If a certificate of the above statement will be of any benefit to you I can truly and cheerfully make it— I am Dear Sir in much confusion and with much esteem

Your Sincere Friend, &c.

JUDSON DANA.

(To Stephen Moody.)

PORTS^M Oct. 26, 1808.

Dear Sir

Let the good Colonel[1] be dispatched with all good speed— to do all the good he can—if he should expend a little cash he will be remunerated— I have here a letter from Crosby[2] on that subject *which letter I agree to*—

I send you some *news*—I incline to think there is something in it—

D. W.

(To Stephen Moody.[3])

PORTSMOUTH, Octr. 21. 1808

Dear Sir.

I have just rec'd yours of the 15, as I arrived in Town from Haverhill. I doubt whether there will be a pamphlet published in this Town—if there be, you shall receive some numbers, as soon as they are out of press— A little book is in the Walpole press.[4]—it will be distributed through Cheshire and Grafton— I think you might obtain some numbers at Plymouth.— Wherever John Shepherd goes Col. Greely must go after him—I think there will be pamphlets at Plymouth & perhaps at Concord the

---

[1] The "Colonel" Samuel Greely, a leading and active politician, father of the late Stephen L. Greely, N. C.

[2] There is a note at foot of this letter by Stephen Moody, which is as follows: "Crosby," I suppose, means Oliver Crosby, of Dover, a leading lawyer.

[3] Addressed to Stephen Moody, Esq., of Gilmanton, a prominent lawyer of New Hampshire. See Bench and Bar of N. H., p. 519.

[4] He probably refers to the pamphlet on the Embargo, which he issued in 1808. See Curtis' Life of Webster, vol. i, p. 95.

first of next week— I wish the Col. would take some & go after Shepherd—or go without them, if he cannot get them—

I think this election very perilous—am glad to hear Gilmanton is like to do better—

Pray keep a look out on the Towns around you.— I consider every thing depending on this election—let us do our utmost to give it a favorable result.

I am Dr Sr. Yours

D, WEBSTER

(D. W. to Fuller.[1])

Dec. 2. 1807

* * *

"If the fates are propitious, I hope I shall be able to afford you a shelter, in a year or two. I have been a young dog long enough, and now think of joining myself, as soon as convenient, to that happy and honorable society of which you are one; the society of married men." * * *

(From Geo. Herbert.[2])

SURRY [Maine] March 13. 1809.

My Dear Daniel,[3]

* * * My dear fellow I should not have written to you so soon— (I will confess the truth.) had it not been that my own affairs are in so miserable condition owing to the vile policy of our enemies[4]—which has as I have before told you made our *poor people at the best* so poor that I cannot have of them what they ought to pay me, without *distressing* them— I might more truly say I can not *have it at all.* Many of our people are pinched even for food & are suffering all the horrors of a famine. One man in Sullivan has had some provisions for sale of late & people have brought their plate, cows, pigs &c. &c. as they had, to barter them for some little food to keep them from starving. Oh my God—where is thy hidden thunder? Oh my country— thou deservest all! Thou hast slighted the warning voice of thy

---

[1] Private Correspondence of Daniel Webster, vol. i., p. 227.
[2] A Dartmouth College friend.
[3] Addressed to D. W., Counsellor at Law, Portsmouth, N. H.
[4] Alludes to the effect of the "Long Embargo."

friends— thou hast sinned against light— Thou deservest all—nay more.— But woe unto them by whom this cometh! It were better for them—that they had not done this—for the way of transgressors *is hard*—& justice *shall surely overtake them!* If I had come via Portsmouth I should certainly have availed myself of your kind offer. as it is, my necessities coming upon me I must send you my note. * * *

Your friend

GEO. HERBERT

Write me an answer soon & your prospects in N. H.

———

(From Sam'l Sparhawk.)

Secretary's Office

CONCORD [N. H.] June 26th. 1811

Sir[1]

I have the honour to transmit to you herewith an attested copy of a Resolve passed at the late session of the Legislature, appointing yourself, Jeremiah Mason and John Goddard Esquires a committee for certain purposes therein expressed.—

Very respectfully Sir Yr. obedt. Servt.—

SAML. SPARHAWK

Daniel Webster Esqr.

State of New Hampshire

In the House of Representatives June 20th. 1811—

Resolved, that the Hon. Jeremiah Mason, John Goddard and Daniel Webster Esquires be a committee to revise the code of criminal laws, and prepare police laws for the regulation of the State prison, in the recess of the General Court, and report at the next Session of the Legislature—[2]

Sent up for Concurrence

CLEMENT STOWRER, Speaker

In Senate the same day, read & concurred—

WILLIAM PLUMER, President

Approved June 21, 1811—

JOHN LANGDON Govr.

Attest   SAML. SPARHAWK Secry

---

[1] Addressed to D. W., at Portsmouth, N. H.

[2] On December 17, 1812, the House resolved that the three members of the above committee receive $100 for services in revising, collecting and reporting the Criminal Code. The journal of the House on that and the preceding day treat the matter further.

(From Geo. Herbert.[1])

ELLSWORTH [Maine] Ap[1]. 20. 1813.

My Dear Daniel.[2]

* * * We are all here in *misery* the distress of this part of the country is inconceivable—already *starving* and *starved* a woman & 2 children are already dead of the famine as I am informed.[3] Many are sick & famishing from want. God preserve us all or we shall all die. Our best livers have already parted with all pretty much that they had for their own subsistance and all in one condition. There is not a cent of money in the country more than provision. It is all drained away & gone. I believe I am the owner of what would in good times be worth $20,000 to me, and I cannot raise a dollar. Can you *now* help me, if you can you will do a deed *of charity*—for all I am worth would not produce $100.

CURSE THIS GOVERNMENT! I would march at 6 days notice for Washington, if I could get anybody to go with me— and enough I could if I had but a commission, and I would swear upon the *altar* never to return till Madison was buried under the ruins of the capitol. All the pleasure I have is anticipating the time when I shall march in armour on the *farthest Georgia* and trample the planters under my feet.— But they must be after all the aggressors in war— But, again they must be *made* such. And how easy that would be, if we were to exercise one hundredth part of the policy *they* have used to bring about this war. I can almost never pardon Boston & the leaders of the Federal interest there, for their pusilanimous and mean conduct in holding back the country from taking even *one* step—when so many are to be taken; some of which are *preparatory* Hence it comes we are *ruined—starved.* And this is a light thing forsooth. "O let the country suffer"—with a mighty careless unconcerned air, as they had no duty to perform but to attend festivals of the table the very *crumbs* of which would afford us relief— I wish to God—if I know myself that Boston was bombarded this moment. I could shrug up my shoulders with much complacency when I saw the *smoke of their torment* ascending up on high— *Thou in thy life time hast had thy good things.* let them suffer— let them suffer! Otis has overcome all the *good sense* and *hu-*

[1] An old college friend.
[2] Addressed to Portsmouth, N. H.
[3] The result of the Long Embargo and the war.

manity of the town òf Boston & Boston has depressed the independent feelings of Mass. & Massachusetts not moving—who else could move till she was ready & how could Mass. move till Boston was ready & how could Boston move till Otis was ready! Heaven preserve us! on *what a slender thread hang* the destinies of nations! The mere breath of *that man* is a more absolute law with Federalists than the ordonnances of Buonaparte are in Paris. It is time things were otherwise— If they are not soon such is our love of life, wives children & selves that I will not answer for the consequences. & our neighbours under the *despotic* government of a *King* enjoy such privileges without *taxation*, as produces them abundance of all the comforts of life. I doubt whether the time will not soon come when we shall determine to live [on] leeks and onions of Egypt, rather [than] hunger, we have no manna rained upon us by the God and they intend to force us to live upon air like chamelions. If so they have a right to expect that we shall change the colour of our coats as soon. And I'll warrant them *we shall*—so help us God! We care for *ourselves.* Shall we care for those whether at *Boston* or *Washington* or any where else who care nothing about us? What is *Country*—& *love of Country* & Liberty? Is *it to stalk about* like *shadows?* and *live on air*—and pay tribute of *more than all we have!* No—! we will not starve if any nation that has wronged us so little as a *certain nation* we can mention, will provide for us. Boston people are *very* wise. If they do not take care they will overshoot themselves—in starving us into reason. I have known a democrat come about in a moment from the violence of his disease to perfect sanity—at least so far as to swear he was ready to take up his musket and fight but what he would have better times. These fellows know no distinction between federalism founded as it was really on democracy and monarchy. but *life is sweet and a pleasant thing it is to see food*—sometimes. you may tame the tiger with hunger till he will lie as still as any other carcass. And may my children rise up and call me cursed if I starve them to death. I tell you friend the timid counsels of Boston and Boston folks will not do for this meridian—I have only to add God send bombardment upon Boston I should admire to see how they will stand it & like it. I am not saying this for the *public* ear I am only uttering to *you* the bitterness of my heart—

But the mail is come   farewell   G. H.
with next mail   I now add my name to this treason.

(To Hon. Moses P. Payson.[1]*)*

PORTSMOUTH. [N. H.] Monday morn.
[June. 1812 [2]]

Dear Sir.

We heard yesterday that Hall was elected Counsellor in Convention, & we are overwhelmed with mortification. If a Federal Legislature has done this. I shall cease to have faith in men. We know no particulars. I never have seen so much indignation expressed on any occasion as is manifested here. If this choice was effected by the infidelity of a few, they ought to be published immediately, that general odium may have some individuals to rest upon, & not attach to the whole. What little Federalism there is in this town is certainly *extinct,* unless some explanation can be given of this most strange transaction.

After the pains & expence to which our people submitted to reject the Portsmouth votes,—they feel *personally* ill treated. They think too, that all confidence among ourselves as a party is destroyed—above all, a Federal Legislature that can so soon forget Josiah Sanborn—what shall I say of it? For Mercy's sake give us some consolation. I can give no answers to the questions put me at every corner of the street.

Yrs.

D. WEBSTER.

(To Timothy Pickering.[3]*)*

PORTSMOUTH, Dec. 11, 1812.

" No event of the kind could have caused me more regret than that my absence, when you were here, should have prevented me the pleasure of seeing you, and of paying you, in person, the respect which I feel for your character.

"Among the consequences which may probably grow out of recent events,[4] I look forward to none with more pleasure than the opportunity which may be afforded of cultivating the acquaintance of one of the *masters* of the Washington school of politics. Wholly inexperienced in public affairs, my first object is to comprehend the objects, understand the maxims, and imbibe the

---

[1] Senator in the N. H. Legislature.
[2] The letter is indorsed June, 1813, but the date 1812 is more probable.
[3] This letter is copied from the Life of Timothy Pickering, vol. iv, p. 223.
[4] The election by which Webster was made a member of Congress.

spirit of the first administration; persuaded, as I am, that the principles which prevailed in the cabinet and councils of that period, form the only *anchorage* in which our political prosperity and safety can find any *hold* in this dangerous and stormy time. If my progress in the science of Washington policy should be in proportion to my regard for its dead and *living* teachers, I shall have no occasion to be ashamed of my proficiency. Intending to visit Boston this winter, I contemplate paying my respects at the place of your residence.

"I am, with the utmost respect, your obedient servant,
"DANIEL WEBSTER."

Webster, the Local Politician

DURING the first ten years of Webster's congressional career he gave little indication of that lofty national statesmanship that so strongly marked the whole of his subsequent career. The welfare of New England was the chief object of his political action. True, he at times rose above mere sectional interests, and stood for a moment on the high plane that was characteristic of his later years, but there was not yet the consistent breadth of vision.

The material here offered tells, with a fair degree of completeness, the story of those years, and adds much to the information already furnished in Curtis' "Life" and in the "Private Correspondence." There is a remarkable flood of light on his first days in the national council. His opposition to the administration is clearly shown. The speech on the Conscription Bill, now published for the first time, contains sentiments very characteristic of this period of his political life. He advocated a doctrine hardly distinguishable from nullification. When he threatens that the state government will interfere, we wonder if Hayne and Calhoun went any further. But we get the healthy Websterian tone at last in the final paragraph, and feel sure that the love of the Union was as strong then as in the later days of the Hayne and of the 7th of March speech.

In choosing a date for closing this period of local statesmanship, I have determined upon the time just preceding the Greek speech. In that memorable speech he rose to the altitude that overlooked the whole field of world politics, and he rarely afterward descended from that eminence.

(To Ezekiel Webster.[1])

Dear E.   WASHINGTON, May 24, 1813.

You will be glad to hear of my safe arrival in this place. We

---

[1] This letter is owned by Mr. Edwin W. Sanborn, of New York. It was written on the first day that Webster sat in the Congress of the United States.

got into this city, so called, Saturday Eve'. The House are getting together this morning. I have marked myself a seat; or rather found one marked for me, by some friend who arrived here before me. I am in good company. Immediately on my left Lewis & Sheffey—on my right, Pearson, Gaston, & Pitkin— I suppose we shall proceed to choose a Clerk, in an hour or two. The House seems to be pretty full.

Adieu. Yrs.

D. Webster.

(To C. March.[1])

Tuesday 12 oclock
[Washington May 25, 1813]

The Message is out—Russian Embassy in front—call for taxes in the rear—*immunity of flag* insisted upon.
if possible I will enclose a copy before Mail closes.

D. W.

(To Edw. Cutts, Jr.[2])

Washington May 26. '13

Dear Sir,
I am much obliged to you for yours of the 19th; as I shall be for all similar favors.

Davis death, with the awful suspicion attending it, I had previously heard. It is in truth a most melancholy affair.

I should be willing to adopt the Judicial system, of which you give a general account, not because I think it the best possible, but because it proposes *some advantages*, & because a change is indispensable. Too much cannot be done or said to convince Federalists of the necessity of attending to the subject.

I hope the Legislature will have spent en° to correct the violent proceedings of Plumer[3] & his Council. I think public opinion

---

[1] Addressed to New York City. As an importer, Mr. March was interested in the "immunity of the flag."
[2] Addressed to Portsmouth, N. H. Edw. Cutts was a prominent lawyer in that city. See Bench and Bar of N. H., p. 301.
[3] Governor of New Hampshire.

requires it; at least, that it w^d well bear it. I thank you for your hint, on the defensible state of the coast. If a fair occasion presents, shall endeavor to make use of it—
Mr Cutts[1] is here. It is generally believed, that an attempt will be made to supersede Mr Otis, as Clerk of the Senate, by appointing Mr C. I understand, pretty directly, that such a project is in being. Messrs. King[2] & Gore[3] have not yet arrived. They are on the road. Bayard[4] has resigned his seat. The Gov. of Delaware is Democratic, but the Legislature have outwitted him, and have contrived to have a session about this time. They met yesterday. They were called together a good while ago, under pretense of providing defense for the Delaware, but the rumor of Mr Bayard's appointment to Russia getting out, they took the liberty to adjourn, to this time. Messrs Wells[5] & Vandyke[6] are the Candidates.

It is generally believed we shall have the *taxes* in some shape. The Western People, some of them, say their Constituents are *eager to be taxed.* An excise, on certain articles, is I think to be expected. Whether a land tax will be voted is not quite so certain.

I went yesterday to make my bow to the President. I did not like his looks, any better than I like his Administration. I think a voter could find clearly en° in his features Embargo, non-Intercourse & War—

The Houes will probably today go into Com^{ee} of the whole, on the Message, & refers its parts to Committees. Dawson[7] & Finlay[8] are the makers of all motions, which are of [ac] count. Finlay makes his from the Journal of the last session, which he holds in his hand & reads. Dawson is as insipid an animal as one would wish to see—

I shall hope to hear from you often, I shall be happy to communicate to you any thing which may be thought to be either important or entertaining.

Yrs with great esteem

D WEBSTER

---

[1] Charles Cutts, Senator from New Hampshire.
[2] Rufus King, Senator from New York, took his seat May 28th.
[3] Christopher Gore, Senator from Massachusetts, took his seat May 28th.
[4] James A. Bayard, of Delaware.
[5] Wm. H. Wells, Senator from Delaware.
[6] Nicholas Van Dyke.
[7] John Dawson, of Virginia.
[8] Wm. Findlay, of Pennsylvania.

(To Chas. March?)

WASHINGTON May 27 (1813)

Dear Sir

The Committees, appointed in pursuance of the standing rules of the House, & also on the several parts of the President's Message were read from the journals this Morning.   Their *constitution* is generally very little pacific— I send you the names of the several Chairmen— A Federal name is now & then put in, to save appearances—

on Electors—Fish, (Vt)
Com. & Manu—Newton[1]
Ways & Means—Eppes[2]
Military affairs—Troop[3]
Foreign Affairs—Calhoun.

Yr—

D WEBSTER

(To Chas. March.[4])

WASHINGTON May 28 (1813)

Dear Sir.

The Elections of Bayley[5] & Hungerford[6] are to be contested by Basset[7] & Taliaferro[8]—

Petitions presented yesterday.— We have had nothing done in the House today.—not in session an hour—& have adjourned to Monday— Messrs Gore & King took their seats in the Senate today— A new Senator is expected from Delaware, *vice* M^r. Bayard— Probably he will be Wells or Vandyke— The Legislature of that State is in session.— I understand the Senate have ratified M^r. Crawford's appointment as Minister to France— I do not understand that the nomination of Minister to Petersburg has yet come before the Senate—

Yr

D. WEBSTER

---

[1] Thos. Newton, of Virginia.
[2] John W. Eppes, of Virginia.
[3] Geo. M. Troup, of Georgia.
[4] Addressed to New York City.
[5] Thomas M. Bayly, of Virginia.
[6] John P. Hungerford, of Virginia.
[7] Burwell Basset, of Virginia.
[8] John Taliaferro, of Virginia.

(To Chas. March.)

(WASHINGTON May 31 1813)

The French news will have no very great effect with our rulers. They will not believe. Some of the first men of the party here insist that the Emperor's loss last Campaign was inconsiderable;—that it was nothing like an overthrow—& not exceeding the ordinary wear and waste of a large army. While Bona lives, some of his worshippers will continue to adore him— The prospect about the Taxes is doubtful. There will be opposition, in the ranks of the Democratic party. The President talked so much about " amicable dispositions," & the effect to be expected from the Embassy to Russia, that some of his party pretend to think Peace so near, that it is unnecessary to lay the Taxes— They are for breaking up the session— Sentiments like these have fallen from Ingersoll, of Philadelphia; Bradly of Vermont, & others— Others talk of a very small tax on whisky—& a high tax on some other articles. Eppes, I am well informed, says, he can find no two agreeing—& that every one is for taxing every body, except himself and his Constituents.—

At present, rely upon it, there is great diversity & schism, among the party—how much of this can be remedied, by caucussing and drilling, it is not easy to say. The prevalent impression on our side of the House seems to be to keep quiet, until we see whether the jaring interests on the other side will be reconciled—

I wish to remit 150 Dols. to Capt Charles Coffin, Portsm°— At this moment I have no money here, fit for remission. I would be obliged to you, if convenient to enclose him that sum, on my account, & I will find something in a few days, which will be proper for remission to you—

I like several of your N. York members very much. Was at M. Vernon, on Saturday, at a dinner party—had [a] very pleasant time— Judge Benson[1] was present—he & I held fast our integrity to the " Murdock "— We insisted it beat " Hills ", & every thing else— The party generally returned Saturday Eve— The Judge staid over Sunday

Yrs   D. WEBSTER

---

[1] Egbert Benson, of New York.

(To Chas. March.)

June 3rd [1813]
Mr. Russell[1] is said to be nominated Minister to Sweden— There are great doubts whether the Senate will concur.— I incline to think they will not—

Sundry Resolutions have been mentd—one, calling for information, on the point, whether Bassano did communicate the Repealing Decree to Russel[2]—

The *Envoys* to Russia are also under consideration—there will be some trouble— The document—or letter—tending the offer of Russia will be asked for.— Whether Gallatin is still Sec. of Treas will be inquired—etc, etc. A very distinguished Gentleman takes the lead in these proceedings in Senate—

A sort of "Budget" was rec'd today from the Treasury— It calls for a loan of 5 millions instead of that amt. of Treasury notes—& insists on the necessity of internal Taxes— It is signed by Wm Jones, as acting Sec. of Treas.

Yrs

D WEBSTER

I suppose not much should be said of the Senate's doings.

—————

(To Chas. March.)

WASHINGTON June 3. 1813
Thursday afternoon— I have just learned that the Senate have *refused* to call for the Russian document by a maj. of 5 Gen Smith,[3] Leib, Lambert etc voted with the Federalists— Giles absent—

I cannot say certainly whether the new loan is 5—or 7 millions—Gov. Strong's[4] speech is more determined than any thing I have seen from him— I expect the tone in Mass. will be high

Yrs   D. WEBSTER

---

[1] Jonathan Russell of Massachusetts, was appointed Minister Plenipotentiary to Sweden in 1814.

[2] On June 10th Webster offered a series of five resolutions intended to bring about a complete investigation of the charge that the United States government had been apprised of the Repeal of the Berlin and Milan decrees (April 28, 1811) by the Duke of Bassano, before the communication of that fact to Mr. Barlow in May of 1812. See McMaster's "History of United States," vol. iv, p. 215.

[3] Samuel Smith, of Pennsylvania.

[4] Caleb Strong, governor of Massachusetts.

(To Ezekiel Webster.[1])

WASHINGTON, June 4, 1813.

Dear E.

If your Legislature pass any Resolves this session, on the War, &c., I hope you will not fail to put in a solemn, decided, and spirited Protest against making new States out of new Ter= ritories. Affirm, in direct terms, that New Hampshire has never agreed to favor political connexions of such intimate nature, with any people, out of the limits of the U. S. as they existed at the time of the compact.

Yrs

D. WEBSTER

(To Chas. March.)

WASHINGTON June 6. (1813)

Dear Sir,

The Committee of W & M have concluded, I understand, to report all the Tax Bills, as they rec[d] them from the Treasury— & leave their discussion & modification to the House. They will probably be in, Monday or Tuesday—

They are so drawn, as to bear most hard on the Atlantic & Eastern States[2]— This was to be expected. The Stamp Tax —for example—is to be imposed, almost exclusively, upon Bank Bills—& notes negotiated at Banks.— The Whiskey Tax will be small—and so contrived, as to be easily evaded— It will be laid, not on the gallon but on the *Still*, according to its capacity —leaving out all under a certain size— Instead therefore of a few great stills, they will have a thousand little ones— Every effort will be made to force the taxes down—but I continue to think their passage a little doubtful— Gallatin made Parish the most solemn assurances of two things— 1. That there w[d] be peace—that he himself had been always opposed to the War —& was now going with a full resolution to end it—2 That the Taxes should be laid— You see in all the Executive Communications, the necessity of Taxes urged.— Nothing of consequence has lately transpired in the Senate—
We were yesterday at the Russian Celebration— It was a

[1] This letter is owned by Edwin W. Sanborn, of New York.
[2] See McMaster, vol. iv, p. 217.

pleasant occasion.— Many persons of Virginia & Maryland, of the first distinction were present— G. W. P. Curtis made an Oration, and Hon R G Harper made an Address to us, at Table, of three quarters of an hour—it was very good—

Yrs

D W

(To Chas. March.)

Monday Afternoon (June 7 1813)

Dear Sir,

We have done nothing today, but hear a case of disputed Election in Tenessee— Taxes not in yet—have just heard of the taking of Fort George, & the loss of Chesapea[k]—

Tomorrow I intend to bring forward a motion, calling for information relative to the famous French Decree, repealing the Berlin & Milan Decrees[1]—

Lest some accident should prevent, you will say nothing of this, till you see or hear more of it. If they chuse to oppose it —& to bring on a general battle, we are ready— Some of your N. Y. members are very good fellows— Grosvener, Shepherd, Oakley, Howell &c, as well as the Judge,[2] are relied on to give us a lift— Hanson[3] is a hero—

Yrs

D. W.

I look anxiously for news from N. H. respecting Senator Mason.[4] N. B. Giles has just taken his seat in Senate, & has put a claw on Gallatin— The President will be hard pushed in the Senate

(To Chas. March.)

(June 8 1813)

Dr Sir,

Nothing done today, save agreeing to postpone the hearing of the Tennessee Election case—

---

[1] Not offered until June 10, 1813.
[2] Judge Benson.
[3] Alex. Contee Hanson, of Maryland. See McMaster, U. S. Hist., vol. iii, p. 553.
[4] Mason did not arrive until June 21st. He was elected during the June session of the N. H. Legislature.

Owing [to] Hanson's ill health, the motion I spoke to you about[1] is not bro't in yet— As soon as he is seen in his place, it will come forward—

Tuesday 3 oclock—

D. W.

(To Chas. March.)

Wednesday—June 9. 1813

We have done nothing to day, of any importance
Hanson[2] *not in the House.*—

I understand some unexpected obstruction has delayed the Taxes in the Committee—

There is much close running in the Senate— It w'd be too much to expect that Gallatin will not be confirmed, but it will be *a close poll*— Giles has opened his severe thunders upon poor Albert[3]—

If we had only three or four more Senators, we should see Madison kick the beam— I shall have a good deal to say to you, on my return

D. W.

(To Chas. March.)

(June 10 1813)
Thursday Afternoon—

D'r March,

The *resolutions* were offered today—they lie until tomorrow for consideration— What the House will do with them, I cannot say— The question to consider them was carried—132 to 28— I have done what I tho't my duty—& am easy about the result— A friend will forward them this Evening to the Commercial Advertizer—in which paper you will be likely first to see them— I ask of you the favor to obtain a few of the papers, & send two or three of them to Portsm° (nobody there takes the paper) & one to each of the following persons—viz. Tho⁵. W. Thompson, Esq. Concord, N. H. via Boston; Ez¹. Webster, Concord N. H.—via Boston—& Isaac P. Davis Esq. Boston— send one to Wᵐ Garland, Portsm°—

---

[1] In respect to Berlin and Milan decrees.
[2] Alex. C. Hanson, of Maryland, who was opposed to the administration.
[3] Albert Gallatin.

The taxes are in today— they make a good many wry faces— they are referred to a Committee of the whole, on Monday— They will make the People stare— Albert Gallatin has not yet got thro' the Senate— After several days discussion, he is committed to a Committee of 5—viz—King, Giles, Anderson, Brown & Bledsoe—*the 3 first are agt. confirming him*— There cannot be much sleep in the White-house about [th] is time— let nothing get into the Newspapers, about the Senate, at present—

Yr's in haste—

D WEBSTER

(To Chas. March.)

(June 11th, 1813)

Friday Eve

We have done nothing today. M^r. Bibb asked me not to call up my Resolutions till Tomorrow. He s^d he was willing to vote for the four first— Whether he really so intends I cannot say. If the party wishes to oppose them, & to give us battle, so be it—

The Senate have decided nothing yet. They have been all day on *Russel*, as Minister to Sweden—& come to no conclusion— Giles has no mercy— It is most probable he will stick with King & Co— I should not be surprised, if they should drive Madison *to* and Gallatin *from* the Treasury—

If any fault is found in your City with my Resolutions, let me know it—

We tremble for New London.[1]

D. WEBSTER

(To Moody Kent.[2])

WASHINGTON June 12 1813.

Dear Sir,

I send you the enclosed report, that you may see how we pass time here. Today we have been wholly occupied with it, & expect to be a day or two longer.[3] The only questions are; "will the House *presume* that the Sheriff *did not* perform his

---

[1] It was in danger of attack by the British fleet.
[2] A much respected lawyer of Concord, N. H. See Bench and Bar of New Hampshire, p. 469.
[3] The contested election of John P. Hungerford, of Virginia.

duty, in having the Clerk Sworn", & "can the name of a man be written, by the initial of his Christian, & the whole of his surname. For example, if, I should put at the end of this letter "D. Webster", is that "entering my name" upon it, or not? On these knotty points, we are much divided. Speaker Clay made a vehement speech, in favor of the report. He said the name must be written at full length, that both names might be given by initials as well as one &c &c— *Col Pickering* ansd. him. He said, it was required that all Bills should be "signed by the Speaker", & he had observed the constant mode of signing to be "H. Clay"— He wished to know, whether this was right or wrong; & if right, whether a public Law is not a matter requiring as much form as a Virginia Poll list— The Speaker spake no more.

Macon[1] was not clear, whether the law wd. presume the Clerk to be sworn, till the contrary appeared; or whether the other assumption ought to take place.

Calhoun made a long speech to prove the essential policy of Virginia, in requiring every voters name to be written at *"full length"*. It was, he said, because there was a land-list, or list of freeholders, & this served to check the votes by—therefore the names were required to be written "at full length" on the polls, so that the same names may be found on the land list.

This Orator was mistaken only in three unimportant points—

1. The land list is not a Check; because every freeholder does not vote in Virginia—

2. The names on the land list are, more than half of them, [are] abbreviated in the same way—

3. The law of Virginia requires no such thing, as that the name shall be written "at full length"— vid. the report.

Sheffey[2] demolished all this nonsense, in a very sensible argument, & strewed the dust of the fabric over those who had raised it— How the House will decide is uncertain— The taxes are reported; not acted upon. *I hope they will pass.*—

All that I have heard from Concord yet, I like very much— My information comes down only to Dr. G's[3] election— Write me, & tell me all the news.

Yrs &c

D. W<small>EBSTER</small>

---

[1] Nathaniel Macon, of North Carolina.   [2] Daniel Sheffey, of Virginia.
[3] Dr. John Goddard, of Portsmouth, elected Senator, but refused the honor. See McClintock's Hist. of New Hampshire, p. 499.

(To Chas. March.)

WASHINGTON June 14. (1813)
Monday—

Dr Sir,

All day Saturday, & all today on the disputed Election in Virginia—   Tax Bills yet not acted on—

When I am more at leisure I will say what I think about the prospect of Peace.   In the meantime, if any thing looking like a repeal of Non Intercourse should take place, I will give you notice—

You must contrive some way for me to get rich, as soon as there is a peace.

Y'r's

D. W.

N. B—The Senate are yet in debate, on Gallatin, Russel etc: Russel was today referred to a Committee, viz. King, Giles, Wells—   Poor Madison!—

I doubt whether he has a night's sleep these three weeks—

(To Chas. March.)

June 15— (1813) Tuesday—

Nothing today—except the Election case, again—(undecided)—& a resolution offered by M'. Pitkin, in relation to the "Distribution of Arms,"—a subject that excites some interest especially in Massachusetts—   I do not know when we shall get on the taxes—

Yrs.

D W.

Nothing, I learn, in the Senate today—Mason is on his way as Senator from N. Hamp—

(To Chas. March.)

June 19. 1813

I have not time to write you any thing in detail; especially as I intend saying a word, on my Resolutions, Tomorrow Morning.

There is no prospect of Non- Importation coming off. I am watching it very closely, & will give you the first hint. The fact is, the Administration are, for the moment, confounded— They are hard pushed in our house—much harder in the Senate— Gallatin not confirmed—a Resolution has actually passed the Senate, that the Office of Secretary of Treasr^y & Foreign Minv ister are incompatible!!— Madison has been several days quite sick—is no better—has not been well en° to read the said Reso- lution of the Senate— the Taxes go heavily— *I fear* they will not go at all— They cannot raise a Caucus, as yet, even, to agree what they will do— They are in a sad pickle. Who cares?—

D. W.

I will steadily watch the Non- intercourse—

(To Chas. March.)

June 21. 1813

Dear Sir,
    The Resolutions[1] have passed, unaltered, except putting in the usual saving in the last Resolution, which was left out by accident.
    The last Resolution passed 93.—to 68. I made no speech— When I came to the House this morning, Calhoun told me, the Motion for indefinite postponement would be withdrawn—his motion to amend withdrawn—& he, & some of his friends should vote for the Resolutions as they are— I of course could not object—& considering the thing given up on their part, I fore- bore to speak— They have acted very strangely— A dozen Motions, made & withdrawn—some pulling one way—some an- other— They do not manage like so many Solomons—
                    Adieu—
                        Yrs D. W.

Hanson, Grosvenor, Oakley, Pearson &c have made excellent Speeches

---

[1] Concerning the Berlin and Milan decrees.

(To Chas. March.)

[Washington] June 22. 1813.
Dear Sir,
    This morning we shall take up the taxes— I have a little draught on New York, which I shall enclose you, either today, or tomorrow—to repay the sum you sent to Portsm°— I expect this week to have occasion to send 5 or 6 hundred Dollars to Boston— If I do, I shall take the liberty to write to you, and if convenient to you to get you to send it on, & receive it when I return home—
    I know not what course the taxes will take—perhaps at night I can tell you better—
                                                    Yrs
                                                    D. W.
                    turn over
    Mr *Rhea*,[1] after my Resolutions passed made a little Resolution calling for information of the P. Regent's Declaration— passed nem—con— The Speaker has appointed me & *old Rhea* to carry the Resolutions to the Palace!!— *I never swear.*

(To Chas. March.)

    JUNE 24— Thursday— (1813)
    Nothing yesterday & today but " taxes "— There is a good deal of objection to the detail—there is great doubt what will be done. Virginia hates a land tax— Dearborn has resigned[2]— Madison still sick— Eppes sick—&c &c— I went on Tuesday to the Palace to present the Resolutions[3]— The Presd^t was in his bed, sick of a fever—his night cap on his head—his wife attending him &c &c— I think he will find *no relief* from my prescription— You will see by today's Intelligence, that the Party are troubled with them. You recollect what R. Smith s^d about his inquiry of Serurier— How will Madison answer the part of Resolutions calling for his correspondence with Serurier? In truth, there never was a party acted so awkwardly, as the Demos did thro the whole of that business—

        [1] John Rhea, of Tennessee.
        [2] Henry Dearborn, commander of the American forces. Madison did not order his removal until July 6, 1813.
        [3] Concerning the French decrees.

The Senate has done nothing yet— They now have Duane before them, for Adj. Gen[1].— They are not in a hurry to appoint any of Madison's Creatures.

The news is, that the British have rec[d] a vast reinforcement in the Bay, and the lower County is greatly alarmed— You will see there has been a battle between a frigate & some Gun Boats

Yrs   D. W.

(To Chas. March.)

WASHINGTON June 26. 1813

Dr Sir,

This day on the Taxes—made some progress— I shall "have to sit again"— *The President is seriously sick.* Not much is suffered to be said on this subject, & I am not disposed to excite alarm, but you may be assured, that he is sick—he has been sick 13 days—& has no symptoms of convalescence— You will of course say nothing of this—

Yrs tr.

D. W.

(To Chas. March.)

WASHINGTON June 26. 1813
Saturday— (1813)

Dear Sir,

We are spending this day in deciding how much money shall be given the Collectors of the Taxes—

Yr Mr Post[1] is making a sensible speech, ag[t] M[r] Speaker Clay, who is for putting the salaries pretty high.— We shall do nothing else today.

It is said the President is better today—this is said every day— I know not how the fact is— Gallatin not yet confirmed—

Nothing looks like repeal of non-Importation. My Brother Mason[2] likes this place a little better than I expected he would. He is pleased, I believe, with his company in the Senate—

Yrs

Give me a daily letter   D. WEBSTER
The British are in great fame down the bay—

---

[1] Jotham Post, of New York.
[2] Jeremiah Mason, Webster's warmest friend.

(To Chas. March.)

Monday— (June 28, 1813)
D'r March,
You are probably tired of receiving letters containing nothing; but I continue to write them. Look at the enclosed; & if you think it worth while, hand it along.

Y'r man Fiske[1] has this day put the Democratic works in no small confusion, by moving a Resolution for a tax on whiskey, to be imposed on the *gallon*, not on the *still*— All the West is in arms. It lies over till tomorrow.

Nothing of any importance has recently occured in the Senate. As to Peace, a part of the Democrats doubtless wish it; a part do not. The West is still fierce for war— Do not credit any report of Mʳ King's opinions without good evidence— I see him sometimes, & think I should know any important sentiment, on these subjects, which he might divulge—

I am fully of opinion, that the Administration now looks forward to its own certain downfall, unless it can have a peace. But if it does make Peace, it will have all the West up in arms ag't it—

Poor Madison does not know what to do. I can tell you, for y'r own ear, that he this day nominated Paul Hamilton, Com. of Loans for S. C.— The Senate will certainly negative it!!— This shows his standing with that body— Never was man sinking faster— It is said today, as it is every day, that he is better, as to his health

Adieu Yrs

D W

(To Chas. March.)

WASHINGTON Tuesday—
(June 29, 1813)
Dear Sir,
We have had the Massachusetts Memorial[1] today—read by Mʳ Pickering—

On the question of printing, a good deal of warmth was manifested—voted to print, 108 yeas—

---

[1] Jonathan Fisk, of New York.
[2] The Remonstrance of the Massachusetts Legislature against the continuance of the war.

The President is worse today— We shall directly take up Fiske's motion to tax whiskey by the gallon— I think it will not pass—tho' my own opinion is, that our friends, one & all, ought to vote with Fiske.   Yrs

D. WEBSTER

Shall draw on you today or tomorrow—

(To Chas. March.)

July 6 (1813)

Dear Sir,

For four or five days I have found myself getting out of sorts, & have determined to stay here not much longer. So late is the period of the session, so hot the season, so languid is every body, that I incline to think we shall have no general battle about the war. Indeed events are proving our positions, faster than it could otherwise be done. M^r. Madison has sent no answer yet— I only intend to wait till Saturday—hope to be in N. York Tuesday or Wednesday—shall go to Mrs Gallops—spend a day with you, & pass on, *taking you with me*—

We have passed the Whiskey tax thr° our House. We shall pass the land tax I think tomorrow— Boerstler's affair[1] makes long faces.

Yrs

D. Webster

(To Chas. March.)

July 10. '13

My dear Friend,

I expected to leave this place Tomorrow, & to be with you by the middle of next week— But understanding that we are to hear from the President either today or Monday, I shall wait a few days longer—

The Senate have decided *against* the Swedish Mission—

Gen. Armstrong is going to the frontier to take the command

---

[1] See McMaster's " History of United States," vol. iv, p. 45.

of our discomforted armies![1]— This is not publicly announced, but I have great reason to think it true.

Your's as ever,

D. WEBSTER

(From Mr. Waldron.)

[About Dec 28, 1813.]

* * *[2] Think My Dear Sir how your bosom would have heaved, what wild distraction would have filled your eye to have so missed poor Grace in the height of the flames & what poor Mrs Websters feelings were we can better imagine than describe.[3]

Thanks be rendered to heaven they with all our friends are safe— My poor mother Sheafe was almost killed by exertion & fatigue & agitation— Friday confined to her bed all day yesterday sat up & is on the recovery they are at Cutts— Mrs Waldron wished Mrs Webster & Grace to spend the winter with us but Mrs Mason would take no denial— When things get a little settled I hope the blackeyed miss & her mother will make us a long visit—

Father Sheafe saved a good deal of his furniture, fortunately they had invited a doz navy officers to sup who had been in 1/2 hour & rendered much service swore they would save the house, stripped to the buff & fought like heroes 'till the flames compelled them to make a precipitate retreat— The real distress & consternation at Portsm° is beyond all discription & I hope something great and liberal will be done for them—you will see how many widows & people in low & middling circumstances have lost all & are unable even to put up a shelter— The N. H. delegation I know will do all they can— I have written to Mr Hale— If Congress offers [to] do any relief for heavens sake dont suffer it to have any political bearing I had rather nothing should be done than that sh[d] be the case— It must be advanced by the N. H. Members—

---

[1] The editor wishes at this point to call attention to an account of an event in Webster's life, related by J. N. McClintock in his History of New Hampshire, p. 496. He says that Webster made a speech urging the people to use spades and build forts to defend Portsmouth against the British. Webster then joined them in the work.

[2] Preceding part is lost.

[3] The fire broke out Dec. 22, 1813. Webster's house, valued at $6,000, and his library were consumed. Webster was on his way to Washington. See Curtis' Life of Webster, vol. i, p. 115.

I pray to heaven that the sympathies & liberality of the whole country may be roused on this occasion & that signal relief may be afforded Y'r Emb. I learn has passed all branches I hope the Federalists did not espouse the measure,

I have time to add only my best regards & respects

(To James Thom.[1])

PORTSMO June 29. 1814

Dear Sir,

The Committee of the W. B. S.[2] have directed me to ask the favor of our Exeter friends to attend our celebration on the 4th. I have written to Mr. Sullivan, & intended to have addressed a similar note to the rest of the Gentlemen individually, but not having time, I must ask you to do me the kindness to present the request of the Committee to them—

Judge Tenney, Judge Peabody, the Messrs Gilmore, Mr Abbot, Col. Rogers, Brothers Tilten & Lawrence &c &c— You will not confine yourself to these names, but it is our wish that as many gentlemen as can with convenience attend should be invited— Of course, you will not expect as much gratification as to be induced to break up any projects which you may have for a celebration of your own— We cannot promise you anything but a good oration from Mr Haven, & a very light dinner with the Society—

Y'rs

D. WEBSTER

N. B.—I think our Reference was fixed for July 6.— If I am wrong, set me right—

(From Mr. Lawrence.[3])

HARRISBURG Decr.

Dear Sir

I must take leave to ask you one question, not for my own

---

[1] Addressed to James Thom, Esqr., of Exeter, N. H., and belongs to the Pennsylvania Historical Society.

[2] The Washington Benevolent Society.

[3] This is probably a copy of Lawrence's letter, *but in* Daniel Webster's hand. There is no date.

satisfaction, but in order to enable me to satisfy others.   Although it has been so often, & so authentically denied, you are aware how many People in Pa. still believe that you were a member of the Hartford Convention.   Will you do me the favor, therefore, to say under your name, whether you were, or were not a member of that body, & give me leave to make such use of your answer, as I may judge expedient.[1]

Yrs with much regard
[Mr. Lawrence.(?)]

(To Mr. Lawrence.[2])

Dear Sir
   I have recd your letter, & very cheerfully answer its inquiry. I was not a member of the Hartford Convention, and had no agency in it, nor any correspondence with any of its members. If you will refer to the Journal of Congress, & to the dates of the proceedings relative to that Convention, you will find, My Dear Sir, that I was in my seat in the House of Representatives in Congress, which was before any proposition to hold such a Convention was brought forward, & that I remained in that seat, until after the Convention had met & dissolved.

(To William Sullivan.[3])

WASHINGTON, Oct. 17, 1814.

Dear Sir
   The papers rec'd today have put us right about the time of your proposed Convention.
   We this morning rec'd the communication of Dallas relative to finances.   He differs in some things from Eppes—He proposes to increase the land tax 100 pr ct. & most of the present internal duties in the same ratio;—& to lay 25 cts. pr gallon on *whiskey* in addition to the present tax on stills—But his great hobby is a bank, of 50 millions—6 millions specie—44 millions

---

[1] See Massachusetts Hist. Soc. Proceedings, vol. vi, page 288, for Judge White's testimony as to D. Webster's connection with the Hartford Convention.
   [2] This letter is in D. Webster's hand and was probably a copy kept by him. It is endorsed "Correspondence with Mr. Lawrence, Hartford Convention."
   [3] This letter is owned by Hon. Geo. F. Hoar.   Mr. Sullivan was an orator and a Massachusetts politician.

stocks—Gov't to own 2 fifths—15 directors—President to appoint 5—& to appoint President &c. &c.

I shall send you the instructions to our ministers which have been published—You perceive that certain parts are kept secret—You will see enough, I think, to be of my opinion, that the British have completely outgeneralled us—

Some of our good friends here are fearful that the Federalists in the Bay State are not sufficiently attentive to the ensuing Election for members of Congress. In whatever event, it would seem to be very important to make the Federalists as numerous as possible. Mr. Wilson has just arrived—I perceive he is a little apprehensive that no measures are taking in his District to secure the election of a Federalist in that District. Would it not be very well for your Committee to write immediately to the active men in that District on that subject It would be excessively disagreeable to have any Jacobins from Massachusetts—We hope also that Mr. Dana may be excused from attendance here hereafter. Pardon me for calling your attention & that of your friends to this subject

Mr. Randolph has been this way & has gone Northward—I did not see him. I understood he was going to Boston. others say to Philadelphia only. It is now confidently said he will be in the next Congress—& that Eppes will decline the contest

I shall be very glad to hear from you often

Yrs

D. WEBSTER

(To Ezekiel Webster.[1])

Oct. 20, 1814.

Dear E.

I left home on the 7th, & arrived here on the 14—just in season to give an unavailing vote on the question of removal. It is probable we shall hear of that question again before the session closes.

I have sent you the dispatches and instructions, The first opportunity, some of our People will tell the Administration what they think of it—You see there is no hope of present peace; probably none while Madison is in power.

The Elections in Pennsylvania have cheered us a little. At

---

[1] The original of this letter is owned by Edwin W. Sanborn, of New York.

least 10 Federalists are believed to be chosen into the next Congress from that State, with Joseph Hopkinson at their head.—N. Jersey made a great gain of Federal votes, thro' the State, but not enough to carry the Election. They lost a Federal Legislature by 44 votes. It is said by the Gentlemen from Virginia, & N. Carolina that in each of those States a majority of Federalists will be chosen for the next Congress. This is perhaps rather too large a calculation, especially for Virginia.

We have as yet heard nothing of the British forces under Lord Hill. It is thought here that New Orleans is his object. If he should take that city, & he will if he tries, & hold it, the Western States in one year would make their peace with England. Of this I have no doubt, from what I see & hear. I rather expect myself, that Lord Hill will first come into the Chesapeake & make a new attempt on Baltimore.

You will see how many plans of taxes are before us. I have not made up my mind definitely as to my own course on this subject. I should be glad of your advice. My present inclination is, not to deny all sorts of supplies, in the present crisis, but to hold myself quite at liberty to vote for or agst. any particular tax. I intend to vote *for* the whiskey tax, agst pretty much all the other internal duties. As to increase of the land tax, I have not decided. That is equal, among States, & is the bitterest pill to the Southern Democrats. Let me have your advice.

Randolph has offered again as a candidate in his old District. Election in April. It is conjectured that Eppes will quit the field.

Yrs

D. WEBSTER.

'(*From Mr. Ezekiel Webster.*[1])

Oct. 29, 1814.

Dear Daniel,

I received yours of the 20th this morning & am very glad to hear that you are at your post. The present will be a session of very arduous & difficult duties, & of very great responsibility. On the subject of the taxes my opinion corresponds with yours. Let them have the whiskey tax. In case any money is to be

---

[1] Daniel's elder brother. For biographical sketch see p. 31, vol. i, "Daniel Webster's Private Correspondence."

voted the administration, the tax on land is perhaps the most equitable. It will bear with a more just & even hand, upon the Southern & Eastern states. The internal taxes perfect the system of "domiciliary vexation". If my hat, my boots, my shoes, my horse, my chaise, my saddle & bridle &c are to be taxed what will be exempted? Most of these taxes I apprehend will operate most injuriously upon New England— For instance the tax upon spindles in cotton & woolen factories, I apprehend more than three fourths of these establishments are this side the Potomac Woolen cloths are almost altogether of New England consumption— Besides I think the faith of the government is somewhat pledged not to tax these establishments. It has always professed its desire to encourage them. The restrictive system depriving us of all importations; they are in some degree very necessary to us. The principal part of the cotton clothes worn in this quarter are of our own manufacture. Many factories with the high price of cotton and under this tax would be obliged to cease their operations.

The proposed tax on leather would likewise be unequal in its operation. It requires not much argument to prove that the same population in New Hampshire have occasion for much more leather than in Georgia.

Of $100,000 proposed to be raised on playing cards, I imagine Virginia will pay her proportion. It is right they should have this tax. Let gamblers be made to contribute to the support of this war, which was declared by men of no better principles than themselves.

I am not pleased with the idea of taxing the "process of law", Let justice be administered *freely*. No man ought to be compelled to pay a tax in order to have his rights.

There are but a very few of the taxes that I should vote for. I am not sure that I should that I should vote for any 'till the administration should change its measures. For what purpose should you put men or money into their hands? You voted last session men & they have been marched to Canada. You voted money & what portion of it has been expended in defending our maritime frontier? With all the men & money asked for, how have they defended the Capitol? It is worthy of remark that the defence of the Capitol under the eye of the administration & all its officers is more disgraceful than any event of the war. It discovers more imbecility and more cowardice. Gen. Hull's surrender was a triumph to it.

I am confident that the people would support almost any attack that should be made on the administration, especially any which should expose their imbecility & their incompetency to fill their offices. The language toward them ought to be dignified, but at the same time it ought to be plain & intelligible. They have as many vulnerable points as their assailants could wish & I want to see them goaded to the very quick. It would be better to lash them "naked through the land" for bringing us into these difficulties, than to unite with them to plunge us into still greater. Reformation ought to come from them. It was told them war would ensue from their restrictive system. The progress & events of the war were likewise foretold— but they still persisted in their measures—and they now acknowledge no errors, nor change any of their measures. Ought they to ask for the support of the opposition in this state of things—no.— They ought not to ask it, and they *ought not to have it.* Every day demonstrates their incapacity & the folly of their measures & furnishes the best evidence for not supporting them. Had not any of the predictions of the opposition been fulfilled, they might with some plausibility expect their support.

I hope an occasion will soon happen, when some of your people can speak their minds of them. I trust it will be done fearlessly.

I feel very anxious that Judge Farrar should assent to be a Candidate. We propose to address a letter to him, signed by all our delegation in both branches. I think it ought to be done immediately.

We are all well. With affection &c

Yours

E. WEBSTER

(To Ezekiel Webster.[1]*)*

WASHINGTON, Oct. 30. 1814

*   *   *

We have a plan for a conscription. I think I have sent you its outlines. The bill is drawn principally on Mr. Monroe's first plan. Of course we shall oppose such usurpation all we can. *   *   *

D. WEBSTER.

---

[1] Daniel Webster to Ezekiel Webster. "Private Correspondence," vol. i, p. 246.

(To Ezekiel Webster.[1])

WASHINGTON, Nov. 29, 1814.

Dear E.

The man in the patent office is searching to see whether Mesrs. Geirishes invention is new. As soon as he finds out, I will let you know. *   *   *[2]

We are here on the Eve of great events—I expect a blow up soon—My opinion is, that within sixty days Govt. will cease to pay even Secretaries, Clerks & Members of Congress—This I expect—& when it comes we are wound up.

Everything is in confusion here. Eppes [changing] Dollar —Dollar [changing] everybody. The Bank bill finally lost— 104— to 49—after a day of the most tumultuous proceedings I ever saw—

The conscription[3] has not come up—if it does it will cause a storm such as was never witnessed here.

In short, if Peace does not come this winter, the Govt. will die in its own weakness.

I have recd several letters, especially from Cheshire, relative to Governor & wishing to know what I thought of nominating *Mason*. What do you think of it?—Would it be popular—decidedly so? My own opinion is he would not *refuse*, if there should be a meeting of Delegates from all the Counties who should agree on him—This *you may take for granted*—but you must not intimate that you have any particular authority for saying so—But who would be Senator?—I cannot agree to Upham, & if I thought that would be the consequence, I would certainly oppose Mr. M's nomination for Gov.—because it may yet happen that the place of Senator may call for a man of firmness & decision.

If we were sure of Vose, [Chamberlain] & W. H. Woodward, or Payton for Senator, I should be very much inclined to support Mason for Governor—Write me fully about this—In the meantime, make no haste to nominate anybody. We shall know many things by Jany 15 which we do not know now.

Yrs

D Webster

---

[1] The original of this letter is the property of Edwin W. Sanborn, of New York.

[2] Cut out by Mr. Sanborn as matter he did not wish published.

[3] *i. e.*, the Conscription Bill.

(An unpublished speech.[1])

Dec. 9. 1814

Mr. Chairman,

After the best reflection which I have been able to bestow on the subject of the bill before you, I am of opinion that its principles are not warranted by any provision of the constitution. It appears to me to partake of the nature of those other propositions for military measures, which this session, so fertile in inventions, has produced. It is of the same class with the plan of the Secretary of War; with the bill reported to this House by its own committee for filling the ranks of the regular army by classifying the free male population of the United States; & with the resolution recently introduced by an honorable gentleman from Pennsylvania, (Mr. Ingersoll) & which now lies on your table, carrying the principle of compulsory service in the regular army to its utmost extent.

This bill indeed is less undisguised in its object, & less direct in its means, than some of the measures proposed. It is an attempt to exercise the power of forcing the free men of this country into the ranks of an army, for the general purposes of war, under color of a military service. To this end it commences with a *classification,* which is no way connected with the general organization of the Militia, nor, to my apprehension, included within any of the powers which Congress possesses over them. All the authority which this Government has over the Militia, until actually called into its service, is to enact laws for their organization & discipline. This power it has exercised. It now possesses the further power of calling into its service any portion of the Militia of the States, in the particular exigencies for which the Constitution provides, & of governing them during the continuance of such service. Here its authority ceases. The classification of the whole body of the Militia, according to the provisions of this bill, is not a measure which respects either their general organization or their discipline. It is a distinct system, introduced for new, purposes, & not connected with any power, which the Constitution has conferred on Congress.

But, Sir, there is another consideration. The services of the men to be raised under this act are not limited to those cases in which alone this Government is entitled to the aid of the militia

---

[1] Daniel Webster's speech on the Conscription Bill made in the House of Representatives December 9, 1814. (See Curtis' Life of Daniel Webster, vol. i, 138.)

of the States. These cases are particularly stated in the Constitution—"to repel invasion, suppress insurrection, or execute the laws." But this bill has no limitation in this respect. The usual mode of legislating on the subject is abandoned. The only section which would have confined the service of the Militia, proposed to be raised, within the United States has been stricken out; & if the President should not march them into the Provinces of England at the North, or of Spain at the South, it will not be because he is prohibited by any provision in this act.

This, then, Sir, is a bill for calling out the Militia, not according to its existing organization, but by draft from new created classes;—not merely for the purpose of "repelling invasion, suppressing insurrection, or executing the laws," but for the general objects of war—for defending ourselves, or invading others, as may be thought expedient;—not for a sudden emergency, or for a short time, but for long stated periods; for two years, if the proposition of the Senate should finally prevail; for one year, if the amendment of the House should be adopted. What is this, Sir, but raising a standing army out of the Militia by draft, & to be recruited by draft, in like manner, as often as occasion may require?

This bill, then, is not different in principle from the other bills, plans & resolutions, which I have mentioned. The present discussion is properly & necessarily common to them all. It is a discussion, Sir, of the last importance. That measures of this nature should be debated at all, in the councils of a free Government, is cause of dismay. The question is nothing less, than whether the most essential rights of personal liberty shall be surrendered, & despotism embraced in its worst form.

I have risen, on this occasion, with anxious & painful emotions, to add my admonition to what has been said by others. Admonition & remonstrance, I am aware, are not acceptable strains. They are duties of unpleasant performance. But they are, in my judgment, the duties which the condition of a falling state imposes. They are duties which sink deep in his conscience, who believes it probable that they may be the last services, which he may be able to render to the Government of his Country. On the issue of this discussion, I believe the fate of this Government may rest. Its duration is incompatible, in my opinion, with the existence of the measures in contemplation. A crisis has at last arrived, to which the course of things has long tended, & which may be decisive upon the happiness of present & of future generations. If there be anything important in the concerns of men, the considerations which fill the present hour are important. I am anxious, above all things, to stand acquitted before GOD, & my own conscience, & in the public judgments, of all participations in the Counsels, which have brought us to our present condition, & which now threaten the dissolution of the Government. When the present generation of men shall be swept away, & that this Government ever existed shall be a matter of history only, I desire that it may then be known, that you have not proceeded in your course unadmonished & unforewarned. Let it then be known, that there were those, who would have stopped you, in the career of your measures, & held you back, as by the skirts of your garments, from the precipice, over which you are plunging, & drawing after you the Government of your Country.

I had hoped, Sir, at an early period of the session, to find gentlemen in another temper. I trusted that the existing state of things would have impressed on the minds of those, who decide national measures, the necessity of some reform in the administration of affairs. If it was not to have been expected that gentlemen would be convinced by argument, it was still not unreasonable to hope that they would listen to the solemn preaching of events. If no previous reasoning could satisfy them, that the favorite plans of Government would fail, they might yet be expected to regard the fact, when it happened, & to yield to the lesson which it taught. Although they had, last year, given no credit to those who predicted the failure of the campaign against Canada, yet they had seen that failure. Although they then treated as idle all doubts of the success of the loan, they had seen the failure of that loan. Although they then held in derision all fears for the public credit, & the national faith, they had yet seen the public credit' destroyed, & the national faith violated & disgraced. They had seen much more than was predicted; for no man had foretold, that our means of defence would be so far exhausted in foreign invasion, as to leave the place of our own deliberations insecure, & that we should, this day, be legislating in view of the crumbling monuments of our national disgrace. No one had anticipated, that this City would have fallen before a handful of troops, & that British Generals & British Admirals would have taken their airings along the Pennsylvania Avenue, while the Government was in full flight, just awaked perhaps from one of its profound meditations on the plan of a Conscription for the conquest of Canada. These events, Sir, with the present state of things, & the threatening aspect of what is future, should have brought us to a pause. They might have reasonably been expected to induce Congress to review its own measures, & to exercise its great duty of inquiry relative to the conduct of others. If this was too high a pitch of virtue for the multitude of party men, it was at least to have been expected from Gentlemen of influence & character, who ought to be supposed to value something higher than mere party attachments, & to act from motives somewhat nobler than a mere regard to party consistency. All that we have yet suffered will be found light & trifling, in comparison with what is before us, if the Government shall learn nothing from experience but to despise it, & shall grow more & more desperate in its measures, as it grows more & more desperate in its affairs.

It is time for Congress to examine & decide for itself. It has taken things on trust long enough. It has followed Executive recommendation, till there remains no hope of finding safety in that path. What is there, Sir, that makes it the duty of this people now to grant new confidence to the administration, & to surrender their most important rights to its discretion? On what merits of its own does it rest this extraordinary claim? When it calls thus loudly for the treasure & the lives of the people, what pledge does it offer, that it will not waste all in the same preposterous pursuits, which have hitherto engaged it? In the failure of all past promises, do we see any assurance of future performance? Are we to measure out our confidence in proportion to our disgraces, & now at last to grant away every thing, because all that we have heretofore granted has been wasted or misapplied? What is there in our condition, that bespeaks a wise or an able Government? What is the evidence, that the protection of the country is the object principally regarded? In every quarter, that protection has been more or less abandoned to the States. That every town on the coast is not now in possession of the enemy, or in ashes, is owing to the vigilence & exertions of the States themselves, & to no protection granted to them by those on whom the whole duty of their protection rested.

Or shall we look to the acquisition of the professed objects of the war, & there find grounds for approbation & confidence. The professed objects of the war are abandoned in all due form. The contest for sailors' rights is turned into a negotiation about boundaries & military roads, & the highest hope entertained by any man of the issue, is that we may be able to get out of the war without a cession of territory.

Look, Sir, to the finances of the country. What a picture do they exhibit of the wisdom & prudence & foresight of Government. "The revenue of a State," says a profound writer, "is the state." If we are to judge of the condition of the country by the condition of its revenue, what is the result? A wise Government sinks deep the fountain of its revenue—not only till it can touch the first springs, & slake the present thirst of the Treasury, but till lasting sources are opened, too abundant to be exhausted by demand, too deep to be affected by heats & droughts. What, Sir, is our present supply, & what our provision for future resource? I forbear to speak of the present condition of the Treasury; & as to public credit, the last reliance of Government, I use the language of Government itself only, when I say it does not exist. This is a state of things calling for the soberest counsels, & yet it seems to meet only the wildest speculations. Nothing is talked of but Banks, & a circulating paper medium, & Exchequer Notes, & the thousand other contrivances, which ingenuity, vexed & goaded by the direst necessity, can devise, with the vain hope of giving value to mere paper. All these things are not revenue, nor do they produce it. They are the effect of a productive commerce, & a well ordered system of finance, & in their operation may be favorable to both, but are not the cause of either. In other times these facilities existed. Bank paper & Government paper circulated, because both rested on substantial capital or solid credit. Without these they will not circulate, nor is there a device more shallow or more mischievous, than to pour forth new floods of paper without credit as a remedy for the evils which paper without credit has already created. As was intimated the other day by my honorable friend from North Carolina (Mr. Gaston) this is an attempt to act over again the farce of the Assignats of France. Indeed, Sir, our politicians appear to have but one school. They learn every thing of modern France; with this variety only, that for examples of revenue they go to the Revolution, when her revenue was in the worst state possible, while their model for military force is sought after in her imperial era, when her military was organized on principles the most arbitrary & abominable.

Let us examine the nature & extent of the power, which is assumed by the various military measures before us. In the present want of men & money, the Secretary of War has proposed to

Congress a Military Conscription. For the conquest of Canada, the people will not enlist; & if they would, the Treasury is ex-- hausted, & they could not be paid. Conscription is chosen as the most promising instrument, both of overcoming reluctance to the Service, & of subduing the difficulties which arise from the de- ficiencies of the Exchequer. The administration asserts the right to fill the ranks of the regular army by compulsion. It contends that it may now take one out of every twenty-five men, & any part or the whole of the rest, whenever its occasions require. Per- sons thus taken by force, & put into an army, may be compelled to serve there, during the war, or for life. They may be put on any service, at home or abroad, for defence or for invasion, ac- cording to the will & pleasure of Government. This power does not grow out of any invasion of the country, or even out of a state of war. It belongs to Government at all times, in peace as well as in war, & is to be exercised under all circumstances, ac- cording to its mere discretion. This, Sir, is the amount of the principle contended for by the Secretary of War.

Is this, Sir, consistent with the character of a free Govern- ment? Is this civil liberty? Is this the real character of our Constitution? No, Sir, indeed it is not. The Constitution is libelled, foully libelled. The people of this country have not established for themselves such a fabric of despotism. They have not purchased at a vast expense of their own treasure & their own blood a Magna Charta to be slaves. Where is it written in the Constitution, in what article or section is it con- tained, that you may take children from their parents, & parents from their children, & compel them to fight the battles of any war, in which the folly or the wickedness of Government may engage it? Under what concealment has this power lain hidden, which now for the first time comes forth, with a tremendous & baleful aspect, to trample down & destroy the dearest rights of personal liberty? Who will show me any constitutional injunc- tion, which makes it the duty of the American people to sur- render every thing valuable in life, & even life itself, not when the safety of their country & its liberties may demand the sac- rifice, but whenever the purposes of an ambitious & mischievous Government may require it? Sir, I almost disdain to go to quotations & references to prove that such an abominable doctrine has no foundation in the Constitution of the country. It is enough to know that that instrument was intended as the basis of a free Government, & that the power contended for is incompatible with any notion of personal liberty.   An attempt to maintain this doctrine upon the provisions of the Constitution is an exercise of perverse ingenuity to extract slavery from the substance of a free Government.   It is an attempt to show, by proof & argument, that we ourselves are subjects of despotism, & that we have a right to chains & bondage, firmly secured to us & our children, by the provisions of our Government.   It has been the labor of other men, at other times, to mitigate & reform the powers of Government by construction; to support the rights of personal security by every species of favorable & benign interpretation, & thus to infuse a free spirit into Governments, not friendly in their general structure & formation to public liberty.

The supporters of the measures before us act on the opposite principle.   It is their task to raise arbitrary powers, by construction, out of a plain written charter of National Liberty. It is their pleasing duty to free us of the delusion, which we have fondly cherished, that we are the subjects of a mild, free & limited Government, & to demonstrate by a regular chain of premises & conclusions, that Government possesses over us a power more tyrannical, more arbitrary, more dangerous, more allied to blood & murder, more full of every form of mischief, more productive of every sort & degree of misery, than has been exercised by any civilized Government, with a single exception, in modern times.

The Secretary of War has favored us with an argument on the constitutionality of this power.   Those who lament that such doctrines should be supported by the opinion of a high officer of Government, may a little abate their regret, when they remember that the same officer, in his last letter of instructions to our ministers abroad, maintained the contrary.   In that letter, he declares, that even the impressment of seamen, for which many more plausible reasons may be given than for the impressment of soldiers, is repugnant to our constitution.

It might therefore be a sufficient answer to his argument, in the present case, to quote against it the sentiments of its own author, & to place the two opinions before the House, in a state of irreconcilable conflict.   Further comment on either might then be properly forborne, until he should be pleased to inform us which he retracted, & to which he adhered.   But the importance of the subject may justify a further consideration of the argument.

Congress having, by the Constitution a power to raise armies, the Secretary contends that no restraint is to be imposed on the exercise of this .power, except such as is expressly stated in the written letter of the instrument. In other words, that Congress may execute its powers, by any means it chooses, unless such means are particularly prohibited. But the general nature & object of the Constitution impose as rigid a restriction on the means of exercising power, as could be done by the most explicit injunctions. · It is the first principle applicable to such a case, that no construction shall be admitted which impairs the general nature & character of the instrument. A free constitution of Government is to be construed upon free principles, & every branch of its provisions is to receive such an interpretation as is full of its general spirit. No means are to be taken by implication, which would strike us absurdly, if expressed. And what would have been more absurd, than for this constitution to have said, that to secure the great blessings of liberty it gave to Government an uncontrolled power of military conscription? Yet such is the absurdity which it is made to exhibit, under the commentary of the Secretary of War.

But it is said, that it might happen that an army would not be raised by voluntary enlistment, in which case the power to raise armies would be granted in vain, unless they might be raised by compulsion. If this reasoning could prove any thing, it would equally show, that whenever the legitimate powers of the Constitution should be so badly administered as to cease to answer the great ends intended by them, such new powers may be assumed or usurped, as any existing administration may deem expedient. This is a result of his own reasoning, to which the Secretary does not profess to go. But it is a true result. For if it is to be assumed, that all powers were granted, which might by possibility become necessary, & that Government itself is the judge of this possible necessity, then the powers of Government are precisely what it chooses they should be. Apply the same reasoning to any other power granted to Congress, & test its accuracy by the result. Congress has power to borrow money. How is it to exercise this power? Is it confined to voluntary loans? There is no express limitation to that effect, &, in the language of the Secretary, it might happen, indeed, it has happened, that persons could not be found willing to lend. Money might be borrowed then in any other mode. In other words, Congress might resort to a *forced* loan. It might take the money of any man, by force, & give him in exchange Exchequer notes or Certificate of Stock. Would this be quite constitutional, Sir? It is entirely within the reasoning of the Secretary, & it is a result of his argument, outraging the rights of individuals in a far less degree, than the practical consequences which he himself draws from it. A compulsory loan is not to be compared, in point of enormity, with a compulsory military service.

If the Secretary of War has proved the right of Congress to enact a law enforcing a draft of men out of the Militia into the regular army, he will at any time be able to prove, quite as clearly, that Congress has power to create a Dictator. The arguments which have helped him in one case, will equally aid him in the other. The same reason of a supposed or possible state necessity, which is urged now, may be repeated then, with equal pertinency & effect.

Sir, in granting Congress the power to raise armies, the People have granted all the means which are ordinary & usual, & which are consistent with the liberties & security of the People themselves; & they have granted no others. To talk about the unlimited power of the Government over the means to execute its authority, is to hold a language which is true only in regard to despotism. The tyranny of Arbitrary Government consists as much in its means as in its ends; & it would be a ridiculous & absurd constitution which should be less cautious to guard against abuses in the one case than in the other. All the means & instruments which a free Government exercises, as well as the ends & objects which it pursues, are to partake of its own essential character, & to be conformed to its genuine spirit. A free Government with arbitrary means to administer it is a contradiction; a free Government without adequate provision for personal security is an absurdity; a free Government, with an uncontrolled power of military conscription, is a solecism, at once the most ridiculous & abominable that ever entered into the head of man.

Sir, I invite the supporters of the measures before you to look to their actual operation. Let the men who have so often pledged their own fortunes & their own lives to the support of this war, look to the wanton sacrifice which they are about to make of their lives & fortunes. They may talk as they will about substitutes, & compensations, & exemptions. It must come to the draft at last. If the Government cannot hire men voluntarily to fight its battles, neither can individuals. If the war should continue, there will be no escape, & every man's fate, & every man's life will come to depend on the issue of the military draught. Who shall describe to you the horror which your orders of Conscription shall create in the once happy villages of this country? Who shall describe the distress & anguish which they will spread over those hills & valleys, where men have heretofore been accustomed to labor, & to rest in security & happiness. Anticipate the scene, Sir, when the class shall assemble to stand its draft, & to throw the dice for blood. What a group of wives & mothers, & sisters, of helpless age & helpless infancy, shall gather round the theatre of this horrible lottery, as if the stroke of death were to fall from heaven before their eyes, on a father, a brother, a son or an husband. And in a majority of cases, Sir, it will be the stroke of death. Under present prospects of the continuance of the war, not one half of them on whom your conscription shall fall, will ever return to tell the tale of their sufferings. They will perish of disease & pestilence, or they will leave their bones to whiten in fields beyond the frontier. Does the lot fall on the father of a family? His children, already orphans, shall see his face no more. When they behold him for the last time, they shall see him lashed & fettered, & dragged away from his own threshold, like a felon & an outlaw. Does it fall on a son, the hope & the staff of aged parents. That hope shall fail them. On that staff they shall lean no longer. They shall not enjoy the happiness of dying before their children. They shall totter to their grave, bereft of their offspring, & unwept by any who inherit their blood. Does it fall on a husband? The eyes which watch his parting steps may swim in tears forever. She is a wife no longer. There is no relation so tender or so sacred, that, by these accursed measures, you do not propose to violate it. There is no happiness so perfect, that you do not propose to destroy it. Into the paradise of domestic life you enter, not indeed by temptations & sorceries, but by open force & violence.

But this father, or this son, or this husband goes to the camp. With whom do you associate him? With those only who are sober & virtuous & respectable like himself? No, Sir. But you propose to find him companions in the worst men of the worst sort. Another Bill lies on your table offering a bounty to deserters from your enemy. Whatever is most infamous in his ranks you propose to make your own. You address yourselves to those who will hear you advise them to perjury and treason. All who are ready to set Heaven & earth at defiance at the same time, to violate their oaths, & run the hazard of capital punishment,

& none others, will yield to your solicitations. And these are
they whom you are allowing to join your ranks, by holding out
to them inducements & bounties with one hand, while with the
other you are driving thither the honest & worthy members of
your own community, under the lash & scourge of conscription.
In·the line of your army, with the true levelling of despotism,
you propose a promiscuous mixture of the worthy & the worth-
less, the virtuous & the profligate; the husbandman, the merchant, the mechanic of your own country, with the beings whom
war selects from the excess of European population, who possess neither interests, feelings or ˙character in common with your
own people, & who have no other recommendation to your notice
than their propensity to crimes.

Nor is it, Sir, for the defense of his own house & home, that
he who is the subject of military draft is to perform the task
allotted to him.   You will put him upon a service equally foreign to his interests & abhorrent to his feelings.   With his aid
you are to push your purposes of conquest.   The battles which
he is to fight are the battles of invasion; battles which he detests
perhaps & abhors, less from the danger & the death that gather
over them, & the blood with which they drench the plain, than
from the principles in which they have their origin.   Fresh from
the peaceful pursuits of life, & yet a soldier but in name, he is
to be opposed to veteran troops, hardened under every scene,
inured to every privation & disciplined in every service.   If, Sir,
in this strife he fall—if, while ready to obey every rightful command of Government, he is forced from home against right, not
to contend for the defence of his country, but to prosecute a
miserable & detestable project of invasion, & in that strife he
fall, 'tis murder.   It may stalk above the cognizance of human
law, but in the sight of Heaven it is murder; & though millions
of years may roll away, while his ashes & yours lie mingled together in the earth, the day will yet come, when his spirit & the
spirits of his children must be met at the bar of omnipotent justice.   May God, in his compassion, shield me from any partici-
˙pation in the enormity of this guilt.

I would ask, Sir, whether the supporters of these measures
have well weighed the difficulties of their undertaking.   Have
they considered whether it will be found easy to execute laws,
which bear such marks of despotism on their front, & which will
be so productive of every sort & degree of misery in their execution?   For one, Sir, I hesitate not to say, that they can not be

executed. No law professedly passed for the purpose of compelling a service in the regular army, nor any law, which under color of military draft, shall compel men to serve in the army, not for the emergencies mentioned in the Constitution, but for long periods, & for the general objects of war, can be carried into effect. In my opinion, it ought not to be carried into effect. The operation of measures thus unconstitutional & illegal ought to be prevented, by a resort to other measures which are both constitutional & legal. It will be the solemn duty of the State Governments to protect their own authority over their own Militia, & to interpose between their citizens & arbitrary power. These are among the objects for which the State Governments exist; & their highest obligations bind them to the preservation of their own rights & the liberties of their people. I express these sentiments here, Sir, because I shall express them to my constituents. Both they & myself live under a Constitution which teaches us, that "the doctrine of non-resistance against arbitrary power & oppression, is absurd, slavish, & destructive of the good & happiness of mankind." [1] With the same earnestness with which I now exhort you to forbear from these measures, I shall exhort them to exercise their unquestionable right of providing for the security of their own liberties.

In my opinion, Sir, the sentiments of the free population of this country are greatly mistaken here. The nation is not yet in a temper to submit to conscription. The people have too fresh & strong a feeling of the blessings of civil liberty to be willing thus to surrender it. You may talk to them as much as you please, of the victory & glory to be obtained in the Enemy's Provinces; they will hold those objects in light estimation, if the means be a forced military service. You may sing to them the song of Canada Conquests in all its variety, but they will not be charmed out of the remembrance of their substantial interests, & true happiness. Similar pretences, they know, are the graves in which the liberties of other nations have been buried, & they will take warning.

Laws, Sir, of this nature can create nothing but opposition. If you scatter them abroad, like the fabled serpents' teeth, they will spring up into armed men. A military force cannot be raised, in this manner, but by the means of a military force. If administration has found that it can not form an army without

---

[1] New Hampshire Bill of Rights.

conscription, it will find, if it venture on these experiments, that it can not enforce conscription without an army. The Government was not constituted for such purposes. Framed in the spirit of liberty, & in the love of peace, it has no powers which render it able to enforce such laws. The attempt, if we rashly make it, will fail; & having already thrown away our peace, we may thereby throw away our Government.

Allusions have been made, Sir, to the state of things in New England, &, as usual, she has been charged with an intention to dissolve the Union. The charge is unfounded. She is much too wise to entertain such purposes. She has had too much experience, & has too strong a recollection of the blessings which the Union is capable of producing under a just administration of Government. It is her greatest fear, that the course at present pursued will destroy it, by destroying every principle, every interest, every sentiment, & every feeling, which have hitherto contributed to uphold it. Those who cry out that the Union is in danger are themselves the authors of that danger. They put its existence to hazard by measures of violence, which it is not capable of enduring. They talk of dangerous designs against Government, when they are overthrowing the fabric from its foundations. They alone, Sir, are friends to the union of the States, who endeavor to maintain the principles of civil liberty in the country, & to preserve the spirit in which the Union was framed.[1]

(To Ezekiel Webster.[2])

WASHINGTON. Jan. 22. 1815

* * *

I have sent you Stockton's and Ward's speeches; also my little talk about the bank.[3] My conscription speech must rest till another day. * * *

D. WEBSTER.

---

[1] See Private Correspondence, vol. i., p. 248. In this letter to Ezekiel, Webster says "after the best reflection which I have been able to bestow" he has decided not to publish this speech on the conscription bill. It is merely mentioned in the Register of Congressional Debates.

[2] Daniel Webster to Ezekiel Webster, "Private Correspondence of Daniel Webster," vol. i., p. 250.

[3] Speech on the incorporation of a bank of the United States, Jan. 2, 1815. The President vetoed the bill.

(To Moody Kent, Esq.)

Dear Sir, [Washington] Dec 22. [1814]

I am glad to hear that that creature will resign his Office, for the good of the State and People. I cannot say whether I would or not accept the office if offered— I was once rather in a temper for it, but of late my opinion is somewhat altered— My hope would be, that if Mr. F. resigns no nomination should be made until there is a new Council. I should not expect H.[1] to agree to any thing that was proper; & therefore think the Govr. should omit the nomination. My indifference to the office does not arise from any wish to be here. I do not intend spending another winter in this Great Dismal.

Who are the People for, for Govr?— If it be Mr. Mason, let them have him—nominate him— I do not think he would refuse, in these perilous times.

We have passed most of the Taxes thro' the House of Reps— A permanent Annual Land Tax of 6 millions is in its last reading this morning.

Things look very bad here, & I confess I have no expectation of their growing better while this War lasts.— The *People* *cannot* pay the Taxes proposed; especially in the South— The Govt. *cannot* execute a Conscription Law, if it should try— It cannot enlist soldiers— It cannot borrow money—what can it do?—

The Govt. *cannot last,* under this war & in the hands of these men another twelve month— Not that opposition will break it down, but it will break itself down. It will go out— This is my sober opinion.

We have had sundry good speeches, which I shall send you in time— I am obliged to you for all your favors— I earnestly beg you to write oftener—letting me know all about the local news, temper of the people &c

Ever Yrs D. W.

(To Moody Kent.)

Dear Sir, WASHINGTON Jan 14— [1815]

I have just recd yours of the 2d & 6th together— I am

---

[1] Probably Isaac Hill.

greatly *surprised* at the resolution taken at the Meeting at Concord— It seems to be a part of the never ending troubles & embarrassments of our State politics— I hope those concerned will *consider*, & re-*consider* their determination— If my information, which is pretty general, is not altogether incorrect, *schism* would certainly follow that nomination—

I have not time this day to say more—but will [write] you again soon— In the mean time I have no objection to your saying to any body, you may think proper, my opinion on this. I am sure it is also the opinion of others here much better entitled to give an opinion than myself— Whether we are all of that opinion I cannot say, but will inquire & let you know. I thought it *settled* & *decided* last June that we were to have a new Candidate for Governor— but it seems nothing can be decided, in the politics of our State.—

In haste Yrs—

D. W.

Nothing yet decisive of the fate of N. Orleans—considerable reinforcements were likely to arrive in season—

(To Hon. Moses P. Payson.)

BOSTON.[1] Oct. 10. 1816.

Dear Sir,

Mrs Webber the respectable widow of the late President of Hanover College, desires me to inquire of you, about some wild lands, taxes &c. in your country. She says she wrote you, sometime ago, enclosing money, & never having heard from you, she is anxious to learn whether her letter miscarried.

I learn [that] Mr Olcott is to be in this place next week, & I hope he will be prepared to adjust my affairs with your "Institution" as Bro. Sprague used to call the Bank. From the symptons which I thought manifested themselves in Rock.[2] County, it appeared to me, that the Feds. in N. H. *have the coming Election in their power*. I do not believe it possible to heal the divisions in & about Portsmouth. I think the *Judge* will not obtain all the Democratic votes in Rockingham, by a great many.

---

[1] In August of 1816 Webster removed from Portsmouth, N. H., to Boston. His first residence was on Mt. Vernon St., at the summit of Beacon Hill.
[2] Rockingham.

It would be a thing to be remembered, & rejoiced at if the Federalists, by a little vigor & exertion, should carry their Ticket.

Yrs.

D. Webster.

(To Jeremiah Mason.[1])

Boston Oct. 29th 1816

Dear Sir

M^{rs}. Webster thinks she cannot be ready for her departure till Monday the 11th & I should think that would be in tolerable season as it w^d give us three full weeks. My plan is to make some bargain for myself & wife to be conveyed to Hartford, independent of your carriage. It is a long & heavy road to Hartford, & I should not think it would be well to add anything to the burden of your new horses, at their first setting out, & over so hilly a road. I can easily take either a hack, or a gig, & in the last case send our baggage by stage. It will be three days, to Hartford, by way of Worcester, & Stafford—& not much less on any road. One day from Hartford to New Haven, & two thence to New York. We shall then have a week to go to & stay in Philadelphia, & another to get to Washington. If we go from here the 7th. or 8th. (Thursday or Friday) as you propose, we shall find ourselves in Connecticut *at a time of the week*, when we could not travel, if we would.

I have written M^r. Coyle, & rec^d. an answer. He is afraid of turning off his old boarders—at least he says so,—& thinks he cannot take us. You know the true reason. Do you know much or any thing of M^{rs}. Hyers? It is the house where Hopkinson & Sargeant lodged last winter. Possibly, when at Philadelphia, we can make an arrangement with them. If you think it useful to write to any body else at Washington at present, I

---

[1] Jeremiah Mason and Webster were friends and mutual admirers through life. Webster believed him to be the greatest lawyer in the United States. He was plain and straightforward in speech and undoubtedly greatly influenced Webster's style for the better. See "Bench and Bar of New Hampshire," p. 502, also Curtis' "Life of Webster," index. For Daniel Webster's opinion of Mason's strength intellectually, see Daniel Webster to J. Mason, Feb. 27, 1830. Daniel Webster had been asked to plead against Mason. "If it were an easy and plain case on our side I might be willing to go, but I have some of your pounding in my bones yet, and don't care about any more till that wears out." "Private Correspondence," i, 488.

wish you would do it—or if you desire it, I will write to Coyle, (knowing nobody else there) to be looking out a place conditionally,—that is, if we like it.

Our daughter is yet not well. She has a tumor on her neck which we thought the *mumps* but it has remained too long for that. It has for some days appeared to be better, & we believe it is going off.[1] We have made an arrangement to leave our children with M^rs. Webber, at Cambridge.

We saw Mary on Sunday. She was well and I think not *homesick* Her instructor told me yesterday that she began well.

I am, D Sir, Yours

D. WEBSTER

(To James W. Paige.[2])

WASHINGTON Dec. 1st 1816

Dear Brother,

We reached this place, called a City yesterday, our journey was pleasant and much less fatiguing than I expected.— We have not yet taken permanent lodging but shall in a day or two. We shall be, and indeed are now on the hilly *Capitol* I should say, very near the house where Congress sits, which is a pleasant circumstance. Mr & Mrs Mason my husband and myself make, what is here termed a *Mess*. Indeed there are to be no other lodgers in the house * * * [3]

Mr W. and myself [meant to go] to a little Presbyterian Church this morning, but our dinner was too late to admit of our going, and indeed if it had not been the case Mr W. is too unwell to go out he went to bed when we dined. I hope it is nothing more than a cold and fatigue.— Write to me soon and let me know how you all get along.

Please to remember me to Mr & Mrs Greenleaf and believe me
ever your affectionate
sister   G. WEBSTER.

---

[1] The daughter, Grace, died early in 1817 of consumption.
[2] Mr. Paige was a half-brother of Mrs. Webster. The mother, Rebecca Chamberlain, married, first, the Rev. Elijah Fletcher, of Hopkinton, N. H. Grace Fletcher was the youngest of four children by this marriage. Mrs. Fletcher again married the Rev. Christopher Paige. James W. Paige, to whom this letter was written, was the third son of this marriage. He became a successful merchant in Boston. See Curtis' " Life of Webster," vol. i, p. 83.
[3] Unimportant matter omitted.

(To James W. Paige.)

My dear Brother, WASHINGTON Dec. 14 1816—
   *   *   *[1] We are in very good health, and the City upon acquaintance is more pleasant than I expected I have twice been to see the ruins of the Capitol it was more splendid than I had imagined; the external which is of stone is entire except the windows; there is considerable remains yet of the architecture, tho broken and defaced. It looks as if it would be at least the work of this generation to repair and complete the whole. There are a number of artisans employed in carving stone; foreigners both French and Italians. There were several at work on the cap of pillars, we inquired how long it would take to complete one cap and they said two months or perhaps longer. The Capitol is directly in front of our lodgings and if Congress sat there it would add much to our amusement to see them pass and re-pass. *   *   *[1]

    and believe me ever Your affectionate

          Sister G WEBSTER

(To Jeremiah Mason.)

Dear Sir BOSTON June 28 1817
   I believe your reasons for resigning are tolerably good,[2] & yet I could have wished that you should have remained. It is, I think, very much to be desired that somebody should be in each House who would be capable of making out a proper course for Federalists to pursue, in those emergencies which will probably arise, in a year or two.

   I fear Mr. King will follow your example, & leave the Senate. Who remains, fit to prescribe any course to us?— I thought also that the few Federalists in N. H. who have much intelligence on the subject, were desirous that you should remain, & that you might, under the circumstances, decide a doubtful question by a regard to their satisfaction & gratification.

   Nevertheless, it is true, that very little political interest exists any where, & that the sacrifices which your situation in Congress required were very great.

---

[1] Trifles about the children omitted.

[2] Mr. Mason acted for four years as Senator from New Hampshire and then resigned.

M[r]. Otis[1] it is said, is balancing, between his two places.   He may try to get thro' next winter, without relinquishing either, but in the end, he must probably quit one, & I have little doubt it will be his seat in the Senate.   Did you know that Hunter was gone to England?—   He has been gone a month.   Has he any object in it? [2]

M[r]. Lloyd is in Philadelphia.   The meetings of the Directors of U S Bank, when they propose to make new Branches &c, is sometime in July, but I cannot ascertain when.   They have a quorum, always, in Philad[a]. and can meet at any time.

I wish you would make Roberts continue his Foul & Lawrence cause till Feb. 9th.   As you will now be at that term, I suppose he can have no great objection.   It would be very convenient for us to have this agreement made, as I do not think we can probably be prepared, at any rate, & it w[d] put M[r]. F. who wishes to attend the trial himself to very great inconvenience.

I found that the College people[3] thought that you made a strong impression, in their cause.   It would be a queer thing if Gov. P's[4] Court should refuse to execute his Laws.   I am afraid there is no great hope of their disobedience to the powers that made them.

I am coming down the coast pretty soon.   I cannot answer for M[rs]. W.   She has a tour to Monadnock in head, where she may be detained some time.

We see Mary sometimes but not as often as we wish.   You have her approbation very decidedly in resolving to quit W.   We talk of nothing but the President's visit,[5] in relation to which we have as much folly as heart could wish.

Yr's always

D WEBSTER

(To Hon. Jeremiah Mason.)

BOSTON, Dec. 8. 1817.

Dear Sir,

Judge Smith has written for a form of citation in the College[6] cause; which I shall send him & write to him for his minutes.

---

[1] Harrison Gray Otis, Senator from Massachusetts.
[2] William Hunter, Senator from Rhode Island (?).
[3] Dartmouth College.
[4] Plummer, Governor of New Hampshire.
[5] Monroe visited New England in 1817.
[6] Dartmouth College Case.   See Curtis' "Life of Webster," vol. i, p. 163.

My wish is to see both him & you, before I go to Washington.
If I should not be kept in town by the Court, as I do not expect
to, I intend seeing you about Christmas or New Year. Every
body will expect me at Washington to deliver the Exeter argument. Therefore the Exeter argument must be drawn out before I go. I will spend a day or two on this subject at Portsmouth or Exeter, if you incline that I should do so.

We must have Richardson's[1] opinion a little before hand if we
can, that we may consider its weak points if there be any such.

Gore & Pierce has not disappointed me. There is not one of
them that I would trust a sixpence with.

I am sorry our College cause goes to Washington on *one*
point only. What do you think of an action in some Court of
the U. States that shall raise all the objections to the acts in
question? Such a suit could easily be brought, that is jurisdiction could easily be given to the Court of the U. States by bringing in a Vermont party.

Yrs.
Dan^L. Webster.

(To Rev. Francis Brown.[2])

Washington March 11. 1818.

Dear Sir,

Our Case came on yesterday,[3]— I opened the argument, and
occupied almost the whole of the sitting in stating the burden of
our complaints.

M^r. Holmes followed and stated the following as his propositions.

1. This Court has no jurisdiction, because the parties do not
live in different states— (we never put the jurisdiction on that
ground)—

2. That the grant of 1769 was not a *Contract*; but the trustees merely officers of Government under the King—.

3. That all Corporations, created by the King, were dissolved
by the revolution.

4. That if the charter were a *contract*, the acts do not *impair*
it.—

---

[1] Wm. M. Richardson, Chief Justice of the Superior Court of New Hampshire.

[2] President and trustee of Darmouth College, successor of Wheelock.

[3] Darmouth College Case.

We have heard him on his three first heads— He is to take up the fourth this morning.— Thus far, there is nothing new or formidable developed.

(all *stuff*)

M^r. Wirt is to follow M^r. Holmes. *He* is a man of talents, and will no doubt make the best of his case—

[part lost] M^r. Hopkinson is to reply, and will make up for all my deficiencies, which were numerous.—

Yours of the 28. Feb. I received this morning. I am glad a suit is to be brought— I am very much inclined to think the Court *will not* give a judgement this term. It is therefore most essential to have an action in which all the questions arise. Pray, therefore take care, that a *proper* action *be properly* commenced, and in the earliest season—in the Circuit Court of N. H.

All I shall at present add is, that from present appearances, I have an *increased* confidence that in the *end* Justice will be done in this cause— M^r. Hopkinson has entered into this case with great zeal,, and will do all that man can do.— [Part lost.] say nothing about *that,* till you hear from me further

Yours truly

D. WEBSTER

(To Jeremiah Mason.)

BOSTON June 29th 1818

Dear Sir

M^rs. Webster has a letter from M^rs. Mason this morning, in which she says nothing as to the *time* of being this way— I have a little occasion, partly of business, & partly for the ride, to go to the Western Counties—say, the first of next week, to be gone 10 or 12 days— I would not go, however, if your arrangements are to be here within that time, as I prefer, very much, our Sandwich expedition & would not let this ride, if I take it, interfere with it. M^rs. W. will not go with me— Be good en° to let me know how you are, & whether you have fixed any plan & time &c

I see that P. is chosen Senator & Bell to be Govr.[1] —This I think, much better than could have been expected— Plummer seems to have been laughed out of the whole—

---

[1] At the New Hampshire Republican legislative caucus in June, Samuel Bell was nominated for Governor and Governor Plumer for United States Senate.

We have no news.   Judge Story's Court was here three days last week— we argued the question of law which I mentioned to you.   The Judge gave no opinion— I think we shall get a favorable decision; viz to this effect: "that if the next of Kin of one domiciled in India & dying there, be here; & funds be found here, which are an undevised surplus (a will having been made in India) and such funds, here be in the hands of an adm'r with the will annexed; and the funds be not necessary for any purpose of the Will in India, nor to pay debts—the Court will decree the adm'r here to distribute; it being a clear case, that the Plf. would be Entitled to distribution in India, if she were to follow the fund there—"

Nothing else of importance was done.   The Judge promised to come & spend a day with me when you should be in town—

Let me hear from you

Yrs

D WEBSTER

(To Jacob McGaw.[1])

July 27, 1818.

"I send you, with great cheerfulness, a sketch of our views of the case in the question about Dartmouth College.   I have never allowed myself to indulge any great hopes of success; but, if even a few such men as Judge Wilde should think that we had made out our case, it would repay the labor.   If you should think there is any merit in the manner of the argument, you must recollect that it is drawn from materials furnished by Judge Smith and Mr. Mason, as well as from the little contributed by myself."

(To Dr. Cyrus Perkins.)

BOSTON Nov. 28. 1818.

Dear Sir,

I am obliged to you for a copy of your ingenious & well written Eulogy on Judge Woodward.[2]   I have but a single fault to find with it; & in regard to that many others would no doubt

---

[1] Taken from the publication called " Webster Centennial," p. 123.
[2] Wm. H. Woodward, secretary of Board of Trustees of Dartmouth College, died Aug. 9, 1818.

differ from me.   The French rhetoricians have a maxim, that, in eloquence, *nothing is beautiful which is not true*.   I doubt a good deal whether the two last paragraphs on your tenth page would bear the test of this rule of rhetoric.— That point, however, being disposed of, according to every man's taste (& there are a great many whose taste, in matters of this sort, does not approve the rule before mentioned) the performance is one which I think does you credit.

I suppose you know what Mrs. Woodward's intention is, relative to the cause at Washington.   The law of the U. States makes provision for summoning Excrs. & Admrs. in such cases; but I do not know, at present, whether the summons must come from the Court at Washington, or whether some equivalent notice may not be given before Court, & have the same effect.   In the first case, some delay would be necessarily created, which, I suppose, is not desirable to either party.

Will there be any agent of the University, at Washington, in Feb'y, authorized to appear for Mrs W. or not, according to circumstances?— One would think this would be very convenient & useful—   If Mrs W. has no motive for not disclosing her intentions in this respect, I should be glad you would write me on the subject—   If she has, of course I wish no information.—   If I do not learn that Mrs W. intends to authorize an appearance for her at W. I incline to think that we must take some step on the subject soon—

Yours
D WEBSTER.

(To Jeremiah Mason.)

WASHINGTON Feb. 24. 1819

Dear Sir

Since I wrote you a day or two since we have been talking a little about the College causes.   In the action ag^t. Woodward, judg't is rendered, *nunc pro tunc*, as of last term.   The other causes will be remanded, without argument or discussion here. If no alteration shall be made in the Verdict, the Circuit Court will know what judg't to render.   If the other side should be inclined to attempt to make a different case, he must offer his evidence & rely on his bill of exceptions, if the evidence should be ruled out, as being immaterial—

In the mean time the opinions in the first cause will be published, & it is not probable that Counsel will see anything left, whereon to maintain further contest. I thought it, upon the whole, a great point gained, to make this arrangement & avoid further discussion here. If they move to set aside this verdict, it will probably only be granted upon condition of acceding to all the facts, on our part, already in the verdict— This will secure us against the expense & inconvenience of going thro our proofs again. But I am inclined to think, that when the Election is over, there will be no great inclination to keep up the contest,— Our Bank argument goes on[1]— & threatens to be long.— Nothing new respecting Bell's cause

Yours as usual

D. WEBSTER

(To Jeremiah Smith.[2])

WASHINGTON Feb 28. 1819

Dear Sir

Judgment is entered in Trustees vs Woodward, as of last term, that the said Trustees do recover of the said Woodward the aforesaid sum of twenty thousand Dollars, so found & assessed as aforesaid; & I have in my bag a mandate to the Superior Court of Judicature of the State of New Hampshire to carry this judgment into Execution. So much for that cause, & the *second argument* therein expected—

As to the other causes.[3] Messrs Pinkney & Wirt have been very much pressed by the agents & partisans here to argue one of these causes, upon the ground of the *new facts*. By the time however, that we approached near the causes, they saw difficulties and their zeal began to cool. It was impossible to agree on definite facts. It was hardly possible to expect any different result than had already taken place, from another argument without new facts. Some of the opinions of the Judges appeared to go so far as to be decisive against them, even taking the new facts

[1] M'Culloch v. State of Maryland. Webster and Pinckney were counsels for M'Culloch. See McMaster U. S. Hist. vol. iv. p. 497.
[2] One of New Hampshire's greatest lawyers. It was said of him that he found New Hampshire law without form and void, and he reduced it to order and harmony. Webster said of him, "he knows more about law than I do or ever shall." See "Bench and Bar of New Hampshire." p. 58.
[3] That is in connection with the Dartmouth College controversy.

for granted. At the same time we heard here the echoes of the clamor in N. H.— that the cause had not been heard on its true facts. I called up the subject a day or two before we should have reached the cause & desired to know from the Counsel whether it was expected to argue one of those causes. This brought on a conversation between Bench & Bar which finally terminated in this that the causes should be remanded by consent; that Def'ts might, in Circuit Court, move to set aside this Verdict if they should be so advised, when the opinion of the Judges in Woodward's case should be read & known— I found this course would be *agreeable* & adopted it at once. In truth I did not want a second argument here, upon an *assumption* of facts. If I do not misjudge we shall have no difficulty in the Circuit Court. We shall not, I trust, be called on to argue on any more special Verdicts— If the Def'dts do not acquiesce in any opinions of the Judge, they must take their course by bill of exceptions.

We are not yet thro. the Bank question. Martin has been *talking 3 ds*— Pinkney replies tomorrow & that finishes— I set out for home next day—

Always with sincere regard yrs

D. WEBSTER

Inter nos:

I do not believe any body expects the College Question ever to come here again. My impression is, that Council here are glad of a convenient mode of disposing of it quietly.

(To Jeremiah Mason.)

BOSTON April 10. 1819

Dear Sir

My own interest would be promoted by *preventing* the Book.[1] I shall strut well enough in the Washington Report, & if the "Book" should not be published, the world would not know where I borrowed my plumes— But I am still inclined to have the Book— One reason is, that you & Judge Smith may have the credit which belongs to you— Another is, I believe, Judge Story is strongly of opinion it would be a useful work, that

---

[1] "Report of the case of the Trustees of Dartmouth College vs. Wm. H. Woodward," by Timothy Farrar, Boston, 1819.

Wheaton's Reports go only into the hands of Professional men, but that this Book might be read by other Classes— &c &c— If it should be decided, at May term, that another cause should go to Washington, I should be very unwilling to have the book published— but I have hitherto had a strong belief we should finish the actions, at May Court— I think so still, but very probably may be disappointed. I should be for pressing the Judge to adjourn for a short time, rather than continue the causes. I think he will feel the propriety of settling the controversy, as far as may be done.

I shall come down, accidents excepted, & very possibly Mrs. W. may attend the same Court— she has not determined, however, as yet, whether she shall go that Circuit. Solicitor Genl. Davis goes down to try *Bullard vs French*. By what I learn he intends to go to issue on a new premise in that case.

In a newspaper Report, I see that M^r. Justice Bayley, of the Kings bench, said lately "—Debt will not lie by indorsee of a Bill of Exchange vs Acceptor, for want of privity."

Yrs.

D W.

(To Jeremiah Mason.)

Boston May 5. 1819

Dear Sir

We arrived, very safely, last night at 8 Clock. Having found a bit of fresh salmon by the way, & finding also a drop of good wine in our chaise box, we had a sumptuous dinner at Topsfield—

As you have little or nothing to do,— according to your own account of yourself, (except looking after the Book[1]) I want you to think of a question or two, which may arise in *Blakely vs Cabot*.

The plf is described as of *Wilmington*, N. Carolina— &c I suppose the Defdt will, or it is possible he will, plead, that she is not of *Wilmington* &c but of *Boston*. Would such a plea be in *disability of the plf*, or to the Jurisdiction?—If the latter, is a plea to the Jurisdiction, like other pleas in this respect; viz; that if an issue of part be joined in it, & found for the plf, the Judgment is to be peremptory, or in chief?

---

[1] See letter, Daniel Webster to Mason, April 10, 1819.

I have not looked at these questions— but seeing it probable they may arise, I should like to get your notion upon them—

I have not been out to learn the news if there be any

Yrs   D WEBSTER

The action vs Cabot must be tried—   I have a hope that the other may not—   Whatever occurs to you, either on the law of the case, or on the General reasoning ab^t. motives, I sh^d. be glad to hear[1]

(To Jeremiah Mason.)

BOSTON Saturday Evening, [May 1819]

My dear Sir

I learn this moment, that you are chosen a Trustee of D. College.   Under present circumstances, I hope, *earnestly*, you will not decline it.   You can relinquish it when you please; but it will do great good, that you should not refuse it.

It will gratify all good people, that you are chosen; & if you hold it but a year, I trust you will accept it—

Yours as ever

D WEBSTER

(To Jeremiah Mason.)

BOSTON May 27. 1819

Dear Sir

Mr Austin read this morning a mass of papers, about the *new facts*—[2]   The Judge thought there was nothing in them, but has taken the papers for a day or two, to examine them before he gives a formal decision.—   He says, he sees nothing which contradicts any part of the recital of the Charter—   We had not much talk about it—   M^r. A read & stated all he chose to do, & the Judge intimated, that the *new facts* had no bearing on any part of the Courts opinion—   *The Slander causes are settled.* How does the Book come on?—   I believe it will never be finished.

Yrs,

D WEBSTER

---

[1] It is to be noticed that Webster very often sought Mason's advice on legal questions, also that of other friends.

[2] In the Darmouth College case.

(To Henry Baldwin.¹)

WASHINGTON Feb. 15. 1820—

Sir

May I have permission to see you, at such time & place as may
suit your convenience, for the purpose of asking you to correct
a misrepresentation, which seems to have gone abroad, respecting
expressions said to be used by me, in a late conversation with you.
I understand it is reported, that I observed to you, that I considered the question before Congress,² as a question of *political
power* & added [that if the free States could carry this question
No such expression used by you or me³—
now, they could hereafter carry any others.]
I am sure I said nothing, in any degree like this, for I never,
at any time, spoke, or thought of this question, as being a fit
question to be decided on such considerations— After some previous conversation, in which you intimated, I think, (what I had
understood before) that your opinion was against the restriction,⁴ you lamented the agitation of the question now, & thought
it not wise in the Gentlemen from the North to have produced it,
since there was the subjects of the Bankruptcy Bill, & other
subjects deeply interesting to the people of the North towards
which it would be desirable to conciliate the dispositions of the
South— To this my remark, by way of answer, simply was,
that I presumed the people of the North, among other considerations, regarded this question as one which affecting their right
*to an equal weight in the political power of the Government, &
tho't they would not* think it reasonable to be called on to surrender this, in order to obtain any favorable act of Ordinary
Legislation. This observation was in reference to the subject of
representation, which I have always supposed to be one of the
objections to making new slave States. I certainly spoke in reference, *solely*, to this mode, in which political power was to be
affected; & if I was understood in any other sense, I was greatly
misunderstood—
I beg you to be assured that I am quite certain that no inten-
tional misrepresentation could have been made by you. On a
subject however, of so much excitement, I am particularly anx-

¹ Representative in Congress from Pennsylvania.
² The debate in Congress upon the admission of Missouri.
³ The line in italics is in Mr. Baldwin's handwriting and the brackets are his.
⁴ *i. e.*, the prohibition of slavery.

ious that no remark of mine may be misunderstood, & must rely on you to correct an erroneous impression, as far as may be necessary so to do, whether it arose from any inaccuracy in my own expression, or any other cause—

With great respect

Yrs   D. Webster..

(From Henry Baldwin.)

Dear Sir

There was no misapprehension of our conversation— It related to slave representation as the subject was referred to in the Boston Memorial. I did not think of any other meaning to the word political power— There was no allusion to any election or office— In relation to the relative importance of this question and the Bankrupt law, Commerce and manufactures I understood you as expressing your own rather than the opinion of the Northern people

Yours with esteem

Henry Baldwin

(To Jeremiah Mason.)

Boston June 25 1820

Dear Sir

The first I saw or heard of the N. H. Resolutions[1] was in M^r. Hale's paper on Saturday. Who sent them to him I know not, & I believe he was altogether self moved in his remarks on that occasion. I met Judge Story at Nahant on Saturday— he had rec^d. a copy from you & we had it read after dinner— I saw that you had been obliged to be quite guarded & yet the whole argument is in it, & some points are put in a new & striking light. We voted it a good thing very unanimously; but then it was after dinner, when if it had not been as good as it was, our patriotism would have prevailed over our criticism. I like very much your allusion to the unparalled unanimity of the slave holding states in Congress & also your Answer to the Virginia arguments, at the top of page 7.— A very excellent argument,

---

. [1] These resolutions drawn up by Mr. Mason were in answer to "The Virginia Report and Resolutions on the Missouri questions" which had been sent to the New Hampshire Governor.

ag^t the notion that the prohibition affects *Sovereignty*, & one which I have not noticed before, is on the third page—

It was a good achievement to bring the N. H Legislature to these Resolves— I entertain much hope of better times from it; & think you must be satisfied that you did quite right in attending the Session, & taking part in the business of the State—

I regret I could not go to Concord, not however for the reasons you state, but because I wished to see you, on other accounts, & to make some progress in M^r. O', business. When you get over your Concord labors, you must come & see us. I expect to be at home all Summer. Mrs W. will not be able at present to leave home, & we shall be in a state of great leisure, if you will come this way & see us.

M^r. Davis tells me he has shipped your wine

Yrs as ever

D. WEBSTER.

(To Jeremiah Mason.)

BOSTON Nov 12. 1820

My dear Sir

I have not been able to come to any definite conclusion, on the subject of votes for vice President. There seems to be no way, yet found out, of ascertaining how it would be rec^d. at Washington, if the votes here should be given for Mr. Adams.[1] I wish you would see your *friend*, on your way to Concord, & ascertain what he thinks of it. Indeed I know no one more likely to be able to learn from the Gentleman himself, how it would suit. There will be a number of us,[2] of course, in this state, who will not vote for M^r. Tomkins,[3] & we must therefore look up somebody to vote for.—

If you can, without inconvenience, I hope you will see the Ex. Governor, as you go to Concord— It is hardly out of your way, I believe— If you learn anything worth communicating, be good enough to write me. Several of our Electors are members of the Convention, & will be here this week— I shall have some conversation with them, and will write you again.

Our Court is adjourned for a Month; so that we have nothing

---

[1] One of New Hampshire's votes was given for J. Q. Adams for President.
[2] Webster was an elector from Massachusetts.
[3] Daniel T. Tompkins was elected Vice-President.

to do but attend Convention—   I shall follow the course which I intimated to you, & which you approved in relation to my concern with the Convention.—

Mary I believe has written to her Mother today— so that you will learn all the news, if there be any.

With many respects to M^rs. Mason

I am, D^r. Sir.   Yours

D. WEBSTER

(To Jeremiah Mason.)

BOSTON July 11. 1821

Dear Sir

I received the enclosed yesterday.   You will of course have seen that M^r. Gales had even *anticipated* your wishes, & *spoken out* on the subject.   What he said you will observe was printed in the Democratic Paper here yesterday.   It seems to me that all this works kindly, & will have the best effect.—   No one can be at a loss now, I think these things are regarded at Washington.

I learned from Judge Story as well as from Yourself that he intends paying you a visit next week—   I have promised to go with him.   We heard last Evening of the death of M^rs. Webster's Mother.   This will probably prevent her going, but I intend to persuade her to go, if I can.   If she should not, I shall try to pick up some companion— probably I think M^r. Everett.

I expect to see the Judge, on his return from Newport, & will fix on the day—   I can go any day, as our Courts are now thin

Yrs truly   D. W.

(To Jeremiah Mason.)

BOSTON July 15. 1821

Dear Sir

In the Intelligencer of the 11th. you will see some very sound remarks on your Resolutions,[1]   They are from the same source, to which my letter was addressed.   I have also a letter from the same quarter, which I shall show you.   It is quite edifying.

---

[1] The resolutions referred to in the letter, Daniel Webster to Jeremiah Mason, June 25, 1820.

Indeed I will, I think, enclose it,[1] tho' I have hardly had time to run over its contents.

I have not heard from Judge S. since I wrote you last. M^{rs}. Webster thinks if I will put off my journey to Monday the 23rd— she will accompany me. I have therefore concluded so to do,— & shall write to the Judge accordingly. If any alteration of this project takes place, it will be by coming on an *earlier* day— I should like much to ride round Winnipissiokee Lake[2] never having yet seen its Eastern shore— I dare say the Judge would like it— The Ladies might have their choice to remain at Ports^{mo}. or go to the Lake but I think they would prefer going

I shall intimate this project to the Judge

Yrs in haste

D WEBSTER

(To Jeremiah Mason.)

BOSTON Sep. 12. 1821

Dear Sir

I cannot say much about this Bank matter till I see you. The short of this is I recommended the appointments which took place,— partly *because* some of the Gentlemen were *impractible* —[1] tho't good would come of it. I tho't it time to break up a sort of *knot*—

There is no sort of necessity of presenting any claim, at the present Session of Commissioners nor any *utility*, that I am aware of— In many cases it has been done, & in a great many

---

[1] The following letter was enclosed:

Dear Sir

The N. H. resolutions were placed amongst the articles for to-days paper, yesterday while I was absent at the Council. Of this I was not aware last evening, and intended them for Monday. I do not think, however, that their appearance this morning should interfere with your purpose; but it would be well, perhaps, if any reward were now made, that it should be rather more comprehensive than was before intended, or was indispensable, had it accompanied the resolutions. But this you must decide on according to your leisure and inclination. It may be not amiss to mention to you, that a letter (received yesterday in my absence, and which I did not see till this morning) from Mr. Webster urges a particular notice of the resolutions, which are certainly very important at this juncture.

Very respectfully yours
W. W. SEATON

J. C. Calhoun, Esq.   Saturday morning

[2] Winnepiseogee Lake, N. H.

omitted; as convenience dictated. Several have been drawn very well, in Portsm°. by M^r. Cutts— I send you a rough copy of one that happens to lie before me, which was altered in some respects, afterwards, in order to set forth the 'case more exactly, but the *formal part* is such as has been most generally used here. Mr Bliss has gone to Washington, & has carried on a pretty large budget of these claims. I cannot say what it may amount to, but most of the claims here go thr°. my hands— It has given me three weeks of hard work to prepare them,[1] & will call for as many more— Judge Story has given judgment in the Volant case here. On the facts, as presented, he entertains no doubt, that the Volant did no more than she was authorized to do, *with or without letter of Marque* We have one difficulty to meet. *Mr. Gill,* who is a party, really or nominally, in the policy I sent you, was our *best* witness here. I believe however we can supply his place pretty well. It will not probably be possible to have a trial in Oct. at Exeter; & therefore you can exercise your own Judgment, as to sueing at that term. I see no great benefit, in it, but shall leave it to you.

My wife & children are well but have not yet come into Town— We expect to gather ourselves in Somerset Street next week

Yrs

D. WEBSTER

(To Samuel Boyd, Esquire.)

Dear Sir   PHILADELPHIA Jan. 3^d. 1822

I intend to have seen you as I passed through New York on New Year's day, but, having an engagement to be here this evening, I had not time. I wish to say something to you confidentially on a subject of some importance. Perhaps you will think my suggestion out of all boundry of reason: if so, say so.

I understand that Chancellor Kent[2] can remain in office but one year.— What is *he then to do?* Not hearing whether he has answered this question for himself, I proceed to make my suggestion with fear & trembling.

Dart. College has no President & it wants one; & the trustees would be very glad I presume to wait a year, & then appoint the Chancellor if it were not altogether beneath his acceptance.—

---

[1] This year was devoted to legal business. Webster was not in Congress.
[2] This letter is endorsed by Webster's literary executors. "Received from M. Kent, January 16, 1853."

I suppose they could offer him these terms viz.

1. $2.000 Dollars salary
2. A long vacation in the winter, say
   " 3 months, which he might spend
   " where he would desire—
3 An exemption of course, from all clerical labors, such as attendance on prayers &c—: all this to be done by the Theological Professor; the President to be in all respects a layman

Now the reason I have for suggesting this, I derive from conversation with the Trustees, & especially with my brother who is one of them.

I promised him to hint this Subject to the Chancellor or some of his friends.—

I commit this to you.   If the thing be without the reach of all probability, burn this letter & say nothing of it.—   If you think otherwise, I wish you would suggest it to the Chancellor in the way you judge best.

I am now going to *Washington* where I shall be glad to hear from you.

I would thank you to write me soon after receiving this, giving your own opinion

The Trustees meet in February, & I should like to have something to say to them on the subject by that time, if anything is to be said.

If you write to the Chancellor, I wish you would nevertheless in the mean time write me your *own* opinion of the matter.

Yours with true regard—
DAN^L WEBSTER.

(From Ezekiel Webster.[1])

Jany. 28, 1822.

Dear Daniel,

I never did like John Q. Adams.   He must have a very objectionable rival whose election I should not prefer.   I think it would be difficult for any candidate to divide the vote in New England with him.   Although he may not be very popular, yet it seems to be in some degree a matter of necessity to support him, if any man is to be taken from the land of the *Pilgrims*.   I should really prefer Calhoun, Lowndes, Crawford, Clinton &

---

[1] This letter is owned by Edwin W. Sanborn, of New York.

fifty others that I could mention—but this is high matter & it is very uncertain what political feeling may prevail three years hence. I am sorry that there was not a better account from Albany. The course you mention is the only one—that our condition leaves—*& that will not be taken.* At least I fear it.

E. WEBSTER.

(To James W. Paige.)

Dear William WASHINGTON, Feb. 6, 1822.

I rec'd your letter yesterday, & am very glad to hear you are all well. Judge Story & Mr. Coolidge arrived safe, Sunday Eve. The Court is now in session,[1] & together with the *claims* keeps me sufficiently occupied— I send a draft for 100 Dolls—thinking it may be wanted to pay taxes; or for some other good purpose. I hope you look out to keep *good fires,* I have a snug time of it. You seem to have little snow yet, but I dare say I shall find enough when I get home. My present expectation is to be home by the 10th of March—I suppose there will be a summer session of a fortnight, or three weeks, which either Mr. Bliss or myself must attend, and that, I hope, will get us thro' the *thickest* part of the bushes.

Eliza's friends, the Misses Inches, arrived here three days ago. I have called to see them, but they were not at home. Tonight is the President's Drawing Room, where they will see all the glory of Washington— I shall not be able to attend.

Give my love all the household. I believe I owe Mrs. W. several letters—not to mention my great debt to *Eliza*—all which I hope soon to discharge.

Yrs truly,

D. WEBSTER.

(From T. H. Perkins et al.)

BOSTON 18 Oct. 1822.

To The Honorable Daniel Webster,
Dear Sir
We the undersigned having been chosen (at a meeting or

---

[1] Webster did not again enter Congress until December of 1823 after six years' absence. During this absence he greatly increased his fame as a jurist and orator.

delegates from all the wards, held at Concert Hall, on Thursday Evening last') a Committee to acquaint you that at that meeting you were unanimously selected to be recommended to the support of their fellow citizens, to represent the District of Suffolk in the next Congress of the United States,[1]

Your obedient servants
COMMITTEE.

(From Ezekiel Webster.[2])

Feby. 10, 1823.

Dear Daniel,

 * * * We are likely to have fine sport here till after March meeting. The nomination of Judge Woodbury puts Hill into hot water. He has not hesitated in choosing his course—& that is to write against the Judge. I think you will be very much edified in reading the Patriot. It will be very refreshing after a severe day's labor. I look on like a spectator at a bull baiting, pretty indifferent who is the conqueror or the victim— I have no tears to shed for either.

It is for some reasons desirable to have Woodbury elected. He would not be under the influence of Hill & Ayer—Dinsmore would be a man of straw merely. Mr. Hill would be the governor in fact. I am of opinion that the Judge will triumph over the General. This is as it should be. The judicial should be above the military power. Let the event be as it will—we are breaking up into new parties, & probably with more accrimonious & bitter feeling, than ever marked the old.

I am yours truly
EZEKIEL WEBSTER.

(To Jeremiah Mason.)

WASHINGTON, March 25, 1823.

My Dear Sir,—

The Secretary of War has, I believe, directed a prosecution to be commenced in New Hampshire, against a man in Boscawen, for fraud & perjury, in obtaining a pension. I understand that he has authorized the District Atty of N. Hampshire to engage

---

[1] See Curtis' "Life of Webster," vol. i, p. 197. He accepted the nomination and was elected, returning to Congress after six years' absence.
[2] This letter is owned by Edwin W. Sanborn, of New York.

your services in aid of the prosecution.   The person accused &
his connexions, & the circumstances of the case which I believe to
be a very gross one, are all well known to E. Webster, but he
would not willingly act in the case farther than necessity might
seem to require; at least, he would not volunteer—If you send
him a blank Subpoena, with a request to insert the names of such
persons as may know the circumstances, he will find no difficulty
in giving names of witnesses—   I take it to be a case of fraudulent giving away of property, to sons & daughters, by deeds still
retained by the grantor.   It is a flagrant case & it will do good
to look it up.   Any instructions which may be sent to E. Webster he will attend to.   You will understand at once, that the
information comes here from him.   He thought it a case too
bad to be connived at:—but at the same time does not wish to be
officious, in other persons concerns, any farther than a feeling of
duty compels.

I expect to leave this place for home about the 10th of April,
& to be home the 20th—   There has been of course little of interest here, since Congress adjourned.   I believe I understand
the opinions of men, most attentive to the subject, on the prospects & probabilities of the Presidential Election.   It seems to me
to be a case, in which we shall be obliged to take some part, & I
shall be anxious to see you, as soon as I get home.   I do not
think there was ever a moment, in which it was more uncertain
who would—or will—be President than it is now.

If I do not go to the Circuit Court at Portland—which I shall
hardly be in season to do—I shall not see you, at Portsmo so
early as I should wish, & hope you will find it convenient to come
to Boston.

I need not say that I am rejoiced at the election in N. Hampshire.   Saying nothing of the comparative merits of the Candidates, the *means* by which the Caucus nomination was defeated,
gives hope of much future good.   We must divide, into Republicans & Radicals; comprising, in the last class, not merely the
reformers, in Congress, but the *intriguers*—the caucus men—
the hot and Exclusive party men, &c.   It appears to me the
public sentiment is ripe for a distinction of that sort.

Give my love to your wife, & all the children—

Yrs, as ever,

D. WEBSTER.

Smith Thompson will be Judge, if he chooses, & I think he
will choose.

(To Jeremiah Mason.)

Dear Sir   Boston Saturday Morning.

I have yours, & also one from the Judge, this morning.   We
shall not fail to be at your House on Tuesday—

I agree with you entirely about J. Q. A's oration.   Such is
the man.   My impression of that Gentleman's character, tho'
high & favourable in some respects, is, in others, so little satisfactory, that I hardly know what to *wish*, in regard to the future.

I think *all* our prospects are *bad*.   My hopes gave out, last
winter; & since then I have felt as if it were *settled*, that we
shall not at present, or for several years, see such an administration of the Government as we can heartily approve.

I left Mrs. W. & the children at the Blue Hills this Morning.
They are quite well.

                                        Yrs
                                        D. Webster.

_____

(To Jeremiah Mason.[1])

                            Washington Nov. 30. [1823]

It appears to me to be our true policy to oppose all caucuses;
so far our course seems to me to be clear.   Beyond that I do
not think we are bound to proceed at present.   To defeat caucus nominations, or prevent them, and to give the election, where-
ever it can be done, to the people, are the best means of restoring
the body politic to its natural and wholesome state.   *   *   *

                                        D. W.

_____

(To Jeremiah Mason.)

                            Washington Dec. 22, 1823.

My Dr Sir

Will you be kind enough to read in a late No. of the Nat. Int.
a Report of the Judiciary Comtee. of H. R. of last year, on the
Subject of the *Courts;* & write me your opinion, freely, thereon.[2]
Soon after new years day we must report some measure on that

_____

[1] Taken from " Private Correspondence of Daniel Webster," vol. i, p. 330.
[2] See Mason's reply December 29, 1823.

subject; & I should be particularly glad to know what you think of the matter.

I incline to think there will be no caucus at present.   Possibly, the course of one of the candidates has been so much identified with a caucus that some *sort* of a caucus will be convened, during the Session,—but, at this moment, I imagine, it would ill succeed, if attempted.   I cannot help having a half-suspicion that some doubt of Mr. Crawfords *health* is entertained; & that *this* has some effect in the postponement of a caucus.   It is said your Mr. Bartlett[1] is in favor of a caucus.   Your other members agt. it.   I suspect this is true, but I cannot vouch for it.

Yrs always,
D. WEBSTER.

---

[1] Ichabod Bartlett, representative from New Hampshire.

Webster, the National Statesman

WHEN *Webster returned to Congress in 1823, after an absence of some six years, he was free to advance his own broad views upon public questions, as he never had been in his former congressional career. He had hardly been in his seat a month before he delivered the famous "Greek Speech" in defence of a resolution which he had offered, providing, if the President deemed it necessary, for the expenses of a commission to Greece. The Revolution in that land had aroused the sympathy of the American people, and this resolution aimed not to entangle the United States in that conflict, but to express American sympathy. Webster chose in his speech rather to utter for the first time his conception of the destiny of the American Union, than to use for rhetorical ornament the classical memories clinging to the land whose wrongs he displayed. This speech then fitly marked the time when Webster, the National Statesman, succeeded Webster, the Local Politician.*

Within a few months he delivered an able and powerful speech against Clay's tariff bill, which was to inaugurate "the American System." New England's interests were opposed, as yet, to a high protective tariff and Webster argued against that which four years later he was called upon to defend because the government's policy had forced New England into manufacturing and thus fostered her interest in protection. From this somewhat sectional attitude on the tariff Webster turned to a task in which his broad views were of great service. As Chairman of the Judiciary Committee he defeated a jealous attempt to curtail the power of the Supreme Court. In the next session he showed an interest in Internal Improvements which marked him for special favor among the people of the West. He defended in a strong speech a bill to continue the great national turnpike, the Cumberland road.

In the political excitement attending the election of John Quincy Adams by the House of Representatives, Webster played a prominent part. During the preliminary struggle between the

95]

several candidates he had favored Crawford, but, when he came to a decision between Adams and Jackson, a man of Webster's character could not hestitate, and, anyway, the sentiment of New England compelled him to support Adams.

Politics out of the way, Webster turned to the much-needed work, for which he could expect no popular appreciation. The task was the carrying through the "Crimes Act," first codifying the whole body of the Criminal law of the United States—a work in which Justice Story rendered great assistance—and then by an eloquent defense putting it through the House. In striving to do a like service, by pushing through the House a bill for the improvement of the Judiciary, he succeeded, where his influence could be effectual, but the bill was defeated in the Senate. Later he also made a futile attempt to pass a much-needed Bankrupt Law.

Meanwhile his relations with Adams' Administration had been friendly, although he was long kept well-disposed by promises that were never realized. Webster tried in the House to carry out Adams' views in respect to the Panama Congress. He declared unconstitutional the attempt of the House to dictate the conduct of the representatives whom Adams might send, and took occasion to make a clear exposition of the "Monroe Doctrine." Again, when Adams' message concerning Georgia's stubborn opposition to the government in regard to the Creek Indians was attacked by the Southern members, Webster defended the President's attitude with spirit. So valuable did he become to the Administration, that Adams opposed his retirement from the House, when in 1827 he, though reluctantly, was prevailed upon by his friends to permit his election to the Senate.

During the three years that preceded his election to the Senate, he had, in addition to a number of powerful legal arguments and the prosecution of the Spanish claims, distinguished himself in private life by his famous Bunker Hill oration and the eulogy on Adams and Jefferson. His visit to Jefferson in 1824 was an event long cherished in his memory.

Hardly had the senatorial dignity been accepted, when the loss of his wife seemed for the moment to crush him and his ambitions. The excitement of public life, however, proved to be the greatest relief that he found from his sorrow. He was soon deep in affairs and after carrying through a bill for the relief of surviving officers of the Revolution was called upon in this session to defend New England's new interest in protection—a change of attitude for Webster which has already been mentioned. After this tariff had been passed, South Carolina strenuously opposed it and threatened nullification. This theory, fostered by Calhoun and ably defended by Hayne, Webster found opportunity to confute in the course of a debate on the Foot resolution, which, though it referred to the public lands and not the tariff, aroused the opposition of the South, and led directly to a debate on nullification. This famous "Reply to Hayne" marks the height of Webster's powers. He there set forth with consummate power the folly of nullification as a constitutional mode of evading the laws made by Congress and approved by the Supreme Court; and he uttered in words that still ring in the Nation's ears his love of the Union.

The next few years of stress, out of which came the combination of interests creating the Whig party, were of greatest moment in deciding Webster's future. They were to decide whether he was to be drawn into party relations with Clay and Adams or with Jackson, Benton and Van Buren. At first there seemed no doubt, because of the very character of the men themselves. Webster's whole past, too, bound him to support the effort to renew the United States Bank, and for a time he was in all things opposed to Jackson. He defeated an administration amendment to give the states authority to tax the bank, and, when Jackson vetoed the bill, Webster denounced the veto. Then, though not in spite, he attacked Jackson's nomination of Van Buren as ambassador to England. But events at once arose which drew Webster into sympathy with Jackson. In November of 1832 South Carolina passed her nullifying acts, and Jackson turned upon her with a proclamation threatening to use the whole power of the Executive to bring her to terms. Webster sustained Jackson in the effort to get through Congress a force bill, which would give him means to coerce South Carolina, and, when Clay offered a compromise tariff which would meet the demands of the recalcitrant state, Webster, on grounds of expediency as well as for economic reasons, opposed. While yet both bills were undecided, Calhoun made a powerful argument for nullification which Webster, sustaining Jackson, effectively answered, and then in a strong speech, approved by the Executive, opposed the Compromise Tariff on its final passage.

Thus for a time Webster seemed Jackson's powerful ally, but the latter's attitude on the bank question soon drew Webster away from him. When Jackson caused the removal of the government deposits from the United States Bank and Clay had offered resolutions condemning the President's action, Webster, submitting like resolutions from Boston, made a speech approving the condemnation. During the long controversy which followed, Webster, attacking Jackson's financial policy, made a series of speeches which no American statesman except Hamilton could have matched. They were exhaustive and masterful in a high degree. Jackson's protest against the action of the Senate was answered by Webster in a most conclusive manner, discussing the powers and duties of the Executive. By this time the estrangement between Webster and Jackson was complete.

In the following presidential campaign, Webster was proposed as a candidate by several states, and in Massachusetts, in spite of his withdrawal from the contest, was given all the state's fourteen electoral votes. In 1837 he made an extended tour of the West, being received with enthusiasm everywhere as he had previously been in 1833. At this time he seriously considered retiring from the Senate, giving as a reason the need of recuperating his finances, which had greatly suffered by his devotion to his duties as a senator. He was dissuaded by everyone from resigning, and yielded to the general wish. After announcing his decision, he was given an enthusiastic reception by his friends in New York, where in Niblo's Garden he delivered one of his most famous speeches, in which he outlined his policy in the problems then before the country. His views on Slavery and his opposition to the Annexation of Texas were expressed in and out of the Senate at this time. He was opposed to the Abolitionists, but when Calhoun offered a resolution to the effect that Congress had no right to interfere with slavery in the District of Columbia, he exposed the fallacy of such a theory and took occasion to review Calhoun's political conduct which he said was aimed at the overthrow of the Constitution. He at this time doubted the wisdom of trying to conciliate the South.

In 1839 Webster made a long desired journey to England, and, upon his return, although he had been nominated for the presidency by the Massachusetts Whigs, yielded to the general wish throughout the country and entered the campaign for Harrison. Everybody wanted to hear him, and he spoke until, as he wrote his wife, his throat was sore. At Saratoga, Bunker Hill, and in New York and Richmond he made the greatest efforts, denouncing and arraigning the recent financial and other errors of the Democratic party.

As a natural result of his great services, he was urged by Harrison to become Secretary of State, and accepted. Upon the death of Harrison, Webster remained as a member of Tyler's cabinet. When Congress reached its open rupture with Tyler over the attempted financial reforms, and when the other members of the cabinet resigned, Webster remained, because the difficulties which confronted the country in its foreign relations seemed to need his masterful hand in order to prevent war. The new material here presented is especially rich in details of Webster's work in settling the several controversies; the closely connected "Caroline" and "McLeod" affairs; the North Eastern Boundary dispute; and the Impressment question. He also secured a long-needed extradition treaty and settled the controversy which had arisen with England because of her insistence upon the "Right of Search" in her attempts to stop the African Slave Trade. While engaged in this work he was incessantly urged by the Whigs to resign, and, when persuaded by his friends, he delivered his famous "Hard to Coax" speech in Faneuil Hall, he was viciously attacked by the press for his temerity. There was at that time a plan to send him to England on a mission concerning Oregon, the only great controversy with England which he had left unsettled, but the Senate disapproved of the plan. In May of 1843 Webster resigned his office and was once more a private citizen with no great desire to return to public life.

A year later when Clay was nominated for the Presidency, after Webster had, in a speech at Andover, approved of him and the Whig principles, the party forgot its anger over the cabinet episode and took Webster again into favor. There was a demand that he return to the Senate, and once more he yielded. During the campaign for Clay he had again expressed his opposition to the annexation of Texas, and upon his return to the Senate offered a resolution that war ought not to be waged with Mexico for the purpose of getting new territory to be added to the Union, and that Mexico ought to be told that the United States did not want her territory. He voted for the Wilmot Proviso and claimed to have invented the doctrine.

In 1848 Webster seemed to be the available leader, but, much as the people admired him, he was not popular, and Taylor, the miliary hero, was chosen, though Webster, on the early ballots of the convention, received votes from Maine, New Hampshire, Massachusetts and New York. He was disappointed and at first was undecided whether to support Taylor or not, but decided to be generous.

Though his record proved him to be a Free Soiler, yet his conservatism kept him a Whig. His real disapproval of Taylor might have furnished an opportunity to leave the Whig party, but he staid, and as letters here presented show, hoped for the office of Secretary of State. In that he was disappointed, and he returned to the Senate to meet the questions whether the territory taken from Mexico should be free or slave, and could the Constitution be extended over the territories. To the last question Webster said no, that it was confined to the states, and he prevailed. Then the South threatened secession, Texas and New Mexico quarreled over their boundary, and California with a free-state constitution asked for admission. A great crisis had come and the national peace and unity was threatened. Clay offered a compromise and spoke in its defence; then Calhoun spoke, and Webster, having deliberately made up his mind what the safety of the country demanded, spoke and "discharged a clear conscience" by what he called his "Constitution and Union" speech, and what became known as his "Seventh of March" speech. Then before the measures of the Compromise had been passed, President Taylor died, Fillmore succeeded him and Webster became Secretary of State for the second time.

During this occupancy of the State Department there were no great negotiations like those of his previous service, but there were some striking episodes in which Webster appeared quite as sagacious and tactful as before. He inherited a controversy with Austria which arose because Taylor had sent an agent to report the condition of the Hungarian revolutionary government, intending to recognize it, if it deserved it. In spite of the fact that the agent reported against recognition, Hülsemann, the Austrian chargé, complained of Taylor's action. Clayton, the Secretary of State explained the object of the mission, and, When Hülsemann sent an offensive reply, Webster, who had succeeded to the State Department, determined to give him a rebuke, which, while stimulating the national pride, would apprize Europe that America was a nation not to be brow-beaten. He suggested among other things that the United States was a country of so vast an extent that in comparison with it the possessions of the House of Hapsburg were but a patch upon the earth's surface. Mr. Hülsemann moderated somewhat under this domineering letter, but later, when Kossuth was enthusiastically received in this country, the chargé was again filled with wrath, and after a correspondence, which is published in this volume, left the country.

In addition to this incident, Webster's skill as a diplomat was fully tried in a controversy with England growing out of the Clayton-Bulwer treaty, and another with Spain resulting from the Lopez invasion of Cuba and a consequent sacking of the Spanish consulate at New Orleans. The Lobos islands affair, some trouble with England about the fisheries, and a dispute with Mexico, also vexed the Administration. In the midst of these troubles, Webster and his friends made the last struggle to secure for him the nomination for the Presidency which he had coveted for so long. Again a military hero secured the nomination and this time Webster refused to support him. Long before the failure to secure the nomination, Webster had shown signs of failing health. Active public life was putting too great a strain upon a body of which he had never taken the wisest care. He had too often subjected himself to a tremendous strain for a short time, preparing for great speeches under fearful pressure. All this tended to break down even his iron frame, and when in the autumn of 1852 the annual catarrhal attack came upon him he was too weak to resist it and the end came.

(To Wm. Plumer.[1])

My Dear Sir   Jan. 9 [1824]
    My little Greek motion will come on, on Monday, week—viz—
the 19th—   I know not what you think of it, but if it meets your
approbation, I wish you would *say something* in its support[2]—
                        Yrs with much regard,
                                        D WEBSTER

(To Nathan Appleton.[3])

Dr Sir,   WASHINGTON Jany 12, 1824
    I transmit you a copy of the bill proposing an augmentation

---

[1] Representative from New Hampshire.
[2] This letter is in possession of the New Hampshire State Library.
[3] See letter dated May 30, 1827, Daniel Webster to Appleton, for sketch of the latter.

of duties, recently reported by the committee on manufactures. I shall be much obliged to you for the communication of such observations as may occur to you, on the examination of this bill.

It is probable that the subject may be acted upon in about three weeks, or a month, and the importance of the subject I hope may excuse me for asking for the benefit of your opinions respecting it.

I am Sir with great regard

Yours   DANL WEBSTER

(To Ezekiel Webster.[1])

feb. 15. [1824]

Dr E.

The caucus assembled last night,[2] & you will see its official details, I presume, as early as you see this.   I think the result *not favorable* to Mr. Crawford.   The meeting was too *thin;* it shows his weakness in the H. & R. & how little chance he has of success, if the vote comes there, as I think it must.   Pray keep all still & silent.   Let the Patriot folks espouse the Caucus Candidate.   It will do wonders & work good in the end, that they should do so.   I hope you will not let the Presidential question make its way into your Spring elections.   You seem to be in a most *disjointed* state.   I fear your friend W. will come in again, simply for want of an opposing candidate.   The last news we had was of Genl. Dinsmore's declin'g.

Genl. Jackson continues to make head, in Penna. & at the Convention, at Harrisburg, three weeks hence, I fancy he will be *nominated*.   If so, it will produce some change of prospects.

Our Steam Boat[3] case is not yet decided, but it *can go but one way.*

Mrs. W. & the children are well, & send a great deal of love. We have had the finest winter here ever known.   It has been as mild as October.   Today we have a plentiful rain.   My wife means to write you herself soon.   Julia & Edward send love to their cousins.

Yrs

D. W.

---

[1] The original of this letter is owned by Edwin W. Sanborn, of New York.
[2] A caucus of the party members of Congress, which was the prevailing method at that time of making nominations for President and Vice-President.
[3] Gibbons vs. Ogden.

(To Jeremiah Mason.)

WASHINGTON Apr. 5, 1824.

My Dear Sir

It is rumored here this morning that *Judge Sherburn* had re-signed; on hearing of this, Judge Livermore has started for the vacant place.   I believe all the Delegation of N. Hamp., with perhaps the exception of Mr. Plumer, *have signed his paper;* that is the style of things here.   Official information of the resig-nation has not been yet rec'd.   *Mr. Parrott*[1] *also has signed the paper.*   Mr. Bell declines, on the ground of *impropriety,* he being a Senator.   I shall know more about it today—but this shews you how things go.   I hope the story of the resignation is not true—what I have mentioned I derive from *confidential* sources.—& you must use it accordingly.

I am your debtor for two letters.   As to the time of my return, I shall press very hard to get home before May is out.   I expect to be obliged to return, say in July, to get my Money, if we pass the Bill this session, & if so I need not, that I now see, remain here after the rising of Congress.   I will write you further on this head & on other things soon.   I scratch this in the House, merely to give you the information above.

Yours very truly,

D. WEBSTER.

(To Jeremiah Mason.)

April 6. [1824]

Dear Sir

I believe I was wrong in one part of my communication yester-day.   Mr. Bartlett has not signed the paper; but is, I learn, willing to do so, on receiving an assurance that the Candidate, if appointed, will remove to Portsmouth—a pledge, I learn, quite ready to be given.   *Mr. Parrott* I believe has rather retract-ed his recommendation, on the ground of its being not perhaps quite compatible with his character as Senator.—After all, I hope there is no vacancy.   Pray tell the Judge that Congress will not, this session, increase his duties.

We are approaching the question—on the Tariff.   I know not

---

[1] John F. Parrott, Senator from New Hampshire.

how it may go, we sometimes have hopes of stopping—but again our fears arise, & exceed our hopes.

Yrs
D. WEBSTER.

5 O'Clock
We have beat them on the *iron* 95 to 90.[1]

(From H. A. Dearborn.[2])

BOSTON, May 4th, 1824.

Dear Sir

I received a letter from a friend in London dated the 6th of March who justly observes:

"Mr. Webster's speech[3] has been received with general approbation & applause. It has been translated into Greek & printed in London, in order to be distributed all over Greece. I am happy that the Demosthenes of America has taken the lead in encouraging and animating the countrymen of his great prototype!"—

I tender my thanks for your wise & magnificent speech on the Tariff. The ground you have assumed is the only one, which history, policy & experience can enable us to maintain, with interest to the nation. I march with you, side by side, in all the route you take. If you are not correct, there is no truth in *induction*, there is no *wisdom* among the learned, there is no *intelligence* to be found in Parliament,—there is no reliance to be placed on the statements of the learned political writers on the currency of nations; in fact we have not any *new lights*, to

---

[1] On the motion to reduce revenue from $1.12 to 90 cents per ton on bar iron, the vote was, however, 99 to 90, in favor of the motion.

[2] Henry A. S. Dearborn, born in New Hampshire, 1783. Educated at William and Mary College. Practiced law in Massachusetts and Maine. Was successively Representative, Executive Councellor and Senator in the Massachusetts Legislature, and in 1831-33 was representative in Congress. Later was Adjutant-General of Massachusetts until 1843. As an author he wrote three volumes on the commerce of the Black Sea, a biography of Commodore Bainbridge, a book on architecture, and a Life of Christ. He was a lifelong correspondent of Webster's.

[3] The "Greek Speech," delivered January 19, 1824. Webster said of it : "I am more fond of this child than any of the family; " referring to all the published speeches. See Curtis, vol. i, p. 205. There are in the New Hampshire Historical Society collection over thirty pages of notes made by Daniel Webster in preparation for this speech.

guide us, since the dark ages, & must grope on with *tyrant* custom & *old precedent*, for crutches.

Your most obt. S't.   H. A. DEARBORN.

———

(To Jeremiah Mason.)

BOSTON May 23. [1824]

DR Sir

I wrote you yesterday.   Last Evening I saw Mr. Hale of Keene— In conversing with him on the subject, I found he entertained the same general impression as others, that the result of the elections was unfavorable.   He said, however, that Cheshire would be 3 or 4 votes better.   He had supposed that Strafford was much changed for the worse.

I perceive he is a good deal friendly to Mr. Plumer.   From what he says, as well as from some other things, I am fully persuaded that Mr. Plumer still thinks he has some tolerable chance. I have told Mr. H (in hopes he might suggest it to Mr. P.) that I did not think your friends would vote for Mr. Plumer—that it was unreasonable to expect it—that your strength was greater than his, or any other candidate who was supposed to be favorable to the administration, & that if they acted on principle, they ought to unite, in your favor.   That Mr. Adams friends could elect you if they chose—that if they did not, I did not see why you & your friends should seek to uphold Mr. Adams' interest by electing Mr. Plumer or Parrott.   In my opinion, this is the right tone; & it ought to be held distinctly to Mr. P. & also to Mr. Parrott; & let the responsibility be on them.   Mr. Livermore will doubtless be a candidate.   It is said, & I incline to think it is true, that Mr. *Bell* would prefer Mr. Livermore's situation to his own, whether this chance of opening the other seat, to be filled this Session also, presents any new views, you can judge.   I am at present a good deal inclined to think that Dinsmoor will be the leading candidate; & if you are not elected it seems probable he may be.[1]

I shall leave town tomorrow for three days.   On my return hope to find a letter from you.   It is suspected an attempt will be made at Concord to repeal the Congressional District Law.

---

[1] See "History of New Hampshire," by McClintock, pp. 541-2.   Mason was defeated.

I think Mr. Fuller will be speaker here.   At least I hope so. The House, I believe, is *Federal.*   Yet I think they will elect Mr. Fuller, & give Mr. Lincoln just such a Council as he may wish.

Yrs   D. W.

Let me know if anything occurs to change the prospect.

———

(To Ezekiel Webster.[1])

PHILADELPHIA, June 5. [1824]

Dr E

I have come so far with Mrs. W. & return today to Washington—while Mrs. W. moves along homeward   She expects to be met by Mr. Paige in New York.   A week, I trust, will suffice for my concerns in Washington, & I shall be home about the 20th of June.

Mr. Crawford is *sick—very sick.*   And recent events have appeared very favorable to Mr. Adams.   In the event of Mr. C's death, (which I anticipate) Mr. Adams will be chosen by the *People* & by a great vote.   If Mr. Crawford survives, I still think Mr. Adams' chance the best, at present, greatly.   Genl. Jackson's interest is evidently on the *wane.*

As to Senator from your State, as you have not the power of making him, it would be idle to give advice, even if I had it. You know my preferences.   If there is not—& I suppose there is not—any chance of choosing the *best* or the *next best,* man—if, in short, it comes to be a question between Gov. Morrill—Gov. Woodbury—& Mr. Parrott—I hope you will choose the latter. Depend on it, he is much preferable to a new man.   He has gone along very well, I think, this session, and I should greatly prefer him to either of the others.   I wrote Mr. Mason on this subject some time ago.

I have not learned yet your choice of Governer.   My Spanish claims come to an end, on Wednesday next.

Yrs
DANL WEBSTER

P. S.

Do not fail to try hard to *District.*   Of present members, I know most, & think the best of Mr. Plumer.   I think you may talk with him very confidentially—& will find him liberal &

———

[1] This letter is owned by Edwin W. Sanborn, of New York.

sensible. If he can be kept in Congress, in my opinion it will be *a good thing*. He will doubtless be at Concord, and I trust you will see him, & converse with him. He is, much less than the rest of mankind—or some of them at least—under the influence of party feeling.

———

(From William Gaston.[1]*)*

KINGSTON No. Car. April 11th, 1824.

My dear Sir

Availing myself of a leisure moment on my circuit, I take the liberty of applying to you for some information on the subject of the Presidential Election. While there was a prospect of electing Mr. Calhoun I felt a strong interest for his success. Since this prospect has vanished my concern in the contest has almost ceased. Still however I have a choice, and would prefer Mr. Adams to either of the remaining candidates. In this State the struggle will be between the Crawford and the Jackson tickets. I believe that the latter if taken up generally by those who would prefer Adams might be made to succeed. What effect would its success have on the final result? If Adams, Jackson & Crawford be the three from whom the House of Representatives is to select, which would get the majority of States, and of what states would this majority be composed? If Adams, Jackson & Clay be the three, how then would the election terminate?

Favour me with answers to these inquiries, and believe me very truly

Yours,   WILL GASTON.

———

(To William Gaston.[2]*)*

BOSTON Sept. 8th 1824

My Dear Sir

More difficult problems were never presented than those contained in your letter (which I suppose you have forgotten) of April last— They were difficult then, & after waiting four or five months, I do not see that time has done much towards their

[1] Judge of the Supreme Court of North Carolina. He probably became acquainted with Webster when a member of Congress from North Carolina, 1813-17. See Webster's answer September 8, 1824.

[2] This letter is owned by Isabel D. Bronson. See letter dated April 11, 1824.

solution— It seems to me vain to conjecture, even now, what will be the result of the election— I have an impression that Mr Adams' chance is best;—but others, close about me, think differently— All New England may be put to his credit—so, I suppose, may New Jersey and the greater part of Maryland— as to the rest, I have no means of knowing in what States his friends may confidently expect votes for him— From the beginning I have supposed the election would come to the H. of R. & still continue of that opinion. If Pennsylvania adheres to General Jackson, & S. Carolina, also, Mr. Crawford, Mr. Adams, & Gen¹ Jackson will come into the House, I should conjecture in the order in which I have named them— If S. Carolina should go for Mr Adams, it might put him possibly at the head of the list, & bring in Mr Clay instead of Gen¹ Jackson. How the election would terminate, in either of these cases, I cannot, with any certainty, foresee— My opinion, however, such as it is, I have already intimated. We are putting to the proof the most delicate part of our system, the election of the Executive— In the absence of such persons as are very prominent, & highly distinguished, for character & service, the choice falls necessarily among a greater number, & among those also whose merits may not be supposed to be very unequal. In such case, local considerations, personal considerations, & hundred other *small* considerations will have their influence. The result, I fear, will be a general failure in the election, by the Electors, in time to come— And the consequence of this will be, as is obvious, a diminution of the weight & authority of the Executive Magistrate, & a continued devolution of more & more of the authority properly belonging to that department on Congress— When we have strong parties again, we shall have a chance for Presidents, who shall be elected thro' their own favor & popularity;—so we may also, if war or troublous times should bring forth great talents, united with great services— Otherwise I am fearful the President's Office may get to be thought too much in the gift of Congress.

In this part of the Country there is no great warmth about the approaching election—

Mr Adams' friends seem to be most numerous; but the other Candidates are neither feared nor greatly disliked, except by the public writers.

Our portion of the Country is at this time exceedingly prosperous, upon the whole; & having had a little excitement from the visit of the good Lafayette, we are going on again in our every day pursuits— Our Congressional elections take place in Nov. No nominations have yet been made— Most of our present members will probably be reelected.— It is *possible* that our friend Mr Mason may be chosen Senator again, from N. Hampshire—but this is only *possible*— The times, tho' tolerably good, are not quite good enough— I fear for that.—

I see Roger Vose now & then. He is as formerly, except that silver locks render his venerable appearance more venerable— He can laugh yet—& cause others to partake in the same exercise.—

Poor Lovat, you know, has been deceased some years— I had a short visit last year from Mr Morris S. Millar. He is what they call in N. York a *Bucktail*— He & Mr Shepherd think that opposition to the war was carried too far!—

We have, My Dear Sir, a great many good people in New England, who would be glad to see your face. Some of us think you bear a resemblance to the better class of Yankees— If you regard this as a reproach, come and disprove it—

Yours always affectionately

DANL WEBSTER

(To Jeremiah Mason.)

BOSTON, Nov. 14, [1824.]

My Dear Sir

A letter has been rec'd in answer to that written to Portsmouth, quite satisfactory as to the writers own wishes & intentions; and rather encouraging as to the general prospect. It speaks of the writers favourable sentiments & good wishes towards the present incumbent, but also of the hopelessness of his reappointment; & says, that when that is fully seen, *his* friends will heartily join in the other object. It mentions as probable the desired success in the H.R.; speaks of the difficulties elsewhere, but hopes they may be overcome, the more easily, as he does not think any *amendment* likely to unite a Majority of the voices. The whole letter is liberal & personally friendly to you, in a high degree. It manifests, moreover, more willingness *to take* a part, than I expected. I have permission to show it to one or two discreet friends, which I shall do tomorrow.

Yrs always,

DANL WEBSTER.

(To Wm. Plumer.[1]*(?))*

MONTECELLO, Decr. 18.[2] [1824]

My Dear Sir   Saturday Morning

If I am inquired for, have the goodness to say I may be expected either on Tuesday or Wednesday morning. We should have left here yesterday morning, for W., but for the rain, which fell in torrents all day. This morning the streams are very full, & we doubt the expediency of setting out.

I have found my visit here very pleasant. It has not only gratified a natural desire to see a distinguished & extraordinary man,[3] but allowed an opportunity for much interesting & instructive conversation—

Yours, with true regard

DAN^L WEBSTER.

The rain fell here yesterday & last night 5 inches

———

(To Jeremiah Mason.)

Dear Sir   WASHINGTON Jan. 25, 1825.

Ohio & Kentucky have agreed, I believe without doubt, to go for Mr. Adams. This makes his election nearly or quite certain. I have thought this might, perhaps, be important enough to write a word to you, to mention it.[4]

We have no other news.

Yrs   D. WEBSTER.

———

(To Ezekiel Webster.[5]*)*

WASHINGTON, Jan. 18, [1825]

I am much obliged to you, for yours of the 10th. It gave me much information that I wanted. I trust you have not forgotten to write me again, having seen Mr. Mason at the Court.

---

[1] There is no address, but the letter was found among the Plummer papers in the New Hampshire State Library.

[2] On this day Webster's son Charles died.

[3] Thomas Jefferson.

[4] For other correspondence on this subject see the "Private Correspondence of Daniel Webster," vol. i, p. 374, Daniel Webster to Ezekiel Webster, also pp. 377-380, Warfield to Daniel Webster and Daniel Webster to Warfield.

[5] The original of this letter is owned by Edwin W. Sanborn, of New York city. Curtis, vol. i, page 236, quotes the latter part of this letter and quotes it incorrectly.

I hope you will pay all proper attention to your approaching election. The Patriot man, I perceive, is very angry, & will be very active. If you save the House, you will save all. I hope that public opinion, even when for Mr. Mason, will have some effect on the People of N. H.

As the 9th Feb. approaches we begin to hear a little more about the election. I think some important indications will be made 'soon. A main inquiry is, in what direction Mr. Clay & his friends will move. There would seem at present to be some reason to think they will take a part finally for Mr. *Adams*. This will not necessarily be decisive, but it will be very important. After all, I cannot predict results. I believe Mr. Adams *might be* chosen, if he or his friends would act somewhat differently. But if he has good counsellors, I know not who they are.

If Mr. Clay's friends should join Mr. Crawford, it would probably put him ahead of Mr. Adams the first ballot—& that being done, I know not what might follow.

I should like to know your opinion of what is proper to be done, in two or three contingencies—

1. If, on the first, or any subsequent ballot, Mr. Adams falls behind Mr. Crawford, & remains so a day or two, shall we hold out, to the end of the Chapter, or shall we vote for one of the highest?

2. If for one or the highest—say Jackson & Crawford—*for which?*

3. Is it advisable, under any circumstances, to hold out, & leave the Chair to Mr. Calhoun?

4. Wd or would not, N. E. prefer a man of the power of Calhoun, to a choice of Genl. Jackson?—

On these, & other similar points, I want your full opinions, by the first of next month.

I shall write you again in a day or two.

Yrs

D. W.

(To Thomas H. Benton.)

Feb. 25. [1825.]

My Dear Sir

I send you Mr. R's[1] original communication of which I keep no

------

[1] John Randolph of Roanoke. See "Webster Private Correspondence," vol. i, p. 258. In 1816 Mr. Randolph had challenged Webster to a duel, and the

copy.   The letter prepared as an answer is destroyed, & no copy preserved.   The correspondence being thus disposed of, I send you a *memo*. of what I am willing that you should now say to Mr. R. & will add that it would have given me pleasure to have said the same at any time.   Our understanding is distinct, I think, that the letters being thus disposed of, no publication is called for, & none is to be in any way authorized by either of us—

Yrs with much regard

D. W.

[*Memorandum.*]

[Feb. 25. 1825]

Mr. W. is willing that Mr. B. should say to Mr. R. that he has no recollection of having said any thing which can possibly be considered as affecting Mr. R's veracity beyond what he said in the H. R.—   If he has used other expressions they must have been about the same time and the same import; he does not now recollect them, and disclaims them.

As to what Mr. W. said in the H. R. he meant only to state that Mr. R. was under an entire mistake, or misapprehension, of the facts; he meant to say nothing more; and neither intended to make, or did make any imputation on the personal veracity of Mr. R.

Dr. Sir,   Senate Chamber, 3 P. M. [Feb. 25. 1825]

The arrangement is perfectly satisfactory. I return the *memo*. that you may put it into your own handwriting.

I go out to dine this evening, and that prevents me from having the pleasure of seeing you til tomorrow forenoon.

Very respectfully, &c.

THOMAS H. BENTON.

(To John Q. Adams.[1]*)*

PRIVATE.

Dear Sir: H. R., Feb. 26, 1825

I received this letter this morning.   You know Mr. Mason's

---

latter in a dignified way refused to accept the challenge. Now Webster again receives a challenge, and the matter is temporarily disposed of, as is seen in the correspondence here presented. See also the letter of Mrs. Webster to Webster, dated March 1, 1825, in this work.

[1] This letter is owned by Charles Francis Adams.

reputation and standing in New England. In the events which have happened in New Hampshire on the recent occasion, he took an active and prominent part. Although I did not expect to receive any letter from him on the subject, and have no reason to know precisely how far he would wish his sentiments to be known, yet I presume he would expect that I would make such use of his suggestions as I might think discreet. And I have thought the best course would be, to enclose the letter itself, for your perusal. You will see that in general, his sentiments are like those which I have expressed to you myself. This note does not require any answer. The letter you may return to me enclosed at your convenience. My private letters correspond with the public accounts, as to the general satisfaction of the people all over the North, at the result of the Election. There are letters also today from Kentucky and Ohio, of a very favorable complexion.

Yours truly,

DAN'L WEBSTER.

(To Ezekiel Webster.[1])

feb. 26. [1825]

Dr E.

I shall stay here probably till 15. or 16. March. Your election will be the 8— Write me Wednesday Eve—the 9th & the letter will meet me here.—Write me again on Monday, the 14. & that letter will meet me in N. York—to which place let it be addressed.

Mr. Clinton is offered the Mission to Engd. If he accepts, Mr. Rush is expected to [be] Sec. Treas. Gov. Barbour Sec. of War. There are some objections to these appointments. Mr. Adams' situation is full of embarrassments, & I know not how he will get along. I retain however a confidence that he will act liberally, & in this hope I rest. Mr. Mason has written me a very sensible & judicious letter, on various topics, which *I have submitted.* I think Mr. Mason will yet be chosen. New influences will begin to bear on the case by June next.

I have a letter from Keene (Mr. Prentiss) saying there will be a *scatter'g* of the votes in that County for M. C. I rather think you have some chance to be chosen—but shall not be disap-

---

[1] The original of this letter is owned by Edwin W. Sanborn, of New York.

pointed if you should not.   Judging from the Patriot, I suppose old heats must be much revived.   If it be so, it is but a
dying effort.

Yrs.   D. W.

(To Jeremiah Mason.)

BOSTON May 21, 1825.

Dear Sir

   Mr. P.[1] you probably saw, in the stage coach.   He has been
here, & says he met you near Newbery Bridge.   We have had a
full conversation with him; & every thing has been suggested,
according to our understanding.   He rec'd the Communication,
as well as could be expected, I really think his present inclinations
are good; but I fear he will not act with sufficient decision.   He
thinks, like the rest, that the chance of success has been a good
deal lessened by the late election; but he does not appear to possess any particular information.   He thinks your Townsman,
Mr. P.[2] has no chance at all—that H.[3] has not *agreed* to go for
W.[4]—that Mr. D's[5] friends will still adhere to him—& he seems
quite doubtful what will be the result.   I have not, in any degree, given him to understand that your friends would in any
event, incline to go for *him*—I have thought best that he should
not expect *that*.   Finally, it is arranged that he will be at C. the
first day—that he will then Communicate freely with *Mr. Oliver
Peabody*, a Gentleman in whom he has confidence.   It will be
necessary that Mr. Peabody should be previously seen; &, being
informed of the Conversation which passed between you & me,
he will know exactly what has been said to Mr. P.

   Mr. Everett has acted extremely well in this business.   I believe also that Genl. D. saw Mr. P.

   The case should be laid before him *strongly* as C & I hope good
may come of it.   I doubt whether he has much influence with
individuals but he could do much to make a general impression on
those who are favorable to administration.

   I have written to Washington.   Mrs. W. finds her sister's family not well & I do not know when she may leave Salisbury,—I
have written her to come down to Portsmouth.   My going there
to meet her will depend altogether on the question whether I can

---

[1] Wm. Plumer, Jr.   [2] John F. Parrott.   [3] Wm. H. Y. Hackett.
[4] Levi Woodbury.   [5] Samuel Dinsmoor.

do any *good* If I can I will come, tho' I cannot come earlier than the 30th inst. I doubt whether Mr. Parrott *can* do anything, if he would.

Please acknowledge receipt of this & let me know what you think. Mr. P. is half inclined to have a conversation with H.

Yrs

D. WEBSTER.

_____

(To Jeremiah Smith.)

Sunday Eve. [May 22. 1825]

My Dr Sir

I send you a few letters &c It would be *queer* if you & I & Judge Story should happen to meet at Niagara. It is possible. The Judge & I intend to set off in that direction ab't June 20th.

Yours always most truly,

DANL. WEBSTER.

_____

(To James W. Paige.)

N York Thursday Morning [Nov. 24, 1825]

D'r. Wm.

We were all so busy yesterday that we let the day slide off without writing to you. I had many ways to go, Mrs. W. was much occupied with her friends & acquaintances. We came here very seasonably to dine on Tuesday—not finding convenient lodgings at the public houses, we availed ourselves of Mr. & Mrs. March's hospitality, & have staid with them. This morning we proceed on our journey.

I hear of some important failures here; but all these things are known to you early of course. The state of things in the mercantile world is spoken of as not being very satisfactory. Mrs. W. will probably write you from Princeton.

Yrs

D. W.

_____

(To Jeremiah Mason.)

WASHINGTON Dec. 11, 1825.

Dear Sir

I do not think there is the least probability that any arrangement will be made to supply, temporarily, Judge Sherburne's place.   When Judges become permanently incapable, they ought to resign.   There is as much reason, at least, for proceeding vs. Judge S. now as there there was for the course which *he* pursued against his predecessor,   But at any rate, no *substitute* will be provided, I presume.   If a vacancy.—should occur, in that office, I will give my aid to support the Gentleman you refer to; unless a new state of things should in the mean time arise. For example, if new Circuit Judges should be created, it might become an object, in our Circuit, to propose a Candidate under such circumstances that it might not be expedient, also, at the same time, to press for the appointment of the person you refer to you as District Judge.

We have done little here yet, & nothing more than you have seen.   There will be opposition to Mr. King's appointment, in the Senate, but it is thought it will not be successful   The opposition, however, is strong, in that body.   A very good temper prevails thr° the mass of our House.   There is nothing of a spirit of *exclusion,* except among some of our N. England worthies, & perhaps a few others.

It was not a bad thing that the friends of Mr. *Crawford,* generally, supported a *Federalist* for the Chair.   Some of my friends thought that I might have obtained some votes for that place, but I wholly declined the attempt.   If practicable to place me there it would not have been prudent.

Virginia, as you will see, is in a great rage with the Message. We think it possible your old friend Mr. Giles may come back again to the Senate;—unless the lot should fall on Mr. Randolph.

Yrs truly,

D. WEBSTER.

––––––

(To J. Q. Adams.[1]*)*

PRIVATE AND CONFIDENTIAL

Feb. 28, 1826

Sir:

These letters were put into my hands this morning, to be used at my discretion.   I venture to enclose them to you for your perusal; and will receive them again, some days hence, when an opportunity may occur.   I have conversed with Mr. Williams

––––––

[1] This letter is owned by Charles Francis Adams.

on the subject, and find him somewhat desirous that Mr. Seawell, *should be appointed,* more specially and most especially, that he should not be *omitted,* in favor of any *other* gentleman, in *his* part of the country.   Hereafter I may venture to make some further suggestions on this subject at some future period; but it is thought convenient in the mean time, that these letters should be presented to your consideration.

With entire regard, Yours,

DAN'L WEBSTER.

|(*To* ——————— (?)¹)

WASHINGTON Mar. 20, 1826.

Gentlemen

I have been favored with yours of the 14th instant, relative to the proposed new Bridge, & another also from Mr. Webbs, accompanied by a Report, made to the Senate, by a Com^ee of which Mr Hoar is Chairman.

In a question, at once so important, & so difficult, I feel extremely unwilling to say more than the emergent occasion requires.   Whether the State Legislature can authorize an *obstruction,* in an arm of the sea, on which a Port of delivery is established, by the laws of the United States; and, if it cannot, whether a Bridge, built for public convenience, & having suitable draws for the passage of vessels is to be deemed an unlawful obstruction, are questions depending on very general considerations, & are of great moment.   Very little has been decided, or discussed, on such questions, except what transpired in the New York Steam Boat cause, with which you are probably acquainted. On the other hand, the rest of the Bridges about Boston, & especially Craige's, seem to stand only on the supposition that the Legislature may exercise such a power.   There is a Bridge, also, over Piscataqua River, at Portsmouth, fifteen or twenty miles below the head of the tide.   There are other similar cases.   It is difficult to draw a line between Rivers, below the head of the tide, & arms of the Sea.   If the commerce of the United States, for its substantial interest & convenience, require a port of delivery at Roxbury, & if a Bridge, with suitable Draws, ought to be considered as a real & substantial obstruction, in the way of such commerce, then it would seem to follow that such Bridge could

---

¹ Copied from the original draft of a letter.

not be lawfully erected.   But I do not feel prepared, at present, to express an opinion on either of those questions.   I might mislead you by doing so; & they are, indeed, questions of a nature as fit to be considered by yourselves as by me.   The Courts of U. S. could not regard the injury to private property.

I am the more willing to be spared from giving an opinion on those points at present, because I do not see how the question can be raised, till the Bridge shall be built, or begun.—The Courts of the U. S. cannot interfere, till some one, lawfully navigating, meets with an unlawful obstruction.—He can then sue, & try the right.   There must be some actual conflicts, between a right exercised under the U. S. & a right exercised under the State, before a ground of action can be laid.

In this view of the case, it is perhaps not expedient that I should do more than to indicate the general nature of the questions, which would come, in my opinion to be discussed, should the occasion be furnished.

(From Henry Clay.[1])

(PRIVATE AND CONFIDENTIAL)

[Apr. 1826]?

My dear Sir

The lapse of time now renders the adoption of Mr. Hamiltons resolution about Panama necessary.[2]   The Senate wants a spur. Respect for it has heretofore induced the President to hold up his message to the house until the Senate voted.   The same consideration continues to operate; but that ought not to prevent the House moving in the matter, if it think proper to do so.   *We* really desire that you should, and, if you see no objection to the course, suppose you take up Mr. H⁹ resolution and pass it for him to day?   I made this suggestion to Letcher, Storrs & one or two others who were at my house last night.[3]

I am Yours faithf⁷

H. CLAY.

---

[1] This letter is owned by Mr. C. P. Greenough.

[2] Refers to the bill "making appropriations for carrying into effect the appointment of a mission at the Congress of Panama."   See McMaster's "History of United States," vol. v, pp. 433-58.

[3] See Curtis' "Life of Webster," i, 266.   Webster made a powerful speech in defence of this resolution, "Works," iii, 178.

(To William Gaston.[1])

BOSTON May 31. 1826

My Dear Sir,

I lose no time in answering yours of the 20th, which was rec^d
'yesterday. Most of the Gentlemen you mention I have the pleasure to know, & know them to be most worthy & respectable persons— Dr Holmes, a distinguished Clergyman, author of the
two vols of "American Annals"; Dr Harris, author of several
respectable publications, among others a "Natural History of the
Bible," which has attracted much praise abroad, as well as in
U. S.; Dr Foster, & Dr Richmond, are all well known to me.
Genl Crane, Sheriff of Norfolk, I know quite well. Mr Morey
is a particular acquaintance— Mr Rodman I know, & Mr Samuel Williams jr, both of New Bedford—I do not know anything
of the Messrs Whitakers either personally, or by reputation; nor
am I acquainted with the characters, or persons of Mr Kimball,
Mr. Ritchie, or Dr Stone— Mr Bailey I have known only from
an intercourse in Congress; & of Samuel Williams Junr. I can
say only that I take him to be a respectable Gentleman, who
was member of Congress many years ago from Bristol County
It will give me pleasure to oblige you, or to serve the cause of
truth & justice by stating, in any form, the general character &
reputation of those Gentlemen whom I have mentioned as being
known to me. They are all equally well known to the following
persons, who, I presume, would cheerfully join me in bearing
testimony to their good character; viz. Isaac Parker, Chf. Justice of Mass: Levi Lincoln, Govr;—Mr Justice Story; John
Davis Esqr District Judge;—I think it likely some of these Gentlemen may know those persons mentioned in your letter, with
whom I have said that I am not myself acquainted.— Any wish
of yours, in regard to this matter, will be complied with, with
great readiness & pleasure—

I thank you, My Dear Sir, for your kind sentiments towards
my poor speech; but much more, I assure you, for the friendly
dispositions which you express towards the Administration &
your disapprobation of this strange opposition— I believe Mr
Adams' feelings and purposes are extremely good. Be assured,
there is nothing in him of narrowness, or illiberality, or local
prejudice— The South, I very much fear, means to quarrel
with him, right or wrong; or perhaps, it may be more charitable

---

[1] This letter is owned by Isabel D. Bronson, of Summit, N. J.

to say that it means to act on the presumption that he must &
will be wrong, & act wrong, in all things.

I trust it will turn out otherwise, however, & that his measures
will be found not unmixed evil— I have long wished to write
you, on these subjects but have been restrained from various
considerations—I know the posture of your state; & how difficult
& dangerous it is, or may be thought to be, to support the measures or approve the conduct of one, with a Community that is
disappointed at his elevation, & hopes soon to see his place occupied by another—

Nevertheless, if you could spare a half hour to give me your
views & feelings fully, I should be very much gratified— You
see on what grounds the opposition places itself— The Leading
Jackson Journals make the great charge to be, *a tendency, in
Mr Adams, to stand well with Federalists*— All this, notwithstanding the Genl's Letter about Col. Drayton, Ingraham, Hous-
ten, & twenty others have repeated these ideas, in their speeches
in Congress— Yet you know whose follower Mr Ingham was,
as late as 1823, & what was the professed principle on which he
who then was (& now is) his leader, acted—

But, My Dear Sir, I will not avail myself of the little opening
which your letter affords, to inflict upon you a political epistle—
I am, however, I confess, desirous of knowing more than I do
know at present, of your sentiments, in regard to public affairs;
& perhaps you will find leisure to tell me frankly what you think,
& something of what you see & hear around you—

It caused me much grief not to be here last summer, when you
did our town the honor of a visit— Your various friends will
be gratified by your remembrance of them—

I am, My Dear, with unabated esteem & regard,

Yours
DANL WEBSTER.

(To Ezekiel Webster.[1])

BOSTON, Feb. 9, 1827.

Dear E.

I carried your wife to Woburn last Evening. She intends
going to Bellerica today, & to be home on Thursday. The
weather, however, is such as may perhaps delay her progress.

---

[1] This letter is the property of Edwin W. Sanborn, of New York.

I wish to see you, on many matters, especially in regard to political matters. Affairs in N. H. are such, evidently, as require *attention*. I have thought very much on the subject, & have an opinion which I can now only state, but should be glad of an opportunity to explain the grounds of it.

1. It will not answer for you, & the Gentlemen who acted with you last June, to *retire* at the present moment. You cannot, I think, with honor or propriety.

2. Confusion & discord will attend all the elections of the next year, unless some understanding or arrangement be made, to unite all the friends of the Admin—

3. There is no obvious mode of avoiding this result, but that of calling public meetings, of all friends.

4. It is uncertain whether the Republican friends of the Admn. (as they call themselves) will take this course, & call such meetings. At least I am afraid it is uncertain.

5. If they will not, still such meetings should be called, in the Papers, & by printed notices, & let all attend who choose.

The *lead* might well be given to the Republicans, so called, if they will take it, If they will not, *others should*.

My opinion is, that you & your friends should signify, *distinctly* to the other supporters of the Administration, that unless *they* will undertake to give that support on liberal principles, you will feel it your duty to lead, in attempting to render such support.

These are the results of my reflections. I wish to talk with you upon them, but I suggest them now, as you will see some of your friends next week.

Mr. Hale of Keene is in town. I have told him, in the plainest manner, that in my opinion, the Federalists will not support the Adams' nominations in the Senatorial Districts, etc. unless they shall be consulted in mak'g them; &, generally, that *they* must either agree to act with the Federalists, or expect the Federalists to act *agst.* them. I added, that unless he & his friends would support the Administration on its own principles, *others* must undertake it & *wd.* undertake it, &c. &c.

I *must* see you, in the course of two or three weeks. Let me know when. you can come. Mrs. W. left Mary remain here, & we shall keep her till you come for her.

Yrs with constant affection,

D. WEBSTER.

(To J. Q. Adams.¹)

H. R. Saturday, 10 o'clock March 3rd, 1827

Sir:

The two Houses have suspended their 18th Joint Rule, so far as to allow bills to be presented to you today, *which shall have passed the Houses by 12 o'c.* Not knowing whether you are informed of this, I now give you the information, supposing you might think it proper for you to be at the Capitol. The H. R. will pass probably, three or four private bills. It has, as you see, adhered to its Amendment, in the Colonial Bill.

Yours as always,

DAN'L WEBSTER.

(To J. Q. Adams.¹)

PRIVATE.

PHILADELPHIA, March 26th, 1827

Sir:

Mr. Walsh is going to Washington tomorrow, of which I give you notice, only to express the hope that you may see him, and converse with him. He seems to be laboring under the influence of feelings, which I think would be changed by a free conversation and explanation. His position at present is one of some influence and his future course, a good deal important. Pray place this note to the account of friendly zeal and anxiety, rather than to that of officiousness, and believe me to be, as

I am Most truly yours,

DAN'L WEBSTER.

(To J. Q. Adams.¹)

PHILADELPHIA, Mar. 27, 1827

Sir:

I hope you will pardon me for troubling you once more on a political subject. However infirm my judgment may be in the matter about which I write, you may yet be assured that every word proceeds from entire singleness of heart, and devotion to that which is the great immediate object of my thoughts, and efforts, the support and *continuance* of the Administration.

---

¹ These letters are owned by Charles Francis Adams.

One of the observables here is Mr. Walsh's entire neutrality, (if it is *entire*) as to the existing contest. This is a great drawback in the means of affecting favorably the public sentiment. It is important, as I think, and as all here think, to bring· him out in a moderate but firm manner, in support of the Administration. He circulates 4000 papers, and his Review also, which is getting an unexpected extent of patronage, opens another field, which might be prudently and usefully occupied, for the discussion of certain principles, now becoming interesting, and on which we must hope to stand, if we stand at all, in this state.

You are aware that there are 40, or 50 thousand Electors in Penn. who formerly belonged to the Federal Party. With these, Mr. Walsh's opinions have great weight, and a majority of these votes is necessary in any calculation which anticipates, that this state may be found in favor, of the continuance of the present state of things. I have now been here near a week, have seen very many people, and have conversed with all. I have seen who are favorably disposed, whether Greek or Jew. I have learned the grievances of the Democratic Press, and what I could do, or suggest in that quarter, tending to promote satisfaction, and ensure active exertion, has not been omitted. The present state of feeling here, is certainly not the best, so far as it has been produced, by the recent appointment. This, I have endeavored by all the means in my power to mollify and satisfy, and I hope with some success. I have endeavored also, to learn the causes of Mr. Walsh's coldness, and to find out what might propitiate his good felings, and secure his efforts. He sees nothing, I believe, to disapprove in the general measures of Government, but certainly is at present in rather an unsatisfied mood, towards the Administration. He is an old and attached friend of *Mr. Hopkinson,* and he feels that Mr. H. as an early and true friend to the President, has been neglected and injured. Mr. Hopkinson himself does not talk in that way, still if something fit for him to receive could be offered to him, I have no doubt it would gratify Mr. Walsh more than anything else whatever. The District Judge of this District, will hardly last long. It is a small office, but I presume Mr. H. would take it. No doubt he is entirely well qualified for it, and would probably be recommended, by nearly all the Bar. I am persuaded a little effort would reconcile all our other friends here, or nearly all, to this measure. Some act of patronage, or kindness, performed at the same time to them, would lead them easily, to acquiesce in it.

The first fruit of such an understanding, if it were found practicable to make it, would I am persuaded, be seen in the appearance of quite a different tone and manner, in the National Gazette. It would heal much of the wound, which is felt in New Jersey, and would suffice even in New England, to awake the activity of many friends. I know not what objections there may be to this arrangement; but it strikes me that the good must greatly over-balance the evil. Friends here, are in sections and parties and unless *union* can be produced, great mischief may, or will ensue.. If things should remain in their present state, I think it more than probable that Mr. Hopkinson will be run for Congress, with or against his consent, in October, against Mr. Sergeant. I see not why the National Gazette and the Press, might not go on well enough, without collision. There are measures of Government for Mr. Walsh to defend, steps of opposition for him to expose, and reprobate generals, good principles to be enforced, &c, &c. The Press, in the mean time, may very well pursue its own course, taking care not unnecessarily to annoy its neighbors. They might thus tend to the same point, although they should not walk in the same road. These ideas, I have endeavored by all means in my power, to enforce on all sides. It is proper for me to add, what you already well know, that Mr. Hopkinson is my particular friend. Make as much allowance for bias, and possible error of judgment on this account, as seems proper to yourself. Be assured only, that I speak as I really think. Again begging you to pardon me for writing on such a subject, and so long a letter, I have only to renew the assurances of my sincere and constant regard.

DAN'L WEBSTER.

(To Ezekiel Webster.[1])

BOSTON, April 4, 1827.

Dear E.

I have seen no New Hampshire Papers, but hear from Mr. Paige that you are to be in the Legislature. I am very glad of it. This is a time for *action*. I wish to confer with you & Mr. Mason. I shall have no objection to return by way of Portsmouth, if you will accompany me.—

I submit for your consideration this course. Early in the

---

[1] This letter is the property of Edwin W. Sanborn, of New York.

session introduce a string of Resolutions, approving of the election of Mr. Adams—& of the general measures of the Administration—& characterizing the opposition as groundless. In support of these resolutions, make your best *Speech*—print it & circulate it thro' the State. So favorable an opportunity to do good & to distinguish yourself, will never occur to you again.

Let me hear from you by return of mail.

Yrs.

D. WEBSTER.

(To Joseph E. Sprague.[1])

BOSTON April 27, 1827

My dear Sir,

I was very happy to find here yours of the 21st, on my return from N. Hampshire the day before yesterday; and rejoice to see today, how well you have begun in Salem. *The thing will go.*

I have letters from Maryland, New York, Ohio, and Washington all giving very gratifying accounts.[2] Indeed there seems to be a general awakening among our friends. I am going to Ipswich on Tuesday, and will endeavor to see you a moment as I go along, say about 10 o'clock.

Yours truly,

DANL WEBSTER

(To Nathan Appleton.[3])

NEW YORK May 30, 1827.

My dear Sir,

I recd yours, enclosing the Govr's[4] letter, which you did right to open & read. From the manner in which he expresses himself, I see little reason to hope that he will alter his resolution.—

---

[1] See letters in Fl. Webster's Edition of "Daniel Webster's Correspondence," vol. i, pp. 414, 420. J. E. Sprague was a member of the Massachusetts House of Representatives and an active politician. In 1829 he was State Senator and in 1830 one of the Governor's Council.

[2] Refers doubtless to the tariff agitation. See McMaster's History of United States, vol. v, p. 247.

[3] At this time a Representative in the Massachusetts Legislature. Later he twice represented the State in Congress. He was a lifelong friend of Webster.

[4] Governor Levi Lincoln. He refused to run for the U. S. Senate. Webster was chosen Senator for Massachusetts in 1827.

Nothing has occurred, since I left home to change the view, which I communicated to you.— If the Govr. *cannot be persuaded*, then a case will have arisen, in which I am content the legislature shall act as its own sense of public interest may dictate. I repeat what I observed to you, on parting, that in my opinion the choice should be made, without loss of time. Enclosed is a letter for the Govr. which I will thank you to hand to him.

Yours very truly

D. WEBSTER

The length of my stay here is as yet a good deal uncertain.

(To J. E. Sprague.)

BOSTON May 23, 1827.

My dear Sir,

I am obliged to you for your letter of yesterday. The opinions you express are in general my own opinions precisely. I see but one way of escaping from our present difficulty, and that is to *prevail* with the governor to be a candidate.[1] To this end a united and vigorous application should as I think be made to him at the very earliest opportunity, after he arrives here. I have explained myself freely on this subject to Mr. Silsbee[2] whom I saw yesterday.

Yours with entire regard

DANL. WEBSTER.

(To J. E. Sprague.)

CONFIDENTIAL.

NEW-YORK May 30 1827

Dear Sir

Your letter was forwarded to me here, and I now return its enclosure under another cover. I left the subject on which your letter treats in this position, namely, that if the Governor could not be persuaded, my friends might dispose of me as they saw fit.[3] Since I left home, I have seen or heard nothing which should

---

[1] For election to the U. S. Senate.
[2] A successful merchant who had represented Massachusetts in Congress and was at this time U. S. Senator for Massachusetts.
[3] In regard to the U. S. Senatorship. Webster was elected.

have any material weight in determining the matter. What I have seen however as far as it goes rather tends to show that I may be spared, without great inconvenience from the place where I now am. I shall probably be home early next week, but in the present attitude of the case I do not perceive that my presence is likely to be important.

Yours truly,

D. WEBSTER

(To Ezekiel Webster.[1])

BOSTON, June 13, 1827.

Dear E.

Daniel arrived safe this morn'g. I have recd. a summons, lawful in form & substance, to attend the Circuit Court in Newport and must set out tomorrow morn'g. Mrs. W. is getting well.

Your Resolution, as to the course to be pursued by yourself & friends seems reasonable & just. *Will your friends stick to it?* If they will remain firm, you will accomplish your purposes; but in such cases some are generally to go on separate account.

If the Adams Republicans of N. H. do not, by this time, see the hopelessness of success, without a change of system, nothing but the utter ruin of their cause will ever open their eyes.

I shall be back on Sunday. Let me hear from you, by that time.

Yours

D. W.

(To Ezekiel Webster.[1])

BOSTON, friday Eve' June 22 '27.

Dear E.

I recd your letter of Thursday morn'g (yesterday) in the even'g, giving an account of the fate of the Resolutions, &c. In the actual state of things it would seem desirable that you should not break up the session without coming to some arrangement as to future political movements. Doubtless the only true course is to rally those, of whatever name or party, who are willing to unite to support the administration without reference to former divisions. If the Republican Gentlemen will not lead in such a system of action, then of necessity the Federalists must. Give

---

[1] These letters are owned by Edwin W. Sanborn, of New York.

them a fair option; if they decline taking a leading part, assume it yourselves.   There would seem to be no other course.

In the present position of things, you are bound, I should think to do something.   It would hazard too much to leave public opinion without a rallying point for another twelve months. For some purpose or another, there should be, I think, a union meeting, more or less public, before the legislature separates.   I cannot see thro' the matter very clearly, but I suppose there must have been many Republican friends of the Administration, who voted with you, & who would not be adverse to *a union*.   How this is to be brought about, those who are on the spot can best judge; but in some form it seems most desirable.

The main purpose of this is to suggest the importance of doing something, which shall produce these two effects; 1. To prevent any impression from the postponement of the Resolutions, that a majority of the Legislature is agst Mr. Adams; 2d. to agree on some system, or mode of action, which shall unite as many as possible of the friends of the administration, in future movements.   It would now seem especially incumbent on *you* to do all you can, and to take the responsibility in regard to these two objects.

As soon as the weather is fair I go off on a little journey with Mrs. W.   Write me often, directed here, & your letters will be sent to me by Mr. Bliss.   I shall be very anxious to learn your proceedings, & to hear of the effect produced by the facts.

Yrs as always,

D. W.

(To J. Q. Adams.[1])

PRIVATE.

Sir: BOSTON, June 30th, 1827

Having occasion to write you today, on another subject, it occurred to me, that it might not be amiss, to use the same opportunity, to say a few words, in relation to the late occurrences in New Hampshire.   The failure of the Resolutions made in the Legislature may, I fear, have some little bad influence elsewhere, but they ought not to be received as evidence of any unfavorable state of feeling and opinion in the State.   It was produced by a difference among friends, which is greatly to be lamented, but which has been threat'g for some year or two, to break out.   A

---

[1] This letter is owned by Charles Francis Adams.

short state of the case is this. Ten or twelve years ago, the Republican Party, having attained *a very small* majority over the
Federal Party, all political contests from that time forward, *on
the former grounds of controversy,* closed. It has never been
renewed by the Federalists, on any occasion. Still, however, the
Republican Party have kept up their organization, and had
their caucuses for nomination, their County conventions, &c.
When the division took place in that Party, between the friends
and enemies of the Administration, a division which became manifest, soon after the election for President, or indeed rather before
that event, each section of the party wished to retain to itself the
character and re-nomination of the *Republican Party.* And to
prove its title to this character, each kept up the same tone of
hostility towards the Federalists, as in the days when there was
a Federal Party. This struggle for what is called the organization and machinery of the Republican Party, has been going on
now for some time, a majority of the members being with the
Administration, but much the greatest portion of management
and activity, being on the other side. Both have constantly disclaimed all Federal aid and cooperation, this was sensible enough
on the part of the opposition, because few or no Federalists would
be expected even if invited to join those ranks. But it was
obviously a good deal dangerous for the Republican friends of
the Administration, because the Federalists constituted, whether
in the Legislature, or in the State, one half, certainly a large
third, of the whole in point of numbers, and their proportion
was still larger in other respects. Yet this course has been steadily pursued, although with such results, as might, one should
think, have inspired a diffidence of its practicability. Mr. Hill's
election for the State Senate last Spring affords an apt illustra-
tion of these results. He was nominated by the Caucus, and
being so nominated the *Journal* would not support anybody else
Federal or Republican. I suppose there is no doubt the Editor
himself, voted for Mr. Hill. At any rate I have been assured
that if he would have opened his paper, to the nomination and
support of any other Republican Candidate, (whose opinions
were friendly) Mr. Hill would not have been elected. Thus far,
in almost every instance, the opposition, tho' a small minority,
has succeeded in obtaining the command of "the machinery and
organization" of the party. I had last Winter several conversations with Mr. Bell on this subject, and expressed to him my
decided opinion, that the true course was to appeal directly to the

people, on broad and popular grounds, with an abstinence from all reference to former Party. He signified uniformly that his own feelings would lead to such a course (and I have no doubt they would) but he was afraid to ask it, as a matter of policy. I believe that in regard to the Federalists, their opinions and feelings were fully made known to Mr. Bell, before the Meeting of the Legislature; that they expressed their entire readiness, and their solicitude, to join in any Measure, calculated to strengthen the Administration, but they stated distinctly also, that if this was expected of them, no mark of *opprobrium* must be set upon them. While they did not wish anything to be done, to show any *union* with them, they still expected that nothing would be done to exclude and proscribe them publicly and offensively. Notwithstanding this, as you will have seen, the meeting which was called, was limited in the terms of the call, ex industria, to the "Republican friends of the Administration". This call did not embrace in its terms, one half in number, or a fifth in talent and character, of all the friends of the Administration in the Legislature. What happened afterwards and by consequence you have noticed. If I had been in my Brother's situation I probably should have supported the Resolutions, notwithstanding the previous proceedings had been conducted in such a spirit. I have made so many sacrifices of feeling, in such cases, that they come easy to me. But it seems he did not desire to brook it. There is not a faster friend to the Administration in the State, nor a more devoted supporter of the President personally, than he is. I may say this, as you do not know much of him, that his weight and consideration with the Community and in the Legislature, are deemed to belong to few. No harm as to New Hampshire politics, will grow out of this business, although as I have before said, its effect elsewhere may be feared. It will, perhaps, impress one salutory truth on the minds of our friends, in that State, to wit, that this Administration, cannot be supported, but upon the merits of its acts, and by a direct appeal to the judgment of the People. I am thoroughly convinced that it cannot be upheld anywhere, by combinations and arrangements, among political leaders. It is the singular fortune (for good or bad) of the Person now at the head of the Nation, that if he has any party disposed to support him, it is the party of the People, Craving your pardon, for the unexpected length of this letter, I beg to repeat the assurances of my sincere regard.

DAN'L WEBSTER.

(From Joshua Phillips.)

ELDREDGE, County of Huron, Ohio.
[Dec. 10, 1827]

Dear Sir,

I hereby inform you that we had a County meeting at the
Court House last Friday for the purpose of Appointing Delegates to meet with others from different parts of the State at
Columbus the last of December to nominate Electors for President & Vice President & to take all laudable measures to secure
the reelection of John Q. Adams

As there is little or nothing said publicly about Vice President
I would suggest the propriety of nominating Daniel Webster
of Boston as a Candidate for Vice President the ensueing election
& you need feel no delicacy in answering me for I am your friend.
Although I was not intimately acquainted with you in New
Hampshire I was personaly so. I have mentioned you as a
Candidate for Vice President to some of my friends & have told
them in addition to other things you would never fight a Duel

Yours respectfully

JOSHUA PHILLIPS

(From Jeremiah Mason.[1])

PORTSMOUTH Jany 9, 1828

My dear Sir

On coming home today from Salem, I received your letter of
26 Decr., which had been lying by several days. I had been
desirous of writing to you from the time I first heard of your &
Mrs Websters sickness at N. York.   *   *   *

I am aware that your sufferings have been excessive & with all
the alleviation of present favourable appearances, if they continue as when Mr. Paige left you, that your situation must still
be full of distress. In case Mrs. Webster still continues in a
condition actually critical, in the opinion of those most competent to judge of it, I do not think that your duty to the public
requires you to leave her to resume your seat in the Senate. Indeed it seems to me that under such circumstances it must be quite
impossible for you to attend to your duties in the Senate, and I
think you ought not to attempt it. Nor do I think you

---

[1] Printed in Jeremiah Mason's "Memoir," p. 309.

ought to return to Washington till your own health is in a good degree restored, & confirmed. But I hope & trust my dear Sir that when you receive this, Mrs Webster may be deemed to be out of danger. If however she should unfortunately be otherwise & that you should be obliged to remain with her (as I think in that case you would,) I much doubt whether that would justify you in *immediately* or *soon* vacating your seat in the Senate. This I understand to be the intimation in your letter. Whether her continuing long in such situation would not render your resignation expedient can be determined hereafter. I most cordially wish under present circumstances that you was out of the Senate. But I do not see how you will justify resigning at *this time*. Your motives will be misunderstood by many of your political friends & misunderstood & misrepresented by all your political enemies. Your resignation would unquestionably be imputed to your supposed dispair of success of the Administration party. I am sure it would be so represented by all the opposition papers in the U. S., and I think it very probable that many not under their influence would believe it. Considering your standing, such a belief might at the present time do the administration & the Country vast injury. I think the injury arising from absence from the Senate would be immeasureably less than from your resignation. Having accepted the place so recently nothing but imperious necessity will be or ought to be considered a justification for resigning it under the present circumstances of the Country. At all events I hope you will not come to a determination to do this hastily. If you find it probable that you must be absent from the Senate the whole or chief part of the present session I think you ought to state your willingness to resign to some of your political friends at Washington & be in some measure guided by their opinion of its expediency. There can be no danger of thereby exposing yourself to the suspicion of wishing to obtain their advice to retain it altho, I doubt not such will be their earnest advice—You are too well known at W. to fear anything of that sort.

After giving you my opinion thus frankly on this point, I think I am bound to say with equal frankness that not only Mrs Websters situation, if it continues to be dangerous & critical, but in my opinion a due regard for your own health, if it be as low & slender as I fear, makes it your duty to remain quietly where you are for the present. I know the calls for you in the Supr. Court will be urgent, but I really fear that any extraordinary exertions with your present feeble health & anxiety may destroy you—If you do return to Washington I most sincerely advise you to abstain as much as possible from occasions of high excitement & exertion.   Such a course under present circumstances cannot injure your reputation.   *   *   *

The prospect is now favourable for our spring elections— There will be greater exertions & excitement than we have experienced for many years.

We shall be very desirous of hearing occasionally how you & Mrs Webster are.   Mrs. Mason joins me in affectionate regards to her & yourself.

        I am my dear Sir most sincerely yours

                                J. Mason

_____

(To Ezekiel Webster.[1])

                    WASHINGTON, Mar. 18, '28.
My Dear Sir

We are exceedingly delighted with the N. Hampshire news. It has caused many gratulations, & rejoicings, among *some* of us, & disappointment & chagrin are very visible on the faces of *others*.   It was really expected here that Genl. Pierce w'd. be re-elected.   Several of the N. H. members had little hopes till I showed them your letter, written after your return from Haverhill.   They esteemed that authentic, & took courage.   They all, I believe—& some, I know—see & feel how much you have aided to bring about this excellent, excellent, result,   I mean to be proud of the old *Natale Solum* after all—(Mary must translate my Latin)—I only beg you, now, *not to lose the fruits of victory.* Follow up the blow.   You know *one thing*, which I have very much at heart.   *Be in season, in preparing for that.*

You will never regret it.

I see a good number of good men returned to the House, Stevens, Farley, Peabody, Chamberlain, Chamberlain,[2] Kent, Abbott, &c. &c.—It looks, too, as if Wallace & Steele were both chosen into the Senate.

I have the pleasure to say that from other quarters the news is most cheering.   Kentucky is now the great point of attention. Her election for Govr. &c. takes place the first Monday in Au-

_____

[1] The original is the property of Edwin W. Sanborn.
[2] The repetition is in the original.

gust. Metcalf vs Barry. This will call out the whole strength of parties, & settle the final vote of Kentucky. It will be a severe contest, but our friends are in good spirits, & high hopes. Recent intelligence is very favorable.

In N. York the Anti-masonic feeling is bearing down everything. Noth'g can stand before it; not even Genl. Jackson. For once, an incident is helping the right side. Mr. Adams *is not* a mason. Genl. J. is.—A delegation from nearly half the State assembled ten days ago, at Le Roy, as an anti-masonic Convention. Genl. Wadsworth presided.—Out of 77 members, 76 were for Administration. They will have a Convention, in the Spring or Summer, to agree on a Govr. It will be Ch. Jus. Savage, or Mr. Granger, of Canandaigua.

I now *believe* Mr. Adams will be re-elected.

I shall send you more of Mr. Wright's speeches, & the other Documents you write for. The Court has adjourned; & I hope to have time to breathe—& to think of my friends.

Pray give my best love to your wife & children.

Yrs. always,

D. WEBSTER

(To Jos. E. Sprague.)

PRIVATE AND CONFIDENTIAL.

WASHINGTON Mar. 22 1828

My dear Sir,

I thank you for your very kind and gratifying letter of the 16th and reciprocate your congratulations on the result of the N. Hampshire election. Most undoubtedly that result is to be wholly ascribed to the judicious arrangements made in the fall for conducting the elections.[1] If our fellow citizens of the Republican party had adhered to their old usages, and gone with the machinery of the *Caucus*, it is certain now that the friends of the Administration would have been outmanaged, overwhelmed, and defeated—all the success is fairly to be ascribed to the *course* adopted, and I am fully sensible that *no man* in the U. S. had done so much as yourself to bring men's minds to agree to that course— Whoever else forgets this *I* shall not— I am persuaded that your efforts have been felt, not only in Mass. but

---

[1] See McMaster, " History of United States," vol. v, p. 6, for the anti-caucus movement.

also very deeply in N. Hampshire and generally throughout the country. I know no one who has done so much The present united force of New England is mainly owing to the course which you have steadily and zealously urged on your Republican friends,— Depend on it— that you have been *abused* because you have been *felt* and that the loud cry against *amalgamation* has originated in the terror which our enemies felt at the idea of a union among their adversaries— You will see Judge Story as soon as he returns, He and I had some conversation, which I asked him to state to you, and to which I ask your particular attention—

As to the mission to England, it is a subject on which I know little and say nothing. I heard what your opinion is, and assure you that you may rest satisfied of one thing—and that is—that nothing will be done as far as I am concerned, but on the maturest consideration and nothing on grounds merely personal. Our friends think that prospects are getting better and better both on this and the other side of the Alleghany. The first great contest is to be I think in Kentucky on the 1st Monday in Augt. If General Metcalf shall succeed by a large majority, the effect will be not only to secure the whole vote of Kentucky, but also to give great courage and activity to our friends elsewhere. In this last point of view even the recent election election in N. Hampshire has done good. We do not enough estimate the effect which an expression of public opinion in one state has in another, however remote. For this reason it is of great importance that the tone in N. England should be united decisive and strong.

Yours always truly
D. WEBSTER.

(To Jos. E. Sprague.)

CONFIDENTIAL.   WASHINGTON April 13 1828

Dear Sir,

I saw Mr. Silsbee's letter received from you yesterday. Your election comes on nobly. From what I see, I shall confidently expect that you yourself will be in the Senate. You certainly deserve to be there from your able and indefatigable exertions in the good cause, as well as from your ability to be useful in that situation. I fear we are getting into trouble here about the *Tariff*.[1]   The House of Representatives *will pass the Bill*—it will be a poor and inefficient aid to wool and woolens, and will [   ][2] the molasses and hemp in it, what shall *we* do with it?   Pray turn your thoughts to this matter a little.

1. Can we *go* the *hemp*, iron, spirits and molasses for the sake of any woolen bill?

2. Can we do it for a poor woolen Bill?

Yours always truly,

D. W.

P. S.   I think the Bill will positively *injure* the manufacturer, (though possibly the "passing" it may help the woolen grower—

(To Jeremiah Mason.)

WASHINGTON March 20th 1828.

My Dear Sir

The practice of asking the advice of friends, in one's own affairs, is a little old fashioned.   I do not think very highly of the custom, myself, still, I now write mainly for the purpose of taxing your good nature with the request, that you will say, in a strait forward way, & few words what you think upon the subject, with which the newspaper have been busy, for some time past.   I do not mean to trouble you for a long statement of *pros* & *Cons*; nor do I mean to anticipate your impressions, by a single suggestion of my own.   You see what all the world sees, & know what all the world knows, of the state of things here, & of *my* present condition—Will it be best for the *administration*, & best for *me* that I stay where I am, or that I go elsewhere?[3]

I care not how *shortly* you speak, but I pray you to speak *freely*

We are in very good spirits, with the news from N. Hamp.   I believe certain Gentlemen here are a good deal disappointed.   It was confidently expected by them, that Genl Pierce would succeed.[4]

We trust he has failed & it seems that our friend Hill[5] is out also.

---

[1] See McMaster's "History of the United States," vol. v. p. 254, *et seq.*
[2] A blank is left here in the copy.   Original not obtainable.
[3] Refers to the talk of sending Daniel Webster to England.
[4] In the contest for the governorship.   John Bell was elected.
[5] Isaac Hill.

Affairs here are wearing rather a better appearance.   The intelligence, from interesting points, is a little cheering.   Perhaps the most important contests or rather one of the earliest of the important contests will be in Kentucky.   The election of Govr &c takes place, in that state, on the first Monday in August.   The whole will turn, mainly, on the administration question.   Metcalf is candidate, for the adm'n'n side, & Barry whom you know, for the opposition.   The result of this election is likely to decide the ultimate vote (*the whole vote*) of Kentucky, & must necessarily have a great operation elsewhere.   If Barry should succeed, by a strong vote, I should give up Kentucky; & with Kentucky, nearly all hope of Mr Adam's reelection.   New York is unquestionably *mending*.   If it goes on, as it is now going, a great majority of votes in that state will be for Mr Adams.

The Louisiana members are to be elected again, in July.   It is believed Mr. Livingston will be left out, & a friend of Admsn [the admistration] elected in N. Orleans.

Judge Story left us two days ago.   The Court has had an interesting session, & decided many causes.   The Judge of our Circuit has drawn up an uncommon number of its opinions, &, I think, some of them, with uncommon ability.

Yrs always truly

D. WEBSTER

(*From Robert B. Campbell.*[1])

WASHINGTON March 25th. 1828.

Sir;

I have received a note from Mr. Randolph to which I am about to send the answer annexed.   In doing so, I am actuated by no desire of becoming a party to any controversy, for I have a repugnance to every thing of the kind.   I do not however feel authorized in refusing to commit to paper, when desired, the substance of a conversation held with a gentleman three years ago four hundred miles from this place.

Yr. Obt. S^r.

ROBERT B. CAMPBELL.

Hon. D. Webster.

---

[1] Representative from South Carolina.

(From Rob't. B. Campbell to John Randolph.[1])

WASHINGTON, March 25th. 1828.

Sir

In reply to your note, my recollection enables me to state only, that on the morning of the last day of the Session of Congress of 1824, the Richmond Enquirer containing your letter to your Constitutents was passing among a few gentlemen who were reading & descanting upon your strictures on the conduct of the committee appointed to investigate the charges against Mr. Crawford.   During this conversation Mr. Webster arrived in the Representative Chamber, when his attention was called to your communication.   While persuing it, he appeared much excited & incensed, repeatedly denounced it as a lye, & asserted that upon the meeting of the House he would proclaim it, in as plain language as a sense of decorum would permit.   Shortly after the meeting of the House Mr. Webster rose in his place, and in words which I cannot now repeat, reiterated the charge of falsehood and concluded by saying if any gentleman could and would convey his meaning in stronger language he would thank him to do so. Having no particular reason to charge my memory with Mr. Websters remarks, they would probably have been forgotten had not their violence forcibly impressed me.

r. Obt. S^r.

ROBERT B. CAMPBELL

(To Jos. E. Sprague.)

HANOVER July 20. 1828

My dear sir,

Your several letters have reached me here, beginning with that addressed to me at Nantucket.   Various things have successively occurred to put the "Address" out of my thoughts, or out of my power.   I intended to have written you on the subject while at Boston, but in truth there were so many other things pressing, and I was under so urgent a necessity to get out of Town, for the sake of a little *rest*, that I omitted it.   Without more of apology

---

[1] This letter accompanied the one written to Daniel Webster by Campbell, March 25, 1828.   See the letters between Benton and Daniel Webster dated Feb. 25, 1825.

I wish now to say that if the paper is drawn up by another hand, I shall be very glad; if it be not and it is still wished that I should do it, I wish to suggest my opinion; according to which I would be willing to make an attempt at an address, that is that it should not be prepared and published till the first of October— or certainly not till September. The main reason for this opinion is that by the 20th of Augt. we shall be in possession of the result in Louisiana and Kentucky, of the pending elections. That result whether favorable or unfavorable will make a considerable change in our condition and prospects and the address would profitably be accomodated to the new state of things.

I leave here for *home* tomorrow or tuesday. I shall be in Boston by Friday or Saturday when I hope to hear from you.

Yours truly

D. W.

(*To Jos. E. Sprague.*)

Saturday Evening. [Aug. 1828]

My dear friend.

I hope you will not come up *tomorrow*, for though I am most sorry to say it I have not yet succeeded to do any thing valuable— I find it exceedingly difficult to say anything which has not been said before. Yesterday and today I have staid in my Study without being able to satisfy myself at all. Tomorrow I will write you again, not expecting to go out of town till *Tuesday*. I have a letter this evening from Lexington (Mr C.) dated the 12th.[1] It is very good— It states in effect as follows namely.— that General M. is elected *by not less* than 1500 votes, that the Lieutenant Governor is also elected. That the late Jackson speaker is defeated in his election. That there are ascertained to be majorities favorable to the administration in at least two of the districts now represented in Congress by Jackson members— That the successor to General Metcalf in Congress is an administration man, and finally that in all probability there are majorities favorable to the administration in both branches of the Legislature

Yours truly always

D. W.

---

[1] The letter from Clay (?) has not been preserved.

(To J. Q. Adams.¹)

BOSTON, Sept. 13, 1828

Dr. Sir:

I herewith transmit copies of two letters which passed in Feb. 1825 between Mr. Warfield, of Maryland, and myself. This correspondence, as far as I know, is the whole foundation of all that has been said about the "Webster pledge". My object now, is to submit to your consideration, and that of those around you, the expediency of publishing the letters. To that end, it would be necessary first, to obtain Mr. Warfield's consent. The publication if made, may be made perhaps by him better than by others. If Mr. Clay had been at Washington, I should probably have written him, on this subject; as I have reason to think that Mr. Warfield has had some conversation with him, upon it. In his absence, I am quite willing, if you think best, that the paper should be handed to Mr. Rust, and published in such manner as his judgment may approve. Mr. Warfield being first consulted. I have only to add the wish, that the mode of publication may be such, as shall not make my appearance in the newspapers necessary, if any publication should be made. It strikes me, that a short note from Mr. Warfield to some editor, transmitting these letters, would be the most eligible manner. But of this a better judgment can be formed by others. If thought better on the whole, that the publication should be authorized by me, I will cause it to be done, if Mr. W's consent be obtained. I do not write to him not knowing his address.

Yours always truly,

DAN'L WEBSTER.

(To Jos. E. Sprague.)

Wednesday Morning. [Sept. 1828]

Dear Sir

I believe you will do well to put this address into other hands at once, and those other hands I am clear should be your *own*. Strike out the thing, and I will go over it with you, if you desire it and make any suggestions which occur to me. I have really been too unwell for these three weeks past to do anything. The

---

¹ This letter is owned by Charles Francis Adams.

letter which you saw yesterday must also be attended to, and in my present condition I can *beg* better than I can write.

Yours faithfully

D. WEBSTER

I shall see you tomorrow if weather and health allow.

(From Ezekiel Webster.[1])

BOSTON, Jany. 31, 1829.

My Dear Brother.

I intend to go to Boscawen Monday morning. I have had a very pleasant week. The children are all well and very happy. It is very good coasting on the common and Edward is delighted.

Mr. Hale tells me that the correspondence between Mr. Adams & "other folks" is now in his press & will be out in a few days. From his account of it I apprehend, the business will not end with the present publication. I trust Mr. Adams' answer will not be satisfactory to anybody. There was never a publication, I so much regretted as Mr. A's "*explanation*" in the Intelligencer. You will see the account of Col. Pickering's death, before this reaches you. Judge Claggett also died very recently.

I can give you nothing from New Hampshire, in addition to what I said in my last. There is a good deal of anxiety here to know what the Senate will do with the nominations now before you.

Yours truly,

E. WEBSTER.

(To Ezekiel Webster.[2])

feb. 23. [1829]

PRIVATE.

Dr E.

I wrote you last eve' at abt. Capt. Stone's business—I will see it attended to, the earliest moment I can leave the Senate.

A prodigious excitement has been produced by the new Cabinet List.[3] It has set all Washington in a *buz*—friends rage, &

---

[1] This letter is owned by Edwin W. Sanborn, of New York.
[2] This letter is owned by Edwin W. Sanborn, of New York.
[3] Jackson's cabinet.

foes laugh. Nobody will say he was privy to it. Nobody justifies it. The clamor, (for that is not too strong a name) became so loud, that we hear today of a change, that is, that Mr. McLean is to be Secretary of War, instead of *Major Eaton.* This will in some matter alleviate the discontents, but still I think they are deep, & likely to be permanent. This very first step of Genl. Jackson presents him his first difficulty, & every other step will repeat it. His friends have no common principle—they are held together by no common tie—& my private opinion is, tho' I do not wish to be quoted for that, at present, is, that Genl. J. has not character enough to conduct his measures by his own strength. Somebody must and will lead him. Who it will be, I cannot say—but I have an opinion—I will write you again soon, I think I see unsettled times before us. Let me know what prospects your election [promises]—take all the care of it you well can.

Yrs. D. W.

(Memorandum.[1])

[Feb. 1829]

Gen. J.[2] will be here abt. 15. Feb.—
Nobody knows what he will do when he does come.
Many letters are sent to him; he answers none of them.
His friends here pretend to be very knowing; but, be assured, not one of them has any confidential communication from him.
Great efforts are making to put him up to a general sweep, as to all offices; springing from great doubts whether he is disposed to go it.
Nobody is authorized to say, whether he intends to retire, after one term of service.
Who will form his cabinet, is as well known at Boston, as at Washington.
The present apparent calm is a suspension of action—a sort of syncope—arising from ignorance of the views of the President elect.
My opinion is
That when he comes he will bring a breeze with him.

---

[1] Evidently sent by Webster to some New England friend. The original is in the possession of Mr. Edwin W. Sanborn, of New York city, which would seem to indicate that Ezekiel Webster was the recipient.
[2] General Jackson.

Which way it will blow, I cannot tell.

He will either *go with the party*, as they say in N. Y., or *go the whole hog*, as it is [vulgarly] phrased, making all the places he can for friends & supporters, & shaking a rod of terror at his opposers;

Or else, he will continue to keep his own counsels, make friends & advisers of whom he pleases, *& be President upon his own strength*.

The first would show boldness, where there is no danger; & decision, where the opposite [virtue] of moderation would be more useful.

The latter would show real nerve, & if he have talents to maintain himself in that course, true greatness.

My *fear* is stronger than my *hope*.

Mr. Adams is in good health, & complains not at all of the measure meted out to him.

Mr. Clay's health is much improved, & his spirits excellent. He goes to K. in March & I conjecture will be pressed into the next H. R.

His chance of being at the head of affairs is now better, in my judgment, than ever before.

Keep N. E. firm & steady, & she *can* make him Prest. if she chooses

Sundry important nominations are proposed, probably to know Genl. J's pleasure.

The above contains all that is known here, at this time.

(To Ezekiel Webster.[1])

Feb. 5. '29.

My Dear E.

I thank you for your letter from Boston, & wish I had any thing good to tell you from here. But I have not. Those events in N. Jersey & Louisiana have quite depressed us. We are beaten, where we had decisive majorities, by private disagreements & individual partialities. The next Senate will contain a majority favorable to Gen. Jackson, at least who have favored his election, even tho' a Delaware or a N. H. member should be removed to the Cabinet. Neither of these however, is likely.

---

[1] This letter is owned by Edwin W. Sanborn, of New York.

There are greater & stronger claimants.   The City is already full of hungry friends, & will *overflow*, before the 3. of March. Mr. Hill [1] & his cavalcade have not yet arrived, but we understand they are on the road; viz Col. McNeil, Col. Decatur, &c. &c.— Mr. Green, of the Boston Statesman, has been here a month, & a Delegation from the other branch of the Jackson family in Boston arrived last night.   It consists of Genl. Boyd, Col. Orne, & Dr. Ingalls.   Most of these persons are doomed to taste of disappointment.

It is not possible Hill can get the P. Office.   He may, very probably, get some little office, such as an Auditorship—and will be kept here, as a supporter, & as charged with the conversion of N. E.   But I incline to think he will lose his importance, as soon as he leaves home.

Gen. Jackson will be here, in a day or two.   I am of opinion his health is very feeble, & that there is not much chance of his lasting long.

We have *done* nothing in the Senate.   It is difficult to foretell results.   With some, especially the *Federalists* who joined Genl. Jackson's cause, there is as much bitterness as you ever saw in the Concord Patriot.

It is eno' to disgust one with all public employment.—

I have spoken to two or three of the N. Hamp. Govt.   They will do what they can.   The outside of yr affairs looks promising enough, but I suppose it is, as you say, very doubtful how the election will go.   It is of great importance, & I hope no proper pains will be spared.—

I shall write you again soon— I hope oftener than hitherto.

Yrs.

D. WEBSTER.

(To Ezekiel Webster.[2])

WASHINGTON, Feb. 26, 1829.

Dr E.

The cabinet arrangements have been announced, & they are as I wrote you.   It is, on the whole, a very *weak* Cabinet; & if it get along, it must be rather by its weakness, than its strength.   If, with *this* Cabinet, Gen. J. takes a high handed course, he will

---

[1] Isaac Hill, of New Hampshire.
[2] The original of this letter is owned by Edwin W. Sanborn, of New York.

not and cannot sustain himself. Hundreds of partizans are & thousands will be, exceedingly disappointed, by the disposition of offices; & clamor and discontent will arise. In Va. especially the Cabinet is *unpopular*—greatly so. Now, under these circumstances, I rather expect Genl. J. will take a *moderate* course —perhaps a *vacillating* one. The elements of dissension will be in the Cabinet itself. Mr. Calhoun, (who tho not nominally in the Cabinet, is likely to be *near* the President) & Mr. Van Buren & Mr. McLean will all be looking out for the *succession*. I think it possible the state of things may be much as it was under the last 4 yrs of Mr. Madison.

We shall have time to *see* & to *know* someth'g before I leave here. The great point, at present, is the N. Hamp. election. Depend on it, this is the turning point. If Govr. Bell should now succeed, there will be little difficulty hereafter. Pray let your friends be wakened up;—& do your best.—

I shall stay here till about the 20 March. By that time, I shall hear from N. Hamp. If it should look likely that you are to be here, I shall leave my *Books* here, so that if I do not come back, you can take care of them. Otherwise, I shall box them up, & send them home,—to be brought back, if I come back. On this point, I have much to say when I see you.

Yrs as ever,

D. WEBSTER.

———

(To Ezekiel Webster.[1])

WASHINGTON, March 2, '29.

Dear E.

Noth'g of importance has occurred since I wrote you last. The Cabinet list stands as it did. There is much dissatisfaction, especially among the Virginia Gentlemen. Yet they must submit. The general idea now is, that Genl. J. will make no great number of *changes*. The cabinet is not strong enough to carry on a mere party administration. This the Genl. will know soon, if he does not know now. I shall stay here till 20th inst. Send me word of your earliest Election returns.

Yrs.

D. W.

[1] The original of this letter is owned by Edwin W. Sanborn, of New York.

(To Henry Clay.)

BOSTON Sept. 24. 1829.

My dear Sir

The bearer of this is William Smith Esquire of Exeter, N. Hampshire, a member of our profession, and a respectable and very well-informed young man— He has been several years a member of the Legislature of N. H. and extensively acquainted in that state.

Having been sick, and his health not yet entirely confirmed, he intends passing the winter under a climate somewhat less stern than that of New England.

He will probably visit Lexington, and I have great pleasure in commending him to your regard and kindness. Willing to be useful to him, on his own account I feel an added motive in my regard for his Father, one of my earliest and truest friends. Him you know at least by reputation.

He was in Congress in the good old times, and not undistinguished there when distinction was worth something, at subsequent periods he has been Ch. Justice and Gov'r of *our* state of New Hampshire.

I am dear Sir always faithfully and cordially yours

DANIEL WEBSTER/

———

(From Edward Everett.)

[Jan 26. 1830.]

*   *   *   "When you come to the standard of the Union, in the peroration look at (what was floating in your mind) Milton's description of the infernal banner, in the lower regions, floating across the immensity of space, which is in turn borrowed from Tasso's description of the banner of the crusades, when first unfolded in Palestine."[1]   *   *   *

Yours ever

E. E.

———

[1] This passage closes a long description of what Hayne had said in his speech on the Foote resolution. It is not dated, but seems to have been written after Webster's reply to Hayne and before the speech was written out for publication.

(From Isaac Munroe.)

BALTIMORE, Feb. 1, 1830.

My dear Sir:

I must beg the favor of you to forward me a copy or two of y'r. Speech[1] by the *first* mail after it is committed to press. I congratulate you most cordially & sincerely upon your triumph, in the most signal manner, not only in the estimation of y'r. friends, but of your opponents, who are forced to acknowledge it. From the date of that Speech I shall date the rise & successful progress of liberal & enlightened principles in our country. The reign of ignorance must be short & the march of intellect most certain.

Very respectfully & truly y'r ob't. Serv't.

ISAAC MUNROE.

(From H. A. Dearborn.)

BOSTON, Feby. 5. 1830—

My Dear Sir,

The glorious effect of your patriotic, able & eloquent defense of New England,[1] & the triumphant support you have given, to the fundamental principles of the constitution, are not confined to the capital of the Union. The aroma comes to gladden our hearts, like the spicy gales of Arabia, to the distant mariner.

Never have I heard such universal & ardent expressions of joy & approbation. You have assumed an attitude, which the adverse times demanded, & nobly braved the storm, that threatened the destruction of our liberties. The dignity & independence of your manner, & the time, all were calculated to produce a result auspicious to our destinies.

I can but feebly announce the tone of public sentiment, which your speech has aroused, & the climactical demonstration upon that wretch, who presumes to act the part of a dictator. You have the warm gratitude of the north & must command the respect of the south & the west.

This is the attitude for a great statesman,—a firm & honest champion of our rights, & institutions. How infinitely low &

---

[1] The reply to Hayne. Only a few of the many letters of congratulation have been selected and those as diverse as possible in the nature of their commendatory sentiment.

[2] In the reply to Hayne.

mean & contemptable, appear the demagogues of faction, when contrasted with such a man in such an imposing attitude.

With assurances of my profound respect, your sincere friend & most obt. St.

H. A. DEARBORN.

(From J. W. Scott.)

COLUMBIA. South Carolina. Feb. 12, 1830.
Sir,

I am a son of New England and proud to claim you as her Champion. The friends of Mr. Hayne will be very active in circulating his 2nd. speech on Foots Resolution and I am anxious to have the antidote to circulate with the bane. You would therefore oblige me by sending me your rejoinder. Receive my warm acknowledgements for your able and manly defence of *my Country*—the Country of Yankees.

With admiration & respect Yours &C

J. W. SCOTT

(From Robert Walsh.[1])

PHILADELPHIA March 8 1830
Dear Sir

I thank you for the fair copy of *the* Speech, which you have had the goodness to send me. You probably know the opinion which I have expressed of it in my gazette; & I will abstain therefore from repeating my encomium. Nothing of the kind was ever sought with so much avidity here, within my knowledge. You may remember how I exhorted you to make *several* great efforts during the session. You are universally read, and the proper impression is widely made in spite of all prejudice and obloquy.   * * *

Dear Sir, Your respectful & affecte. friend & sevt.

ROBT WALSH, JR.

(From James B. Longacre.)

CHARLESTON S. C. March 2, 1840.
Dear Sir

The relations and friends of the late Governor Hayne of this

---

[1] Editor of the National Gazette. He was an author of considerable prominence among the writers of the day.

State, have requested me to publish an engraving from my original Portrait of him, taken in 1830— and it has occurred to me, that the appearance of your name amongst the subscribers, would be no detriment to your fame in the south—

I do not make the suggestion from a consideration of personal advantage to myself, but regarding my occupations as an artist in the light of an attempt to strew flowers on the pathway of our national history, I have thought you would appreciate the occasion I am able to offer you— if my conjecture is correct; I request the favor of a brief note from you directed to this city, expressive of your views, on paper not occupying a larger space than this.

With sentiments of high regard—I remain Your Ob't Serv't &c

JAMES B. LONGACRE

(To James B. Longacre.)

WASHINGTON Mar. 6, [1840.]

Dear Sir,

I understand you are about publishing an Engraving of your Portrait of the late Govr. Hayne, whose afflicting death I learned, with much pain, in Europe last year.

It has been my fortune to pass several years in public life with Govr. Hayne and I have ever entertained for him a very high opinion, as a man of distinguished talents, perfect integrity, great urbanity, and always devoting himself, with singular zeal & fidelity, to the discharge of his duties.

I will be obliged to you to send me a copy of the Engraving.

Yours with regard,

DANL WEBSTER

(To Jos. E. Sprague.)

WASHINGTON March, 16, 1830

Dear Sir,

I thank you for your very kind letter of the 9th of March, as soon as I came home, I will give every degree of attention, to the object about which you write. I am fully, *deeply* impressed with its importance. Prospects, of a favorable character, are opening, far and wide, and I think we shall see things clearly by midsummer.

Boston is your place for the next three or four years.

You are very civil, in what you say about my speech.   It has made much more noise than it deserved.   The *times* favored its impression.   I follow your hint, and shall frank a copy, of a handsome edition to every member of the Legislature.

Things move very slowly here—   The *Printers* not yet acted on, their fate is quite doubtful,

Nothing will be done with the Tariff.

Yours truly

D. WEBSTER

Your numbers on Mr. Cambreling's[1] Report are read and praised by every body,

———

(To Jeremiah Mason.)

WASHINGTON Mar. 19, '30

My Dear Sir

I return Mr. ——— letter Mr. A.[2] did quite as well, in his letter to the Statesman, as could be expected.

We have not yet acted on the N. H. nominations.   I know not whether to decide to reject them, or not,—   Decatur & Cushman[3] are in great danger but would they be succeeded by any body better?   And if Hill should be rejected, should we not have him in the Senate?

Appearances, in various parts of the Country, indicate dissatisfaction wit hthe present state of things.   The stock of patronage is exhausted, & many are left unprovided for, & they are looking out for other parties, & other leaders,   It is admitted, I believe by most, that Mr. Clay is gaining rapidly in the west. Kentucky is doubtless strong for him & as agt. any body but Gen'l. Jackson, he would take nearly all the western votes.   In the mean time, the Anti Masonic party,[4] steadily encreasing in

---

[1] Churchill C. Cambreling was long a representative in Congress from New York.   He had been engaged in mercantile pursuits with John Jacob Astor and had traveled extensively.   As chairman of the Committees on Commerce, Ways and Means and on Foreign Affairs his reports were numerous and excellent.   One report on Commerce and Navigation went through several editions.

[2] Atherton (?).

[3] See Jeremiah Mason to Daniel Webster, Feb. 8, 1830, in J. Mason's "Memoirs."

[4] See McMaster's " History of the United States," vol. v, p. 109-120.

N. York, is breaking out like an Irish rebellion in Pennsylvania.— It goes on with a force that subdues all other feeling.—These things put party calculations at defiance.— The party here are obviously very much alarmed. The adm'n Senators are understood to have held a *Caucus*, three nights ago, & endeavored to unite & rally. Something more of tone & decision has been since visible It may become, *perhaps*, [the cause of] the Confirmation of all the appointments— As to *measures*, they are irreconcilable,— They cannot stir agt. the Tariff, As a means of union & a *necessary* means—they seem now resolved to keep the present President in office thro. a second term.— He now intends to hold on, beyond all doubt. Here again, accidents to his life or health, would produce quite a new state of things— So that, on the whole, I do not think there has been a period in our time when one could see less of the future than the present

I thank you for your civil sayings about my speech. It has made much more talk than it deserves, owing to the topic, & to the times. I hope it is doing some good at the South, where I have reason to think, it is very generally circulated & read.

Yrs very sincerely

D WEBSTER

having cut my thumb, I write even worse than usual.

———

(From D. Fletcher Webster.)

HOPKINTON March 23.d 1830.

My Dear Father,

 * * * I never knew what the constitution really was, till your last short speech. I thought it was a compact between States. I like that last reply better than all the rest; for it comes out so a'propos, and *conclusive* that Mr. H. has nothing more to say. It is the "Cou de Grace" It winds him up; as we boys used to say. I saw in the papers that the Postmaster has made a new construction of the franking law to suit the occasion.

I do not know how it is; but it seems to me to be as plain an usurpation, or misuse of power as ever was.

However, they can only do so three years longer. * * *

Your ever affectionate Son,

D. F. WEBSTER.

(To Hon. Jos. E. Sprague.)

PRIVATE AND CONFIDENTIAL.

[March 24. 1830]

Dear Sir

Can you inform me what summer it was that Mr. Henshaw[1] passed a part of at the *Hermitage*[2] Can you send me a newspaper which stated, long before General Jackson's election how the Boston appointments were to be disposed of, It may be useful to know that Mr. Henshaw, understood what his chance was in case of success, as soon as he returned from Tennessee—

Yours truly

D. WEBSTER.

(To Jeremiah Mason.)

Wednesday Eve' April 14, [1830]

Dr Sir

A feeble attempt was made to day to reconsider Hill's nomination, but as the *rejection* had been notified to the President, it was held to be out of order.— His game, I think, is finished here.— The President has the power, I suppose, of nominating him again; tho' he will hardly be advised to do that, & it would do no good, if he should do so.— nothing could get him thro' the Senate, for any office— The rejection has produced a strong sensation *here* for so small a thing—The poor N. H. members especially are wofully mortified. H. H.,[1] I learn was heard to say he would rather have lost the whole N. H. Election—- Kendall's fate & Noah's not yet decided, they are both doubtful. I incline to think they will both depend on the casting vote of the V. P.—

There was a great party dinner, yesterday, as you will see. The object was to recompose & reconstruct the party, on the Old Jefferson platform.— The thing did not go off well. Many, very many of the party found themselves taken in— *All the Penna. members, having seen, before dinner, what the toasts were, took themselves off!*

I think we shall see some schism grow out of it.—McDuffie's

---

[1] David Henshaw, who was later Secretary of Navy under Tyler.
[2] General Jackson's home.
[3] Henry Hubbard, representative from New Hampshire.

Report, on the Bank Subject, is not yet printed— It is said to be a stiff negative to the President—

I am tired with the Session, & wish myself safely in N. E.

Yrs truly

D WEBSTER

How will Mr. H.[1] appear, should he be prefered for a Seat in the Senate, Since 2/3rds of its members have so significantly manifested their opinion of him. *If he were to come there, they could not speak to him.*

(From Joseph D. Story.)

CAMBRIDGE April 17, 1830

My dear Sir

I was truly comforted by your kind letter, which I received a day or two ago— As soon as I recovered from the severe fatigues of my long & boisterous passage in the Sound, (perilous with all) & had escaped from the throng of kind friends that called on me, I was about writing you— But an entire new direction was given to my thoughts by the horrible murder of Old Capt'n. White at Salem[2]— You are aware that he died childless & that his principal heirs are Mr Stephen White & my Sisters children— It is altogether the most mysterious & dreadful affair that I ever heard of— "Truth is stranger than fiction" has been often said— I never knew any case, which so completely illustrated the truth of the remark as this. Not the slightest trace has as yet been found by which to detect the assassins, (for I am satisfied there was more than one) and we are yet in a darkness rendered still darker by the utter defeat of every conjecture— I have been obliged to go to Salem several times, & every thing there seems in inextricable confusion.

—I never knew such a universal panic.— It is not confined to Salem, or Boston, but seems to pervade the whole community— We are all astounded & looking to know from what quarter the next blow will come— There is a universal dread & sense of insecurity, as if we lived in the midst of a Banditti.

I am satisfied the object was plunder, though it was not prob-

-----

[1] Isaac Hill, of New Hampshire. He did succeed in getting himself elected Senator in 1831.

[2] For a full account of this affair and Webster's part in securing the conviction of the murderers see Curtis' "Life of Daniel Webster," vol. i, p. 378.

ably found, having been removed some time before from the house— It was a deep scheme, by persons who were adepts in their vocation & irretrivably wicked—damned spirits— Its success is astonishing. Its malicious deliberation unparalelled—

Mr White left a Will— He has given many legacies to his relatives; but the bulk of his fortune goes to Mr Stephen White, who will get from 150 to 200 thousand dollars— Three of my nieces will receive about 25,000 each— But of this no more—

I have been in several circles of our friends since my return, all of whom speak in the most gratifying terms of your Speeches— The first effect has not in any degree subsided; admiration & respect seem to have assumed a permanent mastery over all the meaner views of the doubters & the grumblers— There never was a triumph more complete & to all appearance more undisputed— I hear, however, that at the South there is a little rally; but I suspect it is feint—

I met Mr. Prescott[1] the other day & I know you will be pleased to know, that he thinks most highly of your speeches, deeming them all that we could wish & as sound as they are striking. His praise is worth much, for it is considerate and slow—

In respect to the Circuit Court I have no objection to any adjournment, which will suit the convenience of the Bar—. If *after* the R. Island Court it will be agreeable to me— Arrange, as you think best on this subject, remembering only, that our hot weather begins soon after the 20th of June.

All your friends are impatient to see *Mr* Webster, & above all *Mrs. Webster*; & I am quite sure she will be doubly welcomed *home,* for we are quite bent upon making her give up all thoughts that she has any other home than Boston— And Mrs Story and myself are anxious to prove to her, that Cambridge is not more than three miles from town, & a good deal more pleasant & quiet than Pennsylvania Avenue—

I have talked a little with the Saints about a certain thing— They are satisfied with my views, to wait events, & agree that it is not well to say a word until a movement shall be made elsewhere— N England never seemed less inclined to quarrel with her own than now; but she will be wise & frugal of her resources—

The rejection of Hill has given, I believe, general satisfaction— If followed up by others of a like cast, it will do the Admin more good, than any of their measures— Are the re-

---

[1] The historian.

ports of the Birth Day Dinner Arrangements & Developments mere gossip, or true?—

I write you in great haste, being hard driven by business but always Most truly Your friend

JOSEPH D STORY

P. S.   Remember me most kindly to Mr Silsbee & his family— & to Mrs Webster & Julia—   Forget not my admonition about yourself—   Work & think as little as practicable for the present.

———

(To Louis Dwight.[1])

Boston, April 19, 1830.[2]

MY DEAR SIR,

WILL you have the goodness to express your opinions on the following subjects:

1 *What do you think of imprisonment for debt for sums less than one dollar?*

2 *What do you think of imprisonment for more than one, and less than five dollars?*

3 *What do you think of imprisonment for more than five, and less than ten dollars?*

4 *What do you think of imprisonment for more than ten, and less than twenty dollars?*

5 *What do you think of imprisonment for more than twenty, and less than one hundred dollars?*   agt it; at least to 50 Dollars; perhaps to a 100.

6 *What do you think of imprisonment for debt in any case in which there is no evidence of fraud?*

7 *What do you think of imprisonment for thirty days in cases in which the poor debtor's oath is to be taken?*   Useless—

8 *Can Christian imprison Christian for debt, in any case in which there is no evidence of fraud, with a good conscience?* Every Christian must judge for himself, if the law allows it.   I should imprison nobody, for a debt due me, without evidence of fraud.

---

[1] Secretary of the Prison Discipline Society, of Boston, author of a report on the Gaols and Prisons of Massachusetts.

[2] This printed circular was sent by Dwight to Daniel Webster and the latter wrote on the circular and then added the letter.   The printed portion appears here in italics.

9 *Can Christian imprison infidel for debt, in similar circum-*
  stances, with a good conscience?

10 *Is the penalty of imprisonment for debt well proportioned to*
  the aggravation of the offence, in cases where there is no
  evidence of fraud? I think not.

11 *What evils would result from abolishing imprisonment for*
  debt? frauds might, w't very good guards. This w'd
  depend on the modifications, & the substitute.

12 *What benefit would result from abolishing imprisonment for*
  debt?

13 *Have you ever found it necessary to imprison a man for debt*
  due to you personally? I never did it.—

   Please to communicate any facts or remarks, on other
   points, not embraced in these questions, but touching the
   general subject, which you may deem important.

   By answering the above questions, in such manner as you may
think proper, in order to express your opinion on the general
subject of imprisonment for debt, and returning the answer to
me, you will greatly oblige

   Your sincere friend and obedient servant,

                                 LOUIS DWIGHT.

6. question. It seems to me, that when one does not pay his
debts, for example, to his butcher, & baker, & tailor, *he ought
to shew that he is unable, & that his inability is not fraudulent.*—
That is to say, he ought to shew a full & fair excuse, for not paying. It does not appear to me to be enough merely for him to
say that he cannot pay, & then to call on his creditors to *show*
that his inability is merely pretended, or is fraudulent.— The
debtor ought to shew *why* he cannot fullfil his promise—& that
he has not acted fraudulently— When he has shewed this, his
person ought no longer to be held. He ought to be called on,
first, for his own oath, secondly, for any reasonable explanation
of suspicious circumstances, if such exist.— Having done this,
his person ought to be discharged.—

The great remedy for evils of this kind is obvious. Nineteen
twentieths of the whole of it would be relieved, if imprisonment
for small debts were abolished. Small credits are often given on
the confidence of being able to collect, by the terrors of the jail;
great ones never.—

In my humble judgment, two simple provisions would accomplish all that is absolutely required, in Massachusetts—

1. No imprisonment to be allowed, where the debt, exclusive of all costs, does not exceed 50, 75, or 100 Dols.—

2.—Do away the necessity of the imprisonment for 30 days, in order to take the poor debtors oath; and to give to the magistrate, taking the oath such further powers as may be necessary to a full investigation of the fairness or fraud of the debtor's conduct— The Insolvent Laws (not Bankrupt Acts) of England might well be looked to for useful hints on this subject.—

These, My Dear Sir, are very hasty thoughts. They are intended *for your use only, & you must not make them public.* If you wish for any opinions of mine, on these questions, *to be made public,* you must send this sheet back,[1] & let me prepare what I have to say with more deliberation, & express it more fully, & with more care—

Yrs with regard

D. W/

(From Thos. H. Benton.)

SENATE CHAMBER, April 20th. 1830.

Sir,

The object of this note is to inquire whether you have any objection to the publication of the correspondence between yourself and Mr. Randolph in 1825?[2] and, to the promulgation of the verbal agreement which bound each party to contradict any publication, to the prejudice of the other, which came within its knowledge?

Yours, &c.
THOMAS H. BENTON.

(To Thomas H. Benton.)

SENATE CHAMBER, April 20,—[1830]

Sir

I have your note of this morning. What passed on the occasion referred to, in 1825, having taken place under an agreement

---

[1] This sheet was returned and a more formal letter sent, which appears in the sixth volume of Webster's Works [Boston, 1856], p. 533.

[2] See the correspondence of Feb. 25, 1825, between Daniel Webster and Benton.

that no publication should be made authorized by either party, I do not feel inclined, at this remote period, to depart from that understanding. One consideration enforcing the propriety of this conclusion, is, that something of what passed, & which might perhaps be necessary to qualify or explain the rest, was verbal & I have no minute of it—nor have I kept my memory in charge of it.

Yours—&c.

D. W.

(To James Kent.[1])

WASHINGTON, April 27, 1830.

My dear Sir,—

I thank you much for both your letters. They have helped me. I can hardly find a just and reasonable man, who can speak what he thinks, who does not admit that my amendment is right in-principle. Yet party envy, hatred, and malice are most likely eventually to defeat it. We are fallen on evil times, as times are when public men seek low objects, and when the tone of public morals and public feeling is depressed and debased. I hope our children may see a better state of things,—a state of things in which that part of our prosperity and greatness which depends on ourselves may bear some little proportion to the many favors with which Providence has distinguished our country.

DAN'L WEBSTER.

(To H. W. Kinsman.)

MAY 28. [1830]

Dear Sir

There is a treaty with *Denmark*[2] it will be well for you to go immediately to Mr Snelling, & get him to go with you to the other offices, & secure the agency of their claims—

Yrs   D WEBSTER

---

[1] Printed in the Memoir of Chancellor Kent, p. 207.
[2] See Treaties and Conventions, p. 235. Date of treaty was March 28, 1830. Ratified and proclaimed June 5, 1830. Denmark agreed to indemnify American subjects who had suffered by seizure, detention or confiscation by the Danish authorities.

(To Jeremiah Mason.)

NEW YORK June 4, 1830.

My Dear Sir,

I have rec'd here your letter of the 31th of May   Col Upham may address himself, at once to D. B. Ogden.—Let him write without reference to any supposed conversation between Mr. Ogden & any other person; but introduce the Subject as if *de novo,*   He need say nothing, on the Subject of fees; but merely request to have the suit brought in the Circuit Court, & give Mr. O. leave to associate with him any other Counsel whom he may select.—No time, perhaps, should be lost, in having the suit commenced.—

We leave this City tomorrow, if the weather should favour & hope to be home on Monday morning.   Affairs were in a pretty state of excitement, when we left Washington.   Be assured, Maryland, Ohio, & Kentucky are Irretrievably lost to the administration.   Indiana, also, & probably Illinois & Missouri.   Recent events will hasten on the contest, & it will be impossible to restrain the People from bringing out Mr. Clay, as a Candidate, *agt. Genl. Jackson.*   We had a great run of luck especially in the H. of R. the last week of the Session.

I hope to see you soon.   As to my seat, I shall not act suddenly on that subject.   Some time ago you expressed a wish that Mr. Madison might come out agt. this—nullifying doctrine. *That object is secured.*[1]   In due time the public will have the benefit of his opinions, in the most gratifying manner.

I left Washington on Monday, the moment of the adjournment, & came hither without much delay.   At Philadelphia I saw Mr Biddle, & some other Gentleman, & we had a *hearty laugh* at the fortunes which have befallen your puissant accusers, Hill, Decatur, & Cushman—

I suppose you have heard that Woodbury declines a reelection. I believe it is true.

Mr. Harvey told me, coming on, that it was so—& that he had seen the declining letter, or a copy of it—

I am, D Sir, Yrs as ever

D. WEBSTER

---

[1] See Madison to Daniel Webster, March 15, 1830, in "Private Correspondence of Daniel Webster," vol. i, p. 496.

(To Jos. E. Sprague.)

BOSTON June 28, 1830

Dear Sir,

I was at New Port when yours of the 16th was received,[1] and since my return have not had a moments leisure. All I can say is that in regard to the object and subject of it I will do all that is incumbent on me. You know I am not good for the detail of such matters. I do not understand them, I see the importance of the general object, and most sincerely wish to promote it, and wish also, especially, to do whatever may be useful to you. But other heads must plan. If you will come up here, any morning or evening this week, giving me a day's notice, I will lay all other things aside, and have a conversation on the subject.

Let me hear from you.

Mr. C.[2] is well and in excellent spirits

Yours truly

DANL. WEBSTER.

(To ——————.[3])

Senate Chamber, Feby 23d 1831.

My Dear Sir,

I have read Mr. Bridge's letter, and feel some delicacy in complying with the request contained in it. It asks for an opinion on a highly important subject, calling in question the validity of a very important law of Kentucky. I have little desire to take part in such discussions, especially in cases arising in states remote from the sphere of my usual professional practice. Nevertheless, while I remain at the Bar of the Supreme Court, I do not hold myself at liberty to decline engagements in behalf of reputable persons, in cases coming regularly into that Court for decision. You are at liberty, therefore to say to your friends, that I shall not object to being retained in the cause, looking merely to its discussion here, if such be their wish.

There are, however, I think, good reasons why I should refrain

---

[1] Mr. Sprague's letter cannot be found.

[2] Henry Clay. See Clay to Webster, June 7, 1830. "Private Correspondence of Daniel Webster."

[3] Daniel Webster MSS., dictated and corrected by him. I cannot determine who was the recipient.

from giving an opinion, on this great question, as preliminary to judicial proceedings. There would probably indeed, be little value in such opinion, since the clause of the Constitution, which must be the subject of argument, has been so recently considered and interpreted, by the highest Judicial authority, in the Missouri case.

Indeed, sir, whatever my opinions might be, on a full consideration of the case, it seems to me that the respect due from me to the State of Kentucky, & her Law, and to the great interest she must feel in the question, may justly impose on me a forbearance from expressing such opinions, in advance of the regular forensic discussion.

I am Dr. Sir, Your's with true regard,

[D. W.]

(From Stephen White.[1])

New York August 7 1831

My Dear Sir

* * * The day on which you left the Springs I received a letter from Mr S. C. Phillips which ought to have been received several days before. Had you been there I should have asked you to look at it, and if I find a private conveyance will send it you for it is somewhat voluminous— The main object was to ascertain whether you continued faithful to the interest of Mr Clay and tho' written by Mr Phillips—was doubtless expression of the wishes of the Central Committee— On that point I assured him there had, so far as I could ascertain, been no alteration in your opinions or feelings— that on more than one occasion recently I had heard you speak of Mr C. and of his claims in a mode evincing of that disposition— That in my individual judgement our friends should all stand firm for him unless a failure of a Kent'y election or his death, both equally fatal to his success, should call for a new candidate in which event I thought neither yourself or your friends should be unmindful how prominent your claims were when compared with those of any other individual— I then referred him to a letter I wrote Mr Sprague, detailing among other facts the great feeling in your favour uniformly evinced by the prominent individuals of

---

[1] White was Senator from Essex County in the Massachusetts Legislature and a prominent merchant of Salem. Fletcher Webster married his daughter.

all parties wherever you had been and the strong disposition to create a *constitutional party* and to place you at the head of it— While making these remarks however I distinctly stated then as the result of views consequent upon the failure of Mr. Clay, who I presumed would be supported manfully until his defeat, if it should unhappily take place, should lead our friends to adopt some other more popular candidate rather than make shipwreck of our hopes by an obstinate support of men instead of principles— * * *

resp Yours
STEPHEN WHITE

I enclose Phillips letter, *confidentially*

(To Nathan Appleton.[1])

SANDWICH [Mass.] Sept 11 [1831]

My Dr. Sir,

The enclosed is from the keeper of the hotel in which we lodged last session.   The rooms are, two rooms on the second story one pretty large one, in front, one smaller in rear, connected by a door of common size.   This largest was Mrs Websters room to see her friends, and we dined there also, when we had company. The smaller room was used as a study—but we dined in it when quite alone—

2 rooms in the story next above, which are comfortable lodging rooms, and then rooms still higher up for servants.

These rooms would accommodate two gentlemen very well— there would be a lodging room & a reading or sitting room for each & breakfast & dinner could be served in the larger without inconvenience.   But they would not well accommodate three gentlemen without compelling some of them to read & write in their lodging room.—

My expectation is that Mrs Webster will join me at W. about the 10th March—There will be room enough for her.   She talks something of bringing her sister, Mrs Newbold with her, but I regard that as too uncertain to be the basis of any calculation. If Mrs Appleton should accompany you, or join you, there would

------

[1] Hon. Nathan Appleton, of Boston.   He had just been elected a Representative to Congress and was solicitous about obtaining quarters in Washington. He and Webster finally settled at Gadsby's, mentioned above.

be room enough of course for her. If she should not, and your daughter should visit Washington, an arrangement could be made to accommodate her. Under these circumstances shall we engage the rooms? The charge is high for us two; but the omission of corkage (one dollar per bottle) is a considerable diminution. I have had a coloured man as my servant, for many years. The keeper of the hotel furnishes one good one, & these are enough. Mr. Gorham can tell you what rooms & lodgings would cost at Gadsbys corkage included. Gadsbys rooms are much larger & handsomer & his house much nearer the capital. In other respects, at least in some other, I should prefer Barnards. I believe Gadsbys culinary establishment is as good as Barnards. If you will write me a line to say what you think upon all this, I will give Mr. Barnard an answer. For myself I have no strong opinion, either way. The price is high for our own lodging & board, while alone, which so far as my family is concerned, will probably be three months. In general, I have found that somebody wanted the pay, as much as I wanted rooms, and have not engaged them until I arrived. Yet there may be some danger that we shall not find what will well suit us— I shall remain here some few days longer. You may address me at this place

Yrs truly D Webster

It is exceedingly warm here for to day

(To James Buchanan.[1])

Boston Septr. 24, 1831.

Dear Sir,

The decision at the Treasury on our (or more properly on *your*) Act of the last session astonishes me. I had never dreamed of any such thing. If you think the enclosed expression of opinion will do any good, you are at liberty to com [torn]

I thank you for your kind & friendly expressions; & as I did you no more than justice, in regard to your agency in the passing of the Insolvents' Relief Bill, I trust I shall on no occasion do you less. I would express the hope of seeing you at Washington, in the winter, if it were not that such an expression might

---

[1] This letter is in the Buchanan Collection of MSS., belonging to the Pennsylvania Historical Society.

imply an expectation that you are not to be elsewhere, at that time.   Not knowing at all how that may be, I must confine myself to the tender of general good wishes, & to the assurances of esteem & regard.

DANL WEBSTER

———

(From Ambrose Spencer.[1])

ALBANY Oct. 24, 1831.

Dear Sir—

I am sensible that your professional engagements engross all your time, & I would not obtrude upon you, did not public interest prompt me to it—it would give me great satisfaction to know whether our opinions coincide upon the course to be adopted as to the next Presidency—I was appointed a delegate to the Baltimore convention by the national republican convention held here in June last—nothing was done by that body to take from the delegates their freedom of opinion, altho' a resolution was adopted strongly approbatory of the character & qualifications of Mr. Clay—my present opinion is, I shall not attend the convention at Baltimore—it seems to me,— to be apparent, that the convention will nominate Mr. Clay, taking the Newspapers as indices of public opinion—If he should be nominated & accept the nomination, our cause is lost, & Genl Jackson will certainly be re-elected—I am very unwilling to be a party to a course so ruinous to all our hopes; & I am unwilling also to disturb the harmony of the convention by differing from them.

However Mr. Clay's friends deceive themselves by believing he has the least chance of success if Genl Jackson & Mr. Wirt are both in the field?   Mr. Clay at the utmost can gain but 89 votes, namely Massachusetts, Rhode Island, Connecticut, New Jersey, Delaware, Maryland, Kentucky, Ohio, Indiana & Louisiana—the remaining votes are to be divided between Genl Jackson & Mr. Wirt.   I agree that Mr. Wirt would probably obtain only the vote of Vermont, but he would withdraw a sufficient number from those opposed to Genl Jackson to secure his election by the electoral college—admitting this last opinion to be erro-

---

[1] A. Spencer had served in the New York State Legislature both as Representative and Senator, had been Attorney General and later Judge and Chief Justice of the Supreme Court of New York.   He represented the State in Congress in 1829-31.   See Webster's reply to this letter.

neous, & that there will be a failure to elect a President by the college; we know the representatives of a majority of the States, will vote for him in the House of Representatives.

In my opinion Mr. Wirt has gone too far to decline; if however he should, I know enough of the temper & spirit of anti-masonry, to affirm positively, that they will hold another convention, & nominate some one who will not decline. Mr. Clay can not be that man, he can not speak his opinions on masonry & if he could it is too late.

If Mr. Clay would decline before the meeting of the Baltimore convention, or address a letter to that body recommending the nomination of Mr. Wirt & giving his reasons, it seems to me Mr. Wirt would receive the votes of all Mr. Clay's friends. He certainly would if they are governed by principle & not devotion to an individual—in that event there is every probability Mr. Wirt would be elected—give him the votes of the States I have mentioned & to this we may confidently add New York & Vermont & he is elected—

It is not only my opinion, but that of our most considerate & best informed men, that if a union can take place in this state between the anti-masons, & those opposed to re-election of Genl Jackson, they would certainly form a majority of the electors.

I am astonished that an opinion exists that this State will give its vote for Mr. Clay, should Genl Jackson & Mr. Wirt be candidates—the fact is, Mr. Clay in that case would receive comparatively but few votes—Mr. Wirt would receive three times more than Mr. Clay, but Genl Jackson would receive more than either, & thus gain the electoral vote of the State—I feel as confident in these facts, as in any future event ever presented to my consideration—the result of the late elections in Vermont, is decisive of the Presidential vote of that state; the Anti-Masons are the largest party now, & one year hence will form the majority; but at all events Mr. Clay has nothing to hope from that State—

With respect to Pennsylvania, what I have said of New York, applies to that State—there is already a large body of Anti-Masons there, & it is one of the dogmas of that party, sanctioned by experience, that anti-masonry neither goes back nor stands still—there are anti-masons enough there, to defeat all hopes *of* [that] an electoral ticket favorable to Mr. Clay, can be chosen—it is by no means improbable, that the concentration of the Anti-masonic votes with those opposed to Jackson's re-election, in Mr. Wirt, would give him that State— In Virginia too, is there now good hope, that if Genl Jackson & Mr. Wirt are the only candidates, that State may go for the latter—we know there is great defection from Jackson there; Mr. Wirt is a Virginian by birth, & a republican of the Jefferson school, divested of Mr. Jefferson's political errors.   If Mr. Wirt should not command the votes of all Mr. Clay's friends, this loss will I think be made up, by the votes of many who dislike both, Genl Jackson & Mr. Clay—

Of Mr. Wirt's high qualifications, I need not say one word to you who know him much more intimately than I do—his nomination was totally unexpected, but ought we not to hail it as a most auspicious event, if he can be the means of defeating the re-election of a man whose administration, has been a curse to the nation?

Now if it is apparent or even probable that Mr. Clay can not be elected, but that Mr. Wirt can be elected if Mr. Clay declines, ought there to be any hesitation in taking measures to produce that result?   I feel & acknowledge Mr Clays splendid & patriotic services to the country & that he has been most cruelly & malignantly persecuted & slandered; & that he has high claims on his country; but what of all this, when the real question is, by what means a weak, wicked & dangerous man, shall be defeated—I am for the cause & my Country, & am unwilling from mere personal considerations to sacrifice the cause to the man—

If I am laboring under erroneous impressions, I wish to be undeceived & therefore write you with the utmost freedom & candor —I speak the opinions of many cool & temperate friends of Mr. Clay here—if my facts are true it is madness to persist in nominating Mr. Clay, & if persisted in the result will be Jackson's re-election.

It is to be feared that Mr. Clay is deceived by some of his ardent friends as to the vote of New York, he can not be as to Vermont since their recent election—Is it not possible to lay before Mr Clay a true state of facts, that he may take a course to relieve us from the perplexity we are in?   Could he see that his persistence in being a candidate, must ensure the re-election of Genl Jackson, if I rightly estimate him, he would decline in such a way as to transfer his strength to Mr. Wirt.

There are idle speculations, that Mr. Calhoun will be a candidate, & one of the three highest on the electoral tickets—He will not expose his weakness by being a candidate—this is evident from the course of Duff Green—but where is he to gain votes save in S. Carolina?

I could say much more on this all important subject, but I
fear your patience will be exhausted in reading this already too
long letter—

When you & Mrs. Webster were at Saratoga the last summer,
I was quite indisposed, else I certainly would have seen you there
—present me most respectfully & cordially to her & believe me

   With high respect Your sincere friend

                                                    A. SPENCER

(To Hon. Ambrose Spencer.)

PRIVATE AND CONFIDENTIAL.

My Dear Sir   BOSTON NOV. 16 1831

   I wrote you a hasty line, some time ago, to acknowledge the
receipt of your friendly letter of the 24. of October, & promising to give you my thoughts on the highly important matters, to
which it relates.

   I incline to think, My Dear Sir, that it may be a wise decision
on your part, with your present opinions, to abstain from attending the Baltimore Convention; for I am convinced you will find
there, should you go, very little inclination to support Mr. Wirt's
nomination.   Indeed if the members of it should vote to support
Mr. Wirt unanimously, & Mr. Clay should freely concur therein,
I think, judging from what I see around me here, we could not
induce the People, generally, to vote for him.   I am astonished
to hear—but I daily do hear—persons who were never Masons,
& who are, in truth, in their sentiments, Anti-Masonic;—that is,
they disapprove of Secret Societies, say, nevertheless, that between Mr. Wirt, *standing as he now does,* & Genl Jackson, *they
should go for the latter.*   This seems strange, but it is true.   In
this part of the Country, at least in this State, Anti-Masonry as a
sentiment, is gaining ground; but Anti-Masonry, as a political
party, or basis of such party, I do not think is gaining.   Our
people do not feel that Anti Masonry, alone, is a principle broad
enough to save the country, & maintain the Govt.   I think,
further, that with us, Mr. Wirt's nomination has greatly checked
the progress of antimasonry itself.   It has caused dissatisfaction,
& suspicion, in many, in whom nothing of either existed before.
Of your own State you can judge better but I have been all
along apprehensive, that there being no National Republican
candidates nominated, generally, throughout N. York, very

many, who dislike Anti-Masonry, would go over to the Jackson party. I have never thought it possible to get the vote of N York for Mr. Wirt—tho' I am a poor judge, on that question.— He cannot, I think, obtain any votes in N.E. out of Vermont. He has no chance, at all, in Maryland, Delaware, Ohio, Indiana, or Louisiana. And as to Va. I do not think a respectable ticket could be found for Mr. Wirt, in that State, under present circumstances.

I cannot help thinking, My Dear Sir, that Mr. Wirt acted under great mis-information, when he accepted the nomination at Baltimore. I believe I must say, that it is among our misfortunes that Anti-Masonry, in this State, has not fallen into the hands of the most prudent & popular persons. Its course, therefore, with us has not been so satisfactory as it might have been; &, for a like cause, I fear Mr. Wirt had not before him an accurate view of the ground, so far as it respected this quarter. As I observed in my former short letter, I believe Mr. Wirt's nomination has *secured* Genl. Jackson's re-election! I believe he cannot take a vote from Genl Jackson, but may take a few from Mr. Clay; that is, the Vermont votes; but a greater evil resulting from his nomination is, that it greatly discouraged those, who were desirous of producing a change in the Genl Administration, & greatly encouraged the friends of the present President. I hope, indeed, for a different result, but I do not expect it. It is true, the events of the session may produce new aspects of things & I am willing to anticipate the best.

I have thus, my Dear Sir, freely, & in entire and close confidence, expressed my thoughts. You will not find much comfort in them. But let us trust to a kind Providence, & still adhere to the great interests of the Country. We shall at last thus deserve success. I do not fear great mischief from acts of Congress. Our most imminent danger, at present, is from the manner in which the appointing power is likely to be exercised. We must pray for long life for all good men in office, & deeming our country yet too young to be ruined, we must resist evil, whenever we meet it, & overcome it if we can. May Heaven prosper us!—

It will give me true pleasure to hear from you often—& I may prove myself a more punctual correspondent, hereafter, than on this occasion.

[DAN'L WEBSTER[1]]

---

[1] This letter was taken from Daniel Webster's draft of the letter finally sent.

(From Thomas H. Benton.)

SENATE CHAMBER Jan 4. 1832

Sir,

I take leave to invite your attention to a published letter,[1] which Col. Davis will show you, & to say, that he will receive the answer, if any, which you may think the occasion calls for.[2]

Your obt. servant

THOMAS H. BENTON

(To Thomas H. Benton.)

SENATE CHAMBER Jan 4, 1832

Sir,

I have rec'd your note, of this day, and lose no time in saying, that the printed letter enclosed therein was published without the slightest knowledge on my part, that that, or any publication was intended on the subject to which it relates; and that neither the publisher, or anybody else, ever rec'd any communication from me in regard to the subject; much less any authority to publish any thing. From the time of the transaction to the present moment I have never felt at liberty to authorize any publication, nor even to make it the subject of conversation, so far as respected the manner in which it was finally terminated

Yr ob. servt.

DANIEL WEBSTER

(From Thomas H. Benton.)

DAWSON's *No. 2.*
Jany. 4. 1832.

Sir,

Your letter of this day, by Col. Davis, is received, and is very conclusive on the point to which it relates, which, however, did not come within the scope of my object in laying the printed letter before you. My object was, and nothing more, to present a case for the operation of the verbal agreement which bound each

---

[1] The clipping appeared in the New York Commercial Advertizer December 26, 1831.
[2] This is a renewal of the Randolph Controversy of 1825, to which the printed excerpt referred. See the correspondence of February 25, 1825.

party to contradict any publication, to the prejudice of the other, which came to its knowledge.

Your obt. Servant.

THOMAS H. BENTON.

(To Thomas H. Benton.)

SENATE CHAMBER Jan. 5. 1832

Sir;

I have rec'd your letter of last Eve', thro' Hon'bl Mr. Davis. I have no recollection of the verbal agreement, to which you allude; tho' it is plain enough that such an understanding sh'd have been had. Indeed, in the lapse of seven or eight years, many of the circumstances have passed from my recollection. I considered the whole matter as finally settled, & endeavoring to fullfil, with scrupulous exactness, the agreement remaining in writing between us, not to authorize any publication. I have not kept alive the recollection of particulars.

Nevertheless, with or without any agreement, I should wish to do whatever can be fairly required, of the most delicate and honorable feeling; but I would submit to you, or to any other gentleman, whether I can, with propriety, be called on to contradict anything, after what is reported to have been said by Mr. R. recently, in a public speech, which you probably have seen; & which doubtless caused the revival of this matter in the newspapers.

Your Obt. Ser.

DAN'L. WEBSTER

(From Thomas H. Benton.)

DAWSON's Jany 5th 1832.

Sir,

Your letter of this day, through Col. Davis, is received.

I have taken leave to enclose the copy of a note to you of about two years ago, in which the agreement not to publish, and the verbal agreement to contradict, are both recited for the purpose of putting a question upon each of them; also I enclose a copy of your answer to that note, in which no dissent is intimated to the existence of the verbal agreement. Taking the fact of this agreement to be established, the refusal on your part to execute it (for whatsoever reason) may give rise to a question which I do not wish to solve; namely, whether the whole agreement of which it is part and parcel, is not thereby abrogated?

The exception taken in the concluding sentence of your letter, and which may be considered as a plea to the jurisdiction, for inability in the person, would seem to have been waved by the answer in chief which was given in your note of the 4th. For the rest, I have to say, that I have not seen the reported speech of Mr. Randolph; that I know nothing of it, except as mentioned in the printed letter sent to you; that I was disposed to have cut off that part; but did not for fear of misconstruction; that I am acting without the knowledge of Mr. R.; that I limit my present interposition to the part of the original affair to which I was privy; and, that a line, saying that you do, or do not execute the verbal agreement (taking it now to be established) accomplishes the object which I had in view in laying the printed letter before you.

Your obt servant.

THOMAS H. BENTON.

___

(To Thos. H. Benton.[1])

SENATE CHAMBER, April 20, 1830.

Sir;

I have your note of this morning. What passed, on the occasion referred to, in 1825, having taken place under an agreement that no publication should be made or authorized, by either party, I do not feel inclined, at this remote period, to depart from that understanding,

Yours, &c.

DAN'L WEBSTER

___

(To Thos. H. Benton.)

JAN. 6. 1832.

Sir,

I have recd your letter of yesterday. The question cannot be properly put to me, I think, whether I shall execute a verbal agreement, the recollection of which I have already disclaimed, in my note of the 5. inst; because, in an affair of this kind, after so long a period has elapsed, I do not feel bound to act on any

---

[1] This letter was enclosed in Benton's letter of January 25, 1832.

one's recollection, except my own.   The written agreement speaks
for itself, & is unambiguous.   My note to you of April 20th.
1830 does not admit the existence of any other agreement.   Its
only object was to decline altogether, any publication at all.   I
am offering no pleas to jurisdiction—setting up no justification,
or excuse, for not fulfilling every obligation, which I admit to
exist.   The case, at present, requires no such course from me.
On the contrary, I fulfil, to the letter, all that I regard as the
existing agreement, without inquiring, for the present how that
agreement has been kept, on the other side.   I adopt this course,
because I do not intend to say or do anything, which can be made
a ground for departing from the written agreement.

But I do not admit, that as a matter of propriety or of courtesy, I can be requested to contradict anything, so long as the
public speech reported to have been made in Virginia, goes itself
uncontradicted.   I should be thought to entertain very little self
respect, if, with the knowledge of that occurrence before me, I
should be found correcting published paragraphs (not authorized
by me). however derogatory they might be to the character of
Mr. Randolph.   That very speech, & nothing else, as I presume has occasioned the publication of such paragraphs; & whoever decides that question, which you say you do not wish to
solve, will doubtless consider, whether Mr Randolph's Speech, &
those publications which it has occasioned without any agency of
mine, furnish just cause to abrogate the whole agreement.

If it were necessary to give reasons, for declining the publication to which I am invited, it would be sufficient, to say, that if
there were grounds, at the time, for leading the parties, into such
agreement, there are stronger grounds, now, for adhering to it;
because much of what took place has become forgotten, my recollection of the particular circumstances might differ from that
of others, & the Gentleman, principally consulted by me, on the
occasion, is no longer living.—

Your Ob. Servt

(From Thos. H. Benton.)

Dawson's No. 2. Jany. 8. 1832.
Sir;
Your letter of yesterday contains matter which I deem it in-
dispensably necessary to refer to Mr. Randolph.   I apprize you

of this circumstance, because it is fair that you should know it, and to account for the pause which may take place in our correspondence, even if it is not finally closed.

Your obt. servant.

THOMAS H. BENTON.

(To Thomas H. Benton.)

Sir;   Senate Chamber, Jan, 9. 1832.

I have read your note of the 8th instance, & am disposed to consider our correspondence on this subject, is finally closed.

Your, Ot.

DANIEL WEBSTER

(To J. Q. Adams.[1])

My dear Sir: Thursday eve., Jan. 24th, 1832

Does it happen that you can, from recollection, and without the trouble of any research, refer me to any document, or fact, *anterior to Mr. Monroe's Administration,* showing that U. S. in their negotiation with England, had preferred a claim to the admission of our produce into the Brit'h West Indies, subject to the same duties only, as were paid on products of the same kind imported from the Continental Colonies of G. B.? I pray you not to give yourself the trouble of a search, but if anything of this be in your recollection, it will oblige me to have a reference to it.   Yours with entire regard,

DAN'L WEBSTER.

(To Nathan Appleton.)

Dear Sir,   [June. 1832.]

It appears to me you have completely refuted each & every of Mr. McDuffie's propositions— I see no vestige left, of one of his arguments. You will see I have made a mark or two on the 10th, 14th & 17 pages. The speech is a model of close reasoning, on an abstruse subject.[2]

Yrs truly

D. WEBSTER

---

[1] This letter is owned by Charles Francis Adams.
[2] Without date, but was written after reading Mr. Appleton's speech of May 30, 1832, in answer to McDuffie.

(Memorandum.)

Any letters appearing to be double, may be opened to see **if** they contain letters for other persons.

Letter from *Richmond* if it come, may be opened. If it be from Ch. Jus. Marshall & say anything of [illegible] it may be read by Mr. A[1]— & shown, confidentially to J. Davis, Mr. Choate &c.

Letters from Albany (Judge Spencer) from Trenton (Mr. Southard) from Newbern (Mr. Gaston) may perhaps be rec'd., on the same *subject*. If so, they may be read, & shown confidentially, if they will do good.—

———

(From Abraham Van Vechten.[2])

Dear Sir—   ALBANY June 27-1832

The importance of the approaching election is my only apology for seeking to divert your attention for a few moments from the interesting Subjects before Congress, at the heel of a long and tedious session— You are no doubt apprised of the electoral Ticket lately nominated by our Anti-Masonic convention, with a view of conciliating the national republicans[3]— The result will probably be propitious to their wishes, provided it is understood that there will eventually be no collision between Mr Clay and Mr Wirt—On this subject I am interrogated by well meaning & influential men, who are disposed to pursue efficient measures to defeat the present National Administration candidates— May I ask of you to give me, such information as you may feel warranted to enable me to answer the above Interrogatories so as to allay the apprehensions of the timid, and stir up all to vigorous action— You will of course understand that any communication you may make will be deemed strictly confidential, and used by me without disclosing the source of my Information.

I am Dear Sir With very great respect Your Obedt Servt.

AB. VAN VECHTEN

---

[1] Mr. J. Q. Adams.

[2] An able and distinguished jurist of Albany, N. Y. See "History of Albany," Howell and Tenney, editors, p. 132.

[3] See Schouler's "History of United States," vol. iv, p. 83. See also Webster's reply, next letter.

(To Abm. Van Vechten.)

PRIVATE & CONFIDENTIAL

WASHINGTON July 2, 1832

My Dear Sir

I have been much gratified by the receipt of your letter of the 27th June, relative to the recent nomination of Electors, in New York. Indeed, I had already suggested to a friend, before the receipt of your letter, that I would take the freedom to write you, on the same subject. We look on that nomination as being, on the whole, propitious to the great cause of the Country, under existing circumstances, & we all wish its success. I can say to you, in entire confidence, that there is a perfectly good understanding between Mr Clay & Mr Wirt; & that they had a free & friendly conversation in regard to the political state of the country, when Mr Wirt was here; that it is generally understood here that Mr Wirt would be glad of an opportunity to make public his wishes, that the whole voice of all opposed to the re-election of Genl Jackson should be united for Mr Clay; & that such an opportunity is looked for, & is not unlikely to occur, before the day of giving the votes.

I will only add, that every day brings grounds for increased hopes of success, if we can but unite. We hear, today, of a great defection, among the President's friends, in Kentucky, & understand it is likely to be contagious, along the Ohio River.

The Tariff bill will pass, amended, in some respects. The Bank Bill will pass the House, much as it passed the Senate, probably; but it is generally believed, & I have no doubt it will be found true, that the President will negative it.

This will affect Penna—but how deeply, I cannot say.

One the whole, we think all depends on N. York. We cannot doubt, if the great State goes right, the general result will be right. We therefore respectfully, but earnestly, beg of all good men in your State that they will make one *great* effort to save the Country.

I am, D Sir, with m° true regard,

Yrs.

[D. WEBSTER][1]

---

[1] This copy was taken from the original draft of the letter sent.

(To J. Q. Adams.[1])

WASHINGTON, July 7th, 1832
Dear Sir:
   You will receive herewith your various letters, respecting the
Tariff Bill, for the use of which I am quite obliged to you.   I
feel the greatest anxiety that the House may agree to our
Amendments, they raise, I think, no question of principle and
as to measures, and degree, they do not depart further, from the
provisions of the House, than may be accounted for, as the fair
difference of opinion.   In respect to the Amendment on the
Woolens provisions, I fully believe the whole Bill will be haz-
arded, if that Amendment be rejected.   It is certain that several
senators, who voted for the Bill, will go for its indefinite postponement, if its ultimate form shall be the same in which it came
from your House, and I incline to think the number of these,
added to the enemies of the Bill, would make a majority of the
Senate.

   I am, Dear Sir, with regard Yours,

DAN'L WEBSTER.

(From Henry Clay.)

ASHLAND 27th Aug. 1832.
Dear Sir
   Our Kentucky elections have terminated in the election of the
Jackson candidate for Governor by a majority of 1260 votes,
the U. Republican candidate for Lieut. Governor by a majority
of 2506 votes; and in 60 out of the 100 members that compose
our H. of Representatives, as well as in securing in the Senate,
where the majority was against us last year, a majority of 22 out
of the 38 members composing that body.
   We have been so often mortified with the issue of elections in
this state, that I do not know whether you will take any interest
in the causes of our recent partial defeat.   They were 1st the
employment of extraordinary means by the Jackson party, within and without the State.   On this point all their efforts were
brought to bear; and every species of influence was exercised.

---

[1] This letter is owned by Charles Francis Adams.

The patronage and the means of that party were profusely used. 2dly An irruption of Tennessee voters who came to the polls in some of our border counties.   Last year, official returns of all the voters, in all the counties, were made to form a basis for the periodical adjustment of the ratio of our representation.   In some of those border counties, at the recent election, I understand that the *Jackson majorities*, exceeded the whole number of the voters according to those returns.   But we should have been able to resist successfully the joint effect of both the above causes, if it had not been for a third, which operated most extensively. Our candidate was a Presbyterian, and against that sect most deep rooted, and inveterate prejudices exist, the weight of which had not been sufficiently estimated when he was selected.   Owing to this latter cause I believe we lost not less than probably three thousand votes.

But it is less important to dwell on the past and incurable event of our Governor's election than to look forward and provide against future disaster.   The spirit of our friends is unbroken, their zeal is increased in warmth; and they are full of confidence of success in November.   What is more encouraging, they are already engaged in the best plans to secure success.   Far from being disheartened, their recent partial defeat, arouses them to exertion more vigorous than ever; and the exceptionable means employed by their opponents have fired their indignation.   I think there is much reason to hope that the late events will lead to more certain success in November than if we had carried the election of the Governor by such a majority as the other side has obtained.

What is most absorbing of public attention at this time is the Bank Veto.   On that subject our opponents have been much more industrious in the circulation of documents, than the friends of the institution.   The President's message and Benton's rodomontade have been scattered in countless thousands, and time enough to affect the election; whilst on the other side, but little reached us before the election, except Mr Clay's speech, which had a limited circulation, as it arrived only at the moment of the election. A clear, intelligible, popular statement of the case, with a just account of the certain effects of the overthrow of the Bank is much needed.

I hope that our friends abroad will see in our election that the bad issue of it has been neutralized by the good; and that they will derive from it fresh motives to spare no exertions to save the country.

I remain always Faithfully Your friend

H. CLAY.

P. S.   Whilst it would be indiscreet to publish this letter with my name, I request you to show it to Mess Dearborne, Everetts or any other particular friends

H. C.

Why has not your Speech on the Veto been published at length?[1]

———

(To J. Q. Adams.[2])

BOSTON, Nov. 7th, 1832

Dear Sir:

I am quite obliged to you, for your friendly messages by Mr. Charles Adams, although I had never for a moment entertained the slightest suspicion that such a movement as rumor averred to be contemplated, had rec'd or could receive your countenance. In writing to a friend, ten days ago, I assured him that there was not the least reason to suppose that you were knowing to any such intention, if it existed, or would encourage it, if you should know it, and that I did not believe (as I still do not) that any such intention, does in fact, exist anywhere.   In the engagements of the Court I have not found leisure to read *Dermot.* The world will have it, that there is, and *must* be, satire lurking in it, tho' it is admitted to be well disguised.   Mrs. Webster is exceedingly mortified that she has not been able to pay her respects to Mrs. Adams, since she came to town.   Either my engagements at Court or absence in N. Hampshire, have constantly been in the way of such a visit, until this week.   We had ordered the carriage both yesterday and today for a drive to Quincy; but on both occasions, have been prevented by the weather, from executing our purpose.   It only remains for us to render to Mrs. Adams and yourself our hearty good wishes for a pleasant journey to Washington.   Mrs. Webster intends remaining where she is, through the Winter.

I am, Dr Sir, Yours with very true regard,

DAN'L WEBSTER.

---

[1] This letter is owned by Mr. Greenough.
[2] This letter is owned by Charles Francis Adams.

(To Edward Everett.)

WASHINGTON 15" Feby 1833

My Dear Sir,

I will be much obliged to you for a few of your *thoughts,*—
say, a note of the main objections, as they strike you, to Mr C's
measure.[1]   Let me have them tomorrow at 10.—

Having this matter on my hands, and nullification also, I have
more than I can get along with.

Yours

D. W.

(From Silas Wright.[2])

Senate Chamber Monday Morning 25 Feby. [1833]

Dear Sir,

In the afternoon and evening of yesterday I saw most of my
friends in the New York delegation in the other House, and after
very full conversations with them am inclined to think that it is
my duty to vote for the bill[3] upon its final reading, unless something in the course of the proceedings hereafter shall change my
mind.   I give you this information according to my promise and
had designed to have done it at your quarters, but Company at
my room prevented.

Yours &c &c,

S. WRIGHT, JR.

(To Nathan Appleton.)

Sunday Ev.g [Feby. 1833]

My dear Sir,

I cannot well say how much I thought of you, or how mourn-
fully after you left us.   You seem to have had an uncommon
share of wayfaring hardships, preceding a great, perhaps the

---

[1] See Schouler's "History of United States," vol. iv, pp. 97-104. Clay's
measure is referred to.   This is quite a habit of Webster's to call on his friends
for "thoughts."

[2] Representative and Senator from New York, and at this time holding the
latter position.   Later he was Governor of New York.   President Tyler
offered him a seat in the Supreme Court, but he declined.

[3] See the following letter.

greatest of all domestic afflictions. I have tasted of the cup, & know its bitterness you have all my condolence. Your letter from N. Y. was duly rec.d as also yrs from Boston of the 12th. I pray you to make my most kind remembrance to your daughters; they will be doubly dear to you for the recent occurrence & you may well esteem them as blessing to be cherished, & to be grateful for.

Mr. Clay came forward with his bill on Tuesday, as you have seen. It has thrown us into great confusion. I thought it necessary, in the promptest manner, to signify my dissent. The comm^{ee} has met, upon the bill, three or four times, but as yet has agreed upon nothing.

At our last meeting, he, (Mr. Clay) seemed to me, to be half sick of his own measure.[1] I meet it in committee with unrelenting hostility; so does Mr. Dallas. Mr. Grundy would gladly mend it, & turn it into an administration measure. Mr. Calhoun of course, likes it as it is; & Mr. Ring will also agree to it, in its original shape. Mr. Clayton, though quite disposed I think, to go with Mr. Clay, will not agree to it as it is. If Mr. Clay himself is satisfied he can report it as it is, since Mr. Grundy will vote for it, if it cannot be amended— I think it quite as likely as anything, that it will be reported, without amendment, by the votes of Clay, Calhoun, Grundy &·King.[2] There is no chance of getting it thro' the Senate, unamended, nor probably in any shape. In the meantime the H. of R. seems to have come to a standstill.

It does not look as if there was to be any tariff this year. *We shall need you next session, more than ever.*

I have said all I wish on the Nullification matter. It does not seem magnanimous to underrate ones adversary, but, truly, between ourselves, I was greatly disappointed in Mr. Calhoun. He has little argument;—at least so it appeared to me. Mr. Dutton, Mr. Boon, & Mr. Gorham are all here. Mr. Gray has taken your rooms. The Senate holds two sessions, a day, and as the comm-ee on Mr. Clays bill meets in the morning I am kept busy.—

I am, my dear Sir, with most true regard   Yrs

DANL. WEBSTER.

---

[1] Clay's Compromise, as the measure was known. See Schurz's "Life of Clay," vol. ii, p. 16.
[2] Wm. R. King, of Alabama.

(To Henry Clay.[1]?)

CONFIDENTIAL

MARCH 21, 1833.

My dear Sir,

I learned that you called at my residence on the even'g previous
to my departure from Washington. It is a source of regret to
me that I was not at home. It was my intention, My Dear Sir,
if circumstances had furnished a convenient opportunity, to say
a few words to you confidentially, before the close of the late
session upon subjects interesting to the country. Although our
political associations have not been identical, yet, from the good
understanding, & I believe I may say, mutual respect, which has
always existed between us. I flattered myself that you would
not be averse to confidential interchange of opinions upon topics
which must arise, in the course of a short time, & on which public
men will be obliged to act. No occasion however seemed to present itself. I am still desirous of such an interview, &, with
your permission will seek an opportunity to meet with you, before
the expiration of many months.

It is generally understood, as you are aware, that we may not
have you with us, thro' the summer; but the public seems not to
know, (& in that respect I am only as well informed as the public,) at what time your residence at Washington may be expected
to terminate. I would, prefer to see you, before your *final departure* from Washington; I do not mean the breaking up of
your residence in that City, but the final taking leave of your
friends there, if the general expectation is to be realized, by your
leaving the Country for a time. I understood from you, that you
might, perhaps be in the north, in the early part of the summer,
should that happen, & should it also be your expectation to be at
Washington again, after your excursion to the north, a very
convenient opportunity will be offered me of seeing you in the
course of your northern journey. But if you are not to return
to Washington, it will only be left for me, perhaps in making a
trip which I propose to Ohio, to go by the South and return
by the North, instead of the reverse, as I have hitherto intended.
By this change, I shall be able to see you in Washington, provided you should not leave that place earlier than June.

I leave this City in two days, for N, York, where I shall re-

---

[1] This is taken from Daniel Webster's draft of letter sent. Webster has
indorsed this as follows : "Altered so far as to propose his coming to N.
York by April 5th or coming some day in April to meet me."

main until the end of this month.   If you will favor me with a line, in answer to this, addressed to me in N.   I shall be glad to receive it.   But if any thing should lead you to a desire to postpone any answer which you may think it worth while to make, to a later period, please direct to me at Boston.

I will not send this letter, My Dear Sir, without adding, that I find, everywhere, a high & grateful feeling of respect, entertained towards yourself, for the part understood to have been performed by you, in late measures so essential to the honor & well-being of the country, & which have exhibited so much ability and patriotism.

I need not add, that in all this, no one concurs more heartily, than, Sir

Yours—

D. WEBSTER.

(To Matthew Carey.)

BOSTON. May 14. 1833.

D. Sir

I rec'd & read with interest your letter of the 9th of April. In most of what you remark, I entirely concur.   I think there has been culpable negligence on the part of the friends of the Union and the Government, in not laying fully and forcibly before the people the tendency and consequences of the Doctrines of Nullification; & that at this moment it is the incumbent duty of these friends of the Union & Government to resist, by all the usual means of discussions, reasoning & statement of facts, every attempt made, or which may be made, to produce a belief in one part of the country, that the people of the other part are hostile to their interests. & meditate an attack on the security of their property.   These seeds of separation, it appears to me, are now industriously sown; their growth ought to be prevented.

It is but justice to say that in my opinion your various short tracts on the subject of the Constitution, & the attempts at Nullification; have done much good; & would have done more, had they been more widely circulated.   Plain spoken views of these subjects often are more effectual, than elaborate essays.   I hope that you will suffer nothing to discourage you from doing the good that may be in your power, & that others may not be behind you in the disposition to disseminate truth, & thereby up-

hold the government of the Country, in the affections of the people—
                    With regard, Yours
                              [D. WEBSTER.[1]]

(Objects.[2])

[About June 1, 1833(?)]
First, & principal, To maintain the Union of the States, & uphold the Constitution, against the attempts of its enemies, whether attacking it, directly, by Nullification, or seeking to break it up by secession.

2. To support the Administration, fairly, in all its just & proper measures; & especially to stand by the President in his patriotic constitutional principles; & to cherish a sympathy of feeling, & encourage cooperation, in action, with the friends of Union & Liberty, in the South.—

3 To maintain the cause of American Capital, American Industry, & more than all *American Labor*, against foreign & destructive competition, by a reasonable, moderate, but settled & permanent system of protective duties—

4. To preserve the general currency of the Country, in a safe state, well guarded agt. those who would speculate on the rise & fall of circulating paper; & to this end to advocate the renewal of the Bank of U. S. as the best means of promoting this end, and as especially useful, in this part of the Country, as a check against the combination of other monied influences.

5 To resist & oppose the oppression & tyrannical combination of the Regency,[3] & to endeavor to rescue the people from its yoke, & to obtain for us all, as citizens of New York, a right of thinking & acting for ourselves, as Independent freemen, &c. &c.; and to expose the political conduct of those who, to favor their own ambitious designs, are doubtful & hesitating, in the cause of the Constitution, & are ready to sacrifice all its vital powers & objects to its enemies.

6 I oppose, vigorously & unceasingly, all unlawful combinations, all secret oaths, all associations of men, meeting in darkness, & striving to obtain for themselves, by combination & concert, advantages not enjoyed by other citizens of the Republic.[4]

---

[1] This is Daniel Webster's draft of the letter sent.
[2] This heading is the one given by Webster to this memorandum. The date is a conjecture of the editor.
[3] The New York "machine."   [4] This is drawn up by Daniel Webster.

(From Rufus Choate.)

SALEM 12 Aug. 1833.

Dear Sir

I have hesitated whether I should write to you upon a subject in which you can take very little interest, but in which I take, on my own account, a great deal. It has been intimated that some one has represented to you, that I expressed myself in terms of disrespect & unfriendliness of yourself at the dinner of a few of the party on the 4th of July. It would give me inexpressible pain to suppose that you could believe this, lightly as you might regard it; and I cannot suffer the day to pass without assuring you that the representation is wholly false, and—so far as I had the honor to allude to your name, it is the very reverse of the truth.

I was invited to the dinner by those who got it up, and their object was to bring together some of the younger & more effective of the party to keep ourselves in heart & under arms. The late visit of the Cabinet, it was thought was an electioneering operation of the Vice President, to make an impression, & it was supposed to be well enough to counteract the impression—so far as he was concerned. I doubt whether there was any particular unfriendliness to the President; but it was certainly, & unequivocally an anti- Van Buren Dinner. The specific & immediate object was to keep our own ranks; & to see that none of our numbers were carried away by the recent flow of good feeling— Our Jackson men here are Van Buren men.

In all I said, addressed by the way to one hundred of as sincere admirers & zealous & decided political friends of yourself as there are in the United States, my sole purpose was to keep up the spirits, & organization of the party— I went on the ground throughout, that the object of the party in power was to secure the succession to V. B.—and that our business was to hang together & prevent it— Every thing was pointed at him—not even at the President at all—& pointed at him as the leading administration Candidate for the Presidency—aspiring to come in as the regular successor—the declared choice & natural head of the existing organization— I feel the absurdity and impertinence of reporting to you a dinner speech—but it is perhaps due to myself to say, that I asked in so many words, whether— just because Mr. V. B. was among us—shaking hands with our wives &c. &c.—we should forget our old, tried trusty *absent friends*—naming yourself & Mr. Clay—& following up those names with the highest possible expression of fervent love & respect— Whoever has troubled himself to give you an account of this matter will remember this if he was present.

It is hardly delicate, for an obvious reason, to say so, but it is also perfectly true, that in speaking of Mr. Clay, I alluded to him as a retired statesman, and toasted him as the setting sun— in Garricks' common lines. I made no allusion whatever, to his coming forward again, & the impression made upon every hearer would be decidedly, that I considered him to have withdrawn from active statesmanship, & an unsuccessful competition—& wished to do him justice as a character of history—

It is hardly possible for me to express the reluctance I have felt to trouble you with this letter. I will bring it to a close by hazarding one assertion, that there is not a man in this nation young or old, who rejoices more than I do, to see this great breaking out of your fame,—& that there is not an audience to whom it would be so unsafe to say anything cold or disrespectful of yourself, as an audience of National Republicans of Essex[1]— I am Sir With great regard & affection Your obedient servant

RUFUS CHOATE.

(From H. A. Dearborn.)

BRINLEY PLACE, ROXBURY,
August 12, 1833.

My Dear Sir,
I enclose you a draft[2] of the letter I have sent to several gentlemen, & in the course of two days shall have forwarded one to each of the following persons.

Maine. Peleg Sprague & Mr. Brant, the editor in Portland. N. Hamp. S. Bell Mas. John Davis & Bates Rhd Isld. I. Been Jr &c Conn. W. W. Elsworth Vermont H. Seymour N. Jersey T. Frelinghuysen Delaware John M. Clayton Maryland. Ezek. Chambers Ohio. Thomas Ewing Louisiana G. A. Waggaman & H. A. Bullard. N York. Gov'r Pitcher & John A. Collier Penna. Harmar Denny & Col. Watmough. Virginia Carl Mercer North Carolina Lewis Williams of the House. Tennessee. T. D. Arnold, of the House.

---

[1] This letter is owned by C. P. Greenough. "Greenough Coll.," ii, 32.
[2] See the following letter.

If you will suggest any other names to whom I can write with effect, I will cheerfully attend to it. I shall send off all the letters in three days. I enclosed a Courier in each letter.

With the highest respect I offer the most friendly salutations

H. A. DEARBORN.

———

(From H. A. Dearborn.)

BRINLEY PLACE, ROXBURY, August 12, 1833.

My Dear Sir,

From the demonstrations in Virginia & elsewhere it is apparent the Presidential Canvass has been opened, & whether premature or not, it now becomes the duty of every friend, to the Constitution & Union, to fix on some candidate, who will concentrate the votes of all those, of whatever previous party, who are solicitous to perpetuate the republic, in all its vigor & glorious consequences, upon the prosperity of the *Whole People.*

I enclose a Boston Courier, which contains an article expressive of the views of the national republicans & others in this quarter.

From indications from Ohio, Pennsylvania, New York, the Union party of the Eastern States, & other parts of the country, it is evident that Mr. Webster is looked to as the candidate who will rally the most powerful party under the battle cry of *"The Constitution & the Union."*

What is public opinion with you on this momentous subject. Pray write me freely, & let there be an understanding established, by correspondence throughout the country as to the course we shall pursue.

We are at the most perilous & momentous epoch in the history of the nation & it requires the zealous & firm cooperation, of all really honest & patriotic men, to preserve & perpetuate the government, in all its purity, efficiency & glory.

I write you with frankness & wish you to assume the same manner with me.

With sincere esteem & great respect Your most obt. St.

H. A. DEARBORN

———

(To Jeremiah Smith.)

BOSTON Sep. 3. '33

My Dear Sir

The bearer of this is Matthew St Clair Clarke, Clerk of Uncle Sam's H. of Representatives. He is a very good sort of a fellow

—came from Chambersburg, & tells Dutch & Pennsylvania Stories. With all, he is a reading man, with some touch of authorship in him, At present he is, wandering about, looking up old & dust-covered State records, documents, & all that sort of thing. He goes to Portsmouth—then to Epping, to see Govr. Plumer—& I have advised him to top off with a short stop at Exeter.

You will find him intellectual & agreeable & to say sooth, I was willing he should not leave our native state, without seeing the best things in it "Our native State!" What a forlorn & Prostrate State it is! Quantum mutate ab illa! eheu!

Yours, ever, with sincerest regard

Danl Webster

(To Nathan Appleton.)

Washington Jany 17. 1834.

Dr Sir.

You will see that the comptroller has been ordered to track back, on the subject of the cotton duty. I hope the temporary duration of the evil wrought no great injury. We are looking for the proceedings of the Boston meeting. The correspondent of the Atlas is a Mr. Orr (a N. H. man son of a worthy father Col. Jas. Orr, of Bedford, Hills. Co.) a reporter for the Telegraph. It rather looks to me as if there were certain operations going on, not without system to obtain praises for *certain* of our old friends, from Nullifying sources, & *a contra.* I think there is little chance of getting a maj. in house of Rep's. to restore deposites at present. If such a majority should ultimately be found, tho' the President should veto the Resolution for restoration, yet, I think, he must be brought to *some* reasonable terms. I think of saying a few words, on Monday, not as discussing any thing, but simply expressing my opinion, on two or three things— I do this, to repel certain foolish inferences drawn from my silence.[1]

Yrs truly

D. Webster.

---

[1] Webster regarded the situation at this time as desperate. He wrote Milliard Phillips, Jan 25, 1834: " We are at our wits' end here, and cannot see thro'."

(To Edward Everett.)

21" Jany: 1834

We have *adhered*—34 to 13—   take care of the Bill.[1]—

D. WEBSTER.

(To Nathan Appleton.)

FEBY 2. 1834.

Dr. Sir

I send you the documents which you have requested.   I wish I had any thing cheering to say; but Mr. Wrights budget has little hope.   From all quarters of the country, however, the complaint appears to grow louder & louder.   It strikes me at present, that the thing most likely to be done, in season to stop the mischief, is to continue the present Bank 3 or 5 yrs, leaving Congress at liberty to make another after 1836.   We look anxiously for the effect which the recent debate in the Senate (Mr. Wright Jr) may produce at the north.

Yrs.   D. WEBSTER.

(To Jeremiah Mason.)

WASHINGTON March 21, 1834

My Dear Sir

I recd. two days ago yr letter saying that our cause was fixed for 27th inst.   On the 18th. I moved for leave to bring in a Bill, respecting the Bank; a motion, which, in common times does not bring on much debate.   But in the present state of things, debate arises on every question, Mr. Benton is now speaking, on the question of leave; Mr. Wright, Mr. Leigh & Mr Calhoun having spoken at large.   So soon as I can get a vote, I shall set out for home; but it is impossible, I fear, to be in Boston the 27th.

I will write you again tomorrow,   My utmost hope now is to get off on Monday.

Yrs. truly

D WEBSTER

---

[1] See Benton's " Abridgment of the Debates of Congress," vol. xii, p. 252. The appropriation bill.   Everett was in the House of Representatives at this time.

(To Edward Everett.)

FRIDAY EVE: May 9" 1834.

My Dear Sir,

I have been on the point of writing you this week, but we have had a report, every day, that we might expect to see you here. Today, I hear the same report; but write you to let you know, in case my letter finds you in Philadelphia, that we are all alive yet.

I learn your Committee act as a secret Committee. Have they a right to do that? The general rule is, that every Committee is an open Committee unless it be originally constituted as a secret Committee. I doubt much whether a Committee can, by its own authority, impose secrecy on its members.

I wish you would write me to say (unless it be a secret) how long you expect to be in Philadelphia.— I will write you, on some things, if you are likely to remain some days.

In the month which has elapsed since I saw you, things have, as I think, in a considerable degree manifested their probable tendencies.

I hope you sometimes see Mr E Chauncey.

Yours truly

D. WEBSTER

(To James W. Paige.)

WASHINGTON Decr. 11. 1834

Dear William

I found a letter here from you, & wrote the next day to Mr W. desiring him to shew you my letter. I was yesterday given to learn, by a letter Mr Kinsman rec'd. from Mr White, that Mr W. is not coming here. I had fully expected to see him on the 15th.—& I fear my wife will be still more disappointed, as I believe she relied on him, as her beau from N. York.—

—We are as yet doing little here, except talking about the French business.[1] I think there is no great disposition to go to War in haste, although every [one] sees that France has acted rather cavalierly— She is clearly in the wrong.

I am very anxious to hear from you, & to know how you all are. If your own leisure does not permit you to write, ask Har-

---

[1] Because of the failure of France to pay the spoliation indemnity. See Schouler's "History of United States," vol. iv, p. 184.

riet to write a good long letter, & tell me all about everybody, & everything.— I shall look for Mrs Webster to be here the first of next week, if she can get a beau—

Yrs truly always,

Danl Webster

————

(To Nicholas Biddle.[1])

Decr. 19. [1834]

Dr Sir,

I have yr favor of the 15.—Tomorrow, I intend to send you a remittance of 1500, or thereabouts. If it do not go tomorrow, (as I trust it will,) it cannot go for two or three days; but it will go.—

Mr Fletcher has a blank, by which he can renew Mr A's note. The note, you know, is secured by stock.—

The Bank Report has made Mr Benton, & the Globe, & all the K. C. full of wrath. They say Mr Webster wrote it—now Mr W. did not write a page of it.—Mr W. you know, had sense enough to leave the whole investigation to Mr E. & Mr M.[2]— Every thing relative to your affair stands well. Nothing is said of loans to Directors, & all that is said abt. loans to members of Congress is true & just—& as it should be.—The Report acquits the public men of the country, of all sides, from any such influence over their conduct as the Bank could exert.

We have nothing new here, abt. French affairs. Our latest intelligence, is in the N. Y. papers.

I am always truly Yrs

D. Webster

The Senate does not sit today, (friday) & the House is on private bills.

————

(To A. G. Stevens.[3])

Washington, Jan. 1, 1835.

Dear Sir:

I have written to Mr. Kelley to-day endorsing notes, &c, and desiring him to close the bargain with Mr. Shaw for the pasture.

---

[1] Mr. Chas. Roberts, of Philadelphia, kindly loaned this letter.
[2] Ewing and Mangum.
[3] This letter is in the possession of Arthur Stevens, of Concord, N. H., who kindly furnished a copy.

I rely entirely on your judgment & his in the matter, & hope it will be brought to a conclusion soon.— We shall now be likely to have pasture enough; perhaps more pasture than hay.—

The cattle which were bought last fall did pretty well. The best bargain was that for the steers, of Mr. Babcock. The oxen which were had of Mr. Noyes of Boscawen, turn out well. Most of the cattle were sold. The 4 year old & two year old steers we kept.—

I wish you to keep some of your young stock, (if not the whole) rather better than is usual in the country. I would like to have at least one pair of steers raised every year, which might grow to some size— The heifer calves of the Durham breed, should also be well kept. If you should have a full blooded one, this year, let it run with the cow.

In general, I believe it is better to keep but little stock & keep it *well*.—

I wrote sometime ago to Mr. Kelley, respecting the repairs of the house. If that business is undertaken, as I hope it will be, you must see that everything is so arranged that the house will be done & in readiness for me and my wife by the first of June— I should be glad you would write me on these matters.—

You will wish to know what is the prospect of a quarrel with France.— It is somewhat uncertain & must remain so until we hear from France. Congress will not take any hostile step at present.— The danger is, that France may be either angry, or alarmed, when she sees the President's Message, & may take some measure, which will make matters worse. On the other hand, we have some hopes that France will have agreed to pay the money, due by treaty, before the Message reaches Paris—

Mrs. Webster & Julia desire remembrance to your wife & daughter.

Yours,
DANL. WEBSTER.

(From H. W. Kinsman.[1])

Jany. 18 /35

Dear Sir

I will give you a little chapter of the secret history of matters here— There are, as you are probably aware, among the whigs

---

[1] A member of the Massachusetts Legislature from Newburyport.

three parties, viz— Those Who are more friendly to Mr. Clay as a candidate than to yourself ; Those who prefer you ; & wish to make a nomination forthwith and, those, who, although you would be their first preference, yet wish to wait to take up the strongest whig candidate who may appear in the field— These are all honest, sincere whigs. There is, however, besides, a set of *waiters upon Providence* who at present hail from the whig party, but who are ready to attach themselves to any party in which they can become conspicuous ; these last are generally opposed to you at heart, although they do not deem it prudent to say so openly, & they have occasioned us considerable embarrassment by their management & secret whisperings with the first & last mentioned portions of the Whig party. All the delay in our proceedings has arisen from this source. At the preliminary meeting on Friday evening, which I mentioned in my last, your immediate nomination was advocated by T. Parsons, F. Dexter & M. N. Hale and also by Mr. Gray & Mr. Baylies— It was opposed by A. H. Everett, who said that your prospect was hopeless ; that we, by nominating you should take a course fatal to the influence of the State, & perhaps ruinous to the cause ; that unquestionably some more popular candidate would be taken up by the Whigs, & we should then, being pledged to support you & not being able to recede, be placed in a very embarrassing position ; he affected to doubt, notwithstanding his brother's letters were read, whether Mr. Clay had yet declined & c. &c. Chapman of Greenfield, also opposed an immediate nomination, he is, I think, a good whig, but his *bump of self-esteem is* very strongly developed, as the Phrenologists—would say,— his ground was that Mr. Clay could not have declined— he said he had recently been at Washington, had frequently seen Mr. Clay, & conversed with him, & that that gentleman had not mentioned to him (Mr. Chapman) that he intended to decline being a candidate, he therefore could not believe it &c &c—

Roberts of Salem, was also inclined to the opposition, he is also a good whig, but a very soft one, his whig principles are not yet burnt into him, & hardly any other principles, & he has withal such a desire to appear honest, fair & courteous, that he is almost willing to yield the very question in dispute to his adversary, for the sake of being called generous & candid, From this discription you will perceive, that it was better for us that he should *begin* on the other side, as he did, & come over to us in a *candid, fair, courteous* & *gentlemanly manner*, as he also did— It was with a view to make these men operate in our favour by putting them into a conspicuous situation, that they were all, with Mr. Shaw who professes to be favourable, put on the Committee so that they cannot bolt, or get out of the traces, without being noticed, although I am apprehensive that their policy was carried too far—The committee ought to have been so numerous, as to have given us a majority of assured friends— We hope, however, by keeping a vigilant eye upon their proceedings, that we shall be able to finish the business this week, and if there is any flinching, any hesitation on the part of the Committee, in calling the proposed meeting, it will be called nevertheless by others—

In this state of things we were much troubled by the premature assignment of the time for the election of a senator, a movement which has every appearance of having been concealed—

Our present plan is, to have a meeting Tuesday or Wednesday evening, of which the President of the Senate is to be made Prest. & the Speaker, Vice Prest., & if everything goes on according to present expectation you will hear by the last of this week the result—

Yrs.
H. W. KINSMAN

(To Jeremiah Mason.[1])

WASHINGTON, February 1, 1835.

My Dear Sir,—

I received your letter yesterday, and the mail of today brings intelligence verifying your prediction that Mr. Davis would be elected Senator. So far as regards the filling up the vacant seat in the Senate, nothing could be better. I hope all the evil will not happen, which is expected or feared, arising from the difficulty of finding him a successor in the administration of the executive government of the State. I do not think Mr. Adams will ever again consent to be a candidate; certainly not against Mr. Everett; and Mr. Everett and Mr. Bates are not men to suffer the harmony of the State to be disturbed by a controversy among their personal friends. I am still most anxious that all fair means should be used to settle this masonic and anti-masonic quarrel in Massachusetts. You have little idea how much it re-

---

[1] Reprinted from Jeremiah Mason's "Memoirs."

tards operations elsewhere. The reported debate in the Whig
Caucus, on the subject of the Bristol Senators, is industriously
sent to every anti-masonic quarter of the Union, and has excited
much unkind feeling, and thereby done mischief. We are endeavoring here to make the best of Borden.[1] Our anti-masonic
friends in Congress will write to him, advising him not to commit himself to any course of public conduct, till he shall come
here and see the whole ground. The nomination appears to
have been done as well as it could be. I mean, of course, in the
manner of it. No fault is found with it by our friends, so far
as I know. Measures are in train to produce a correspondent
feeling and action, in New York, Vermont, and some other States.
The Legislature of Maryland is now in session, and I have seen
a letter today, which says, that if Mr. Clay were fairly out of
the way, that Legislature would immediately second the Massachusetts nomination. Mr. Clay does nothing, and will do nothing, at present. He thinks—or perhaps it is his friends who
think—that *something* may yet occur, perhaps a war, which
may, in *some* way, cause a general rally around him. Besides
sundry of the members of Congress from Kentucky, in addition
to their own merits, rely not a little on Mr. Clay's popularity, to
insure their reelection next August. They have been, therefore,
altogether opposed to bringing forward any other man at present. Public opinion will, in the end, bring out these things
straight. If Massachusetts stands steady, and our friends act
with prudence, the union of the whole Whig and anti-masonic
strength is certain. Everything indicates that result. Judge
McLean already talks of retiring. His nomination seems coldly
received everywhere. Unless Indiana should come out for him,
I see no probability of any other movement in his favor. Mr.
White's nomination is likely to be persisted in. Neither you nor
I have ever believed it would be easy to get Southern votes for
any Northern man; and I think the prospect now is, that Mr.
Van Buren will lose the whole South. This schism is calculated
to give much additional strength to our party. If Mr. W.
appear likely to take the South, it will be seen that Mr. Van
Buren cannot be chosen by the people; and as it will be understood that Mr. White's supporters are quite as likely to come to
us, in the end, as to go to Van Buren, his course will lose the
powerful support which it derives, or has derived from an assured

[1] Nathaniel B. Borden, Representative in Congress from the Fall River
District, Mass.

hope of success. The effect of these apprehensions is already visible. The recent attempt to shoot the President is much to be lamented. Thousands will believe there was a plot in it; and many more thousands will see in it new proof, that he is especially favored and protected by Heaven. He keeps close as to the question between White and Van Buren. I have omitted to do what I intended, that is, to say a few words upon that part of your letter which relates to myself, more directly. In a day or two I will make another attempt to accomplish that purpose. Mr. Taney's case is not yet decided. A movement is contemplated to annex Delaware and Maryland to Judge Baldwin's circuit, and make a circuit in the West for the judge now to be appointed. If we could get rid of Mr. Taney, on this ground, well and good; if not, it will be a close vote. We shall have a warm debate on the Post Office Report, the Alabama resolutions, and other matters; but I think my course is to take no prominent part in any of them. I may [say] something against expunging the Journal.

Yours truly,

D. Webster.

(To Edward Everett.)

PRIVATE March 2d, 1835.
Dear Sir,
    There is great complaint here, of the neglect of the House of Representatives of *all* important business. I give this hint, so that friends should not concur in any course, which shall occupy what remains of the time of the House, farther than is absolutely necessary on the French subject.[1]

Yours

D. W.

(To Edward Everett.)

May 31" 1835.

Dear Sir,
    I must not omit to express my thanks for the Resolutions; and more especially, to signify my entire and hearty concurrence in their tone and spirit, without reference to the particular nomina-

---

[1] Mr. Everett was in the House of Representatives.

tion.   The Citizens of Boston, I think, have placed their feet on solid grounds of principle and patriotism, and whatever may betide the Country, they will have no dereliction, or backsliding, wherewith to reproach themselves.

I am bound off for Washington, on Tuesday morning.   There being two or three things to speak about, I intend calling at your house this evening, between six and seven o'clock, for a few minutes.   I desire this the more especially, as I may now hope to see Mrs. E.   But there are several friends in town, and as they may call in, in the P. M. it is quite uncertain whether I may be able to leave home; so that if you have any engagement out, pray do not keep yourself in, in expectation of my call.—

Yours truly

D. Webster.

(From Wm. W. Stone et al.)

Hon Daniel Webster   Boston August 14th 1835
    Dear Sir

At a preliminary meeting of a number of Gentlemen opposed to the late proceedings of the advocates for the immediate abolition of slavery at the South, of which meeting the Hon Harrison G. Otis was chairman, it was voted, that a public meeting of those citizens of Boston who do not approve of those should be called at Fanueil Hall on Friday afternoon the 21st instant at 4 O'Clock,— We, were appointed to make arrangements for that meeting, and knowing the desire of the community to hear you on the very important occasion we respectfully invite you to be present, and address the Citizens.—

We have the honor to be with great respect

Your Obt Servants

Wm. W. Stone,

Dan. D. Broadhead,

Wm. Gray.

Committee

(To Mrs. Caroline Webster.)

Washington Decr. 23 [1835]

My Dear Wife,
    I have today recd yrs of Saturday, & while I write this I

presume you are returning from Plymo. I hope you had a good time, as the weather was fine. In your letter you speak of your going as being a little uncertain— but I trust you went, & was sorry to see you undecided about it. You were doubtless expected, & found yourself, I dare say, well treated.

The fire in N. York has excited a great deal of attention here yet I do not believe its effects are half as serious as at first supposed. In a month, it will cease to be talked about. I do not hear that any of our family friends have suffered much.

We have nothing of interest going on here. Everybody is looking for Mr Barton's[1] arrival to bring us news of our French affair. I grow more & more fearful of trouble in that quarter. Mr. Clay has lost his only remaining daughter. He is much affected by the intelligence, & has not been in the Senate since it was recd.—

The President has a party tomorrow Eve'—viz card enclosed.—Mrs Carroll seems to think you ought to be at Washington. Several persons inquired yesterday for Julia, having seen "Miss Webster's" card, about in various places. I suppose it is Mrs Lindslys sister.

I am pretty well arranged, now, in my lodgings, & get on well— Dr. Sewall calls often, & always inquires for Mrs. Webster. I have not been out—have invited no company—& occupy myself with common Congress matters, & with some preparation for the Court— ....though in the Court, I have not a great deal to do this year, & wish I had less. No Ch. Jus is yet nominated but it is expected Mr Taney will be the man.

I hope Miss Ogden was pleased with the Plymo. Celebration. Did they give her any parched corn?—

Yrs ever truly

D WEBSTER

(To Mrs. Caroline Webster.)

WASHINGTON Decr. 28. 1835

Dear Caroline,

I have recd a nice long letter from you this morning, written the day after your return from Plymo, & am happy to learn that you had so agreeable a time. I hope Sally Ogden will admit that she has had one good New England winter frolic.

[1] Thomas P. Barton, Secretary of Legation in France.

I hope none of you took permanent colds. Nothing has happened here, of any interest, since I wrote you. The President's party, I forgot to mention. I was not present, but understand it was something quite new, & *went off* as you New Yorkers say, very brilliantly— There was dancing, in the East room, a sumptuous supper in the dining room, & so on.

We are expecting a Comee. here from NYork, for aid. If anything passes the H of R. the Senate will readily concur, but I doubt whether Mr Cambreling & his colleagues will get along any thing of much value.

Mr. Clay has not been in the Senate, since the intelligence of the loss of his daughter. It appears to have affected him very much.

I enclose you a check for $350, to pay Mr Wells', & Mr Knights' bills. If it be not enough, you must use some of your own checks, & let me know. Why do you send me this bill for the *Observer?*—It is a paper, you know, taken at your request— If you do not wish it to be taken longer, I do not.—Please send the bill to Mr Fletcher, & ask him to remit the 5.50, or whatever else is due, & stop the paper.

I am very happy to learn by Mr Daniel Le Roy's letter which I enclose that your family suffered little by the fire.

Yrs ever truly

DANIEL WEBSTER

(To Mrs. Caroline Webster.)

Sunday, Jan. 10. '36

Dear Caroline

I recd. your letter of the 5th yesterday, but today we have no mail north of N. York. Judge Story arrived last Evening, in good health, but bad spirits. He thinks the Supreme Court is *gone*, & I think so too; and almost everything is gone, or seems rapidly going.

We are in a state of some excitement, about the French business. The President is warm, & warlike, Mr. V. Buren more pacific; & on the whole, there is, as we learn, a good deal of division in the Cabinet. The extensive preparations made by France alarm some of our wise ones, who heretofore have thought Genl Jackson might do anything with impunity. We shall have the message, tomorrow, or on Tuesday, Mr Barton is not yet here, but is expected tomorrow. Mr Langdon is here. Congress is not at all prepared for war; but nobody knows what might be done if Genl. Jackson should sound a loud war note. As soon as we get the message and I can see what is likely to happen thereon, I shall write you on the subject of my visit home There is nothing to prevent it, but this French business.

The Commodore's[1] Family are all well, & send love. I dined with them yesterday. Your inquiry about Mrs Agg reminded me of my duty & I called yesterday to see her, but she was out. I have seen her only at the President's, on New Year's day. They live with Mrs Carlisle, in C. Street.

I am glad, very glad, you find so much occupation, in lectures, visits, parties &c. It is your first real mixture with Boston Society. I hope you will make the most of it. Give my love to the family, & let me know what Dr. Reynolds thinks of Edwards' eyes. H. Thomas wrote me that Edward thought them a good deal better.—

Adieu! for this day.

Yrs ever   D W.

_____

(To Mrs. Caroline Webster.)

WASHINGTON, Sunday Morning
Jan 24. '36

Dear Caroline

I wrote to Fletcher on Thursday— Yesterday & Friday, I was so much occupied in Court, & with Court Business, I had no time to write.

You will see that there is a good deal of heat here. Mr. Benton, & others of the Senate, have attacked the proceedings of last Session— I have felt bound to defend, or help defend the Senate— this has led Mr Adams to attack us, in the House, in the most violent manner, & to bestow an especial portion of his wrath & bitterness on me. He has the instinct of those animals, which, when enraged, turn upon their keepers, & mangle those who have showed them most kindness. The members of the Mass. Delegation are exceedingly indignant, & most of them will tell him what they think of him, before the matter is over. He may be alluded to, also, in the Senate, but not by me. You will see the debates.

---

[1] Commodore Chauncey.

The weather is exceedingly cold & raw— I feel its effects in that thumb which gave me so much trouble, some years ago. I write this morning, not without difficulty. In other respects I am quite well.

I imagine Mr. Southard, Mr Clayton & Mr Ewing may take part, in this Debate that is going on, & say something to, or abt., Mr Adams & his speech.— The House, I understand was disgracefully disorderly, on friday, & when Mr Adams abused *me* well, some of the members, I believe principally those from the State of New York, clapped him— & then the galleries hissed.— this, you will see, must have been all very decorous & proper.

For a considerable of next week (I mean this week) I must be in Court. My business there now presses me rather hard.

I send you a lot of invitations, that you may see what is going on. I have been to no parties I like very much the pleasure of staying at home, & sitting by the fire, thro' an evening, & never find it dull, tho' I am alone.

Some day this week, I must make a dinner for the Mass. Delegation— They will much miss your Ladyship, from the head of the Table.

It is now, I think, four days, since I had a letter from you; but the mails are so irregular, that perhaps the next may bring me three or four. Today, we have no papers from New York.—

With love to you all, I am, Dr wife—

Ever yrs

D. W.

(To Mrs. Caroline Webster.)

WASHINGTON friday—Jan. 29. [1836]

Dear Caroline

There is no doubt England has tendered her good offices, by way of mediation, in order to reconcile the differences between the U. S. & France. Such, it is understood, was the purpose of the despatch recd. by Mr Brodhead, & which has been communicated to our Govt. The President held a meeting of the Cabinet yesterday, but no positive decision was had on the subject. The general opinion, today, is that the offer will not be declined, & that some how or other an adjustment will grow out of it. The hope of continued peace, at the present moment is strong.

Brother Daniel LeRoy arrived here [last] Eve'.' He came, I believe, with little other object than to see how things are going.

I find he is very despairing about Mrs Newbold [1] He proposes to stay a few days. I should be glad to have him here, but he seems to prefer a Hotel, where he will have an opportunity of seeing more persons, & hearing more news.—

Mr & Mrs C. H. Warren arrived here two days ago. They stay with Mr & Mrs Davis & at Mrs Coyle's— I have endeavored in vain to see Mrs Warren, as yet. Dr Wainwright doth not yet appear.

Today, the Mass. Delegation dined with me, *with some exceptions.*— It is my only effort to raise a dinner, of any magnitude, & I doubt how we shall make out.—

Mr Evans made a famous speech yesterday. I did not hear it, but it is universally praised. I understand he told Mr. A. that he had lived to become "the scorn & derision of his enemies, & an object of pity to his friends."

I was in the House this morning. Mr A. was not there. they said he was probably at home, writing out his speech—or else digesting what he heard yesterday. He has more to hear yet.

The weather is clear, & very cold— This morning is the coldest I have felt this year—

Adieu!

Ever yrs   D. Webster

It is four days since I have heard from home. We do not get a mail as often as any other day.

(To Mrs. Caroline Webster.)

11 o'clock. A. M. Tuesday, Feb. 2. [1836]

Dear Caroline

I have just recd your letter of Friday, which has altogether relieved my anxiety. I hope you will not delay, for so many days, hereafter, to write to me. If you are too busy, there are Fletcher & Julia, to say nothing of Sally Ogden, who may just as well be writing to me, as sitting at the window looking at the sleighs.

My cold is much better, this morning. I sent for Dr Sewall, last Eve', after writing to you, & the Dr. knew how to deal with it.

I shall go to the Senate, but not stay more than an hour.

Yrs truly

D Webster
(over)

---

[1] Sister of Mrs. Webster and Daniel LeRoy.

Evening

Mr. Buchanan finished his speech this forenoon.   It was rather belligerent; that is, it followed the President's example, & recounted all the wrongs of France.   Nevertheless, he expressed great confidence that the mediation would result in Peace.

Mr Crittenden made a very good Speech.   He is for Peace. So that, on the whole, pacific sentiments prevail.

(To Edw. E. Marshall.)

Dear Sir,   WASHINGTON Febry 6". 1836.

In the year 1833 the late Chief Justice Marshall wrote two letters to Mr. Everett, now Governor of Massachusetts on the subject of Masonry, and Masonic oaths.   Those letters express opinions, which the Chief Justice is known to have communicated to others, and Mr. Everett was desirous of publishing one or both of them, or so much thereof as related to the foregoing subjects.   But the Chief Justice desired the letters to be considered as confidential, and that no public use should be made of them.

It has occurred to Mr. Everett that in consequence of the lamented death of the Chief Justice, there probably exists no longer any reason for withholding these letters from publication. Yet he feels a delicacy in consenting to give them to the public, without the permission of the representatives of the Chief Justice.   The fact of the existence of such letters is known, and very solicitous application is continually made to Mr. Everett for their publication.   Mr. Everett has recently written to me, upon this matter, and it is in consequence of this letter, that I write you this, for the purpose of asking whether you and your brother see any objection to the publication?   I may add my own wish, that the letters might be made public, since the sentiments they express are precisely such as I hold myself.   Copies of the letters are in my possession, and if you should think it necessary, in order to guide your judgments in this matter to peruse them, I will transmit them, for that purpose.

I pray you to accept my sympathy, for the loss of your great and good Parent.   Taught to respect him, from my earliest manhood, I have for twenty years, witnessed his judicial labors, and studied his character, with constantly increasing admiration.

With much regard Yours.

DANL WEBSTER

(To Edward Everett.)

MARCH 12" 1836.

Dear Sir,

I enclose you Mr. Marshall's answer to my letter, and Mr. Leigh's endorsement, which will speak for themselves.

I think Mr. L. has decided right, though I could much have wished for the publication of the Chief justice's letter. However, the *fact* of the letter will gradually get out, and by and by, the letter itself, perhaps, may properly appear.

I suppose there can be no objection to my showing the letter, occasionally, to a friend.

Yours D. W.

(To Mrs. Caroline Webster.)

WASHINGTON, Tuesday morng Feb. 9 [1836]

Dear Caroline,

I this morning have recd your letter of the 5th friday—which shows that the mails are regularly delivd.— I am glad to hear you are all well. It would give me much pleasure, I assure you, to partake of some of those little suppers, which appear so good in your letters. They are articles, of which I have seen no specimen, since I left home. Early in March, I hope to taste a potato, in Summer Street.

My cold is getting better, so that I go [to] the Senate, in fair weather, but I am obliged to be very careful. I have not been to an evening party, this winter—& only once to dine, viz at Mr Van Buren's, on Saturday. It was a dinner, I presume, mainly intended for the Judges. He lives in much the same manner as when Secretary of State; perhaps not quite so well. I wished to go last Eve' to Mrs. *Flander* White's last *Soiree*, but dared not venture out. The President has another great party on Thursday—

Mrs. Cass, as you will see has her third rout, the 18th. They say Mrs Cass must be preparing to make her husband a foreign minister.

Mr & Mrs Warren are yet here. They leave on Saturday. I should not be surprised if Charles & I should give them & Mr & Mrs Davis a little dinner, in my study, on Thursday or friday.

Mrs & Miss Chauncy are well, and always send their love. I

have not seen Mrs Lindsly for a month.   Dr. Sewall calls sometimes but not very often.

I am about writing to Edward.   It is now so cold, & it may
be so long before winter breaks up, I am indifferent about his
going to Hanover till I come home, if I should be able to come,
as I expect, early in March.   I see nothing to prevent me, now,
as no change is likely to take place, for some time in our French
affairs.

We must soon hear from Mrs Newbold—

Truly Yrs
D WEBSTER

(From Thomas G. Pratt.[1])

HOUSE OF DELEGATES ANNAPOLIS Feb 24th. 1836
Hon. Daniel Webster

Sir;

In a debate which occurred in the House of Delegates today,
your speech and the speech of Mr Binney delivered in Baltimore
shortly after the removal of the Deposits from the Bank of the
U. States, were assigned as the remote causes of the recent riots in
that city.   You were represented by Mr McLean one of the Delegates from the City of Baltimore, as having on that occasion,
"exhorted the people of Baltimore, to redress their grievances,
peaceably if they could, forcibly if they must".   As no report of
your speech has been made & Mr McLean having avowed himself
responsible for the correctness of the language imputed to you;
you will gratify your friends here, by stating whether he is correct in his statement and if recollected, what was the language
used by you upon that occasion.   The same charge was made
against Mr Binney, to whom I have addressed a communication
similar to this—

Very Respectfully
THOS. G. PRATT.

(To Thos. G. Pratt.)

WASHINGTON Feb. 27. 1836

Sir,

I have recd your letter of the 24th.   Nothing could have sur-

---

[1] Mr. Pratt was at this time in the Maryland Senate.   Later he was Governor of that State and Senator in Congress.   See Webster's reply, February
27, 1836.

prised me more than the representation which you say was made in the House of Delegates of my remarks, at Baltimore, after the removal of the Deposits.

I uttered no such sentiment as is imputed to me, either in the words said to have been used by me, or any other words; nor any equivalent sentiment, nor any sentiment at all resembling it. There is not the slightest ground, in anything said or insinuated by me, on that occasion, for this gross misrepresentation.   I can also speak to the same effect, & with equal positiveness of Mr Binney's remarks, for I was near him, & heard every word he said.

I am, Sir, respectfully, Your ob. Servant
[D. WEBSTER.][1]

(To H. Hunt.)

PRIVATE AND CONFIDENTIAL.

Sir   WASHINGTON Feb. 29. 1836

I recd your letter, as Secretary of the Association of Native American citizens &c, some days ago, & have no objection [of] to the interchange of opinions, on the subject to which it refers.

I am not prepared, however, to give an immediate & formal answer to your letter, as some of your questions are of great importance, & deserve to be well considered.   In truth, in the part of the country in which I live, aliens are so few, that no great attention has been excited by their naturalization.   I have been made acquainted however, with the shocking abuses which have been committed under the naturalization laws in New York; abuses, which in my opinion imperatively demand correction, either by new laws, or new modes of administration.

I expect to be in New York, in ten or twelve days, & should be glad of an opportunity of seeing you.

Yours with regard
DANL WEBSTER

(To Mrs. Caroline Webster.)

Dear Caroline   MAR. 6. 1836 Sunday Morning.

This is a very fine morning, which I hope you are also enjoy-ing.— It is warm, & summer like, and fills me full of the hopes

---

[1] This is copied from the original draft of the letter sent.

of home.   I shall wait only to hear that the Boat has run *once.*—
intending to go the second trip.—   My cold has melted off, & I
am quite well.—

Everything is very dull here.   Mr. Tyler has resigned, and
Mr Leigh[1] says he shall resign next fall.

All the news I have heard this month is that Mrs. Lindsley
tells me that our friend Mr Posts is inclined to make love to
Harriet Webster—& that Genl M'Comb[2] has written a play;—
which was performed on friday night—called *Pontiac*—   I will
tell Charles to send it to you.

I am going out today with Mr Agg to dine at his cottage—I
shall be glad to get a breath of air.

I incline to think I shall bring Charles along, but am not certain—

I must stay a day or two in N. Y. as well as in Philadelphia,
either going or returning, hoping to have a little business in each
place.

I send you a copy of Mr Clayton's Speech.   It is pretty severe.
Mr. Robbin's was an excellent Speech, which I suppose will also
be printed in pamphlet form—& I shall send it—

I hear much of Sally's two rival beaux?—   Which does she
mean to smile upon?   Give her my love; though I fancy I am
too far off to be much remembered *at present* —

Ever Yrs

D WEBSTER

(To D. Fletcher Webster.)

WASHINGTON, Mar. 14. '36

My Dear Son,

I have yours of the 10th.   The difficulty in getting home is
not in the Sound, but in the more Southern waters.   No Boat
runs yet from Baltimore—both the Chesapeake Bay & the Delaware river are covered with thick-ribbed ice.   The weather, however, is warm today, & seems to indicate rain; so that I hope to
be able to sail, in a few days.

It gives me great delight to hear, that you have learned how to
sit still, & read a Book.   If you have really accomplished that,
you have certainly made your fortune.

I am sorry there is so much fault found with Govr. Everett.

---

[1] Benjamin W. Leigh, of Virginia.   [2] General Alexander Macomb.

I am sure he means well, & acts always in good faith towards his friends.   It is strange any rumours should exist of coolness between him & myself—   There is not the slightest foundation for them.

I regret to hear of Caroline's illness.   She must be careful of herself.   Give her my love, & say to her that I hope to find her well next week.

I wrote yʳ mother yesterday, & all the news, since occurring, is, that Wm. LeRoy, the midshipman, was here yesterday, on his way from Norfolk to N York—

He is in fine health, & a fine looking young man.

Yrs always, affectionately

DANL WEBSTER

(To Mrs. Caroline Webster.)

SENATE, Friday Morning April 29. '36

My Dear Caroline,

I recd your letter of Monday Eve this morning.   Fletcher has not arrived, but I shall look for him this Evening, or tomorrow. We have had a week of mild growing weather—a remarkable mixture of moisture & warmth.—

Today we hope to finish the land bill, if Mr Benton should not wear us all out, by an endless speech—which he threatens to do. If we finish the Bill, I think we shall adjourn to Tuesday, to give time for the officers of the Senate to take up the carpet, clean the chamber &c. for warm weather.

I have some thoughts of running down the river, 25 miles, to a place of Genl Mason's where his son John lives—a great shad fishery, & return on Monday.   It now looks, however, like rain; & if that should come, I shall stay at home.

I imagine you will find it necessary to establish your headquarters in N. York at Mrs Edgars, especially as Mrs Dan'l. Le Roy appears in bad health.   It will be agreeable for you to be with your father.   I think you will find it pleasant [to] come to N. York sometime next week, or the early part of the week after—   You will of course let me know when to write you at N. York—

Commodore Chauncy had a party to dine yesterday—   I did not make one—   It is much pleasanter to have the afternoon to walk about, that is, all that is left of it after a short session.   My health is at present very good—but I wish I had Sorrel here. I hate to ride a hack horse, & cannot afford the expense of buying one. I think I may hire one, under Tweedy's advice, for the session.—

I shall of course write to you as at Boston, till I hear to the contrary—

Adieu!—love to Julia—how can you get on, with so small a household— I should think you would do well to break up, as soon as you can conveniently—

Yrs ever truly

D WEBSTER

(To James Watson Webb.[1])

WASHINGTON May 6, 1836.

My Dear Sir,

My son is quite obliged to you, for giving him a letter to your brother.[2]

As to the subject of your two letters, My Dear Sir, all I can say is, that I pray you to follow the course, which you think duty & honor point out. I have certainly no desire that any effort should be made for me, under circumstances which leave no hope that *good would be* produced by such effort.

I estimate highly your assurances of continued confidence & attachment, & shall never forget the regard & kindness which you have manifested, so long & so readily. But in the present state of things, I pray you to feel fully at liberty to act for the good of the Country, and the cause, without reference to any expectation, which you may suppose I have heretofore formed, & to be assured, that in so doing you will meet my entire approbation. You probably saw my letter to the Whigs of the Massachusetts Legislature. It spoke my undisguised sentiments. I should have withdrawn from the canvass altogether, but for the state of affairs in Massachusetts, & the opinions of friends there.

I could very much desire to pass an hour with you, on this & some connected subjects. Are you not to be this way?

[DANL WEBSTER]

---

[1] New York journalist; editor of the Courier and Enquirer. He was one of the most enterprising newspaper men of his day. He had also a most creditable military career.

[2] Probably Henry L. Webb, of Illinois.

(From Samuel Houston.)

COLUMBIA Texas 20th Nov 1836

Dear Sir,

I take pleasure in presenting Genl Santa Anna, to your friendly & distinguished attention. He will visit the Capitol of the U. States, under peculiar circumstances, and tho' we have been antagonists in war, as he visits my native land, it will be matter of singular gratification for me to know, that those whom I had the honor to act with, in exalted station, have received and treated General Santa Anna, with the respect, and kindness due to his distinguished, Genius, rank and character.

Whatever kindness you may find it in your power to bestow, upon the distinguished guest of the U. States, will reflect honor, upon Texas, and place myself, with others who are struggling for Liberty, under lasting obligations.

It will afford me felicity to receive your Commands.

I am with high regard Your friend & obt Servt.

SAM'L HOUSTON.

(From D. Fletcher Webster.)

DETROIT [Michigan] Feby 24th. 1837.

My dear Father

* * * I regret that you will lose the bridge case—perhaps you may be mistaken— I cannot but hope so, more especially as it may be, as you say your *last* case. You don't know what strange emotions I felt at learning that you really mean to resign to your seat in Congress,[1] although I was prepared for it by your conversation with me just before I left, yet the knowledge that it was decided on, gave us a shock. Caro. could not refrain from tears— "She was glad of it, yet it will be so strange not to have him there—what will become of us all!" I felt the same too, but I sincerely rejoice at it— I rejoice to learn that you have withdrawn from that body, now so fallen, of which in the days of its highest splendor & renown "pars maxima fuisti" with all honour to yourself & that with full capacity to enjoy & improve it, you retire to leisure which you have a thousandfold earned and for many reasons need and in the enjoyment of which

---

[1] See Webster's "Works," vol. i, p. 341.

you will be blessed by the kindest wishes & regards of all honest men.— "Famam bonam, certamque domum reportas."

Mother wrote me a day or two before you, of your intention. She will be very happy at the decision— We all rejoice on your account, while all regret it on their own. * * *

[D. F. WEBSTER]

(To Edward Everett.)

WASHINGTON March 4" 1837.

My Dear Sir—

I do not think Mr. Davis has any wish to be a Judge.

I would not, certainly, embarrass you, by too warm a recommendation of Mr. Hoar; and feel the force of the local considerations, suggested by Mr. Curtis. Mr. Wells, I believe, would make an excellent judge. You must, of course, collect the general sentiment of friends, and to a great degree respect it. I regret these local feelings; but they do exist, and have much influence.

The Inauguration went off, I thought rather coldly.

Yours truly

D. WEBSTER.

(From D. Fletcher Webster.)

DETROIT [Michigan] Apr. 5, 1837.

My dear Father,

It is a long time since we heard from you, except through the papers, indeed, I ought to be content with that. We have read of your reception in New York[1]— I must let "expressive silence muse" my thoughts of it.

I am constantly asked whether or no you mean to resign & I answer not at present.[2] I hope you have not changed your ultimate purpose. * * *

The people are all very anxious to see you out here.[3] It would be prudent to let me know if you can when you will be

---

[1] See "Works of Daniel Webster," vol. i, p. 339.

[2] See letter of Fletcher Webster to Daniel Webster, Feb. 24, 1837—note.

[3] Webster made a trip through the West in the summer of 1837. In his correspondence are letters from Western legislatures—Kentucky, Ohio, etc.— giving him urgent invitations to accept their hospitality. Louisville, Russellville, Michigan City, Detroit, Toledo, Erie, Pa., and Rochester, N. Y., sent him flattering letters to the same effect.

here, that I may make arrangements for lodgings, for there won't be room to turn round from May to November. We mean to give you a good reception. Our City authorities are, alas! all Tory, but that will not have the slightest influence. * * *

Your most affectionate son

DAN'L F. WEBSTER.

———

(To Benjamin D. Silliman.[1])

WASHINGTON Jan. 29, 1838.

My dear Sir

I recd your letter this morning, for which I am much obliged to you.

I do not know whether I can find here a copy of my speech, in 1830, on Foote's Resolutions. If I can I will send it to you.

I think you would be very safe in adopting, in your House, an Anti Texas Report. As to Slavery, I think it very safe to adopt a Resolution, condemning Mr. Patton's Resolution. Whether it will be best to go farther, you who are on the spot, can best decide. My own opinion is, that the anti-slavery feeling is growing stronger & stronger every day; & while we must be careful to countenance nothing, which violates the Constitution, or invades the rights of others it is our policy, in my opinion most clearly not to yield the substantial truth, for the sake of conciliating those whom we never can conciliate, at the expense of the loss of the friendship & support of those great masses of good men, who are interested in the anti-slavery cause.

I send you enclosed a copy of a letter lately addressed by me to Mr. Peck of the H. of R. It states shortly the opinions, which I hold, & am ready to express, on the general Slavery questions. I refer you, also, to some remarks of mine, published in the Intelligencer, upon Mr. Clay's substitute for Mr. Calhoun's 5th Resolution.

We begin the proceeding on the Sub Treasury Bill to-morrow. It will probably pass this House, without amendment, by 2 or 3 votes. Its fate in the other House is greatly more doubtful. The decision on the Mississippi Election is expected to day or tomorrow. The Sub Treasury Bill may, perhaps, be a good [deal] dependent on this decision.

---

[1] Mr. Silliman was a New York lawyer, at this time a member of the State Legislature. Later he rose to great prominence as a New York politician.

I will look round for a copy of my speech of 1830, & write you again in a day or two.

Yrs truly
Danl Webster

━━━━━

(To Mrs. Caroline Webster.)

July 4, 1838 Wednesday Mor'g.

Dear Caroline

I recd yrs of Friday Eve', last night, I was glad to hear you were safe home. We are here yet, quarrelling about these everlasting questions, and I see no end, but the end of the session. Mr. Curtis did not come to dinner yesterday till 10 clock, altho we had invited the Commodore[1] & his son, & two or three other friends to dine at 5. At ten, Mr. C, Mr. Hoffman, Mr. Jenison, & Mr. Biddle came home to *dinner*.

The weather is intolerably warm. I never knew such a succession of hot days—there is no going abroad a step, in the sun.

I dare not say a word about the time of getting home, because you say I am so apt to disappoint you. I shall be sure to leave Washington as soon as I can, & to hasten home as fast as I can—but I must stay some days in N. York—how many, I do not know.

But few members have left yet. I look for Col. Perkins who is away to-day. He comes here, & then goes to Wheeling—Nothing further from Fletcher—but hope to hear today.

I hope you & Julia are safe & *cool*, down at Marshfield.

Yrs ever lov'ly
D. Webster.

I have a letter from Mr. White—he thinks he shall see me, here, or at N. York—but I do not depend on it.

━━━━━

(To Mrs. Caroline Webster.)

Washington July 6, 1838.

Dear Caroline.

I had some idea of getting away today, but my colleague utterly forbad it, on acct. of a Harbor Bill, pending in the Senate.

---

[1] Commodore Chauncey.

The weather has changed, at last, & today the wind is northward, & cool. I feel much better for it. I think my health improves daily. If it were not so late, & if I were not so anxious to get home, I would go to the Warrenton Sulphur Springs, for a week. But as it is, & having indispensable business in N. Y. I must go northward..

Col. P returned hither last evening. He passed a week with Mr. Page's party at the Hot Springs. By yesterday's mail, too I recd the enclosed letter from Mrs. P.

Nothing new here, of any interest, except that Mr. Grundy[1] is appointed Atty. Genl., in place of Mr. Butler—to go into office Sep. 1

Mr. Curtis continues to improve, but is obliged to work a little too hard.

I have heard nothing of yr. horses—if they have not arrived, I suppose you have looked up some other pair for the present.

Yrs alway, truly

D. W.

(From Nicholas Biddle.)

PHIL^A. Sepr. 6, 1838

My dear Sir

I stated to you last year my views in regard to Texas, and you then thought that if the plan of annexation to the U. S. could be abandoned, every consideration of feeling & interest would conspire to make us desire its prosperity. That question is now settled. Mr Jones the new minister arrived two days ago in Phil^a and he is instructed to withdraw the proposal of Union. This troublesome part of the question being thus disposed of, I am much inclined to think that if their loan of five millions were taken in the United States it would be far better than if they were obliged to seek it in England. I do not however wish to mix myself with the political contests of the day; nor to interfere in matters which have been the subjects of party warfare and I should like to have the benefit of the opinions of judicious friends before doing anything final in respect to it. Will you then say, whatever you feel at liberty to say on the questions, Whether it would not be greatly for the interest of our common country that Texas should continue independent of all foreign nations—that

---

[1] Felix Grundy, of Tennessee.

she should be protected by this country & not be permitted if possible to owe her prosperity to any other aid than ours.   Say too
whether your opinion is that Texas can maintain its independence
or whether in the last extremity this country would permit her to
be conquered or reconquered. and being free whether you think a
loan to her would be perfectly safe.   You will readily understand by the strain of these remarks that I am predisposed to
serve Texas because I believe I should benefit our country by it—
but before taking any decisive step I should wish to have your
judgment because I know that your opinion will be an impartial
& a patriotic one.   If any circumstance public or private indis-
poses you to answer I request that you will not answer.   But if
you incline to speak—speak—for I think the occasion worthy of
you and so speak that if when I have decided I should want the
benefit of your judgment to sanction my course I may have it &
use it publicly or privately.   I will only add that what you say
I wish you to say quickly.[1]

With great regard Yrs

N. Biddle

(To Henry Cowperthwaite.[2]*)*

Dear Sir   N. Y.   Sep. 27. 1838 Thursday morning

Parlour No. 14 is rather dreary this morning, inside & out.
It has ceased to rain, but the fog is about as thick as cream. And
yet the Stonington Boat was in at 7 'clock this morning, to my
utter surprise.

I felt concerned for you yesterday, as the day was so very
bad, for a gentleman with a cold, & an inflamed throat.   I hope
you kept dry, & reached home safe.

The "New Concern" opens today.[3]   I was out, to meet a considerable number of Gentlemen last Eve', & this was the general
topic.   Some said the individual Deposits, today, would be very
great; others feared that the Institution would be so annoying to
the powers at Albany, that they would yet seek to embarrass it, although it was not easy to see how they could do so.   All agreed
it was an important operation, promising to be useful, & likely to
produce a *sensation*, right & left.

---

[1] This letter is owned by Mr. C. P. Greenough.
[2] This letter is in the possession of the Pennsylvania Historical Society.
[3] See Schouler's "History of the United States," vol. iv, p. 292.

I shall not get away today, on account of the weather—& if I hear anything worth telling in Wall Street, upon the go off of the new Bank of the U. S. in N. Y. will write you a line.

I am acting on the *presumption* (I agree I am *presumptuous*) that when you go into the Marble House this morning, you will cause a *trifling error* to be corrected, in Mr. Andrews account.

God bless you—

D. WEBSTER

(Memorandum.[1])

MAR. 10. [1839]

I happened to hear, near the close of the Session, that Mr. Poinsett had expressed, in presence of the Pres't. an opinion favorable to sending me on the Special mission to England.

I heard it intimated, also, ab't the same time, that the President might think my notions too much inclined to a *war* aspect.

I therefore called on Mr. P.—told him what I had heard, & said that I wished to say a few words to him, expressive of my opinion of the course the minister ought to pursue merely for the purpose of justifying his favorable opinion. I read to him this memorandum. He expressed himself as pleased with the suggestion, in general, and asked me for a copy; which I sent him on the 9 Mar.

D. W.

(A Scheme for the Settlement of the Northeastern Boundary.[2])

[APR. 1839]

1. That the negotiation should be opened, & conducted throughout, in the most friendly spirits, treating all the arguments & suggestions of the Br. negotiators with entire respect.

2. But that an immediate and final settlement of the question should be urgently proposed, upon considerations and motives, which address themselves equally to both parties.

3. That informal & friendly interviews should be sought, with the Br: Negr. & the members of Her. M's Cabinet; which inter-

---

[1] Found among Webster's papers and owned by Edwin W. Sanborn, of New York.

[2] A scheme submitted by Webster to Poinsett in 1839. See "Curtis' Life of Webster," vol. ii, p. 2. It had been suggested that Webster negotiate this treaty in England.

views should be carefully used, to accomplish the following purposes.

1. To satisfy the English Agents & the English Govt. of the intrinsic weakness of their case, upon the orig'l question, under the Treaty of 1783.

2. To satisfy them as far as possible, that they overate the importance of this Territory to England. To suggest, that England cannot feel anxious for it, merely as so much land, since in the Provinces of New Brunswick land now is, & for many years to come must be, out of all proportion to population; and that as affording a better communication between Halifax & Canada, it is to be considered that no great communication, by land, between those points can exist, under any circumstances; or at least, not for half a century; that England can seldom have occasion to move troops, on that route; that if she sometimes have such an occasion, there will be no objection to it, in time of peace, although the U. S. should own the land; and that, in time of war, we should prevent such a movement, if we could, whether She, or we, owned the territory. Perhaps, in this connexion, a right of passage, might be thought of, as fit to be made a Treaty Stipulation. I imagine however, that it is not merely a communication from Province to Province that England desires, so much as it is a general strength'g of her frontiers, by widen'g its breadth, East of the St. Lawrence, at this point, and giving compactness & continuity to her possessions.

4. To take an early opportunity, in the formal correspondence, of presenting a clear & concise, view of the merits of the original question would not be amiss, if the course of correspondence should seem to make a place for it.

5. To bring England to take her ground; either, that she asserts a line, conformable, as she alleges, to the Treaty, as she did before the Dutch arbitration; or, that she insists, that the description in the Treaty is so indefinite, that the boundary cannot be found, by any attempt to pursue its requisitions.

6. If she shall take the first course, & set up such a line as heretofore, then how utterly impossible it is to reconcile that line to the plain & clear demands of the Treaty.

7. If she adopt the latter branch of the Alternative, and insist that the Treaty line cannot be found, controvert this, by the arguments, appropriate to the case & among other things, that ridges, or heights of land, are not of infrequent use, in fixing lines, on this Continent; that the English Govt. has, in other

cases, prescribed such boundaries; that the U. S. have done the same thing, in many treaties, without practical inconvenience; & then as an important matter of fact [then] urge the actual result of the late survey under the authority of Maine.

8. But, however the argument may stand, it is probable that England will not, gratuitously, yield her pretensions; & something must be yielded by us, since the subject has actually become matter of negotiation.   A conventional line, therefore, is to be regarded as a leading & most promising, of adjustments. With a view to this, before he leaves the country, should have an interview with the Govr. of Maine, & her Delegation in Congress. He & they should examine the map carefully, & consider the whole subject maturely, & they should be called on to say *what* conventional line Maine would approve.   This interview might be had, without form, or announcement, but it would take time, & should be done as soon as convenient.

If conventional line should be agreed on, in London, it should be one of the conditions of the Convention, that the Prest.'s ratification should be postponed here, till Maine had given her consent; & that her Majesty's ratification should be postponed till ratification should be made in U. S.

9. To the suggestion that this Territory cannot be (which suggestion should only be made in informal conversation) of much importance to Great Britain, her negotiators would doubtless reply, that, if so, neither could it be of much importance to the U. S.—   This would furnish a suitable opportunity to explain the nature of our political Institutions, the limited authority of the Genl Govt, the natural tenacity with which a State clings to what it considers its rights of soil &c; & to suggest that for these & similar reasons, the desire for peace, which is really felt by the Cabinet of W. ought not to be measured precisely by what it feels itself authorized to propose, &c &c.

10. In the informal conversation which may take place, suggest & urge strongly the great expense, & perhaps the serious difficulty, to both Government, of preserving quiet, along the whole line of frontier, thro' another Winter, if this controversy be not settled, or some progress made in its adjustment.

11. If a Conventional line cannot be agreed on, propose a joint commission of survey. &c. of two Comms. on a side, who if *they can agree*, shall ascertain the Treaty line, & mark it, definitely.   But this to be without an umpirage.

12. If this be not agreed, propose, that each party shall, by

itself, appoint a Commissioner of Survey, to ascertain the fact, whether the treaty line can be ascertained, or not; that these Commissioners shall act separately; that they shall perform the duty, as early as possible, that each Commission report to its own Government, & copies to be interchanged, the reports to be made by ————— next, & the negotiation, mean while, adjourned, & transferred to Washington.   I suppose however, that if this course were agreed to, the survey could not be accomplished, the ensuing summer; as the British ministry will probably be very much engaged until the close of the session of Parliament, which will probably not terminate before August; & it may [be] doubtful whether, earlier than that, any thing could be agreed on.

If nothing else can be done, another reference, or a joint Commission with an umpirage, is to be thought of.   This however, to be the last resort, unless U. S. Govt. be already committed ôn the point.

13. Finally, that if an agreement cannot be arrived at, in some of these modes, or in some other which may be suggested, the negotiation to be broken off, with an expression of deep regret, & an intimation that the Govt. of the U. S. fully believing in the easy practical ascertainment of the Treaty Bound'ry, will cause a careful & accurate survey to be made, by a Commission of high character, appointed by itself, & acting with authority to explore the country, & following the terms of the treaty ascertain the Boundry under oath; that in the spirit of amity, it will communicate the result of this survey to the British Govt, expressing, at the same time, its own sense, of what the case, as it shall then be presented, shall demand.—

———

(From Lewis Cass.[1])

Paris 23d June, 1839.

My Dear Sir—

I perceive by the papers you are in England, and I suppose you will take a good look at your fatherland before you extend your journey further.   But I trust you intend to visit France,

---

[1] Lewis Cass was then the American Minister at Paris, and this is his letter to Webster in London.   The letter was taken from a newspaper clipping in the possession of C. E. Bliss, of Bangor, Me.   The editor has, however, seen the original in the collection of C. P. Greenough, of Boston.

and I write to say that I shall be happy to see you here and contribute to make your residence agreeable. There is much to interest you in Paris, and I will play guide for you. I am sure you will not regret the little time which a brief tour through France will cost you. Mr. Fish, who has promised to send you this letter, is an American clergyman. I am happy to introduce him to you, for he has high qualities, moral and mental, and is the most eloquent man I ever heard in the pulpit. Mrs. Cass joins me in the tender of respectful regards to Mr. Webster, and with the hope that we shall have the pleasure of seeing him in Paris.

With sincere regards I am, dear sir, truly yours.

LEW CASS.[1]

(From Charles Sumner.)

ROME, June 24, 1839.

Allow me to give you joy on this occasion and to say how happy I am as an American to know that you are in England. It has happened to me to see English society quite widely and to enjoy in no moderate measure that hospitality which it understands so well. I can truly say that your distinguished name has gone before you, and that you will find large numbers of the best people who will be anxious to make your acquaintance.[2] Lord Lansdowne and Holland inquire of me about you with great interest. Lord Fitzwilliam has the first volume of your speeches in his library and he told me with what pleasure he had read your discourse at Plymouth. * * * Renewing my salutations and wishing you great joy in Europe, I am, my dear sir, Very faithfully yours,

CHARLES SUMNER.

---

[1] See Daniel Webster to S. Jaudon, dated "1839," among "Personal Finance" letters.

[2] Daniel Webster to Edw. Curtis, Liverpool, June 3, 1839; Daniel Webster to I. P. Davis, London, June 24, 1839; Daniel Webster to Hiram Ketchum, London, July 23, 1839; Memorandum, London, July 30, 1839; Daniel Webster to Ticknor, Lowther Castle, Aug. 21, 1839; Daniel Webster to Mrs. Lindsley, Scotland, Sept. 6, 1839. The above letters, describing the visit to England, may be found in " Private Correspondence of Daniel Webster," vol. ii, pp. 46, 50, 58, 60, 63, 67.

(To Judge Wilkinson.¹)

LONDON, July 4, 1839.

My dear Sir:

I have had the pleasure since I came to England to make the acquaintance of Mr. Sandback, of the House of Sandback, Tinne & Co. of Liverpool. These Gentlemen are connected with the Colony of Demarara and are desirous of knowing if free black labor could probably be obtained in the U. S. and be employed in that Colony. I have ventured to refer Mr. Sand(b)ack to you.

He will write you at length upon the subject, and I need only add that he is a gentleman of character and reputation.

I am, Dear Sir, With much regard yours

DANL WEBSTER.

———

(Memorandum.²)

[LONDON.] Wednesday, July 10. [1839]

We all breakfasted at Mr. Lockhart's.

Present, beside ourselves, Mrs. Rogers & the two Miss Alexander's. Mrs. Millman & her sister. Lord Ashley, Lord Mahon, Sir Henry Ellis & Rev. Mr. Millman, Prebend of Westminster.

2. Dined at Lord Brougham's with Lord Wharncliff Lord Stuart De Rothay. Lord Nagert. (etc) Lord Chief Justice Tindall. Sir Arthur Paget. Mr. Leader, M. P. F. B. Kerr, Law Commissioner. Basil Montagu. The Atty. Genl. Baron Dashe. Mr. Eden. Mr. Shafts.

In the Even'g, we all went to a concert at Prince Esterhazy's— where were assembled the general society of London.

---

¹ This letter is owned by the Hon. Geo. F. Hoar. The letter is written to the agent of the American Colonization Society, Buffalo, N. Y.

² In Webster's handwriting. Among his papers there are several spasmodic efforts to keep a diary of his experiences abroad. The original of this is the property of Edwin W. Sanborn, of New York. During his visit Webster made the acquaintance of Coleridge, Wordsworth, H. C. Robinson, Duer, Sir Chas. Fellows, Count Montalembert and many other distinguished persons. See Curtis' Life of Webster, vol. ii, pp. 8, 89, 125. There are among Mr. Greenough's papers letters from Thos. Hodgkin, Wm. Vaughn, W. F. Webster, J. Devereaux, J. Alexander, A. Stevenson and John Miller, eminent Englishmen, who wrote him invitations, etc., during this visit.

(To Nathaniel (?) Coffin.¹)

MARSHFIELD Saturday morn'g [1840?]

Dr Sir

I was called from my office suddenly, yesterday before I had an opportunity of saying one or two things to you.

I hope you are all impressed with the importance of preparing *Resolutions*, for Worcester with care.

It is a crisis; & it calls loud for both decision & prudence. Can you send me a copy of Mr John Van Buren's speech, at F. Hall.

Yrs   D. WEBSTER

———

(From D. Fletcher Webster.)

SALISBURY [Illinois] Mar. 16th, 1840.

My dear Father

* * *² I have made a short trip among the Tuckers—Harrison goes pretty well,—but the ignorant & obstinate Pennsylvanians with whom the Country abounds call the Whigs *Federals* & join Harrison with them; and it is difficult to teach them their error in the latter respect, and impossible to correct their dogheaded prejudices in the other— Still I think he will carry the state.   We have a meeting tonight in Peru & I am to make an address. * * *²

Your affectionate son,

D. F. WEBSTER

———

(To Peter Harvey.)

MAY 24, [1840].

Dr Sir

The salmon arrived safe, & was good, but it did not get here till Saturday, instead of Wednesday or Thursday.   These transport cars cannot be trusted.   If I try again, the box must be put into the passenger train, under the care of somebody, who can b'g it right on.   When salmon gets down to 25 d's, if Mr. Appleton could get me one quite fresh, especially a Merrimac River one, & could sent it with despatch—I shou'd like it—all which you may say to him.

¹ This letter belongs to the Pennsylvania Hist. Soc.
² Minor family matters omitted.

We shall probably pass the Bankrupt Bill thro the Senate—voluntary only—& without including the Banks— Look out for my little speech[1] in the Nat.-Int. of Wednesday.

Yrs. D. WEBSTER

Mrs. Webster sends her love.

────

(To D. Fletcher Webster.)

My Dear Son   WASHINGTON May 31, 1840.

I have recd your letter of the 18th of this month, & also Caroline's, enclosi'g one to her father. I am glad to see that the Whigs are stirring, in your quarter. Your Senators, I believe are confident that the vote of the state will be given to Mr. Van Buren, but Mr. Stuart thinks otherwise. Our intelligence is encouraging, from all quarters, & I have no doubt, or very little, at present, that Genl. Harrison will be elected.

You seem to be hesitating about comi'g East. No doubt, it is a subject demandi'g due considerations. You seem also to think that you prefer Peru to any place East, except N York or Washington. I believe you can get along in N. York, but there is not a very extensive field of local practice, in Washington. It is, however, a good spot for practice in the Supreme Court, & I believe money is occasionally made by attention to claims pend'g before Congress. But for political objects, neither N. Y. or Washington is so good as Boston, or Lowell. In either of these last, you would go immediately into the State Legislature, & have a chance to show yourself. And in either of them, you would by diligence & hard labor get along. Middlesex is not full of talent, & I should esteem Lowell quite a good place, for a promising & resolute young man.

Perhaps you will not find yourself ready or able to make up your mind, definitely, until I see you. Much ought to depend on what you think of the healthfulness of Peru. My property in the west will want attention from somebody, & since Ray's death I have thought of no way but of putt'g it with your management. At any rate, I must see you, in the course of the season, & we must settle upon someth'g. If you could send your family East, at the same or as little expense as you can send

[1] Refers, no doubt, to the speech in the Senate, May 18, 1840, on the proposed amendment to the bill establishing a uniform system of bankruptcy. See Works of Daniel Webster, vol. v, p. 3.

them, & support them, at the North, we will find a corner for them at Marshfield till autumn.   I do not know the arrangement of your courts, & therefore cannot say when you yourself can best leave home.   Many things depend on the result of the ensuing election.   If that should go against us, I should know pretty well what to do myself, & what to recommend you to do. If it should go for us, different questions would come.   I hope you will think of all these things, & write to me often.

Yours affectionately
Danl Webster

Is there any other place in the West, where you think you can do better than in Peru?

(From D. Fletcher Webster.)

My dear Father,   Peru, [Ill.] June 30th, 1840.
     *   *   *   I made a pretty good speech at Rocksport and a very good one, for me, at St. Louis.   *   *   *
     P. S.   What can I say, my dear Father, to your letter of June 13th, in which you speak of the letter recd by Mr. Clay? The applause was given to the *son* not the individual or his speaking— So it was in Missouri; whenever I appeared to speak they cheered your name.   I did my best but it would be too complimentary to say of me
     "Sequiturque patrem non passibus acquis."   it was a "non sequitur" at all.   D. F. W.

(To Mrs. Caroline Webster.)

Wilmington Thursday mor'g Oct. 1, [1840] 8 o'clock.
Dear Caroline
     I arrived here last night, and as I intend leav'g for Baltimore this P. M. shall have no moment but this to write you a line. Mr. Bayard & family recd me with all kindness.   F. is with me, at least as far as W.—   My cold is a good deal better, tho' I feel *sore* from my effort in speaking in N. Y.[1]—   I shall have little to say here today, & as the weather is fine hope I shall not suffer.

Yrs   D. Webster.

I expect to find letters tomorrow mor'g at Washington.

---

[1] Refers probably to the speech in Wall Street, Sept. 28, 1840.   See Works of Daniel Webster, vol. ii, p. 58.

(To Geo. W. Nesmith.[1]*)*

FRANKLIN Oct. 25 [1840] Monday—

My dear Sir.

It is with unfeigned disappointment & grief, that I find myself unable to attend your meeting today. The state of my health absolutely confines me to my room.[2]

I was not only willing, but anxious, to close my efforts in the great contest now going on by an Address to the citizens of my native town & of the towns in its vicinity. But Providence has ordered it otherwise.

I confess, my dear Sir, I feel an interest in the result of the election in New Hampshire, far beyond the importance of her electoral votes. Those votes, indeed, cannot affect the result. The question is already substantially & fully settled. Genl. Harrison will be elected by a majority never witnessed before, in any contested election for the Presidency. I have lately passed through many of the Atlantic States; I have information from other states, as correct, perhaps, as that of any other gentleman.— And my opinion is, that, if New Hampshire chuses to stand out and refuse her vote to Gen. Harrison, among all the old Thirteen States, that accomplished the Revolution, she will find but one state by her side; and that is the state of South Carolina. Some believe that Pennsylvania may be an exception to this remark; I do not think so. But, if it should turn out to be the case, it cannot possibly affect the result. And, then, look to the West, to the majorities in Indiana in Kentucky, & now the overwhelming majority in Ohio. No intelligent and candid man can doubt or deny, that the whole country is going, as by one consent, for Genl. Harrison. It is not, therefore, for the *cause*, but for the *State* itself, that I feel so anxious for the result of the approaching election in New Hampshire. Genl. Harrison, & all his friends, have been treated, in this state, by the Administration Press, and administration orators, with more calumny, slander, & wilful & wicked falsehood, than in any other part of the Country. The whole country sees this,—and cries out, "foul Shame upon such miserable detractors!" But suppose all this should succeed, what would be the consequences? It would only be to place New Hampshire in an attitude of angry, bitter personal

---

[1] Of Salisbury, N. H.

[2] See the letter of Daniel Webster to Mrs. Webster, Oct. 26, 1840, where this is further explained.

opposition to the new President. It would only be, on this account, to expose herself, further, to the disapprobation & reproach of the Country. It was my intention, on this & on other topics to address my fellow citizens today. I had hoped that some of the honest farmers of the vicinity, who have hitherto supported the measures of the Administration, would do me the honor to attend. And, if any such should be present, when this letter shall be read, I pray them to pause, to reflect & to consider; I would ask them, what desirable object, if they could secure Mr Van Buren's reelection, they propose to themselves! But then, that is *impossible.* He cannot be reelected. And, therefore, I would ask them, with still greater fervor & earnestness, what possible advantage they propose to the State by placing it in opposition to the New Administration!

My dear Sir, I am wearied even with the effort of dictating this short letter. My best wishes will be with you; and with those eminent townsmen of yours, who are to address you today. I am distressed in not being able to hear them, and to join them, in as fervent an exhortation to the people who may be assembled, as it might be in my power to make. May Heaven prosper our State; and enable her citizens, one and all, to see their own best interests.

Yours truly
DANIEL WEBSTER

(To Mrs. Caroline Webster.)

CLAREMONT, [N. H.] (8 O'clock.) Oct. 22, '40.
Dear Caroline.

I came here yesterday, in the rain, & found the town overflowing with people. There was a large meeting in the Eve'; but it was in the church. I remain pretty well; quite as much so, as when I left home. This mor'g I go to Hanover by way of Windsor, & to Oxford this Eve'g.[1]

I am now at Mr. Brighams, where I have rec'd the kindest reception; & am off in 5 minutes.

Yrs truly
D. WEBSTER.

---

[1] Webster was making a campaign tour in the interest of Harrison. See his letters to Mrs. Webster, dated Oct. 26, Oct. 27 and Oct. 28, 1840.

(THE NEXT SENATE.[1])

[Dec. 3. 1840.]

We have seen in several of the Papers calculations of the strength of the respective parties, in the next Senate. None of these agree exactly with our own estimate. To us it appears likely that parties will stand, in that body after the third of March thus:

Whigs		*Tories*	
Maine	1	Maine	1
Mass.	2	N. Hamp.	2
R. I.	2	N. Y.	1
Vermont.	2	Pennsylvania.	2
Con't	2	Georgia	1
N. York.	1	Alabama	2
N. Jersey	2	Louisiana	1
Delaware	2	Arkansas	2
Maryland·	2	Missouri	2
Virginia.	2	Illinois	2
N. Carolina	2	South Carolina	1
Georgia	1	Ohio	2
Louisiana..	1	Mississippi.	1
Mississippi.	1	Tennessee	1
Tennessee.	1		—
Kentucky	2		21
Indiana	2		
Michigan..	2		
South Carolina	1		
	—		
	31		

thus giv'g a majority of 10—to the Whigs.

We believe the Legislature of Tennessee does not assemble till Decr. of next year; so that after the 3rd of March—next, one seat of that State may be vacant, till the ensu'g Session of the Legislature.

Mr. Williams of Maine, Mr. Wright of New York, Messrs. Buchanan & Sturgeon of Penna; Mr Lumpkin of Georgia, Mr. Mouton of Louisiana, Mr. Walker of Mississippi, Mr. Allen &

---

[1] This paper, in Webster's own hand, was not dated, but from internal evidence is doubtless as given.   See Niles' Register, vol. lix, p. 217.

Mr. Tappan of Ohio[1] &, very possibly, two members from Illinois, will be Tory Senators sitt'g for Whig States. And it is possible, indeed that the two Alabama Gentlemen may be in the same predicament. How they will deport themselves, under these circumstances, remain. They are, we believe all of them, great sticklers for the right of instruction. To some of them, we doubt not, the benefit of inclination will be communicated, in full measure.

We think of no Whig Senator who will be found opposed in sentiment, to the State he represents, unless perhaps Mr. Preston[2] may come within this predicament. How this may be, we shall see, when we know how S. Carolina disposed of her electoral vote, the day before yesterday. Her other Senator, Mr. Calhoun, has been at great pains, at divers times, to "define his position." On this occasion, we take it for granted, he will assist the State to define hers ———— as to his own position, the worthy Gentleman may give himself no further trouble. That needs no definition by him, now. His own acts, & events, have defined it quite clearly. Noth'g can be said of it, but that it is absolutely ludicrous. We should think it probable a general smile would pervade the Senate & the galleries, when he shall walk in, to take his seat. Never was there an instance, in which political crookedness met with a more sudden & awful retribution.

(To Theophilus Parsons.[2])

WASHINGTON Jan. 28. 1841.

My Dear Sir

There can be no objection to any temperate, tho' firm, expression of opinion, by our Legislature, on this Boundary question.[3] Yet, it behooves us to consider what the present state of the subject is.

By the treaty of Ghent, it was admitted & acknowledged, that the question of the N. E. Boundary, was a question, on which

---

[1] Reuel Williams, Silas Wright, James Buchanan, Daniel Sturgeon, Wilson Lumpkins, Alex. Mouton, Robt. J. Walker, William Allen, Benjamin Tappan, Wm. C. Preston.

[2] A Boston member of the Massachusetts House of Representatives. Webster had been asked (Dec. 1, 1840) to become Secretary of State under Harrison.

[3] Such a resolve was approved by the Governor, March 13, 1841. See Massachusetts Acts and Resolves, 1839-42, p. 420.

the two Governments might not agree; & it was stipulated, in the treaty, that in that event, the question should be made matter of arbitration, by a friendly Power.— an arbitration was had— the arbitration decided—but his decision satisfied neither party, & both rejected it.   The parties, then, as it seemed, were referred back to the stipulation in the treaty, & were to try another arbitration.   A negotiation, preparatory to such other arbitration, is now in progress between the two Governments, but has not, as yet, terminated in a Convention.   This is the actual state of thi'gs.

It might have been better to have avoided the necessity of this second arbitration, & to have proposed a line by compromise. In my opinion, that might well have been thought of.   But no such attempt was made, on either side.   The negotiation for explanation, arbitration, &c must go on, unless something shall occur to break it off till a convention is concluded.

The real ground of complaint is the dilatoriness of the proceedings, & the consequent postponement of the final adjustment. On this point, a Resolution, in proper terms, but with a firm tone, might be useful, & certainly would be proper.

I do not see, therefore, on the whole, that the proposed Resolutions can do more, than,

1st. To express a strong sense of the right of our side of the case; & 2d

2. To complain of delay, & urge the high importance of hasten'g the negotiation to its close.

I have not yet seen the Governor's message, but you will perceive, by what I have written, that I concur in the views which you express.   We must avoid alarm'g the country with the fear of rupture, at the same time that we assert our rights finally, express proper confidence in our own Govt.—& urge the importance of an early settlement of the dispute—

Yrs with great regard,

[D. Webster]¹

'(From Chas. Francis Adams.)

Boston, January 26, 1841

Dear Sir:

A few days since Governor Davis when transmitting to the

---

¹ This copy is taken from the original draft of the letter.

Legislature the resolutions of the States of Maine and Indiana upon the question of the boundary, took occasion to comment upon that subject in such a manner as to lead many members to suppose that some very formal reply was proper and ought to be made.

The Message was in the first instance referred to the Joint Standing Committee on the public lands of which Mr. Kinsman and I are members, but yesterday it was taken from them on the ground that a larger and a special Committee was more suitable to the importance of the case, upon which Mr. Parsons and three others in the Senate with myself and a proportionate number of the House are placed. And Mr. Parsons insists upon making me responsible for a report.

Perhaps it is as well to say that in the whole business my name has appeared without the slightest agency direct or indirect of my own. But if it should so happen that I must be responsible for the action proposed to the Legislature, it is very desirable to me that I should be informed of the opinions of those who have heretofore guided the policy of the State and who are for the future to guide that of the Nation. It is generally understood that the foreign affairs are to be in your hands under the next Administration. Now it is not my wish to do any act which should have the slightest effect to embarrass you in your future management of the Negotiation. Neither is it my desire to assume on the part of the State any extreme position beyond what may be contained in stating the general principle involved. In such cases, I am well aware of the importance of proceeding with caution and deliberation. And it is for this reason alone that I have ventured to intrude upon your attention.

Should you have any suggestions to make either as to the nature and extent of the report itself or as to the character of the resolutions to be proposed, it would give me pleasure to receive them—and even if I should not be charged with the duty, which is not yet certain although probable, (the Committee not having been assembled as yet) I will take care that the person who does it shall have the benefit of them without loss of time.

I will only add, that I have also written to my father on this subject,

      I am Sir, With respect, Yours, etc, etc,

                (CHARLES F. ADAMS)

(To C. F. Adams.)

WASHINGTON, Jan. 30, 1841

My dear Sir:

I have rec'd your letter of the 26th, & am happy to find that the important & delicate business of the Boundary falls into the hands of an able & discreet Committee. In answer to a letter from Mr. Parsons, I wrote him yesterday, stating my general views on the subject, & as he is with you on the Committee he will doubtless communicate the letter to you.

I cannot say that I think the business is in a very promising train. The two Governments have agreed to enter into a negotiation, as you know, for a joint Commission, but this negotiation, so far as I can learn, makes very slow progress. It must, nevertheless, go on, as a manner of settlement already agreed to, & all due pains should be taken to hasten it.

As suggested in my letter to Mr. Parsons, I see little more to be done by the Legislature at present, than to make a firm & temperate expression of its settled opinion in favor of the right of our side, & rather a warm & urgent remonstrance against all unnecessary delay in bringing this dispute to a close.

I do not look for any further communication on the subject from the President at this session.

When I wrote to Mr. Parsons, I had not seen Gov. Davis's message. I now find, that he has referred to the report of the British Commissioners, a paper, very bad in its spirit, & shallow & miserable in its reasoning. There can be no harm, probably, in your giving that, in a report, such a Review as it deserves; but I recommend that the direct proceedings of the Legislature, by way of Resolution, be confined to the two points above mentioned.

I am, Dear Sir,[1] With much true regard, Yours

DAN'L WEBSTER

(To John Davis.)

WASHINGTON, Feb 10. 1841

Sir:

Events being likely to take place, which will necessarily cause my retirement from the Senate, I have thought it proper that I

---

[1] This letter is owned by Charles Francis Adams.

should anticipate their actual occurrence, for the purpose of enabling the Legislature to fill the place, should such be its pleasure, during its present session.[1]   *   *   *

(From John Tyler.)

TUESDAY. [1841]

Dear Sir—

     *   *   *   I can no longer tolerate the Intelligencer as the official paper.   Besides assaulting me perpetually, directly and indirectly, it refuses all defensive articles, as appears by the Madisonian of Saturday.   There is a point beyond which one's patience cannot endure.[2]   Most truly yours,

J. TYLER.

(To Wm. H. Seward.)

Private.

DEPARTMENT OF STATE, WASHINGTON, March 17th 1841.
My dear Sir:

     The President has learned, not directly, but by means of a letter from a friend, that you had expressed a disposition to direct a *nolle prosequi* in the case of the Indictment against McLeod,[3] on being informed, by this Government, that the British Government had officially avowed the attack on the Caroline as an act done by its own authority.

     The President directs me to express his thanks for the promptitude with which you appear disposed to perform an act, which he supposes proper for the occasion, and which is calculated to relieve this Government from embarrassments and the Country from some dangers of collision with a foreign power.

---

     [1] The remainder of this merely formal letter to John Davis, the Governor of Massachusetts, may be found in the Washington newspaper. the Madisonian, vol. iv, No. 63, Feb. 23, 1841.   Webster entered on his duties as Secretary of State March 4, 1841.
     [2] This letter was taken from a newspaper clipping in the possession of C. E. Bliss, of Bangor, Me.   The editor has, however, seen the original in the colleclection of C. P. Greenough.   Webster was then Secretary of State.
     [3] See Schouler's History of the United States, vol. iv, p. 397.   In a letter of Seward's to Webster, dated March 22, 1841, Seward positively denied the least intention to enter a *nolle prosequi* in the McLeod case.

You will have seen Mr. Crittenden, whom I take this occasion to commend to your kindest regard.

I have the honor to be, Very truly, Yours

DANL WEBSTER[1]

(From Washington Irving.)

TARRYTOWN, April 2d, 1841.

My dear Sir,

I trust you will excuse the liberty I take in speaking a word in favor of a gentleman at present employed in your department. Mr. George Washington Montgomery. His father was once American consul at Barcelona and he himself passed much of his youth in Spain. I became acquainted with him in Madrid when he rendered me essential services when I was preparing the life of Columbus. I found him a fellow of most upright, honorable and reliable character; a good scholar, and well acquainted with the modern languages. He writes Spanish correctly and elegantly and has published works in that language which have gained him a reputation in Spain. Mr. Forsyth who knew his merits and was acquainted with his family, gave him various employ; and at one time sent him on a confidential mission to Guatemala; of which expedition, on his return he published a very interesting account. * * *

Ever my dear Sir Very respectfully & faithfully yours

WASHINGTON IRVING

(To John Tyler.)

Private.

[ABOUT JULY 1841].

To the President.

My Dear Sir

I think I have learned, pretty fully, the real object & plan of open action, of these "Hunter's Lodges," "Patriotic Societies," &c which are in existence all along the Northern frontier, from Maine to Wisconsin.

1. They are in constant correspondence with the disaffected in Canada; & these disaffected persons come over the line, & harrangue them, in their secret meetings.

---

[1] This letter has been printed. See Daniel Webster's Works, vol. v, p. 134; also Daniel Webster's Diplomatic and Official Papers, p. 285.

2. They do not expect to be able to invade Canada, with any hope of success, unless War breaks out *between Canada & the United States; but they desire that event, above all things,* & to br'g it about will naturally join in any violence, or outbreak, if they think they can do so, with impunity. They may even attempt violence upon McLeod, should he be discharged by the Courts, or on his way from the Prison to the place where the Court shall be sitt'g.

The aggregate of the members of all these clubs is probably not less than ten thousand. Cleveland is rather their Headquarters.

3. If war breaks out, these persons do not propose to join the forces of the United States, but to unite themselves to the disaffected in Canada, declare the Provinces free, & set up another Government.

I am told that Regimental officers are already designated, for the command of these volunteers.

That such as above described is the real state of thi'gs, there can be no doubt.

It is evidently full of danger, & I am quite surprised at the apparent ignorance, or supineness of the Govt. of N. Y., who represent, evidently, that there is no danger of any violence—

Our duty, is, I think, in the first place, to have officers all along the frontier, in whom we have confidence, & to let them understand that there is danger.

In the next place, it becomes us to take all possible care that no personal violence be used on McLeod. If a mob should kill him, war w'd be inevitable, in ten days. Of this there is no doubt.—

I regret that the Atty Genl. did not go on, & confer with McLeod's counsel, notwithstand'g the postponement of the trial. They appear to me to be men of no great force, & who place their main reliance on b'g able to prove an *alibi* for their clients. But such a defence does not meet the exigency of the case, nor fulfil the duty of this Govt.

I must pray your early consideration of this subject, & shall be glad of an opportunity for consideration, & for tak'g your direction—

[D. WEBSTER's][1]

---

[1] This is taken from the original draft of the letter in Daniel Webster's hand.

(To Joshua A. Spencer.)

Private.

WASHINGTON, July 15, 1841.

My Dear Sir:

I have to acknowledge the receipt of your letter of the 12th instant.

Officially, I have of course no advice to give, on the subject of further proceedings in McLeod's case.   But my private opinion is clear, that the true course is to go to trial, the earliest possible opportunity.

Yours with regard,

DANL WEBSTER.

(From John Tyler.)

[JULY 20, 1841?]

Private files.

I send you my Dear Sir, a draft of such a message as I am in-clined to send to the Senate—

Read it—weigh it—and tell me your views concerning it freely fully and candidly—

The cabinet without reference to the Envoy, think it a capital move, and for myself my highest aspiration is to be the maker, under Providence, of a lasting, & permanent peace—who can do this great work but yourself—

Most truly Yrs

J. TYLER

(To Mrs. Caroline Webster.)

WEDNESDAY EVE' Aug. 4. [1841] 8 O.clock P. M.

Dear Caroline

I was not well when I left you, this mor'g, & had a hot time up. But after I arrived, & got cool, & dressed, I felt better, & am now pretty well.   On my arrival, I went immediately to the President's, & staid till 3 o clock—

It looks lovely enough, here.   We are having a fine shower, & nobody in the House but Fletcher & myself.   I learned no news this mor'g—not a word said about the Bank.—   The H. of R. is still in session, debatg that subject.   In the Senate, nothg done but to consider the Fortification Bill.   The late sitting of the House intimates a disposition to press the Bank subject through, this week.— nothg is yet heard of the Delaware—

I have met with Dr. Lindsley. He says the City is very healthy; that Capitol Hill is a healthy place, for this season; but that if I cou'd go into the Country, three or four miles, so as to come in & go out eve'y day, it would be better. If I feel unwell, I shall follow his advice.

I pray you to see Mr. & Mrs Bates, & to give them my kindest regards. I have sent Despatches to Mr. Stevenson to go by Mr. Bates.—

We miss you very much—& miss Grace also, who I hope is a good girl—& we send her six kisses—not to say that we miss Ann— George is trying to find out about my things—& to be familiar with the bureau—

Nobody has come in this Eve'—as it rains hard; and as the House is still sitt'g. I have been look'g over the English papers, recd today—& Fletcher is engaged with his French— If this reaches you before Miss Seaton leaves you, pray give her my remembrance & regards— If it ceases to rain, F. will go up to see her mother—

Yrs affectionately always

D. WEBSTER—

I have no private letters of any consequence from England—

(To Mrs. Caroline Webster.)

MONDAY MOR'G Aug. 16. 1841.

Dear Caroline

A week has run away, without my writ'g to you. It has been an anxious week, on acct. of the Bank Bill; but the question is settled, & a Veto will be sent in today. I hardly know what may the consequences, but the general feeli'g is not so much irritated as it was a week ago. They may perhaps try another Bill, with modifications. Some of Mr. Clay's friends are particularly angry, & this makes it doubtful whether any thing will be done. It is feared, also, that the fate of this measure may have a bad influence on the fortunes of the Bankrupt Bill, & other measures. On the whole, we have an anxious & unhappy time, & I am sometimes heart sick. I hope Congress will get away in a fortnight.

I send you the Intelligencer of this mor'g, that you may read the account of our trip to Annapolis. The President did not go, as the Senate did not adjourn over, & he was much engaged. There were very few ladies—Mrs. Crittenden, Mrs. Clark, Miss White, Miss Yeatman, &c

Yesterday mor'g I rode out to Mrs. Aggs, as the day was cool and agreeable. I generally ride to the office, in the mor'g & sometimes walk home when it is not too hot. My health is good, except that my rheumatic shoulder troubles me a good deal.

I have thought it best to invite the Whig members to a *man* party, tomorrow, in order to keep them in good temper. Charles is to buy some hams, & bread, &—no ices, & no fruits, & set them on the table down stairs—where people may help themselves.

The House gets along, pretty well. Of course the painting inside is not yet finished, as it takes time for the paint to dry.

I notice what you say about papering the rooms— You may have it arranged as you please. I will write tomorrow, say'g what day Mr. Stubbs will be in N. Y. about the carpets. He has been sick & is now out again.

Fletcher may find it necessary to go to N. Y. on account of Mr. White's death—but he has not yet made up his mind, not having heard from Mr. Paige.

It is likely that Capt. Clements will break up here, the first of next month. When I shall go, if I cannot go North by that time, I know not. If Mr. Whitewell takes the house, as is expected, I presume your thi'gs can all remain where they are.

I will try to write you again tomorrow.

Yrs ever

D. WEBSTER.

(To `Mrs. Caroline Webster.)

THURSDAY 3½ o'clock [Aug. 19 1841]

Dr Wife

Fletcher has written you a word, to say that Mr. Stubbs would be at Astor House, next Wednesday morn'g. I am well but most dreadfully hard worked. The Bankrupt Bill is signed—another attempt will probaby be made for a Bank. The Whigs appear to be in great spirits.

My party went off well—almost all were there.

Yrs   D. W.

(To John Tyler.¹)

11 o'CLOCK, August 20th, [1841]

My Dear Sir:
I am promised a copy of the paper (the bill) by twelve o'clock, or a few minutes after, and have left a messenger to bring it immediately to me.   It is uncertain whether anything will be done to-day, but I understand there is a strong desire for immediate action.   The alterations which I suggested were assented to at once, so far as the gentleman himself was concerned to whom the suggestions were made.   *I have done or said nothing as from you by your authority, or implicating you in the slightest degree. If any measure pass, you will be perfectly free to exercise your constitutional power wholly uncommitted, except so far as may be gathered from your public and official acts.*
I am, most truly and faithfully, yours,

DANIEL WEBSTER.

——

(To Peter Harvey.)

3 o'CLOCK
Sept 10. [1841]

Do the Whigs of Mass think I ought to quit—or ought to stay? ²

Yrs   D. W.

——

(Editorial on writing letters to the president.³)

SEPT. 25. 1841

It is plain enough that the ex-Secretaries⁴ take the President at great disadvantage.
They write him letters which they know he cannot answer, because the President of the U. S. cannot enter into such a correspondence.

---

¹ Copied from the printed letter in " Letters and Times of the Tylers," vol. ii, p. 85.
² In Tyler's cabinet.
³ This editorial appeared in the administration paper, the *Madisonian*, No. 471, Sept. 25, 1841, and the original, in Webster's handwriting, is among Webster's papers.   The inference naturally is that he wrote it.   In other cases he speaks in his letters of having written editorials.
⁴ In the original this is " retiring Members."

They use weapons, therefore, which they know *he* cannot use.

In the next place they undertake to state Cabinet conversations, which *he* regards as confidential, and to which *he* cannot refer, without violating his own sense of propriety and dignity.

Having thus placed the President in a position in which he cannot defend himself, they make war upon him; and this, we suppose, will be called high-mindedness and "chivalry!"

(The ex-members' publications abbreviated.[1])

SEPT. 25 1841

We should more readily incline to suppose there might be some reason for the retirement of the four members of the late Cabinet, if they could agree on such reason among themselves. But, unhappily, they entirely differ, each has a ground of his own, & no sooner does one come forth to show his cause than another follows with a different showing.

Mr. Ewing, who leads off, rejects the Veto, as ground of resignation, & goes out on "personal indignity."—

Mr. Crittenden follows, & having no complaint to make of personal indignity, he goes out on the Veto—

Then comes Mr. Badger, who does not go out, on the Bank question, but because the case is one of "a measure, embraced, & then repudiated—efforts promoted, & then disowned—service rendered, and then treated with scorn and neglect"—

That is to say, Mr. Badger resigned because the President trifled with his Cabinet.

But now hear Mr. Bell—

"Nor was it because the President thought proper to trifle with or mislead his Cabinet, as there is but too much reason to believe he intended to do, in the affair of the late Fiscal Bank that I resigned my place.—

There were other & pre-existing causes, for such a course, &c."

What these "other & pre-existing causes" are, or were, Mr. Bell does not inform us. In regard to these, the world is yet to be enlightened.

Placed in the shortest form each Gentleman, with his cause of resignation, stands thus—

---

[1] In the *Madisonian*, No. 471, Sept. 25, 1841, appeared this editorial, entitled "The Ex-Members' Publications Abbreviated." Among Webster's private papers the original manuscript, in Webster's hand, was found.

Mr. Ewing................personal indignity
Mr. Crittenden.............Veto
Mr. Badger................trifling with the Cabinet.
Mr. —————— ....other & preexisting causes.

Or the matter may be fairly represented, by stating each one of the several alledged causes, & seeing who concurred in it—
In that view, the case thus—
"Personal Indignity"—
Assigned by Mr. Ewing; not alledged by any body else.
"Veto"—assigned by Mr. Crittenden, expressly renounced by the rest
"Trifling with the Cabinet"—the substance of Mr. Badger's ground; expressly repudiated by Mr. Bell, & alledged by nobody else—
"Other & pre existing causes"; alledged by Mr. Bell, alluded to by nobody else, & of which the world is yet in utter ignorance.
We cannot suppose that these Gentlemen could have a weak affectation, each to give a separate reason for himself; and since they so entirely differ among themselves, we think the inference fair, that there was *no* plain, substantial cause, for breaking up the Cabinet, such as the public mind can readily understand & justify— Time will show what opinion the Country may come to; but of one thing we feel entirely confident, & that is, that when the passions of the moment shall have passed away, the revealing of Cabinet secrets for the purpose of attacking the President, is a proceeding which will meet with general condemnation.

(From John Tyler.)

WASHINGTON Oct. 11. 1841

My Dear Sir;
I have pleasure in saying that the Cabinet is now full. Mʳ Spencer Mʳ Wickliffe and Judge Upshur will be here early this week— Each man will go steadily to work for the country— and *its interests* will alone be looked to— I congratulate you in an especial manner upon having such co-workers. I would have each member to look upon every other, in the light of a friend and brother— By encouraging such a spirit I shall best consult my own fame, and advance the public good— My information from all parts of the country is encouraging, and altho' we are to have a furious fire during the coming winter, yet we shall

I doubt not, speedily recover from its effects— Our cause is too plainly before us to be mistaken— We must look to the whole country and to the whole people—

The letters from Stevenson and Hughes are full of interest— The swearing in the M^c. Leod case is hard against him—but Mr Spencer's opening speech inspires me with confidence— That gotten over and you will have the honour of a final adjustment of all other difficulties— I shall truly rejoice in all that shall advance your fame— I gave you a hint as to the possibility of acquiring Texas by treaty— I verily believe it could be done— Could the North be reconciled to it would any thing throw so bright a lustre around us? It seems to me that the great interests of the north would be incalculably advanc'd by such an acquisition— How deeply interested is the shiping interest? *Slavery*—I know that is the objection—and it would be well founded if it did not already exist—among us—but my belief is that a rigid enforcement of the laws against the slave trade, would make in time as many free States, south, as the acquisition of Texas would add of slave states,—and then *the future,* (distant it might be), would present wonderful results.

I shall leave here in as few days as I can for my quiet home, to meditate in peace over a scheme of finance— In whatsoever you do upon that subject, remember always my difficulty which, Ewing Bell & Co. to the contrary, have given me from the first more pain than either of them can have felt— The day for attempt at compromise has pass'd however, and we must take good care to trim well our sails for the voyage which lies before us— The more simple the agency to be employd the better— We have no surplus nor are we likely to have for some years— and may be regarded as living "from hand to mouth"

I pray you to accept the sincere assurance of my confidence and warm regard

JOHN TYLER

P. S. Since writing the above the proceedings at the Syracuse convention have reached me— What a low and contemptible farce— You were right to remain in the Cabinet, *quoth Filmore & Co*—and yet these very men united in forcing Granger to retire.

I learn by a private letter that in secret session M^r. Clay was proposed for the succession and supported by Filmore[1]—

---

[1] This letter is owned by Mr. C. P. Greenough.

(To D. Fletcher Webster.)

Private.

MARSHFIELD, Octr. 25, 1841.

My Dear Son

I have reason to think that some very meddlesome people, in Portsmouth, N. Hamp. are interferi'g with the Navy Agent, at that place in regard to his selection of a Bank, for the deposit of the public funds, entrusted to him.

I will be obliged to you to say to the Secretary of the Navy that Genl. Upham, the Navy Agent, is entirely trust-worthy, & discreet; & that I should regret that any change, in the arrangements made by him, should be thought advisable, at least, before I shall have an opportunity of seei'g the Secretary.

Yrs.

DAN'L WEBSTER

(To D. Fletcher Webster.)

PHILADELPHIA Saturday, [Nov. 13, 1841].

My Dear Son,

I arrived in this City yesterday P. M. & was obliged to stay over today,—I now fear I am in unexpected difficulty, as I cannot learn of any train of cars, or boat, likely to leave tomorrow, till midnight. I do not feel well enough to make a night passage; so that it is uncertain whether I can reach Washington earlier than Monday night—if possible, I should prefer goi'g directly to our own house— Let Charles meet me, at the cars—

Yrs D. W.

(To John Tyler.)

Nov. 25, 1841.

My dear Sir,

I rec'd your note last evening by Mr. Blackford.[1] Mr. Semple[2] has signified his wish to return to the U. States. Mr. Blackford, therefore, can be nominated to fill his place, if you so incline.

You think I propose "hard conditions" as connected with this appointment. Of course, my dear Sir, I only intended to call your attention to the true state of the case.

---

[1] William M. Blackford, of Virginia. He was appointed.
[2] James Semple, Chargé d'Affaires to the Republic of Colombia.

In addition to the five Charges, already appointed from the South, Mr. Hilliard[1] expects to go to Brussells making six & Mr. Blackford's appointment will make seven.

You know that these appointments are eagerly sought & that there are pressing Candidates from many states, especially the two good states of Vermont & Connecticut for neither of which have we done anything.

I suppose Mr. Blackford must be provided for, but if so, other offices I think, should be distributed in other places. As to Consuls we must remember that out of the three most desirable consulships a citizen of Georgia holds one—(Havannah) a citizen of Virginia another (Hanse): & I do think it w'd give dissatisfaction to appoint Mr. Haggerty to the third. It would give offense to many who did what he did not—give time, pains & trouble to effect the Revolution of 1840. I really think it much better for the administration to have Mr. Schuyler where he is than to recall him & appoint Mr. Haggerty in his place. These things are stated for your reflection; &, as you say "we can talk about them" hereafter

Yrs faithfully

DAN'L WEBSTER

(The Message.[2])

[Dec. 1841]

Should a *quorum* be found in attendance in both Houses of Congress on Monday, the Message, according to usage will be transmitted on Tuesday.

Of course we know nothing of what the Message will contain; but we know that the Chief Magistrate is actuated by a sincere desire to do his duty, & that it must therefore be his desire, & his object, to recommend such measures to Congress, as the good of the Country requires. That the message, whatever it may be, will be fiercely & coarsely attacked, there is no doubt. So reckless has a portion of the Press become, that nothing else can be expected. Indeed the more merit the Message may have, the more sure it will be to meet assault and condemnation, in certain quarters. In proportion as it is likely to be acceptable to the

---

[1] H. W. Hilliard, of Alabama.
[2] An editorial evidently written by Webster for the administration organ. The manuscript is in Webster's hand.

Country, in that same proportion will *party* dog it, from the Metropolis to every point on the frontier. All this we are prepared to see. But it is our purpose, in this article to address ourselves to that portion of the Public Press, which is really free & independent; and God be thanked that there is such a portion of the Public Press, & that it is increasing, every day.

We appeal to this part of the Press to give the message a full insertion, a candid reading, & fair commentaries. But above all, that they publish it, that they circulate it, & that the People may have an opportunity to read & judge of it, unprejudiced and unprepossessed by condemnation of it, in advance.

But it is our higher purpose, on this occasion, to appeal to the People themselves, to the great community of American Freemen, to judge the conduct of the Government, established by themselves, with fairness & candor. It is *their* interests which are at stake; it is *their* country, which is to be benefitted by a good, or injured by a bad administration of public affairs. They are competent to judge, & to form just opinions. We intreat them to judge for themselves. It is often said, that the Present Chief Magistrate is a President without a party. If this be so, it would seem more reasonable that all should judge of his acts, free from the malign influences of party spirit. Let him be judged by his conduct.

It is usual that reports from the Departments having the principal expenditure of the public money, that is to say, the Departments of War, the Navy, & the Post Office, accompany the President's Annual Message. These reports give an account of the administration of the respective Departments, for the past year. We invite the attention of the People to these reports. Let not their length, if they should be long, deter any one from going through them, who wishes to be truly informed of the progress & present state of public affairs. They may not be so vivacious & racy, as speeches in Congress, or the commentaries of the Press. But being founded on facts, & official documents, they may be quite as useful in enabling the people to form a just opinion of the administration of the Govt. It sometimes happens, that the commentary is read, without a previous perusal of the texts; & there are but too many Newspaper Editors, who are disingenuous enough to write & publish harsh & violent denunciations of public papers, without publishing the papers themselves;—a degradation, we believe, to which party has not fallen, in any quarter of the civilized world, except in the United States. Here again we appeal to the *Independent Press;* the Daily Press, the Penny Press, the Magazines, to every Editor conducting any journal which professes to treat of public affairs, that they give the Country, *the People* a fair (chance).

We would fain address a similar request to those members of Congress, who feel duty to the Country to be a higher obligation than attachment to Party. We know there are many such, and the hour is come, as we think, for reflection & sober thought, with them all. Recent occurrences must have convinced every thinking man, that the public mind is not in a temper to second mere heated party efforts. There is a vast number of the People, of all parties, who doubt, whether party success, to which ever party it should fall, would afford assurance of relief to the suffering interests of society. They think that mere party power, exerted angrily on one side, & opposed angrily on the other, can never achieve that relief. They think, that the business of the Country, the industry of the Country, the currency of the Country, & the public faith & general honor & reputation of the Country, can never be restored, but by the common efforts & cooperation of sober & patriotic men of all parties.

Every man must see, in the circle around him, that this is a growing sentiment, among those, who have no interest, separate from the general interest of the Community.—

The administration can have no object but to advance this general interest. It desires & seeks to advance it. Without too much retrospect on the past, or anticipation of the future, it proposes to consider things as they are, & apply the best practicable remedy. Let its recommendations be considered fairly & candidly. If found erroneous, let superior wisdom correct them; but let neither the personal objects of individuals, the selfishness & recklessness of party, or the fierceness of animosities arising from the past, deprive the People of the benefits of good Government & useful administration.—

If this great Country, so rich in resources, so young & vigorous, so full of all the means of prosperity & happiness, be suffered to continue in its present depressed & ruinous condition, for want of wise & provident legislation, a heavy responsibility must rest some where. The President, we doubt not, is resolved, that this responsibility shall not fall on him. At the head of a Republican Administration, seeking to conduct the Government on the true principles of Liberty, justice, prudence & Frugality, & anxious to do everything in his power to remove the causes which, at the present moment, operate so injuriously upon all the great interests of the Country, he will not have it to be said that he has shrunk from any thing, which the crisis demands.

(A message prepared for President Tyler on the Tariff.[1])

[Dec. 1841?]

The reductions of the duties on imports, provided for by the act of Mar. 2, 1833, will all have taken place after the 30th day of June next. From that day, no duty will exist on any imported article exceeding 20 per centum, ad valorem, and the act declares that all such duties shall thereafterwards be paid in ready money, and shall be assessed upon the value thereof at the port where the same shall be entered, under such regulations as may be prescribed by law. The laws at present in force, laying ad valorem duties, make the cost in the foreign market the basis, on which such duties are to be calculated, making certain additions, however, to the amount of that cost. The legal effect of the Act of Mar. 2, 1833, is to repeal all these laws; so that unless Congress [shall] at its present session shall prescribe regulations for assessing the duties upon a valuation at the port of entry, or pass some law modifying the last mentioned act, no ad valorem duties can be further collected.

It is obvious, also, that the act of Mar. 1833 contemplates no other than ad valorem duties, in any case, whatever; because whether a specific duty, that is to say, a duty of so much per ton, or per cent, or per yard in which the amount could not always be known; since it would depend on the cost of the article, whether a specific duty exceeded the rate of 20 per cent ad valorem, & the fluctuations of price might carry a specific duty beyond the limit of 20 per cent tomorrow, although the same duty was within the limit today.

The act is peremptory, in two entire provisions; 1st, that after June 30th all ad valorem duties shall be reduced to 20 per cent; and, second, that the duties shall be assessed on a home valuation, & it is not to be disguised that these two provisions bear to each other the nature of equivalents, or mutual considerations.

It would not be contended, as the under-signed supposes, that

---

[1] This paper is in Webster's handwriting, and is indorsed in the words of the heading and dated 1842. The date, however, is probably wrong. Tyler treated this subject in his message December 7, 1841.

the Act of 1833 stands more free from the legal effect & operation of subsequent acts of Congress than any other law; yet that there are very grave reasons, doubtless, why any modification of it which is esteemed necessary, should take place by general consent. It was proper at a time of considerable agitation, & conflict of opinion, & was the result of a spirit of conciliation & compromise. If experience, or a change of circumstances, shew the necessity of modifications, those modifications should be attempted in the full exercise of the same spirit. The maintenance of harmony & good will, & the general acquiescence & satisfaction of the people ought to be regarded as objects of great importance, in the imposition of all taxes. The undersigned feels himself bound frankly to declare his opinion to Congress, that sooner or later, the interests of all parts of the Country will be found to require some modifications of the act of 1833.

In support of this opinion, the undersigned suggests, in the first place the great, if not the insurmountable difficulties of establishing a home valuation at any port, without running the risk of producing such diversity, in the estimates of value, as shall not only lead to great practical inconvenience, but interfere, also, in effect, with the constitutional provisions, that duties & imposts shall be equal in all the States.

In the second place, the undersigned cannot think it will ever be regarded as a wise policy, by any part of the Country, to augment the amount of revenue, if public exigencies should require such augmentation, by raising duties on all articles, including those of absolute necessity, to the full extent of twenty per cent, pressing that limit, at the same time, as an absolute barrier against higher duties on all articles, even those of the merest luxury.

In the third place, the undersigned feels the strongest conviction, that looking to the security of the revenues, & the prevention of frauds, & especially on the supposition, which he believes to be well founded, of the impracticability of a home valuation, every reason of propriety and prudence requires that duties should be made specific, wherever from the nature of the subject they can be so framed. If in political economy, any thing is to be regarded as settled, either by the judgment of the best writers, of the practice of enlightened commercial nations, it is the usefulness & importance of specification, & discrimination, in the imposition of duties of customs.

Finally, the undersigned will not conceal his opinion of the probable effect of the future operation of the act of 1833 upon the manufactures & general industry of the Country, particularly if no home valuation be established, & no equivalent found for the benefits intended by that provision.

The undersigned fully acknowledges that all duties & taxes are to be laid with primary reference to revenue, & the wants of the Government; he fully admits, too, that no more revenue should ever be raised than such as is necessary for the economical administration of the Govt; but within those limits, and as incidental to the raising of such revenue as is absolutely necessary, the undersigned entertains the fullest conviction, that such discrimination may be made, & specific duties imposed in such manner, as that while no parties of the country will suffer loss or inconvenience, a most beneficial degree of protection may be extended to the labor & industry of the Country.   To produce this result, the undersigned thinks it only necessary to lay & collect duties in the usual & approved mode; to specify, where specification is practicable; to discriminate, where discrimination may be useful, & to reject arbitrary limits, & the idea of a forced & unnatural uniformity—

In expressing the opinions which the undersigned has thus the honor of submitting to Congress, in his first official communication to the two Houses, he has proceeded under the influence of the fuller conviction & feeling that the whole Country, is one Country; that the interests of its several parts, are not essentially adverse,—a truth, most triumphantly established, by the fact of the unparalleled growth & prosperity of all these parts, under the care & protection of one Government; that of all nations upon earth, the United States are, in their variety of soil, climate, production & polity, most suited to benefit one another, not only by free internal intercourse between each part, but also by the establishment of uniform external relations; & that therefore a policy which shall embrace the interests of all parts is the only true policy for the Government.

Slight local inconveniences may here & there be felt, under any system; but, in general, a comprehensive & well adapted policy will not fail to promote the interests of all.   It is true, that such is the extent of our territory, & such the variety in our products, natural & manufactured that what would be wide-spread foreign commerce, on the Continent of Europe, becomes domestic with us, all carried on, under one general system, which gives, at the same time, uniformity to internal & external intercourse.   And the

fortunate & happy experience of half a century teaches us, that
this system is practicable, notwithstanding its extent, & that there
is no serious opposition between the interests of the various portions of the Country.

The opinions which the undersigned has expressed, relative to
the operation of the law of Mar. 1833 & to what is required for
the protection of the industry of the country are his own opinions.
He has felt it his duty to lay them before Congress, frankly,
under the responsibility of his official station, & the duty expressly
enjoined upon him by law; & he cheerfully submits them to its
consideration, since to Congress belongs the power of making
such new laws, or so modifying those which may exist, as the
public good shall seem in its wisdom to require.—

(From Thurlow Weed.)

PRIVATE.

ALBANY, Dec. 18, 1841.

Dear Sir,

The President has triumphed not only over his enemies but over
himself. It is a great Message. Now God grant to Congress the
wisdom to act in the spirit of your Letter in the National Intelligencer of Agust, [six] and all will be well.

If Greeley, who is "all honest and true" (we can sing again!)
takes hold of the Madisonian, he will reflect whatever is useful
and salutary from the President, the Cabinet and the Congress,
to the People.[1]

Very truly yours,
THURLOW WEED.

(To Edward Kent.[2])

PRIVATE.

WASHINGTON Decr. 21st. '41.

Dear Sir

I have this mor'g recd your private letter of the 15th inst.
Its contents are important.

I may say to you the negotiations for a Convention to settle
the Boundary Question can hardly be said to have, made any
positive progress, since last year.

---

[1] This letter is owned by Mr. C. P. Greenough.
[2] The Governor of Maine.

Mr. Forsythe's counter project, deliv'd in Aug. 1840, recd no answer until just before Ld.Palmerston went out of office,in Aug. 1841.   It was then amen'd, & this answer has reviewed the subject, & other correspondence will ere long take place between the parties. The interest of both parties undoubtedly requires a compromise, & I have no doubt that the position which Maine has assumed is the only obstacle to br'g'g such compromise about. The English Govt. cannot treat with us about a compromise, unless we say we have authority to consummate what we agree to; & although I entertain not the slightest doubt of the just authority of this Govt. to settle this question by compromise, as well as in any other way, yet in the present position of affairs, I suppose it will not be prudent to stir, in the direction of compromise without the consent of Maine.   I am very glad to learn that it is probable that your land agent will give some accurate idea of the value of the land North of the St. Johns.

Suppose England should be will'g *to pay* for the land north of the River, & leave the question of its navigation to be settled hereafter; or suppose she should be will'g to let our line run from the monument to the mouth of the Eel River; & then up the St. Johns, & so through the Lakes?

I should be very glad of your thought, on these and on all other points; but incline for the present to think with you, that perhaps the easiest mode of gett'g the parties together for a compromise may be the creation of a commission.

I hope this may be done this session of Congress.

Yr truly
[D. Webster]¹

(The Exchequer.²)

[Jan. 1842]

There appear to be clear proofs of a growing disposition in the public mind to give the Exchequer, a chance, & a trial.   Many persons approve it, altogether, & among them some of acknowledged ability & experience; & many others, feeling that something ought to be done, see no prospect of success in any other attempt.

But this dispassionate tone & tendency of public sentiment

---

is not allowed to take its free course. Efforts are repeated, in a certain portion of the Press, to prejudice the public judgment, by renewed railing against "John Tyler."

We find the following paragraphs in the New York American of Friday last.

(Excerpt sealed here.) [*A virulent attack on the Exchequer & J. Tyler*]

So barefaced a proposition to place great measures of National Legislation on mere party grounds has seldom been avowed, even if such a motive has sometimes had unacknowledged influence, on the conduct of individuals.

"John Tyler"—to use the respectful appellation of the American,—is President of the United States. He was chosen to the second office, by the People, & came to the first, in the Constitutional mode of succession.

But the American considers John Tyler as not of his party, nor of the party of Whigs. He has no confidence in him, & presumes they have none; and therefore he calls on them not to concur in passing such a law, as, so far as appears, he would be willing they should pass, if its provisions were to be carried into effect by one of their own party. This is the very *ultraism*, of party spirit. It is an open & broad avowal of that preference of party, & party objects, over Constitutional provisions, & the will of the People regularly declared, which has undermined free Institutions in other cases, & is very likely, at some day to undermine them in others.

It is noth'g to the Editor of the American that "John Tyler" is President, by the election of the People, & the provisions of the Constitution. It is nothing that the Constitution has conferred on him the same power as on other Presidents, & to be exercised under the same responsibilities. It is enough for him to know, that a measure, necessary to the public interests, might place the nomination of a dozen individuals to office, in the hands of John Tyler. On this account he opposes the measure, & is willing to leave the public interests to shift for themselves. If a favorite of his party could have the appointment, he would be for the measure. If his favorite candidate was President, he would not hesitate. But this not being the case, he admonishes the Whigs in Congress, not to trust to the Constitutional organization of the Government, not to leave other Departments of the Government, to their own Constitutional responsibility, & the exercise of their own Constitutional powers; but they, the Whigs, having a majority in Congress, should interfere with the arrangements of the Constitution, & refuse to the Executive the exercise of powers, which, if he were of their party, they would gladly confide to him. Now what is this, but placing party considerations above the Constitution? What is it, but advising one branch of the Govt. to distrust, & resist, the ordinary exercise of its powers by another Branch?

There is as much evidence that the President enjoys the confidence of the People, as that the members of Congress enjoy it. He is President, holding his place in pursuance of Constitutional provisions; they are members of Congress, by provisions of the same authority. But because he happens, as may happen, not to have *their* confidence, the confidence of the People shall go for nothing, & *they* will not trust *him*, with the exercise of the powers properly belonging to his office.

These are the ideas of the proper duty of Departments, in a goverment, organized upon the plan of a distinct division of power, among its several branches, which the Editor of the American entertains, & which he takes pains to urge upon his friends in Congress.

For the same reason, there should be no courts; because "John Tyler," President tho' he be, should not be trusted to nominate Judges. There should be no army, & no navy, because he could be trusted with the nomination of their officers— There should be no appropriations for the foreign service abroad; for how can the Whigs of Congress trust "John Tyler" to nominate foreign ministers?—

It has been supposed, that by the provisions of the Constitution of the United States, the Govt. might go on, even if the various Departments should not harmonize, in regard to all political questions.— It has gone on, more than once, amidst great differences of political opinion, between different branches. Until now, party purposes have been kept within some limit; & members of one Branch have not been publicly admonished, & urged, by the public press, to pursue party ends, not only to the greatest prejudice of the public interests—to the rejection of measures admitted to be for the public good, but to the obstruction & resistance of powers properly belonging to other Departments; in other words, to the general derangement of the Government, under its Constitutional organization.—

So much for the *theory*, or principle of the objections set up by the Editor of the American to the Exchequer.—

Now it appears to us, that there would have been a great deal more, both of good sense & patriotism, if the Editor of the American had addressed his friends to the following effect.

"Whigs of Congress, do your duty! If the President shall violate his, you will not be answerable. You constitute the Legislative power; see that that power is properly exercised. See that all useful laws are passed. He holds the Executive power; if he shall abuse it, on his head be the responsibility, & on him fall the condemnation. If you think the Plan of an Exchequer to be such, as that, *if properly carried into operation*, it would relieve the Country, adopt it, adopt it, at once. Adopt it, without hesitation. Prove your own supreme devotion to the public good. Clear yourselves of consequences. A crisis, an ordeal, is at this moment, before you. The Country looks, earnestly, & anxiously, to see how you will bear yourselves in it. Follow your·duty, your own duty, your peculiar duty, your *constitutional duty;* & if a flame should be kindled, seven times hotter than that of Nebuchadnezzar's furnace, still, so acting, you will go through it, & whoever else may be scorched or consumed, as for you, the smell of fire will not be on your garments."—

(From Lord Ashburton.)

PRIVATE.

THE GRANGE 2nd Jan'y 1842.

My Dear Sir,

You will hear by this opportunity, and probably not without some surprise that I have undertaken to cross the Atlantic at this stormy season of the year as a special messenger of peace & I would not make my sudden appearance at Washington in this my new character of a diplomatist, without sending you a few lines to say that I am coming— My advanced period of life, not unaccompanied by some of its infirmities, has for some time imposed upon me the duty of retirement, and I felt myself justified in declining to form part of an administration just formed by my political friends with whom I have been in habits of confidence and intimacy on public matters. Under these circumstances, it is not without some reluctance, that I have suffered myself to be persuaded that I am a person likely to be of service in the important task of setling the difference which seems to stand in the way of that which all men of sense and honesty have most at heart, a good and cordial state of peace and good will between our great countries— In short I am making preparations for my early departure.

A Frigate is preparing for me at Portsmouth I hope to start before the month is out, and by the end of February or early in March to make my appearance at your seat of Government.

I confine myself for the present simply to the communication of this fact. I hardly need add that I should not have yielded to the pressing solicitations of my friends but for the very strong impressions of the importance of the service, and that the confidence and full powers of my government afforded the best chance of performing it, meeting as I am sure I shall with a corresponding disposition with the existing enlightened Government of America.—

The principal aim and object of that part of my life devoted to public objects during the 35 years that I have had a seat in one or the other House of Parliament has been to impress on others the necessity of, and to promote my-self, peace and harmony between our countries; and although the prevailing good sense of both prevented my entertaining any serious apprehensions on the subject. I am one of those who have always watched with anxiety at all times any threatening circumstances, any clouds which however small may through the neglect of some or the malevolence of others end in a storm the disastrous consequences of which defy exaggeration—

I shall be most happy, my dear Sir, to cooperate with you in this good work— since my appointment was made the President's speech has reached us, and although it gives us a longer catalogue of differences than I could wish, I flatter myself that many if not all will vanish on a candid explanation and discussion, and I am strongly confirmed in that hope by the plain and cordial expressions by which they are accompanied. The material interest of the two countries call loudly for peace and friendship, but what to my mind is of infinitely greater importance I believe the moral improvement and the progressive civilization of the world depend upon it.—

But I will not begin my first attempt at Diplomacy with overabundant professions of which I hope I shall shortly prove the sincerity. Lady Ashburton[1] will not be able to accompany me.

---

[1] Alexander Baring (Lord Ashburton) married the daughter of William Bingham, of Philadelphia.

She would much wish once more to visit her native country but her
health and domestic duties make this impossible.

I am, my dear Sir, with great truth Yours sincerely ever

ASHBURTON.

(*From Lady Ashburton.*[1])

BATH HOUSE Jan. 12 [1842]

My Dear Mr. Webster

I take great credit to myself for the discretion which has hitherto checked my impulse to write to you, at the risk of appearing
unmindful of the very gratifying proofs of your recollection, I
have received on various occasions; for in truth I had little to tell
you beyond the gossip of London society at a moment when I
knew your time and attention were absorbed by the most important affairs. I cannot however now resist troubling you with a
few lines to say how fully we concur in your description of Mr.
Everett, who is in every respect calculated to sustain the high
opinion *now* entertained of American Statesmen, & to inculcate
the regard of all those who have the advantage of knowing him—
I should have made his acquaintance as a country woman, but I
can now boldly urge my claim to his consideration as an acknowledged friend of yours—a privilege I am so apt to boast of, that
it is gratifying to my vanity to have it confirmed by you— Mr.
Everett's brief visit to the Grange was not made under the most
cheering circumstances, for my *heroic patriotism* has been sadly
depressed by the prospect of a long suspension of our domestic
happiness, to say nothing of the great anxiety we all suffer about
Lord Ashburton's health, which I fear will be sorely tried in a
tedious voyage at this inclement season— These honors were
thrust upon him as the person most zealous in the cause of America, & most sanguine as to the possibility of settling the long
pending differences between the two countries. God grant that
his best hopes may be realized & that I may see him return with a
treaty of peace in his pocket— It will go far to compensate us
both for the sacrifices we are about to make. At all events pray
treat him kindly, & meet his advances with the same friendly feelings he carries towards you, for to borrow your own significant
phrase "if you dont like him, we can send you nothing better."

He will embark in the warship about the 25 of this month, &

---

[1] The daughter of William Bingham, of Philadelphia.

I hope he will have no difficulty in finding a suitable House at Washington— Mr. Bates has promised to write to secure one— Had the season been more propitious I should much have liked to accompany him, & to have seen the vast improvements which have taken place in my native country during an absence of forty years— Adieu my dear Mr. Webster & pray believe me to be your truly obliged

A. H. ASHBURTON

(To John Wilson.[1])

WASHINGTON Feb. 9, 1842

Dear Sir

I have rec'd your letter of the 29th of January. While I very much lament that you do not approve of recent steps, taken here, in regard to the important subjects of currency & finance, I have no right to complain, nor would I desire you to withhold your opinions, however they may differ from mine. The state of the Country is known to us all; we all know the failure, thus far, of all attempts at relief; and yet, for one, I have not thought it a part of duty to give up hope, or relax all effort. I certainly concurred in the President's recommendations of the plan now before Congress; & this you think inconsistent with former opinions of mine. On this part of your letter, I will say a word or two. Genl Jackson's proposition, so far as it was stated by him, was for a *Bank,* founded on the credit & revenues of the Govt, & to carry on the *Common business* of a Bank; that is to say, it was to be a Bank of Loans & Discounts.

Now the plan suggested by the President proposed no *loans*— no *discounts,* in the way of common Bank operations. It seeks to help the country, by furnishing exchange, as far as its means, & a due regard to safety, will allow.—and beyond this, it refrains from all loans or advances to individuals. This distinction appears to me to be broad & clear.

I cannot help hoping, on the whole, that you will come to the conclusion that the plan before Congress is the most likely to be useful to the Country, of any thing that can now be suggested.[2]

Yrs respectfully

DANL WEBSTER.

---

[1] Addressed to General Wilson.
[2] This letter was written in reply to a long letter reproving Webster for inconsistency in matters of national finance.

(To Reuel Williams.[1])

WASHINGTON Feb. 2, 1842

Dear Sir,

Recalling the conversation which passed in the Department between Mr. Evans and yourself, & me, & also the short interview which I had with you at the Presidents, I now beg leave to address you, on the important subject of those conversations.

Lord Ashburton may be expected in this country by the first of March, fully empowered & instructed to discuss and settle definitely every subject in controversy between the United States & England.   At the head of this list stands the dispute covering our North Eastern Boundary, & I suppose this will be entered upon, immediately upon his arrival.

You are aware that a negotiation had been going on between Mr. Forsyth and Mr. Fox, for many months, before the late change of administration.   In the progress of this negotation, the parties had arrived at an agreement for a joint commission, with an ultimate reference to arbitrators, appointed by the Sovereigns, or Heads, of other Governments, in case necessity for such arbitration should arise.   On several matters of detail the parties differed, & appear to have been interchanging their respective views & opinions, projects & counter projects, without coming to a *full* (final) agreement down to Aug 1840.   Various causes, not now necessary to be explained, have [arrested the progress of the negotiations at that time] prevented any further considerable progress, since that period.   (& no efficient progress has since been made in it.)

It seems to be [have been] understood on both sides, that one arbitration having failed, it is [was] the duty of the two parties to proceed to institute another, according to the spirit of the Treaty of Ghent, & other Treaties, and (I suppose, that) unless some new course be adopted the pending negotiation will be immediately pressed to its conclusion.

But I think it highly probable that Lord Ashburton will come prepared to agree to a conventional line of boundary, on such terms, & conditions, & under such compensation, as may be thought just and equitable.   It is the conviction of the high probability of this, (although we have no authentic information

---

[1] R. Williams was a prominent lawyer of Maine, and was a Senator from that State from 1837 to 1843.

to that effect) that leads the President to desire that the attention of the Government of Maine should be immediately & seriously turned to this subject, with a view of learning whether it might not be useful for that Govt. to make itself, to a certain extent, and in a certain form, party to the discussions & conclusions, which may be had between the Govt. of the United States & that of England.   The Treaty for a conventional line, if one should be agreed upon, must of course be between the United States & England, & could be submitted for ratification only to the Senate of the United States.   But agents or commissioners of Maine might represent her interests & wishes, in the negotiation, with an understanding that no exchange of Territory, or other proceedings to make a new line by agreement, would be adopted without their express assent.   Their commissioners would of course correspond with their own Government, and as they would be possessed of the, fullest local information, & well acquainted with the interests, sentiments, & wishes of the People of Maine, an arrangement entered into with their consent, if happily such an arrangement could be made, would be likely to give satisfaction.

I pray you to have the goodness to confer on this subject with Gov. Fairfield, & other Gentlemen, & learn their opinions.   You will see that time presses, as I suppose the Legislature of Maine will adjourn in a month.

It was deemed of so much importance that this subject should be brought under consideration in Maine, that, with the President's approbation, I have concluded to write to some Gentleman of High character in Maine, inviting his attendance here immediately, to confer upon the means proper to be adopted, & should probably have addressed myself to Chief Justice Weston. But as you are now on the spot, it has been thought better to communicate with you, in the first instance.   If you & other Gentlemen should be of opinion that it w'd be useful that a suitable person should come here, at once, to confer with the President, & this Department, more freely & fully than may be done by correspondence, we should be very glad to see him; & though I have great respect for Judge Weston, founded on long acquaintance, yet if his engagements will not allow him to visit us, any other Gentleman will be agreeable whom Gov. Fairfield & yourself may select.

It is our purpose, to put the question in the fairest manner to Maine, whether she will consent to be satisfied with a conventional line, & all the other terms & conditions, which commissioners of her own appointment shall have approved. And it is but candid to say, that for many reasons, some of which are obvious to all, no negotiations for such a line will be opened, or entered upon, without an express previous consent on the part of Maine, to acquiesce in any line, with all its terms, conditions, & compensations, which shall have been thus previously approved. I hope the Government of Maine will think favorably of what I have now suggested; since it is my opinion, that in all probability, five or six years will elapse before the line of the Treaty of 1783 can be ascertained, by proceedings under a convention for a joint-commission and an ultimate arbitration. It will be our duty, however, to press the conclusion of such convention as soon as possible, unless the Government of Maine should think it incompatible with the honor & interest of the State to concur in measures for an earlier settlement of the whole question.

Allow me to hope for an early acknowledgment of the result of this communication.

[DANIEL WEBSTER][1]

(From Reuel Williams.)

PRIVATE AND CONFIDENTIAL.

AUGUSTA Feb 12 1842

Dear Sir

Since writing to you some days ago I have endeavored to ascertain what may be expected from the Legislature of Maine in reference to the boundary question.

The point of honor, and consistency on the part of the Legislature, are in the way of arriving at what might be satisfactory to both Countries.

Maine is confident of the justice & validity of her claim as advanced and insisted upon by her, & has no wish to change the Treaty line. Still I believe she would release to Great Britain such portion of the territory in controversy as the convenience of the latter may require, on an offer of other territory in exchange, or other suitable equivalent. In her view, Great Britain has interposed an unwarrantable claim to a portion of her territory, & has taken & now holds part of it by military force.

To open a way to a friendy adjustment of the question, it

---

[1] This copy was taken from the original draft of the letter in Webster's hand.

would seem that Great Britain should first withdraw all military occupation of the territory in controversy & then a proposition from her for an exchange of territory and equivalents would be met & carried out by Maine in a friendly spirit.

Aware of the difficulties urged by the Government of Great Britain as standing in the way of her proposing a conventional line & equivalents to a party not authorized to agree to & establish such a line, the members of the Legislature, as well as the Governor of Maine, as far as I can ascertain, would agree to any course which can be honorably adopted to afford the parties an opportunity of understanding the objects and views of each other, & of arriving at a settlement of the long pending question of boundary, if possible, without resort to arbitration, indicated by the last, as well as the present administration, as the only remaining course to be adopted.

If the information proposed by the general Government would enable you to propose to the Governor of Maine, or the Legislature, a specific line of boundary; yielding to Maine territory, privileges of navigation or other benefits equivalent to the territory which might be yielded to Great Britain, in lieu of the line described in the Treaty of 1783, it would be well received, & acted upon by the Legislature as the General Government might justly expect from one of its members.

If that cannot be done, then I think an appeal to Maine, as indicated in your letter, would receive grave consideration & be acted upon with a strong desire to adopt the measure, if it shall be deemed consistent with the honor and just pretensions of the State.

Suggestions are made by some that alltho' Great Britain has heretofore proposed to treat for a conventional line *it is not* known that Lord Ashburton will be so instructed, and that Maine should authorize Commissioners to consider & agree upon a conventional line & its terms, & then learn that no such line or terms were to be *proposed by England,* Maine would then be placed where no American could wish to see her placed.

While I have thus given you the views of the dominant party in Maine, as fairly & fully as I can, it should not be forgotten that much will depend upon the course of the Whigs. Neither party, as such, will be inclined to encounter the united efforts of the other upon this great question. If the Whigs shall, as I think they will, sustain a reasonable proposition from the general government for authority to settle the question upon just grounds

& with proper limitations it seems to me that the object may be attained; but I speak from appearances & not from authority. The Legislature propose to adjourn about the first of March.

I am very respectfully Your obt. servt.

R WILLIAMS

_____

(To Reuel Williams.)

PRIVATE AND CONFIDENTIAL.

WASHINGTON Feb. 18, 1842

My Dear Sir

Your letter of the 12th. was received yesterday. The disposition which appears to animate Govr. Fairfield, & the other Gentlemen with whom you conferred, is such as to give hope, I think of favorable results. Nothing is more earnestly desired by the President than to terminate the Boundary controversy in a manner honorable, satisfactory, & useful to Maine, & to the whole Country.

You remark that it is suggested by some [here mark, as quoted on page 3 "that although" &c to the words "her places"] I have no further information to give, as respects Lord Ashburton's instructions. All we know is, that Lord Aberdeen informed Mr. Everett that Lord Ashburton would be clothed with full power to discuss, & definitely settle, all questions pending between the two governments.

I have no doubt, whatever, that his instructions will give him the fullest authority to agree on a conventional line. But if Govr. Fairfield & other Gentlemen think that more positive assurance on that point is necessary, before any step be taken by Maine, then of course nothing can be done before the Minister's arrival. It may be proper to take this view of the subject, & it would not become me to make any objections; altho' for my own part, I should have preferred that a different view might have been taken.

I regret that Govr. Fairfield & his friends should be of opinion that any points of honor & consistency, on the part of the Legislature are in the way of arriving at what might be satisfactory to both Countries. It is true that Maine is confident of the justice & validity of her claim, & certainly I think this a well founded confidence. But it is equally true that England has evinced, on her side, no less confidence. Maine thinks that England has interposed an insurmountable claim to a portion of her Territory, & the Govt. of the U. States thinks that Maine in that opinion, is entirely right; but England asserts, on the other side, that the U. S. & Maine have interposed an insurmountable claim to a portion of her Territory; and these conflicting opinions & assertions of right must be, in some way settled & adjusted. It is true that England occupies or protects a part of the disputed Territory by armed force, but it is equally true that the United States occupy & protect another part by an armed force also, and this last force was placed in position, at the request of the Govt. of Maine. Indeed if I remember correctly, Maine assented, in the year 1839, that the question of possession should remain as it then stood; that is, that Great Britain should hold one part, Maine not acknowledging her right, & that Maine should hold another part, England not acknowledging her right. The spirit & general principle of this understanding between Maine & the Govt. of New Brunswick has governed the conduct of the Govt. of the United States, in all subsequent measures respecting the possession of the disputed territory; the principal alteration, that of substituting U. S. troops for the posse of Maine having been adopted, as I have already said, at the request of Maine. I make this remark, My Dear Sir, with no other view than that of expressing the hope, that on more reflection, & upon full consideration of all the circumstances, the Govt. of Maine may not find any obstacle founded on considerations of honor & consistency from concurring, in the manner suggested in my letter, in a proceeding, having in view the establishment of a conventional line, if the British Minister should in fact bring with him proper authority for such a purpose.[1]

I am, My Dear Sir, with true regard, Yours obedient servant,

D. W.

(To Samuel Rush et al.)

WASHINGTON Feb. 19, 1842.

Gentlemen:

It would give me much pleasure to join you, in your proposed commemoration of the Birth Day of Washington, but public duties deprive me of that satisfaction.

Every revolving year evinces, more & more clearly, the wisdom,

---

[1] This copy is taken from the draft of letter sent.

& virtue, & patriotism of that illustrious man, and instead of
offering you any sentiments of my own, to be announced at your
celebration, will you allow me to transcribe a paragraph from
his Farewell Address.

(Here copy as marked, pp. 57, 58.)[1]

There is no one of these sentiments, Gentlemen, which does not
enter into my conviction, & sink deep in my heart.   They have
constituted & so long as I live, will constitute, the principle of my
political conduct, whether in public or private life.   If we can
maintain these sentiments, if we can keep their lodgment high,
secure, & unshaken in the affections of the American People, we
need not fear that patriotism & good counsels will lift the Country triumphantly out of all difficulties, & carry it ever on in its
bright career of prosperity & renown.   But if these sentiments
shall be abandoned, we may be assured that there will come consequences, amidst which I know not on what plank Patriotism
itself may hope to stand, for its last effort, or how the voice of
the wisest commander may expect to be heard, above the howling
of the storm.

Your invitation intimates Gentlemen, that the company will
be composed of the Friends of President Tylers Administration.
Of that Administration, its character, its purposes, or its prospect of success, it may become me to say little.   In the events
which have happened, & amidst the circumstances which surround
it, It asks one thing from the American People; & that is, a fair
trial.   If they will protect it against the effects of unjust denunciations in advance, & judge of its merits or demerits, as they may
be disclosed in the sequel, it will have no right to complain, &
so far as I am concerned, will not complain of the final judgment
of the Country.

Let it be judged by its measures; by the degree of care it shall
manifest to maintain the honor & interests of the United States in
their Foreign Relations; by the disposition it shall evince towards
a reasonable provisions for public defense, on the land & on the
water; by its recommendations on the great subjects of revenue
& finance; by its cooperation in all practicable means of retrench-
ment & reform; by its impartial regard to all interests, & all
parts, of the Country; and, above all, by its remembrance, or its
forgetfulness, of the solemn admonition of Him, whose now glorious name & services you commemorate, that the main pillar of our

---

[1] Webster's instruction to his amanuensis.

Independence, Prosperity, & Happiness will ever be found to be that "UNITY OF GOVERNMENT, WHICH CONSTITUTES US ONE PEOPLE."[1]

I am, Gentlemen, Your obliged friend & fellow citizen

[D. WEBSTER]

(To Pearce & Bullock.)

WASHINGTON 11th. March, 1842.

Gentlemen

I have recd your letter of the 8th of this month, & read its contents with great interest. I shall take occasion to have parts of it published, without your names, that the facts which it mentions may get before the public.

I do not know what views on the whole subject of our reciprocity treaties may be now entertained, or hereafter adopted, by our Branch of the Government of the United States. But writing as a friend in confidence I may say to you that I have looked at the operation of these treaties, with extreme concern for the last three or four years.[2]

Yours very respectfully,

D. W.

(From Joseph Story.)

CAMBRIDGE March 26, 1842.

Dear Sir,

Accidental circumstances have prevented me from before answering your letter of the 17th instant. I now do it with great pleasure.

The first part of your Inquiry is whether the Law of Nations does not make a difference between the case of ordinary fugitives from justice and the case of persons committing offences upon the high seas. I am not aware that any such distinction has ever been made theoretically or even practically, except so far as Piracy (which I will presently consider) may be supposed to constitute an exception. Offences committed on the high seas are exclusively cognisable by the Courts of the Nations, to which the ships on board of which they have been committed, belong. Such

---

[1] This letter is taken from Webster's draft of letter sent.
[2] Taken from Daniel Webster's original manuscript.

ships are treated as being subject to the municipal laws of their own country, and to none others.   No other nation has any right, or duty to take cognisance of, or to punish such offences.   And on this account, as the offences are merely municipal, no distinction has been taken between fugitives from justice, violating municipal laws, on the ocean, and those violating those laws on land. This case was a good deal considered in the case of U. S. v. Palmer (3 Wheat. R. 610) and U. S. v Klintok (5 Wheat. R. 144) and U. S. v. Furlong (5 Wheat. R. 184)

But wherever the Crew of a Ship of any nation have usurped the command thereof, and assumed the character of pirates, there, the general rule has been that *all* nations may take cognizance of, and punish their subsequent piratical acts; for the ship has then lost her national character.   This was expressly held in U. S. v. Klintok (5 Wheat. R. 610) U. S. v. Smith (5 Wheat. R. 154) and U. S. v. Furlong & als. (5 Wheat. R. 144) and U. S. v. Holmes (5 Wheat. R. 412).   It has, therefore, become a common practice for all nations to take cognizance of and to punish piratical offences, although committed on board of Ships, which originally belonged to another foreign nation, the Ship having by force, or usurpation lost her national character.

But although every nation is deemed thus at liberty to punish piracy, whenever the pirates are brought within its own dominions, it is by no means uncommon for a nation, under such circumstances, to remit the offenders for trial to the Country to which the Ship belonged.   This, however, has always been understood to be a matter of comity and discretion, and not of national duty. Several cases have occurred in the Circuit Court, in my circuit, where this has taken place.   Thus in the case of U. States v. Tully; the Prisoners were arrested in St. Lucia, and sent to the U. States and were there tried and convicted.   The case of U. S. v. Ross was a case where a South American Govt. (I forget which one) sent home the offenders for trial.   But the most striking case was that of U. S. v. Gibert 2nd Sumner R. 20, where the British Government ordered the Spanish Pirates, who plundered the Brig Mexican, of Salem, to be sent to Boston for trial and they were accordingly sent and tried and convicted.   The offenders were originally arrested by British Officers in Africa, and were sent to England, and then were by order of the British, sent here, and a British officer as a witness accompanied them.   See 2 Sumner R. 24 NOTE.   This was understood at the time to be, not a matter of duty, but a matter of discretion and comity.

Your second question is, as to what cases I recollect as to sending persons of the last description (that is, offenders on the high seas) home for trial, and particularly what I remember of the case of the Plattsburg.

I have already stated several cases in my Circuit; and I believe more have occurred; and in cases of municipal offenders, I have a strong impression that American Seamen have been often sent home who have committed crimes of a malignant character; such as murder, revolt, and manslaughter. But I cannot recall the particular cases. A search in the Clerk's office of the Circuit Court in Boston, would, I doubt not, present many such. I doubt not that many cases have occurred in other Districts, especially in New York. In respect to the case of the Plattsburg, I suppose you refer to that case, as it came before the Supreme Court, and is reported in 10th. Wheaton R. 133. You will there find all the facts stated at large. If there be any other case of the Plattsburg involving other facts, it has not as yet occurred to my memory.

The real question, however, in the Creole Case is not a question as to the delivering up of fugitives from Justice, as of property, and property coming by the *vis major* and involuntarily into a foreign port. Suppose the case had been one of Shipwreck, and the Cargo had been ordinary goods, no one could well doubt that in the present state of civilization every nation would feel itself bound by the general doctrines of comity and humanity and justice to protect and restore such property and to give a right of reclaiming it from wrong doers. The question then is reduced to this, whether there is a sound distinction between that case, and the case of Slaves, who are property and held as property by their owners in America, and are by the *vis major*, or by shipwreck found in a foreign port. It is certainly true, that no nation held itself bound to recognise the state or the rights of slavery, which are recognised and allowed by any other Country. And if slaves come *voluntarily* into a Country with the consent of their masters, they are deemed free. The only point left of my argument seems to be, whether the like privilege applies, where they are in such Country by the *vis major*, or by shipwreck. I have always inclined to think this must be deemed matter of comity, which a nation was at liberty to concede or refuse, and not a right of another nation to claim or enforce as strictly arising under the Law of nations. Could an action be maintainable in a Court of Justice to enforce a right to Slave property in New

England or any other non slaveholding State in a case not covered by the Constitution, or by a Treaty? The argument, ab inconvenienti, may be addressed with great force to Great Britain on this subject; but it strikes me to furnish a ground for mutual Treaty Stipulations as to slave property and the slave trade, fit to be pressed, in negotiations, although difficult to support as a positive public right independant of Treaty. See the Amistad 15 Peters. A, and the Penna Slave Case in Supreme Court last term.

Believe me most truly, yours.

JOSEPH STORY.

(To Edward Everett.(?)

Private

WASHINGTON Mar 30" 1842 10 P. M.

My Dear Sir,

I have only time to say that your despatches, *to* the 3rd, were rec'd this evening, and have been glanced at, but not read. Lord Ashburton as yet is to be heard from; but he is not out of time, according to other passages recently made from your side to ours. Mr. Clark's house is taken for him, and is in readiness.

We have some excitement here at this moment from the new attempt of Mexico to reduce Texas. The want of all due preparation on the part of Texas, renders it possible that the Mexican troops may overrun the Country; but I have no belief they can hold it. There is also a good deal of feeling in the United States, about the manner in which certain citizens of ours, who say they are non-combatant followers of the Texan expedition to Santa Fé, have been treated by the Mexican authorities. I hope, however, we may be able to keep the peace.

Congress is doing nothing, at least, no good thing. Endless debate, and personal quarrels are the order of the day. The foreign relations of the Country are ticklish enough; but our domestic condition is terrible. We are now enjoying the rich fruits of the Compromise Act of March 1833. Almost the only symptom of returning sense among us is found in the very general idea now prevalent, that there is no course left but to lay duties in the old way, discriminating and specific, abandoning all notions of universal *horizontalization* in such things.

Mrs. W. desires her best regards; and I am obliged to place this

at once into the hands of Charles Brown or lose the chance by
the Boston Boat.

Yours,

D. WEBSTER.

(From Joseph Story.)

My dear Sir,   CAMBRIDGE April 19, 1842

I have been very busy with cases in bankruptcy and other
matters or I should have answered your last letter before this
time. I now send a sketch of three articles of a Treaty upon
three of the critical points, to which you have directed my attention—(1) fugitives from Justice—(2) vessels with slaves going
into British ports by stress of weather &c. (3) Acts done under
Government orders like McLeod's case &c.

As to the first I have taken the 17th Article of Jay's Treaty
of 1794, as my main guide, as far as it goes. But it stops short
of pointing out how the surrender is to be accomplished, (as I
think it should be) through the judicial power, which gave rise
to the senseless popular clamours in Jonathan Robinson's case.
I have added the proper provision.

As to the second, I have drawn it up with considerable fullness,
and directness meaning to meet the difficulty in language calm
and yet clear; with the proper grounds as to the right of examination into the character of the persons on board, whether properly held as slaves or not, to prevent public odium and clamour.

As to the third I can only say, that considering the importance
to our national peace and Security, it is more properly a matter
for treaty stipulation, than for an act of Congress. I hope
therefore it may be adopted. The first part of the clause is
vital to its just operation by excluding the judicial action where
the act is clearly authorized by the Sovereign. This will cut up
the difficulty by the root.

If I had more time I would probably have given more finish
to the phraseology; but you can easily amend and alter it. I
am sure the provisions are in *substance* right and will reach the
evils.

In the article about fugitives from Justice I have put in the
crimes only, which most usually occur, and will be likely to call
for the interposition of the Government for extradition. If you
think it too broad, you can strike out any part of the enumera-

tion, you may think best.   I have purposely excluded political offences, as involving very debatable matters not to say also, that they might hazard the ratification by our Senate from popular clamours.

I am very anxious to have all our difficulties with Great Britain settled for I love peace, and I wish well to G. B. as well as to my own Country; and I have not the slightest doubt, that all matters may, if met in the right spirit be settled honourably for the interests and permanent peace of both Countries.   I will therefore, hold myself ready at all times to aid your efforts, whenever you may think I can be of any real use in accomplishing so desirable an end.

In my judgment we ought to accede to the Treaty of the five Powers as to the search of Slave vessels and to suppress the Slave Trade.   That Treaty is exceedingly well drawn, and most carefully weighed.   We might do so by a single article, merely referring, as to the *modus operandi*, to the provisions of that Treaty, and agreeing to have them regulate our article as far as they are applicable.

I confess that I despair of Congress; and I believe this is becoming a very pervading feeling among all our intelligent men. If we are to be saved at all, it must be by different counsels; and by the Executive taking, as to our foreign affairs, a bold and firm ground, but conciliatory.

I regret, that our Ministers, Cass and Wheaton, should intermeddle with these matters uncalled for.   They have a tendency to embarrass our negotiations; and I am surprised that they should write without orders, and thus inflame, if not misdirect the public mind.   I have seen Cass's pamphlet, but not Wheaton's. Cass's pamphlet is calculated to do much mischief here as well as in *France*.

Believe me most truly Your's

JOSEPH STORY

———

(To Edward Everett.)

PRIVATE

WASHINGTON, D. C. 28" April, 1842.

My Dear Sir,
There is one fact of very considerable importance which I omitted to mention in my last private letter bearing upon the convenience or inconvenience of ceding to us the strip of land

west of St. Johns; and that is, that the British authorities are constructing a road from Fredericton directly across the country to the Great Falls of the St. Johns; so that for communication between New Brunswick and Canada, there will be no occasion to cross the river nor indeed to come near it below those Falls. Please explain this to Lord Aberdeen.

Yours always
DANL WEBSTER.

(To Waddy Thomson.[1])

PRIVATE.

WASHINGTON June 27, 1842.

Dear Sir,

That part of your despatch No. 1 relative to California, & your private letter to the President of the 9th of May have been considered.   There is no doubt that the acquisition of so good a port on the Pacific as St. Francisco is a subject well deserving of consideration.   It would be useful to the numerous Whale Ships & trading vessels of the United States, which navigate the Pacific, & along the Western Coast of America.   It would in time probably become a place of considerable trade, having a good country around it, but colonization & settlement could not be expected to advance in that region, with the same spirit and celerity, as have been experienced on the Northern Atlantic Coast. In seeking acquisitions, to be governed as Territories, & lying at a great distance from the United States, we ought to be governed by our prudence & caution; & a still higher degree of these quali-ties should be exercised when large Territorial acquisitions are looked for, with a view to annexation.   Nevertheless, the benefits of the possession of a good Harbour on the pacific is so obvious, that to that extent, at least, the President strongly inclines to favor the idea of treaty with Mexico.   The claims of citizens of the United States against the Mexican Government are large. The amount of those already awarded, as you will see by another communication by this conveyance, is upwards of two millions of dollars; another large amt. failed of being awarded, as is sup-posed, only because the umpire did not feel authorized to act upon them, after the expiration of the time limited for the dura-tion of the Commission.   There are still other classes of claims,

---

[1] Thomson was appointed Minister Plenipotentiary to Mexico in 1842. From 1835 to 1841 he represented South Carolina in Congress.

of various descriptions, but amounting in the whole to a large aggregate. You are at liberty to sound the Mexican Govt. upon the subject of a cession of the Territory upon the Pacific, in satisfaction of these claims, or some of them. Although it is desirable that you should preserve the Port & Harbor of St. Francisco as the prominent object to be attained, yet, if a cession should be made, St. Francisco would naturally accompany the Port. It may be useful, however, for divers reasons, that the benefit & convenience of the Port itself should, at least for the present, be spoken of, as that is chiefly desired by the United States. I do not think that England has any present purpose of obtaining that important place, or would interpose any obstacles to the acquisition of it by the United States. What may be the wishes of France, in this respect, I cannot say. You will please proceed in this matter very cautiously, & quite informally; seeking rather to lead the Mexican Secretary to talk on the subject, than to lead directly to it yourself. You will be particularly careful not to suffer the Mexican Govt. to suppose that it is an object upon which we have set our hearts, or for the sake of which we should be willing to make large remuneration. The cession must be spoken of, rather as a convenience to Mexico, or a mode of discharging her debts. By no means give countenance to any extravagant expectations, content yourself with sounding the Government, endeavor to hear, more than you say, to learn more than you communicate; & apprise us promptly & frequently, of all that may occur on the subject.

Your project of visiting California this season can hardly be realized, as it is likely that your presence will be required at your post.[1]

I am, Dear Sir, with much true regard, Yrs.

[D. W.]

(To John Davis.?)

PRIVATE AND CONFIDENTIAL.

WASHINGTON, Jul. 15, 1842

Dear Sir,

I enclose herewith the copy of a letter addressed by me, on the 2nd instant, to Mr Williams, one of the Senators of Maine, now

---

[1] This copy is taken from Webster's draft of the letter.

on a visit to his own residence in Augusta, & to which I beg leave to call your attention.

In the settlement of the Boundary Question, Massachusetts has an interest, as well as Maine, inasmuch as a moiety of the public lands lying in the latter state belong to her. The right of territorial sovereignty, however, is exclusively in Maine; & it is this consideration, I presume, which has caused something more of excitement & concern in the question to be experienced in the one State than in the other. But the interest of Massachusetts is not to be overlooked; & it is for that reason, that I now address you. You will see the suggestion, which I have made thro' Mr Williams to the Gov. of Maine, & I now submit the same proposition to the Consideration of the Govt. of Massachusetts.

If a conventional line be agreed upon, as very probably may be upon conditions, which, while perhaps generally useful to the whole Country, & highly important to Maine, may be of less positive advantage to Massachusetts. That this may be so, you will readily perceive. And yet, I suppose, that Massachusetts, anxious for the settlement of so distressing a question, & finding her own interests reasonably provided for, would not interpose any objection, founded on narrow considerations.

Under these general views, I submit to you the propriety of considering the proposition which I have communicated to His Excellency, Gov. Fairfield, as a proposition which may be, also, to be acted on by the Govt. of Massachusetts. I entertain no doubt, whatever, that Lord Ashburton will bring with him full power to settle the Boundary Question by agreeing on a conventional line. He may be expected here, according to my information, in less than a month. As yet, I have no answer from Mr. Williams, further than that he has recd my letter, has shown it to Gov. Fairfield, & other Gentlemen, & that he will write me again soon. I shall communicate to you, in confidence, all I learn, and as soon as I hear it, from that quarter. It may, perhaps, be as well for Maine to take the lead, if anything is to be done; (tho' of that you will consider) and if the Govt. of Maine should think favorably of the suggestion, & act upon it, the Govt. of Massachusetts will decide whether it will adopt a similar course.

I should be glad to hear from you, at your earliest convenience; am with the most sincere regard,

Yours

[D. WEBSTER][1]

---

[1] This letter is taken from the original draft in Mr. Webster's hand.

(From Isaac C. Bates.)

JULY 19. 1842
* * * [He acknowedges Webster's letter of the 16th]
"You agree with me in opinion, that the proceeds of the public
lands ought to be distributed among the states.   This you know
is the opinion of Massachusetts." [1]   * * *

=====

(To ——————.)

Private

SATURDAY MORNING July 30. [1842]
My dear Sir,
    I feel exceedingly mortified at feeling obliged to call your at-
tention to a very extraordinary paragraph in the Madisonian of
this morning.
    How it is possible, at a moment when we have points of so much
importance pending with the British Minister that a paper supposed to enjoy your confidence should publish respecting him
such horrible libels.   I am mortified to death.
                                            Yrs truly
                                                    D. W.

=====

(From Lord Ashburton.)

private

SUNDAY 31 July 1842.
My Dear Mr. Webster.
    Using the words of Walter Scott when he sent one of his works
to his publisher—I send you my Creole—D—n her.—
    I leave her in my original sheets to save time, believing that
you can read my scrawl.—   Pray see if you think I could mend
this case with a view to conciliation.   I have treated it quite
fairly for I really believe it would be best settled in London.—
I also believe something satisfactory may & should be there settled.
    Would it be well to leave extradition to be settled at the same
time?   The questions are more or less connected.   I have no
objection to either course.   I congratulate you on the return of

---

[1] This is an excerpt from a letter owned by Mr. Greenough (in folio Mass.
i, a–b).

breathing weather. I really believe that if yesterday's had continued I should not have lived to sign any treaty with you, which is now the great object, as it is likely to be the fifth act of my life.

Ever, my Dear Sir, Yours Truly

ASHBURTON.

(From John Tyler.)

AUGUST 1. [1842]

Dr Sir

I have read your letter on impressment with great interest and pleasure. It occurred to me that it would be proper to press the principle, so as to settle the matter as well on land as at sea— hence the view is somewhat enlarg'd— You will remember the case alluded to of prisoners captured in Canada— While this doctrine of perpetual allegiance exists the naturalized citizen goes into the service with fear and trembling—and I have thought that it would be well to extend the argument so as to embrace the case stated.

You will do with it as you please.

Your paper is plain in its proposition and conclusive in its reasoning. It is a question on which this govt. can hold no other language.

Yrs truly

J. TYLER

(To Fletcher Webster.)

AUG. 5, 1842

Dear F.

I recd this morning yours of the 3rd, & in the enclosed have said to the President what occured to me, in relation to the two remarks which he speaks of. I cannot answer the Portugeese Minister till I receive.

1st. The Treaty with Portugal; 2. The Tariff;
both of which please send me immediately.

I shall endeavor to answer your communication & return the papers promptly, to prevent accumulation. Letters marked *private*, Mr. H. Derrick will know what to do with, & the rest you can dispose of.

Your mother came to town with me last evening, & will depart tomorrow P. M.

                                             Yrs   D. W.

The weather has been adverse, & I do not believe the Warships have yet got to Sea:

───────

(From John Tyler.)

                                          Aug. 8, 1842.
Dear Sir;

I have delayed sending in this paper to day from a desire that you should look over it before it went—   The other gentlemen saw its outline on Saturday when I deeply regretted your absence   Suggest if they occur to you, any amendments on a separate paper.

How deeply do I regret that I cannot have your full concurrence in this proceedure.[1]   But a Clay Congress can only be met in the way proposed—nor can the independence of the Executive or good of the country be otherwise advanced.

If you could return it to me immediately after reading and suggesting changes, it would enable me to have it copied and off of hand this Evening.

                              Most truly yours
                                          John Tyler

───────

(To John Tyler.[2])

Confidential

                                     Aug. 8th. 6 o'clock. [1842]
My dear Sir;

I have gone over your paper, twice & must say, that if the thing must be done, you have given the best reasons for it.

But I must still say, my dear sir, that in the present awful state of the Country, amidst these violent factions looking to consequences likely to spring up in every quarter I would give almost my right hand if you could be persuaded to sign the bill.

At the same time it is my opinion that the conduct of Congress in uniting these two subjects is wholly indefensible.

───────

[1] This letter refers to the veto of "An Act to provide revenue from imports, and to change and modify existing laws imposing duties on imports and for other purposes."

[2] This is taken from Webster's *draft*, which he kept as a duplicate.

What you state in the first & third head of your reasons, is most just & most important. I feel the force of your remarks on this part of the case & am willing to give you every assurance of my entire disapprobation of the conduct of the two Houses in this respect. It is calculated to give to our legislation a violent spasmodic, factious character.

Nevertheless in the present state of affairs I should *sign the bill*.

You will find in the accompanying paper some suggestions which you will look at & give them what weight you think they deserve.

Yrs truly

[D. W.]

(To John Tyler.)

Aug. 8, 1842

My Dear Sir;

Your note gives me the most sincere pleasure— Let what come that may, the affair settled with England, and we shall have cause for unmixed joy. Take my best thanks for your zeal and industry in accomplishing this important matter.[1] Tomorrow at tea I shall be glad to be surrounded by the Cabinet.

But I would rather have you ponder over the idea of separate conventions for each subject. Many friends think that a single Treaty is best. Reserve this if you can for tomorrow.

Yrs J. Tyler

P. S. I fear the extradition article, but we will confer tomorrow.

(To Mrs. Caroline Webster.)

Tuesday 3 o'clock. [Aug 1842]

My Dear Wife

I write a word, only to say that I am well. We are in a great of uncertainty & excitement, & I know not what a day may bring forth. The President is not in good health, & is under a good deal of worry & excitement. I suppose Congress could hardly sit beyond next week.

[1] Refers to the completion of the Webster-Ashburton Treaty. See message of August 11. 1842. "Messages and Papers of the Presidents," vol. iv, p. 162.

Fletcher is well, & we are both exceedingly busy. We breakfasted this morning with Mrs. Lindsley—all well. The general health of the City is good. I wish you had a supply of our peaches.

Mrs. Agg sent me a letter for you, which I forward. Before you receive this you will have seen Mr. Stubbs. I direct this to A. House. You will write me I hope before you leave the City for Morrisiana

What an awful scene at Syracuse!

Yrs.

D. WEBSTER

(To Mrs. Caroline Webster.)

Dear Caroline,   TUESDAY, 3 1/2 o'clock, Aug 1842.

Another day has passed off without important occurence. I have been at the office all the morning, and in tolerable health. Yesterday Mr. Stubbs told me about your purchase. I directed him to order on the 3 principal carpets, and to put one on the study, so that four rooms will be carpeted at once. I thought it as well to defer the other for a while, as the whole was a pretty large sum, and perhaps we could manage for what remains, either here or in Boston.

I was at the President's this morning. He seems quite feeble, and is very much embarassed and harassed. If we get another veto, I know not what will become of us.

I follow your good advice, keep in night and morning, get exercise when I can, and "spatter water" every morning. I am glad that you are off for Marshfield. Oh, that I could go with you. I am really worn down with care and uncertainty, and should hear with pleasure tomorrow that the world of politics had no more for me to do in it. 5 o'clock—I am all alone and am going out to walk

Yours   D. W.

I shall not write you again, until I hear where you probably may be.

(To John Tyler(?).)

My dear Sir,   SUNDAY MORNING [August 28, 1842]

I thank you for your obliging note. Our success in the Senate was signal, indeed.[1]   Mr. Derrich will call on you, about one, today, for a necessary signature & will be off for England to-morrow morning.   He will be back with the Queen's ratification by the time I have done making *chowder* at Marshfield, & we can then have the Treaty published & proclaimed.   Meantime, I suppose the Senate will remove the enjoinder of secrecy from the correspondence on the subject of the "Caroline", the "Creole." & "Impressment;" and will see what the public say, on these matters.

I shall come to see you tomorrow—evening.

Yours truly
DANL WEBSTER.

Yr paper will be returned this P. M.

(To D. Fletcher Webster.)

A. HOUSE, N. Y. Sep. 4. [1842]
Sunday morn'g. 8 o'clock.

My Dear Son,

I arrived at 2 o'clock Saturday, having suffered most severely the whole three days with my cold.   I think I have had it worse, but hope it will not last long.

Lord Ashburton was just setting sail, or rather the Boat was just carrying him out of the harbor, as I crossed the ferry yesterday.   So I did not see him.

I find here several communications from you.

Mr. Adams must be quite wrong in regard to the Mexican business   Nothing is more common than to authorize expenditures, & pay out money by Resolution.[2]   *Search the Statute Books;* and at any rate pay Mr. Thompson's bill.

You speak of a note, of which the Seal was broken by Mr. Seaton, but which I do not find; & his disappointment, but do not state the cause.

Your mother is at Robt. Morris'.   I am going out this morning, to return in the Evening,—if Mr. Curtis arrives meantime, shall probably leave for Boston tomorrow Eve.

I was exceedingly mortified, at the manner in which the Presi-

---

[1] On August 26, 1842, the Senate ratified the Ashburton Treaty.

[2] In a letter of J. Q. Adams to Fletcher Webster the former had questioned the constitutionality of that action.

dent was treated at the Ashburton Dinner. I believe it was principally owing to the awkwardness of the presiding officer. If I were present on any such occasion, I should make known my opinion of good manners.

Yrs.

D. WEBSTER.

(From R. B. Minturn et al.)

Private

Hon. Daniel Webster   NEW YORK Sept. 28, 1842
    Dear Sir,

We have heard with much concern that there is a probability of your resigning the situation in the Government which you have filled with such eminent advantage to the Country— We beg that you will bear with us in expressing to you the feelings of deep regret with which we have rec'd. this intelligence, and that the earnest desire we feel that such a decision may be averted will excuse us in saying to you, that if you can see your way clear to remain in your present position, upon a footing satisfactory to yourself, we believe that you will render the most essential service to your Country, and secure the support and gratitude of all who regard the true welfare of the Nation— We are, With great respect, Your most obt servts.

R. B. MINTURN
M. H. GRINNELL
JON. GOODHUE
RUSSELL H. NORRIS
JNO. A. STEVENS
GEORGE CURTIS
P. PERITZ.

Mr. Geo. Griswold has authorized me to say that he concurs in the wish above expressed.   R. B. M.

(To D. Fletcher Webster.)

MARSHFIELD Oct. 4, 1842.

Dear Fletcher;

By the Steamer arrived at Boston, I have recd. some English letters, but none, either official or private from Mr. Everett or Mr. Derrich. I suppose the package from London may have gone to Washington, or I may find it in Boston tomorrow.— If gone to Washington please send them here. If the President shall have returned, he will of course desire to see the Despatches.

I have a letter from Genl Cass. He desires permission to return home. Please mention this to the President, but to nobody else.

Yrs. D. WEBSTER

(*To D. Fletcher Webster.*)

MARSHFIELD Oct 5 1842.

My Dear Son;

The English Despatches were sent to me, this Evening, and have looked them over, sent to you what were for the Department, and packed and sent off other person's letters.

I send you a despatch from Mr. Everett, and a private letter, both of which please show the President.

I enclose also Genl Cass' letter, which you will please lay before the President, and take his orders (upon). He will probably direct you to write a civil answer, thanking the Genl. for his faithful and useful services abroad, and yielding to his wishes to return to the Country.[1] It ought, I think, to be rather a *cordial* letter, as I believe Genl C is coming home with some expectation of acting a political part.

The President will readily give the proper directions.

Tomorrow morning I leave for New Hampshire.

Yours affectionately
DANL WEBSTER.

Continue to write me regularly as Healy will forward the letters.

(*To D. Fletcher Webster.*)

MARSHFIELD, Oct 6. Wednesday Evening 5 o/clock. 1842.

My Dear Son;

The Acadia arrived in Boston yesterday, at 3 o/clock, and Mr. Zantzinger has brought me down the foreign letter bag. I send to you every thing belonging to the Department except copies of Mr. Stevenson's correspondence with Lord Palmerstone on the subjects of the Caroline and the African Seizures. The corre-

---

[1] See McLaughlin's "Life of Lewis Cass," p. 185.

spondence on these subjects is voluminous, and I retain it a day or two for perusal. You will find a duplicate from Mr. Stevenson, and a letter written by Mr. Christopher Hughes in London, marked for the President's perusal, which please lay before him. I have not opened the newspapers, but you will see by the letters that the McLeod affair, is the great subject of interest in England, so far as we are concerned. Mr. Zantzinger returns to town with the bag in the morning.

Your's affect'ly

D. W.

(To D. Fletcher Webster.)

My Dear Son   FRANKLIN [N. H.] Oct 15, '42

We have been here now a week, in admirable weather, & I have traversed the mountains, & vallies, to great advantage to my health. My catarrh has disappeared, & I feel in all respects well. I go to Boston on the 19th, & if Mr. Derrich shall have arrived, with the Treaty, I shall make haste to Washington.

There is nothing new in this quarter. You see what a dust my speech has raised.[1] It is no more than I anticipated. I am sorry the Intelligencer acts so foolishly; but that is its own affair. The Speech is printing in pamphlet form, in Boston, & will be widely circulated. I have directed an early copy to be sent to the President.

As they send me no newspapers, I know not what has been going on, for the last ten days; only that I see there is no reason to doubt whether the Whigs have not lost Maryland. On arriving at Boston, I shall see the state of things—meet Mr. Cushing & other friends, & write you again.

Your mother has enjoyed this visit very much, & her health is excellent. Mr. & Mrs. Paige have been a week with us, & left us yesterday. The season has been good, & the crops abundant. The whole scene, & all its associations, are interesting to me. I like much to be here, & sometimes I think it may probably happen that I shall end my days in the spot of my first remembrances & consciousness.

Yrs affectionately

DANL WEBSTER

---

[1] Speech at the reception in Boston September 30, 1842. See "Works of Webster," vol. ii, p. 117.

(To D. Fletcher Webster.)

Dear Fletcher,   Boston October 19, 1842
    The Britania arrived yesterday, but brought no Mr. Derrich,
& no Treaty. I am not a little disappointed at this, as Lord
Ashburton arrived and as early as Septr. 23— We have no
public despatch from Mr. Everett, but from his private letter I
am led to suppose, that the delay, in regard to the ratification,[1]
was occasioned, first by Lord Ashburton's proceeding to his own
residence, on arriving at Portsmouth, instead of proceeding immediately to London, & secondly the absence of several members
of the Govt. from London, on visits to their respective residences.
Mr. Everett expresses no doubt of the ratification of the Treaty,
altho. it appears that a writer in the Chronicle, supposed to be
Lord Palmerstone, attacks it vehemently, & calls it Lord Ashburton's capitulation. We may look for Derrich by the next
Steam Ship.
    I have just returned from N. H. & shall wait no longer for the
Treaty, but proceed to Washington next week. Give my best
regards to the President. The result of the election in Ohio
creates surprise & astonishment, with the proscriptive Whigs in
this quarter. But it need surprise no man of sense. New York
will follow suit, without doubt; & if Govr. Davis can get thro.
in this State, with such a load as he has to carry, he will do well.
It is obvious, that the political power in the Country is falling
back, into the hands of those who were outnumbered by the
Whigs, in 1840. All this was to have been expected, from the
violence & injustice which have characterized the conduct of the
Whig leaders.
    The state of things, now certain to exist three weeks hence, will
call on the President, & all who wish well to his administration,
to consider deeply & seriously of what shall be done for the
future.
                                   Yrs affectionately
                                        Danl Webster

(To D. Fletcher Webster.)

Private   Oct. 20, 42.
Dear F.
    I write you, under date of yesterday, a letter, such as, that if

---

[1] See Curtis' "Life of Webster," vol. ii, p. 150 et seq.

you see fit, you can send to the President, respecting the Treaty, &c. &c.

I had no letter from Derrich, but looked into his note to you. You had better not show that note to the President, as he might think Mr. Everett had not pressed for an early ratification of the Treaty, as urgently as he might have done.

Yrs truly

D WEBSTER

(To D. Fletcher Webster.)

OCT. 20, '42

Dear Fletcher

I return the Mexican papers. On the whole, I regret that the negotiations had not been left to be carried on in Washington, under the President's own eye; but trust Mr. Thompson will get successfully through it.

Your's

D. WEBSTER

(To D. Fletcher Webster.)

Private

BOSTON Oct. 20, '42

Dear Fletcher,

I quite regret that any room should exist for an inference, that in my speech I represented the plan of the Exchequer as my own. I meant only to defend it, & to say that I approved it. If there be danger of misapprehension on this subject, I will take occasion to put all right.

Please say this to the President.

Yrs   D. W.

(To D. Fletcher Webster.)

N. YORK Nov. 3, 1842

Dear Fletcher

Your mother & I arrived this morn'g. We shall probably stay a day or two, & it is most likely I shall then leave your mother here. It is hardly probable that I shall stay long enough for Derrich's arrival, but he may come.

I have seen many friends, this morn'g, who seem in good spirits, but there being no particular news. I am glad to see the Madisonian[1] so effective.

If I should not leave tomorrow, I shall write you again.

Yrs affectionately

DANL WEBSTER

(From Lord Ashburton.)

Private

THE GRANGE Jan. 2, 1843.

* * * Jan 7.[2] I had thus far left my letter unfinished as there was no immediate opportunity of sending it and in the meantime the President's speech reaches us.[3] On reading what concerned my transactions I could hardly believe my ears until I read it over deliberately a second time. The deliberate approval of Genl Cass' interference and the insinuation, for so I apprehend that I must understand it, that our cruising article was the result of our consideration of what is miscalled the right of search,—the further assertion that the practice of visiting in cases of suspicion is the only assertion of a right of search in a different form,—these are startling propositions and I am at a total loss to conceive what could have so entirely confused and upset all facts and all reasoning on this subject since I left Washington. It was not without reason that we deprecated Genl Cass' return during our negotiations, for he seems to have got fast hold of your cabinet and to have treated this subject so as best to answer the purpose of the knot of mischievous persons in Paris who have been seeking to embarrass their own government and disturb the peace of the world. But I will not pursue this subject; fortunately for me my diplomatic character has ceased, and I may leave the troubles of the world to others. I shall confine myself to defending my own character in disclaiming all allusion to the right of search in our cruising article, and in stating that no demand was made on me growing out of that supposed grievance, and no intimation given me from any quarter that the last explanation of what was to be the conduct of our cruisers on the

---

[1] The administration newspaper.

[2] This part of Ashburton's letter to Webster was omitted (without indicating the omission) by Fletcher Webster in his edition of Webster's private correspondence. See vol. ii, p. 162.

[3] See " Messages and Papers of the Presidents," vol. iv, p. 195.

African coast was otherwise than satisfactory. I need hardly
tell you that any thing I may say or do on this & all subjects
connected with America will be always to promote peace and allay
irritation, but I can not deny that your Presidential speech has
made European politicians of all parties and all countries stare
with unusual surprise.

There is another paragraph on a subject with which I have no
concern upon which I can not refrain from asking a few words,
with a view to correct an evident mistake. You are aware that I
studiously avoided during my mission all interference with, or
even discussions about, your Federal or state finances, loans or
Tariffs. Until my return home I did not know that a Gentleman
had been sent to Europe by your Treasury to negotiate a loan.
This gentleman asked an interview with me but before the appointed day came round he returned home, despairing, I believe,
of success. I did not therefore see him, but I should certainly, if
I had seen him, have given him the best advice and assistance in
my power. But what I wish to observe upon is the very mistaken
notion which, if we mistake not, seems to have obtained that there
must have been some sort of combination among capitalists to
force some settlement of the state debts by refusing credit to the
federal government. I think you must know enough of the world
of business to know that this can have no foundation. Any single
individual losing half his fortune in state debts may object to risk
the other half with the general government,—but there can be
no combination among these capitalists, & any one would employ
his funds, if he could do so advantageously, without caring one
straw about what had happened to his neighbors. It is true that
the greater number do not discriminate; and Massachusetts—
New York—& federal credit, which in my opinion is as good
as any in the world, are mixed up in the public mind with Michigan, Missouri, &c. There is necessarily much ignorance but
there has not been, nor can there well be, any conspiracy.—I shall
be watching anxiously though with little personal interest, what
you do on this subject of credit. If you are wise you will set it
right as fast as you can, for your means for the purpose are
superabundant. Good credit is indispensable for a country acting
upon the wise principle of using it for emergencies only. At this
moment money is raising here for Canada with British guarantee,
at 108 p'c't for a 4 per cent stock. Your federal government
could borrow here any time at the same rate but for the late loose
practices. I wish our finances were on as sound a basis as yours.

might be; but then nobody, whatever may be the difficulty, talks or thinks of repudiation. All this however is as well known to you & to those about you as to me, so I will spare you further useless common place on the subject. My object in touching it at all was to explain the mistake about combinations & conspiracies.   *   *   *

ASHBURTON.

———

To John Quincy Adams.[1]

DEPARTMENT OF STATE January 9th, 1843

Sir:

In answer to your inquiries this morning, I have to say, that from the nature of the case, the Department is not able to give an exact estimate of the probable expenses, of a mission to China. The expense of repairing to the place, will, of course, exceed that of proceeding to a Court in Europe, a sum at least equal to that allowed Ministers at other Courts as an annual salary, it is presumed, will be deemed reasonable; the Commissioner, or Minister, will need the services of an American Secretary, and a Chinese Secretary or Interpreter; and what may be the extent, of necessary contingent disbursements cannot well be foreseen.

If the Committees and Congress see no objection to such a course, it appears to the Department that an appropriation of a sum, in gross, say $40,000 for the expenses of a mission to China, might be a useful mode of providing for the expenses of the mission at its inception.

I have the honor to be

Your obed. Servant,

DAN'L WEBSTER

———

(From John Tyler.)

[FEB. 1843][2]

Dr Sir

Sir Robert Peel's speech renders the publication of the cor-

———

[1] This letter is owned by Charles Francis Adams.
[2] The correspondence was submitted Feb. 24, 1843. See "Messages and Papers of the Presidents," vol. iv, p. 229. Peel's speech, which is referred to, must be the address of February 2, 1843, in which he comments on the President's message.

respondence with Cass more urgent. Every day's delay will injure us. Let the whole blast be at once over.

Y'r's.

J. TYLER

(To D. Fletcher Webster.)

[FEB. 1843]

My Dear Son,
    Let not the persons interested in the repeal of the Bankrupt
Law despair. Stand firm, all friends. Stronger gales than this
have been met with, & ridden out. If a repeal Bill comes to the
President, we shall see what we shall see.

Yrs   D. W.

(To Jared Sparks.[1])

MARCH 11, 1843.

    * * * As to the boundary subject, you understand it
well. What is likely to be overlooked by superficial thinkers is
the value of Rouse's Point. England will never visit us with an
army from Canada for the purpose of conquest; but if she had
retained Rouse's Point, she would at all times have access to Lake
Champlain, and might in two days place a force within two
days' march of the city of Albany. The defence of the country,
therefore, would require a large military force in that neighborhood. * * *

DANIEL WEBSTER.

(To Jared Sparks.[2])

MARCH 11, 1843,

    * * * As to the conduct of the negotiation, there is one
point on which I wish to speak to you very freely, even at the
hazard of a well-founded imputation of some vanity. The grand
stroke was to get the previous consent of Maine and Massachusetts.[3] Nobody else had attempted this; it had occured to

---

[1] Taken from the "Life and Writings" of Sparks, vol. ii, p. 413.
[2] Taken from Sparks' "Life and Works," vol. ii, p. 403.
[3] To the Northeastern Boundary agreement.

nobody else; it was a movement of great delicacy, and of very doubtful result. But it was made, with how much skill and judgement in the manner, you must judge; and it succeeded, and to this success the fortunate result of the whole negotiation is to be attributed. * * *

"You notice the great majorities with which, after all the high-sounding notes of opposition, the appropriations for the treaty passed both houses. There is probably no instance of a similar approach to unanimity. In the Senate four votes were found against it, in the House, about forty. * * *

D. WEBSTER.

(To Jared Sparks.[1])

MARCH 18, 1843:

* * * In the 'London Morning Chronicle' of February 6th you will find some observations about the map.[2] I am blamed, not for not showing the map, but for expressing confidence in the claim. Now, in my letter to Lord Ashburton I argued the question on the terms of the treaty, and you know that Lord Brougham has said the terms of the treaty sustained our rights; and I know that Lord Aberdeen has said the same thing, though I am not at liberty to say so publicly. Now, what is the value of the evidence of the map, such as it is, against the admitted plain sense of the treaty? Any lawyer would say 'Nothing.' * * *

DANIEL WEBSTER.

(To D. Fletcher Webster.)

APRIL 9, 1843.

Dear F:

I came down yesterday, & last eve' rec'd various things from you to which I shall attend as fast as possible. I wish the Despatch could be published extensively. I believe it will stand fire. All as usual here. Some signs of spring. Another *map* is found in N. Y. important to the right side.

Yrs   D. W.

---

[1] Taken from Sparks' "Life and Writings," vol. ii, p. 404.
[2] The famous "red line" map.

(To D. Fletcher Webster.)

Dear F.   APRIL 16 [1843]

Things look all right ab't China. Here is Mr. Warren Delano Jr. of Canton, a fine young man, going to China, in July, & wishes you to go with him, & *live at his house while you stay in China!*—& proposes other good things. Keep all this to yourself till I see you Tuesday.

                                        Yrs   D. W.

Don't let Brown have anymore money, till I go to W.

———

(To John Q. Adams.[1])

DEPARTMENT OF STATE

Dear Sir: WASHINGTON, May 7th, 1843

I observe an Amendment of the Bill making appropriation for the civil and diplomatic expenses of Government, has been adopted in the Senate, as a proviso for the appropriation for the contingent expenses of foreign intercourse in the following Words, viz: "And provided further that no part of this appropriation be applied, after the 1st July next, for compensation to separate Agents, appointed without the consent of the Senate; or any act of Congress authorizing it, for receiving or transmitting despatches (see House bill 74 as amended by the Senate, page 32 lines 827 to 831 inclusive.) I hardly know what is meant by *separate* agents and rather suppose the word intended to be used was *Diplomatic,* and that the word "or" should come in (line 830) before the words "for receiving it." It is to the latter part of this Amendment, that I have ventured to ask your attention, viz: so much as is embraced in the following words, "or for receiving or transmitting despatches." I take leave to send you a copy of a communication addressed by me yesterday, to the Chairman of the Committee of Ways and Means on this subject. I presume such a prohibition would hardly be enacted, under a full knowledge of the circumstances of the case, and the consequences of such a prohibition. I have ventured to hope, that, as your experience both in this Department, and abroad, has been such as to make you fully acquainted with the subject, you

---

[1] This letter is owned by Charles Francis Adams.

would take some pains to set the matter right in the House of Representatives. Should this amendment be adopted by the House, the charges usually arising from this part of the service, must either be transferred to other connected heads of appropriation, or serious obstruction would be likely to be met with in the modes of carrying on foreign correspondence, at an important moment in our affairs. You will see how repugnant this provision is, with all former appropriations under this head, and the constant practice of the Government; and with the law which authorizes the accounting officers of the Treasury to settle accounts of such appropriations upon the President's certificate alone.

I have the honor to be
> D'r Sir
> > Your obedient Servant,
> > > DAN'L WEBSTER.

(To Mr. Bigelow et al.[1])

WASHINGTON, Jan. 23, 1844.

Gentlemen:

Circumstances have not allowed me an opportunity, until the present moment, of answering your letter of the 18th of December.

In that letter, you expressed the belief that a proposition might probably be presented to Congress at its present session, for the annexation of Texas to the United States; and you desire to know my opinions on the constitutionality of such a message; its probable effect on the character and future action of our government; its tendency to promote the cause of freedom, or to strengthen the bonds of slavery; and, in general, the consequences which may justly be expected to result from the annexation to the United States of a large slave-holding country, not only to American liberty, American Industry, and the continuance of the Union itself, but, also, to the great cause of human knowledge, virtue and happiness, in the United States, in Texas, and throughout the world.

At the time when your letter was received, I indulged a strong hope that no such proposition would be made in Congress, or would proceed from any other quarter. I deem it quite unfortunate that a topic, so certain to produce great excitement, should

---

[1] This copy was taken from the original draft of the letter in Webster's hand.

be added to the other causes, operating at the present moment, to create diversities of public opinion.

As an intention has recently been manifested, however, of making the annexation of Texas to the United States a subject of discussion in Congress, I lose no time in answering your letter, and in complying with its request.   The answer is quite at hand.

In the early part of the year 1837, it was generally understood that a proposition was about to be made to the government of the United States for the annexation of Texas to the United States.   Having occasion, in March of that year, to address a political meeting in the City of New York, upon the interesting topics of the day, I could not, consistently with my sense of propriety and duty, abstain from a full expression of my sentiments on that subject.   I take liberty to transcribe the remarks then made by me.

(Extract.)[1]

I need hardly say that these opinions remain entirely unaltered.

Five months after these remarks were made, that is to say, on the 21st of August, 1837, the Minister of Texas, Mr. Memucan Hunt, addressed a letter to the Secretary of State of the United States, submitting a direct proposition for the annexation of Texas to the United States.   This letter recited, at much length, the history of the separation of Texas from Mexico, and set forth, very fully, the advantages, which it was supposed could accrue to the United States from that annexation.

On the 25th of August, Mr. Forsyth, the Secretary of State, answered this letter;—and the following is an extract from that answer.

(Extract.)[1]

From that time until quite recently, the subject has been withdrawn from public attention.   The war between Mexico and Texas is not yet concluded; although active hostilities have ceased, and a truce is understood to have been agreed upon.   In the meantime, Texas has maintained itself, as an independent sovereignty, and has extended its relations with the nations of the world.   If in the judgment of the government of the United States, there were insuperable objections, even to entertaining

---

[1] The extracts are not given in this draft, nor are they indicated by page or paragraph.

any negotiation on the subject of annexation, seven years ago, it seems to me that time and events have served only to strengthen such objections.

The Constitutional authority of Congress to admit new states into the Union, formed of Territories not belonging to any of the states, at the adoption of the present form of government, is an important point in your inquiries.

The Constitution of the U. S. provides that "New States may be admitted by the Congress into this Union but no new states shall be formed or erected within the jurisdiction of any other state; nor any state be formed by the junction of two or more states, or parts of states, without the consent of the legislature of the states concerned, as well as of the Congress."

It would seem very reasonable to confine this provision to states to be formed out of Territories already belonging to the United States, and in regard to which the old congress, by accepting the cession of territory from individual states, and agreeing to the proposed terms of cession, had already stipulated that they might be created and admitted into the Union. Any other conclusion would be forced, & immature; and would imply that the framers of the Constitution, & the People, were looking to the admission of their territories, although those which they then had were, one half a wilderness, & the other half very thinly peopled. It is not at all probable from the history of the states, from the circumstances in which they were placed in 1789, or from all that is to be learned of mens opinions and expectations at that day, that any idea was entertained, by any body, of bringing into the Union, at any time, states formed out of the territories of foreign power. Indeed much jealousy was felt towards the new Government, from fear of its over-bearing might & strength, when proposed to be established over the thirteen states. This jealousy, it is easy to believe, would have been heated into more decisive, & perhaps successful opposition, if it had been understood that projects of enlargement of boundaries, or Territorial aggrandizement had been among the objects contemplated by its establishment. And it is one of the unaccountable eccentricities, and apparent inconsistencies of opinion, that those who hold the Constitution of the United States to be a compact between States, should think, nevertheless, that the government created by that Constitution, is at liberty to introduce new states, formed out of foreign territory, with or without the consent of those, who are regarded as original parties.

By the Convention with France of the 30th April, 1803, Louisiana was ceded to the United States, with this condition, "The inhabitants of the ceded territory shall be incorporated in the union of the United States, and admitted as soon as possible, according to the principles of the federal constitution, to the enjoyment of all the rights, advantages, and immunities of citizens of the United States: and in the mean time they shall be maintained and protected in the free enjoyment of their liberty, property, and the religion which they profess."

It is now known to have been Mr. Jefferson's opinion, at the time, that an amendment of the Constitution was necessary, in order to carry this stipulation into effect; and it is known, also, that such was the opinion, ably and earnestly maintained by distinguished persons in the government. The treaty, however, was ratified. No amendment of the Constitution was proposed, and in 1812 Louisiana was admitted into the Union, as a state, upon the same footing as the original states. All branches of the government concurred in this act, and the Country acquiesced in it.

In the year 1819, a treaty, was concluded with Spain for the cession of Florida. This treaty followed the precedent of that with France, and contained this stipulation. "The inhabitants of the territories which his Catholic Majesty cedes to the United States, by this treaty, shall be incorporated in the Union of the United States, as soon as may be consistent with the principles of the federal constitution, and admitted to the enjoyment of all the privileges, rights and immunities, of the citizens of the United States."

Florida has not yet been admitted into the Union, but the treaty was ratified, the cession accepted, according to its terms, and the people, as well as the public authorities, have acquiesced in the contract, for twenty years, and given it the sanction of their approbation.

Louisiana and Florida, therefore, are settled cases. The admission of one, and the agreement to admit the other, at a proper time, are facts, are acts done, and as such must have their full effect. But it does not follow that they are precedents for the annexation of Texas. Important differences are pointed out, between the cases, in Mr. Forsyth's letter; and others might be suggested. But it is enough to say, that what has been done, on at best a very questionable right, and in a case of strong and urgent necessity, is no sufficient warrant for a similar proceeding, in a case in which no such necessity exists, and in which both the right and the expediency may be very properly considered, on the original and independent grounds belonging to them.

I am certainly of opinion, with Mr. Jefferson, Mr. Madison, Mr. J. Q. Adams, and other eminent men, that the Constitution never contemplated the admission of New States, formed out of the territories of foreign nations; and while I admit, that what has been done in regard to Louisiana and Florida, must now be considered as legally done, yet I do not admit the propriety of proceeding farther, and admitting, not a territory, ceded by a foreign nation, but a foreign nation itself, with all its obligations and treaties, its laws and its institutions, into the number of the States, which compose this Union.

The broad question proposed by you of the probable, general influence of the annexation of Texas, upon American liberty and industry, the continuance of our Union, and the Universal cause of knowledge, virtue, liberty, and happiness, is a question full of intense interest, and which suggests thoughts and reflections, well worthy to engage the deepest attention of intelligent minds. It is not to be doubted, that the continuance of the American Union, and its prosperity and success, under its present form of government, is a matter of high moment to all mankind. It is one of the most cherished hopes and reliances of that universal cause of which you speak, the cause of human knowledge, virtue, liberty, and happiness. And he is a bolder reasoner than I am, who has satisfied himself that this government may be continued indefinitely, either to the North or to the South, without endangering its stability, and its duration. It is true, that under the beneficent operation of the practical principle of maintaining local government for local purposes, and confiding general interests to the general government, the ends of political society are capable of being fulfilled, by the same free and popular system, and the same administration, over a large portion of the earth. This is the result of our experience; but our experience is the only instance of such a result. A monarchical and arbitrary government, may extend itself to the full limit of its military means. Under such a government, society is kept together by pressure from above, by weight of the Government itself, and the strength of its arm. But how obvious it is, that in free, elective systems, the political society exists and coheres, & must exist and cohere, not by superincumbent pressure on its several parts, but by the internal and natural attraction of those parts; by the assimilation of interests and of feelings; by a sense of common country, common political family, common character, fortune and destiny. Not only the organization of such systems, but also their continuance by means of periodical popular elections, necessarily requires intercourse, mutual conference and understanding, and a general acquaintance among those who are to unite in such elections. When individuals are to be selected for high situations in government, and to exercise an influence over the happiness of all, it would seem indispensable, that a general, if not a universal confidence should be inspired, by knowledge of their character, their virtues and patriotism. It certainly may be very well questioned, with how much of mutual intelligence, and how much of a spirit of conciliation and harmony, those who live on the St Lawrence and the St John would be expected in sincerity, to unite in the choice of a President, with the inhabitants of the Banks of the Rio Grande de Norte and the Colorado. It is evident, at least, that there must be some boundary, or some limits, to a Republic, which is to have a common centre. Free and ardent speculation may lead to the indulgence of an idea, that such a Republic may be extended over a whole hemisphere. On the other hand, minds less sanguine, or more chastened by the examples of history, may fear, that extension often produces weakness, rather than strength; and that political attraction, like other attractions, is less and less powerful, as the parts become more and more distant. In this difference, between ardent speculations, and cautious fears, it seems to me to be the truest wisdom to abide by the present state of things; acknowledged, since that state of things is on all hands, to be singularly happy, prosperous and honorable. In all points of view, therefore, in which I can regard the subject, my judgment is decidedly unfavorable to the project of annexing Texas to the United States. "We have a Sparta," said the old Greek; "Let us embellish it."

We have a Republic, Gentlemen, of vast extent & unequalled natural advantages; a Republic, full of interest in its origin, its history, its present conditions, & its prospects for the future. Instead of aiming to enlarge its boundaries, let us seek, rather, to strengthen its Union, to draw out its resources, to maintain & improve its institutions of Religion & Liberty, & then to push it forward in its career of prosperity & glory.

I am, Gentlemen, with most true regard, your obliged friend

D. WEBSTER

(To Peter Harvey(?).)

WASHINGTON Feby 13, 1845 Thursday morning
Dear Sir

I have leisure enough, at present, to write to friends, if I knew anything to be told, in regard to passing events. There seems no certainty as to what is to happen here within the next fortnight, although there are surmises & conjections, in plenty, & perhaps, on some points, there are probabilities. The new president is expected today, &, in due time, he will of course, solve mysteries, so far as he is concerned. As to the Cabinet the general impression now is, that it will be *new*, from top to toe. I think that very probable, as discrimination would be invidious, & I believe all the present incumbents are quite willing to serve their country still longer.

The Texas debate, begins in the Senate today. In all probability, the result will be postponement, & a provision for further negotiation. It is said Genl. Jackson does not like the proposed form of annexation. He says it is a *whig* measure, & Texas must stay out till she can get better terms.

There is no doubt some degree of truth in this; & very likely Mr. Bentons plan suits the General better than the pending resolutions. Oregon remains as it was. I think the measure will stop in the Senate. There is no more of the session remaining. than will suffice for the debate on Texas, & the passing of the necessary appropriation bills. Mr. Calhouns friends, what few there are of them, will be for laying Oregon on the table. On the other hand, some Western whigs may feel obliged to vote for the measure. It seems understood, that the English minister has made sundry propositions, *but has rec'd none* among others he has offered an arbitration, leaving it in the option of the United States to designate, out of all the Governments of Europe, that one, which shall arbitrate, itself, or appoint arbitration. I believe I shall take advantage of a few days leisure to go north as far as N. Y.

Yrs very truly

D. WEBSTER.

P. S. The last edition of the "Cabinet" seems to stand thus
Mr. Calhoun—State to remain for some time or else Mr. Walker.

Gov. Marcy Treas.

Wm. V. Butler Ken.—war. It may be A. J. Donaldson.

Franklin Pierce N. H. Navy.

Romulus Grundy, or Cave Johnson—P. M. G.

———

(To Peter Harvey.)

My Dear Sir   N. Y. Feb. 18, '45.

I shall take care of Mr. John Wards Drft.

I do not know exactly how the Court was divided in Milne[1] case. Judge Story, I have no doubt, held the Mass. acts void, & so must every other constitutional Lawyer. I never knew anything about these laws, till I looked into the case at Washington; & was quite surprised, at their provisions, & their apparent repugnance to acts of Congress. Every thing may be said of them, which Massachusetts says agt. S. Carolina. I shall not leave this City, probably, before Monday.

Yrs.   D. W.

———

(To D. Fletcher Webster.)

Dear F.   MAR. 2. [1845]

I arrived last night. I think I shall be able to write you good news about your little affair, tomorrow. Perhaps Mr. Curtis may write today. I begged him to inquire of Mr. Evans, & give you notice.

Love to C. & the babies.

Yrs.   D. W.

I have read your letter, & shall write abt its contents tomorrow.

Luchanan, for State Walker for treasury— So much is certain

———

(To D. Fletcher Webster.)

Dear Fletcher   [MARCH 1845] Saturday 3 o'clock

Mr. Bates is much as yesterday. No *worse*. Dr. Parker[2] confirmed, tho' not without some *wriggling*.

---

[1] Milne vs. City of New York, vol. xi, Peters' Reports. See the letter of Daniel Webster to J. Prescott Hall in Curtis' "Life of Webster," vol. ii, p. 374.

[2] Dr. Peter Parker, appointed secretary and interpreter to the American legation, China.

There is a good deal of coolness between "brethren of the same principle," That is evident.

Yrs

D. W.

(To D. Fletcher Webster.)

MONDAY MORG Mar. 3. [1845]

My Dear Son

I wrote you a hasty note yesterday. I now find, that a proper communication was sent to the com^{ee}. of the Senate, from the State Department, respecting the arrears of the China Mission. A proposition of appropriation was inserted, by the Senate, as an amendment to the Civil & Diplomatic Bill, from the H. of R. This item, with other amendments of the Senate, was disagreed to, by the H. of R.—& a com^{ee}. of conference appointed. The Comee. on the part of the House is Mc. Kay, Dromgoole, & that amiable person, Garrett Davis.— On the part of the Senate, Evans, Barrow, & Benton.

The Committee met yesterday, & agreed on some points, & left this undecided. The Gentlemen of the House opposed it, for no other reason but general opposition, so far as I can learn. —They meet again today. Mr. Evans will do what he can, & I have also written a note to Mr Barrow— I have also despatched a note to Mr. Cushing, who does not know what has been done, suggesting to him the necessity of paying some attention to the matter.—

I know not what the result will be—

I saw Mr. Cushing yesterday. He said he had recently filed 2 Despatches, to do up the business of his mission, one, to set forth the obligations he was under to the other Gentlemen of the Mission; & one, to discharge a similar duty towards the Naval officers.

I will go to the office the first opportunity, to look at the first of those; & also to inquire about the letter of instructions, &c.—

Mr. Bancroft[1] came on, yesterday, & they say it is settled, that he is to be Sec. of the Navy.

D. WEBSTER

---

[1] George Bancroft, the historian.

(To D. Fletcher Webster.)

WASHINGTON Mar 5. 1845.

Dear Fletcher

It was impossible to get your appropriation thro' with all our efforts.

In the first place, the recommendation from the Department, tho' well enough, was not entirely *specific,* & this gave the enemy a handle.—

In the next place Mr Kay & Garret Davis were obstinate as mules, & bitter as possible. Mr. Cushing went to see Mr Kay, & the latter *promised* to withdraw opposition, but broke his promise. Mr. Curtis, Mr. Crittenden, Evans, Choate, &c did what they could—but to no purpose—

It is no great matter. The only evil is delay. You may want the money next year, perhaps, as much as this. Mr. Cushings reference to you, in his despatch is in these words, or very nearly

"Mr. Fletcher Webster, as Secretary of the Mission,[1] was of great & important service, not only in the discharge of the ordinary duties of his office, but also by the performance of several official duties, which the peculiar nature of the negotiation, made necessary."

He says he is very sorry the Drawings have not arrived, so that you could have them, & expressed the greatest readiness to furnish any thing he could, to your use—

I fear our session will be longer than I expected. They say it will take Mr. Polk a week to find out what is the actual condition of things, as left by Mr Tyler.

Yrs truly

D. WEBSTER

The Instructions, letters &c—were sent from the Department to the President—whether he sent them to the Senate, I do not yet know— I will enquire about the matter today.

———

(To D. Fletcher Webster.)

MONDAY NOON IN SENATE [Mar. 9, 1845]

Dear Son

The instructions &c are in the President's hands—I will send a copy as soon as possible.

———

[1] To China.

It is said Mr Polk means to give Mr. Almonté as mild & amiable an answer as possible.

Yrs affectionately

D. W.

————

(To Fletcher Webster.[1])

[MAR. 11. 1845]

R. M. Armstrong of Tennessee, said to be a respectable man, will be consul at Liverpool.

—A Mr *Davis* is to be Surveyor of the Port of Phila. in place of Mr *Cooper*

—So much for Mr Polk's *gratitude* to Mr. Tyler.

————

(To D. Fletcher Webster.)

WASHINGTON Mar. 12. 1845

Dear Fletcher,

It is certain that a considerable degree of dissatisfaction prevails with a certain portion of Mr Polk's supporters at the Cabinet arrangements, & other appointments, made or expected.

At the head of the aggrieved, stands Mr Calhoun. Mr. Calhoun professes to be greatly delighted with an opportunity of returning to Private Life; but nevertheless makes no secret of his feelings, as to the *manner* in which it has seemed fit to others, that he should relinquish the seals of office. He thinks that manner, unkind, discourteous, & even decidedly disrespectful. The two Carolina Senators are equally disaffected, & Mr Woodbury, probably, is behind neither, as he seems very much neglected. He is the more disturbed, I think, at seeing Mr Allen of Ohio putting forth pretensions to be considered as *Leader* of the Party, in the Senate.

I doubt, however, whether there be enough of dissatisfaction to make anything like a *breach*, at present. Mr Calhoun's area is a very small one, almost wholly confined to South Carolina, & Mr Woodbury is not followed much at the North.—

Mr. Polks Inaugural says nothing of the existing *Tariff Law,* viz the Act of 1842.— But it is certain, some modifications, or alterations, will be recommended by Mr. Walker, at the Com-

---

[1] Unsigned, but in Daniel Webster's hand.

mencement of the next Session.   Taking this for granted, I think our friends, who are interested in the preservation of the system, may very well take some steps, during the summer, to produce just impressions, by communicating facts & information to the Secretary—   Mr Walker is a good tempered & accessible man; he professes to be no general enemy to protection; a Pennsylvanian, by birth & education, he is not without sympathies with the good people of that State.   He is new in office, ardent, & sanguine; & like other persons of that temperament, & in that situation, hopes, confidently, that he may be able in some manner, to reconcile jaring interests and opposing opinions.   Care ought to be taken, that while getting his materials, & before making up his report to Congress, he should be put in possession of full and accurate information.   I think, that the Gentlemen, concerned in manufactures, should, through the aid of a Com^{ee}, or by some other agency, set to work, at once, to prepare a View, or Statement, showing the operation of the Law of 1842 upon the principal manufactures, and what parts of it might be altered, & to what extent, without injury.   I am sure he would receive such a communication very kindly.   If you have opportunity, you may suggest this, to Mr Appleton, Mr Paige, or other friends.

After the receipt of this, you may address me at the A. H. New York—

I hear from Mrs Bates, that Mr Bates was a little easier last night, but that there was no material change.

Yours affectionately
DANIEL WEBSTER

(To D. Fletcher Webster.)

Dear Fletcher   New York Mar: 24. 1845.

I left Washington Thursday afternoon, the 20th, immediately on the adjournment of the Senate   No great political event occurred, after Mr Almonté's[1] demand of his Passports; & it will be two months before we can learn how Mexico takes the Resolution for Annexation.   In the mean time, recent information would seem to show that Texas herself is not too anxious for the proposed espousal as she was expected to be.   I am not surprised at this intelligence; for I had reason to know, before I left Washington, the Govt. was quite apprehensive, on this point.

---

[1] The Mexican Minister.

One great stimulating agency, in the Annexation subject, was the interested activity of the holders of Texas Stocks. The stipulation agt. paying her debts has of course cooled the zeal of these persons.

It is time, that Mr Tyler, in eager haste, sent off a despatch, announcing the determination of our Govt. to act under the first Branch of the Resolutions, & to bring Texas finally in by an act of the two Houses. This was done, under a belief common to most people, & fully expressed by Mr Calhoun, that if *negotiations* were entered into, under the second branch, Texas could not come in by Treaty, & so not without the consent of two thirds the Senate. But I have reason to believe that in this opinion Mr. Buchanan differs from Mr Calhoun; & that it is the determination of the President and the present Administration to bring Texas in by law, a joint Resolution of both Houses, whether Texas accepts the old terms, or negotiates for new.

So it is likely there will be a struggle in either House, next session.

The President will send somebody soon to Mexico; but whether a sole minister, or a joint mission, I do not think is yet decided. I should not be surprised if Mr Cushing should be employed on that service. The China mission has given him reputation, & he has one point of qualification, not found in everyone, that is, a knowledge of the language. You will receive this as my conjecture, only; but my opinion is, that such an appointment is very probable.—

I recd your letters here; rejoice that you are all well; & expect to be in Boston in two or three days.

Yrs affectionately
DANL WEBSTER

(*From John C. Spencer.*[1])

Hon. Daniel Webster   Albany, June 5, 1845.

Dear Sir,

* * * I feel peculiar pride and exultation in the masterly and incontrovertible vindication it [the Treaty of Washington] has received from the only man who was capable of exhibiting its difficulties and its vast importance.

---

[1] John C. Spencer represented New York in Congress, was Secretary of War under Tyler, and later Secretary of the Treasury. He was a prominent lawyer and achieved fame in the work of revision of the laws of New York.

And yet, you will pardon me for saying that there was one ·branch of the difficulties and obstacles to a successful termination of that negotiation, which *you* have not noticed, and which you could not well notice, altho the ability, temper and tact required to overcome them—were at least equal to what was demanded by the adroitness of Lord Ashburton and the skill of the British ministry. I allude to the organized opposition then existing in the State of Maine, to any surrender of territory, stimulated by a party, with which you could have no political association, and no influence;—and also to the position of the Senate,—nearly one half of the members ranging themselves with a party which certainly felt under no political obligations to you for its recent defeat at the Presidential election,—and the other half, with two or three exceptions, boiling with rage because you would not desert the country to avenge the quarrels or minister to the ambition of Mr Clay. And two thirds of these men were to be conciliated and bro't to support a Treaty which was to place the *cope*-stone on the pillar of your renown! I well know how you dealt with these refractory spirits and how they were bro't in one one by one to sustain a measure which most of them would gladly have defeated. You had four parties to negotiate with,—the British Ambassador, the State of Maine, the Senate of the United States and the President. The third in this Series was the most difficult to deal with. That part of the negotiation, I suppose never can be written. If it could be, in my opinion it would command the applause and gratitude of your countrymen in a greater degree than any other part.

I am very glad to hear that Mr. Tyler has done you and himself justice in the matter of the Secret Service fund, and that this calumny at least is likely to recoil on the head of its inventor.

With great respect

Your most obedt. Servt.

J. C. SPENCER.

———

(*To D. Fletcher Webster.*)

Dear F.   JUNE 21—[1845] Sunday 1 O clock

It may be that Ld Aberdeen gave a hint to Mr. McLane of a readiness to *mediate*, but I do not suppose that Mr. Pakenham is authorized here, to make such an offer.[1]

---

[1] Alludes to the Oregon controversy.

Since writ'g you yesterday, I have thought it would be best to go to Marshfield, on friday, *by the 9 Oclock Boat*—& have written to Mr. Weston to that effect. So, on arriv'g, I shall probably go to Tremont H. for breakfast.

D. W.

(From Henry Wheaton.)

BERLIN, 26 Nov. 1845

My Dear Sir,
As you will before this reaches you have taken your Seat in the Senate, I write these hasty lines merely to call your attention to two matters which will come before that body in the Executive Council at the opening of the Session—
The first is the Treaty of Extradition with Germany[1] which was concluded here in January last, with some few alterations in your original *project* arranged with von Boenne (?) on which (though I had no doubt myself) I consulted our Government, & under its instructions adopted them— As it is substantially the same arrangement with your treaty with Lord Ashburton, I presume it will encounter no difficulty in the Ratification— Any correspondence relating to it ought to be communicated with the Treaty, & if anything should be accidently omitted, you will (of course) call for it— The correspondence fully explains the nature and object of the alterations, which though not very important you will perhaps think real improvement— They were suggested by the Prussian " *Justice-Minister*,"—to make use of a Jeremy Bentham term—
The second matter to which I refer is a little Convention between the U. States & Saxony for the mutual abolition of the Droit d'Aubaine & taxes on Emigration in the two Countries[2]— This treaty is one of a Series on the same Subject which I have negotiated with different German States, 20 which have already been ratified by the Senate. It differes in one particular, from the others in giving a little more power to the subject of Saxony as to purchasing & holding lands in the U. States in return for the abolition of taxes on emigration by which we gain in the amount of capital brought over by the emigrants. This is a matter of more importance than might be supposed, as the number of emigrants is constantly increasing, consisting of rich

---

[1] See Treaties and Conventions, p. 45.   [2] Ibid., p. 981.

peasants, who bring with them several millions of florins— The point is fully explained in my Despatch accompanying the Convention to which I beg leave to refer you, & to request you to explain the matter to the Senate when the question comes up.   *   *   *

I have the honor to be ever truly your obliged friend,

H. WHEATON.

(*To D. Fletcher Webster.*)

DEC. 11. 45 Thursday Eve'

My Dear Son

I arrived last night, just in time to bear my part in the argument of my first cause. Today I have been in Court, all day, excepting 15 minutes in the Senate.— I shall speak either tomorrow or Monday. It is an important cause from N. Y. respecting the State tax on passengers—

I have seen nobody except the Senators, & the Court.

Friends in the Senate were glad to see me, as they look for important business soon. They seemed sober. As soon as I learn anything, I will write you. As yet, I have seen & heard but little, out of the Court room.— I am at Ademan's—& well lodged for the present.

Yrs

D. W.

(*To D. Fletcher Webster.*)

PHILADELPHIA,

Hartwell, No. 13 Dec. 25. 1845 Christmas Day, 4 o'clock in the Morning.

Dear Fletcher

I arrived here last evening, & write this, that I may put it into the mail, at N. Y. if I get there in season this P. M. If the weather be mild, I mean to go to Boston on Saturday. But I shall write you more fully tomorrow. Court duties will call me back immediately; but I must see You, & if storms & tempests prevent me from getting to Boston, you must be prepared to come South & find me where you can.

I hope Caroline and the Children are well, & all happy. My own health is excellent. Let Mr Healey know that I am *in itinere*.
                        Yrs affectionately
                                        DANL. WEBSTER
F. W.
    Remember me, at 30 Winter Street, & 63 Summer Street. I hope you will all enjoy, with grateful hearts, a happy Christmas. Kiss the whole circle for me.

———

(*To D. Fletcher Webster.*)

                                        JAN. 12. '46
Dear F.
    I have recd the answer—signed it, sworn to it before Judge Nelson, & dispatched it.
    I also hear from N. Y. that the expected letter has gone to Boston.
                        Yrs   D. W.
    In Senate today, Allen *notice*[1] put off, till Feb. 10.
    Ayes 32. Noes 18—a pacific augury.

———

(*To Nathan Appleton.*)
PRIVATE.
                        WASHINGTON, Jany 12, '46.
My dear Sir.
    I cannot learn any particular reason, which has induced the Intelligencer to retract its *confidence*, in the continuance of peace. I have seen Mr. Gales today. He seems vexed at the " ruffian spirit " as he deems it, manifested in the H. of R. You will see that the Senate has postponed the subject, by ayes & noes to Feby. 10, by a majority of 14. 2 or 3 of our friends being absent, viz Morehead, Huntington, & I think one other. My own opinion is that there is not at this moment, a majority greater than 5 or 10 in the H. of R. the future may and will, probably, much depend on what we hear by the next Steamer. There is, certainly, rather a sober feeling on the subject, prevalent with the majority,—of the Senate. If things remain as they are, no

—————

[1] Concerning the famous charges of Allen against Webster's honesty while in charge of the Department of State under Tyler.

resolution to give notice will pass this body, at present, at least.

Something is in progress, on the point which I mentioned to you, but what may be its success I cannot say. There is not *perfect* temper on either side. Mr. B[1] is cold, stern, repulsive, & not very gentle. Mr. P.[2] seems nettled, & a little excited. He seems to think his antagonists sharp, captious, & not always quite respectful. I have had several conversations with Mr. C.[3] He is not likely to change his course.

Yrs truly
DANL WEBSTER

(To D. Fletcher Webster.)

JAN: 14. 46

My Dear Son,

Yrs was recd this morning, stating the receipt of the N. Y. letter. Mr B. & Mr Curtis are now here. I can only say I shall be infinitely obliged, if matters can be brought at once to a successful close.

Mr Polk said to a friend of mine last night, *that he had not the slightest apprehension of war.* The administration must either have some assurances from Mr Mc Lane, of the absolute disposition of England to keep the peace under all circumstances, (which I do not believe) or else it must have a curious notion of the tendency of its own measures, & the declaration & speeches of its own friends.

Still, I do not believe there will be war. Mr Allen's *non interference* Resolution was laid on the Table, today.

Yrs affectionately

D. W.

Pray write me daily, the more especially as your family are not well.

(To Nathan Appleton.)

WASHINGTON, Jany 20, 1846.
Tuesday Ev'g

PRIVATE.

My dear Sir,

The news from England has undoubtedly had some effect here. It is generally considered that the new ministry, especially if

---

[1] Buchanan. [2] Polk. [3] Probably Calhoun.

Lord Palmerston should take the seals of the foreign office, will probably be less pacific towards us than Sir Robt. Peel's govt.— I think it has been clear for 3 or 4 days, that the debate in the house begins to falter & lose interest. I do not think the violence exhibited there altogether pleasing to Mr. Polk. He seems to have expected that he would have been indulged in a *monopoly* of patriotic professions & self gratification. I am quite sure that he & some of his cabinet feel quite uneasy, at the present moment, in view of the blaze which they themselves have kindled.

You are now probably wiser than we are as the Steamer will be likely to have arrived. I look with great interest to the state of things in England. What is to be Sir Roberts relation to the new ministry? Can he go with Lord John for the repeal of the Corn laws, without separating himself from the conservative party, entirely? I confess I regret his retirement. I fear it will be long before a wiser, abler, or better man will be at the head of English affairs. In regard to a private matter, which I intimated something of to you, in Boston, I can now say, that *something* has been done, which can hardly fail to be useful, hereafter & done just in time, as the news of yesterday might have prevented it. We are in the midst of a very heavy fall of snow.

D. W.

(To D. Fletcher Webster.)

JAN. 27. [1846] Tuesday 3 o clock

Dear Fletcher,

The most important occurrence of today is, I think, Mr Bentons Speech against Mr Fairfield's Navy Bill. Mr. B. denounces the measure, as a war weapon, when, as he insists, *all indications are for peace.*

His Speech will have some effect, I think, & give the war party trouble.

I believe Mr Buchanan will leave the Cabinet, & go upon the Bench. There is—certainly—a difference between him & the President. The latter is much the most pacific. Probably Mr. Mason, at present Atty Genl, will take Mr Buchanans place. Everything looks more and more like *peace*— But then comes the great struggle about the Tariff.

Yrs truly

D. W.

(To Nathan Appleton.)

PRIVATE.

JANY 29. Thursday 2 o'clock

My dear Sir.

We grow daily more pacific. Mr. Spaight has, today, followed up Mr. Benton, & Mr. Bagley in a decided anti-war speech. He denies that our title to all Oregon is plain; says England has rights there which must be respected, &c. I imagine the Cabinet is projecting something, or considering some offer. The altered tone of the Union is remarkable; or would be, if it did [not] so frequently vibrate from side to side. Two equally pacific speeches in the H. of R. today, Mr. Holmes & Mr. Ewing, the new member from Tennessee. I wish I felt no more alarm about the *Tariff*, than I do at the present moment about *war*.

Yrs truly

DANL. WEBSTER.

(From Lord Ashburton.)

LONDON, Jan. 1846

My Dear Mr Webster.

Mr Spencer Ponsonby the son of my old & good friend Lord Roxborough is about to visit Washington where he will probably be connected with our Legation. He is himself an amiable steady & intelligent young man and I am anxious that he should have the advantage of being known to you. Excuse therefore my giving him these few lines of introduction.—

Mr Ponsonby will explain to you, as far as a young Diplomatist dare explain any thing, the strange confused condition of parties here. Six weeks ago I should have said that my friend Peel was the strongest Minister this Country ever had, and was likely to hold the Government for life or at least till he was tired of it, but the scene has changed, a conspiracy called the Anti-corn Law League has frightened men who should have had better nerves, and some Coxcombs called Political Economists have turned the heads of our younger people and we are throwing overboard all protections & running a race of what is called free trade, surrounded as we are by nations who like yours will have no free trade with us. I am very much opposed to all this, and hold mainly to the doctrines of your speech in Faneuil Hall on your Tariff, but the measure is likely to pass from a singular combination of passions & interests which it would take me a much longer letter to explain than you would like to read. In the conflict however the ministry will probably be shipwrecked, our whigs, who stoutly support free trade, will take the first opportunity to trip them up while the anger & disappointment of their own friends will render the task easy. This is my speculation and the only opposite chance is that there is no man or set of men having sufficiently the confidence of the Country to take their place. In the meantime all interests are flourishing & prosperous, and I need not tell you that we are pacific if you will let us be so, for though we care as little, or probably less, than your men of sense do about Oregon we cannot afford to be kicked.—

This Oregon dispute was mainly invented before we settled the Maine boundary, and when it is closed some new grievance will soon be opened. As long as we are neighbors on the great Continent which you begin to think should wholly belong to you we shall never really be friends, and I have long wished we could find a decent Excuse to let the work of Annexation be completed.—

Pray let me occasionally hear from you my Dear Sir & present my very best respect to Mrs Webster.

Yours ever

ASHBURTON.

'(To John Tyler.)

WASHINGTON Mar: 5. 1846

My Dear Sir,

You have probably seen a very extraordinary statement, made by Mr. C. J. Ingersol, in a speech in the H. of R. on the 8th or 9th of February, respecting communications from me to Gov. Seward, in the Spring of 1841 relative to the affair of McLeod.

I have no recollection of having written any private letter to Govr. Seward, on that occasion; yet I may have done so; but I am sure never such a letter as Mr. Ingersol states.

I must, at an early day, take some notice of these remarks. I think I should not have written any thing to Gov. Seward, private or public, on such a subject without first showing it to you, or to Genl. Harrison, if before his death. I beg now to inquire what you recollect, or whether you recalled any thing connected with the subject.

I wish also, particularly, to inquire whether the correspondence between Yourself & Gov. Seward, relative to Mr Spencer's acting as McLeod's counsel, &c &c was left in the Department of State or was retained by you. If left in the Department I think of calling for copies of it, if you see no objection. I remember we all were of opinion that you answered the Govr's Complaints, very satisfactorily.

I am, My Dear Sir, with continued good feelings. & good wishes, Yours truly

DAN WEBSTER

(From John Tyler.)

SHERWOOD FOREST Chs City County Va. *March 12, 1846*
My Dear Sir;
Your letter of the 5th March did not reach me until last night, and I delay not a moment in answering it— I have not the slightest recollection of your having written any letter to Gov. Seward during the pendency of the McLeod case— During your absence from Washington on a short visit to Boston a letter was received by me, in my official character, from Gov. Seward asking me to forbid Mr. Spencer, the U. S. D. Attorney for Western New York, from appearing in the defence of Mc Leod— I did not deem it necessary to await your return to Washington and answered the Governor's letter under my own signature— This led the way to a correspondence of some length between us, which as it related to a public matter and one at the time of much interest, I deemed it best to have placed among the files of the Department of State—where it no doubt is now to be found, and is subject to the call of any Senator—

Mr Ingersoll's remarks in the House escap'd my observation, but upon seeing Mr. Dickenson's statement in the Senate, I was upon the point of writing to you and requesting a call for my correspondence with Gov. Seward but was rendered silent by the knowledge of your presence in the Senate and my belief that you would best understand what the exigency of the moment might require— My desire is that the call should be made.

Concerning the whole of that business the administration of which I was the head, has nothing to fear— The peace of the Country when I reached Washington, on the 6th day of April 1841, was suspended by a thread, but we converted that thread

into a chain cable of sufficient strength to render that peace se-
cure, and to enable the Country to weather the storms of faction
by which it was in every direction assailed—
With some regard,
I am Dr Sir Yrs &c
JOHN TYLER

(To Robert C. Winthrop.[1])

NEW YORK March 20th (1846)
Dear Sir,
   I have read this morning your speech upon "Oregon" & can
not omit to say how much it gratified me.   Mr. Ingersoll I think
is well paid off; nor does his countryman in the other end of the
Capitol appear to be fareing much better.
   There is a good deal of panic here about Texas—   It is well
the country took the alarm when it did, as there is more hope of
stopping the progress of the measure than if it had proceeded
farther.   From what I see in the American this P. M. a Mr.
Todd, bearer of despatches seems to have been a good deal
talkative on his road home.
   I shall be quite glad to hear from you especially if anything
important touching Texas should become known.—
Yours truly
D. WEBSTER

(William H. Seward to R. M. Blatchford.[2])

AUBURN March 23d 1846.
My Dear Blatchford,
   Although I have been some days at home, I have not until now
been able to look into the matter arising from Mr. Ingersoll's
Speech.
   I suppose Mr. Webster may have spoken long before this, and
therefore these papers may be unnecessary.   If he had written to
me directly I should cheerfully have furnished him with any information in my power,—and of course you can state to him the
contents of this.

---

[1] The Massachusetts orator and statesman.   He represented the State in
both Senate and House of the United States Congress.
[2] Mr. Blatchford was one of Webster's warmest friends, and the latter was
evidently sounding Seward through the former.

The points in Mr. Ingersoll's remarks touching Mr. Webster are 1. That Mr. Webster wrote the Governor of New York a letter, marked "private", in which the Governor was told that he must release McLeod or see the magnificent commercial emporium, the City of New York laid in ashes—

2d. The Governor asked when this would be done? The reply was, Forthwith—Steam force will undoubtedly destroy N. Y. if McLeod be not released. But said the Governor the power of pardon is vested in me and even if he be convicted he may be pardoned. Oh no! said the Secretary, If you ever try him you will bring destruction upon yourselves— The Governor was not entirely driven from his course by this representation.

3d. The next step taken by the Administration was to appoint a District Attorney who was to be charged with the defence of Alexander McLeod (Spencer)—and a fee of $5,000. was put into his hands for this purpose.

4th. The application to the New York Supreme [Court] for a habeas corpus, by Spencer, to discharge Alex McLeod.

5th. The Marshall was about to let him go when he was told by the Court that if he did so it should be at his peril &c

6th. The passage of the Act of Congress, taking away from the State Courts Jurisdiction in Cases like McLeod's.

The Assembly of this State on the 18th of May 1841, called on me for the correspondence with the Federal Executive in the case of Alexander McLeod, and for information whether any arrangements whatever had been entered into by the Executive with the Federal Executive, in reference to that person.— This Resolution will be found on the Assembly Journal of 1841 at page 1228—

McLeod was then before the Supreme Court, on a Habeas Corpus,

On the 19th of May 1841, I replied to the Resolution by a Message of that date— Assembly Document 1841 No. 292.

I stated in the message that no arrangement whatever, of any kind, or for any purpose, had been entered into by the Executive Department of this State with the Executive of the United States, concerning McLeod.

I informed the Legislature that McLeod was then before the Supreme Court on a writ of Habeas Corpus, with a view to his discharge from costody— That I had no knowledge or information concerning the application for the writ, or the proceedings thereon, except what had been read from the newspapers—

That the proceedings first became known to me when the prisoner passed through the City of Albany on his way to N. Y. City in custody of the Sheriff in obedience to the writ of habeas corpus—

That the Attorney General of this State was thereupon immediately instructed to resist the motion for the discharge of the Prisoner, and at the same time I had remonstrated with the President of the United States against the appearance of the District Attorney of the United States as Counsel for the Prisoner— And the Attorney General of N. Y. was then attending the Court.

23 pages accompanied the Message—

No 1. The letter of the Governor to the Chief Justice of N. Y. dated Feb 15, 1841, requesting him to hold the Court of Oyer and Terminer to try McLeod.

. No 2. A letter from Mr. Forsyth, Secretary of State under Mr. Van Buren, to the Governor, transmitting the original correspondence between Mr. Fox and Mr. Forsyth, of December 1840—

These letters are Nos. 3, 4, 5, 6, 7, 8,

No. 9, was a letter of the Governor to Mr. Forsyth, Feb. 27, 1841, approving the decision of the President (Van Buren) in regard to McLeod, and pledging the State to support that position.

No 10, A Letter from John Bell, Secretary of War to the Governor transmitted by Major General Scott, directing him to make a requisition of troops to keep peace on the frontier.

11. The Governor's reply to the Secretary of War complying with the requisition for troops.

12. A Letter from the Chief Justice of N. Y. March 15, 1841, saying that the trial of McLeod was unavoidably postponed—

13. A Letter from the Governor to the Chief Justice—

14. Letter from same to General Scott—

15. Letter to the Attorney General at Lockport March 18, 1841.

16. A Letter from the Governor to Mr. Webster, informing him that McLeod's trial would not come on at that term of Court.

17. A Letter from the Governor to Mr. Webster, dated March 22, 1841 after Mr. Crittenden's visit on consultation with him, and referring to the renewed demand of the British Government for the surrender of McLeod—and reaffirming the previous determination of the Governor on that subject.

No. 18, 19, Report of Willis Hall Attorney General, and Letter of the Governor to Mr. Webster, transmitting it to him?—
No. 20. A letter from the Governor to the President of the U. S. protesting against Joshua A. Spencer (Dist. Atty. U. S.) appearing in behalf of McLeod in Supreme Court.
No. 21. The President Tyler's reply.
No. 22. Correspondence with Lord Lyndenham.

When I was in New York City early in March 1841, Mr. Fillmore met me there on his way home from Congress, told me he was requested by Mr. Webster to hurry on to meet me, and see whether I, with Mr. John C. Spencer (Secretary of State of N. Y.), could not devise some plan to get McLeod discharged— He told me that despatches had been received by Mr. Fox from his government, and their effect communicated by Mr. Fox to Mr. Webster, which was that war would follow a refusal to discharge McLeod, and that conditional instructions were already understood to have been given to a squadron then on or near the Coast. Mr. Fillmore told me Mr. Crittenden the Attorney General of the United States would be in Albany in a few days charged to communicate on the part of the Government of the United States with me—
I proceeded to Albany and found there a letter from Mr. Webster, marked "Private", dated March 17th 1841,
I send you a copy of this letter
Mr. Crittenden arrived at the same time—say March 21, or 22— He held a consultation with me, in presence I think of Mr John C. Spencer and perhaps of Mr. Collier.
In that interview Mr. Crittenden submitted to me his instructions from Mr. Webster, together with a copy of the renewed correspondence between Mr. Webster and Mr. Fox in which the latter demanded apparently an immediate discharge of McLeod, and the former admitted that he ought not to be detained.— Mr. Crittenden in behalf of the Federal Government and in the spirit of his instructions (afterwards published) asked me to surrender McLeod to the Federal Government— I inquired the consequence of refusal? He said that of course War would follow, as the correspondence of Mr. Fox implied I asked when —on what event, whether if we refused to surrender McLeod, or if we proceeded with the trial of McLeod or if he should be executed. Mr. Crittenden replied "if he was executed." I answered Mr. Crittenden that I thought his instructions did not present that point. He thought they did: but on looking at

them found it otherwise. He then authorized me to assume that War was not to come unless McLeod should be executed.

I then assured Mr Crittenden, first, that McLeod could not be convicted because, I had undeniable evidence, that he was not guilty— Second—that if convicted wrongfully or rightfully, yet as the crime was pronounced by the Governments of Two of the most enlightened nations on earth to be merely a constructive one I should deem it my duty in that case to interpose my Constitutional power to prevent the sentence from being executed. The result was my adherence to my decision that McLeod should not be surrendered but should be tried by the Courts of this State.

With these explanations Mr. Crittenden was satisfied—and he promised to communicate these views to the President and to Mr. Webster. He assured me also that in his opinion the Administration would approve of my decision, and would suffer the proceedings in relation to McLeod to take their course.

I replied to Mr. Webster's private letter by a letter marked private, a copy of which I send—and by a public letter I reiterated the same decision—

The papers submitted to me by Mr. Crittenden were then considered private, because not yet made public at Washington.

At the next meeting of the Legislature, January 1842, I transmitted to that body all these papers except the letter marked private; together with the correspondence between myself and the President and Secretary of State and other officers relating to the proceedings against McLeod.

All these papers will be found in the Assembly Documents No — for the same year 1842.

Neither Mr. Crittenden nor any other person wrote to me the result of his report after his return to Washington. I learned by the Debates in the British Parliament that the Government of the United States adhered to the policy expressed in the correspondence submitted to me by Mr. Crittenden, instead of adopting that I had proposed to him. I advised Mr. Crittenden while he remained at Albany that Mr. Spencer was Counsel for McLeod and therefore ought not to be appointed District Attorney, unless that relation should be discontinued, He was nevertheless appointed. There is a long published correspondence between the President and myself on that occasion. It is well understood that Mr. Spencer received $5000. from the British Canadian Authorities

In regard to the application made to the Supreme Court of the State of New York for the Discharge of McLeod—the proceedings are notorious, and the Correspondence is full of them. I know nothing of the Marshall's being about to let the Prisoner go—and his being threatened by the Court that if he did he should fill the prisoner's place—but I remembered that the Sheriff of New York expressed a doubt about receiving him into custody and the Court obliged him to do so—with some such menace—

Of the passage of the act of Congress in regard to the Jurisdiction of the State Governments, I have no information, other than what is public.

My dissatisfaction with all the proceedings of the Federal Government on this occasion, was not secret. It is expressed in all the Correspondence.

You know how much I was misapprehended at Washington when it was said as it was all over the Country and in Europe that I was determined to sacrifice McLeod, or at least to involve the Country in War. I appealed to Mr. Crittenden by a private letter to vindicate me with the administration, and recalled the whole transaction to his mind in which I had given him assurances to the Executive that McLeod could not in any event be executed, and so in no event could there be war. He however made me no reply. I appealed to the President (Tyler) and sought to disabuse his mind.

But all was of no avail.

I have never affected any secrecy in this matter The Administration of 1841 took its ground and I mine. They were well understood to be different grounds.

After a proper time of disclosures I have never made any secret of my vindication—— Mr. Ingersoll asked me for the facts—— I gave them to him as I have done to a thousand others, without reserve, I did not indeed expect him to use the statement where and as he did—— But I expressly stated that I affected no confidence—— It is not for me to examine on this occasion the accuracy of his report of my convention with him.

This letter written hastily is so far private that it must not pass out of your hands nor be copied—— It may be shown to Mr. Webster or any friend of his under this injunction.

    I remain Dear Blatchford

        Very truly yours

                WILLIAM H. SEWARD

(From John Tyler.)

SHERWOOD FOREST Charles City County Va. April 21. 1846
My Dear Sir;
Your letter dated the 14 Inst. reached me by our last mail
and I lose no time in acknowledging its receipt. The disposition made by yourself and Mr. Bartley of the call for the
correspondence between Gov. Seward and myself was altogether
appropriate— I desire its publication merely as a matter of
history and as containing an explanation of my course upon the
subject to which it related.
I read with much satisfaction your speech in answer to the
objections urged to the Treaty of Washington, and unless I am
totally deceived I think you have put them forever at rest, at
least with the Country— I am also pleased to learn that you
design the publication in a more durable form than at present
exists, of the correspondence to which the negotiation gave rise—
To yourself I am disposed to leave the selection of such documents
as may properly enter into the compilation. Having full confidence that whatever is done will be best calculated to develop
the feelings and motives of the administration— My opinions
on the right of search and most of the other questions involved,
were plainly expressed in my messages to Congress.
I have reviewed the whole procedure, from time to time, in
association with the final result and I cannot withhold the remark,
that if we had consummated no other act than the Treaty, we
should have better deserved any other fate, than the violent and
unjust denunciation to which we have been subjected.
The Newspapers had brought me acquainted with the proceedings of the H. of R. touching the secret service fund, and I
regarded them as quite extraordinary— Who submitted the
paper to Mr Ingersoll's inspection I cannot as much as conjecture
Mr. Stubbs the confidential agent of the fund, had the exclusive
possession and knowledge of them upon my leaving Washington,
and I do not think that he would have volunteered to make them
public— As to the disposition which the President may make of
the House resolution I certainly have no feeling, and I doubt
not that you are equally indifferent— This fact I think it
proper to mention lest it should escape your attention, that Mr.
Van Buren with not one half the weighty matters to dispose of
that occurred during my time left a balance of but $1600—of
the fund, all of which was consumed in payment of engagements

made by him prior to his leaving office— Swetszer and Tappan for example received upwards of $10,000 for bearing despatches &c to S. American States— My balance exceeded $28000— Considering the many important negotiations which were consummated, and matters disturbing to the tranquility of the U. States which were quieted, I think I have a right to be regarded in any other light than as wasteful and extravagant—

Truly Yrs—

JOHN TYLER

(From Francis O. J. Smith.)

26—WASHINGTON ST BOSTON, Apr. 30/46

My Dear Sir—

According to the published accounts of Ingersoll's slanders, the vouchers in the State Department so far as I am concerned are eroneous beyond $1500— But that error is easy of correction— I write now only *to assure you,* that I am ready to bear testimony, if need be, in the fullest manner to your vindication, & explain, in a way to put your assailants to shame, all that concerns my agency as to the Boundary question—

I say this, as I suppose you may desire to know on what to count, amid the treacheries and ingratitude of this censorious age—

Ever truly & devotedly
Your friend & Obt Servt, in haste

FRANCIS O J SMITH

(By Peleg Sprague.)

BOSTON May 27. 1846

I hereby certify that in May 1842, at the particular request of the Hon. Daniel Webster, then Secretary of State of the United States, I went from Boston to Augusta in the State of Maine, to be present at the meeting of the Legislature of that State, which had been convened by the Governor for the purpose of considering and determining the question, whether Commissioners should be appointed to represent that State at the then proposed negotiation between the United States and Great Britian respecting the North Eastern Boundary—

The purpose of my Mission was to represent the views of the Secretary of State to the Governor and the Legislature—

For this purpose I called on the Governor at different times, and the subject of appointing such commissioners having been referred to to a very large Committee of the Legislature; by their invitation I met that Committee and, in a full and free conference, endeavored to make known to them the views of the Secretary, and particularly as to the importance of appointing Commissioners with full power.

After my return to Boston, and some time in the Summer of 1842, I received from Mr. Webster, then at Washington the Sum of two hundred dollars, by check on the Merchant's Bank of Boston, as I think, for which I gave no receipt, but acknowledged it in a note to Mr. Webster.

The above sum, was, in my judgment, not more than a just and reasonable compensation, for my services and expenses.

Double the amount would not have induced me at that time, in my then state of health, to have made the journey had it not been connected with the public interest.

PELEG SPRAGUE

(Memorandum on the Ingersoll Charges.[1])

[1846]

Mr Ingersoll   3. charges.
1.   Unlawful use of the contingent fund.
I wholly deny it. The statement is indistinct, but substantially false.
1.   *I* had no power of directing the money to be placed in my hands.—

The course was this. Very important things were pending, calling for small expenditures out of the fund, from time to time. The President saw fit to give an order, for small amounts, from time to time, to be accounted for, by me, as vouchers were recd.— Leaving no considerable sums in my hands, at any time; although it would of course sometimes happen, that sums were paid, & vouchers not recd. till afterwards.

The President never gave a certificate to cover a dollar, till he was satisfied—& I only took them [vouchers] to

---

[1] These notes are in Webster's own hand.

show him that the money had been duly applied, to objects stated & approved by him. We were not of course careful to get such vouchers, as if we were to settle an account before an Auditor. All was confidential, & intended to be secret.

Then, in the first place, it is not true that I *directed* the Accountant to place money in my hands. The direction was the President's.

2.   There never was such a sum as 15,000, or anything like it in my hands at once. When one small sum was exhausted, or new uses were expected, the President directed the necessary payment to me, & not otherwise. I know not how this alleged sum of 15,000 is made up; as it is three times as much as the whole amt. covered by the President's Certificate, while I was Secretary of State.

3.   It is utterly false that I ever drew a dollar, of which the President was ignorant. I could not draw a dollar, of my own authority, & never did. Nobody but the President had authority.

He is disbursing agent of this fund. See opinions of Atty. Genl.

4.   The money paid to Mr. Crittenden was paid by order of President Harrison, in May 1841. It probably stood w't. [without] a voucher, for sometime, but afterwards Mr. Crittendens receipt was taken, the item carried to the *public* account of the expenditure out of the Contingent fund, & was published, in course, in the Treasury accounts. This is as I remember that transaction.

5.   Alexander Powell's employment was in 1841.

—It was of a secret nature, & it is altogether wrong, & a breach of the faith of Gov't. to publish his name. He rend. valuable services on the frontier, connected with the preservation of the peace of the Country.

6.   F. O. J. Smith never was sent to the Frontier. He was employed, in the negotiation at Washington 1842.

7.   Mr Ingersoll says; there is a credit of cash returned, $5.000—& asks why return it, if taken for a *public* purpose? The answer is, simply, because it turned out not to be wanted. Not being wanted, it was of course to be "returned," & not kept. —I have no recollection of this; but if such a " return " appear, that must have been the reason.

8.   As to the balance of 2.290 agt me, on the " closing of my accounts." This cannot be true. If it means only, that at a particular time this sum was not covered by vouchers, it may be

so, or it may not; but if it means that this sum was a balance in my hands after deducting all payments actually made by me, & all charges on the fund, then it is not true.

9. As to the 17.000 dollars said to be in my hands, "agt. former usage," I can only say that I know not how it is pretended that this amt. is made up; nor do I know what the " former usage " was. I only know that I acted as the President directed; applied all that was applied, to objects authorised by him, & rendered him such returns & vouchers, as satisfied him, as to all amounts which were to be covered by his Certificate.

10. Corrupting the *Party Press* (what party?)   As to this, I can only say that I never directed a dollar to be paid to any Editor, Printer, or other person connected with the press.— I have no recollection of any such letter as is said to be found from Mr Smith— Nor has he any letter from me, requesting or approving any " corrupting of the Party Press."—Mr. Smith had been a member of Congress; was a reputable man in Maine, & had the confidence of the leading public men, & the popular party. His services were thought to be important; they were all honest, so far as I know, and I am sure, so far as I intended. It cannot be right, unless in a case of *high importance* to drag his name before the public, as connected with a transaction in which the *law* promised him confidence & secrecy.

As for my justification, it is enough to say, that in all the other cases, the money was paid by the Presidents direction.

11. I do not remember the report of Mr Royce.— I recollect purchasing various maps & Charts—some of them at high prices —one especially—which I had become acquainted with in 1838— & which I learned the British Consul then wished to buy—at almost any price, as it had a *red line* on it—supposed to have been placed there, by Mr *Jay.* I bought this, at my own risk, in 1838—afterwards gave it to the Agent of Maine, Mr C. L. Davis, who paid for it. At the time of the Treaty it was sent to the Dept.— Mr Davis was refunded what he had paid for it— & the map is now in the Dept.

My correspondence with Mr. Stubbs, and the papers will shew how the account was settled. The President never wrote me on the subject at all. I believe Mr Stubbs said, in one letter, that the President was anxious to see the account settled—which was very proper. Mr. Tyler was cautious, as to making expenditures from the contingent fund—& used much less of it than his predecessor. See his letter to me.

(A Proposed Retraction by Mr. Ingersoll.)

Whereas the Honorable Charles J. Ingersoll, in his speech on the Oregon question in the House of Representatives, on the 9th of February last, made certain charges against the Honorable Daniel Webster respecting a private correspondence alledged to have taken place between him and the Governor of the State of New York in March 1841 on the subject of the imprisonment of Alexander McLeod; And Mr. Ingersoll on the 9th instant, in the House of Representatives made other charges against Mr Webster respecting certain alledged transactions in the Department of State, and Mr Ingersoll having made known to the undersigned that those charges were founded on information which he has ascertained to be entirely without foundation in truth and feeling a desire, voluntarily and promptly to do ample justice to Mr Webster, it is proposed by Mr Henry D. Foster of the House of Representatives, on behalf of Mr Ingersoll, that latter will rise in his place in the House to day and make the following statement, towit, " It will be recollected by the House that in my remarks on the Oregon question on the 9th of Feby' last I made certain charges against the Honorable Daniel Webster respecting a private correspondence which I had been led to believe had taken place between him and the Governor of the State of New York in the month of March 1841 respecting the imprisonment of Alexander McLeod— It will also be recollected by the House, that on the 9th instant I made other charges against Mr Webster alledging that certain transactions had taken place in the State Department at the time he was Secretary of State— Now, in justice to Mr Webster and to myself I embrace the earliest opportunity to say that the charges to which I referred were founded on information which I have since ascertained to be entirely erroneous—that I was entirely misinformed—and that I therefore withdraw those charges altogether, and with pleasure retract any derogatory expressions towards Mr Webster made on either occasion, by which they may have been accompanied " It is therefore proposed on behalf of Mr Webster by T. Butler King and Robert C Schenck of the House of Representatives that on tomorrow tuesday the 14th inst— That Mr Webster, with the published remarks of Mr Ingersoll before him—will rise in his place in the Senate and say:—" Mr President, It was with unaffected pain, as I then stated, that in the remarks which I made in debate here a few days ago, in reply to the Hon Senator for New York (Mr Dickinson), I felt compelled to notice and comment on a speech made by the Hon Charles J. Ingersoll of the House of Representatives, an extract from which had been published by the Senator from New York with his speech. Now sir, I recur to that subject for another and more agreeable purpose.

I find in the report of proceedings yesterday in the House of Reps., as published in the Union newspaper of last evening, that Mr. Ingersoll has done me the justice to state publicly, in explanation to the House, that the charges which he had made against me in that speech of his on the 9th of February last, in relation to a correspondence with the Gov. of New York in 1841, as also other charges & averments, in relation to my conduct when I was Secretary of State, which he made in the House of Reps. on the 9th of this month, on occasion of his offering a certain resolution of inquiry as to the expenditure of the secret service fund, were founded on information which he has since ascertained, & became satisfied was entirely erroneous; & that he has withdrawn therefore altogether those charges as groundless, & has retracted the expressions derogatory to my character with which they were accompanied. In this state of the case I am ready to meet that retraction of Mr Ingersoll in a like spirit. I take this opportunity therefore of saying to the Senate, that my remarks & comments upon Mr Ingersoll & his speech which I made here, having been founded entirely upon his charges & averments in regard to myself, the occasion being taken away, those remarks & comments fall to the ground; & may be forgotten with the cause & circumstances which produced them—"

[Handwriting changes here.]

This paper was drawn up after a conference and consultation between Mr Henry D Foster, who had been requested by Mr Ingersoll to act for him—and myself, After it was drawn I placed it in Mr Foster's hands to be shown to Mr Ingersoll— In a day or two he returned it, saying that Mr Ingersoll thought that Mr Webster should begin any explanation, which might take place— I told him that was impossible— Two or three days afterwards the subject was again revived between us, and terminated in a similar result. On none of these occasions did Mr

Foster, say or intimate, that Mr Ingersoll had any objection to make the declaration, which in this paper it was proposed he should make, provided Mr Webster would begin the explanation— To this Mr Schenck and myself decidedly objected, and therefore my intercourse with Mr Foster, on this subject ceased.

T. BUTLER KING.

(Hon. R. C. Schenck's statement in regard to Mr. Ingersoll.[1])

I acted with Mr King, in behalf of Mr Webster, in the attempt to adjust the difficulty between Mr Webster & Mr Ingersoll— wrote the latter part of the paper prepared for that purpose as above—was present at the second named interview with Mr Henry D. Foster, & concur with the statement of Mr King in relation to what then transpired. Mr Foster said, Mr. Ingersoll thought that Mr Webster should make the first explanation—this Mr King & I agreed was inadmissible. Mr Foster made no other objection, in my hearing, to the form or terms of the adjustment proposed.

ROBT. C. SCHENCK.

(From Francis O. J. Smith to Fletcher Webster.)

BOSTON May 8th. /46

My Dear Sir—

On Monday last I met our Mutual friend at Portland— I had previously written your father, of my readiness and ability to explode Ingersoll's slanders— Give yourself no apprehension so far as I am concerned— My early letter to your father will cover more vouchers, than he has filed, if need be—and bring the Govt. in his debt— But this is *inter* nos, until I see you.

I think it best to force the Govt. to summon me— I have not yet been summoned—& dont wish to put myself in the position of a volunteer— But the Committee will readily appreciate the propriety of calling on me for explanation. They don't yet see Ingersoll's false scent.

I have not yet seen your father—will if needful— But I know

---

[1] This heading is indorsed on the back of the paper.

so well what is needed, you may trust all to the facts of the case, & my discretion, until I have occasion to see you. The world, the present as well as future, will see in this whole matter, nought but the envy of greatness, as in other days it was the envy of justice, that furnished a moving pretext of persecution.

In haste, yours truly

Francis O. J. Smith

(To Edward Curtis.)

Boston May 9, '46 Saturday 12 o clock

My Dear Sir

I came up from Marshfield last Eve', & found letters here from yourself, Mr W. & Fletcher.— The latest & most direct, was from Mr W. who said the Comee. had done nothing more than to summon Mr Stubbs, to appear before them on friday, (yesterday)— The N. York mail is not in, yet, today, as there was a heavy fog last night—

My purpose is, in conformity to your suggestion, to proceed immediately to Washington— I shall leave Boston on Monday Morig—& N. Y. (nothing happening to prevent) on Tuesday Morning, with Mrs W. & Mrs Curtis—& get to Washington as soon as we can.

I have seen Mr F. O. J. Smith. He thinks I have great reason to desire that the Comee. should send for him. He says everything is properly *straight*, & states a good many useful particulars. But I am, still, of opinion that we should, for the present, express no wish on the point of his being called.— *I shall bring on copies of his entire correspondence with me.* |

If I get a letter this forenoon, I will answer it; but just say to F. & Mr Winthrop, that I may not have time to write them today. I am really "rundown" with calls & visits, I have been so much whirled about that I am more fatigued, than when I left W.—

I am glad to learn from Mrs W. that you are comfortably *lodged*, in W.

Probably I shall hear from you at N. Y.

Yrs ever sincerely

D. W.

(To D. Fletcher Webster.)

WASHINGTON May 17. 46 Sunday mor'g.

Dear Fletcher

I rec'd your letter yesterday mor'g, the first, after having arrived home.

I was a little sorry not to find you here, but do not know that your longer stay could have been useful.

On the retirement of Mr. Petit, there arose a controversy about Chairman.[1] Mr Vinton succeeded Mr Petit, accord'g to usage, but Mr Brinkerhoff moved that the Com^{ee} elect a Chairman. This slight on the Mr. Vinton would probably have drawn him from the Comee.— After several meet'gs, in which little or noth'g was done, the question of charg'g a Chairman was decided, yesterday, in the negative, Mr. Davis vot'g agt. it.　So Mr. Vinton remains Chairman.

The Committee, as I believe, have as yet summoned nobody; nor have they yet done with Stubbs, who, I suspect, does not behave as he ought.　I believe there are only a few small matters, connected with F. O. I. Smith's accounts, that the Committee are not satisfied about.　But this I do not know for certainty.　Probably Mr Smith will be sent for—　We shall know tomorrow.

Yrs ever

DANL WEBSTER

———————

(To D. Fletcher Webster.)

My Dear Son　　　　WEDNESDAY MOR'G May 20. '46.

I wrote you a hurried note yesterday.

After it was decided, by the vote of Mr. Jefferson Davis, that Mr. Vinton should remain at the head of the Commee, the examination went on fairly.　Brinkerhoff, from Ohio, one of the majority, moved to choose a chairman, say'g it was a "party Comee," and ought to have a party man, at its head; or to that effect.　This Mr. Davis, whom I do not know, appears to be an honorable man.

The original mover of the mischief was Stubbs.　He volunteered to go to Ingersol, & give him information, upon some

———————

[1] Chairman of the committee to examine the charges of Mr. Ingersoll against Mr. Webster.

matter touching the McLeod case; and then intending to disclose
secret papers, but this led to Ingersols coming to him, & b'g let
loose among all the vouchers & papers touching secret service
money &c. &c. &c.   Stubbs has been thoroughly examined, by
both Committees, & has been compelled to do me justice.——
     I understand that on Monday the Com^{ee} came to the conclusion,
that they would call Mr. Tyler, & Mr. F. O. J. Smith, & nobody
else, for the present.—— They want to know what the latter
meant by "operat'g on the Press" &c; & thought it proper that
Mr Tyler should have an opportunity to state, to them, whether
he justified or sanctioned these expenditures.   He cannot but
answer affirmatively, since there is his name, nor do I suppose
he has the least inclination to evade any th'g, or to do me injustice.   He will probably be here, by the end of the week.   Mr
Smith is expected here tomorrow.
     After all, we must not be too sanguine of the result.   It is a
greater point with the party to injure me, & a little one to protect Ingersol.   Every party effort, we may expect, will be used,
to prevail on the majority of the Com^{ee} to report someth'g, unfavorable.   Nevertheless, the temper does appear, as I am well
informed, to be materially changed.   The subject has ceased to
be talked of, in a great measure out of doors.   The Com^{ee} will
hardly meet again till next week.
     As to a meet'g in Boston, it might be very well, if the Resolu-
tions were guarded.   They might be.   1st. That the Country
b'g in actual war, must be defended, & its rights & interest maintained, whatever opinion be sustained, of the necessity of its
commencement.
     2. That so long as the war is waged for National defence, or
public rights & interests, & appears not connected with in-
justifiable purposes of ambition, or desire of aggrandizement, or
acquisition of the Territory of other States, by arms, the Govt
should be supported, in carrying it on, & in br'ging it to a speedy
& successful termination, by all truly patriotic men, witht. distinction of Party.

D. W.

(To D. Fletcher Webster.)

Private.   MAY 25, 1846.
Dear Fletcher,
     Mr F. J. O. Smith has got thro' his examination, & I believe all
is very well, in that respect.   Mr Tyler will be here, in a few

days, & I have no doubt will act fairly, & in a friendly manner. Indeed, he cannot do otherwise, since there is his name.

There is one th'g—& only one—that I am in doubt about— It is relative to Mr Sparks.— I have a sort of recollection, that he charged a very low compensation, for his journey to Maine— that I paid it—that I thought it quite too low—that I asked Mr Tyler to increase it—whether he did—or if he did whether I ever handed the additional sum over to Mr Sparks—and forgot— or omitted it— I cannot say. I do not know that any th'g appears about this—but if an additional sum was allowed Mr Sparks, & he has not recd it, he ought to receive it— I may have occasion to write you again on this subject, to-morrow.—

I think Judge Sprague was paid $200— Please ask him how that was— I believe no receipt was found—please ask him to say, in a Certificate, that he made a journey to Maine, at my request, on business connected with the North Eastern Boundary, for which he rec'd from me, at the time, $200—

Please attend to this by return of mail.

Yrs   D Webster

(To D. Fletcher Webster.)

FRIDAY. 3 O clock. (May 29, 1846)

Dear F.

Mr Tyler has finished & signed his Deposition. They say he has cleared every th'g up—tak'g the whole on himself—&, as Mr Curtis says, "has given Mr. W. quite a character."—

—I rec'd yrs enclosing the *Certificate* this mor'g—all right— I will write again respect'g Mr S.—

All well, at home.

I rather suppose the inquiries of the Comee are *closed*, now; tho' I do not know it.

Yrs ever

D. W.

(To D. Fletcher Webster.)

MAY 31. 1846. Sunday mor'g.

Dear F.

Mr Tyler has got thro. with his evidence before both Com^ees— His testimony is full, complete, & conclusive. He differs essentially from Stubbs; & Stubbs' conduct appears so bad, that if Mr Buchanan has any sense of justice, he will turn him out of office.

I doubt whether the Com'ees. or Mr Ingersols Comee will take any more evidence. They may examine Upton, perhaps; if they should he can do hurt. Mr Tyler has closed up all that business about the Virginia Smith.

I look upon the whole th'g as now thro', and perfectly well through. How the Comees will report—that is, whether all the members will agree, or whether each Comee will have two reports—majority & minority—I cannot say. It is of no importance, since the evidence will fully satisfy the public, both of the propriety of every th'g done by me, & of Ingersoll's rascality, both in his charges, & in his mode of rumaging for evidence.

I dont yet hear from our good friend Mr P. H.[1]—but suppose I shall tomorrow.

Yrs D. W.

———

(To D. Fletcher Webster.)

Sunday (May 31 1846).

Dear F.

The Com.ee will report tomorrow. Four members, viz. Messrs Vinton, Davis, Jones & King, agree.—one, Mr. Brinkerhoff dissents. The Report of the four repudiates & negatives all Ingersolls charges; that of the 5th imputes noth'g, of unfaithfulness or corruption; but talks about delay in settl'g accounts, & other trivial th'gs.—so I understand.

The majority recommend the papers to be sealed up, & kept secret, till the House otherwise order.

D. W.

———

(To D. Fletcher Webster.)

JUNE 1. 1846.

Dear F.

It seems now well understood that the administration expect to come to terms to England soon. I believe there is no doubt that instructions have gone to Mr McLean, of such a nature as Mr Polk supposes will prove satisfactory to England. Persons in Mr. Buchanan's confidence, certainly understand this to be so.

---

[1] Peter Harvey.

The 54.40[1] men are a good deal cast down.   Mr Buchanan says he has no doubts, now, that the dispute will be settled on 49; tho' this wd. have not have been the case, had he not claimed to *54.40.*

It is certain, too, that the President expects favorable accounts from Mexico—that is, that the Govt will *treat;* & perhaps in the mean time come to an armistice.   Probably Genl Taylor will remain where he is till *October,* as the rainy & sickly season sets in next month.   If this is resolved on, there will probably be no more fighting in that quarter,—at present.

On the other hand, an expedition has gone agt. Santa Fe, & no doubt our Squadron on the Pacific will dash at Monterey, &c. &c.—   These occurrences *may* prolong the war.   Such is my fear—

Yrs   D. W.

(To D. Fletcher Webster.)

Tuesday June 10. 46. 1 O clock

Dear F.

The Report is in—& so is Brinkerhoffs minority report—a minority of *one.*   This last is said to be poor, weak, & contemptible—& can do no harm—both are ordered to be printed—

It is Cabinet day; & probably the Cabinet are now getting up a message to accompany the British offer, to the Senate.   It is sure to come; & in all probability will be in tomorrow.

D. W.

(To D. Fletcher Webster.)

JUNE 13. [1846]

Dear F.

You see that the Union says the Oregon business is finished in the Senate, & undertakes to give the *votes.*   If he knows any th'g he probably got it from the President, or Mr Buchanan— If he is correct, there wd. be no further cause of fear, about this matter.—

As to Edward, I believe Mr Smith is at the North, & that Edwards presence here is not now pressingly necessary.   I hope he

---

[1] i.e., the extremists' claim for the northern boundary of Oregon.

is looking well after employment in the Water works.   His services as Captain or Col. are not likely to be soon called for—
—As to Mr Greenough, when I go home, I will take somebody along from N. Y. to help finish up that business—
—I think a treaty will be sent in, & finished, next week.   In which case, I shall push right for Boston—
As to Mexico, the idea here is, that the war will not last long. The settlement with England will tend to settle it—
We shall have the President's views about revenue, &, in answer to the Senate's call, early in the week, as is expected.   It is thought there will be an issue of T. notes

Yrs truly

W.

(To D. Fletcher Webster.)

Sunday, P. M.—(June 1846?)

Dr. F.
   The Telegraphic has told all the news—   The Treaty will be signed & sent in tomorrow or next day—so, as I told you, the Oregon question is at an end.—
   Tomorrow the President will answer the call of the Senate— He will recommend a tax on tea & coffee—say 20 or 25 per cent—*& an issue of T. Notes.*
   Of course, we have no news here today.

Yrs affectionately

D. W.

(From Edward Everett.)

(Confidential.)

Cambridge 6 July 1846.

My dear Sir
   Yours of the 3d reached me on Saturday.—   I sincerely wish it were in my power to undertake the proposed review of the negotiations at Washington.[1]   So strong is my desire, on every occasion, to comply with your wishes, that nothing but a real &

---

[1] The Ashburton Treaty.

overruling necessity prevents my undertaking it. But the pressure of my duties here,—great & severe beyond my expectation,—makes it impossible for me even to think of any thing else.—Instead of two or three hours daily, in which I was told the routine of the work could be gone through, I find the whole day, from five in the morning till ten at night, too short for it, and my vacation, instead of being a season of repose which I greatly need, is filled up in advance with reserved labours. Instead of time for literary pursuits, I have not had two hours reading since I came here, and the quality of my work is worse than its amount, being that of an usher and a police magistrate combined.—

You may remember that you repeated to me, (when I was balancing about accepting the office),[1] what you had said to Judge Story relative to the Law School, that it would kill me. But instead of standing it, as he did, fifteen or twenty years, I feel already as if rottenness had entered into my bones.

But there is now no retreat. The step was false, but irreparable,—at least till its nature & effect upon my health & spirits are too apparent to leave any ground of doubt as to my duty, & then it will be too late.—

You must not mistake the purport of this querulous strain.—It is in perfect good faith. I have not the slightest wish to return to public life, & had made up my mind at all events to leave it.— Nothing would have induced me to encounter the coarse violence, into which our party contests have degenerated. My wish was for strictly private life, and leisure for carrying out some literary plans.— I allowed myself to be over persuaded, and I must abide the consequences. I deeply regret that one of the first of these is to hold back, for the only time, I believe, in my life, from anything which could however slightly promote Your Service.—

With constant attachment Yours,

E. E.

(To Nathan Appleton.)

My dear Sir   N. Y. July 8, 1846.

The state of the Tariff bill at Washington is such, that we shall need the advice of our best informed & most prudent friends,

---

[1] President of Harvard College.

next week & the week after, & I write this, to bespeak your attention, & to express the hope that we may hear from you & your
neighbors as fully as possible.   It would be very well, I think if
some intelligent Gentlemen from Boston could spend the next ten
days at Washington.

Information on many subjects, will be very much needed.   The
first practical question is, shall we make any attempt at amendments?   My own impression rather inclines towards two conditions.   1st. That we cannot make any thing of this bill, at all
likely to satisfy the country, unless we can alter its *advalorum*
principle materially, and I doubt whether we can do this, and
consequently, it is doubtful policy to propose amendments.

2d. That our best chance of killing the bill, is, to put to the
vote, *just as it is.*   I should like to learn what is thought in your
circle, on these points.

With whatever chance of successful opposition I think we
ought not to let the occasion pass, without attacking the whole
principle of the bill, & exposing the follies of its detail.   Pray
take the trouble to *book me up* in these respects.   Since 1840 I
have not been brushed up, on Tariff subjects.

My purpose is to oppose it

1st. as being wholly unnecessary, the tariff of 1842 having
established a system, good for revenue, & good for protection; &
disliked by none but theorists, or abstractionists.

2d. Because a universal *advalorum* rate, is absurd, at this
stage, in the advancement of political science, & if practicable,
even, with proper guards, there are no such guards.

3d. Because it will destroy or injure, interests, which ought to
be protected & preserved.

4.   Because, if it have the effect expected from it, of a greatly
increased importation, it will seriously affect the business of the
country, derange exchange, & finally disturb the currency.

I go south this P. M.

Yrs truly,

D WEBSTER.

(From James Kent.)

NEW YORK July 13—1846.

My Dear Sir

I ought before now to have thanked you for your Pamphlet
containing your conclusive & admirable vindication of your con-

duct in the Ashburton negotiation. I read your Speeches &
triumph over the foulest calumnies with the highest Interest &
Pride. But my inducement this moment for this Epistle was not
that benefaction, but to let you know how exceedingly I was
gratified with a long extract from your Son's oration at Boston
on the 4 of July, in respect to the follies of the day. It is clear,
strong, pungent and stringent & written in the best style &
spirit. I was very much struck with the good sense & truth.
There is a mental epidemic abroad in the land. It infests every
thing, Religion, Politics, Law, Physic, political economy &c—
men are now crazy with one idea only in matters of Reformation,
It shows itself eminently in abolitionism, Philanthropy, Temperance, Law Reforms, Punishment & *annexations*. Mr. Sumner's Oration was beautifully classic & eminently benevolent, but
his mind is diseased manifestly so on certain subjects. Your son
displays a most sound & powerful mind, & I beg leave to congratulate you on so distinguished a Paper from your Son.

Yours truly & affect.

JAMES KENT

(To James K. Mills.[1])

WASHINGTON July 16 46

My Dear Sir

I recd your obliging letter yesterday, & have complied with its
suggestion.

I was never more at a loss to guess about the result of a pending measure, than I am about the fate of the Tariff vote. I
have yet some *hope*, & shall not give that up, till the very last.
You will see, in the proceedgs of the Senate today, Mr Dix's motion about the Harbor Bill. This matter will *affect the Tariff
Bill*, one way or another, very much. A good many things seem
in agitation. I cannot clearly foresee the result, but will keep
you advised, how things look.

Yr truly

D. WEBSTER

---

[1] A prominent local politician of Boston.

(To ——————(?)

FRIDAY 5 O clock. [July. 1846]?

Dr Sir

The greatest objection to the proposed amendment, which I have yet heard, comes from Ohio, & is founded on the idea that *wool* will not be decently protected.   Pray tell us how that is— I wish Mr Saml Lawrence was here, or some other wool man.— Mr Simpson seems to understand the subject, but it is thought possible that his notions, in regard to wool & woolens may run in a particular line.

Yrs truly—

D. W.

(To James K. Mills.)

TUESDAY July 21, 46.

Dear Sir,

I think it will be submitted in this form.   Every man of business here—Whig or loco—Mr. Lamb, Mr. Simpson, Mr. Marlow, Mr. Peck of N. Y.—Mr. Chambers of Pa. &c &c—all, are *for* the proposition.   Many Whig members *are agst it*—possibly, more or less on political grounds.   I am sorry to say Mr Evans is rather violent against it—at least, abundantly decided.   I think Mr. Davis is *favorable* to it.   I shall keep off any *vote*, till Monday.   If you have opinions, in Boston, please express them to Whig Senators.   If *all* the Whig Senators go for this I have great hopes of carrying it.

Yr   D. W.

(To James K. Mills.)

Private.

JULY 21. 1 Oclock. [1846]

My Dear Sir

I wrote you a note, two hours ago, enclosing a proposed amendment, &c—   I hope to send you, by same mail, some printed papers, tables &c—

Now, you & your friends—& my friends must look these things over.—& *say what is best.*   My wish is to do good, & save the Country.   I care nothing for consequences to my own popularity. If I can defeat this infamous Bill, & retain the principle, & the principal provisions of 1842, it is glory enough for me.

If the present bill should pass, in its present shape, *when can we repeal it?* Certainly, not by this Congress. And though we might carry the House of Representatives, the Senate *will be stronger against us, a great deal, than it is now.*

I wish Mr. Appleton would write to Mr Winthrop; if he be in Boston. If not, I wish Mr. Winthrop might hear from other friends.

The true difficulty—here—or at least one of them—is, that there are those, on both sides, who think much is to be made, hereafter, out of the Tariff, as a *political topic.*

Yrs most truly

DANL WEBSTER

(To James K. Mills. (?)

WEDNESDAY 3 O clock [July 1846.]

Dear Sir

I wrote to Fletcher this morn'g, a letter to be shown to you.—
Noth'g of interest has arrived today, that I know of. Some motion, or motions, will be made from the other side. I shall vote for any th'g, likely to put off the evil day.

Yrs   D. WEBSTER.

(To James K. Mills.)

Private & confidential.

SUNDAY 3 Oclock. [July 1846]

My Dear Sir

Things change their appearances so often, that ones hopes & fears, respecting the final result, successively predominate every hour. There is now reason to apprehend that Mr. Jarnagin has been induced to *promise* his vote for the Bill. If this be so, as I shall hope it is not, we must do our utmost to obtain help from other quarters, as our chance will be much diminished of killing the Bill, on a direct vote. Mr Niles speaks tomorrow. He will probably propose some amendment. If it be no very important one, such as to gain new support to the Bill, I shall be for agreeing to it, that the bill may go back, (necessarily) to the House, where I learn there is now some slight hope of putting an end to it.

We may try a general postponement of the Bill, or a postponement of its operation to the first of March next. If we can do nothg else, & the worst comes to the worst, I think, somewhat seriously, *of proposing a compromise.*

What wd our friends say to such an amendment as this, viz: "Strike out all the Bill after the enacting clause, & insert

"That from and after the passing of this act there shall be a reduction, on all duties now established by law, whether specific or *advalorem*, of 25 per cent; & at the expiration of 5 years from the passing of this act, a further reduction of 8-1/2 per cent—" I wish you, if you see fit, to show this to friends, & signify to me their general impression *by return of mail.* I do not by any means know that such an offer would be accepted. But it is possible. Perhaps a reduction of 33-1/3 would be insisted on, to begin with, & 17-2/3 more (50 in all) after the 5 years. Perhaps *nothing* of this sort can be done. All I know is, that Mr. Calhoun is much troubled, & his present feeling rather leads to a *settlement* of the question.

I shall hope to hear from you by Thursday mor'g, & shall defer speaking, at large on the subject, till that day.

Yrs very sincerely

DANL WEBSTER

Under the expectation that the Bill may get back to the House, members there must be looked after.

(To D. Fletcher Webster.)

WASHINGTON July 29. 46.
Wednesday mor'g 6 O clock.

My Dear Son,

I wrote you on Monday mor'g, that if all things went, thro that day, as was expected, the Tariff Bill would be killed. But in all probability, you will hear of its final passage, before you receive this letter. I will therefore explain to you how we have been disappointed.

Every thing depended on Mr. Jarnagin's vote. If he could be brought to act against the Bill, its fate was sealed. I was supposed as much influence with him, as any body, & I exerted it, as

far as I could. I wrote him two private letters, as argumentative, & as persuasive as I could make them. The last of these he
showed on Saturday, to some Whig members from Tennessee; &
on Sunday, all the Whig members from Tennessee called on him,
& he agreed that the Bill should not be permitted to pass. He
wished, however, to br'g the Vice President to the necessity of
a cast'g vote. I was desirous of gett'g some amendment into the
Bill, so that if it should pass the Senate, there might be a chance,
still, to defeat it in the House. Hav'g settled with Mr. Jarnagin,
what the course should be, & how his vote should be given, Mr.
Gentry & Mr. Ewing of the Tennessee Delegation came to me,
in the afternoon of Sunday, to communicate Mr. Jarnagin's
resolution. To prevent all mistake, & make the matter sure,
I drew up a memorandum, A which I now enclose. Messrs Gentry & Ewing carried this to Mr. Jarnagin, & read it to him.
He agreed to it, & promised to vote accordingly ; with one immaterial alteration, which was, that my motion should be to strike
out, not the whole, but a part of the 9th Section of the Bill; &
that part he marked on the Bill, with his pencil.

Thus things stood, when I wrote you last Monday. I went
to the Senate that mor'g, and curtailed the residue of my speech,
in order to br'g things to a close, before accidents should turn
up. I had given notice, that I should conclude with a motion
to postpone the Bill till the next session of Congress. But this
I changed, in pursuance of the agreement, into a motion to
amend. And now came quite an unexpected interference. While
my motion was pending, Mr. J. M. Clayton made a motion, which
by the rules of proceed'g, displaced or superseded mine; viz, a
motion to commit, with certain instructions which you have seen.
This motion he did not choose to withdraw. Everybody saw it
was perfectly useless, but the Whigs could not well vote against
it. Mr. Jarnagin voted for it, & it prevailed. I understand Mr.
Clayton says that Mr. Jarnagin assented to this. Others say,
that Mr. Clayton importuned Mr. Jarnagin to countenance the
motion, & support him in it. I know not how this was. But
the proceed'g led to fatal consequences. The success of this
motion necessarily put off further proceedings to the next day,
Friday, which was yesterday. In the Eve'g of Monday, Mr.
Jarnagin's Whig friends could not find him any where till 10
Oclock. He had been at the Presidents, & when Mr. Gentry saw
him, at that hour, he did not incline to talk. Yesterday mor'g,
early, I saw Mr. Gentry, & with his concurrence, & indeed at his

suggestion, I wrote Mr. Jarnagin a third letter, as strong as I could make it, stat'g how much I was grieved by the proceedings of Monday, & beseeching him to relieve both himself, his Whig friends from the distressing condition in which they were placed, by a resolute & immediate conformity to the agreement of Sunday Eve'g. To this letter, I recd an answer, which I herewith enclose. This answer showed that all ground of reliance on his vote was now taken away.

On the meet'g of the Senate yesterday Mr. Lewis moved to discharge the Committee from the consideration of Mr. Clayton's instructions. You will have seen the proceedings. The motion prevailed, by Mr. Jarnagin's own vote. No doubt, he had promised so to vote, the night before. This decision gave me an opportunity to renew my motion to amend, which I did, & the motion prevailed, not by Mr. Jarnagin's vote, for he did not vote on the question; but by Mr. Benton's vote. And thus amended, the Bill was engrossed by the casting vote of the Vice President. Mr. Jarnagin declin'g to vote, & finally passed by the vote of Mr. Jarnagin.

If the manner of proceeding, which was agreed on, on Sunday Eve'g, had been permitted to be carried out, so that we could have brought on the final vote before the President & Cabinet had had an opportunity of a meet'g with Mr. Jarnagin, I have no doubt the Bill would have been defeated.

But at the meet'g at the Presidents, on Monday Eveg, means were found to fix Mr. Jarnagin's vote for the Bill. Yesterday mor'g at 10 Oclock, I saw Mr. Walker at the Capitol, & found him well apprised of Mr. Jarnagin's ultimate purpose.

I would not impute any corrupt motive to Mr. Jarnagin. There are means of influence not generally esteemed positively corrupt, which are competent to produce great effects. But he falsified his promises, & has thoroughly disgraced himself, forever. As to his pretended respect for his instructions, it is all an after thought. He has said, twenty times, that he cared nothg for instructions. Besides, on his speech on Mr. Clayton's motion, he took great pains to prove that his instructions did not reach the case of such a Bill as this.

I must now say a few words, on another subject.

You are aware that the amendment to the Bill, proposing to reduce certain duties 25 per cent, &c. was at first cooly rec'd at Boston. The idea of an amendment in this form, & to this effect, originated with Mr Edward Curtis. The amendment B was proposed, by him & myself, with the aid of Mr. Chambers of Philadelphia, Mr. Lamb & Mr. Simson of Boston, & other Gentlemen, concerned in the various interests.   After more full & particular information, the project obtained more favor in Boston, & every where among business men.   I have already given you my reasons for be'g in favor of this proceeding.   It was, clearly, the proper measure, & ought to have been adopted.   I think that Mr. Davis, reluctantly, the R. I. Senators cheerfully, Mr. Thomas Clayton & the two Maryland Senators willingly enough, would have supported the measure.   Mr. Crittenden, Mr. John M. Clayton, Mr. Huntington, Mr. Berrien, Mr. Mangum, & the two New Jersey Senators warmly opposed it, and greatly to my disappointment & regret, so did Mr. Evans, also. These Gentlemen gave different reasons.   Mr. Huntington & the N. Jersey Senators insisted that the proposed amendment would not give sufficient protection.   Yet, every man of business from their own States, said it did.   Mr. Crittenden's objection was, in the first place, that he wished the administration to make it its own Bill, and to make it as bad as it pleased.   In the second place, he said, there had been an understanding, that we should not propose amendments.   As to this, I never supposed the understanding went farther than this, viz; that we should not propose particular amendments, in favor of particular interests, so that, if these were adopted, the Bill might become less objectionable to some, but still be not satisfactory to all.   There never was any understanding that we should not, if we could, make the Bill acceptable to all the protected interests, & then pass it, if we could.   This, we might have readily accomplished.   My amendment, which amended so as to be someth'g more favorable to woolens, was the precise measure proposed.   This would have been carried, with the assent of the Whigs.   Mr. Walker not only told others, but said to me, he was willing to take it, was satisfied with it, & if the Whigs would agree to it, so that it passed, he should feel it to be his duty, in his next official communication, to say, that this ought to be considered as the *settlement* of the Tariff controversy.   But the Whigs would not listen to it.   You will have seen, in the Debates, the spirit which prevailed, especially in Mr Crittenden's speeches.   The political Press exercised a mischievous influence.   Looking itself only to political effect, it stimulated, highly, public men, who were look'g in the same direction.   Members of the House took an interest against the proposition, especially Mr. Grinnell; & none of them

would give it a help'g hand. Some of these Gentlemen expressed
the utmost confidence, that if the Bill could be sent back, it would
fall in the H. of R. Mr. Lawrence's last letter to me, (which he
will remember) written after having just come from state street,
said the opinion seemed to be, that the proposition might better
come from the other side. This had some influence with me; but
the truth is, that find'g the unwillingness of the Whigs to come
in & form a proper & *permanent* Tariff, I had fallen back upon
efforts to prevent the passage of the present bill, altogether,
rely'g chiefly, upon the chances of securing Mr. Jarnagin's vote.
This hope held out till yesterday mor'g, & then failed leav'g no
time [to] rally upon the projected amendment.

Mr. Niles exhibited unexpected proofs of vigor, & ability, &
acted like a man, throughout.

The Bill will be finally disposed of in the House today. The
administration expects to carry it by three of four votes. It is
barely possible, that they may be disappointed.

I wish you to show this letter to Mr Lawrence, & Mr Mills, &
then preserve it, with its enclosures.

I need hardly add, that I am sufficiently tired & fatigued, as
well as annoyed & distressed, by these results of things.

Yours affectionately

D. W.

(*Memorandum.*[1])

— motion to strike out the 9th Section—   A
   Mr. J. to vote *for it*.
— it will [be] then be struck out—
—then, motion to engross— Mr J. not to vote— If the
Vice President votes *for* the Bill, then Mr. J. to move to lay the
Bill on the table.—

This memorandum was carried to Mr Jarnagin Sunday Eve—
July 26.—by Mr Gentry. He read, & declared in presence of
Mr. Gentry & Mr. Ewing that he would follow the course & give
the votes, as herein stated.

B

Strike out the first 5 sections of the Bill and the 7th, 8th, and
9th sections, and insert:

"That from and after the first day of December next, there

---

[1] This memorandum, in Webster's hand, belongs with Daniel Webster's letter
to Fletcher Webster of July 29, 1846.

shall be a reduction of *20 per cent* of the duties, whether specific or *ad valorem,* now imposed by law on articles of imported merchandise whereon duties exceeding 30 per cent *ad valorem* are now charged; excepting Brandy and other spirits distilled from grain or other materials, and wines; provided, nevertheless, that duties on articles, now charged with duties higher than *30 per cent,* shall not be reduced below *30 per cent.*

Small tax on tea & coffee.

(*From Spencer Jarnagin.*[1])

Dear Sir   [JULY. 1846][2]

After a patient examination of all the circumstances with which I am surrounded, after hearing and duly considering all the arguments of friends, it is with pain I have to say, with my view of duty, I cannot concur with them, or conform to their wishes— I shall refuse to vote upon the engrossment of the bill, and leave its fate to be decided by Mr Dallas, but I cannot vote to postpone it, for reason I will give in the Senate— In this I have every thing to loose, and nothing to gain, save having done what I believed to be right, and if it brings upon me abuse of friends, and seals my political fate, I cannot help it. I shall go into the ranks and do battle for principle.

Your friend
SPENCER JARNAGIN.

(*To D. Fletcher Webster.*)

Dear Fletcher,   WASHINGTON Aug. 1. 1846

I have no doubt it would be agreeable to Mr. Westcott to receive some civility, from Boston, on account of his remarks upon Ingersol's slander. Probably, he would accept a dinner; *certainly* would be glad to be invited. If you & other friends think best, let an invitation come, before the 10th.

I am well—and beg'g to write out my Tariff Speech, & to get ready to go home

Yr affectionately
D. W.

---

[1] United States Senator from Tennessee.
[2] " Rec'd [Tuesday] Monday mor'g, 9 O'clock. D. W." is indorsed on the back of this letter.

(To D. Fletcher Webster.)

TUESDAY Aug. 4—[1846]

Dear Fletcher,

Beyond all expectation, the Bill for the Old French claims will probably pass the House today[1]—(I believe it has passed)— Give notice, immediately, that you propose to act as agent for claimants, before the Board— Set all yr friends immediately at work. I will help you do the business—& so you may say— though not publicly—stir quick.

D. W.

(To D. Fletcher Webster.)

AUG 6, '46.

Dear F

There is no doubt the President is desirous of putt'g an end to this Mexican War; but how to do it is the question. We hear noth'g at all from Mexico—not one word;—& when she will speak, no one knows. The President I have no doubt is anxious to hear from her, but she is silent.

Meantime, our troops are gett'g impatient, as well as in some degree sickly— Camp duty is not what they listed for. Persons acquainted with country think it would be a hard job to march to Mexico—& the army is not strong enough, at present. The expenses are goi'g on enormously. So there is good reason for our Govts' desir'g *peace,* as I have no doubt they do. But the question is what shall be the next step? Shall an armistice be proposed? Shall an extra mission be sent?— Shall the army push on, & fight its way through?— Is it str'g enough for this, & well enough supplied? *Will the money hold out?*

In my opinion, the prospect of a speedy peace is not very flattering, yet I hardly expect much more hard fighting— Mexico is an ugly enemy. She will not fight—& will not treat.

Yrs affectionately

DANL WEBSTER.

(To D. Fletcher Webster.)

NEW YORK Octr. 28. '46.

Dear Fletcher

I have felt obliged to decline the invitation to be at Faneuil

---

[1] The bill was vetoed by Polk Aug. 8, 1846.

Hall, on the Eve' of the 6th.— There are several reasons—
One is, if I speak at all, I must address the Gentlemen whose letter was presented by Mr. Dimmock.

But another is. I must attend to my own affairs, there be'g, as you know, some things to be provided for shortly.—

I wish you would send me two or three copies of my Speech at Baltimore, May 1843.[1]

Yrs affectionately

D. W.

You may read my letter to Mr. Stevenson, as it says someth'g of the state of things here.

———

(To D. Fletcher Webster.)

WASHINGTON Decr. 10. '46.

My Dear Son

I have recd yrs of Monday, I am not aware that I have any paper, respecting the Spanish case, which was not left in Boston. Mr Pendleton is here, & has promised me information on the present conditions of that part of the Macedonian's case, which is yet undecided.

My present purpose & expectation is, to arrive at Boston on Friday, the 18th, mor'g or Eve, accord'g to the weather, & to be ready, on Saturday, to consult with other counsel on the causes which stand for Monday the 21st. Of this, you may inform Mr. Bowditch, & Mr. Bartlett. If anything should happen to put off the causes, let me know. You may calculate that I shall leave Washington on Monday Eve'—be at Phila. Tuesday noon—at N. Y. Wednesday noon, & thro' Thursday—and, as before said, in Boston on Friday.

My speech is to be published in Pamphlet form,[2] forthwith. You will see how much the President quotes me.

I am well, but we have very bad weather.

Yrs affectionately

DANL WEBSTER

---

[1] Not published in the Works of Daniel Webster, but appeared in the National Intelligencer, May 27, 1843. See also Daniel Webster's Private Correspondence, vol. ii, p. 196, for Webster's comment on this speech; also Works, vol. v. pp. 135–137.

[2] Probably the speech on the Tariff, July 25–27, 1846. See Works, vol. v, p. 161.

(To Edward Everett.)

WASHINGTON. Dec. 10" 1846

My Dear Sir,
The memorial forwarded to me by Mr. Eliot,[1] was presented yesterday, and will be referred as soon as the committees are appointed. I shall ask Mr. Evans to endeavour to hasten it through the committee, and have little doubt it will pass the Senate.

It is my expectation to be in Boston two or three days the week after next, and should be very happy to be able to have an hour's talk with you, some evening.

I pray to be most kindly remembered to Mrs. and Miss Everett.
Yours always truly
DANL WEBSTER.

(From Sherrod Williams.)

(Confidential.)

FRANKFORT Ky Jan. 14th 1847.

Hon. Daniel. Webster
My worthy friend I am a member of the Kentucky Legislature now in session, and am Chairman of the Committee on Federal relations, to which Committee the subject in relation to the Constitutional right of the President of the United States to appoint the Commander of the state volunteer militia in the present war with Mexico is referred for the purpose of enabling you to understand Clearly the subject to which I desire to call your attention I enclose you a copy of the resolutions.[2]   will you be so good and kind as to give me your views in relation to the subject and if you can spare that much time from senatorial duties to throw your opinion into the shape of a report, you know that I have great confidence in your opinions generally

---

[1] A memorial from Harvard College asking to be allowed to bring into the United States a telescope bought in Bavaria without paying the duty fixed by the last Tariff act.

[2] The following resolutions were inclosed:

1. Resolved, That the Committee on Federal Relations inquire into the constitutional power of the President of the United States to appoint and commission officers of any grade in the Volunteer Militia, when called into the service of the United States.

2. Resolved, further, that the said Committee inquire whether in the late exercise of that power by the President of the United States, the constitution of the United States and the rights of the States have not been encroached upon.

and more especially upon great constitutional questions I would
rather rely upon your opinion than the opinion of any man dead
or alive.   *   *   *

Your true friend

SHERROD WILLIAMS

(To Sherrod Williams.[1])

[JAN 1847]

The Militia, is the Militia of the several States, & is not an
armed force, belonging to the Genl. Govt.

Nevertheless, the Constitution of the United States gives Congress power "to provide for calling forth the militia to execute
the laws of the Union, suppress insurrection, & repel invasions"

The Act of Congress, of the 28th of February 1795, was
passed, in order to carry this constitutional power into execution.
It enacts "That whenever the United States shall be invaded, or
be in imminent danger of invasion, from any foreign nation, or
Indian tribe, it shall be lawful for the President of the United
States to call forth such number of the militia of the State, or
States, most convenient to the place of danger, or scene of action,
as he may judge necessary to repel such invasion, & to issue his
orders for that purpose to such officer or officers of the militia
as he shall think proper."

Similar power is given to the President by the same act, in
cases of insurrection, to call forth the militia, on the application
of a state; & also to call forth the militia, when necessary, to execute the laws of the United States.

The President has the power of deciding when an invasion exists, or is threatened, so as to make it proper to call out the
militia.

This power was frequently exercised, dur'g the last war with
England. On the call of the President, it is the duty of the
Executive Government of the State to order out militia, in Regiments, Battalions or Companies, as called for; & the troops so
ordered out, are bound to obey.

This is the only *compulsory* military service at present known
to our laws; all enlistments into the army, being *voluntary*.

The power of the President to call forth the militia b'g limited
by the Constitution and the Act of Congress to the three specified

---

[1] This copy is taken from Webster's draft of the reply to Williams.

cases of Invasion, Insurrection, or forcible resistance to the laws; it has not been resorted to, in the present war with Mexico, because the service is a foreign service.

The Volunteer Regiment, Battalions, & companies, which have tendered their services, & been rec'd in carrying on the present war, are placed on a peculiar ground. They do not belong to the regular army of the United States, nor are they militia, called out in pursuance of the Constitutional provision.

They are voluntary Corps, either such as were previously organized, under the militia laws of the state, or such as have been formed and organized for the occasion. In either case, they are officered by the State Govt.— But then the law of last session enables the President to appoint Superior officers, to command the Volunteer corps. It is difficult to say that this is unconstitutional; because the whole matter originates in a call, which leaves it optional with the militia to come forth or not. The whole proceed'g is rather anomalous, as the troops are not regular troops, nor are they militia, called for, & ordered out, to meet the Exigency provided for bv the Constitution. In short, this invitation for the service of Volunteer corps, is but a mode of raising, expeditiously, a temporary or provisional army, destined for a short service. It is officered, in general, by the state authorities, and should be so, in all cases, as far as possible; yet, as the service is voluntary, as the militia corps may enter into it, or not, at their pleasure, I cannot say that it is unconstitutional for the Genl. Govt. to retain & exercise the power of appointg the High Field officers who shall command them, or to place them under the command of officers of the regular army.

This mode of rais'g troops is suited only to such occasions as are expected to require only a short service. Toward the end of the late war with England, & when it was feared the war might still last, for some time, the volunteer system was pretty much given up; so inconvenient was it found for troops, serv'g under state commissions, to be act'g, for any great length of time, mixed up with, & subordinated to troops of the regular army.

The great advantage of the Volunteer service, is, that it is generous, & patriotic, entered into more for the hope of honorable distinction, than from the hope of pay; & that it gives men, what they like, an opportunity of bear'g arms, under officers of their own choice. This should be preserved, as far as possible, so long as the volunteer system is resorted to at all. If the system is voluntary, let it be voluntary throughout. For the Volunteer corps have a voice, in the appointment of their highest, as well as their lowest officers. Let him be known to them, & be an object of their confidence, who is to lead them to the cannon's mouth, or scal'g the walls of the enemy's (fortification). To place others, by the appointment of the President of the United States, over the heads of their own officers, degrades the volunteers, & depresses their patriotic ardor. They take the field, with the proud hope of serv'g their country, & doing honor to themselves. As their objects are not mercenary, so their character & conditions should not be subordinate. If, in a moment of emergency & peril, their patriotism & love of country have called them to arms, let the honors, as well as the dangers of the field, be theirs. In the past conduct of the Volunteer corps, we find ample assurances for the future. Never did officers or men submit to evils & privations more patiently; never did officers or men, behave more gallantly before the enemy. The veterans of years, have not stood more firmly under a raking fire from the enemie's batteries, or plunged, more daringly in the closest, thickest, & hottest personal conflict with the foe.

In the opinions of the Committee, the House ought to adopt the following Resolutions:

Resolved, That in accept'g volunteer militia corps, into the service of the United States, it is consistent with the true spirits of the Constitution, that the officers of such corps, of every grade should be commissioned by the State authorities.

Resolved. That for the purposes of a war, the employment of volunteer corps, is the best & safest mode of rais'g troops: most consistent with our Republican Institutions, most agreeable to the People, who regard large stand'g armies as dangerous, & especially important, as it prevents the accumulation of an enormous military patronage in the hands of the President of the United States.

It may be, that they are right, who think that it would have been better, if the volunteer corps had been raised, by direct enlistment, for a short period, with a right to designate their officers, but such officers, nevertheless, to be commissioned by the President of the United States, thus raising a provincial army, enlisted for a short period, with officers designated by themselves, instead of accepting the services of the militia, in bodies already exist'g, or organized for the occasion. But the Govt. has not adopted this course; it has called for militia Volunteers; & hav'g done so, & invited them into the field, it ought not to withhold from them any part of the honors or distinctions to which they are so well entitled.—

(To D. Fletcher Webster.)

WASHINGTON Jan. 25. 1847.

Dear F.

It is true, as you wrote me, that Edward has been badly treated. On the one hand, I think the Whigs in the Legislature are act'g quite injudiciously, & on the other the party, locofoco spirit, prevail'g among the officers is mean & miserable. Edward must take care to act with propriety, & look to the end. I have some doubts whether his Regiment will be ever filled. Bounty is given to enlistment into the regular service, for no longer term than volunteer enlistments.

John Taylor writes me that he has p'd you $200 dollars; I suppose it is the same about which you wrote me. I hate to lay any new tax on Mr. Harvey, but if he could pick up a few more fees, I should be glad, as I have put off a thing he knows about, here, until April 1st & can put it off no longer. If you think it not pushing his kindness too far, you may show him this.

I hope you will [look out for] a just provision for the volunteers, without gett'g into any heats or quarrels upon the matter. The wisest th'g w'd be for Massachusetts *not* to act very differently, in this respect, from other States.

Yrs affectionately

DANL WEBSTER

(To D. Fletcher Webster.)

WEDNESDAY 10 Oclock [Feb. 1847(?)]

Dear Fletcher:

The Peace rumours continue, & there must be someth'g in them. The Administration expects no more fight'g. They have someth'g, upon which they are now deliberati'g, & expect someth'g more, soon. They have lost all *haste*, about their proposed measures. It is possible they may be disappointed; but it is certain they expect peace.

Yrs   D. W.

(To D. Fletcher Webster.)

WASHINGTON Saturday Feb. 6. 1847.

Dear Fletcher

I recd yr letter, yesterday mor'g, & was greatly relieved & gratified by it.   I trust all is well.   I wrote to Edward yesterday, & may write him again tomorrow—

I have read your speech.   It is a very good one, & well spoken of here, by all who have read it.   I suppose there is no help for it, but it is true, that, in some things, our Whig policy in Mass is quite narrow.

Yrs   D. W.

Mr. Walker's policy is;—if he can get Congress [to make] to grant a tea & coffee tax, to propose a loan; if not, to get along, as well as he can by T. notes

---

(To D. Fletcher Webster.)

WASHINGTON Feb. 7. 47. Sunday mor'g.

Dear Fletcher.

I recd your letter of the 4th this mor'g & am quite glad to know what is going on among you.   I perceive by the newspaper that the House has mitigated its infliction on Potatoes, by striking out 64, & insert'g 60.   This will crowd them a little less, in the half bushel.

Your letter gives me the very first information I have recd respecting the choice of a Senator.   If the present incumbent is out of the question, as you state, my notion of a successor is exactly like yours.   Mr. Winthrop must wait a little, & Mr. A.[1] might be my choice.   Govr. B.[2] nevertheless, is a good man, & would make a good Senator.   Nobody could object to him.   He is true, & able, & experienced.   Nor could the election of Mr. Hudson be objected to.   He is quite an able man.   I suppose his location is not quite far enough west.

If Gov. B. be elected Senator, I really hope my old friend Lt. Govr. Reed may be chosen, at least for once.   He is prudent & discreet, sensible & modest, & has been a steady, good man, in public life for thirty years.   If he has no great positive popularity, he is yet a man whom no one can find fault with.   How-

---

[1] Probably Geo. Ashmun.   [2] Governor Briggs.

ever, I am not the best judge of these things, & you Whigs of the Legislature will set them all right, I have no doubt.

The Massachusetts law laying a tax on passengers, is now under discussion in the Supreme Court. It is strange to me how any Legislature of Massachusetts could pass such a law. In the days of Marshall & Story it could not have stood one moment.

The present judges, I fear, are quite too much inclined, to find apologies for irregular & dangerous acts of State Legislation; but whether the law of Massachusetts can stand even with the advantage of all these predispositions, is doubtful. There is just about an even chance. I think, that it will be pronounced unconstitutional. Mr Choate examined the subject, on Friday, in an argument of great strength, & clearness, Mr. Davis is on the other side, & I shall reply.

P. S. I have your kind letter, say'g that there had been a small caucus, in which Mr. D. had 50 votes out of 80; but that nothing was definitely settled. Mr. Davis' motives were quite good, in the course he pursued about the Wilmot proviso. But it was not fortunate. He is a man of good principles, & generally very good sense. It does not become me, to interfere, in any manner, in the pending election, or to express any preference, or any opinion. I wish all the members of the Legislature to know that to be my feeling. All I have said above, is to this effect; vz. that if Mr. D. is not to be re-elected, & if position (in the east end of the state) excludes Mr. Winthrop, then Mr. A. presents himself to me as prominent, though both Gov. B. & Mr. Hudson are also among those, who are excellently well fitted for the office.

———

(To Thomas D. Grover et al.)

WASHINGTON Mar; 1. 1847.

Gentlemen,

I had the honor to receive, this morning, your very friendly letter of the 27th of Feby, inviting me to a Mass Meeting of the People of the First Congressional District, in Pennsylvania, on the Evening of the 5th instant, to testify their sense of services, rendered in procuring a Provision by Law for a Floating Dock Basin, & Rail-Ways, for the Philadelphia Navy Yard.

I fear, Gentlemen, that I owe the favor of this invitation to too partial an estimate, which your worthy & dist nguished Representative has formed, of the value of my cooperation, in that measure. I did no more than to support, with some zeal & decision, an appropriation, which I deemed essential to the Public Service, & eminently due to the interests connected with the Navy, in Philadelphia. My aid is not to be compared, in importance, with that of others; least of all, with that so ably & so perseveringly rendered by Mr Levin himself.

I fear, Gentlemen, that it will hardly be in my power to reach Philadelphia by the Evening of the Fifth. I must therefore pray you to congratulate the Meeting, in my behalf, on the accomplishment of so desirable an object; & to express to all your fellow citizens, there assembled, my respects, & thanks, & hearty good Will.[1]

DANL WEBSTER

(To D. Fletcher Webster.[2])

WASHINGTON Mar. 17. '47.

Dear Fletcher,

I am detained here, beyond all my expectation, but the business is important, & at an important stage, & I must see it thro. I shall be able to stay but a day or two, in Boston; that is to say, if I go south at all, for I ought to leave this place by the first of April. I cannot go at all, unless progress be made, in my matters, of which Mr. Mills & Mr. Thayer have charge. I wish you would see Mr. Thayer, & let him know how short my stay must be. I wrote to Mr. Mills, sometime ago, to the same effect.

I regret that Mr Harvey has not been this way. He is my reliance, for every thing kind & useful. I hope that by his aid, I may be able to pick up a few fees, to help pay the expenses of my journey. So much has been said about this journey, that I must now undertake it, if possible.[3]

1/2 past 3 O clock.

I have been with Mr C. to the Depts— Yr papers were linger'g in the Treasury, but we have hastened them along. A Warrant has gone to the Treasurer, & Mr McCulloch said the remittance would be made, in course, tomorrow.

---

[1] This letter is the property of Mr. Chas. Roberts, of Philadelphia.
[2] In Webster's handwriting. but unsigned.
[3] Referring to the tour into the South, which he did take in April and May.

(To Edward Webster.)

WASHINGTON, Feb. 5. 1847.

Dear Edward.

I write you this, in the hope you will get it before saili'g;[1] & I trust I shall hear from you every day till you sail, & also on your first touching land, any where; & after that as often as you shall know of conveyances.

I feel interest, of course, My Dear Son, in your success, in your new call'g. I am afraid of no unbecom'g conduct, no fear, on one side, & no foolish recklessness on the other. But I know the accidents of war; & what I fear most of all, is the *climate*. Pray study to guard agt. the effects of climate, in every possible form. Take good care of Henry. There is no one else he w'd have gone with. I shall write you constantly.

Yᵣ affectionate father

DANL WEBSTER

(To Edward Webster.)

WASHINGTON Feb. 22. 1847.

My Dear Son

We hear of your hav'g been tow'd from the wharf on the 18, but such has been the weather that I rather suppose you are at this moment on anchor in the outer Harbor.— I get Adjutant Genl Jones to forward this, that you may receive it at Brazos. We are quite well. Noth'g of political importance has occurred, for the last few days. A warm Debate has spr'g up in the Senate, between Mr. Benton & Mr. Calhoun, but I do not know that any thi'g important will come up of it. Fletcher is afraid you committed an indiscretion in tak'g a letter from Curzon (?) to Genl Almonte— I should think you had better rid yourself of it. I suppose it is only a common letter, but an American officer should not have in his pocket a letter to one of the enemy. I trust you will write me, from Brazos, & on all occasions, afterwards, whenever you can. We shall be full of anxiety to hear from you, & you must gratify us as frequently as possible. Henry's Family are all well.

Yrs affectionately

DANL WEBSTER

---

[1] Edward was on his way to join the army in Mexico.

(From Edward Webster.)

BRAZOS Santiago March 17th 1847.

My Dear Father—

We arrived here night before last, after a very pleasant and quick passage of 19 days; and we are lucky enough to have no sick men. We march this morning for the mouth of the river, and then we take steam boat for Camargo, we are to await the orders of Gen Taylor— A part of the Carolina Regt left yesterday and the last three companies of Virginia Regt. arrived last evening—

Henry is quite well, and sends his love to Aunt M— and George, he has been a little home sick, I think— We are all in good spirits and hope to have something to do—

Excuse this as it is written on my knees, with every body speaking to me.

with much love to all—
your affectionate son

EDWARD WEBSTER

(To Edward Everett.)

PRIVATE.

WASHINGTON Mar. 21" 1847

My Dear Sir,

There are two topics, on which I have intended to trouble you, for half an hour, on my return to Boston. But that return has been so long delayed, and the necessity of an early departure on a proposed visit to the South is so pressing, that if I reach Boston at all, my stay can only be for a day or two, and my interview with you, if I shall have one, must be brief. I have thought it might be well, therefore, before hand, to signify the subjects about which I wished to converse with you.

Some friends of mine have collected my official letters and papers, written while I was Secretary of State, and propose to publish them immediately, in a handsome volume. You are acquainted, in general with all these; and especially know everything, connected with English questions. In your private letters to me, you spoke kindly and favorably of some parts of the correspondence with Lord Ashburton, and quoted flattering sayings of other persons. You were also in the way of knowing what impression, if any, was produced, on the Continent, as well as in England, by the letters on Impressment, Maritime Law, Right of Search, &c. &c.

Now it has occurred to me, that out of your own correspondence, and from other sources, you might possibly extract something, which it might be well to print, in the volume. This is the first matter, on which I wished a few moments of your reflection. You know, that owing to the quarrel between the Whigs and President Tyler, the Treaty of 1842, and the correspondence accompanying it were more coldly received, by our Whig friends, than perhaps they might have been under other circumstances. Probably you have noticed, that in France, Prussia, and elsewhere, where jealousy of English maritime ascendancy prevails, the papers on the subject of Impressment etc, were favorably received. Some of them, I think also, were well spoken of in Parliament. Your private letters to me are all safely boxed up at Marshfield. Whether you kept copies of such letters, I do not know, but I can easily put the originals into your hands, and will endeavor to do so, by the first of next week.

The other subject is not of so pressing a nature. It is this.

Fifteen or sixteen years ago, a collection of my speeches was published, to which you was kind enough to contribute an introduction to the second volume. That collection has been extended to three volumes, and contains speeches of a date as late as 1840. There are more recent productions, enough to make another volume. It is now proposed to publish a new Edition, to include all; with notes, some furnished by myself, and the rest by other hands. It is intended to leave out the law arguments, and to insert any miscellaneous or popular matter, in their place, which may be found.

What I now wish to ask, is, that you would consider the propriety of enlarging the introduction, to meet the new contents of the volumes, and be a sort of introduction to the whole.

If you will give this subject a few moments thought, before I see you, I will be greatly obliged to you.

Yours always truly

DANL WEBSTER

(To Benj. F. Perry.[1])

WASHINGTON April 5. 47

My dear Sir

I wrote a short & hasty Answer to the very flattering invitation from your town.[2] I am well aware, My Dear Sir, to whose active friendship I am particularly indebted for this signal proof of respect.

I am afraid, My Dear Sir, that too much may be expected from me, in your quarter in the way of public speaking. I must really beg of you, not to raise expectations in that respect.

Yrs very truly

DANL WEBSTER

(To D. Fletcher Webster.)

SUNDAY April 18 [1847]

Dear Fletcher:

I have yrs this morning. I think I shall be able to give some idea, tomorrow, of the time of our departure—& shall write, in the morning, to Col Perkins, & Mr Frothingham, as well as to you. Pray get yr Bill thro, about the appointment of officers in the Volunteers.

Genl Taylor's popularity seems to spread like wild fire. They say it is likely to break down party division entirely, in the south and west.— The administration & its friends are attempting to induce him to come in, since they hardly expect to be able to keep him out, as a " no party " man.— So that they, who now have the offices, may keep them. Hence, it is well to place him in opposition to the Administration, not only as a *Whig*, but as a Whig attempted to be injured, & kept down, by Mr Polk & Co—

rc'd Int. of yesterday

Yrs D W.

We are all—that is *both*—quite well—

---

[1] Mr. Perry was at this time an active politician of South Carolina, opposed to nullification and secession. He was later Governor of the State. See B. F. Perry's " Reminiscences," p. 62, for an account of Webster while in South Carolina.

[2] Columbia, S. C.

(To D. Fletcher Webster.)

APRIL 21. '47.

Dear Fletcher;

I am glad you do not discontinue your correspondence, & hope you will consider me as being here, until you hear I am gone.

I believe we are pretty much out of Mr. McCulloch's hands, at last, but he has done us all the mischief he possibly could. His report against Mr. Jebb's old claim is unfair, disingenuous, bitter, & endless.— How long Mr. W. will take to come to a decision, or what the decision will be, I have no idea, at present. We all wait.

This horrid delay will of necessity cut short my journey. It will be too late to go to N. Orleans.

It is now likely, if I can get away in a week, that I shall pass the mountains, in N. Carolina, or Georgia, into Tennessee, & then home by the Ohio. Before I leave, I shall lay a plan, & let you know. I am quite sorry Mr Buckingham acts so strangely—

Your proposition is not only right, but necessary.

Mr. Schouler is a good man. Please say to him, I am glad of his purchase, & shall be happy to be useful to his undertaking.

All well

D. W.

(To D. Fletcher Webster.)

WASHINGTON April 27, 1847.

Dear Fletcher

I have been to the War office, but can do nothing for the Mass. Volunteers. The 10 Regiments are all filled. There must be an election of some sort, where the Regiment is.—

I am off tomorrow. Our *case* is to be decided, positively, on Monday the 10th. Mr. Berrien & Mr Russell stay to take care of it. What little may be coming to me, will be placed to my credit in Bank, & I shall be informed— I hope then to be able to remit, for Mr Weston, & some other little things, in Mr Heeley's hands— I have made out to scrape together a little travelling money, though I hardly know how—

If you write on receipt of this, address me at Charleston, where I shall be till the 10th & then in Savannah till the 15— I shall write you from all places where we stop a day.—

Affectionately Yrs   **D. W**

(To D. Fletcher Webster.)

NORTHAMPTON July 5. Monday P. M.
[1848?][1]

My Dear Son

I thank you for yr letter, & am glad all are well. I am safe here, but have had some cold, for three days. I think it is goi'g off.— We shall have a long cause, & I prescribe to myself patience, moderation, & coolness. We begin tomorrow.

Mr. Schouler is right. If Genl Taylor did that letter then the case is free from all embarrassment. We cannot support him— I am willi'g to hope, for the present, that he did not do so foolish an act. We shall see.

Mrs. W. says she goes to M. tomorrow, & takes down Dan, which is all right.

If I have English papers, keep them in Boston.
—Love to the Ladies of your family.

Yrs affectionately

D. W.

(To D. Fletcher Webster.)

MARSHFIELD, Sep. 26. (1847)
Sunday morning.

My Dear Son;

It seems impossible for me to go up today; and as I intend being at Springfield, I suppose my being a little sooner or a little later, at Boston, is of no importance. Unless the storm shall prove of unusual duration, I think you may fully expect the Major and me, at dinner tomorrow, either at your house, or Mr. Paiges.

I shall probably go to Springfield in the early train of Tuesday.—

---

[1] The year is not written in dating this letter but the allusion to Taylor's letter would seem to place it in 1848 though possibly the famous " Allison " letter (April 22, 1848) is not referred to.

I wish the letter to Mr. Curtis to be placed in his hands, as early as possible.   Mr. Healeys suggestion is of great importance—   The matter of the Resolutions should be closely seen to—.

Please send Mrs. Bell this note, at once.   I should be glad if all the notes could be delivered this evening.—

I shall not prepare any long speech for Springfield—a few words, of exhortation and encouragement will be all.

Yours

D. W.

(From Edward Webster.)

NEW ORLEANS Nov. 10th—1847—

My Dear Father;

You will be surprised to learn that I am still here—but there has not been any way for me to go—   My horses were sent to the Steamer Alabama, yesterday, and my trunk was on its way, when the Quarter Master sent me word, that if I could wait till today, he would give me a better place for my horses—so I concluded to wait.   It makes no difference, as we shall have to wait at Vera Cruz—till a sufficient force can be collected to move with towards the City—   Gen Butler arrived yesterday—   I was introduced to him, and he promised to give me some thing to do, when we arrive in Mexico—   I go to day by the Galveston—   Gen Butler will leave tomorrow—   On account of the long delay here, I was obliged to draw on you for $100.00—which I hope will be the last time I shall trouble you in that way—   The weather is oppressively warm, thin clothes are very comfortable. The town is filling up very fast, and it begins to look busy.

With my best love to Mother

I remain your affectionate Son

EDWARD WEBSTER.

(To D. Fletcher Webster.)

FRIDAY MORNING Dec (7) 1847.   11 O'clock.

Dear F.

I received your note this morning, and am glad you made a good stir among the children of Marshfield.— I have sent by this mail, "bills for the relief of Sylvester Prince and Rufus Hathaway "— I also send $100., by mail, to " Mr. O. Rich, Fish and Provision Dealer, Federal Street near High Street, Boston.

Yesterday we finished the argument in the New York Passenger tax case, and were to have begun the Boston cause, but Mr Choate has a turn of sick head-ache.

The case comes on, on Monday. In these cases, I have no doubt, whatever, that the law is with us; but where the Court may be, I know not.

I am glad to hear from your family, and a letter every day, or day or two, long or short, will be always most acceptable—

I have seen nobody, nor been any where, but to the Court room and back.

Your's affectionately

D. W.

Is it not time to hear from Edward? I get quite uneasy about him.

————

(From Edward Webster.)

City of Mexico, Decr 8th 1847.

My Dear Father—

We arrived here this afternoon, and I have just learned that a train will leave for Vera Cruz, to morrow morning— We have made the march in nine days from Perote, to this place, a distance of 170 miles—and have lost but two men from our Regt. At Puebla, we joined Gen Cushings Brigade, which was composed of the 1st Pena the Mass—the 4th Ohio and a Regt of recruits— Our Regt made as good an appearance as any in our entrance into the City to day— We are quartered in an old college, which we hope to leave in a day or two—

The news to night—is that a portion of the forces will [on] move to Cortrera (?) in a week—and that Genl Cushings Brigade will form a part, in that case, in all probability I shall still retain command of the Regt— I have not had time to see more of the City, than I noticed in marching through this morning— I intend to give you by the next mail a sketch of our march—

With much love to Mother—

Yours affectionate son   EDWARD

(To Edward Everett.)

WASHINGTON Jany. 29 1848.

My Dear Sir:

I have received yours of the 26th this morning.

It strikes me as being doubtful, whether you should deal with the subject of the maps.[1] It would not be without interest, but if gone into at large, would necessarily require a good deal of preface. If the principal facts could be stated, in an abridged or condensed form, I should like it; but whether that can be done, I do not know. I am rather inclined against the usefullness of a full and minute description.

The proof sheets are sent to me here. In looking over one of them this morning, I find that in my letter to Genl. Cass I ventured to suggest, that our Treaty, so far as it respected the right of search &c, on the coast of Africa, or rather substituted a new and different provision might be adopted elsewhere. You are aware what has been since done, in Europe, and would naturally take some notice of it.

My letter to you, and by you communicated to Lord Aberdeen, in which I discussed the attempt of Mr. now Sir Charles, Wood, and Sir Robert Peel, [to distinguish] between " Visitation " and " Search ", was I think never answered. You remember that Lord Brougham denied any such distinction.

If I can help you in anything, please command me. I suppose you have Mr. Gallatins paper, read before the New York Historical Society, respecting the *maps.*

Are you regularly supplied with our current documents here?

Yours always truly

DANL WEBSTER.

(From B. B. Tibbs.)

MONONGALEA COUNTY Va. Feb'y 1st 1848.

My Dear Sir.

I have the honor of communicating to you that your high and very commendable policy during the present Administration is duly appreciated in North western Virginia And that at a meeting of your fellow country men I have been empowered to express the same to you And also to enquire, whether it would be agree-

---

[1] i.e, in getting out the book concerning the Webster-Ashburton treaty.

able to you for your humble fellow citizens to use your name in connection with that of our ever Gallant and worthy Taylor, in the coming Presidential canvass.You may deem this premature, but allow me to say, that it will not be used any farther at present than a few of the discreet and politic Gentlemen of our party, and whom I here represent, may think prudent. Some are unwilling that instruction should be given to our representatives in the national convention whilst others strenuously urge that we cannot omit this opportunity of testifying our consideration &c &c

Excuse my uncerimonious and hasty epistle.

Very Respectfully

B. B. Tibbs

──────────

(To Peter Harvey.)

WASHINGTON Feb. 4. '48

My Dear Sir;

I recd your kind letter of the 15. Jany. & have left it unanswered so long, by reason of engagements, which have occupied my time. The Petition, respect'g the weight & measure of goods, I presented & explained to the Senate. There will be no difficulty, I think, in that Body, in agreeing to a proper amendment of the law.

I shall be very happy to be retained, by Mr. Belknap, who is an old friend. I have a payment to make the 14th of this month; and as Mr Belknapp is a man deal'g in so large affairs, that the amount of a Lawyers Retainer makes no great change, in his operations, even tho' money be "tight," perhaps, at your suggestion, he would place the fee in your hands, before that time.

I have been thinking, for a week or two, of say'g someth'g on the condition of the country. But almost all the Whigs in the Senate wish to speak, & generally desire me to hold back. Besides, I hardly wish to fall into the middle of a procession of Speakers, half a mile long, ahead, & equally long behind. We have had good speeches.

I know not what to make of the Peace rumours. The Administration talks one way, one day, as I fear, & the other the next. Before I address the Senate, I wish to see whether we are to have peace, or whether the war is to continue.

Mrs. W. as you will have learned, has gone to Boston. I feel concerned about Mrs. Appleton.   Let me hear from you, when you can.

Yours always truly

DANL WEBSTER

━━━━

(To D. Fletcher Webster.)

Dear Fletcher   FEB. 19. (1848(?)

   This note is for the last of the acceptances for the Eastern lands— You must try to beg & borrow, & take it up, as you alone are now interested.   I am very hard run— Edward's dft will be paid, & it will require all I have here.   I hope to get some small things soon, but have seldom met with such constant disappointments.

   You said, sometime ago, that our invaluable friend, Mr. Harvey, was com'g this way.   It appears he does not show himself. I was in hopes he might have picked up a few fees, as that Southern debt, which he knows about, annoys me so as to keep me awake at nights.   But I should be most glad to see him here, fees or no fees.

   I have a kind of feel'g, that we shall have peace in the Spr'g, though I can scarcely give the source of it.   I shall make a short speech early next week.   Send on Mr. H. to hear it.

Yrs

D WEBSTER

━━━━

(From Chas. W. March.)

Dear Sir   WASH. April 2—[1848]

   I received in due time from Boston your frank covering Mr Ketchum's letter to me.   It seems he is not satisfied with Mr. Everett's essay upon your services as Sec'y of State, & wishes me to prepare another.   But for his suggestion that I should consult you upon the subject, I should hardly have supposed him in earnest.

   The little I can do, you know, will be cheerfully done.   If you deem it necessary, I will come on during the month, & with your guidance, prepare what Mr. Ketchum wants, or anything else necessary to the attainment of the desirable object we have in view— I shall await the direction of your wishes.

The Tribune, I see, copies the numbers of "Whig from the Start," & I have no doubt they will gain general circulation & command general approval. Mr. Ashmun & myself are gladdened this morning with an editorial in the Boston Courier, not only written with ability, but with more than Mr. Buckingham's usual policy. A few such will do much good. The iron seems sufficiently heated & all that is necessary for shaping our ends is a succession of well-directed blows. Your friends, in my opinion, occupy the position that in our school-boy days we were wont to take in one of our sports—one of us would stand still & firm till the whole school linked hand-in-hand together surrounded us in a series of concentric circles— So will the whole school of Whigs—Clay men, Taylor men, Scott men, Courier men,—do now, if this centre stand firm.

Mr. Giddings told me a day or two since he was ready for one to come out for "Webster for Pres. Corwin for Vice Pres." giving the South to Taylor I am not so confident but that such a move would be our best—& even save a *check-mate*— Corwin I have reason to know, is ready for such.

I send you per mail a parcel of your R. I. argument.[1] I think I will retain the rest, unless otherwise directed by you, till I can find an opportunity of sending them by some one going East.

Fletcher's friends here are much gratified at the complimentary notice that appears in the Boston papers of his effort on the Boundary question before the Legislative Committee.

*   *   *   Raymond's edition of your speech did not reach us till after Houston's was generally copied; which is to be regretted as it was more full & accurate.

I will write soon again

Every Truly & respy Yrs

CHS. W. MARCH.

(From Millard Fillmore.)

ALBANY, May 2d, 1848.

My Dear Sir,

Your private note of the 24th ult. came to hand, yesterday, and I avail myself of the first leisure moment to reply.

[1] An argument made in the Supreme Court of the United States on the 27th of January, 1848. See "Works," vol. vi, p. 217.

You can not have had more cause to regret the coolness that has some time existed between us than myself. The cause of it I never suspected until informed of it by our mutual and esteemed friend Mr. Fessenden, some four years since, when we accidentally met at the Astor House. I was not aware of the letter to which you allude, addressed by me as chairman of the committee of Ways & Means to you as Secretary of State which you deemed (and no doubt truly) disrespectful. I trust you will believe me when I say that nothing of the kind could have been intended. My duties were so varied and laborious that I was compelled to intrust to the clerk of the Committee the task of writing the letters to the departments, from general directions. He generally wrote them after the adjournment of the committee for the morning and while the house was in session, and brought them to me in my seat for my signature. I had seldom time to do more than sign without reading them; and in this way the accident must have occurred of sending a letter which never would have been sent, had I supposed it contained a word or phrase, that could by any possibility have been tortured into seeming disrespect.

I am gratified to know that you are already appraised of the substance of what I have now related, and to be assured that the explanation is satisfactory and that I still enjoy a portion of your respect and esteem, which I can assure you I value very highly.

I am frank to say there is no man in the nation for whom I have entertained, and still entertain, so high a regard. My respect has bordered upon veneration, and my esteem upon admiration, and though this estrangement to which you allude, has prevented all correspondence and intercourse, yet it has not prevented me from noticing and admiring your uniform high and statesmanlike course in the Senate which has uniformly met my entire approval.

I sympathize with you most deeply in your domestic afflictions, and would that it was in my power to offer consolation, but that must come from a higher source.

I write in much haste without time to copy and beg leave to subscribe myself

Your devoted friend

MILLARD FILLMORE

(To D. Fletcher Webster.)

MONDAY EVE' May 15. '48.

My Dear Son:

I have recd yours of yesterday, & a parcel of speeches from Mr Kingsbury, which I have franked, & shall send off by this mail.

—It will give me pleasure to oblige a son of Mr Shaw, & a daughter of Genl Lyman; & I shall not fail to remember Col. Andrews.—

I cannot comply with Mr. Ketchum's suggestion to frank the "address." It would be out of character.

—Whatever I can properly do, I am ready to attempt; but I must maintain an elevated position

Yrs   D. W.

(To D. Fletcher Webster.)

ASTOR HOUSE May 25. 48. Thursday mor'g

Dear Fletcher

We must leave Albany to Mr. Ketchum, or to chance.

Mr Clingman M. C. is here. He is a member of the Convention. He says if a Northern Candidate be nominated at Baltimore, many Southern Whigs will see the necessity of nominating a Northern Whig, at Phila. He is among the No. I rather think he has some preference, not very decided—for Genl Scott.

I should be glad to see you, & one or two Boston friends, as soon as you can arrive, leaving Boston when your trial is over.

We go South this mor'g.

Yrs   D. W.

(To D. Fletcher Webster.)

WASHINGTON June 8. 48.

Dear Fletcher;

I have yrs of yesterday, 11 O clock. Before you receive this, matters will be all over. We shall get a Telegraphic dispatch, doubtless, this P. M.

This letter to Mr. Blatchford is *highly important.* It respects Marshfield. If he be not gone, put it immediately in his hand. If he shall have left, direct it to him at N. Y. without loss of time.

Yrs affectionately

D. W.

(To D. Fletcher Webster.)

WASHINGTON June 10. 1848.

My Dear Son;
We heard all the news yesterday; & I have yours, this morning.[1]

I think you did right to go straight home. I shall get away as soon as I can, without appearing to be in a hurry.—

As to the future, *keep entirely quiet till I see you.* I suppose there will be an *emeute;* but it may be quite a question, whether you & I, & our particular circle of friends had not better stand quite aloof. That is my opinion, at present, and until we see into things farther than we can at present. There will probably be enough others to do the work. At any rate, nothing can be gained by sudden action, or movement; & therefore by no means commit me, or yourself, or our especial & personal friends, till we meet, & can consult. Mr. Ketchum advises strongly to a course like this.

Mr Ashmun has not reached Washington, nor has any body else, that I can hear of. If I see any body, I will write you again tomorrow.

Yrs affectionately

DANL WEBSTER

(To D. Fletcher Webster.)

JUNE 16. 48.

Dear Fletcher
I have looked over the article & believe I wrote a great part of it; but I cannot separate what I wrote from what I did not write. What makes this a matter of any interest?— I really do not comprehend—

—I cannot get away before Monday, & would not go then, but

---

[1] Refers to the outcome of the Whig Convention at Philadelphia, where General Taylor received the nomination for President. See Curtis' "Life of Webster," vol. ii, p. 339 et seq., for Webster's action.

from Mr. Frothinghams *relentless* pressing about his mortgage: as I am wanted here next week, to keep along a Bill for paying scrip of Mexico, &c— But Mr F. will not give way, even for a week—& I shall therefore leave Monday—if noth'g further be heard.

Yrs affectionately

D. W.

(To D. Fletcher Webster.)

Dear Fletcher   WASHINGTON June 16. 48.

I shall endeavor to steer my Boat with discretion, but it is evident, that I must say something, or else it will be said for me, by others.   And I can see no way, but acquiescence in Taylor's nomination; not enthusiastic support, nor zealous affection; but acquiescence, or forbearance from opposition.   This is in accordance with what I said to the Whigs in Boston, viz. that I should not recommend Genl Taylor to the People, for President; but that if he were fairly nominated by a Whig Convention, I should not oppose the nomination.   I must stand here.

This northern movement will come to nothing respectable. Our best friends in Ohio have made up their minds to support Genl Taylor, & think he will carry the State.   Mr. Corwin, who has just returned from that State, is of the same opinion.   In N. Y. there seems to be no *Whigs*, opposed to the nomination, except Mr. Clay's friends.   The old Abolition party will adhere to *Mr Hale.*

The Barnburners intend, some of them to br'g forward Mr. Van Buren for President, & Marcus Morton for Vice President. Others nominate Mr Wilmot for President.   Meantime, there is certainly, at this moment, a fire spreading for the Whig nomination.   How long it may continue to burn, I cannot say, but at this moment it is rather fierce.   There is an entire confidence among the Whigs, that Taylor will be chosen; & many Democrats are of the like opinion.

I would send you some letters I have recd, if it were not for fear of accidental discovery or publicity.   I attach no great importance to them, but they show, to some extent, what is the true state of feel'g.

We set forth, Monday Eve'.

Yrs affectionately

D. WEBSTER

(To D. Fletcher Webster.)

My Dear Son;   WASHINGTON June 19—48

I am sorry that I cannot see my way clear to follow your advice, entirely. It appears to me necessary, that I should express, publicly, either acquiescence, or dissatisfaction, with the nomination. I have already said, often that I should not recommend Genl Taylor; but I have said, too, always, at the same time, that I should not oppose his election if nominated. Beyond that, I propose to say nothing, except in favor of the general Whig cause.

These Northern proceedings can come to nothing useful, to you or to me. The men are all low, in their objects. The abolitionists will adhere to Mr. Hale. The Barnburners will nominate Mr. Niles. If the Conscience men, at Worcester, were to ask to put me on their Ticket, what w'd it all come to?— I could not consent to that, with so little show of strength as they now put forth. On the other hand, suppose I acquiesce in Genl Taylor's nomination— He will, or will not, be chosen— If chosen, (as I incline to think he will be) it may be for *your* interests, not to have opposed him. As to *mine*, it is quite indifferent. I have, for myself no object whatever.

If he is not chosen, things can stand no worse.

Then, on the general ground; it seems to me I must not, in consistency, abandon the support of Whig principles. My own reputation will not allow of this. I cannot be silent, without being reproached, when such as Cass is pressed upon the country—

I agree, it is a difficult & doubtful question; but I think the safest way is, to overlook the nomination, as not being the main thing, & to continue to maintain the Whig cause.

We shall see; but I think we shall come out right.

Yrs affectionately

DANL WEBSTER

I take the cars with this.

Take care of these letters, *& keep them private.*

(To D. Fletcher Webster.)

IN THE SENATE, Monday 2. O clock. (Aug. 6 1848)

Dear Fletcher

I have talked with several persons this morning. Mr. Grinnell,

just returned from N. Bedford, says, the Whigs, generally, &
a good many Democrats, of *property*, will vote for Gen. T.¹ to
keep out Gen. C.²—thro fear, that the latter will bring on *War*,
with some nation or another—

—On the other hand, both the Senators from Pa., think Genl
T. has no chance in Pa. They say Cass is popular—& party
lines strict, & well observed. I shall gather up opinions here,
& write you, from day to day, & *write you daily*, till I leave
for home. We hear a rumor of a meet'g in Boston, Saturday
Eve', but no particulars. I suppose it is a mere rumor. Holding
back, for the present, is a position, not without its advantages.

Yrs   D. W.

(To D. Fletcher Webster.)

PRIVATE.

Dear Fletcher.   SUNDAY MORNING (Aug. 13), (1848).

Somebody is needed here, of sufficient character & force to go
directly to leading Whigs in Congress, from the South, & tell
them what can be done at the North, & what cannot. I do
trust Mr Stevenson, with others, will be here by Thursday. No
time should be lost, if it be possible for them to come.

I suppose you will leave Tuesday P. M.

Yrs   D. W.

(To D. Fletcher Webster.)

ASTOR HOUSE, Wednesday 2 Oclock. [Aug. 16 1848].
Dear F.

I have got on, so far; & may stay here a day, or so, to rest,
as I have been quite feeble—a better air today brings me up a
little.

I found yr letter at Phila.— I have made no speeches, & shall
make none. Still, I hardly understand yr earnestness on that
subject. Other friends do not write in that strain.

We must talk the matter over. I feel, every day, more & more
inclined, to withdraw altogether.

Your mother is well, & sends her love. She, too, has suffered
from the heat.

Affectionately

D. W.

------

¹ General Taylor.   ² General Cass.

(To D. Fletcher Webster.)

ASTOR HOUSE Wednesday 12. [Aug. 16 1848]

Dear Fletcher

I recd yours, this mor'g, & shall endeavor to follow your sagacious advice.

Mr. K. breakfasted with me at 7 this mor'g. He is to be in this House till June 7.—

—I have talked with Mr Grinnell, Mr Hoffman, Mr Nelson, &c. &c. &c.— They are in a state of mind, at present, which makes it important to consult & conciliate— They are not badly disposed. They are going, in force, to Phila. I hope you will come along in season, with other Boston friends, & see them here.

I hear nothing from Albany.—but will write you again, before leav'g this City.

I shall go tomorrow. morning.

Yrs   D. W.

(To E. Rockwood Hoar.[1])

MARSHFIELD, Aug. 23d, 1848.

My dear Sir

I am greatly obliged to you, for your kind and friendly letter; you overrate, I am sure, the value of my speech,[2] it was quite unpremeditated and its merit if any consists I presume in its directness and its brevity. It mortified me to see that some of the newspaper writers speak of it as the "taking of a position"; as if it contained something new for me to say. You are not one of them my dear Sir but there are those who will not believe that I am an anti slavery man unless I repeat the declaration once a week. I expect they will soon require a periodical affidavit. You know that as early as 1830 in my speech on Foote's resolutions, I drew upon me the anger of enemies, and a regret of friends by what I said against slavery, and I hope from that day to this my conduct has been consistent. But nobody seems to be esteemed to be worthy of confidence who is not a new convert. And if the new convert be as yet but half converted, so much the better, this I confess a little tries one's patience. But I can

---

[1] This letter is the property of the Hon. Geo. F. Hoar.
[2] Speech on "TheExclusion of Slaveryfrom the Territories." See "Works," vol. v, p. 302.

assure you in my own case it will not either change my principles or my conduct.

It is utterly impossible for me to support the Buffalo nomination, I have no confidence in Mr. VanBuren, not the slightest. I would much rather trust Genl. Taylor than Mr. VanBuren even on this very question of slavery, for I believe that Genl. Taylor is an honest man and I am sure he is not so much committed on the wrong side as I know Mr. VanBuren to have been for fifteen years. I cannot concur even with my best friends in giving the lead in a great question to a notorious opponent to the Cause, besides there are other great interests of the Country in which you and I hold Mr. VanBuren to be essentially wrong, and it seems to me that in consenting to form a party under him Whigs must consent to bottom their party on one idea only, and also to adopt as the Representative of that idea a head chosen on a strange emergency from among its steadiest opposers. It gives me pain to differ from Whig friends whom I know to be as much attached to universal liberty as I am, and they cannot be more so. I am grieved particularly to be obliged to differ in anything from yourself and your excellent father, for both of whom I have cherished such long and affectionate regards. But I cannot see it to be my duty to join in a secession from the Whig party for the purpose of putting Mr. VanBuren at the head of the Government. I pray you to assure yourself, my dear Sir, of my continued esteem and attachment, and remember me kindly and cordially to your father.[1]

Your's etc.

DANL. WEBSTER.

(To D. Fletcher Webster.)

PRIVATE.

THURSDAY 2 O clock [Sept. 1 1848]

Dear F.

I see no way but to *fall in*—& acquiesce— The run is all that way. We can do no good by holding out.— We shall only isolate ourselves— Northern opposition is too small & narrow to rely on—

I must say *something, somewhere*, soon.— My purpose is, to

---

[1] Was a Judge of the Supreme Court, and in 1869 became Attorney-General under Grant.

enlarge on the necessity of a change of Administration, to say something of the North, & its expectations—&, on the whole, to express a hope for Taylor— I must either do this, or go right into opposition.

D. W.

(To D. Fletcher Webster.)

WASHINGTON. Tuesday noon Decr 26. 48.

My Dear Son;

My rheumatism seems going off, & I hope to get away, either this afternoon or tomorrow. I have written Mr. Geo. T. Curtis not to let the Patent cause wait for me.

Saving & excepting a stiff back, I am quite well. I suppose I took cold, in the Court room, on Friday. When I finished, the heat was suffocat'g, the thermometer being at 90. The Court immediately adjourned—all the doors & windows were opened, & the damp air rushed in. I did all I could to protect myself. It was just such an exposure, which caused Mr Pinckney's death. He had been arguing, against me, the cause arising on Gov. Dudley's will, the first case, I think in 10 or 11. Wheaton. He came into court next morning, pale as a Ghost;—spoke to me, went to his lodgings at Browns, & never again went out alive.

I argued my cause well enough, & if I were not always unlucky, now adays, in such cases, I should think I saw a glimmering of success. But tho' we shall get 4 Judges, I fear we may not a 5th.

Yrs affectionately.

I am reading Lord Campbells Lives of the Lord Chancellors. If you have credit enough, run in debt for the Book, & read it the first thing you do.— Do this, careful & thoroughly, & you will imbibe a new love for legal studies.

(To D. Fletcher Webster.)

MONDAY 2 O clock.
[Feb. 1849]

Dear F.

Nobody can tell what will be done with the *License laws*, so great is the difference of opinion on all these subjects on the Bench. My own opinion is;

    that the License laws will be sustained;[1]
    that the passenger law of Mass[2] will *not* be sustained.

This, however, is opinion merely.

We are just break'g ground in the Senate, on the war, the acquisition of territory, &c. Mr Calhoun will probably come out tomorrow.— I shall say someth'g anon; but for 14 days I have been sitt'g here, in Court 4 /. hours every day. We hope to beat our adversaries in the Luther (?) case.

Yrs truly

D. W.

All well.

(To Peter Harvey. (?))

SUNDAY MORNING, 8 o'clock. [Feb. 1849.]

My Dear Sir—

I passed half an hour last evening with General Taylor. He was pleasant and social enough and by no means of such a harsh and stern countenance as the pictures represent him. Our conversation was general. He said nothing to me or I to him of cabinet appointments. It was said last night that he had signified his purpose to decide nothing for two or three days. The last rumor gives Mr. Binney to the treasury and Mr. Lawrence to the navy. I am perfectly satisfied it was arranged some time ago with Mr. Crittenden that Mr. Lawrence should come into the cabinet if Mr. C. could put him there. Everything indicates this. It is not unlikely that the end may be accomplished. Everybody of sense and character here is the other way of thinking, but I fear that Mr. Crittenden's opinions and views will not be easily overcome by all that others can say and do. General Taylor means well, but he knows little of public affairs and the life of a public man. He feels that he must rely on somebody—that he must have counsel even in the appointment of his counsellors, and regarding Mr. Crittenden as a fast personal friend he feels safest in his hands. This, I think, is the present state of things. What may be the result I do not know, and it would be idle to conjecture. The various cliques with their committees and debating are around him in force.

----

[1] See Howard's Reports, vol. v, p. 504.   [2] Ibid., vol. vii, p. 283.

Of course they feel different ways. The main hope for a favorable issue of things must be that in this scrambling he may lean to the judgment of his secretary of state.

You had better burn this letter.

Yours truly,

D. WEBSTER.

(*To D. Fletcher Webster.*)

PRIVATE.

MONDAY EVE, Mar. 26, '49.

Dear Fletcher

Things go *badly*. It turns out, that the President, sometime ago, I know not how long since, *promised* the office of Dis. Atty. to Mr Lunt. As far as I can learn, this promise was extorted by Mr. Gentry, & other members of the Philadelphia Convention. I saw the President, today, & he said he had made the promise. He said at the same time that he meant to do something for Mr Fletcher Webster. I told him, at once, that Mr. L. was not fitted for the office, by his Professional standing; that I said that, upon my responsibility, I should stand to it. He said he should bring the matter before the Cabinet; & if the Cabinet was not satisfied with Mr Lunts qualifications, he would not be appointed. He expressed himself entirely satisfied with your testimonials, & had noth'g to object, but *his promise.* I repeated my opinion of Mr L's want of qualification, & said I should probably express that opinion, in writing, & lay it before the Cabinet.

Thereupon, we parted, I afterwards saw Mr Clayton, & Mr Ewing. As far as I could judge, they knew noth'g of his *promise.* Mr. Ewing thought I had better suggest delay, & see what could be proved agt. Mr. Lunt's qualification. For the moment, I was rather inclined to adopt that course; but, on reflection, think it not consistent with my character—

The President has seen your testimonials. He is satisfied with them. He knows my wishes. He knows my opinion of Mr. Lunt's qualifications;— And there I shall leave the matter, without seeking for statements, or affidavits, against Mr Lunt.— I shall see Mr Clayton, & Mr Ewing, in the morning; & authorize them to say, in Cabinet Council, what I said to the President.— He will then take his own course— I shall ask for no time, nor for any thing else. Something was said by somebody about a

" charge ship for you," To which I answered, you sought no such employment. In the meantime, Mr Rantoul's resignation is in my pocket. I shall enclose this to Mr Curtis, & ask him to read it, & then forward it to you. I shall charge him to show it *to no human being*, & I charge you, not to communicate it, even to your wife, or to Healey. Keep every thing to yourself. They may find something else to satisfy Mr Lunt. Let them take their own course. I shall ask nothing, for you, or myself— Of course, I will write you again, tomorrow:—to accompany this, & perhaps thro the same channel.

Yrs affectionately
DANL WEBSTER

―――――

(To D. Fletcher Webster.)

WASHINGTON Mar. 29. '49. 1/2 past 2 O clock.

My Dear Son.

Mr Seward has seen the President again today. He says the President expresses very friendly feelings—that nothing is in the way but that unlucky promise— He says *that promise was made to some Massachusetts people, as well as others.* I have no doubt A. L. has had a hand in the whole matter. The President said he would see if nothing else could be found satisfactory to Mr Lunt, & his friends. If not, then something should be found for you. He repeated, that if well founded objections to Mr Lunts legal & Professional qualifications appeared, they would be decisive.

I think Mr Ashmun would join in a letter to the President, confidential, urging that Mr Lunt's standing at the Bar did not justify the appointment. Mr Choate ought to join, but suppose he is too timid. What would Joseph Bell, Prest. of Senate, & F. B. Crowningshield, Speaker of the H. of R. say, to joining in a confidential letter? Or any other respectable person, known here.

I shall remain here for better weather. We are in the midst of a violent snow storm.

Yrs affectionately
D. W.

Last night I felt not a little disturbed. Today I feel better.
By all means, observe absolute silence & secrecy.

(To D. Fletcher Webster.)

WEDNESDAY 1 O clock Mar. 28. '49.

My Dear Son

It has rained all the morning, like a torrent, & I have not been out of the House.— Nor have I heard a syllable since I wrote you last, yesterday.

Mr. Winthrop, as you know, has certified that Mr Dexter, Mr. Lor'g, & Mr C. P. Curtis, constitute the very front rank of the Boston Bar.

Now, if some of these Gentlemen would join Mr Ashmun in a private & confidential letter, saying that Mr Lunts professional standing is not what it should be, for so important an office, & in which he is to meet such able opponents, I incline to think it would settle the matter. Something else would then be found for Mr Lunt.

Indeed, I very much wish that Mr Ashmun & Mr Curtis would come on here.

Can you suggest this to Mr Ashmun?— He might look a little after his Brothers matter.

Tell Mr Healey that his friend S. J. T. will abide, for the present.

Yrs affectionately

DANL WEBSTER

(To D. Fletcher Webster.)

TUESDAY MOR'G 10 Oclock—[March 29 '49].

My Dear Son

I did not mention in my letter last night that Gov. Seward, who has been extremely kind, went with me, yesterday to the President. I staid in the Ante Room, while he went in, & spoke to him. I then went into pay my respects, & Mr. Seward & I came out together. While going down stairs, he told me the result of his interview. I then went back, alone, & spoke to the President; expressed my regret, & disappointment; & added, that in my opinion Mr Lunt was not fit for the office. He then stated, that he had been induced to promise it to him, by the urgency of members of the Phila. Convention— That he must, in compliance with his word, bring his name before the Cabinet, that if the Cabinet thought him not qualified, he should make another nomination.　I then went to Mr Clayton & Mr Ewing.　Mr Clayton said at once, it was Mr Gentry's doings.　Mr. Ewing thought I had better ask for a postponement, for a month, to be able to show Mr Lunts unfitness—　At first, I thought I would do this: but have altered my mind, & wrote a note this morning to Mr Clayton to the following effect.

viz.

That I wish him to communicate to the other members of the Cabinet the opinion which I expressed to the President, & to him, respecting Mr Lunt's qualification for the office;

also,

Requesting him to inform the President, and the Cabinet, that I was authorized to say, that Mr Choate would take the office, if offered to him.　I did this to raise, a plain question, viz. whether the President would prefer Mr Lunt, not on account of Massachusetts support, but on account of Tennessee & Louisiana support, to Mr Choate.　Mr Seward has now gone up with this letter, & I should not be surprised, if he should show it also to the President, for he, Mr Seward, is very thoroughly friendly, & Persevering.

The President gave to Mr. Seward, as I believe I stated last Eve', the same reason for his promise, which he gave to me; that is, the application of members of the Phila. Convention.

I have little doubt the matter will be postponed, for some time. And if plump & strong declarations from authentic quarters could be produced, agt. Mr Lunt's fitness, on the direct ground of want of sufficiently high standing at the Bar, the members of the Cabinet, I have no doubt, would all be glad to reject him.　A confidential letter, to this effect, from any judge, or other source, to the President or Mr Clayton, I presume would produce the effect.　But whether any such thing can be obtained, I know not—

I shall cause it to be suggested, that it will be much easier to find a charge'ship, or something else, for Mr Lunt, than to find any other office than this, for you to take—

I send these letters thro Mr Curtis, in order that having read them, he may forward them, together with his advice; or, if he can, that may run down to Boston for a day & see you.

Yrs affectionately
DANL WEBSTER

I shall remain here, sometime.

(To D. Fletcher Webster.)

APRIL 12. '49. Thursday mor'g—6 O clock.

Dear Fletcher

I wrote you a hurried line yesterday.   As nothing more was expected from Boston, I thought it best to go & see the President.   He seemed in good humour, & we talked the matter over. The thing had not been before the Cabinet.   He had not seen the letter, respecting Mr Lunts Professional standing, but had heard there were such.   He said he had been assured he was competent, & therefore made the promise.   I told him I thought it would be well, if it could be done, to avoid raising such a question before the Cabinet, & afterwards before the Senate.   That it wd be better to give Mr Lunt something else, if there were any thing which would satisfy him & his friends.   He assented to that.   He said he had told all the Cabinet, what he had told me, that he intended to give someth'g to Mr. F. W.   We then spoke of the Marshalship.   He said that was not promised, that he knew of, & he would ask Mr Ewing to look up the papers.   I stated the reasons why you preferred the other office, but said I should be satisfied with any thing, not disparaging, which should arrange all interests.   At this stage of the conversation Mr Ewing came in.   We continued the conversation.   Mr Ewing said he must leave the City on Monday, to go to Ohio for his family, & should be gone a fortnight, and could not possibly take up this subject before his departure.   We had a good deal of further conversation; & it was finally agreed that the thing should rest, till Mr Ewing returned, & until I went to Boston. So it stands, Mr Johnson spoke to Mr Ewing on the subject, in the morning, & asked who were candidates for the Marshalship. Mr Ewing said he did not know & did not care.   I presume his inclination is fixed.   So is Mr Johnsons; & I look for no opposition in the Cabinet.

Now—I think one or the other may be had, & ought to be made certain.   I do not know who are candidates for the Marshall's office.   But it is best to be *strong,* if we are obliged to go for that.   I recommend that Mr Healey, & other friends get up a *strong paper,* signed by the Electors, & members of Congress, & some other well known men.   It might be somewhat after the enclosed form.   Mr Fearing should sign & add "Electors" &c.— There should be twenty or thirty strong names. It wd not be amiss to have this done, right off.—   Then, when I get home. I will see whether Mr Lunt will take some thing else, & leave the Atty's place to you; & if not, we will see what is next to be done.   Let us secure the Marshalship.   That will be a great office for you. Its duties may be performed very much by Deputy—   You can practice in the State Courts, & so keep your hand in, in the Law—

Now, take my advice—& let such a paper be signed.   Begin with Mr Fearing, & let him go to Mr Livermore—get the names of members of Congress, where you can.   Let there be weight enough to satisfy the President, over all other comers.—

I am going to Norfolk, to return in a few days—say abt the 18—& on the 23. I hope to leave for home.

I am glad your wife & children are all safe at Marshfield.

The true policy, in regard to your office, now is *to keep still*— & go on & get strong names—   It is said Mr L. has written letters, full of indignation at the delay.

Yrs affectionately—

D. W.

'(To D. Fletcher Webster.)

MONDAY MOR'G April 16. '49

My Dear Son

Mr Lunt, I take it, is a cross-grained person, & at the present moment, probably, particularly sour, & angry.   He is doubtless a difficult subject, for negotiation—   Yet, he sees that delay has occurred, & will find more occurring.

If he has much sense, (which may be doubted) he will see that he may encounter difficulties in the Cabinet, & more in the *Senate*. Possibly, these considerations might lead him to think of some other place, if there was any channel of communication, through which useful suggestion could be made to reach.   I know, my-self, nothing of his associations.   You can think of these things.—   I wish you to continue to write to me, as usual, until you hear from me to the contrary as my letters will be forwarded.

It is dreadful cold—ice last night a line thick.

Yrs affectionately

DANL WEBSTER

(To D. Fletcher Webster.)

MONDAY—2 O clock April 2. (1849).

My Dear Son

Mr Ashmun has written me an excellent letter.   Mr. Winthrop a very fair letter, in favor of Mr Geo. T. Curtis, if you are out of the way—*not otherwise.*

—You will not be out of the way.   Mr Johnson has written Mr Choate.   If Mr Choate's letter comes strong & plump, it will settle the matter.   But he should not only speak strong as to Mr Lunt's want of standing & qualification, but should go strongly for you.   He does no good—to any body—& only harm to you, by holding out any hope, or giving any assistance to Mr Brinley—

Yrs   D. WEBSTER

TUESDAY April 3. [1849] 12 O clock

My Dear Son

I hardly know whether I have much to say today.   I told you Mr Johnson had written Mr. Choate.

I have reason to think Mr Brinley is sick of his position, & will help us, if he can.   Mr Evans will also have a free talk with Mr Ewing.   I trust we may weather the storm; but wd not have had so much anxiety for any thing in the world, connected with myself.   We are all pretty well.   The claimants under the Mexican Treaty are coming in upon me, thick, to take charge of their claims.   They think I am a rising young man.

We have no Boston mail today, but shall hear from you tomorrow, & know all that has been, as yet, done in Boston.

Mr Choates answer we shall look for on Thursday.

Yrs, My Dear son, always affectionately

D. W.

(To D. Fletcher Webster.)

WEDNESDAY 1 O clock. [Apr. 1849]

My Dear Son;

I have your two notes of Monday, and, as the Merchants say, "note contents."   Tomorrow, I presume, we shall hear from

Mr. Choate & others, & then, I presume, we shall know all that can be done.

It looks to me, at present, as if Mr Lunt could *not* be appointed. But I cannot tell what may happen. I shall be glad when the business is over, for it has worried me, prodigiously.

Yrs affectionately

D. W.

————

(To D. Fletcher Webster.)

THURSDAY 3 O clock [Apr. 1849]

My Dear Son

A letter has come from Mr. C.—but I have none from you, except one about Gloucester matters— I do not hear of letters from Mr Fearing etc—but have not inquired. I suppose they must have come—Mr Evans will give a strong letter, & also speak personally.

I do not know what will be the result, but it will be difficult to appoint Mr Lunt—

He ought to be persuaded, if he has any friends, to go for some other place.

Yrs affectionately

D. W.

————

(To D. Fletcher Webster.)

PRIVATE.

SUNDAY MOR'G.

Dear Fletcher,

I have yours of Friday. Mr. Johnson was to see the President, yesterday, & see if he could arrange for a conversation on your subject, tomorrow— I suppose he saw him; but he went immediately to Baltimore, before I heard the result.

Mr. Evans is taking an active & friendly part; but I do not know whether any thing will change the Presidents purpose. I think not. I presume that Lunt writes directly to the President, & tells 40 lies about us all—

Whether he would give you the Marshall's office I cannot say. But I feel as if we should be obliged to take hold of Mexican claims, & passenger taxes, & get some money. I will take care of the first, if you will push the last—

—I will keep you informed; tho' I am quite doubtful as to

having any good news—only think of Mr Clayton's appointing M-L. Davis Express Agent at N. Y.!

Yrs   D. W.

(To D. Fletcher Webster.)

Sunday 2 O clock

Dear F

Mr E. is quite hopeful of your affairs—much more than I am. The difficulty—& the only difficulty—is the *promise*—Mr Lawrence can do no harm now. It is the *promise*. If the President cannot fairly extract himself from that, he will fulfil it, at all hazards, as I suppose. We shall see in a day or two—

D. W.

(To D. Fletcher Webster.)

PRIVATE.

April 11 [1849] Wednesday

My Dear Son;

I have been to H. Q. (?)— You will have one, or the other— I am sure of that— *But nothing will be done, till I get home.* Keep the Peace, profoundly— Mr Ewing is *flatfooted*. I will write, at more leisure tomorrow. I dare not trust the wires—

Yrs affectionately

D. W.

(To D. Fletcher Webster.)

Thursday 2 O clock [1849]. .

My Dear Son;

The Superintendence of Attys & marshalls is transferred to the Home Dept.— That is favorable. I have seen Mr Ewing, & Mr Reverdy Johnson, today. It looks, now, as if some agreeable result might be arrived at. *Pray keep entirely still—& silent.* Gov. Seward is going to N. York, & I think he will run down to Boston. He proposed, of his own accord, to do so. I shall write to you every day, also to Mr Curtis—

Keep absolutely silent   Mr Lunt has gone home.   —We are sure of time enough to arrange things.

Yrs affectionately

Danl Webster

(To D. Fletcher Webster.)

SUNDAY 2 O clock (1849)

My Dear Son:
I recd. Mr Curtis despatch yesterday, & answered it. I believe somebody will write to somebody today.— Yet it would
have been better if Mr Choate & others had come forward, without waiting to be written. There came word to me today, from
some subordinate official quarter, that the *Marshalship* was a
better office than the Attorney ship—that Mr F. W. might have
it; & if he wd not take it, Mr Lunt must. I do not know how
high the spring was, from which this rumour, or suggestion,
proceeded.

In point of profit, no doubt, the Marshalship is worth twice
as much as the other office. It is especially important, just now
as the Census is to be taken—& many assistants, of course, appointed.

There seems to be no Boston mail today. I have no letter, but
hope to hear tomorrow. I think, that some how, things will
work themselves clear— If not, you must go to work, & cut
your own fodder; & I shall be relieved from a good deal of labor
& responsibility.

Give my love to Mr Curtis. I fear he suffers from his kindness. —Remember me also to Gov. S. if with you.
Yrs affectionately

D. W.

Your mother sends her love.

———

(To D. Fletcher Webster.)

BALTIMORE, Tuesday, April 24. 49.

My Dear Son
I arrived here from Norfolk this morning, & shall go North
tomorrow; & hope to be in Boston, Saturday Eve'g.

You will have considered what it will be best to do, in your
case. Mr Ewing will return, I suppose, sometime next week; &
on his return the matter must be settled, I suppose, some way.
My opinion is, that if we can, we must persuade Mr Fearing to
go Washington, taking Mr Harvey with him.

I have no hope that Mr. Lunt will come into any arrangement.

I trust you will have made up your mind on what will be a proper course by the end of this week.   I wish Mr Ashmun would go to Washington.

I must return to Washington the 1st of June.

Yrs affectionately

DANL WEBSTER.

(To D. Fletcher Webster.)

Dear F.   [SPRING OF 1849 ?] Sunday P. M.

Depend on it, Mr Hudson's letter will make a great noise here, & be run thro all changes, in both Houses.   Genl Taylor places almost all his removals, on the ground of interfering with politics.   I never knew so rash a proceed'g.

I am a little rheumatic today.

Yrs   D. W.

(To Thomas Ewing.)

My Dear Sir;   BOSTON May 1st 1849.

I do not find, on inquiry, that Mr. Lunt has, as yet, manifested any disposition to waive his claim to the office of District Attorney for Massachusetts.   He states, that the President made a promise, some time ago, to give him that office; & that he is inclined to insist on, or that he expects, the performance of that promise.

It is extremely painful for me to oppose whatever the President feels bound to do, or to make the performance of his promises disagreeable, or unpleasant to him, by any act of mine.   He, & his cabinet have already the means of knowing, pretty well, the state of things, & the state of opinion, in Massachusetts, in regard to this appointment.

The bearer of this is the Honorable Albert Fearing, late Whig Elector for this county.   No man understands our political affairs here better than he does, & no man enjoys, in a higher degree, the confidence of the Whigs of this State.   He will seek an opportunity to see you, and will be glad, also, to have a personal conversation with the President.

I am, My Dear Sir, with very true regard

Yours always

DANL WEBSTER.

(Memorandum.)

[MAY 1 1849]

Mr. Fearing will know, very well, what to say to the President; but, among other things, he may, perhaps, in his discretion state; That there has been a general expectation, & wish, that F. W. should be appointed Dist. Atty.

That he is generally acceptable to, & popular with, the Whigs of Boston, (if Mr. F. thinks so) & that the leading men of the Bar, (Mr Loring, Mr Dexter, Mr Curtis, Mr Simmons &c) recommend him.— That there is a prevailing opinion, at the Bar, & with the public, that Mr L's professional standing is not such as to make it proper to appoint him to that office—

—That a great majority of the Boston Bar, & nearly all the leading members are Whigs, & took an active & efficient part, in Genl Taylor's Election.

—That it is supposed many of them might feel dissatisfied, with the *comparison* which the public might naturally draw, from Mr. Lunt's being selected, in preference to some of themselves.

—That there is no Whig who has been thought of, as a Candidate, (unless Mr Brinly be an exception) who has not expressed his entire readiness to stand out of the way, if Mr F. W. is a candidate.

—That it might be naturally supposed, that if—Mr Lunt understood, that the case gave the President embarrassment, he would, at once, take some other, & better place—

—That it is highly important, & desirable, to the Whigs of Boston, & the whole State, that controversy & schism, on this subject, should be avoided; so that no question may be raised, any where, upon the propriety of Mr. Lunt's nomination to the office—

—That as to Mr F. W. himself, he would regret to be the occasion of any difficulty; & so far as he is himself concerned, he leaves it to friends to suggest, what place shall be assigned to him, if it be the pleasure of the President to appoint him to any office. It may also be suggested, that it might be well to ask, *confidentially*, of Mr Winthrop, & Mr Greely, whether in their opinion, Mr. Lunt's appointment would be generally satisfactory, or whether it would be otherwise—

There are letters with Mr Ewing, or Mr Johnson, from Mr Choate, Mr Evans, & Mr Ashmun, respect'g Mr Lunts Professional standing. No doubt, others to a similar import, might be had for asking for.

—Finally, it might be put to Mr. Ewing, as a question for the exercise of his discretion, whether, in his judgment, it would be well—to fill the office by the appointment of a man, who has no considerable Massachusetts support, & who relies, mainly, on a promise said to be made by the President, to persons out of Massachusetts, & in no way connected with that State—

(To D. Fletcher Webster.)

FRIDAY MOR'G 4 O clock May. 1849

My Dear Son;

I recd yours by Beals Express this Eve'g— I am glad you going on, by all means, & hope you will do something. Take care how you commit me to support Mr Lunt.— I feel quite anxious that Mr Curtis should go with you. He can do more than any body else— If Genl McNeil is not to be removed, had you not better take the marshal's office, if you can get it? Do not hasten back, while there is a chance of doing any th'g.

D. W.

Be sure to see the President yourself, & have a free talk with him— Do not fail in this. I am quite sure you will make a favorable impression—& you should br'g things to some point, if you can.

All well here— I shall write to your mother today.

D. W.

(To D. Fletcher Webster.)

WASHINGTON Sunday 3 O clock
[May. 1849]

My Dear Son,

Letters were recd from you yesterday, and again today, respect'g Genl McNeil, & a little about California— Mr Curtis will go to the President, tomorrow,—if he does not I shall, & read your letter, & ascertain what the President means to do. Before I go to bed tonight, I will try to write to Mr Harvey; but not in season for this mail—

There is nothing new about appointments— Few nominations, of persons appointed in the recess have yet been reported from Com.ees At present, we are engrossed by Bradbury's Resolution,

Cass' Resolutions, & Clays' Resolutions, upon neither of which do I propose to say a word. I am in the Court, for 4 days, beginning tomorrow, & then a little respite—

The fish were so good, that if the weather be cold when you receive this, you would send me " a ditto of your last respects—" viz. 2 good cod, & *one or two good* cusks

I am glad to hear from Mr Weston that your road goes on well.

Yrs   D. W.

_____

(To D. Fletcher Webster.)

TUESDAY MOR'G 8 O clock [1849]

Dear F.

Mr. Curtis saw the President yesterday, & read him your letter. He appeared to be quite pleased with it, said, those were " high sentiments," & that he appreciated them. He said there [were] difficulties, but he inclined to think he [would] reappoint Genl McNeil. Mr. Curtis seemed quite pleased with the interview.

Yrs Affectionately

D. W.

_____

(From D. Fletcher Webster.)

NEW YORK May 8. 49.

My dear Father,

I met Mr. Curtis this morning. He was rather opposed to my going to Washington at all—

He said it looked as if I were begging & that all the papers would remark upon it. However I shall hold my course. I mean to go see for myself.

He says that Mr. Ewing thinks that there is not much to choose, on the score of *acceptability to the public*, between Mr. Lunt & myself, & I hear from another quarter that that he supposes *Mr. G. T. Curtis* to be more fit for the place than either of us.

I want Mr. Fearing to write, if he will not go on, & tell Mr. Ewing that Mr. L's appt. is not acceptable & mine is, that is if he thinks so.

I shall write to him to that effect. Mr. Curtis thinks he had better not go on & on the whole I don't care to have him. Coming from New York he would be likely to give rise to many remarks, if he interferes in a Boston appt. He says he will write Mr. Ewing.

I mean to have a plain talk with Mr. Ewing and if I have an opportunity with the President.

I shall not remain long, unless you write me to do so. Mr. Curtis says I had much better not.

Mr. G. T. Curtis is a good lawyer, but he does not need the place and his manners are most unpopular, nor do I know of any claim he has to it, whatever. Besides he is not in my way.

I wish very much Mr. Fearing would either go or write— I do not believe that the administration knows what they are about in this matter & no one in Boston seems to dare to tell them.

Yr affectionate Son
FLETCHER.

Mr. Lunt has left at the Dept. Judge Shaw's letter, in which he says something about Mr. Lunt's able argument &c &c.

Could you not write Judge Shaw & ask him if he meant to recommend Mr. L. informing him of the use to which Mr. L. has converted his letter. It seems to me you could perfectly well do this.

Judge Shaw I have no doubt would disclaim such intention & that might be of service.

F. W.

———

(From W. H. Furness.[1]*)*

Dear Sir,   PHILA. Jan 9. 1850

Pardon this intrusion, & the boldness implied in this address. I deprecate the appearance of presuming to give counsel to you whom I regard with sincere admiration. But I must have the folly of the presumption, for I cannot but obey the impulse, that I have very long felt, to express to you, Sir, my deep conviction that if Daniel Webster would only throw that great nature, which Heaven has given him, into the great cause of the world, the cause of human Freedom, his fellow-citizens, his fellow-men, would behold such a demonstration of personal power as it is seldom given to the world to witness. And yet no one would be more surprised than he. You have given evidence,

---

[1] Furness was an eminent Unitarian clergyman, a voluminous writer upon religious subjects and an enthusiastic exponent of the anti-slavery movement.

which has filled us all with pride, that you were made for great things, for far greater things than any office; but we do not know, Sir, how much you are capable of. You do not know yourself, & it is impossible in the eternal nature of things that you ever should know, until, with a devotion that makes no stipulation for yourself, you give yourself utterly to the Right.— You once said of a professional friend, "that when his case was stated, it was argued." Of no man can this be said with more entire truth than of you. If, taking Liberty for your light, you cast your broad glance over the history & state of the Country, if seeing, as many think you could not fail to see, how Slavery has *interfered* & is *interfering*, not with the property, but with the rights, with the inmost hearts of freemen, making them its tools & supporters, you were then to tell the country, in that grand & simple way in which no man resembles you, what you see, *stating the great case*, so that it would be argued once for all & forever, you would not only render the whole country, North *and* South, the greatest possible service, but you would be conscious of a compensation in your own being, which even your great power could not begin even to compute. The service of great principles is not a whit more beneficent in its results to others than in its influence on those who undertake it. They may witness no results to others. They may possibly subject themselves to inconvenience, to suffering. But the redeeming, ennobling effect on themselves they cannot miss. We have seen again & again how it regenerates ordinary men. What then must be its influence on one whom nature has made great?

But I will not trespass any further. Accept I pray you these few feeble words as an expression of the earnest personal interest of

Yours faithfully & respectfully[1]

W. H. FURNESS

(From Charles W. March.)

My Dear Sir.   NEW YORK Januy 9, 1850.

Not bad employment, for I am sending a bottle of Ceylon, Just

---

[1] For the reply see Private Correspondence of Daniel Webster, vol. ii, p. 353. In this reply Webster deprecates slavery, but says: "I cannot co-operate in breaking up social and political systems, on the warmth, rather than the strength. of a hope that, in such convulsions, the cause of emancipation may be promoted."

separated from the lees, it is fit for immediate use. This same Wine on a former occasion I believe, performed no unimportant service. If it could be again useful in giving peace and security to the South, how happy many would be made. I used to tell my friends in Carolina that if they wanted a man at the head of affairs who could carry out the Compromise of the Constitution, they need not look far beyond the very one to whom this note will be addressed.

I am ever, and with true
regard, Sincerely Yrs
CHARLES MARCH

(To Fletcher Webster.)

WASHINGTON Jan. 25, 1850

My Dear Son
I should be glad to aid you, if I could, in your wish to join Mr. Harvey in a little enterprise to California— But, really, I have no money, nor could I raise any, now, in any way that I know of. I should be willing to give a note, for not a large sum, payable about the end of the Session, say 4 or 5 months, if that would be of use to you. I have earned a good deal of Money, within the last year, but it has all been paid away, either on Mr. Frothingham's mortgage, or on those old debts, which we once thought had been provided for.

The Court, with a short recess, will probably sit here till July. I have a good deal to do in it and hope to get some fees.

As to the Mexican claims, things look fair, at present; but nothing can be pocketed from that source for some time.

I do not hear when the Passenger causes are to be tried.

I hear nothing from Mr. Ticknor, in answer to the letter written to him, when you were here.

Yours affectionately
DANL. WEBSTER.

(To D. Fletcher Webster.)

WASHINGTON Feb. 1, '50.

My Dear Son
The fish came in good order, & were perfectly delicious. It seems more like living, than anything we have had for a good

392 LETTERS OF DANIEL WEBSTER

while. I send you a draft on the Bank here, for $40. Pay $20 to Mr. Rich, & keep the other twenty to pay for the fish sent, & for other fish that may be ordered. I recd. your Telegraph last eve about the $500 draft—all right—

As to petitioning the Legislature, in regard to the passenger tax business, I think it is better to wait a while, till we see what the Legislature of New York shall do, who have the subject now before them, & with whom better sense, as well as better feeling, seems to prevail.[1]

Mr. Munroe, the Superintendent, is now here, & I have seen him, & told him that he will find no assistance here till the State leaves off its belligerent legislation. The Bill which has passed the Mass: Senate was drawn last year by Mr. Joseph Giles, " to get round the decision of the Supreme Court," as he himself, I understand, avowed. While that disreputable policy prevails, Mr. Giles & his fellow laborers may be assured that the chance for favorable measures here is small. Mr. Healey may safely hint that, to whomsoever he pleases—

The Co^mee, the two Aldermen are also here, & I shall see them, probably today—I incline to think Mr. Munroe will write to Boston, today, advising, forbearance, & proper temper * * *
[Torn off.]

(To Peter Harvey.)

WEDNESDAY, 13, Feb. [1850]
My Dear Sir
I have been engaged, since 5 o clock this morn'g, on a Mexican claim, with the exception of an hour in the Senate— I must put off my " political letter " till tomorrow. Meantime, I wish to say, *for your own Govt.* that there will be no disunion, or disruption. Things will cool off. California will come in. New Mexico will be postponed. No bones will be broken—& in a month, all this will be more apparent[2]—

I recd. your Telegraph last Eve'; & thank you, most sincerely.
D. W.

---

[1] See Curtis' "Life of Webster." vol. ii, p. 373. Both New York and Massachusetts passed laws imposing a tax upon vessels bringing alien passengers, on account of every passenger brought into the State. This was declared unconstitutional.

[2] Does Webster not refer to his proposed Constitution and Union speech delivered on March 7, 1850?

(To Fletcher Webster.[1])

FEB. 24. 1850

My dear Son

I am nearly broken down with labor and anxiety. I know not how to meet the present emergency or with what weapons to beat down the Northern and Southern follies now raging in equal extremes.

D. W.

———

(Notes of 7th of March Speech.[2])

Causes which have so suddenly produced this state of things.
War declared May '46.
Armies over run Mexico—& siezed the Capitol—
Navy siege her ports
—Feb. 48 Treaty—& cession of her Provinces—
—900 miles of coast on Pacific
—Revolution in California, meanwhile, July 1846
—Col Fremont
Soon as War known, U. S. flags hoisted—
Great numbers rushed to Mexico, in '46, '47.
 In Jan. 48 Mormon discovd. gold—
Same winter, or spring, Suttlers & Marshall's discoveries—
In May '48 digging commenced.
—Success incredible. Larkin letters, June 1, & 28.
Col Mason's Rept. Aug. 17, 48
On the peace, a new rush—
1000 large vessels—70,000 passengers.
Amt. of gold remitted—& amt. merchandize
via Aspinwall—6 Steamers—4 or 5 small ones
—Trade & revenue   15 millions of gold to
Congress passed no law   U. S. & England
                                   2 or 3 to Oregon
                                   a great deal at home

---

[1] A copy of this note, in the possession of Edwin W. Sanborn, of New York, is all that the editor has seen.

[2] These notes are in Webster's own hand, with the exception of several passages which are excerpts from speeches made in the past. These excerpts were copied by some one for him. Curtis' "Life of Webster," vol. ii, p. 403, says there was "but little written preparation" for this speech, only "two small scraps of paper." There were, in fact, twenty-eight sheets of foolscap.

California called a Convention—Formed a Free Constitution —chose Senators & members of Congress, & now asks for admission.

—Her Constitution excludes SLAVERY—

—War raged for Territory—expected to be Slave Territory— Events have decided the matter otherwise & hence the present controversy, & the present excitement[1]

Slavery

The North regards it as a great political & moral evil, &, in its nature, founded in wrong.

Slavery has existed from the earliest times.

Oriental, Jewish, Greek, Roman, Feudal

There is no positive injunction agt. it, in the old Testament or the new.

The Theocracy of the Jews tolerated it

—The religion of the Gospel deals little with the political relations of men.

—The teachings of Jesus Christ are addressed to the hearts & consciences of individual men.

—They seek to purify the soul, & to regulate the life   But it cannot be doubted, that the principle of Slavery is opposed, in the abstract to the meek spirit of the gospel.   It is founded in the power of the strongest.

It is conquest, a permanent conquest of man over man.

It is against the law of Nature.

It is like unjust war, or any other form of oppression or subjugation

These are the sentiments of the North.

—It is probable many in the South are hardly prepared to deny these truths in the abstract

—But, in general, they are accustomed to it ; born & bred where it exists, & taught to consider it as no wrong.

And they are honest, & conscientious, in this.

No doubt, there are thousands of men, deeply religious, & whose consciences are as tender as those of any other Christians, see no way for them but to treat their slaves with kindness & humanity

They are far from thinking, that in all cases manumission would be useful to the Slaves themselves—

---

[1] The above is endorsed "History of Events that have led to the Present State of Things."

The Methodist Church equally conscientious, in both branches.
I have read their proceedings, & lamented the result.
When religious excitement takes place, men run to extremes—
                         Algebra
Abolitionists.   Fault finders, with the sun.
Impatient waiters, on Providence.
They do not enough heed St. Paul.
—Mr. Butler—War-horse!
—They think they can draw light from angry clouds—
—*They want candor, & charity*
And not willing to leave things with him, who sees the end
from the beginning.
How Slavery was considered, in 1789; & reason of changes.
In 1789, when Constitution adopted, everybody regarded Sla-
very as a great evil.
The Sentiment stronger in the South, or oftener expressed,
because the South had more of it.
It is called now, an "Institution", a "good," a "blessing" a
"Religious, moral, & social blessing—
Then, it was denominated a "blight," a "blast," a "mildew,"
a "curse"—
Mr. Campbell's Speech—see his extracts
The Ordinance of 1787—all the South agreed to it
Contemporaneous with the Constitution
I honor the liberality of Va—
80 millions of Dollars
The truth is that in Aug. '87, v. Association of 1774
1. Provision was made for limiting the importation of Slaves,
& it was believed that Slavery would gradually die out.
Mr. Madison & others thought the time allowed too long.
2. That the Prohibition should be laid on all the Territory—
Mr. Madison's reason for omitting the word.
3. Slavery, as it existed in the States, should not be interfered
with in.
In the first Congress, this was all reaffirmed, as I have stated
Before—
The whole Country unanimous, in all this.
But now: *What has caused the change?*
In the North a stronger religious feeling, & a horror at seeing
Slavery increase—
In the South, *Cotton*—
In 1790—Cotton hardly exported—

—Sudden growth of this created eagerness for acquisition of Slave Territory—

Cession of Georgia............1802
    "   Louisiana 1803
    "   Florida 1804

And Finally *Texas.*
This, the great Consummation.
And now my Genl. proposition.
"There is not a foot of land, in any State or Territory of the U. S. the character of which, as to free soil or Slave soil by some law—

1st. as to Texas. read the clause of the 2 Resolution—read it. Now what is to be said ag't this?
Nothing can be stronger
Mr Bell's Joint Resolution adds nothing to it—   And, looking to the difficulties of getting any prospective Resolution thro' the House, I think it best to adhere to *practical* measures—& make no resolution for the future—
I am obliged to Mr Clay—& Mr Bell
—But, refering to the difficulties of the case, I prefer to follow the President's recommendations.
But now
Texas was brought in by Northern & new England votes— in both—
But for these votes, she mus'. have staid out.
New England could have kept her out—
But N. E. Bought her—
Con. N. H. & Maine. And New York. —
Mr. Dix & Mr. Niles—voted for Texas *& then turned Free Soilers—*
If they were here now, could they apply Wilmot?
They helped to bring in every foot of Slave territory this side the Rio Grande—& then turned Free Soilers
Then set up the symbol—The empty symbol of the *Wilmot Proviso.*
—as a gentleman careless of his stables.
This matter is now absolutely settled by Law.
So much for Texas My Previous votes[1]

vid next sheet, page 2

---

[1] Endorsed "No. 3—How slavery was considered in '89 and acquisition of Texas."

Now as for California & New Mexico
This is all Free Country by the Ordinance of Nature. There
is no slave there, in our sense of that word, & never can be—
It is an arid formation, & scenery—
Immense Mountains, & deep valies—
Especially New Mexico
—Mountains with white tops—parched *vallies*—*no culture,
but by Irrigation*
Wilmot, here, would be perfectly without effect.
Inquire of the California Senators—& members—
—Inquire of any Body—
It is a point of honor with the South—
I do not wish to show power, merely wound this point of honor
I follow the example of Mr Polk, in Oregon
My proposition, then is proved.
1. As to Texas
2. As to California & New Mexico.
Then what is the value of Wilmot—
I wish to be distinct—
I shall not vote for Wilmot,
in New Mexico—
Nor in Texas.
As to Texas, I shall not violate faith, & repeal the Law of Con-
gress—
As to New Mexico, & California—
I will not reaffirm an Ordinance of Nature, or attempt to re-
enact the Will of God.
Speech at Niblo's Garden 1837
Admission of Texas 1845
        "   Three Million Bill Mar 1. 1847
        "   Springfield Sept 27. 1847
        "   In Senate Mar 23. 1848
        "   Oregon Bill Aug 12. 1848[1]

———

(Extract from Speech in Senate March 23, 1848.)

I am against the creation of new States. I am against the
acquisition of Territory to form new States.[2] And this, Sir,

[1] Endorsed: "Various speeches, 1837 to 1848, chronologically arranged."
[2] See, for an interesting evidence that in his immature days Webster did desire the acquisition of territory, an essay on the acquisition of Florida, Dec.
25, 1800, found in Massachusetts Historical Society Proceedings, vol. xi, p. 329.

398 LETTERS OF DANIEL WEBSTER

is not a matter of sentimentality, which I am to parade before mass meetings, or before my constituents at home. It is with me no matter of declamatory regret or expressed repugnance.

It is a matter of firm unchangeable purpose to yield to no force of circumstances that have occurred or that I may consider likely to occur; and therefore I say, Sir, that if I am asked to-day, whether for the sake of peace I will take a treaty that brings two new States into this Union, on its Southern Boundary, I say No—distinctly No! & I wish every man in the United States to understand that to be my judgment and my purpose?"

And now—as to the aggressions complained of.

1. By the South ag't. the North

—Fugitive slaves

In this the North is not without blame. The duty is particularly enjoined by the Constitution. No man can, consistently with his oath, attempt to evade it, get around it, or help defeat it. I think the language is addressed to the States— "shall be delivered up— I do not admit all that Mr Berrien said, abt. persons taking slaves— That is more doubtful—vid the words   I shall vote for Mr B's (?) Bill

2 Resolutions of Legislatures.

Mr. Holland

3 Abolition Press, & abolition societies.   —what I think of abolition societies, & the Abolition Presses—

I have expressed my opinion heretofore. They have done nothing but mischief—

—State of feeling in the So. Compared with 1832—

They have recd. money eno. to purchase the liberty of all the Slaves in Maryland.

—by contribution on the People—the result all bad   But the *Press is free.*   It cannot be restrained & Speech is free.

Nothing is said, in the Legislature, nor by the Press, on either side, more violent than is said every day in Congress.   *Our Debates have corrupted the Vernacular tongue*

2. Southern aggression

1. The eagerness for New Conquests—for new Slave States

2 The zeal with which Slavery is pressed, & the contumely bestowed on Northern Labor.

Northern Grievances.

1. The South has changed Slavery, from the character in which the Constitution tolerated it, & the South acknowledges it, in 1789,—i.e., an evil to be tolerated, till it should wear out; into

a cherished institution, to be strengthened & increased by all possible means.

2 The South lavishes as much abuse on the Free Labor of the North, as the North does on the Slavery of the South.

3. The South inclines to War, & conquest, eagerly, in order to obtain more Slave Territory

4. The So. insists on carrying her local law into the Territories, instead of the general law

5. The South, tho quite a minority, insists on making her interests paramount—

Southern list of grievances, & aggressions

1. The ordinance of 1787.

2. System of Revenue which impoverishes the South

3. Destruction of the original equilibrium

4. The Govt. Construes its own powers.

5. Abolitionism, & the interference of Northern Legislatures respecting fugitive Slaves

Mr. Doroney. (?)

"Northern Labor."

Educated—enlightened—free—ear'g wages—independent—or living on its own Capital.   4/5 of all ppy. in its hands.

Is this to be compared to absolute ignorance, & abject Slavery—

No wonder the North feels indignant

No wonder that it sometimes feels, that the power is in its own hands.—

―――

(Speech of Aug. 12, 1848.)

Let me conclude, therefore by remarking, that while I am willing to present this as showing my own judgment and position in regard to this case, and I beg it to be understood that I am speaking for no other than myself, and while I am willing to offer it to the whole world, as my own justification, I rest on these propositions—

First that when this Constitution was adopted, nobody looked for any new acquisition of territory, to be formed into slaveholding States.

Secondly: That the principles of the Constitution prohibited, and were intended to prohibit and should be construed to prohibit all interference of the General Government with Slavery as it existed and as it still exists in the States.   And then that looking to the effect of these new acquisitions, which have in this great degree enured to strengthen that interest in the South by the addition of these five States, there is nothing unjust, nothing of which any honest man can complain, if he is intelligent; and I feel there is nothing which the civilized world, if they take notice of so humble a person as myself will reproach me with, when I say, as I said the other day, that I had made up my mind, for one, that under no circumstances would I consent to the further extension of the area of Slavery in the United States, or to the further increase of Slave Representation in the House of Representatives.

Secession.

I am utterly astonished at the idea—

Secession is disunion— Who is for disunion? It is worse than nullification, because more insidious, & asserts that the Union may be severed, without breach of law

"Peaceable Secession." We shall see no such miracle

—Dismemberment of this Republican Empire without commotion!

—Breaking up of the fountains of the deep, without ruffling the surface—

—Planets starting from their spheres, & jolting agt. each other, without producing the Crush of the Universe.

—Voluntary & peaceable Secession!

All such ideas are founded in a totally incorrect idea of the Nature of the Govt.

It is a Govt. instituted by the People—not a confederacy of States.

It has just as popular a basis, as the State Govts—

This is too plain to be disputed.

It claims the allegiance of individuals & holds them to that allegiance by their *oaths*—

It does judge, in its proper Department, of the extent of its own powers.

If it did not, it could not exist. *This has been always so.*

All officers, National & State, must take an oath to support this constitution.

Now, where is secession to begin? Who is to take the first step? —What is that step to be?

It must be some violation of law.

To secede from the operation of law—is to resist the law.

The object is to separate the Slave states from the free

It cannot be done
Take the case of the Mississippi Va. & Maryland.   Who to
possess & defend the Chesapeake
What States is it to embrace
Where is the frontier of Slave Confederacy to be.
What States are to join the Confederacy?—
What is to be America?—   The flag, the Eagle—
—What is become of the Army? the Navy? the public lands?
Where is this City to belong?
The States must have standing armies
They must have separate systems of Commercial regulations
They must plunge into chaos
I am sorry Mr. Calhoun suggests the possibility of secession.
It affects the honor & credit of the Country.   There can be no
such thing.
Secession is civil, & servile war—
There can be no secession—
Nashville Convention
Mr. Windham
The dismemberment of America!
How wd. it strike Europe!
And the way to prevent this, is, *to restore the equilibrium.*
To give the *minority* as much power as the *majority.*
This is impossible.
I agree, there may be a case, in which a majority so oppresses
a minority, as to justify rebellion & revolution.   But, then, it
must be rebellion & revolution—
Within a Govt., founded on the preamble of majority, the
majority must rule.
Any attempt to give equal forces to majorities & minorities is
plainly preposterous—
There will be no secession, or either disruption of the Union
by any causes now existing
—The South enjoys all her original guaranties, & securities—
The complaint is, that the North has outgrown her.
And she wishes the major vote to be placed, still in her hands.
Boundaries & Constitution of California—
& Constitution
1 Boundaries
2. Constitution
Case of Mexican Treaty—
3 There now two observations to make.

1st. If Texas shall be inclined to dispose of a part of her vast domain bordering on New Mexico to the United States, at a reasonable price or for proper compensation, I know no objection to making the purchase and paying the same out of the public Treasury—

2d. In speaking of the Slavery of the coloured race in the United States, I have expressed no opinion upon the manner in which it might be practicable & for the benefit of all parties to reduce the number; but it has occurred to me that a system of colonization, undertaken by Govt.

Conclusion.

I have gone thro'. If I can serve the Country, with these opinions—ready to do so— If not, still glad to have expressed them

We need no amendment of the Constitution —

We need only a just administration of it

We need forbearance & moderation—

3 Tennessee

Let us raise ourselves to a just conception of duties.

The maintenance of this Constitution is one of the greatest trusts conferred on man.

It is a great, popular, Constitutional Govt. defended by Law, & Judicature, & the love of the People

Its daily respiration is liberty, patriotism, & the public good

—No monarchical throne presses its parts together

—No military power encumbers, with crown lands.

All kind influences, have favored it

The world admires, what we enjoy

Let us show ourselves equal to the demand, which this high trust makes upon us.

—Let our Comprehension be as broad as the country

—Our aspirations, as high as her destiny!

—Not pygmies, where men are wanted—

—Let us make our generation a subject of admiration hereafter, in a strong & bright link of this glorious chain.

—The world has nothing to contemplate, surpassing this our America, in its present grandeur & its prospects for the future

Every day, this fortune, head resplendent, increases in brightness

Every morn'g, the horizon is gilded with new beams—

Meantime, a vast accession of Territory—

So that this vast Territory is marked, on the one side, & on the other, by the two great seas of the world

We realize, on a mighty scale, the description of—Achilles' Shield

:Now the broad[1]

———

(From Calvin Hitchcock.)

RANDOLPH Mass. March 13, 1850.

Hon. Daniel Webster,

    Dear Sir;

I give you many thanks for your late speech. The inquiry has arisen in my own mind, as a professed student and expounder of the Bible, what was the *ratio legis* of such prayers as Leviticus 25:44, 45. From the fact that the Jew has to *circumcise* his bondman thereby taking on himself a covenant obligation to give him the same *religious* instruction which he was bound to give his *son*, and from the well known treatment of bondmen by pious Jews from Abraham downward, in this particular, and the good effects of this treatment, especially on the servants of David, I hold to the following suggestions.

1. It was important to secure human belief in the Messiah, in all ages, that the Jews should remain a separate people till his advent.

2. So important was the monotheism, and other doctrines of the Jews to the souls of men, which they would not *go forth* to carry to other nations, on account of their *distinctive* character, that the love of God enjoined it upon the wealthy Jew to *bring in*, by purchase, those already bondmen, among the Gentiles, for their *religious benefit*.

There was probably no other way to bring them to the knowledge of the truth, as to retain them under its influence, except

---

[1] These notes have been given in full because of the insight they afford into Webster's method of preparation for a speech. They are written in a hurried, nervous hand, with irregular lines and half-spelled words. In different collections of Webster's papers the editor has seen the original notes for nearly all of Webster's formal speeches. The notes for the reply to Hayne are scattered. Part of them are in the New Hampshire Historical Society collection, part in the possession of C. P. Greenough, of Boston, and part are the property of Hon. Geo. F. Hoar. For interesting testimony upon his method of work see Private Correspondence of Daniel Webster, vol. ii, p. 232. See A Memoir of Robt. C. Winthrop, p. 111, for the story that Winthrop called the night before March 7th and found Webster dictating his speech to his son Fletcher. The notes here printed are in Webster's own hand.

by purchase, and the perpetuity of the relation.   Was not this
the ratio legis of Jewish proselytism?

3. When Christ gave the common *Go* ye *into* all the *world,* and
preach the Gospel *to every creature,* was not this a destructive
blow at the *rationem* legis of purchasing bondmen? and if so,
and it was so understood by the Jew, who received the word of
Christ, who seems to have been well versed in the science of
proselytism, was it not the most effectual repeal possible of the
Law itself, as it existed among the Jews?   We are not now to
bring men *in,* to teach them saving truth, but *to go* and carry
the Doctrine *to them;* and will not this explain the reason that no
specific statute is contained in the N. T. against slavery? [1]

Pray, Sir, excuse the liberty of the above hints.   I am not a
technical abolitionist, and perhaps *ought* therefore to think and
say the more.

Your most sincere friend,

CALVIN HITCHCOCK.

———

(From Edward Curtis to Peter Harvey.)

WASHINGTON D. C. March 15th. 1850

My dear Sir—

All your letters have been very interesting and very cheering—
We do not see the Atlas, but learn from the other Boston papers
that it shows its teeth—very well—the day will soon come when
its bite will not hurt Mr. Webster nor his great speech—

All you can do at home to strengthen & sustain Mr. Webster,
makes his speech so much the more powerful & useful—   It is
very important that the people should pack into Faneuil Hall
some night, and say they approve of it—   The wave of approbation & applause from the West & South, in the shape of letters
and Newspaper laudation is strong, and the waters are yet rising.   Don't let the Faneuil Hall meeting fall through—   Get
out Mr. Everett, if possible.   In a letter to Mr. Webster, Mr.
Everett says he will attend such a meeting, if his health permits.
'Tis important that Mr. Everett should take part.   His repre-

---

[1] This letter is important because of its indication of the nature of the arguments offered by the clergy in this crisis. See Webster's reply, Private Correspondence, vol. ii, p. 359.   At the same time James R. Lowell was writing
to a friend: "I should like to tack something to Mr. Webster (the most
meanly and foolishly treacherous man I ever heard of) like the tail which I furnished to Mr. John P. Robinson."   Letters of James R. Lowell, vol. i, p. 187.

sentation is National, & so have been his politics.   From his life, his learning, & his eloquence, as well as his public character, there is great good to be had from his voice & face—

I wish I could send you the tons of Southern & Western papers that are filled with glorification of the Speech—they would do you such good—   The letters from Clergymen all over the Country and from. Democrats in all the States concurring in the strongest approbation of the Speech have filled Mr. Webster's Office, so that there is no room to sit down.   If Boston wd. give $250, I wd. guarantee & pay $250 from New York, to be devoted to the purchase of Speeches to be sent by Members of Congress through the length & breadth of the land—   That sum ($500), would procure at Washington prices, *Five hundred thousand Copies*, and no better seed can be sown among the people.   A great *Union* & Webster crop would spring up from that kind of planting—   What do you say?

Your's truly
EDWARD CURTIS.

(To D. Fletcher Webster.)

WASHINGTON Mar: 21, '50

My Dear Son;
I think the idea of a letter is a very good one.   If it come, I shall write an answer, and, as you say, "take up a few stitches." On receipt of this, please call on Messrs Redd'g 260 & see how they get on, with their edition.   I shall send copies of the handsome edition to the members of the Legislature, under my own frank.

The clamor for Speeches, So. & West, is incredible.   Two hundred thousand will not supply the demand.

Yrs affectionately
DANL WEBSTER

(To Peter Harvey.)

FRIDAY, 3, P. M. [Mar. 22, 1850 (?)]

Dr Sir
Letters come in thick; & all one way.   As soon as we can get a decent Edition out, I mean to send a copy to the members of the Mass. Legislature, & every Judge, Lawyer, Justice of the peace,

Doctor, & Clergyman in the Commonwealth.   And I would send thousands more, under my own frank, if I could afford it.   But other people will send many also.

Yrs

D. W.

(Edward Curtis to Peter Harvey.)

WASHINGTON D. C. 22d. March 1850

My dear friend—

We are greatly gratified to hear that you are going ahead with a good letter,[1] & that the best of Boston will sign it— Perhaps that, in some respects, is better than a Meeting at Faneuil Hall—   It will give Mr. W. a chance to trip you less in reply, & to clap in anything omitted—   The letters of thanks, admiration & glorification daily recd. by the mails, would astonish you—   Mr. W. will have a specimen of a good edition gotten up here—   I expect to hear from you, in reply to a line written the other day.   Mr. W. has a bad cold but is in good spirits.

Truly yours,

E. CURTIS.

(From T. H. Perkins et al.[2])

MARCH 25, 1850.

To the Honorable Daniel Webster.

Sir;

Impressed with magnitude and importance of the service to the Constitution and the Union, which you have rendered by your recent speech in the Senate in the United States on the subject of Slavery, we desire to express to you, our deep obligations for what this speech has done and is doing to enlighten the public mind and to bring the present crisis in our national affairs to a fortunate and peaceful termination.

As Citizens of the United States we wish to thank you for recalling us to our duties under the Constitution, and for the broad, national and patriotic views which you have sent, with the weight of your great authority and with the power of your unanswerable reasoning into every corner of the Union.

[1] Referring probably to the letter of March 25, 1850, signed by about 750 citizens of Boston.

[2] This was taken from the original address.   See Boston Daily *Advertiser*, April 3, 1850, for this letter with about 750 names.

It is, permit us to say, Sir, no common good, which you have thus done for the country. In a time of almost unprecedented excitement when the minds of men have been bewildered by an apparent conflict of duties, and when multitudes have been unable to find solid ground on which to rest with security and peace, you have pointed out to a whole people the path of duty, have convinced the understanding and touched the conscience of a nation. You have met this great exigency, as a patriot and a statesman; and although the debt of gratitude which the people of this country owe to you was large before, you have increased it, by a peculiar service, which is felt throughout the land. The desire, therefore, to express to you our entire concurrence in the sentiments of your speech, and our heartfelt thanks for the inestimable aid it had afforded towards the preservation and perpetuation of the Union. For this purpose we respectfully present to you this our addresses of thanks and congratulation in reference to this most interesting and important occasion in your public life.

T. H. PERKINS et al.

(Edward Curtis to Peter Harvey.)

WASHINGTON 28—March. [1850]

My dear friend—

We are getting along here pretty well with distributing the Speech. More than one hundred thousand Copies have been printed & sold in Washington. Our chief anxiety is to see your letter & its suggestions, at the earliest possible day. How shall we get the Speech extensively circulated in Mass. since your Whig Committee is [in favor of the] Atlas? So far as I learn the most vindictive of all opponents are in Mass. Cannot something be done to distribute to all the towns of Mass *some copies* of the Speech? If Reddings Edition be too good & too dear, then a cheaper edition might be gotten up. In New York, I will be responsible for a most thorough circulation. The money to do it with, is now, chiefly, subscribed, & the showering of the interior of New York with that speech will begin next week.

This letter is written at the dictation, & in the presence of Mr. Webster, in his office.

Truly your's

E. CURTIS

(From Edward Curtis to Peter Harvey.(?))

WASHINGTON *12"* April [1850]

My Dear Sir—

You told me I might depend on 300 from Boston to be laid out in speeches—

I have got rising of $1200 worth of Speeches and my $700 from New York will not pay it— I can send you any amount of Speeches (cost one cent) that you may want out of my purchase, in return for your money— You say you can distribute from Boston— Is it not better to have them go to the people of Mass under the frank of Mr. W. He franks any amount wanted. Some people think he don't sign his name on the speeches quite so well as he used to, but it does very well, though only written *by his authority*, that is the fashion in the Senate, but I think it best to mention it to nobody—so don't—

Mr. Webster goes for California separate & alone, & apart from all other questions, & has set that matter right in the Senate to day.

The Gold Watch & Chain are here[1]—the latter about as big as your leg, above the knee,

We shall have a burst up in the Cabinet of old Tayler, in a few days I think—

Clayton & Crawford will probably set out for their respective homes, having done enough for their Country, & Galphin Claimants to be entitled to discharge— * * *

———

(To Peter Harvey.)

THURSDAY 3 o'clock April 1850.

My Dear Sir,

I received your very acceptable note this morning, but have not time to honor it today. Mr. Curtis or myself will write you tomorrow. I do not care what a portion of the Press may say, if we can only get the Speech into the hands of the People.

It is impossible to meet the demands here, under some time.

Yrs.   D. WEBSTER

---

[1] Referring to a gift to Webster by some prominent New York men. See Daniel Webster's Private Correspondence, vol. ii, p. 361.

(To D. Fletcher Webster.)

[Apr. 3 1850]

Private   IN COURT, Wednesday 1/2 past 2

My Dear Son

I have recd. yrs, & will send 1000 Speeches by Express to-morrow.—

The Senate has vote to send a Comee. with Calhouns remains to Charleston— Of course, I shall be much pressed to be one— *Should I go—?* think of it, *two days*, & say little to anybody— & then send me a Telegraphic Despatch—saying "aye" or "No"— But think deep.

Yrs   D. W.

(To D. Fletcher Webster.)

WASHINGTON April 8, '50

Dear F.

I shall not go [to] the South,[1] on the whole, First, because it might be thought I was carrying my Southern courtesy too far, considering my age & status: Second, because I should hear a great deal of commendation of Mr. Calhoun's particular opinions, in which I could not concur, & to which I could not, decently reply: Third, because I shall [have] no better time to go home—

If I am well, & nothing happens, I shall be with you, sooner than you expect. I shall go right down to Marshfield, & if I stay at all in Boston, shall stay on my return.

Yrs   D. W.

Is there any objection to my coming now? or soon? I mean to get the answer off tomorrow.

(Edward Curtis to Peter Harvey.)

WASHINGTON—21, April 1850

My dear Sir—

Mr. Webster expects to leave Washington on Friday next, on his journey to Boston. He will lodge, that night, at Baltimore,

---

[1] That is, with the congressional committee accompanying Calhoun's remains.

and on Saturday reach New York, where he will pass Sunday. On Monday, the following day, the 29th. inst, he will proceed by the Rail Way to Boston.   If his friends intend to notice his arrival in Boston, in any public manner, Mr. Webster's arrival by the Rail Way train will be at a convenient hour, & it is thought that a public reception or greeting may well be gone through with at the Depot in Boston, immediately on his arrival—   If anybody shall address him, on behalf of the People, as he alights from the Cars, it may be well to let Mr. Webster have a note or idea of what is likely to be said, by the Boston speaker—   Mr. Webster expects you to reply to this, by addressing *him* a letter at the *Astor House,* New York—   If you have a word to say here, & reply to this on receipt of it, that reply will reach us on Friday morning & before Mr. Webster goes—   Mr. W. will depend on hearing from you at the Astor House—   If the idea put forth some time ago, of a public reception has gone to sleep don't take any trouble to awaken it.   Mr. W. would incline to enter Boston, like other people, unless the public feeling demand some demonstration, as the prints have suggested.

Very truly your's

EDWARD CURTIS.

P. S.   Mr. Webster's letters of congratulation are from the distinguished men of all parties & all parts.   The mail today brought a very remarkable one from the North—   Mr. W. will tell you about it—

(To D. Fletcher Webster.)

IN THE SENATE, Wednesday, 24. of April (1850) My Dear Son

I recd. yrs. this mor'g.—   The Com^{ee.} of 13 will neither do me or any body else any harm; nor need be alarmed at anything touching Mr. Clay.   I rather suppose the course of proceeding, in California & the Territories, which I proposed in a Speech some ten days ago, will be followed.

My expectation is, to leave this City on friday P. M. & reach N. York on Saturday Eve'—   To stay at Astor House, till Monday Mor'g, & be in Boston on Monday Eve, on the N. Y. train—

I think I shall stay over Tuesday, in Boston—& go to Marshfield on Wednesday—   Stay there till the close of the week—so as to leave Boston, on my return hither, about the 6th. or 7th. inst.

I am glad that things are alive at Green Harbor.

Yrs. D. W.

(From Richard Rush.[1])

SYDENHAM, near Philadelphia, April 26, 1850

My dear Sir,

Pray accept my best thanks for the beautiful edition of your speech.   I was going to say it now comes before the public in a form worthy of it—but no I wont; for if we come to that, it ought to be printed on leaves of silver in letters of gold.

I remain my dear Sir, yours very faithfully, and obliged,

RICHARD RUSH.

(From Thomas G. Clemson.[2])

BRUSSELS May 5th, 1850

My dear Sir,

The consolation & satisfaction, which Mrs. Clemson & myself derived from reading the remarks it pleased you to make in the Senate,[3] on the death of our venerated parent, the late Hon. J. C. Calhoun, is sufficient cause, I am convinced, for the liberty I now take, in expressing to you our gratitude for the feeling manner in which you did justice to the long & emminent life, passed & ended in the service of our common country.   May we hope that what he has left may endure, to its usefulness & glory.

If you could feel & say so much of his public life, what must we, of his family, feel, when to all that, we add a boundless love and admiration for the manifold virtues he exercised in the bosom of his dearly beloved family.

He there practised a world of goodness & tender philosophy, unknown to the public, the loss of which we can not yet realize

It was my lot, in the discharge of my humble duties, to be far from him when he closed his eyes, & to have been denied the melancholy satisfaction of soothing his dying moments.   May

---

[1] This letter is owned by the Hon. Geo. F. Hoar.   Only a few of the many letters of congratulation on the 7th of March speech have been included, and those representative of varying interests.

[2] Son-in-law of John C. Calhoun.

[3] See Webster's Works, vol. v, p. 368.

those you love, Sir, surround you at that awful moment, & thus be spared our sufferings. But I hope that time is still far distant. That you may long continue where you are, "to serve your country," is the prayer of your friend &

obedient servant

Thos. G. Clemson

(To Peter Harvey.)

Astor House Saturday Morning May 11 6 o'clock
My Dear Sir,
    * * *¹ The New Yorkers have sent Mr. Curtis seven hundred dollars, for the distribution of the Speeches,² all of which and a good deal more has been expended, and the demand is far from being satisfied. If our Boston friends feel like doing something in the same way, it would like keeping up. It might be best to send whatever might be collected to Mr Curtis, who, I doubt not, is already a good deal in arrears with the Printers. * * *³

Yrs truly
Danl. Webster

(To J. Prescott Hall.)

Washington May 18. '50

My Dear Sir
    I love you sincerely, & always receive what you say, not only kindly but thankfully. I feel neither indifferent, or distant towards our good President. He is an honest man, & a good Whig, & I wish well to his administration, for his sake, & the Country's. But what can I do? He never consults me, nor asks my advice; nor does any one of his Cabinet, except Mr Meredith. His Cabinet was wholly formed, originally, without asking any opinion of mine, & while some are friendly enᵒ others are cross-grained towards me, & excessively jealous. I shall support, cordially, the President's measures whenever I can; but I have been in Public life some time longer than the President, or any of his

---

¹ Personal health comments omitted.
² Seventh of March speech in pamphlet form.
³ The remainder of this letter appears in Fletcher Webster's edition of his father's correspondence. This paragraph was omitted without indicating the omission.

advisers, & suppose I shall not be much blamed, if on great public questions, I feel as much confidence in my own judgment as I do in theirs. Personally I esteem the President, & like him very well. But I cannot, like Mr Truman Smith, and Mr Seward, swing my arms in the Senate, & proclaim myself a champion for the Administration, in regard to all it has done, does now, or hereafter may, could, should or would do.

The truth is—My Dear Sir, that with a good deal of regard for some members of the Cabinet, the Country has not confidence in it, as a whole, nor has the Whig party. Hence I fear, that the administration is doomed, & the Whig Party doomed with it— Nevertheless, I shall do all I can to avert the catastrophe—

My Dear Sir—You have sometimes very hot fires at the Astor— Throw this letter, immediately, into the very hottest of them.[1]

Yrs   D. W.

(To Peter Harvey.)

WASHINGTON May 29, 1850.

My Dear Sir,

The Courier and the Daily Advertiser, should lose no time in coming out decidedly, in favor of *some* plan of adjustment and settlement. They should, at first, take strong ground against carrying on the foolish controversy about Slavery in New Mexico—, further, and should rebuke such politicians as Mr. Mann and Mr. Hale, with emphasis. They may be assured that the side of Union and conciliation is getting to be the strong side. Mr. Linus Childs of Lowell, is here, and he is as strong as a lion in favor of a compromise. He talks to the Massachusetts members strong; and has written for other Massachusetts men to come on and join him.

It is just as I knew it would be, with the Whig Senators of the South. They will not give a single vote for the Tariff until this Slavery business is settled. A very leading individual among them, told Mr. Childs yesterday, that so far as depended on him, and his friends, the Lowell mills might and should all stop, unless the North quit this violence of abuse—and showed a disposition to be reasonable in the present exciting questions. I believe I told you this a month ago.

---

[1] This letter is owned by Mr. C. P. Greenough, of Boston.

Depend upon it our Northern members are getting into a tight place.   If they defeat a compromise, their responsibility will be great.   If they oppose it and it still should succeed they will not belong to the class of Peace makers.

I believe Mr. Childs tells them some plain truths.   I write again soon.   We have no Boston mail this morning

Yrs truly

DANL WEBSTER

(To Peter Harvey.(?))

WASHINGTON May 29, '50

My Dear Sir

Will you have the kindness to ask Mr. T. B. Curtis to sign & endorse this, & request Mr. Haven to place proceeds to my credit. My acceptance of his draft for $500 becomes due on Saturday, & will of course be paid

Yrs truly

D. W.

I have not heard how you like my letter. Mr. Mann[1] does not like it.

(Edward Curtis to Peter Harvey.)

WASHINGTON D C 30 May 1850

My dear Sir,

Mr. Webster showed me your letter suggesting that *I* should manage the speech money—   I am willing & expect to pay twice the amount that any man has subscribed, but as I wrote you, I can't stand the whole—   We have sent off, an immense number of the Speeches, & have now nearly twenty thousand Copies in the folding room—   * * *

Have you seen anything of Hosea Mann's "hoss". You will, if you come across him, be at liberty to put on a halter, upon

---

[1] Horace Mann. Webster here facetiously alludes to Mann's well-known antipathy to compromise, and to the fact that in the " Newburyport " letter Webster had ridiculed his knowledge of the Constitution.

taking out a Habeas Corpus, but don't undertake to bridle him, without a Jury Trial.[1]

Let me hear from you

Truly your's

EDWD. CURTIS.

————

(To D. Fletcher Webster.)

My Dear Son   FRIDAY MOR'G 7 O clock [June, 1850]

I do not think we can arrange the inscription for Dear Julia's monument till I go home.   We must have three monuments, one for Julia, one for Edward, & one for your mother.   I incline to have them all of the same pattern, but the last mentioned rather larger, so as to bear the names of Grace & Charles.   These monuments might all be in preparation, & when I am next at Marshfield we will arrange the inscriptions.

I shall not get away till we finish the present business.

It is now warm, but I keep as cool as I can.

Your mother had a headache yesterday, but is pretty bright this mor'g.

I hope you will write every day, & let me know how Caroline & the children are.

I suppose my Medford[2] letter is printed, & that you have seen the Bill ab't fugitive Slaves, which was in my Drawer when I made my Speech—[3]   The rod came safe to hand.   I shall hardly use it, unless for a perch, or a small rock, at the Little Falls.

Yrs affectionately

DANL WEBSTER

Give my love to Mr. A. & his children, & Mr. Paiges family.

————

(To Peter Harvey.)

Dear Sir,   WASHINGTON, June 2, '/50

I wrote you this morning, and now have your letter of Friday.

---

[1] This letter and others which follow from Curtis to Harvey have an importance aside from the information they contain, because Edward Curtis was practically Webster's mouthpiece, being intimately acquainted with all his plans and ideas.

[2] To the citizens of Medford, June 3, 1850.   See Daniel Webster's Works, vol. vi, p. 563.

[3] He must refer to his 7th of March speech, and his bill was a modification of the Fugitive Slave bill then discussed and of that finally passed.

The Editor of the Courier is all right in his final idea; let him come out, clear and strong, and follow the matter up— He will thereby gain readers and friends. All our friends, who can write, ought to aid him, if he should need aid. But he writes very well himself.

Mr. Stuart's [1] pamphlet is here, and we have read eighty pages of it. It is capital, capital. It is one of the most important productions of our time, and I think will make a great and durable impression on this generation. Abolitionism cannot stand before it. He must get a copy-right, and the book ought to be published, in thousands and hundreds of thousands. I wrote in my letter this morning that we are in a *crisis:* we are so, if "conciliation" makes no progress. I do not know how, even the appropriation bills for the support of the Government are to be got through. Will not the Whigs of Massachusetts think of this?

Yrs   D. WEBSTER.

(To Peter Harvey.(?))

IN THE SENATE—Monday June 3, '/50

My Dear Sir,

The Courier article of Saturday is admirable indeed. I have already heard it spoken of highly, here. Let the Editor follow up his hand.

The Atlas whines, and growls, and abuses people. It reasons nothing, it argues nothing. It only rails at Mr. Webster. It denies no fact, It controverts no matter of law. "An old whig" is dead and buried. There is no discussion in its columns, no fair opposition to other men's opinions. But it rails and rails. Its present topic seems to be, that Mr. Webster's Newburyport letter contains matters derogatory to the Commonwealth of Massachusetts. He derides the State, and holds her up to the reproach of other States; and she must be defended.

God keep the poor old Commonwealth, if the defence of her character and conduct, is to rest on the Atlas!

Mr. Webster assaulting the honor of Massachusetts, and the Atlas defending her! Who would not hasten to the scene, and look on, to see the end of such a contest.

Now according to our apprehension, Mr. Webster has never

---

[1] Moses Stuart, of Andover.

said one word, derogatory to the character of Massachusetts. He has too much respect for himself, if not for the State, to do any such thing. The State has honored Mr. Webster. It is generally thought, we believe, that he has not dishonored her. It is not likely that the efforts of the Atlas will shake the confidence of either of them, for the other.

Yrs always
DL. WEBSTER

(To Peter Harvey.)

THE SENATE, 2 o'clock Tuesday—[June 4, 1850]

Dear Sir

You will see by the Intelligencer, that I have laid my proposed "fugitive Slave Bill" before the Senate. It is printed, in word and letter, just as it was, when lying in my Desk the day I made my Speech.[1] I sent my letter to the Gentlemen of Medford,[2] yesterday.

Mr. Stuart's Book has arrived, and I have read a part of it. If I do not mistake, *it will make a great impression on the public mind.*

I hope I may be able to run up to Harper's ferry about Thursday—but it is uncertain.

Yrs   D WEBSTER

(To Fletcher Webster.)

WASHINGTON June 10, 12 o'clock. [1850]

My Dear Son;

I recd. yr's this mor'g, enclosing one to yr mother; we are well, but your mother is greatly distressed by Mrs. Morris' death. She was greatly beloved.

I hope you will get along with Mr. Coffin, without a quarrel. Of course, he can do nothing here, unless he steals a march.

Mr Harvey writes me about political matters. You see my little Medford letter—I am now writing one for the Kennebeck

---

[1] The 7th of March speech.

[2] In a letter dated "The Senate, June 3, 1850," Webster wrote Peter Harvey: "In the midst of a considerable warm debate I have, at my desk here, written an answer to the signers of the Medford letter." See Works of Daniel Webster, vol. vi, p. 563.

people,[1] with a little more care.— It will go down East, in a day or two.

Mr. Benton is speaking on his motion for Indef. p-ponement.

Yr   D. WEBSTER

(Daniel Webster Toast.[2])

JUNE 17, 1850

"Bunker Hill Monument,—May it crumble to the dust before it shall look down upon a country dishonored, disgraced, and ruined by the breaking up, by sacrilegious hands, of that Union which has secured its liberty, fostered its prosperity, and spread its glory and renown throughout the world."

(To the Citizens of New York.[3])

WASHINGTON, June 19, 1850.

Gentlemen:

Your letter has been received and read with very strongly excited feelings. The terms in which your approbation of my speech of the 7th March is expressed, are so warm, and so mingled with sentiments of personal regard, that when I look at the names of the persons who have given utterance to those sentiments, I feel that what will become me most, is, to confine my answer to the expression of my profound thanks, and to the assurance, that your letter will be treasured up among those memorials of respect which are to be most cordially cherished by me to the end of life.

I am, gentlemen, your highly obliged fellow-citizen and obedient servant,

DANIEL WEBSTER.

(To Samuel Lawrence.)

Confidential

My Dear Sir,   [JUNE 18, 1850]

It is the opinion at the *White House*, today, that the Com-

---

[1] See the Works of Daniel Webster, vol. vi, p. 566.
[2] Sent to the company celebrating the seventy-fifth anniversary of the battle of Bunker Hill. Printed in Hist. of the B. H. M. A., p. 349.
[3] This letter is taken from a newspaper clipping cut from the Traveller, June 27, 1850, and now in possession of the Harvard Library.

promise Bill *will become a law.* I cannot say myself what the result may be. The Mass. Delegation could settle the whole question, *this day.*

I have read the letter from Lawrence, signed by 300 good men. I hope, (with Mr. Hudson's permission) that the business will go on, as fast as may be convenient; *for this is the very moment.* Should not the papers be sent to others of the Delegation, and not to me? Do not mention what I have said about the White House.

Yrs

D. W.

_____

(To Rev. Hubbard Winslow.)

My Dear Sir— WASHINGTON, June 23, 1850.

I am quite obliged to you for your kind and encouraging letter. What is to come of the present commotions in men's minds I cannot foresee; but my own convictions of duty are fixed and strong, and I shall continue to follow those convictions without faltering—*"Nil time, nisi male facere."* [1]

Yours with true regard,

DANIEL WEBSTER.

_____

(To Peter Harvey.)

Dear Harvey JULY 9, '50

I have yrs this morning, & shall expect another tomorrow— Mr. Eliot's nomination[2] is excellent. *Make him* accept. We want him here. I am mortified abt. Mr. Marstons recall. I knew nothing about it.

Yrs D. W.

_____

(D. Fletcher Webster to Peter Harvey.)

Private

Dear Harvey, WASHINGTON July 15, 1850

I wrote you yesterday before I had heard any thing direct from *Fillmore.* I have heard today.

---

[1] This letter is taken from a newspaper clipping in the collection of C. E. Bliss, of Bangor, Me.

[2] For Representative in place of Robt. T. Winthrop.

He has decided on nothing—not even the removal of the present Cabinet; though public opinion will probably effect that.

He will likely enough offer Mr. W. the State Dept. but not, I am inclined to think in such a way as he would accept it. Mr. F. does not seem to be aware of the crisis—I infer from what I heard that he would prefer Winthrop to Webster— At all events, if he doubts on this point it shows that he does not take that view of matters which almost every one else does.

It is enough to determine my own opinions as to what Father ought to do, to know that Mr. F. hesitates a moment— Don't you think it decisive?

The universal truth that men like to be surrounded by none greater than themselves is like to be made manifest in this instance.

Mr. F. says he is wholly uncommitted, & means to remain so for some days as to all points of his policy.

This puts a new face on things, & the conduct of parties interested must be changed accordingly. Mr. W. will hold himself aloof—take "high ground" as Livermore says & wait events.

Please show this to Mr. Haven, & I would not to any one else except Mr. Paige—

Yrs   F. W.

Mr. Clay is very anxious to have Father go into the Cabinet. This alarms me— He would not do it unless he thought it would dispose of Mr. W. out of his way.

I am afraid of the kisses of an enemy.

F. W.

(Memorandum.[1])

[JULY 11. 1850]

Sec of State,	x	x
Do. " Treas.	Mr. Graham [2]	Vinton.
Do. " Interior	Mr. Graham.	
Do. " War	Mr. Bates,	
Do. " Navy	Mr. Conrad,	(Graham) [3]
P. M. Gen.	Mr. Pennington.	(Dayton) [3]
Atty. Gen.	Mr. Crittenden.	

---

[1] Guaranteed an exact copy by G. J. Abbott. It was written first in Daniel Webster's hand.

[2] The erasure of Mr. Graham's name was in the original.

[3] Graham and Dayton are written in lead pencil.

This will come near being a North Eastern appointment, & is better, I think on that account.   Mr. Bates is well known, not only to the People of Missouri, & Iowa, and I believe highly respected by the Whigs in those states.   This point, I think, is better than one farther South especially if there shall be a member from Louisiana.

I will call between 1 & 2 o'clock.

                                                            D. W.

────────

(To Millard Fillmore.)

Private

                              WEDNESDAY, 1 o'clock. [July 12. 1850.]
My Dear Sir,
   So far as I hear the "First Message" is quite well rec'd.   No doubt it will give satisfaction to the North, and, I believe also to all the *Union men* of the South.
   Gen. Foote commended it strongly in the Senate.

                                          Yrs. truly
                                              DANL. WEBSTER.

────────

(To Millard Fillmore.)

Private

                              FRIDAY 4 o'clock. [July 19, 1850]
My Dear Sir,
   I acknowledge my stupidity, in not at once appreciating the value of your suggestion, in relation to giving the P. Office to Mr. S. B. Ruggles.[1]   I was thinking of the appointment of village Postmasters, and little interior mail routes, &c. &c.
   I forgot that a high duty of that official this day is to arrange communications with foreign countries, & propose large plans, or execute them, for postal intercourse with all the world.
   I believe he is the very man; & I have reason to think he will take the office.
   I shall see you before six o'clock.

                                          Yrs. truly,
                                              DANL. WEBSTER.
I know him to be entirely independent of all *cliques.*

───

   [1] Webster had now accepted the office of Secretary of State, and his advice was sought in these matters.

(To D. Fletcher Webster.)

DEPT. WEDNESDAY 2 O'clk.
[July 24 (?) 1850]

Dear Fletcher

I have hardly done anything today but sign Passports, & Certificates, & let all the world know, at home & abroad, that I am Sec. of State.   This, you know, is a necessary, but a tedious business.

It was rather [thought] this morning that there was more chance for the Compromise, than there was a day or two ago.

Yrs affectionately

———

(To Millard Fillmore.)

DEPARTMENT OF STATE, July 30, 1850.

Is it not time the answer to the Governor of Texas was prepared, considered, and accomplished?   The Legislature of Texas meets at Austin on the 12th. prox.   I shall in the course of the day, send a draft[1] for your examination.   It will be well, I think, to put in as many soft words as we can, to soothe the irritation of Texas, which seems to have taken offence at the military aspect of the proceedings at Santa Fe.   I doubt whether the President expected Col. Mc'Call to take the lead in forming a State Constitution for New Mexico, or to act in that respect in his military character.

Nevertheless, it is desirable that we should avoid every thing which might look like a reprimand to him.   I think it will be necessary to send the answer by express.

Yours truly,

DANL. WEBSTER.

———

(To Peter Harvey.)

WASHINGTON Friday August 2, 1/2 past 3. [1850]

Dear Harvey,

I have found time to write a short line to Mr. Fearing.[2]   *He must come;* we want him and must have him.   I pray you take

---

[1] See Webster's Works, vol. vi, p. 479.
[2] Probably Albert Fearing, a wealthy Boston philanthropist.

no denial. In the times which are coming, and in the business which is before us, his mercantile knowledge would be of very great importance.

Besides he is a practical man, who seeks only to bring about good results. He does not spit in a man's face, or knock him down, and then say, "Kind friend, be good enough to give me your vote, in a matter essential to my well being" We are all busy—I hope we shall straighten things out, but I cannot tell.

Yrs always truly
DANL. WEBSTER.

(To Millard Fillmore.)

Private.

My Dear Sir, DEPT OF STATE. Aug. 3, 1850

Some things will keep me here until a little after 10 o'clock; and in the mean time I wish the papers in your hands may be read to the other Gentlemen. It is important that all of us should bring our minds seriously & independently to the subject.

And in regard to yourself, particularly, I wish you to take nothing out of courtesy to me.

The crisis is important, all the North is in commotion at the loss of the Compromise Bill. A good message from you would do a world of good.

Yrs truly
DANL WEBSTER

(To Millard Fillmore.)

My Dear Sir, TUES. MORNING Aug. 6. 1850

On examination & consultation, I thought it best that the letter to Governor Bell [1] should be from *me* by *your* direction. It is sent by bearer for your perusal, if you think another perusal necessary. It has been carefully revised, & examined, and no alterations made except to accommodate the language to the Writer.

The Message will be ready in twenty minutes. I will bring them up. I hope they may reach the two Houses before 12 o'clock.

Yrs. always
DANL. WEBSTER.

---

[1] Governor of Texas.

(To Samuel Lawrence.)

WASHINGTON, Aug. 10, '50.

My Dear Sir,

I thank you for your letter. Mr. Eliot's nomination was an excellent one. He & you were among the very first to write me, after the 7th. of March, that the People of Massachusetts would support me.

The Machine of the Government seems beginning to move again. The Senate, as you see, has passed the Texas Bill, & the House is getting on with the annual appropriations. Abolitionism & disunion are a little less rampant.

Yrs

D. WEBSTER.

I like your letters. They are short, & to the point.

(To Peter Harvey.)

AUG. 14 (1850) 3 o'clock P. M.

Dear Sir

I have your letter, & thank you for it. The very best thing in the world would be for you & Mr. Fearing to come on here, for two or three days. The weather is growing cooler— Give your votes for Mr Eliot, & then come South. You will easily adjust all the things about which you write.

Yrs   D. W.

News from the Capitol, is, that Mr. Ashmun is making a masterly speech, in answer to the Southern Extreme Doctrines, &c. on the Texan question.

(To Peter Harvey.)

WASHINGTON Aug. 16, '/50

My Dear Sir,

I received a letter from you yesterday, and two others today. They are all interesting and excellent. Mr. Curtis devours them, as if they were bits of ripe watermelons. I think your conversation with Mr Draper was exactly right. He is personally friendly—but has had quite inadmissible ideas on some subjects.

Mr Clay's conversation was strong, I wish he could be induced to visit Boston and see our Whig friends.

I have written Mr. Eliot to be here by Wednesday. His vote will be needed. I wish there was hope for Mr. Thompson. I much like the decision of Mr Mills If a few other important men will follow his example, things will soon come right.

Yrs truly
DANL WEBSTER

The Cabinet is now complete.

(Edward Curtis to Peter Harvey.)

WASHINGTON, 16th. Aug: (1850)

My dear Sir—

You see how gloriously every thing has gone thro. the Senate; but after all, there is great danger that all will be lost in the House, by the perverse opposition of a few Northern members— Nobody has had any hope of Horace Mann, but all the other members now here from Massachusetts except the Rev. Orrin Fowler of Plymouth District are expected to vote in favor of peace and conciliation, by voting for the Bill to settle the boundary between Texas & New Mexico, & for the other Bills from the Senate. It is of the utmost importance to gain every Northern Whig vote that can be gained— The Bill first in order, of all the Bills from the Senate now pending in the House, is the Texan boundary Bill—our friends are waiting to rally their forces to vote upon this Bill,—and will not take the question until after Mr. Eliot gets here. My purpose in writing to you, now, is to request, if you know any Boston people who are acquainted with the *Revd. Fowler,* that you should get letters written to him urging him to vote for the Boundary Bill—being a clergyman he may well go in for peace & harmony— If you cannot reach Mr. Fowler you will do good by getting the Courier to print an article or two calling upon the Representatives from the Bay State to sustain the Administration by voting in favor of the Boundary Bill. If we can any way get the Revd. Orrin how well Massachusetts would stand—Rockwell, Grinnell, Ashmun & Duncan, you know, are all right.

It is possible that Mr. Upham may be elected & get here in time— We hope he is not coming here to take part with Mann & Giddings—

Yesterday I dined with General Scott. All the Cabinet were present— They are very agreeable & cheerful persons—

Mr. Webster appears among them, like a father teaching his listening children— Even, Genl. Scott, who has never been known give way to any person in conversation, any more than to an enemy in Battle, was full of deference, and maintained a reasonable silence.

The weather is warm here, but not so scorching as it was last month— I have given Gideon the Printer a draft on you for that $250— We have had so many of the Speech of the 17th. july printed & distributed, that I am now in debt, over & above your $250, to the tune of Four hundred & twenty five, which I fear will have to be paid out of my very small private purse. But I have great consolations—many hundreds of thousands of Mr. W's. letters & speeches have been sent all over the land—the seed taken root, & I see it springing up every where, & promising an abundant harvest in due time.

I am glad to observe that you speak well of the rich in your parts— If they were here to see how incessantly Mr. W. labors, (& has labored all the session) how patiently he goes about to convince men of the error of their ways, and does convince & convert them, how the present good prospects of the Country for conciliation & internal peace are distinctly the result of his exertions, & how cheerfully he gives up Marshfield for the hot rooms of his small dwelling house at Washington, they would feel that they can never pay for such services.

I am glad to say that although the great heat has on some days prostrated him, Mr. W. has had no malady, and is as well, & active & cheerful as ever I knew him to be.

Your's very truly
EDWD. CURTIS:

(To Denning Jarves.)

WASHINGTON D. C. August 19. '/50.

Dear Sir

I have received your favor of the 17th inst. informing me that you have done me the honor to send to my residence at Marshfield, a flint glass Bowl, the largest ever made in any part of the world, and that you design it as a gift to me, and a token of your respect for myself, and of your confidence in my public conduct during my past life.

I have no doubt that this is a brilliant specimen of American art, and it is not the less welcome to my house, certainly, for your having named it the "*Union Bowl.*"

But I am most especially indebted to you, for the kind opinion you entertain, of my public services in the Senate, during the present session of Congress— For any exertions I have made to promote conciliation and peace throughout the Nation, I can derive no more satisfactory reward, than the approbation of the people of Massachusetts whom I have represented and our fellow citizens, generally, throughout the country.

It is now many years, My dear Sir, since you and I first formed an acquaintance with each other, at the beautiful village of Sandwich, to which place I went for the trifling but healthful operation of fishing in "Marshpee Brook;" you, to establish a most important manufactory. As those years have rolled on, I have had equal pleasure in cultivating and cherishing your friendship, and in witnessing the great success of your undertaking. It is not from a stranger, therefore, nor from one indifferent to me, but from a friend long known and esteemed, that I accept the present which your kindness bestows. And I offer you in return my warmest thanks.

I am dear Sir, Very truly your obt. st.

DANL. WEBSTER

(To Millard Fillmore.)

MONDAY MORNING, 9 o'clock—Aug. 26, 1850.

My Dear Sir,

I had an attack of rheumatism yesterday, caused, I suppose, by the late weather, & I doubt, as I was obliged to take medicine, whether I shall be able to leave my house today.

I have been through much of the subject of the appointment of a Secretary of the Interior, & will state, with your leave, my present impressions.

In the first place, I think it very important to find a proper man in Georgia. That seems to be the fit location, on all accounts, & as the Whigs of that State doubtless feel a good deal of mortification at the manner in which Mr. Crawford has closed his career,[1] the selection of another Head of Department from the State would probably be very well received by them.

Charles J. Jenkins is a Lawyer living in Augusta, not far from forty years old, of good standing in his profession, & of excellent character in all respects.   He may not be, and I presume is not, so distinguished a Lawyer as Judge Berrien, or Judge Law, and, in some respects, not quite equal to another Gentleman, whom I shall next name.   But I understand he is emulous, industrious, and very confidential.   I saw a good deal of him at Augusta in 1847—and was much pleased with him. He was then Speaker of the House of Representatives in Georgia, & had, at that time, a very agreeable family; but his wife, & both his children, all he had, are since dead.   He has very amiable and gentlemanly manners.   In his present condition, I presume he would accept the appointment at once,

Charles Dougherty is a highly respectable Lawyer, &, I believe, a very good Whig.   He has a family, is forty seven or forty eight years old, & lives at Athens.   Not so likely, perhaps, to accept the place as Mr. Jenkins, yet probably he would accept.   He was a candidate for the Senate against Mr. Berrien, and in the Whig caucus Mr. Berrien led him but one vote.

I would suggest to your consideration, My Dear Sir, the appointment of one of them, unless objections, not now known to me, should be stated against one or both, as I know Mr. Jenkins, &, as I believe that on the whole, he would be the better appointment, I should prefer him.[2]

Yours, sick or well,

DANL WEBSTER

(To Millard Fillmore.)

TUESDAY MORNING, September 3d. 1850

The bearer of this note is William J. Hubbard, Esquire, a highly respected gentleman of the bar in Boston.   Mr. Hubbard is the Head of the Executive Committee of the Board of Foreign missions, & in that capacity has lately been addressed by Mr. Judd, late Commissioner from the Sandwich Islands to this Government.   The letter was written at Panama and refers to an

---

[1] Referring to the "Galphin claim" scandal. See Rhodes' History of the United States, vol. i, p. 202.
[2] Alexander H. H. Stuart finally took the office.

expected visit of certain French ships of War to the islands with
no very peaceful purpose. Mr. Hubbard will show you a copy
of this letter. He had also a letter from Mr. Judd written at
the same time, which is sent herewith. England has offered to
mediate between France and the Sandwich Islands, which offer
France declines, as would seem from Mr. Judd's letter.

On the 5th of July last, Mr. Rives was instructed by this Department to offer the mediation of this government for the purpose of adjusting the controversy. At the time the instruction
must have reached Paris, however, he had just left there on a
visit to England where he expected to stay several weeks, & we
have heard nothing from him upon the subject. He was at
Edinburgh on the 9th of August under which date he wrote me
from that city. I send the letter to you for your perusal
although I believe it has already been in your hands. It makes
no mention of the matter of the proffered mediation.

I should attend Mr. Hubbard in his call on you to day, but
my cold is very bad and I ought to be at home.[1]

Yours, always, truly,
DANL WEBSTER.

(To Don Mariana Arista.[2])

WASHINGTON 3d. September 1850

Sir:

I have received your Excellency's communication, under date
the 19th. of July last, announcing that as President of the Geographical and Statistical Society of Mexico, you had done me
the honor, at a meeting of that Body held on the 18th of July
to propose me, and that I was chosen, a corresponding member.
Your Excellency's letter was also accompanied by a Diploma and
by a printed copy of the regulations of the Society.

In reply, I have the honor to acquaint your Excellency, that
the distinction thus conferred, is cordially accepted.

The utility of such Associations is generally acknowledged,
and I trust that the labors of yours, in collecting and diffusing

---

[1] Accompanying this letter is a note of G. J. Abbott, who was at this time
Webster's private secretary. A summary of the Sandwich Islands question
appears in the New York Express; the article was prepared after a conversation with Mr. Webster by E. Brooks. Mr. Abbott does not inform us of the
date of this article.

[2] President of the Mexican Republic, a year later.

Statistical and Geographical information, especially with reference to your own magnificent country, will be viewed with lively interest by intelligent men of all nations.   The judicious manner in which your Society has been organized and the eminent, Mexicans who appear to have taken part therein, are favorable omens for its success.   It will at all times be a pleasure to me to do any thing which I can, officially or personally, towards contributing to that success.

I avail myself of this occasion to offer to your Excellency the assurance of my high regard.

D. W.

(To Millard Fillmore.[1])

SEPTEMBER 11 1850.

My Dear Sir,

Mr. Samuel Adams is what he represents himself to be an old merchant of Boston; and he is quite a respectable man, under no bias, I suppose, of politics, or party, such as would lean him to any considerable misrepresentation.

The Collector of the Customs at Boston is Philip GREELEY, Jr. He is rather a young man, not many years ago a merchant of the firm of Guild & Greeley.   The House failed; Mr. Greeley having nothing to do, was employed as Secretary to the "Whig Central Committee."   He is active and plausible, and not content without some information.   In this situation, he made friends, & forstalled opinion, so that when a change of administration came, he presented a very large list of names, and many of them very respectable, as a candidate for the collectorship.   I had no idea he would be appointed because Gen. Taylor told me he should restore Gen. Lincoln.   Mr. Greeley ought not to have been appointed.   He did not possess the proper weight of general character & reputation.   His firm have neither paid their debts or compounded with their creditors.   It is true that he is sued for small debts; and I have understood has lately taken the poor debtor's oath.

In politics, he adheres to the Boston Atlas, which is just such another "Whig" paper as the Albany Evening Journal.   Very

---

[1] This letter and a number of the kind have been given as examples of Webster's criticism of men proposed for office.

likely the Senate may reject the nomination. If that should happen I should recommend the nomination of Mr. Ashmun.

He would take the office, as he means to retire from Congress. He is one of the most popular men in the State. He has substantial friends in Boston, to give his bonds, &, in my opinion, much more *effect* would come from his appointment than from that of any other person.

The Postmaster at Boston is William Hayden, a man of fifty, or upwards, and was many years Auditor of the city. He is a very upright, honest man, & is regarded as a good man of business. He is a sound Whig, & quite right, on pending questions. But he is sometimes blunt, in his manners. He was in the Legislature of Massachusetts, at the time of Gen. Jackson's death & made some remarks on that occasion, which were in very bad taste. On this ground there is opposition to him, and he may be rejected. There really was no malice operating to produce what he said, but it indicated indiscretion.

I have not heard any complaint of the manner in which he has discharged the duties of his office. As to his "fondness for evening festivals" I have never heard anything of that kind alleged against him. He would not have been my choice for Postmaster, yet I have rather wished he might be confirmed; and it was perhaps on my recommendation that General Rush reported favorably on his nomination.

If Mr. Hayden should be rejected my present opinion is, that the best recommendation for the place would be that of Geo W. Gordon. Mr. Gordon was appointed Postmaster in 1841, & a year or two after removed by Mr. Tyler. I believe his conduct in office was universally acceptable. When he was removed he was complimented with the Consulship at Rio from which Mr. Polk recalled him.

There will be time, if there should be rejections to consider of what I have suggested.

Yrs always truly

Danl Webster.

(To Millard Fillmore.)

Sunday morning (Sept 19 1850)

My Dear Sir,

The Bill, settling the Texan boundary passed, as you will have seen, on Friday, through the Senate by a good vote. The California Bill will probably pass the same body tomorrow.   So far, so good.   The Govt. seems to get a little power of motion. Gen. Cass says, that there has been no administration, since March, '49.   That since that time, the Ship of State has had no headway : but that She now begins to feel her helm.

The Texan Boundary Bill will be violently opposed in the House, by the usual concurrence and cooperation of Extremes. It is said, Gov. Seward is taking great pains to defeat it.   The Massachusetts vote, I presume, will be equally divided.   Ashmun, Grinnell, and Duncan for the measure, Mann, Allen, and Fowler, against it.   For my part, I much prefer to see a respectable Democrat elected to Congress, than a professed Whig, tainted with any degree of Free Soil doctrines, or abolitionism.   Men who act upon some principle, though it be a wrong principle, have usually some consistency of conduct; and they are there- fore, less dangerous than those who are looking for nothing but increased power, and influence, and who act simply, on what seems expedient, for their purposes, at the moment.

I see a good many of the members every day, and do all I properly can, towards helping the good work on.   I hope we shall succeed, but expect a good deal of controversy yet.   I hope the Editor of the Courier will come immediately on here.   I think we owe a great deal to his independent spirit, and inde- pendent conduct.   I should be most happy to make him known to the Department.   He well deserves all the help he can fairly get.

I looked for a letter from you both yesterday, and today, but none came.

Yrs truly
D. WEBSTER

No word yet from McKennan.

(To Peter Harvey.[1])

Private
WASHINGTON Oct. 2, '50

My Dear friend;
I feel well, & in good spirits.   My cold is going off, & al- though it leaves me weak, my eye & head are clear, & that awful depression which accompanies the disease has disappeared.   It

---

[1] This letter is owned by A. F. Lewis, of Fryeburg, Me.

will return, occasionally, for a fortnight, perhaps; but not for long visits.

My main relief, however is, that Congress got thr° so well. I can now sleep onights. We have gone thr° the most important crisis, which has occurred since the foundation of the Government; & whatever party may prevail, hereafter, the Union stands firm.

Faction, Disunion, & the love of mischief are put under, at least, for the present, & I hope for a long time. Another effect of recent occurrences is the softening of political animosities. Those who have acted together, in this great crisis, can never again feel sharp asperities towards one another. For instance, it is impossible that I should entertain hostile feelings, or political acrimony, towards Genl Cass, Dickinson, Shield, Bright, Rusk, &c. &c. in the Senate. We have agreed, that as we are never likely to be called on to act in a matter of so much moment to the Country, again, so we will not mar the joy, or the honor of the past, by any unnecessary quarrels for the future.

Another thing is not altogether improbable. And that is, a remodelling of Parties. If any considerable body of the Whigs of the North shall act in the spirit of the majority of the recent Convention in N. York, a new arrangement of Parties is unavoidable. There must be a Union Party, & an opposing party under some name, I know not what, very likely the Party of Liberty.

Many good men among our Whig friends of the North could not make up their minds to renounce their old ideas, & support the great measures. Very well; & if, now that the measures are adopted, & the questions settled, those will support things as they now are, & resist all further attempts at agitation & disturbance, & make no efforts for another change, they ought still to be regarded as Whigs. But those who act otherwise, or shall act otherwise, & continue to talk about Wilmot Provisos, & to resist, or seek to repeal, the Fugitive Slave Bill, or use any other means to disturb the quiet of the Country, will have no right to consider themselves either as Whigs, or as friends of the Administration. Because there is one thing that is fixed, & settled, & that is, that the present Administration will not recognize one set of Whig Principles for the North, & another for the South. In regard to the great questions of Constitutional Law, & Public Policy, upon which the Whig Party is founded, we must all be of one faith, & that can be regarded as no Whig Party in

N. York, or Mass., which espouses doctrines, & utters sentiments, hostile to the just, & Constitutional rights of the South, & therefore such as Southern Whigs cannot agree to.

You will be glad, that I have reached the bottom of the 4th page.

Yrs truly   DANL WEBSTER

———

(To Millard Fillmore.)

BOSTON, Oct. 19th 1850.

My dear Sir,

Since writing you this morning I have received your obliging letter of the 14th instant.   I think Mr. Crittenden's opinion is entirely sound in all points, and I understand that Judge Woodbury, in a charge to the Grand Jury, in this City last week drew the fugitive slave law to their attention, recommending in the strongest terms, their enforcement of its provisions.   I hope to get this charge published.

It may be true that all the provisions of this Bill were not expedient, but I think that some Bill & that an efficient one, had become necessary.   If, I get such health as to enable me to address a public assembly, I shall say something on this whole subject.

As to the Charge-ship at Brussells, Mr. Bayard informs me by letter, that if He has the appointment, he should like to proceed to his post early in December—   As there is no vacancy & one must be made, & as there is no emergency calling for the change I think it would be on the whole, more prudent to make no appointment till the meeting of Congress.

In the meantime I shall write to Mr. Derrick today, requesting him to speak to you on the subject, and with your permission, to write to Mr. Clemson, that a change is contemplated, as soon as Congress shall again assemble, and that in the meantime he may retain his present situation & fulfil its duties until his successor shall arrive.

Mr. Walsh has written a very dissatisfied letter a copy of which I enclose to you.   When we last spoke upon the subject, I had nobody in my mind for that place, but Mr. Goodrich, who, you know, was very anxious for it, nor have I thought much of any other person since.   But there are some things respecting Mr.

Goodrich which I wish to enquire about before I am prepared to recommend him—

I send you a copy of the last letter from Mr. I. B. Clay. It gives me some embarrassment— He expresses a willingness. to return to Portugal, provided his return can be made "with all honor," at the same time he says that in his opinion, Portugal ought to make some acknowledgment of wrong done in the cases in which she proposes to pay, or at least to withdraw the virtual protest she made— It may perhaps, be inferred from this, that he would make it a point of honor to obtain one or the other of these things from the Government of Portugal; and if so, a great protraction of the negotiation is to be expected. In my judgment our true course, as practical men, it to pay no regard to her protests, by which she does dishonour to no body but herself, and to accept, as we have accepted, her actual offer, and to proceed at once to the preparation and execution of the proper convention. It is to be considered that Mr. Clay would not be quite cordially received by the Portuguese Government, if he were to return to Lisbon.

Under these circumstances the question arises, whether it is best to direct Mr. Clay to return immediately to Lisbon & complete the negotiation, upon the simple basis of the actual offer, without regard to any acknowledgment expected to be made by Portugal, or any withdrawal of her protest, or whether it is best to signify to him, that he may consider himself recalled at his own request, with the intimation, that proper public notice will be taken of the fidelity and ability, with which he conducted the negotiation, while in his hands—either of these courses would be honorable, perhaps both equally honorable, to Mr. Clay. All this is for your consideration. If you feel ready to come to a decision on the point, you may signify that decision at once to me here, or perhaps things may remain ten days longer as they are without much inconvenience, by which time I hope to see you. My own inclination of opinion rather is, that it is better that Mr. Clay should return home, and his successor be at once appointed; but there are causes which may perhaps influence my judgment in this respect improperly, and I therefore prefer leaving the matter entirely to your own discretion.

As to an Agent to St. Domingo, we will be prepared to act upon that as soon as I reach Washington—

I know not what we can do about California Judges. I fear no fit men will take the offices at the Salaries now provided. Mr.

Healy has not absolutely decided, but I am afraid he will decline. I shall know in a day or two, and I will endeavor to learn whether there is any body in this region fit for the office, who will accept it.   Perhaps some fit man without a family may be found.

Yours always truly—

Postscript—Sunday noon Oct 20th— I am better today in health & strength than I have been since I left Washington & hope another week will complete my recovery.   They talk of asking me to an Union meeting at Concord, New Hampshire—

(From Millard Fillmore.)

WASHINGTON, Oct. 23. 1850.

My Dear Sir,
      Your letter of the 19th came to hand yesterday, & I am much gratified to hear of your improved health.

I have received a copy of Judge Woodbury's charge on the *Fugitive Slave Law,* and the Report of Judge Grier's opinion in a case before him, all manfully sustaining the constitutionality of the law, and manifesting a determined resolution to carry it out. I have also just received a joint letter from Judge Grier and Judge Keane, stating that a case has occurred before a commission in Pa. where the execution of a warrant under that act was "forcibly and successfully resisted; the posse summoned to aid the officer having refused to act," and "inquiring whether upon the recurrence of an obstruction to his Process he will be entitled to call for the aid of such troops of the U. S. as may be accessible."

This you perceive presents a very grave and delicate question. I have not yet had time to look into it and regret much that so many of my cabinet are absent, and especially yourself and the attorney general.   These judges ask for a general order authorizing the employment of the troops in such an emergency; and I am disposed to exert whatever power I possess under the constitution and laws, in enforcing this observance.   I have sworn to support the constitution.— I know no higher law that conflicts with it; and that constitution says, "the President shall take care that the laws be faithfully executed."   I mean at every sacrifice and at every hazard to perform my duty.   The union must and shall be preserved, and this can only be done, by a faithful and impartial administration of the laws. I can not doubt that in these sentiments you are with me. And if you have occasion to speak I hope you will give no encouragement, even by implication, to any resistance to the law. Nullification can not and will not be tolerated.

It seems to me, with all due deference to your superior wisdom that the true grounds for our friends to take is this; that the law, hav'g been passed, must be executed. That so far as it provides for the surrender of fugitives from labor it is according to the requirements of the constitution and should be sustained against all attempts at repeal, but if there be any provision in it endangering the liberty of those who are free, it should be so modified as to secure the free blacks from such an abuse of the object of the law, and that done we at the North have no just cause of complaint.

We must abide by the constitution. If overthrown, we can never hope for a better. God knows that I detest Slavery, but it is an existing evil, for which we are not responsible, and we must endure it, and give it such protection, as is guaranteed by the constitution, till we can get rid of it without destroying the last hope of free government in the world. But pardon me for saying so much. I thought possibly you might desire to know my sentiments, and I can assure you, I am very anxious to know yours, as to the answer to be given to the Judges' letter. I will, finally, send a copy of it.

I will add something in another letter.

With the highest consideration & Respect, I am in great haste

Truly yours
MILLARD FILLMORE.

(To Millard Fillmore.)

FRANKLIN, N. H. Oct. 24, 1850.

My Dear Sir,

I have been here five days, with evident improvement; but am concerned to say, I am not yet strong, nor has my cough entirely ceased. In dry weather I feel nothing of it, but it returns with rain and damp,—I shall have to go straight to Washington, as soon as I feel any way able.

The politics of Massachusetts are in a state of utter confusion.

Many Whigs are *afraid* to act a manly part, lest they should lose the State government.   They act a most mean part in their courtship of abolitionism.

You see from Mr. March's letter, how the Whig State Committee Convention (?) is acting.   With this Committee, the Atlas most vigorously cooperates, 'tho' it endeavors to save appearance, & so do Greely & Charles Hudson, especially the latter. Seven imported Unitarian Priests are now candidates for public office—viz. members of Congress; besides a host of others who offer for the Legislature,—   These are all free soil, or abolition men.   The Postmaster at Lowell is represented to be a brawling abolitionist,—preaching daily, the duty of resistance to the fugitive slave law,—I shall inquire into this—when I return to Boston.

I have been able to make a draft of a reply to Mr. Hülsemann, which I hope you will approve.

I have also made some notes for that part of your Annual Message which may relate to foreign affairs.

Yours always truly Whether sick or well,

DANL WEBSTER

(From Millard Fillmore.)

WASHINGTON, Oct. 28. 1850.

My Dear Sir,

I have yours of the 24th. from Franklin, N. H. and am greatly gratified to hear of your improved health; and hope soon to learn that your cough has entirely left you.   I infer that you have not received my letters of the 23d inst. addressed to you at Boston. We have had two Cabinet meetings, the last this morning, on the authority and duty of the president to use the Military force in aid of the civil officer to execute the fugitive slave law, and have concluded when, necessary, to do it.   We were somewhat embarrassed by the legislation of Congress on the subject, in 1807. and subsequent acts, which would seem to imply that this was a power to be conferred by Congress, but after a careful examination of the subject, I came to the conclusion that it was an inherent Executive power enforced by the constitution, when it made the President commander in chief of the Army and Navy, and required him to take care that the laws be faithfully executed. In this, however, the whole cabinet were not agreed, some think that the Marshall might summon the Army as citizens and part of the *Comitatus*, but all agree that the aid should be given, and the only question was when? We concluded to give it to the Marshall whereas, he was unable to sustain the laws by the civil authority, and to the special deputies in the same cases when a judge of the District or Justice of the Sup. Court, should certify that in his opinion it was necessary. This direction is given to the commanding officer of the Marines at Philadelphia.

Congress having authorized the Marshall to provide temporary jails, where the Sheriff refuses to admit the U. S. prisoners, we did not think it advisable to grant the use of the Receiving ship at Boston for that purpose. But I mean at all hazards to do my part towards executing this law. I admit no right of *nullification* North or South. My object however, has been to avoid the use of military force as far as possible, not doubting that there is yet patriotism enough left in every State North of Mason's and Dixon's line to maintain the Supremacy of the laws; and being particularly anxious that no state should be disgraced, by being compelled to resort to the army to support the laws of the Union, if it could be avoided. I have therefore commenced mildly—authorizing this force only in the last resort, but if necessary, I shall not hesitate to give greater power, and finally to bring the whole force of the government to sustain the law. But the mail is closing and I can not say more.

I have also yours of the 25th inst. and am gratified to hear that you are preparing an answer to the Dist. Atty. of Missi. and to the Austrian minister.

I can sympathise with you in the melancholy feelings which are inspired by looking upon the grave of your ancestors and kindred but I hope soon to welcome you back to the busy scenes of active life where your absence is so much deplored and your counsels so much wanted

I am truly your friend

MILLARD FILLMORE

(Have not time to read over.)

———

(To D. Fletcher Webster.)

NEW YORK, Tuesday 12 O'clock November. 3. [1850.]
Dear Fletcher,

I see with much pleasure that Mr Sumner declines. This, I suppose will break the force of the new opposition to Mr. Win-

throp, and so render the meeting on Friday Evening less important.   I can see nobody today, on account of the Election, and
the rain.   It is understood here, that the Banks do not touch Mr.
Walker's loan.   They would do it, probably, but for that most
miserable of all pieces of Legislation, the Sub. Treasury Law.—
   If anything should be known of the State of the polls, at the
closing of the mail (1/2 past 3 O'clock) I will give you another
note.
   Mrs. W. and Julia would have gone home today if the weather
had cleared.   But at this moment, it is thick, rainy and foggy.—
                                        Your's
                                        D. WEBSTER.
                        ─────────

(To Wm. Prescott, M. D.[1])

                                        MARSHFIELD Nov. 7. '50
Dear Sir,
   I have rec'd your letter of the third instant, which is quite
proper, & respectful, but really I must be excused from answering the question proposed.   I have not time at present to say
even so little as you propose, respecting myself.
              Very respectfully yr. ob. servt.
                                        DAN'L WEBSTER.

   I ought to add my sincere thanks, for the kind manner in
which you speak of my public services.   My object has been, &
is, to preserve the Institutions of our Fathers; & I feel, deeply,
that those institutions can only be preserved by conciliation, &
the cultivation of friendly sentiments between the different parts
of the country.   What my efforts have cost, or may yet cost, me,
is of little moment.   If the country is benefited, I have my
reward.
                        ─────────

(To Millard Fillmore.)

Private & confidential.
                                        (BOSTON) Nov. 15. 1850.
My dear Sir.
   For two days I have been endeavoring to do something to put
this business of the attempt to arrest Crafts into a better shape.
We are unfortunate here, the District Attorney here has no tal-

─────────
[1] This letter is in the possession of Judge Corning, of Concord, N. H.

ent, no fitness for his place, & no very good disposition. The Claimant, in this Craft case called on him for assistance or advice, which he declined to render. This claimant or agent has used no great discretion, but has acted clumsily. It became immediately known, that a person was here, to arrest slaves; & it is supposed, I cannot say how truly, that this news spread from Mr. Lunt's office. Mr. Lunt's associates with him in nearly all his business a young lawyer, by the name of Sauger, This Mr. Sauger is rather clever, of much more ability no doubt than Mr. Lunt, & is a professed & active free soil man, as you will see by one out of a string of resolutions introduced by him into a political meeting at Charleston.

[Here the resolutions are pasted into the letter.]

The Marshall, Mr. Devins, is, as I believe very well disposed, but I fear not entirely efficient. I sent for him yesterday, & told him he must either execute his warrant or give some good reasons for not executing it, & that that reason should be made public, in order that persons interested in the matters, at the South, might not have it in their power to say that U. S. officers in the North were not disposed to do their duty.

The Marshall has obtained the opinion of Mr. B. R. Curtis on the subject of the Fugitive Slave Law. It is well drawn & argues well that which hardly seems to require any argument. The opinion, however will do good. Mr. Curtis' reputation is high, & his opinion will silence the small lawyers. It will be publish in the Courier of Tomorrow at my request.

I am sorry to be obliged to say that the *general weight* of U. S. officers in this District is *against* the execution of the Fugitive Slave Law. I hear this when I go into the streets from every sound Whig, and every Union man I meet. Mr. Greeley, the collector, is more than indifferent, and Mr. Hudson, without any doubt, has acted for the election of Mr. Mann, with all his power. Our General State Whig Committee has been, & is composed of just such men. The Atlas has lent the aid of all its force, in the same direction, & Mr. Mann's re-election is fairly enough to be attributed to the joint operation of these agencies.

I do not wish to annoy you with these local matters, in the midst of your pressure under other & greater duties; but ere long the condition of the public offices of the U. S. in this District must be inquired into.

Yrs. always
DANL WEBSTER.

(To B. F. Ayer.[1])

BOSTON, NOV. 16, 1850.

My Dear Sir,—

When I received yesterday the invitation of the committee to attend the meeting at Manchester, my expectation was, that I should immediately leave this city, and I contented myself, therefore, with a very brief reply. The weather having detained me for a few days I have time to write a more respectful acknowledgment of your communication, and to express more distinctly as well the gratification it would afford me to attend the meeting as my pleasure that such a Convention is to be convened. A 'Union Meeting, without distinction of party,' holden in the largest town or city in the State, can hardly fail to be attended with good consequences. There is evidently, abroad, a spirit of disunion and disobedience to the laws which good men ought to meet, and to check if they can. Men are to be found who propose as their own rule of conduct, and recommend the same rule to others, 'peaceable resistance to the laws'; that is to say, they propose to resist the laws of the land so far as they can do so consistently with their own personal safety. Their obligations to support the Constitution go for nothing; their oaths to act, if they hold any public trust, according to law, go for nothing; it is enough that they do not, by forcible resistance, expose themselves to dangers and penalties. This is, certainly, quite a new strain of patriotism. We have never before this day known such sentiments to be circulated, commended and acted upon by any who professed love for their country or respect for its institutions. A still more extravagant notion is sometimes advanced, which is, that individuals may judge of their rights and duties, under the Constitution and the laws, by some rule which, according to their ideas, is above both the Constitution and the laws.

You and I, sir, and our fellow-citizens of New Hampshire, have not so read the books of authority, either religious or civil. We do not so understand either the institutions of Christianity or the institutions of government. And we may well value more and more highly the government which is over us, when we see that the weapons aimed against its preservation are also, for the most part, equally directed against those great fundamental, moral

---

[1] This letter is taken from a newspaper clipping from the Liberator, Dec. 13, 1850. It is headed " Letters from the Sham Patriot and Betrayer of Liberty."

and political truths upon which all good government, and the peace of society, at all times, must essentially rest.

I have the fullest belief, sir, that in the State of New Hampshire, this disorganizing spirit will meet such a rebuke as shall put it to flight. The representation of the State in Congress generally supported the peace measures of the last session, and by these measures I doubt not the State will stand. It is time that discord and animosity should cease. It is time that a better understanding and more friendly sentiments were revived between the North and the South. And I am sure that all wise and good men will see the propriety of forbearing from renewing agitation, by attempts to repeal the late measures, or any of them. I do not see that they contain unconstitutional or alarming principles, or that they forbode the infliction of wrong or injury. When real and actual evil arises, if it shall arise, the laws ought to be amended or repealed; but in the absence of imminent danger I see no reason at present for renewed controversy or contention.

My dear sir, the Union will be preserved, and the laws will be obeyed and executed. Let us take courage, and that sort of courage which prompts men to a resolute discharge of their duties. We will save the Union for our own sake, for the sake of the country, for the honor of free governments, and even for the benefit of those who seem ready, with ruthless hands, to tear it asunder. I am, my dear sir,

With true regard, Your friend and obed't servant,

DANIEL WEBSTER.

(To Millard Fillmore.)

BOSTON, Nov. 16 '50

My Dear Sir.

You will see that the N. Hampshire Whigs are all right. We can kill off Freesoilism, in the whole of N. England, by energy & decision.

We have been ready to take the Sound Boat this evening- -but the weather will not allow.

I rejoice greatly that Pettigrew has taken the Att'yship. He is fit for any thing.

Yrs always truly
DANL WEBSTER

(To Millard Fillmore.)

MONDAY, DEC. 2 1850

My Dear Sir

No doubt exists of forming a *quorum* in each House to day, & I incline to think it will be well to send in the message, if the Committee shall come to you with the ordinary announcement, before the hour be too late.

There is enough of *nullification* reading in the papers of the morning.[1]

Yrs truly

DANL WEBSTER.

_____

(To Millard Fillmore.)

3 O'CLOCK. [DEC. *2* 1850]

My Dear Sir

I learn from sundry sources that nothing could be better than the manner in which the message was received, so far as could be judged by the two Houses.

The most absolute attentiveness was observed, & general satisfaction very evident.

In my judgment, My Dear Sir, you have laid the foundation for a distinguished and fortunate administration—no matter what South Carolina may say or do.

Yrs truly

DANL. WEBSTER.

_____

(To J. S. Spencer.)

WASHINGTON DEC. 21, '50.

My dear Sir,

You are quite at liberty to publish my letter,[2] if you think proper. If you value it so highly as to desire to preserve it, I have thought you might like to have it in my own handwriting. The letter was dictated to my clerk, who happened to take a copy. I did not peruse the manuscript, & in the enclosed have altered a

---

[1] An omitted phrase from one of Webster's letters to Blatchford, Dec. 10, 1850, reads: "And northern fanatics are encouraged to pour forth, more and more, their loathsome ebullitions." See Private Correspondence, vol. ii, p. 406.

[2] Published in *New York Observer* Feb. 6, 1851.

word or two. The date was omitted in the copy. Dr. Cox called to day, but I was not at home. I hope both to see & to hear him before he leaves Washington.

I am obliged to you for your little volume of "Sketches," which I have not yet opened, but shall not fail to read.

I am, my Dear Sir, With my true regard Yours

DANL WEBSTER.

———

(To Asabel Huntington.)

WASHINGTON Decr. 21. '50.

My dear Sir.

I thank you cordially for your friendly letter,[1] which I value highly, as I know your good judgment, and have no doubt of your sincerity—

I can not well describe to you, my dear Sir, what my feelings were, for five months, during which no one of my colleagues manifested the slightest concurrence in my sentiments, and at the same time I knew that sincere men, and good Whigs, at home disapproved, or doubted. It was natural enough that the speech of March 7th should produce a shock. The letter which I enclose with this I rec'd this morning, and send it only that you may see that other zealous Whigs were as slow and cautious as yourself.

You may return the letter, as I have not answered it— It is but a specimen of several hundreds.

Yours truly

DANL WEBSTER

———

(To Millard Fillmore.)

WEDNESDAY, 11, o'clock. Jan. 11, 1851.

To the President,

The last balloting yesterday left Sumner in want of *ten* votes. His wants seem to be increasing.

Yrs truly always

DANL WEBSTER.

---

[1] A rather belated letter approving of the 7th of March speech, with the confession that he at first disapproved. Huntington was later Mayor of Salem, Mass.

(To Millard Fillmore.)

My dear Sir,   [JAN. 1851] [1]?
     I was informed by a member of Congress yesterday, "that Mr
Webster had been with the President at least one hour every day
for the last ten days, that their interviews had no witness, &
that it was well understood that it related to the next Presidential
election, & the candidates &c." I replied that all this was news
to me, that I did not recollect that a word about *Candidates* at
the next election ever passed between the President & myself, &
certainly never a word upon the point of *our* being candidates.
My "informant" was Mr. Gentry. He had picked the matter
up in the Hotel.

Yrs always

D. W.

———

(To Millard Fillmore.)

DEPARTMENT OF STATE, Washington Jan. 17. 1851.
My Dear Sir,
     There is a person by the name of Gilbert Russell of whom I
know little who is talking very loudly and angrily against me at
the Hotels because, as he says, I refuse him liberty to see certain
[papers] of his in the Department, & of my answer. Very likely
he may go to you on the subject.
     In order that you may perceive the nature of the case I send
you a no. of the "Republic,"—the allowance of the claims, which
were supported by these papers, having become a matter of newspaper discussion.   The claim was presented under the authority of an act of Congress by Wm. Cort. Johnson, an administra-
tor of the claimant.
     It is understood that many persons are interested in the amount
recovered.   You will see by Mr. Russell's letter that he appears
to have no interest in the matter himself, but his object is to prove
forgery, & perjury, in the parties & witnesses, & wilful wrong
in the late Secretary of State, & the late Attorney General.
     Now in point of fact the papers are not in the Department,
After the claim had been allowed, Mr. Clayton ordered all the
papers, as I learn to be carefully sealed up, & safely kept.
     When attacked in the Union he took the papers to his House,

---

[1] This letter is indorsed by G. J. Abbott, Webster's private secretary:
"Without date, but sometime in Jan., 1851."

probably to make out his Defense, as it appears in the Republic, & they have never been returned to the Department.

All this is a matter of no great importance, but as I supposed you might hear of it, I have thought it might be well to put you in possession of the particulars.

Yours always truly

DANL WEBSTER.

(To Millard Fillmore.)

DEPARTMENT OF STATE Jan. 19th. 1851.

My Dear Sir—

I think the instructions to Mr. Hatch were pretty clear before, at least I meant they should be, but to make all sure, I have added your words, "but you will stop at remonstrance until further orders" The change of purpose from sending a Charge d' Affaires to sending a special Agent is explained in the letter.

Yours truly always

DANL WEBSTER.

(To Millard Fillmore.)

WEDNESDAY 1 o'clock Feb. 11. 1851.

To the President

My Dear Sir,

I send the draft of an answer to the Senate for your perusal and consideration.

I send also the Boston Daily Advertiser & Boston Courier. Read in the first the cards of Marshal Tukey and Mayor Bigelow; in the second a good leader.

Yours

DANL WEBSTER

I am obliged to go to the Capitol for an hour.

(From Mr. Hülsemann.[1])

NEWPORT R. I. 27 July 1850.

To Honorable Dan. Webster Secretary of State

Sir,

I beg leave to add in this private note a few observations to

---

[1] This letter precedes by about a month the famous letter of Hulsemann which called forth Webster s still more famous reply. See Webster's Works, vol. vi, p. 488.

the official answer of yesterday, by which I acknowledged the receipt of your communication announcing your appointment to the Department of the State.

Although the records of the State Department do not contain any correspondence between your predecessor & myself on the difficulties, which have, for the last 8-9 months, interrupted the till then friendly intercourse of our respective Governments, it is probably known to you, that the untoward mission of Mr. Dudley Mann and the language employed by the late Administration, concerning it in the President's message & in other published documents, have been repeatedly the objects of serious remonstrance on my part and by order of my Government. Since the beginning of those proceedings I have abstained, though, at the earnest request of Mr. Clayton, from making any official communication in writing, because I wished to avoid whatever might embitter the difficulties, & which was to be apprehended from the communication to Congress, and publication in the newspapers of the correspondence, which must have been at that time of an unfriendly character. I have no doubt, that Mr. Clayton himself would acknowledge, that during the whole of last winter I have personally done all I could, to *smoothen down* as much as possible the difficulties, which have grown out of that question.

In such matters the change of persons facilitates naturally an arrangement; besides the question itself has become a matter of history, & has no more any political bearing; & the well known pacific and conservative character of President Fillmore, as well as the experience, which during your former direction of the State Department, all foreign Governments have had of your just and judicious management of diplomatic affairs,—all these circumstances induce me to hope, that a frank conversation with you may bring about very easily an understanding between us, which will prove satisfactory to my Government. I shall, for that purpose, present myself at the State Department, as soon as I understand, that the more pressing business during the last weeks of the Session of Congress has passed away, & you will be more at leisure; in the meantime I expect also to receive some answers & instructions from home, connected with this question.

I have the honor to be, Sir, very respectfully
Your Obedient servant

HULSEMANN

(Memorandum.[1])

There was no correspondence between W. Clayton and W. Hülsemann about Hungary— All that did pass was in conversation. He did submit a copy of the instructions he received from Prince Schwartzenberg, but was compelled by W. Clayton to withdraw them, and scared from making a communication to the Dept. as he was required and ordered to do in his instructions by the language which W. Clayton used on more than one occasion.

(G. J. Abbot[2] to D. Fletcher Webster.)

WASHINGTON April 22d. 1854.

My Dear Fletcher,—
In answering your note the other day—I noticed just as I sent it off, that I had omitted the principal part, as the player man did the character of Hamlet.

I have signified to Mr. Everett your desire to see his Draft of the Hülsemann letter.

It will give you some satisfaction, especially, if you see three or four, of the eight or ten other Drafts that were made, and which show the labor which Mr. Webster expended in the preparation of it.[3] My eyes are still weak.

Yours always truly,   G. J. ABBOT.

P. S.   I still am obliged to use Mrs. Abbot's hand—
Mr. Everett you know has the "Draft" with two or three others, all much interlined.

(Wm. Hunter to D. Fletcher Webster.)

Private.

WASHINGTON, May 3, 1854.

My dear Sir;
This morning's mail brought me your letter of the 1st instant. The following is my reply.—
Late in the office hours of the 3d of October, 1850, the day your father started for the north, he came to my room in the

---

[1] This memorandum is in Fletcher Webster's manuscript.
[2] Webster's private secretary during his last years.
[3] This and the three following letters refer to the controversy over the authorship of the reply to Hulsemann.

Department, directed me to prepare a draft of an answer to Mr. Hülsemann's note and to send it to him at Marshfield. He particularly mentioned one point which he wished made in the answer, as to what he supposed to be the illiberal course of Austria in regard to Mr. Mann's mission to Hungary in comparison with that of Spain with respect to the missions of the special agents from this country which were sent to her colonies in this hemisphere after they had declared their independence. He accordingly ordered me to examine the records for the purpose of ascertaining the facts as to this. Your father seemed to be very indignant at the threat in Mr. Hülsemann's note to treat Mr. Mann as a spy, and his feeling on this point suggested the passage in my draft of a threat on our part to bombard Trieste and Venice in case the threat of Austria had been carried into effect. That passage I tried to express in your father's words as well as I could recollect them. His directions were brief and in the ordinary course of business. The draft was prepared as soon as other engagements would permit and forwarded to Marshfield. I heard nothing more of it and your father never mentioned the subject to me again. When, however, after his return to Washington, the answer to Mr. Hülsemann was sent, I noticed that it was very different from the draft I had prepared. I knew nothing of this answer until it had been communicated to Mr. Hülsemann. Mr. Chew, who, upon my recommendation, your father took with him to the north as his private secretary, probably knows more about the answer during its progress and until it was issued, than any body else. He never, however, said anything to me on the subject, and my confidence in his discretion is such, that I do not believe that he ever breathed a word in regard to it to any one. I have been told, that some of the newspapers have stated that the answer as signed was prepared by me. This statement did not come directly, or indirectly, from me. There was a clerk in the Department who knew that I prepared a draft and he may have had the indiscretion to mention the fact out of the Department. Before there was any public controversy in regard to the authorship of the answer, I was on several occasions asked if I was not the author. To this I sometimes replied that I had made a draft of an answer, but I never claimed the authorship of the note as it was signed.

I am not sure that there is a single sentence in the answer as published identical with my draft. Inasmuch, however, as I should be obliged to rely on my recollection only, I would not undertake to affirm this. Possibly my draft may still be among your father's papers.[1] If so, I could at once identify it.

Hoping that this statement may prove satisfactory, I remain,

Yours truly,

W. HUNTER.

_____

(Edward Everett to D. Fletcher Webster.)

Private.

32 SUMMER STREET 8 May 1854.

Dear Sir,

The only contingency which occurs to me as likely to make a public explanation relative to the authorship of the H. letter desirable or necessary at present is the surreptitious re-publication of the pamphlet printed last summer or of the introductory note to it.— As one copy at least obtained by inadventure or accident (tho' Mr. Marvin says he cannot conceive how) has got abroad, such a re-publication may take place. In that case, a statement from you of the nature intimated by you might be expedient. I shall remain here this week:—and if you will draw up and send a statement as you would deem it expedient to make if necessary, and favor me with a sight of it, while I am at home, I might perhaps make some suggestions that would be useful.

With much regard, Sincerely yours,

EDWARD EVERETT.

_____

(Edward Everett to Fletcher Webster.)

Private.

32 SUMMER STREET, 11 May 1854.

My dear Mr. Webster,

I have not yet been able to lay my hand on the duplicate of your father's letter to me of 20 Oct. 1850, which you think you handed to me.—

In the meantime I enclose you a copy from the letter received by me, which,—like the duplicate,—is in Mr. Chew's handwriting.

With much regard yours

EDWARD EVERETT.

_____

[1] For details as to the controversy over this famous letter see Curtis' Life of Webster, vol. ii, pp. 535, 536. The various drafts and a pamphlet on the subject written by Edward Everett are to be found in the New Hampshire Historical Society Library.

(From Wm. Hunter.[1])

WASHINGTON Oct 4. 1850

Dear Sir:

In compliance with your order, I enclose a copy of President Taylor's Message in regard to Hungary. After reading Hülsemann's note,[2] it strikes me that we should not hesitate to receive and answer it, though its tone is sufficiently arrogant and saucy to justify us in requiring him take it back, were such a course deemed most advisable. It may, however, be so easily answered, and the answer, if embracing proper topics in proper form, may be made to tell to such advantage on the public ear and to the public mind, that we must try and do our best.

You can rely upon any aid which can be afforded to you by

Your obedient servant,

W. HUNTER.

———

(From Wm. Hunter.)

Dear Sir,   WASHINGTON, 15th October, 1850.

I send a draft of an answer Hülsemann's note. You will notice that it touches all the points which you mentioned. The subject is of the highest importance, looking both to the foreign affairs and the domestic politics of the United States. It should therefore be well considered. It is perhaps, also advisable that the reply should be promptly given. If you concur in this, Mr. Chew can at once transcribe your answer and it may either be sent to Mr. Hülsemann from Marshfield[3] direct, or through the Department.

Very truly, and humbly, Your obedient servant

W. HUNTER.

———

(From John M. Clayton.[4])

NEAR NEW CASTLE, Delaware, January 12th 1851.

My dear Sir,

Since the publication of your admirable letter to the Chevalier

---

[1] Clerk in the Department of State.
[2] The note dated Sept. 30, 1850. See Webster's Works, vol. vi, p. 488.
[3] Webster was at this time in Marshfield.
[4] Webster's predecessor as Secretary of State.

Hülsemann,[1] I have felt it my duty to write to you something on the subject, not merely to express my thanks for that letter, which no true American can read without pride and gratification, but to correct two errors in the Chevaliers letter to you, of which you could obtain no information through any other source than your predecessor in office.

The first mistake of Mr. Hülsemann, to which I wish to advert, will be found in that passage of his letter, in which he virtually affirms that his reason for not discharging such a missive upon me, as he addresses to yourself, was, that he had not received instructions in sufficient time before the death of General Taylor. Now, although he never communicated his instructions to me, *officially*, yet he left them with the chief clerk, not for the purpose of being laid before me officially, but for the purpose, I suppose, of obtaining the opinion of Mr. Derrick, as to the expediency of communicating them officially to me. Mr. Derrick obtained a copy of them, which is inclosed for your perusal. He (Mr. H.) read to me about the 27th of December. 1849, in an unofficial manner, one or two passages from them, which convinced me that his Government had improperly obtained a surreptitious copy of my instructions to Mr. Dudley Mann, to which fact I called his attention at the time, with the intimation, that he addressed me on the subject officially, as he threatened to do, I would enquire into the mode by which his Government obtained a copy of one of my letters, confidentially addressed to an American Agent, which at that time had not been published. He left me with the declaration that he would write to me, as he afterward did to you. But when I saw him, after the lapse of a few weeks, he informed me that he had changed his mind, and should write me no letter on that subject.

The second error of Mr. Hülsemann, which I wish to note, will be found in his statement to you, that I had informed him, that the only object of Mr. Mann's mission was to obtain information. I repeatedly stated to him, that the President's object was to recognize the Independence of Hungary, in case that Independence, should be found to be established on a permanent basis, sustained by a durable Government, capable of performing the functions of a Member of the family of Nations. I endeavored to explain to him, and defined verbally the course which the American Government has pursued towards other Nations when

---

[1] See Webster's Works, vol. vi, p. 491.

struggling into existence,   But he denied our whole doctrine, and seemed to have worked himself up into a passion, which forbade discussion.

Wishing you all health and happiness and many more such victories over the Agents of Despotism, I have the honor to subscribe myself,

Very sincerely and truly Yours

JOHN M. CLAYTON.

(To John M. Clayton.)

My Dear Sir,   WASHINGTON, Jany 15th 1851.

I was yesterday just about enclosing you a readable copy of my correspondence with Mr. Hülsemann, when I received your acceptable and friendly letter of the 12th. Be assured, My Dear Sir, that it gave me pleasure to defend the conduct of General Taylor's administration in this important particular: & I am quite happy if you think that Mr. Hülsemann & the Cabinet of Vienna have been satisfactorily answered.

I am quite glad to receive the paper which Mr. Hülsemann left with you.   It is certain, that he had obtained, somehow, a sight of Mr. Mann's instructions: I presume, also, that Mr. Hülsemann had received, subsequently, other instructions.   This would seem to be properly inferred, from the introduction to his letter.

We have not heard from him, since receipt of my letter.

I am, My Dear Sir, with regard, and all good wishes,

Yours truly

DANIEL WEBSTER.

(Mr. Schwarzenberg to Mr. Hülsemann.[1])

Sir,   VIENNA November, 5th 1849.

Your reports, including that of October 23d. marked No. 27. have been punctually received.

You have transmitted to me the New York papers containing allusions, which, although mysteriously worded, still treat of the matter as a positive occurrence,—to the fact of a United States Agent having been despatched to Vienna, with orders to watch for a favorable moment to recognise, in the name of his Govern-

---

[1] This is an official translation of the original letter.

ment, the Hungarian Republic, and to conclude a treaty of commerce with the same.   The fact is but too true; and the information we possess on the subject, has reached us from such a reliable source, that we cannot indulge any doubt, as to a proceeding, which, at first, we found it so difficult to credit.   How could we, in fact, reconcile that proceeding, with those principles of International laws, so scrupulously adhered to by Austria towards the United States?   Was it in return for the friendship and confidence which we have never ceased to manifest towards the Government of the United States, that the latter was waiting impatiently for and sought to hasten the moment, when it could profit by the downfall of the Austrian Monarchy, and sell a few bales of cotton more at the expense of her existence?   The Statesmen who have been concerned in the mission of Mr. Dudley Mann have betrayed very narrow and selfish views, and evinced moreover great ignorance of the true state of things, of the resources of Austria, and her tenacity in defending her just rights.   Even Lord Palmerston himself, who certainly cannot be charged with being a partisan of Austria, has acknowledged how vastly important it was for the equilibrium of Europe and the tranquillity of the world, that this power should be preserved in all its integrity.   Was it supposed in New York that our resources were exhausted, and our purpose to struggle against the revolution turned aside?   Was a hope entertained that after a contest of six months' duration, and after having been assured, that in case of need we should not call upon Russia in vain, to assist us, that we would come to terms with rebellious subjects?—We who have struggled for twenty-five years against the French Revolution? At that epoch, all right minded people applauded our devotion to the principles of order and our perseverance in defending them: To-day they have likewise manifested an anxious desire, that we might come out victorious from the struggle in Hungary.

The following is what we have learnt, beyond the possibility of a doubt, in regard to the steps alluded to, as taken by the United States.

In the course of last June, Mr. Dudley Mann, a Sort of *Attaché* to the American Legation in Paris, received from one of the most influential members of the government, a confidential despatch, which was to serve him for instructions, relative to the mission he had to fulfil both at Vienna and in Hungary.   He was ordered to repair hither and to ascertain whether the insurrectionary movements in Hungary were sufficiently matured, to

456   LETTERS OF DANIEL WEBSTER

justify the immediate recognition of the latter, as an independent power:—to endeavor to have an interview with Kossuth and with the agents of that *illustrious man:*—and finally, if he forsaw any chance of success on the part of the Hungarians, to invite them to send a diplomatic agent to Washington, who would be promptly recognized.   The interest which the United States had in opening the earliest Commercial relations with that newly born republic, was represented in Mr. Dudley Mann's instructions, as a sufficient cause to justify the mission.

There is one circumstance which has greatly added to the profound regrets which that mission has caused us; in Mr. Dudley Mann's instructions, the intentions of President Taylor were alluded to, and mention was made of the *Iron rule* of Austria.   It would have afforded us much gratification to have looked upon General Taylor as a stranger to all this kind of intrigue and we were pained to see the head of the American Government sharing in those errors, which malevolence had disseminated in regard to us, but which have never been seriously entertained even by those who had at first believed in them.   You are now in possession of the truth, in regard to the grave circumstances to which you allude in your reports.   You will be convinced that the explanations given you by Mr. Clayton were neither complete nor of a character to satisfy us.   We might then insist upon a more explicit declaration and disavowal on the part of the Cabinet of New York; but we will allow our old friendship for the United States to prevail; and we are willing to consider the step of which we complain as an individual fallacy and a mistake on the part of some member of the American Government, in order to avoid the necessity of making such charges in our relations with it, as would be at variance with our wishes.

You will please, Sir, to regulate your language in conformity with this despatch, the contents of which, if you think it proper, you may even communicate to those whom it may concern.

Be pleased to accept, Sir, the assurances of my perfect consideration.

F. Schwarzenberg.

(From Millard Fillmore.)

To the Secretary of the State   Jan'y 16. [1851.]
My Dear Sir,
I have read & herewith return, the copies of Mr. Clayton's let-

ter, and yours to him and the Austrian Instructions of the 5th. of Nov. 1849. to Mr. Hülsemann.

I am a little surprised at the change made in the printed copy of Mr. Mann's instructions. But as you suspect, they must have had access to the original.

I noticed, you changed the original Draft of your letter and denied the use of the phrase *"iron rule,"* and supposed that you had made a mistake at first. But if I recollect right they predicated their complaint—on the correspondence, as published. If so they cannot go behind the printed copy; and we at last are free from any imputation of mutilation.

Truly yours,
MILLARD FILLMORE

(To Jacob Harvey.)

BOSTON Feby 17 1851

The following Communication has been received at this Office, by Telegraph, from Washington

For J. Harvey—

Was it by connivence or by absolute force?—did the Marshal do his duty—answer[1]

D. WEBSTER

(To Millard Fillmore.)

[FEB. 28 1851]

To the President
    My Dear Sir

I have asked F. Webster to make a draft of a letter to Mr. Marsh— Here it is— Can you get time to run it over?[2]

Yrs   D. WEBSTER

---

[1] This telegram refers to the famous Shadrach rescue. See Rhodes' History of the United States, vol. i, p. 210.

[2] This letter is endorsed by Fillmore as follows :
"A capital letter which I have read with much pleasure." M. F.
There follows also a second endorsement by F. Webster to his wife :
"I told you I was going to write this letter. *   *   *
I enclose this because it will please you,   *   *   *
Y'r own FLETCHER."

* *Can this refer to the famous letter to Geo. P. Marsh, concerning the Hungarian refugees?*

(To Luther Severance.[1])

[*Private*]

(MARCH 1, 1851).

Sir;

I have written you a regular official despatch, setting forth the principles of policy which will govern the Administration here, in whatever respects the Government of the Hawaiian Islands.

I now write you a letter of private instructions, made necessary by suggestions contained in your communication by Lieut. Johnson.

In the first place I have to say, that the war making power, in this Government, rests entirely with Congress. And that the President, can authorize belligerent operations, only in the cases expressly provided for by the Constitution and the laws. By these, no power is given to the Executive to oppose an attack by one independent nation on the possessions of another. We are bound to regard both France and Hawaiia, as independent States, and equally independent, and though the general policy of the Government, might lead it to take part with either, in a controversy with the other, still, if this interference be an act of hostile force, it is not within the Constitutional power of the President, and still less is it, within the power of any subordinate Agent of Government, Civil or Military. If the Serieuse had attacked Honolulu, and thereupon the bandalia had fired upon the Serieuse, this last act would have been an act of (violence) against France; not to be justified: (in fact, if not disavowed at Washington, it would be an act of war.)

In these cases, where the power of Congress cannot be exercised beforehand, all must be left to the redress which that body may subsequently authorize. This, you will constantly bear in mind. But at the same time, it is not necessary that you should make known (enter into these explanations with) these sentiment to the French Commissioner, or the French Commander.

In my official letter of this date, I have spoken of what the United States would do in certain contingencies. But in thus speaking of the Government of the United States, I do not mean the Executive power, but the Government in its general aggregate, and especially that branch of the Government which possesses the war making power. This distinction you will carefully observe, and you will neither direct, request, or encourage any

---

[1] The United States representative, at that time, in Hawaii.

naval officer of the United States in committing hostilities on French vessels of war.

Another leading topic in your letter, is the proposed contingent surrender, by the Government of the Islands, of their sovereignty, to the United States, or their annexation to this country.

This is a very important question, and one which you will readily see, rises above any functions, with which you are charged. It may indeed, be very proper for you in this case, as well as in all others, to communicate to your Government, whatever the Government to which you are accredited desires to be (have) so communicated but it is (very important) that on a question involving such deep interest both domestic and foreign, you should, yourself, altogether forbear from expressing any opinion whatever, to the Hawaiian Government. You will see by my official letter, which you are at liberty to communicate to that Government, the disposition of the United States to maintain its independence; beyond that, you will not proceed. The act of contingent or conditional surrender which you mention in your letter (as having been placed in your hands) you will please (to) return to the Hawaiian Government. In this case, the Government of the United States, acts upon principles of general policy; it will protect its own rights. It feels a deep interest in the preservation of Hawaiian independence, and all questions beyond this, should they arise, must be considered and settled here, by the competent authority. You inform us, that many American citizens have gone to settle in the Islands; if so, they have ceased to be American Citizens, (The American Government (must of course feel an interest (in them not extended to foreigners; but by the Law of Nation (they have no rights further to demand the protection of this Government. (Whatever aid or protection might under any circumstances be given them; must be given, not as matter of right on their part, but in consistency with the general policy & duty of the Government & its relations with friendly powers).

You will therefore, not encourage in them nor indeed, in any other, any idea or expectation that the Islands will become annexed to the United States. All this, I repeat, will be judged of hereafter, as circumstances and events may require, by the Govt: at Washington.

I do not suppose there is any immediate danger of any new menaces from France, still less, of any actual attack on the Islands by her Naval Armament. Nevertheless you will keep us constantly and accurately informed of whatever transpires.

Your account of the prosperity of the Islands, and the fiscal condition of its Government, is interesting, and you can hardly be too full and particular in such statements.

Mr. Allen, is at present, quite unwell, at Boston; so soon as he is able, he will return to his post, and Lieut: Johnson will take this despatch to Panama. If Mr. Allen's illness should continue, for any length of time, which we hope may not be the case Lieut: Johnson, will be directed to return without him.[1]

I have the honor to be with regard,

Your obedient Servant

[DAN'L WEBSTER]

(To Henry S. Foote.[2])

Sir, DEPARTMENT OF STATE. Washington March, 1851.

In the conversation which passed between us the other day in favor of superseding the existing provisions by law authorizing the appointment of Charge' d' Affaires to Guatemala and Nicaragua by the appointment of a Minister Plenipotentiary to be accredited to the States of San Salvador, Honduras and Costa Rica, You are aware that a Minister Plenipotentiary from Nicaragua has already presented himself and it is expected that the other States above mentioned will send diplomatic agents of some grade to this country soon.

In conformity with your request, I have, now, the honor to submit herewith estimates for the appropriation necessary to be made for the purpose of accomplishing the object.

I am, Sir, respectfully Your obedient servant

DANL WEBSTER

(To Peter Harvey.)

BOSTON, March 7th. 1851.

The following Communication has been received at this Office, by Telegraph, from Washington

---

[1] This is the original draft of the letter sent.
[2] Senator from Virginia and chairman of the Committee on Foreign Relations.

For Peter Harvey Esq

Meet me in New York Tuesday next at 5 o'clock P. M.—Say confidentially to Mr. Green that I am willing to leave all matters to the judgment of himself—Mr. Appleton, S. A. Eliot, Mr. Haven. Mr. Henshaw & yourself.

DANL WEBSTER

(To Millard Fillmore.)

Private

To the President   MONDAY MORNING March 17, 1851.

My Dear Sir.

I believe you are acquainted with Mr. John S. Biddle of Philadelphia. He has long been a prominent member of the Whig party in that city, and heretofore generally acting with Mr. Clay's friends.[1] He is a staunch & firm friend of the present administration, & supports its measures, cordially. He was candidate, not by his own procurement, for the appointment of Collector, when the appointment was given to Mr. Lewis; & I suppose a great preponderance of the real & true Whig influence was in his favor. But the interest of the *North American,* & the Gentlemen connected that circle procured the nomination of Mr. Lewis, against him.

Mr. Biddle has been recently appointed appraiser at large, an office which probably he will be unwilling to accept. I have known him long, & think highly of him, & on these Pennsylvania topics now pending, he speaks very sensibly, & with apparent candor. He proposes to call & pay his respects to you to day, & as he is well informed, & I believe worthy of confidence, I write you this to describe his standing & position in case you should wish to converse with him.

Yrs. truly always,

DANL WEBSTER

(From Lewis Cass.)

(Confidential).

BUFFALO March 18, 1851.

My dear Sir,

I have just perused your letter to Mr. March,[2] and tho' not

---

[1] Not at the last election.

[2] Concerning the liberation of the Hungarian refugees.

much given to the *melting mood,* yet I paid it a tribute, I have seldom paid to an official document, and I cannot resist the temptation of telling you how highly I approve its sentiments and its language.   It is a glorious model of an American State paper, and if I were mean enough to envy anything you do, I should surely envy you the authorship of this letter.[1]   Go on and be not troubled at the attacks made for your attachment to the union, for that is the cause of those onslaughts.

Your old friend

Lew Cass.

(To the French Minister of Foreign Affairs.)

Private.

Washington March 19, '51.

My Dear Sir,

The sudden and unexpected recall of M. Bois le Comte, caused us not only surprise but very considerable regret.   His intercourse with the Govt. has been very agreeable, and his whole demeanor such as to command our respect.   The enclosed paragraph which I cut from the columns of the Nat. Intelligencer, expresses truly, I believe, what is here the universal opinion and feeling.

The withdrawal of M. Bois le Comte's pleasant family from our little Washington circle will create a considerable chasm.

We look with interest for the coming of M. Sartiges, whom we understand to be a diplomatist of ability and much experience.

I am, my dear Sir, always with much regard—

Yours

[D. Webster]

(From M. R. Brenner et al.)

Mar 20. 1851

* * *   [They request him to take part in a Clay celebration][2]   * * *

---

[1] See the next letter, Daniel Webster to Fillmore.
[2] Webster endorsed the letter, "Write a handsome letter of apology—very *handsome.*"

(Hiram Ketchum to Peter Harvey.)

(Very private).

SATURDAY March 22d 1851.

My dear Sir

I recd your letter some time ago, and am glad that you showed my communication to you to Mr Webster.

I have seen him since, during a short business trip to Washington, but said not a word on the subject of politics. The President, Mr. Webster & Mr. Hall have been put in possession of my views, clearly and earnestly expressed. They have been entirely disregarded, at which I take not the slightest offence, being fully aware of the falability of my own judgment, and having not the slightest claim of right to influence the Administration by my opinions. One thing however, is certain, and I wish here to record it for your remembrance, that my advice has not been lightly given, but I have pondered well all that I have said to the rulers of my Country, and it has been given with the same feeling that I would have advised my father, when I had a father.

With equal sincerity and deliberation I now say to you that, in my judgment, the President will be without a party in this State in less than sixty days, unless his line of policy is changed very soon. I would say this to the President, and to Mr. Webster but for the fact that I have already urged upon them so much advice, that self respect will not allow me to say more, unless called upon. Such urgence would indicate a feeling on my part, which might be misconstrued, for the *Searcher of Hearts* knows that I am quite as independent of them or the administration, as they, or it, can be of me.

If the President is destroyed here, Mr. Webster will be, for he is regarded as the adviser of the course, which I am sure, unless new & unexpected events occur to give another direction to public opinion, will leave the President—not without admirers & well wishers—but without an organized party in his native state.

I have taken leave to urge upon Mr. Webster the propriety of going right, as I regarded the right, and let Mr. Fillmore take his own course, on his own responsibility. This too has been disregarded,—for the best—I hope.

In the choice of U. S. Senator in this State Seward has triumphed, *by the help of the administration at Washington,* and the administration I have not the slightest doubt has been cheated, by those who exult in the success of their schemes.

Yrs very truly
HIRAM KETCHUM.

(To Millard Fillmore.)

To the President,   MARCH 23. 1851.
    My Dear Sir.
    I think you will be gratified to read this note from James B. Campbell Esq:—a gentleman I have often mentioned to you.— I wrote him, lately & asked him this question: "Can you *guess* what the first step is, which the "seceders" propose to take, as the actual commencement of secession."

Yours truly,
DANL WEBSTER.

(To D. Fletcher Webster.)

ELM FARM, [Franklin, N. H.]
Thursday Eve' [April 1851 (?)]

Dear Fletcher,
    I have recd yours today, & will answer it tomorrow.   Mean time I learn that a com.ee is to be here on Saturday, about R. R. celebration,[1] &c.—
    —Please send me up a green goose, & some good chickens,— a couple of pair—if you can do so by any train, tomorrow, friday—otherwise it will be too late.

D. W.

(To Millard Fillmore.)

PHILADELPHIA, April 4. 1851—

My dear Sir,
    I left Washington not very well, Monday evening, & lodged at Baltimore.   The next day at twelve o'clock reached Harrisburg.   The weather was wet and being under the influence of

---

[1] Referring to the completion of the New York and Erie Railroad, see vol. ii, p. 533, of "Daniel Webster's Works," for the speech on this occasion.

some diarhaea, the dampness of the weather & the limestone water made me a good deal sick. I met the Legislature that evening at 7 o'clock.

The next day, Wednesday, was very rainy, but I saw several friends, such as Cooper, Randall, Brown, &c. They were in apparent good spirits, but all impatient for action, several of them will be at Washington about the 15th inst. They all say that Gen. Johnson is a free soiler, & that he is laboring with all his might to prevent the passage of the act to restore the jails of Pennsylvania to the use of the United States. He says such an act will kill him. There was a supper on Tuesday evening, after my interview with the legislatures; and after I had retired he made a speech, which, it is said, was pretty much an answer to my speech in the State House.[1] You will have seen Mr. Pitman, who will tell you all about this.

I came from Harrisburg, here, on Wednesday afternoon, in a rainstorm, & over the roughest railroad, I suppose, in the United States. We arrived here at midnight, I was quite unwell through yesterday, & unable to see any one to day; however I am pretty well, & propose to go to New York, tomorrow, & thence to Boston.

Yours always truly,
DANL WEBSTER.

(Rufus Choate to Geo. Lunt, District Attorney.[2])

[APR. 1851]

Dear Sir,

I see by the evening papers, that the Grand Jury have returned their indictments.[3]

I should (take) great pride & pleasure in assisting in these important trials in Court, but I find on a survey of my engagements that it will not be practicable, certainly not so to assist in the earlier ones. I cannot feel a doubt that you will triumphantly vindicate the law of the land and the honor of the bar.

I am most truly Your obedient serv't.

R. CHOATE.

---

[1] This speech has never been published

[2] Copy of a letter enclosed in Mr. Webster's letter to the President, of April 4, 1851.

[3] Against the persons concerned in the rescue of Shadrach.

(To Millard Fillmore.)

PHILADELPHIA, April 4" 1851.—8 o'clock A. M.
To the President,
   My Dear Sir,
   Mr. Choate has withdrawn from the assistance of Mr. Lunt, in the rescue cases,[1] I learn this from a copy of a note from [left blank in copy] to Mr. Lunt which the latter has sent me, & which you will find with these papers, & from a letter from C. P. Curtis which I also enclose. I have telegraphed Fletcher Webster requesting [left blank] to ask Mr. Choate, to tell me confidentially, for the benefit of the President and myself, *why he withdrew.* I presume I shall get an answer this morning. I wrote to Mr. Lunt that he was authorized to employ Mr. B. R. Curtis or Mr. Choate. As to Mr. Hutchins I say, I believe him competent; but he may name to me any other person.; but that I do not think Mr. Sauger is a proper person to be employed.
   Mr. Sauger is known to have been all along, a Free-soiler, or worse.

             I am always truly—

                 DANL WEBSTER.

(To Geo. Lunt.[2])

To George Lunt, Esq.   PHILADELPHIA, April 4" 1851.
   Your letter of the 31 March has been forwarded to me here, & having perused it I transmit it to the President. I quite regret Mr. Choate's withdrawal from the rescue cases, & am at a loss for the reason. In the same letter in which I authorized you to employ Mr. Choate, I also authorized you to employ Mr. Curtis (B. R.) if you preferred to do so. As to Mr. Hutchins, I suppose him quite competent; if you think otherwise, I will hear your suggestions of some other persons; but Mr. Sauger does not appear to me to be a proper person to be employed.
   I proceed to N. York to-morrow, on my way to Boston, & shall hope to see you immediately on my arrival.
   These causes are of the utmost importance. We wish them conducted by the best talent & experience of the bar. Not wishing to embarrass you in the slightest degree, nor to interfere

---

[1] *i. e.,* rescue of Shadrach.   [2] District Attorney for Massachusetts.

with your official responsibility, we wish you still to have the very first assistance which the Profession can furnish. You must be fully aware of the consequences if just decisions should fail to be obtained through any want of skill on the part of those who manage the trials.

Yours respectfully,
DANL WEBSTER.

(To Millard Fillmore.)

NEW YORK Tuesday morn'g April 6: 1851.

My Dear Sir.

I arrived here yesterday to dinner; pretty well, but have seen but few persons, not having felt inclined to admit many comers.

My late attack was severe, and has a good deal reduced me. I propose to stay here through tomorrow, & proceed to Boston on Tuesday, & to Marshfield just as soon as I can arrange the matter of the Rescue trials.

You doubtless have heard how the State case stood, at the adjournment yesterday.

I hardly think the Commissioner was *bound* to hear an argument [omitted in copy] a law which both the Judges of the Court appointing him, had declared constitutional. The Fugitive is safe enough & I presume there will be no attempt to rescue him.

I expect trouble in finding proper counsel to assist Mr. Lunt. The same reasons which induced Mr. Choate to retire, will probably induce others to be unwilling to undertake. The truth is Mr. Lunt is not a very agreeable man to be associated with. He is not a good lawyer, theoretic or practical: and, at the same time, he is opinionated, self willed & obstinate. The members of the bar feel he has no right to hold the office; & as the present case is such, that a voluntary appearance may be viewed as, in some degree odious, the leading men may not feel inclined to come to the aid of the Government for a mere fee. This, I suppose to be the truth of the case, altho I shall know more about it when I reach Boston, as it might not be expedient to appoint another person attorney, at the present moment, I have thought it best, as you will have seen by my letter to Mr. Lunt, to suffer him to select assistance for himself, with this limitation only that no known abolitionist like Mr. Sauger, should be employed.

This will leave the responsibility where the law leaves it, & if the trials miscarry, through the want of skill & ability, we shall then have a plain case to deal with.

I shall of course write you from Boston.

Yrs always truly

DANL WEBSTER

(To Millard Fillmore.)

NEW YORK, 1 o'clock April, 1851.

My Dear Sir—

I sent Mr. Derrick [omission in copy] for you this morning. I have seen Mr. Hall and Mr. Evarts today. They are busy in looking up the proofs, & think they shall be prepared to arrest several offenders, tomorrow or Monday.

I doubt whether we will ever be able to restrain these lawless people[1] until some of them landing in Cuba shall be roughly handled by the Spaniards.

We hope to be in Washington Sunday morning.

Yrs always truly,

DANL WEBSTER.

(To Peter Harvey.)

Bains Chemical Telegraph.

BOSTON, Apl 7 1851.

This Despatch has just been received from N. York *For* P. Harvey

No reception. I will come up from Marshfield Shall see you Tuesday evening

DANL WEBSTER

(To Henry W. Hilliard.[2])

NEW YORK, April 7. 1851.

My Dear Sir

Before leaving Washington for the North, I had two con-

---

[1] Referring to the proposed Lopez expedition to Cuba which was then preparing and against which the government was making all reasonable opposition. See Rhodes' "History of United States," vol. i. p. 217.

[2] Hilliard represented Alabama in Congress (1843-51).

versations with the President respecting your letter to him & to me. We both united cordially in the opinion and feeling that you are competent to represent the country honorably abroad, and that it would be advisable to find you a suitable situation. But our power at the present moment is very much limited. The missions are all full, and no more than one vacancy is expected in the course of this year; and even that is not provided for by an appropriation & an outfit. That is Russia. Now as to this mission, the President feels bound to give it to Pennsylvania. Pennsylvania is a large state, and she gave her entire vote for the Whig candidates at the late election, she has no minister of the cabinet, no foreign mission, no highly honorable appointment held by any of her citizens. It is difficult to overlook her claims. New Jersey is in a similar position, tho she is a much smaller State.

Under these circumstances, My dear Sir—with the most sincere desire to place you in an honorable post abroad—the President does not see how it can be done at present.

Will you allow me further to suggest, My Dear Sir, that this term of administration is already half out, if you should now be appointed, and the next election should bring a political change you might be recalled before you were warm in your seat. We have another struggle to go thro. In that contest you will be needed. You will be wanted in the election and *especially* wanted in the convention, by which a candidate, under whatever title, may be designated. You need not doubt, that so far as depends on me, if success attends our efforts, you will be put in a better situation, than amidst the snows of Russia.

I should be glad my dear Sir to hear from you often, and to know your sentiments on all political matters— I expect to be back at Washington by the 20" at furthest. I have already spoken of the friendly disposition of the President towards you— and I think him entirely sincere.[1]

Yours with assured regard

DANIEL WEBSTER

---

[1] In vol. xiii. p. 138 39, of the New Hampshire Historical Society Collection, there is an eight-page protest by Mr. Hilliard because he was not given the mission to Russia or Prussia. He threatens the loss of his influence for the Whig party in Alabama.

(To Millard Fillmore.)

BOSTON April 9" 1851.

To the President.

My Dear Sir.

I arrived here yesterday at 5 P. M. all the way from N. Y. with less fatigue than might be expected, the road all the way is fair & smooth.

The Commissioner[1] has adjourned his decision till Friday the 11th.— I was quite sorry to learn this, but I suppose he wished to take pains with an opinion, & tomorrow, the 10" is Fast day, & all business of course, suspended. The fugitive is safe;[2] the proofs are clear; & the Marshal will move south with him on Friday.

Immediately on my arrival, I sent for Mr. Lunt, The matter of Mr. Sauger is as I told you. He lives in Middlesex, and attended a meeting there last fall at which anti-Fugitive slave bill resolutions were adopted. Mr. Lunt says he did not know it, till he learned it from me. I thought it best not to dispute the point; and as Sauger has diligence and ability, and as Mr. Lunt does not propose that he should appear to take part in the trial, I told him he might employ him.

As to leading arguing counsel, the difficulty is a question of precedence, Mr. Lunt feels that holding the official station, he ought to lead; Mr. Choate is not willing being at the Head of the Bar here to act a subordinate part to Mr. Lunt. I think we could manage to have the aid of B. R. Curtis' services, if his engagements allowed. But they do not. He is a member of the Legislature, which is likely to sit till the middle of May, & after the Senate questions is over, (if ever it shall be over) he is prepared for a public discussion upon Administration matters.

I shall make some other arrangement, probably to suggest to Mr. Lunt the employment of Mr. Lord of Essex Co. & a very fit man, & would be quite acceptable to Mr. Lunt.

The trials come on the 26 inst. It is of great importance to convict Wright.

In an hour I go to Marshfield, & shall write you from that cold & bleak shore.

When you write me please address me at Boston.

---

[1] George T. Curtiss.
[2] Thomas Sims, a Georgia Slave. He was finally returned to slavery.

You will see that an anti-slave law convocation was held here yesterday.

Yours always truly
                                    DANL WEBSTER

The marvels of the moment, are, Rantoul's[1] somerset, Seward's letter.

(Resolutions of Boston Common Council.)

CITY OF BOSTON,
In Common Council, April, 17 1851.

Whereas, Faneuil Hall has been "consecrated" and dedicated to the use of the inhabitants of Boston upon all suitable occasions," and Whereas the exclusive custody of the same is exercised by the Board of Mayor & Aldermen of this City; and Whereas, this branch of the Government has learned with great surprise, that the Mayor & Aldermen have denied the respectful petition of a large number of the Citizens of Boston, for the use of said Hall for the reception of the Hon. Daniel Webster; and Whereas this Board is unwilling to be compromised by the action of the Board of Mayor & Aldermen in this case, or to be identified therewith, therefore,

Resolved, That the Common Council deeply regret the action of the Board of Mayor & Aldermen in closing Faneuil Hall against the Hon. Daniel Webster, our illustrious fellow citizen, whose high official position, whose unwavering attachment to, and unwearying defence of the Constitution, whose long service in the Senate of the United States, and whose untiring efforts in support of the Union have justly endeared him to the whole people of the United States.

Resolved, That while this Board would not interfere with any rights which the Mayor & Aldermen may have over Faneuil Hall, it cannot but consider their action in the present instance, unprecedented and injudicious,—calculated to increase rather than diminish the public excitement.

Resolved, That it would have given to the Common Council of the City of Boston the highest pleasure to have met our distinguished fellow citizen in Faneuil Hall, to exchange congratula-

---

[1] Robert Rantoul, Senator from Massachusetts. appointed in Webster's place after the latter went into Fillmore's cabinet. Webster here refers to Rantoul's speech made at Lynn, Mass., April 3, 1851, in which the latter went over wholly to the anti-slavery doctrines. See "Memoirs, Speeches and Writings of Robert Rantoul," p. 729.

tions with him, & hear him once more address his friends and neighbors in support of Law, Order, the Constitution, and the Union.

And the said Resolutions having been read twice, were unanimously passed by yeas & nays:—each one of the forty three members present answering in the affirmative.

Ordered, that a copy of the foregoing Resolutions be transmitted to the Hon Daniel Webster.

Ordered that said Resolutions be printed.

FRANCIS BRINLEY,
President.

(From Francis Brinley.)

COMMON COUNCIL ROOM. Boston, April 18th. 1851.
Dear Sir,

I have the honor to transmit a certified copy of the Preamble and Resolutions[1] adopted by the unanimous vote of the *Common Council* of this city at their session of last evening, in reference to the refusal by the Board of Mayor and Aldermen of the request of your friends for the use of Faneuil Hall.

One of the Rules of the Common Council provides that "in all cases the President may vote." I cheerfully availed myself of recording my "aye" on the passage of the Preamble and Resolutions. It is with great pleasure I transmit an attested copy of them, by direction of the Board.[2]

I remain very sincerely your friend & obt. St.

FRANCIS BRINLEY, President.

(From H. A. Dearborn.)

HAWTHORN COTTAGE Roxbury April 19, 1851.
My Dear Sir,

I have read your elegant letter to the Committee of Invitation,

[1] See the document on page 471.

[2] For an account of this whole incident see Rhodes' "History of the United States," vol. i, p. 213. An omitted passage in Webster's letter to George S. Smith, *et al.*, April 15, 1851, throws an interesting light on Webster's attitude in this matter : "I am now only anxious that the country should not draw any inferences from it [the closing of Faneuil Hall] unfavorable to the disposition of the people of Boston toward the Union, and their resolution to maintain at all hazards the constitution and the laws of the United States." See "Private Correspondence;" vol. ii, p. 429.

to visit Boston, with indignation, at the despicable attempted insult, & the highest gratification for the dignified manner in which a stern rebuke has been given to the inconsequential imbeciles, who have disgraced the City,—as well as for the decided & lofty spirit you have evinced to pursue, in the future, the same firm & independent course, for which you have been distinguished, during the most perilous crisis of this nation, since its existence.

The extraordinary & infamous conduct of one of the branches of the City Council, in relation to an invitation to the President, & by the refusal to grant Faneuil Hall to your friends,[1] has excited such indignation, among all classes of the people, as will result in a far deeper interest in you, & an augmented appreciation of the immensely important services you have rendered the whole country, & a more determined disposition to do you that justice & honor to which you are so preeminently entitled; while the traitors, who have basely attempted to produce a rebellion, will be execrated through all time.   *   *   *

H. A. DEARBORN.

(From Henry B. Rogers et al.)

APR. 21. 1851

Hon. Daniel Webster,
      Secretary of State.

Sir,
    In compliance with an order of the City Council, passed this day with entire unanimity, we have the honor of inviting you, in the name of the City of Boston, to meet and address your fellow Citizens in Faneuil Hall at such time as may be most convenient to you:— And, in behalf of the Corporation, of the Citizens generally, and of ourselves, we beg leave to assure you that your acceptance of this invitation, should it accord with your feelings and convenience, will be peculiarly gratifying at this time.

With the highest respect & consideration, we remain,

Your very obt. Servants,

---

[1] In a letter to Griswold, *et al.*, there is a passage omitted in the letter as published in "Works of Daniel Webster," vol. vi, p. 595, which it is too bad to lose in this connection. Webster therein says, "If I go to New York to meet you and other friends of the Union, to confer on dangers escaped, or dangers still pending, no doors will be found closed either against you or against me."

(To Henry B. Rogers et al.)

Gentlemen   Boston April 23—1851

I have perused the paper which you did me the honor to place in my hands yesterday; & I have to say, in reply, that it is not my purpose to address my Fellow Citizens in Faneuil Hall during this visit to Boston[1]

I have   *   *   *

[D. Webster]

(To Peter Harvey.(?))

Secret   May 4″ 1851.

My dear Sir,

I have something to say of which I dare not give the least hint in writing: And it may be necessary that I should see you or some other Boston friend in a fortnight.

D. W.

———

(From Hiram Ketchum.[2])

31 Wall St Monday May 5, 1851.

My dear Sir

You have doubtless seen the invitation to you to visit this City signed by more than 5000 citizens.

A Committee of 31 gentlemen have prepared and signed a letter addressed to you, to be forwarded with the original invitation. Mr. Griswold just called to inform me that he should put the letter in my hands today, to be sent in any manner I should see fit.   I shall send it by a special messenger, probably to-morrow.   *   *   *

The names attached to this letter are not unknown.   Of the letter itself it becomes not me to speak.

In all this matter I shall not appear to the public to be a prominent actor—Mr. Griswold, your friend, is the prominent man.
*   *   *

Yrs truly
Hiram Ketchum.

---

[1] Endorsement on back of this letter, "Original draft of reply to Common Council of Boston, April, 1850, declining to appear in Faneuil Hall."   See, however, "Curtis," vol. ii, p. 500.

[2] This letter is owned by the Hon. Geo. F. Hoar.

(To D. Fletcher Webster.)

MAY 5, '51

Dear Fletcher:

I wrote yesterday a letter to Mr. Harvey,[1] for his own perusal, & to be shown to other friends.   You will of course see it, & will probably be of opinion that it contains about all which I ought to say.   Depend upon it, I shall trust no interest of mine to the State Com^ee·   It is in the condition of things as well as in the character of the Comee itself, that it's greatest object will be to establish a Whig Govt. in Massachusetts; & to this end, it will be ready to sacrifice all National Considerations—

Yrs affectionately

D. W.

(To D. Fletcher Webster.)

WASHINGTON May 9, '51.

My dear Son,

I have your letter.   Your view is entirely right.   Expose fully the basis upon which the Atlas proposes to refound the Whig Party of Mass. and show its utter absurdity.   Ask Mr. Haven[2] to show you a letter which I have to day written to him.

Yours affy,

DANL WEBSTER

I hope to see some of you, in N. Y. Monday.

(To Thomas Corwin.[3] (?))

(Private & Confidential)

(1851)

My Dear Sir;

Th⌐ Whigs of this State owe their recent misfortunes, especially the reelection of Mr. Horace Mann, very much to the support given to him by certain Whig papers, at the head of which

---

[1] The letter to Harvey has not been printed and has not been found by the editor.

[2] The letter to Mr. Haven has not been published and the editor has been unable to find it.   This letter and succeeding letters have to do with the efforts to get Webster nominated as Whig candidate for president.

[3] Secretary of the Treasury.

is the Boston Atlas. Other causes concurred, & among these other causes one is, the favor shown towards Mr. Mann's election by certain officers of the Custom House— This last subject may be attended to hereafter; but my present purpose is to request that the patronage of your Department may be altogether withdrawn from the Boston Atlas.

The reliable Union Whig Papers in this City are; the Boston Daily Advertiser; & the Boston Courier. These are large Daily Papers, ably conducted, & entirely sound— The *Bee* is a penny paper, of great circulation, & of good principles. About the Country papers, I will inquire, & give you information hereafter. Meantime, it is safe to say, that the Spr'gfield Republican is a highly respectable & thorough Union Paper.

Yrs with true regard

[Dan'l Webster]

(To Peter Harvey.)

Washington, June 3, '51.

My Dear Sir:—

I am obliged to you for your letter of the 6th. No doubt, what has been done in Boston is entirely right and wise, and I shall always be satisfied with whatever course judicious friends adopt. The general views put forth in the Courier of Saturday are exactly such as I entertain. The danger is, as there shown, that national objects will be postponed to local objects, and that Massachusetts may thus close her high character as a leading, constitutional member of the Union.

The policy of placating the Abolitionists has been long practised. It has always failed; and the state committee has my opinion, if it was thought worth preserving, given two or three years ago, that by yielding more and more to Abolition notions, the Whigs were only strengthening an enemy who would soon become their master.

We are having nothing new here. There is at this season, and in the recess of Congress a sort of leisure, in the pressure of affairs; and as the weather is not warm yet, we get on very well.

Yrs. always truly,

Dan'l. Webster

(To Thurlow Weed.)

Private

My dear Sir, WASHINGTON June 9, 1851.

Your kind and friendly letter, adressed to me at Cambridge, was returned to Albany, and placed in my hands, while sitting at dinner [torn out] gave it to my man, who mislaid it and it was not looked up until after my return to this city.

I thank you for your invitation to dine, and should have been happy, had I not been engaged otherwise, to have met at your house, with the officers of the State Government of New York, I have met the Governor, the Secretary, the Comptroller &c in public life, have always voted with them, and always entertained, and still entertain for them all, high regard. Whether anybody in or out of New York, would be scandalized by my association with those Gentlemen at your table, is a matter, into the probability of which I should not enquire.

I regret my dear Sir, that your relations with the Administration, are not more confidential and cordial. But so far as the want of cordiality arises from occurrences, personal or local, in by-gone times and happening between you and others, you may be quite well assured, that *I* do not partake in it. I am happy to learn what you say of your [opinion in] respect to myself, you are well aware my dear Sir, that you and your friends, especially those of them who live in the city, were Gentlemen in whom I placed unbounded trust, personal and political, down to the time of the nomination of Genl. Taylor. It would not be frank in me, not to say, that the lead taken in that proceeding in the City of New York—gave me dissatisfaction and uneasiness. But I cherish no resentment, and shall be happy, happy indeed, if things shall take such a turn, as that we think alike, and act together hereafter. Alienation and difference, and distrust, between me and my old New York friends, has caused me more regret than almost any other political occurrence.

I pray you to present me to your friends about you—and believe me with regard—truly yours

DANIEL WEBSTER

(To David Henshaw.)

My dear Sir WASHINGTON June 11 '51

Your friendly and very acceptable letter has remained quite too long unanswered, from several causes.

It is certainly strange enough that the Board of Aldermen of Boston should make or should have made, no distinction between those who wish to confer together to support the Govt. and those who meet in a sort of Pandemonium, to overthrow it. Fortunately, however, the public opinion seems to have rebuked with sufficient severity, the folly of those Gentlemen.

I believe my dear Sir, that the political men of lead and consequence, of both the great parties, are sound on great Constitutional questions. They are *National,* and justly appreciate great national objects. But there are thousands in each party, who are more concerned for state, than for National politics; whose objects are all small, and their views all narrow, and then again this abolition feeling, has quite turned the heads of thousands. Depend upon it, indeed I dare say you think so, as well as I, there are many men at the North, who do not speak out what they wish, but who really desire to break up the Union. And some of these are men of influence and standing and are or have been in public life.

I thank you my dear Sir, for your favorable opinion of my political conduct for the past year or eighteen months. I need hardly say that I value your appreciation highly, because I know that you are a competent judge, and that you have no interest or bias to mislead you.

Things begin to look better, there is evidently a reaction in the South; some impression has been made in N. York, Most of the New England States are now pretty right on the Union question; and Massachusetts who has so strangely bolted from her sphere, may I hope be brought back to it. On the whole I believe the worst is past. Whenever you have leisure to write me, I shall be glad to hear from you. Whatever sentiments may have divided us, formerly, we are now together, in feeling and judgment, on the great question of the day: and it will give me pleasure at all times to correspond and to confer with you.

With entire respect, Yours truly

DANIEL WEBSTER.

(To Edward Curtis.)

Private & Confidential.   WASHINGTON June 9, '51.

My dear Sir,

Please to give me the name of a man, the fittest, within your knowledge to be Naval Officer. He must be a firm and energetic friend to the present Administration; not too old, altogether trustworthy, and enjoying public confidence.

Having thought of this subject a day or two, send me the name of such a person.

Yours truly

Entirely confidentially. DANIEL WEBSTER.

(To the Lowell Committee.)

WASHINGTON June 12 '51

Gentlemen:

It afforded me much pleasure to receive your kind letter of the 30th May inviting me in behalf of the citizens of Lowell to visit your city and address them, on the fourth of July.

Few things afford me more happiness than to see the return of that day, hailed and welcomed, with so much joy as it is by the citizens of the *United States*

The great boon which our Fathers attained by wisdom, patriotism and fearless Resolution without a United General Government—they have sought to guard, secure and perpetuate by a cordial Union of the States, under a Constitution itself the wonder of the world and an object of veneration to all lovers of human Freedom. Union and the Constitution, may they continue to shine together the two great lights in the American firmament till "The stars shall fade away, the sun himself grow dim with age and Nature sink in years." At some future day when the heat of the earth is past—

I shall be glad to avail myself of your farther request and pay you a friendly visit I thank you again for your kind letter, and remain with true regard—your most obliged friend and servant.[1]

[DAN'L WEBSTER]

(To D. Fletcher Webster.)

Dear Fletcher JUNE 16, 1851.

We have no news. The President thinks of going to Old Point, this week, for a few days— On his return, I shall make

---

[1] In Webster's hand.

a strong effort to see Marshfield, for one day, & Franklin for another.   But I do not know how it may be.

I was glad to learn that you thought well of Albany.[1]   It was pretty good for the last running.   I have corrected it, with some care, & think there will be a handsome Edition of it, by itself, dedicated to the Young men of Albany—& the endorsed quotation subjoined.   How will that do?—   I am well, & have no great work to do.

There is nothing to complain of but the confinement.

—I did not see Mr. S.—(?) Chase.   All such letters of introduction you had better send to your mother.   She can attend to them better than I can, & would be glad to do it.

Write to her as frequently as you can.   It helps to keep her in spirits.

Yrs affectionately
DANL WEBSTER

(From Chas. W. March.)

PHILADELPHIA, June 21st, '51.

Dear Sir

Our friends here seem to be apprehensive that Scott will receive the nomination at Lancaster, if any nomination be effected. Some of the Whigs think, as the Democrats made no nomination, none had better be made on our side.   Perhaps, as an alternative, our friends will insist upon the latter.   We shall lose the State at this election probably, whatever be the action of Lancaster, but not by such a majority as to discourage the Whigs in the Presidential campaign.

I hope you will see that Mr. Sargent forwards to each member of the N. H. Legislature, a copy of your Hülsemann letter, and your New York speeches, so that they all be perused and digested, before your arrival in Concord.   So far as the North is concerned, I feel confident, your late speeches will have a stunning effect upon your political opponents.

I have written Cutler at Portsmouth to have all things in readiness for your presence in New Hampshire.   Even if you do not make a speech, your presence at this juncture will gain thousands of proselytes.   I think it also advisable that, while in New

---

[1] Referring to his "Speech to the Young Men of Albany," delivered May 28, 1851.   See "Works of Daniel Webster." vol. ii. p. 569.

Hampshire, you should make a visit to Portsmouth, that your old friends of Rockingham County may have an opportunity to renew their allegiance, and so I have written Col. Cutler. You may depend upon it, Sir, that your personal appearance is all that is necessary to confirm the influence of your late political action.

I wish it were proper (and it may be) that your rebuke of Mr. Lawrence for the expressions of his speech in relation to the Catholics might be published. I find from their newspapers as well as from conversation with individuals that their minds are a good deal excited. Mr. Lee (Jno. Lee of Maryland) told me nothing could make you more popular among them. Could you not reply to some call from them; so as to satisfy them. * * *

Ever most respy & truly yrs

CHAS. W. MARCH.

(To D. Fletcher Webster.)

SUNDAY 1/2 past 10 o'clock [June 22, 1851]

Dear Fletcher;

After writing you this morning, I recd two letters from you, for which I thank you. I shall now go to Marshfield, before I go to N. H.— I will push right off for Naumkeag, Marspee, Waltquoit, Red Brook, or elsewhere in those foreign parts.

This morning after breakfast, & before church, that is, between 1/2 past 7 & 11 o'clock I struck out the whole frame & substance of my address for the 4th of July.[1] I propose to write it all out, which I can do in three hours, and to read it, & to give correct copies at once to the printers. So, if I find a trout stream in Va. I shall not have to be thinking out "Venerable men," "Venerable men."

Your mother wrote Caroline yesterday, & sends you her love today.

Yrs affectionately

DANL WEBSTER

---

[1] The " Address Delivered at the Laying of the Corner-stone of the Addition to the Capitol," on the 4th of July, 1851. See "Works of Daniel Webster," vol. ii. p. 595.

(From J. C. Spencer.[1])

ALBANY, June 23, 1851.

My dear Sir,

I am ashamed that you was obliged to telegraph me today to know whether your letters of the 13th inst. were received. The newspapers had announced your intended departure for Boston and Marshfield, and I waited to hear of your arrival at Boston.

Besides, I really had nothing useful to say. I sounded some gentlemen on the subject of Printing an appropriate edition of the Albany speech,[2] but found such an indisposition to provide the funds, that I could make no progress. * * * I ought to add as a mere act of justice to your Albany friends, that the cost of the reception here (some $1200) taxed them to the measure of their present feeling of ability. * * *

Allow me before I close, to mention a curious anecdote connected with the N. Y. clique, which was the subject of some observations I wrote to you;—a clique professing devotion to you and using your name and their pretended associations with you, to subserve the views of Mr. Seward and to promote his abolition objects.

During your recent visit you made to New York and while you put up at the Astor House, Mr. Hasbrouck late Speaker of our House of Assembly, called here to see you, and was told by Mr. Stetson that you was quite unwell and had retired, and that Mr. Curtis and your son were then with you scratching your legs! Mr. Hasbrouck loitered about the Hotel, until Mr. Curtis accidentally came up, and asked him to go with him to your room, which he did, and found you as well as ever you was in your life. I think this occurred on your late arrival at N. York with the President.

The fact is, a Surveillance has been kept over you at the Astor, so as to prevent your seeing any one whom the clique did not desire you to see. There was a double object in this—that you should suppose you had no friends but these gentlemen, and that you should not hear truths that might not be palatable to them. I think this fact will explain a great deal. * * *

Most respectfully, and truly, your friend

J. C. SPENCER

---

[1] The eminent New York jurist, Secretary of War and of the Treasury under Tyler.

[2] The "Address to the Young Men of Albany."

(From Fletcher Webster.)

JUNE 27, 1851.

* * * He has come over, among other things, to get specimens to fill up the blank space in our American part of the show & will take out, on board the "Daniel Webster," which Mr. Train has given him for the purpose, everything that he can get, worth showing.

He says they don't know of any American in Europe but you, & that the Austrian Commissioner is afraid to join the others in a plan to come over here with their goods, on account of the *Hülsemann letter!*

F. W.

(To J. de Marcoleta.)

Private

WASHINGTON, July 10, 51. Thursday morning.

My Dear Sir

I had the pleasure to receive your private note last evening and quite concur in the suggestion it contains. I should be very glad of a full, free and frank conversation with you & Sir Henry Bulwer as to our Nicaragua affair. The only difficulty is as to terms. Sir Henry is now sick, and I must go west. I shall return not many days hence, and in the mean time shall have opportunity to reflect upon the several questions which I think I now pretty well understand. We must all have a little patience.

I am dr sir with much regard your obt st

D. W.

(To Millard Fillmore.)

To the President   TUESDAY 3 o'clock.

My Dear Sir—

I have seen Mr. Crampton, who had already seen these Greytown proceedings in the Newspapers. He thinks it quite unfortunate, that any such attempt should be made, and that no doubt it is time that the British Commander on that station, has orders not to permit Greytown to be taken possession of by any other Government, or the flag of any other Govt. to be raised in it.

He thinks, however, that such joint instructions, or advice may be given from this place as shall avert the danger.

We are to take it into consideration, and I will report to you by 10 o'clock tomorrow or earlier.

Yours truly
Danl Webster.

(To Luther Severance.[1])

Washington July (14) 1851

Sir:

Your two confidential communications, to wit, one bearing the several dates of March 11", 12", 16", 17", 18", and 21"; the other bearing date of the 8" April, have been duly received, submitted to the President, and by him considered.

They relate to a subject of great importance, not only to the Hawaiian Government and its citizens, but also to the United States.

The Government of the United States was the first to acknowledge the National existence of the Hawaiian Government and to treat with it, as an independent State. Its example was soon followed by several of the Governments of Europe: and the United States, true to its Treaty obligations, has in no case interfered with the Hawaiian Government, either for the purpose of opposing the course of its own independent conduct, or of dictating to it, any particular line of policy. In acknowledging the independence of the Islands, and of the Government established on them, it was not seeking to promote any peculiar object of its own. What it did, and all that it did, was done openly, in the face of day, in entire good faith, and known to all nations. It declared its real purpose to be, to favor the establishment of a Government, at a very interesting point in the Pacific Ocean, which should be able to maintain such relations with the rest of the world, as are maintained by civilized States.

From this purpose, it has never swerved for a single moment; nor is it inclined, without the presence of some necessity, to depart from it now, when events have occurred, giving to the Islands, and their intercourse with the United States a new aspect and new importance.

---

[1] At this time Commissioner to the Sandwich Islands. He had represented Maine in Congress (1843–47).

This Government still desires to see the Nationality of the Hawaiian Government maintained, its independent administration of public affairs respected, and its prosperity and reputation increased.

But while thus indisposed to exercise any sinister influence itself, over the counsels of Hawaiia, or to overawe the proceedings of its Government by the menace, or the actual application of superior military force, it expects to see other powerful nations acting in the same spirit.   It is therefore with unfeigned regret, that the President has read the correspondence, and become acquainted with the circumstances occurring between the Hawaiian Government and M. Perrin the Commissioner of France at Honolulu:

It is too plain to be denied or doubted, that demands were made upon the Hawaiian Government, by the French Commissioner, wholly inconsistent with its character as an independent State; demands, which if submitted to in this case, would be sure to be followed by other demands, equally derogatory, not only from the same quarter, but probably also, from other States: and this would only end, in rendering the Islands and their Government, a prey to the stronger Commercial nations of the world. It cannot be expected that the Government of the United States could look on a course of things, leading to such a result, with indifference.   The Hawaiian Islands are ten times nearer to the United States than to any of the powers of Europe.   Five sixths of all their commercial intercourse is with the United States; and these considerations, together with others of a more general character, have fixed the course which the Government of the United States will pursue in regard to them.   The annunciation of this policy, will not surprise the Governments of Europe, nor be thought to be unreasonable by the nations of the civilized world; and that policy is, that while the Government of the United States itself faithful to its original assurance, scrupulously regards the independence of the Hawaiian Islands, it can never consent to see those Islands taken possession of by either of the great commercial powers of Europe; nor can it consent, that demands, manifestly unjust and derogatory and inconsistent with a bona fide independence shall be enforced against that Government.

The substance of what (is here) said, has already been intimated, with sufficient explicitness, to the Government of France; and we have the assurance of his Excellency, M. Sartiges, Minister of the Republic of France, near the United States, that that

Government has no purpose whatever, of taking possession of the Islands or of acting towards them, in any hostile or aggressive spirit.

A copy of this letter will be placed in the hands of the French Minister, here; another copy will be transmitted to Paris; and another copy, you will please to communicate to M. Perrin the French Commissioner, upon the appearance of any disposition on his part, or on the part of any French Naval Commander in the Pacific Ocean, to proceed to hostilities against the Government of Hawaiia, for the purpose of enforcing the demands which have been made upon it, on the part of France.

Your confidential communications Nos. 6, 7, 8, & 11 have been duly received &c.

(Have Nos. 9 & 10 failed to arrive? They were not among the papers you sent me.)

The Navy Department will receive instructions to place and to keep the naval armament of the United States in the Pacific Ocean, in such a state of strength and preparation, as shall be requisite for the preservation of the honor and dignity of the United States and the safety of the Government of the Hawaiian Islands.

I have the honor to be

very respectfully your obt. Servt.

[D. W.]

_____

(From Charles Stetson.[1] (?))

NEW YORK, July 28, 1851.

Dear Sir,

Allow me to hope that your present sojourn in the East will enable you to show to the world, what many have affected to doubt, that Daniel Webster, *on the right track*, has a *personal* political influence, independent of *friends*, or *committee men*, sufficient to secure full blooded Union men as representatives of Mass. in her *State* Councils, at least; and to set aside the Januses like Winthrop, &c. who are, in my opinion, infinitely more dangerous than the, so-called, free soilers. The "all things to all men" policy has been too long pursued by political aspirants in Mass; and *Whig State Convention*, with their shuf-

---

[1] The letter is signed simply C. S., but the writer is probably the proprietor of the Astor House.

fling addresses have finally produced the bastard "Free Soilism."
The Whig Party, *when the child was born*, stoutly denied the
paternity; but the Court of Public Opinion, after a patient hearing, has compelled it to pay for its support.

To remedy past, and to prevent future evils, the State must be
sponged clean; a new party must be formed, upon *Union* principles; and all *suspicious persons* excluded from the leadership.

I should consider such a task, accomplished by your agency, as
the greatest of the triumphs of your political life.

I have the honor to be, Yours Respy

C. S.

(To Millard Fillmore.)

[10 Sept 1851](?)

To the President,
    My Dear Sir

I came down from Franklin on the 8th with rather bad luck.
To avoid the heat, I took the evening train, which met with an
accident that delayed us, & kept me out till late at night. I
took cold and was not well yesterday, but am pretty well today,
& am going to Marshfield by the Hingham boat, & a carriage, I
avoid the cars as much as I can. * * *1

You will see by the enclosed letter from Mr. C. P. Curtis that
Mr. B. R. Curtis will accept the place,2 if offered to him. I shall
write you again on this subject the moment I have seen Mr.
Choate or heard from him.

We are all horror-struck this morning by the terrible news of
the death so suddenly of Mrs. Crittenden.

Yours always truly

Danl Webster.

(From Mr. Hülsemann.)

Sept 30th. [1851]

Our Government had consented before to the embarkation of
the larger number of the refugees under condition, that they

---

[1] The omitted portion of this letter may be found in Curtis' "Life of Daniel
Webster," vol. ii, p. 531.
[2] The "place" was that of Associate Justice of the Supreme Court of the
United States to which Curtis was, in fact, appointed.

should never return to Turkey. Sometime after the Divan addressed themselves again to our Government requesting we should also consent to the liberation of Kossuth and the rest; but we did not think, the time had come as well on account of the tranquillity in Hungary not long enough re-established; and because Kossuth's going to England and to the U. States might serve to increase the excitement and hatred of his partizans against us. But we did not wish to prolong the inconveniences, which Kossuth's presence [at] Kutaiah caused them, beyond the necessary time; but there could be no doubt about the Turkish Government being bound, not to proceed to their liberation *without our consent*, which they had besides recognized by asking us to give our consent.

Of course we were very disagreeably disappointed, when towards the end of June the Turkish Ministry informed our Charge d' Affaires, verbally, that they intended to set Kossuth and his companions at liberty in the beginning of September. Without entering into the question of right, the Turkish Ministry declared in a confidential way, that having been isolated by the interruption of diplomatic relations on our part, and that of Russia, they had been obliged to look for support elsewhere, and for that purpose they had been obliged to make certain engagements. Who those Powers were, who interested themselves for these Refugees, was easy to see; Mr. Webster's letter[1] to Mr. Marsh & Lord Palmerston's speech in the House of Commons indicated the United States and the English Government; it was also clear, that the French Government had followed the English in this occasion. It is though our opinion, that the English Government, took the principal part in prevailing upon the Turkish Government, to break its obligations to a third party, to give us just cause of complaint, and to injure the most essential interests of Turkey by this proceeding against us.

At the reception of this news we suspended the departure of A. Richburg as Internuncio, and instructed the Charge' d' Affaires to advise in a friendly way the Turkish Government not to execute that project. We received the first certain news of the Turkish Government being decided to execute that intention, from Mr. Brown, about the end of July, to whom the Turkish Minister had given the information, that Kossuth should be set at liberty in the beginning of September, he having an interest in

---

[1] March 28, 1851. See Webster's Works, vol. vi, p. 591.

knowing that true state of things on account of the Mississippi being intended to convey them to the United States, and he having written to the Commodore, to send that steamer, and as the Turkish Minister had said, that the Austrian Government had not consented, Mr. Brown wished to learn, how it was? Mr. Klezl answered, it was by no means with our consent.

Mr. Klezl asked the Turkish Minister, who could not deny the assurances given to Mr. Brown, and Mr. Klezl in consequence of that delivered to him a protestation, 29 July.

That protestation has been highly approved by our Government. The Turkish Government though followed the advice of those who interfered in this business, and announced officially on the 16th August to Mr. Klezl that the Refugees would be sent out of the Turkish Teritory in the beginning of September, saying that the keeping of them was very troublesome, that as long as Hungary was now quiet, they had fulfilled their obligations, but that now that necessity did no more exist. So they undertook to judge our own interior concerns. Mr. Klezl repeated his protest and made the Turkish Government answerable for the consequences of their proceedings.

According to the news received in Vienna, Kossuth went on board the Mississippi the 7th September, being received with military honors, and he making a speech to the Crew, which was answered with three shouts. The same day he was condemned to death in Pesth and his name put on the gallows.

We hope, that the American Government, true to its own official declarations, will do, what depends from [upon] them, to permit Kossuth and his partizans from abusing his asylum for the purpose of exciting new disturbances. We would have wished, that the American Government, after having been advised of the Turkish Government not being at liberty to act without our consent, had not offered again the means of transportation. But it is not our object to pursue this recrimination, though it be very well founded.

And we see with real satisfaction Mr. Webster's despatch of 28th February, where he praises the Turkish Government, for having taken individuals, who were dangerous for neighboring States, away from the frontiers. The United States in offering to these refugees an Asylum, take to some extent the place of the Turkish Government, and what Mr. Webster says about the duty of Turkey, not to permit those foreign Refugees to give cause of uneasiness to other Countries; Mr. Webster expresses the expectation, that those men will remain quiet. We wish it too, but we do not expect it, least from Kossuth, who always during his captivity never ceased to labor for new disturbances.

We rely also upon the proclamation of the President concerning Cuba, and expect that, if it should become necessary, the United States Government will act upon the same principles.[1]

(From Mr. Hülsemann.[2])

WASHINGTON CITY 4th Nov. 1851.

Mr. Hülsemann, having met in an English paper with the correspondence which he had occasion to refer to the other day, takes the liberty to enclose it to the Hon. Secretary of the State.

To the Honorable Daniel Webster Secretary of the State.

WASHINGTON CITY, Saturday morning,
15th Nov. 1851.

From Chevalier Hülsemann
    Private

Mr. Hülsemann presents his respectful compliments to the Hon. Secretary of the State, and takes the liberty of recommending the enclosed and underlined article to his attention.

Mr. H. *has before this had* occasion, to mention to the Honorable Secretary that he found it inconvenient, that his conversations in the State Department, either with Mr. Webster himself or with persons belonging to the Department should be—and falsely too—printed and commented upon in the Baltimore Sun, the Philadelphia Ledger and other papers by a notorious individual, whose presence or admittance into the Department or into any private house, is by no means creditable to those, who admit or employ such a person.

CHEVLR. HULSEMANN.

---

[1] Mr. Webster has endorsed this, "This is furnished me for my private use only." December 5. 1851 Kossuth landed in America. For an account of his reception see Rhodes ' History of the United States," vol. i, p 232.
[2] Enclosed clipping from Evening Mail, Wednesday, October 1st : Southampton. "The liberation of Kossuth."

(To Mr. Hülsemann.[1])

Private   DEPARTMENT OF STATE,
Washington 15 Nov. 1851.

The Chev. Hülsemann,

    Mr. Webster's compliments to Mr. Hülsemann— He will inquire into the evil or impropriety to which Mr. Hülsemann, in his note of this morning, adverts, and endeavor to correct it for the future.

[DAN'L WEBSTER]

(From Mr. Hülsemann.)

AUSTRIAN LEGATION
Washington December 13th. 1851.

Mr. Secretary of State

    I have had the honor of communication to you verbally, and at different times, the views of the Imperial government, respecting the arrival of Kossuth.[2] The intentions avowed in the despatch which you addressed to Mr. Marsh, under date of the 28th of last February,[3] and which amounted to *an offer of an asylum to Kossuth, in order that he might spend the remainder of his days quietly in this country, renouncing all political agitation, for the future*, were perfectly in accordance with my instructions. On the first of November last on the occasion of a communication relative to Kossuth, you told me distinctly, Mr. Secretary of the State, that, in the event of your being called upon to make him an address, the scope of your remarks would be, to extend to him, *the offer of an asylum.* This mode of treating the subject, debarred all discussion, and induced me, at the time, to touch but lightly upon the remonstrances which we might have urged, in relation to the diplomatic steps that have preceded the liberation of Kossuth—steps, which were entirely irrelevant to the interests of the United States, and of a character calculated to complicate the relations, already very much involved, between the Imperial Government, and that of the Sublime Porte.

    Independently of those assurances, I had reason to hope, that the extraordinary proceedings of Kossuth, on board the Mississippi, and in the Mediterranean ports, the details of which, you

---

[1] This is unsigned, being the original draft of the note.
[2] See Rhodes' "History of United States." vol. i, p. 231.
[3] See "Works of Daniel Webster," vol. vi, p. 591.

had, yourself, communicated to me, would not be lost sight of. The information I had the honor of imparting to you on the 28th of November last, was corroborative of the fact, that a conflict had arisen, between the high discipline of the American Navy, and the ridiculous claims of a revolutionary pretender, who was constantly striving to abuse the flattering hospitality of which he was the recipient, and endeavoring to compromise the flag of the United States, by throwing the fire-brand of civil war into those countries, which he visited, in the course of his peregrinations in the Mediterranean. The whole tenor of Kossuth's conduct, on board the Mississippi and in England, indicated already a fixed determination, on his part, not to accept the asylum, which the United States had designed for him: for he boldly proclaimed, that he was coming over to this country, with a view of driving the United States to assume an attitude of declared hostility, against the policy of the Continental powers of Europe. These preliminary demonstrations, which, however, were full of meaning, by reason of their being manifestly at variance with the policy, which has governed the United States, since the administration of General Washington, had given me a first hope that the Federal Government, would drive this man, who was meddling with so much audacity with the foreign relations of the Union, back into nonentity. But this has not been the case.

The reception in New York, and the Municipal ovations of which he has been the subject, were deemed to have no international bearing; they were looked upon, as the inevitable consequence of a thoughtless enthusiasm. This was not the case, however, with the Federal Government. It was, therefore, with the utmost regret, that I heard of the unusual honors which had been paid to Kossuth, by the Federal Army and Navy. A Superior Officer must announce to Kossuth, that he was instructed to treat him with all the marks of distinction, which belonged to the most elevated rank, in the army, and, if I am not mistaken, to raise him, thereby, upon a level with the President himself. In the last Message, he is designated as Governor; and Congress, in its deliberations, unreservedly bestows upon him, the title of Governor of Hungary, which that political Mountebank has the insolence of arrogating to himself, while he takes the liberty, even, of using the official seal of Hungary.

The honors which have been paid to Kossuth, have only been the means of increasing his audacity, and have induced him to make a sort of appeal to the people, which I quote, for the purpose of showing the subversive tendencies of the same, and its tone of antagonism towards the executive power of the Union. The address which he caused to be published, on the day of his entrance into New York, and which is designated as a *manifesto*, affords evidence, that the honors, which were no doubt only intended as an excess of civility, by those who ordered them to be paid, are looked upon and represented by him, as an acknowledgment of his absurd pretensions. Allow me to insert here, the passage alluded to from the address in question.

"So I confidently hope, that the Sovereigns of this Country, the people, *will make the Declaration of Independence of Hungary soon formally recognized*, and that it will care not a bit for it, if Mr. Hülsemann takes tomorrow his passports, *bon voyage* to him. But it is also my agreeable duty to profess that I *am entirely convinced that the government of the United States shares warmly the sentiment of the people in that respect. It has proved it* by executing in a ready and dignified manner, the resolution of Congress, in behalf of my liberation. It has proved it by calling on the congress to consider how I shall be treated and received, and even this morning, I was honored, *by the express order of the government, by an official salute from the batteries of the United States, in such a manner, in which, according to the military rules, only a public high official capacity can be greeted.* Having thus expounded my aim, I beg leave to state, that I came not to your glorious shores to enjoy a happy rest—I came not with the intention to gather triumphs of personal distinction, but because a humble petitioner, in my country's name, as its freely chosen constitutional chief, humbly to entreat your generous aid."[1]

It is in the midst of full peace,—It is after the lapse of some years, since the rebellion was put down,—it is at the very moment when Hungary is beginning to recover from her misfortunes, that it is sought to raise a pedestal to a fallen idol, in order to give him a fresh chance of ruining his country. My government appreciates these impotent efforts, at their proper value, and I only comment upon them, for the purpose of pointing out their unseasonableness and impropriety.

The Imperial Government, frankly and sincerely wishes to maintain the best relations with the United States. It makes a very great allowance for the institutions and usages of this coun-

---

[1] A newspaper clipping. Clipping is enclosed with the original report of Kossuth's speech.

try; but, at the same time it relies upon the wisdom of the executive power. I am willing to believe that the President disapproves highly of this crusade of Kossuth against all Sovereigns of Europe: and I flatter myself, that the military honors which have been paid to him on his arrival, and which seem to have turned his head, will not be continued. I attach some importance to these demonstrations, and I shall be obliged to you, Mr. Secretary of the State, if you will let the President know that I desire to be informed, whether these Military honors will be renewed, after the public declaration of Kossuth, that he looks upon them, as affording evidence, that hostile projects against Austria, are approved of by the Government of the United States.

I beg that you will honor me with an answer; and I very much wish, that said answer, may be of a character to convince my government of the friendly intentions of the government of the United States: it will put an end, I hope, to all apprehension, that the movements of this agitation, may encompass the object in view; and that by inducing the Government of the United States to become a party to any hostile demonstrations against Austria, Kossuth may succeed in seriously compromising the amicable relations existing between the two countries.

I avail myself, of this occasion, Mr. Secretary of State, to renew to you the expression of my high consideration.

HÜLSEMANN.

(To the Chevalier Hülsemann.[1])

Private.

[16TH DEC. 1851.]

The undersigned has received the Chevalier Hülsemann's note of the 13th instance. This note does not appear to be a private, but an official communication, and the undersigned finds in it with no little surprise a reference to supposed private and confidential conversations between the Chevalier Hülsemann and the head of this Department and also to letters in the Department which, if shown to the Chevalier Hülsemann at all, were shown to him in strict confidence. The Chevalier Hülsemann is now informed that so long as these references to matters entirely confidential remain in his note, it can receive no answer.

The undersigned has the honor to be, with due consideration, The Chevalier Hülsemann's very humble servant.

D. W.

---

[1] This was taken from the original draft.

THE NATIONAL STATESMAN 495

(From the Chevalier Hülsemann.)

Private.   AUSTRIAN LEGATION
                              Washington 17th December 1851.

The undersigned in answer to the private note directed to him under the date of yesterday by the Hon. Secretary of State, begs leave to observe, that, if for some reason or other the United States Government wish not to expose to the public the correspondence concerning Kossuth's conduct on board the Mississippi, he has no objection to consider as confidential, what has passed between Mr. Webster and himself in that respect. But as for the official though verbal communications, which the undersigned, as Charge' d' Affaires of his Majesty the Emperor of Austria, had in consequence of special instructions received from his Government, the honor to make to the Hon. Secretary of State in an interview at the State Department, appointed beforehand in writing for that purpose, and the assurances, which he received from Mr. Webster in answer to those communications, it is not practicable, to consider them as confidential.

The undersigned takes this occasion to assure the Hon. Secretary of State of his high consideration.

                                                     HÜLSEMANN.

(To the Chevalier Hülsemann.)

Private.   DEPARTMENT OF STATE,
                              Washington, 18th. December, 1851.

The Undersigned has the honor to acknowledge the receipt of the Chevalier Hülsemann's note of yesterday, and has again to say that he has had no conversation with The Chevalier Hülsemann upon the subject referred to, but such as he considered strictly confidential.

The Undersigned presumes that he could have said nothing in any such conversations which he would wish to qualify or explain; but the different recollections of the parties as to what was actually said by them might lead to great inconvenience if the substance of the conversation were not stated in writing at the time and so stated as to conform to the understanding of both.

The Undersigned has the honor to be, with due consideration, The Chevalier Hülsemann's very obedient servant,

                                                     DANL. WEBSTER.

(Hülsemann to President Fillmore.)

LEGATION D'AUTRICHE Washington

Monsieur le Président,   le 8 janvier 1852

Mr Webster a déclaré hier publiquement en presence du Président du Sénat, du Speaker du House of Representatives et du fauteur des calamités de la Hongrie, qu'il ferait des voeux ardens pour l'émancipation la plus prompte et la plus absolue de ce Royaume. Ce langage si extra ordinaire, si déplacé et si inconvenant de la part du Ministre des Affaires Etrangères ne me permettant plus d'avoir aucun rapport avec lui, je me trouve par suite de ce marque de courtoisie internationale dans la necessité, de m'adresser directement au Président des Etats-Unis et de faire ainsi une derniere tentative pour le maintien des bonnes relations entre les deux Pays.

L'hostilité de Mr Webster à l'egard de mon Gouvernement ne date pas d'hier. Sa note du 21 Decembre 1850 était un manifeste révolutionnaire et un appel fanfaron à tous les perterbateurs de la paix publique en Europe Mon Gouvernement devait à la dignité, de ne tenir aucun compte des prétendus argumens contenus dans une note si extraordinaire pour le fonde et pour le forme, et qui dans le fait n'était qu'une volumineuse amplification sur les perfections démocratiques, destinée à augmenter la popularité de son auteur.

Plus tard Mr Webster, fidéle à son rôle, a pris l'iniative pour l'envoi du Mississippi; et pour combler la mésure, sans aucune provocation, sans aucune prétexte plausible il encourage publiquement une partie intégrante de l'Empire d'Autriche a la rébellion et cherche par là à attirer de nouvelles calamités sur la Hongrie.

Ayant fait par ordre du Gouvernement Imperial plusieurs communications à Mr le Secretaire d'Etat sur l'arrivée de Kossuth, Mr Webster m'a donné le assurances le plus positives, que dans sa conduite il ne s'eloignersit point de l'esprit de sa dépeche du 28 fevrier à Mr Marsh; il m'a même dit, que s'il se trouvait dans le cas de faire un discours, il suiveait la ligne politique tracée par cette dépeche et qui se resume dans *l'offre d'un* asyle à Kossuth; ces assurances, que Mr Webster m'à données au Département d'Etat, sont en contradiction manifeste avec le discours qu'il a prononcé hier. Quelque temps après l'arrivée de cet individu j'addressai à Mr Webster ma note due 13 Decembre, mais je suis encore à attendre sa réponse.

J'abandonne à l'appreciation impartiale de la partie saine des populations des deux mondes la partées des honneurs rendus a un homme, dont la déplorable célébrité a été fondée sur les ruines et la desolation de la Hongrie; mais je ne puis, Monsieur le Président, garder le silence sur le discours statistico-politique et intentionnellement hostile au Gouvernement Imperial, prononcé hier par M^r le Secretaire d'Etat.

Desirant faire une derniére tentative en faveur du maintien des bons rapports entre les deux Gouvernemens, j'ose vous prier, Monsieur le Président, de vouloir bien me faire part de la manière, que vous jugerez la plus convenable, si vous approuvez le langage et les voeux emis par Mr le Sécrétaire d'Etat. Si la réponse n'etait pas telle, que jai lieu de l'esperer, je vous prierai, Monsieur le Président, de considérer alors mes fonctions diplomatique comme suspendues.

J'ai rendu à mon Gouvernement un compte exact de tout ce qui s'est passé ici; j'ai transmis aujourd'hui même à Vienne le discours prononcé hier par Mr Webster, et je vais informer de suite S. A. le Prince de Schwarzenberg de ma presente démarche[1]

Je suis avec le plus grand respect, Monsieur le Président,

Votre très humble serviteur

HÜLSEMANN.

(*To Charles J. McCurdy.*[2])

DEPARTMENT OF STATE,
Washington, 15th January, 1852.

Sir.

Your despatch of the 13th ultimo has been received, and I sent you a hasty answer in reply. I now wish to write you more at length and in a private letter. The newspapers will have informed you that Kossuth is now here. Both he and Madame

---

[1] The editor does not hold himself responsible for the correctness of the French in the above document. It is reproduced *verbatim et punctatim*, from the original which was given by President Fillmore to Webster. This letter brought about an interview between Hülsemann and President Fillmore which was unsatisfactory and April 29, 1852, Hülsemann sent an official letter to Webster announcing his withdrawal from the United States. See Doc. 92 of Senate Documents, 1st Session of 32d Congress. vol. ix. where also will be found Webster's comment upon Hülsemann's conduct, in a letter to C. J. McCurdy, who represented us at the Austrian Court.

[2] The United States Minister to Austria.

Kossuth are in good health. Ever since his arrival at New York, he has been treated with the kindness due to his character and his misfortunes. I have caused a copy of extracts of your despatch to be communicated to him. In reply, he has addressed me a private letter, requesting me to instruct you to protect the persons, to whom you refer, which you will of course do, so far as you can with discretion and propriety. This, however, you will understand as implying a due regard to your official situation, and the duties due from you to the Government at Vienna. All that has been done, or will be done, at this Department on M. Kossuth's request, will be merely in compliance with the dictates of humanity and charity.

I enclose extracts from Kossuth's letter[1] to me, making other requests which I hope you may be able to have complied with, but in regard to all these things, you will be careful to act with prudence, and to do nothing which can give even cause of offence to the Austrian Government. The six hundred dollars referred to have been invested in the purchase of a bill on England, which is herewith enclosed, drawn by Corcoran and Riggs on George Peabody of London, in favor of William Hunter of this Department by him endorsed to you.

There is reason to fear that the Austrian Charge' d' Affaires near this Government, does not feel entirely satisfied with what has occurred with Louis Kossuth. You are aware of the whole history of the case. In February last, a Despatch was addressed from this Department to Mr. Marsh, at Constantinople, instructing him to intercede with the Sublime Porte for the relief of Kossuth and his companions. This Despatch you are acquainted with, and it is not necessary, therefore to state its contents particularly here.

On the third day of March last, both houses of Congress passed a Resolution, which you have also seen: it is in these words:—

"Whereas, the people of the United States sincerely sympathizing with the Hungarian exiles, Kossuth and his associates, and fully appreciate the magnanimous conduct of the Turkish Government in receiving and treating those noble exiles with kindness and hospitality, and whereas, if it be the wish of these exiles to emigrate to the United States, and the will of the Sultan to permit them to leave his dominions, therefore,

Resolved by the Senate and House of Representatives of the

---

[1] These were not with this document.

United States of America, in Congress assembled, That the President of the United States be, and he hereby is, requested to authorize the employment of some one of the public vessels which may be now cruising on the Mediterranean, to receive and convey to the United States, the said Louis Kossuth and his associates in captivity."

In pursuance of this Resolution orders were given by the Navy Department, a copy of which is enclosed, together with that portion of the President's Message referring to our Foreign relations.

On his arrival at New York, the Two Houses of Congress, welcomed him to the country and to the Capitol by Joint Resolution. He was introduced by Committee to Both Houses, and was presented by me to the President. On this last occasion, he addressed the President, and I send you herewith a copy of the President's reply.

Members of Both Houses of Congress invited him to a Public Dinner which took place on the 7th day of this month. I attended it, with other members of the administration. You will have seen an account of this Dinner and the speeches of the gentlemen present; and I draw your attention particularly to those of General Cass and Mr. Douglas

I send you herewith, also, a revised copy of my own Speech. Mr. Hülsemann wrote a letter to the President complaining of my speech. This, you are aware, was a very irregular proceeding, because being a Charge' d' Affaires only, and as such, accredited to this Department, he had no official right even to ask an interview with the President; much less to address him in writing. The President, however, waived ceremony and sent him word that he would be glad to see him. Mr. Hülsemann came; and the President stated to him what is contained in a paper accompanying this marked No. 3.

These three Papers, viz: the President's Message; his reply to L. Kossuth, and his statement to Mr. Hülsemann, state fully and clearly, the principles which govern him and his Administration, in his intercourse with foreign States. And it may be well for you to make these repeated declarations known to the Austrian Government.

As was stated by the President to Mr. Hülsemann, I went to the Dinner in no official capacity, but simply as an individual; and it is not easy to see why Mr. Hülsemann had more right to complain of my presence than that of other gentlemen. At any rate, my attendance at the Dinner was my own act, my speech there made was my own individual speech, and the President is in no degree answerable for either.   I do not know to what extent Mr. Hülsemann means to manifest his dissatisfaction. Probably he will be of opinion, upon full observation and consideration, that the President and the members of his administration were more staid and abstinent; in the respect paid by them to Kossuth, than were other leading men in the country.   You may say, in as explicit terms as you may judge proper, that neither the President nor his Cabinet countenance any such thing as "intervention," or involving the Government in European wars, from causes affecting only the nations of Europe.   Public men in this Country, as well as private men, are accustomed to speak their opinions freely.   This belongs to our system, and although in this respect individuals may sometimes be indiscreet, yet there is no where any power of control; and there are some public men, as well as private individuals, who are ready to take a part in the troubles, and in the wars of other States.   It is believed however, that the sober sense of the country will settle down on more prudent and pacific ideas.   While there is no probability that the Government will lend aid or countenance to Kossuth, there is no reason to suppose that the amount of private contributions made for him will be large.   On the whole, the enthusiasm felt for him is not increasing; and having visited most of the large Northern Cities, where there has existed the greatest readiness to subscribe, his success elsewhere is not likely to be distinguishd.   And I venture to say, that the "Intervention" feeling will doubtless subside gradually and rapidly, if nothing should take place, calculated to kindle it into a new flame.

 I feel it my duty to say one thing in justice to myself, as the author of the Letter of February 28th, to Mr. Marsh, as well as in justice to the President who, of course, authorized the letter; and that is, that on instructing Mr. Marsh to intercede for Kossuth and his Associates, we contemplated no other future for him, or them, than that they should come here and remain in the country as quiet and unoffending Exiles.

 You are at liberty to communicate in conversation, as much of the contents of this private letter to the Austrian Minister of Foreign Affairs, as you may think prudent and useful; and I enclose herewith a copy of a recent despatch to Mr. Rives, at Paris, which you may also make known to Prince Schwartzenburg, as another and a recent statement of the principles which govern the Government of the United States in its foreign relations.

Since writing the foregoing I learn, that Mr. Hülsemann has declined an invitation of the President to a diplomatic Dinner, to be given on the 22nd.[1]

I am, Sir, very respectfully, your obedient servant,

DANL WEBSTER

<hr>

(From Chas. W. March.)

NEW YORK Nov. 14 '51.

Dear Sir

Mr. Ashmun writes me to-day as follows: "The sky has decidedly a blue look since Monday & there is not much hope of a favorable change. Tho' we shall keep a bright look out till the 4th Monday. We have had a three days fight here equal to that of Paris, & the Whigs worked like Saints—but to no purpose. Tomorrow night we eat a supper, at which I shall bring Mr. Webster into the field. Bates (W. G.) has raised 20 delegates for the Convention from Northfield. It is not to be disguised however that the result of this election will operate heavily against our movement."

Mr. Ashmun's opinion as to the result of the last election *upon Massachusetts* is doubtless correct. It will be difficult to get up much enthusiasm after the late defeat, so recent to the minds of men. But I cannot think that Mr. Winthrop's defeat can injure the good cause out of Massachusetts, nor there, but for a season. It will, on the contrary but enforce the necessity of getting upon your platform, out of the state. Mr. Winthrop is generally regarded as a free-soiler and opposed to your views, and his success would have been more fatal than his defeat. * * *

Ever most respy & truly Yrs

CHAS. W. MARCH

<hr>

(From Chas. W. March.)

NEW YORK Nov 23, 51.

Dear Sir

We have here quite good accounts of the meeting at Faneuil

---

[1] See Senate Documents, 1st Session, 32d Congress, vol. ix. Doc. 92, for letter Hülsemann to Daniel Webster. April 29, 1852.

Hall on Tuesday next.   Depend upon it, it will be a grand affair. A gentleman who arrived here last night tells me, that the Democrats will be present in full number.   A large number of Democrats go from Lynn, and in fact many from different parts of the State.   This is a feature of future great advantage.   If we can lay down a platform broad enough and strong enough for the honest of both parties, we have nothing to fear.

I beg to take the liberty of remarking that the public mind is very sensitive on the question of the right of search.   The letter which I wrote while in Washington, has been variously criticised, by the Democratic press, with some severe strictures, as evading the real question.

I had quite a long and interesting conversation last night with Mr. Geyer, the new Senator of Missouri.   While he says, that there is no man in the country, he would be more glad to see President than yourself or for whom he would work with more earnestness he is obliged to confess that Mr. Fillmore is the first choice of the Whigs of Missouri.   His course since he has been President has gained their good-will.   But he says that you are its second choice and that you are gaining daily upon the affections of Whigs and Hunker Democrats, between whom he thinks there will be a union before the Presidential election.   While Gen. Scott, he says, has not, to his knowledge, a political friend in the State, Mr. Geyer also says that if you satisfy the public mind, as you doubtless will, in the Spanish-Cuban affair, and "on the right of search" the track will be clear for you.

Geo. Wilkins Kendall has just come in from New Orleans.   He says, that the case of Thrasher[1] is exciting the deepest interest in the whole South and even may be the "cry" of the coming campaign.   Thrasher has been so kind to the American captives in Havana, has supplied them with so much money, has been so bold and been personally reckless in his attentions to them, that his imprisonment and supposed condemnation have raised a vehemence of popular feeling, difficult to be controlled.   That Mr. Thrasher may have gone farther than even an active expression of sympathy towards these deluded men, I have no doubt.   But at the same time, proof of the most positive kind of his connection with the invasion of the island will be required to quiet the public feeling at the South—and I fear even that will not avail.

I hope you will pardon me for any inferences that may be

---

[1] See Curtis' "Life of Webster," vol. ii, p. 557.

drawn from my suggestions. But I know that you have gained greatly upon the public mind from the supposition that you have refused to make any concession to the pride of Spain, even against the President, and I know also that you have it in your power to greatly promote the increasing tide in your favor.

It is probable that I shall leave here Tuesday night, & be with you Wednesday morning.

Ever respy & truly Yrs
CHAS. W. MARCH

(From Fletcher Webster.)

BOSTON Nov 29, 1851.

My dear Father,

I enclose an extract [1] from a letter of Judge Huntingdon of Indiana written to a gentleman of this town.

It was shown to me I suppose for the purpose of communicating its contents.

Perhaps if any occasion offers it would be well to write Mr. Huntingdon & send Mr. Key a speech or something.

Yr affectionate Son
FLETCHER WEBSTER

(Extract.)

"You know that if I have a wish stronger than another it is that the Country should make Mr. Webster President of the U. S.

I have never failed to improve every opportunity offered me of making a friend for him & I have hailed with most heartfelt joy every sign I have seen in any quarter favorable to his prospects.

But I fear that Mr. Webster does not always second with the best effect the efforts of his friends. I never hear from him in answer to my own letters, but of this I do not complain, but on more than one occasion I have introduced gentlemen from the West to him by letter, gentlemen who are ready to unite in any movement to advance his interests who have returned chilled by his cautious and cool reception.

I will mention an instance.

---

[1] See the following letter.

Judge Key of the Commercial Court of Cincinnati, a man of talent, young, ardent, and idolizing Mr. Webster almost as much as I do, connected with all the Keys & Marshalls of Ky. & Ohio came down purposely to visit me on the subject, to see if by concert with the leading young men of Ohio & Indiana we could not set the ball in motion.

He gave me the names of the leading men in Ohio who were anxious for it.

But he had never seen Mr. Webster & determined to visit Washington for that purpose. I gave him a letter of introduction, a general letter telling him if an opportunity offered to have a full conversation with Mr. Webster. I have not seen him since nor has he written to me but I have understood that he presented the letter was coolly but politely received, took his leave and never went back again. Judge Key is perhaps the most popular young man in Ohio &, withal, one of the most shrewd. A half dozen kind words from Mr. Webster, would have made him his Champion. Now I well know the kindness of Mr. Webster's heart & I dare say he is annoyed continually by such introductions, but Key is a modest & a sensitive man. I had told him of the warmth of Mr. Webster's heart when he once knew a man worthy of his regard & suppose he looked for some token of recognition especially as my letter assured Mr. W. of his devotion to him.

Now the amount of all this is that I can never learn from Mr. W. or from any friend in his confidence what line of policy ought to be adopted here &c &c"

―――――――――

(From Chas. W. March.)

New York Dec 2, '51

My dear Sir

I went to Springfield Saturday evening, for a consultation with our friend Mr. Ashmun. He is in great spirits and says you could carry Mass. with 20,000 majority. The last election has turned out precisely *right*. Winthrop's defeat, while it removes from your friends the opprobrium of a connection with freesoilism, will excite the Whigs to a glorious triumph next year. In Springfield, every whig fought like Coeur-de-Lion and every whig is a Webster man.

Ashmun insists upon an immediate organization of your friends here, as in Massachusetts. I regret exceedingly Mr. Curtis's doubtful health, for he is head and shoulders above all your other friends here. Still, he must lay out a chart, and we will steer by it. Each day your strength increases, and if Mr. Fillmore be not induced by Southern Promises to persevere in a canvass, your name will be irresistible.

I hope to be pardoned for saying that this outrage upon the Prometheus[1] by the English Brig skilfully managed will "bring down the house" in your favor. There is deep excitement on the subject here among all classes. If you could repeat the Hülsemann letter, we shall have but little to contend against.

Ashmun longs to be with you, and will be, at the earliest possible moment. I may wait for him here, till Friday, unless Mrs. Webster needs my escort earlier.

We have turned the Democratic flank upon the Compromise Measures, and the Herald says, it is all owing to your efforts. I will see Bennett before I leave and try to have an understanding with him.

Ever most respy & truly yrs
CHAS. W. MARCH

———

(To Millard Fillmore.)

DEP'T OF STATE 8 Dec/ 1851.

To the President,
  My Dear Sir,
  I have read Mr. Thrasher's[2] letter, & shall be very happy to see you in regard to it, *at your house*, at the first fair hour. The difficulty in Thrasher's case is what I have already suggested to you. He went to Havana for the purposes of a permanent residence, as far as appears. He has actually resided in the city I suppose fifteen or twenty years pursuing his private affairs under the protection of Spanish law. These facts seem to impress upon him the duties of a temporary allegiance to the Spanish crown, & if he has been treated only as a Spanish subject would be treated under the like circumstances, I do not see how the government of the U. S. can interfere in his behalf. He seems to have chosen for himself, & he cannot be at the same time a Span-

---

[1] See Curtis' " Life of Webster."
[2] See Curtis' "Life of Webster," vol. ii. 557.

ish & an American citizen. All this, however, we must confer about, & when I go home this evening I will look up the law of temporary allegiance.

Yours truly, always,

DANL WEBSTER.

(To D. Fletcher Webster.[1])

Dear Fletcher,   THURSDAY, 3 o'clock.
    It appears that the letter which I wrote, for the President to sign, to the Emperor of China, was afterwards altered and signed by Mr. Upham, as Secy.——I shall look into this. If there is any plagiarism, I will expose it——I have written to Mr. Marcoe for a copy of my letter.

D. W.

(To Millard Fillmore.)

To the President,   WASHINGTON, Dec. 19, 1851.
    My Dear Sir,
    I will read Mr. Green's paper in the course of the day. I know not what he refers to by charging me with suppressing a part of Mr. Rosa's[2] correspondence. The matter shall be looked into as soon as Mr. Hunter returns.

Yrs truly,

DANIEL WEBSTER

(To Millard Fillmore.)

1/2 PAST 5 O'CLOCK.
My dear Sir,   [Dec. 21. 1851]
    I learn by telegraph from Baltimore that Kossuth will not come hither till Tuesday. His company is 14 persons and he has signified to the Senate Committee that he will require 4 parlors & 8 lodging rooms. They are engaged at Brown's. I expect Mr. Hunter between 6 & 7 o'clock.[3]

D. WEBSTER.

---

[1] This letter is owned by Edwin W. Sanborn of New York.
[2] M. de la Rosa, the Mexican Minister at Washington.
[3] On December 22, 1851, Webster wrote Fillmore significantly, "Mr. Hunter is quite official and *diplomatic*."

(To Abbott Lawrence.)

WASHINGTON, December 29, 1851.

My dear Sir,—

I ought to have written you long ago to thank you for your private letter, accompanied by the memorandum of a conversation between you and Lord Palmerston, but incessant occupation has not allowed me time. What you said to His Lordship corresponds exactly with my own sentiments and opinions, and also, I believe, with those of the President.

You will have seen the Message before you receive this, and that part of it which relates to our foreign relations will have shown you the ground on which I stand, with the entire *concurrence* and *support* of the President, and the other heads of department. You perceive how difficult it is to prevent these lawless invasions of other countries, but we shall do all we can. One of our great sources both of present difficulties and future dangers, Mexico, has a miserable government, is full of factions, and with finances utterly deranged. Her very weakness is threatening to us. I fear her whole frame of government may fall to pieces, inviting aggression and exciting cupidity in all quarters. If I were confident such a line of policy could be steadily carried out by the United States government, I should think it deserved great consideration,—whether it would not be wise in us to uphold Mexico and save her government from disunion, for the reason that it is better for us that Mexico should be able to maintain an independent government, than that she should break to pieces and fall into other hands, even though those hands were our own. This whole subject gives me great uneasiness.

I am very anxious to hear what Lord Palmerston says about the case of the *Prometheus*. Depend upon it, there will be no security for the continuance of peace in that quarter, until the British withdraw from Greytown. The notion that British officers and agents hold that place only in behalf of the Mosquito King, and as his agents, strikes some people as being ridiculous, and others as being an offensive and provoking pretence. I am quite at a loss to know what importance there is in the retention of this miserable town by England, to justify all the hazards of collision which her continued possession of it will certainly entail upon her and us. When Sir Henry Bulwer went to England I looked for his speedy return, and I thought we should be able to bring matters to a final and amicable settlement. I hope you lose no proper opportunity of urging the necessity of such a settlement upon the attention of Lord Palmerston. At the present moment, no part of our relations with England is so critical and so ominous of evil as this petty business.

You cannot fail to see how very probable it is that a more warlike administration than that which now exists is likely to come into power fifteen months hence. There is not only existing among us a spirit favorable to further territorial acquisition, but a zeal also for intervention in the affairs of other states, of a fearful character and already of considerable extent.

This spirit has gained great strength and vivacity from Kossuth's visit and speeches. At one time the whole—or nearly the whole—city of New York seemed quite crazy. The fever however is abating. It has met cooling influences from sober minds, North and South. I suppose it will be revived here, to some degree, as Kossuth comes here to-day, and a large section of the Democratic party intend taking advantage of his presence to bring the country, if they can, to the doctrine and the practice of intervention. I am sure you see, and I wish others might see, the expediency and importance of settling everything connected with England without delay.[1]

Yours always truly,
DANIEL WEBSTER.

———

(To William C. Rives.[2])

[31 DEC. 1851]

Your despatches have been regularly received up to the 18th of this month.

The movement made by the President of the Republic of France, on the second instant, created surprise here, as well as with you, not only by the boldness & extent of its purpose, but also by the secrecy with which preparation for it had been made, the suddenness of its execution, & the success which appeared to have attended it. Events however had already arisen, sufficient to notify sagacious observers, that the Government of France had arrived at the brink of a momentous crisis. No one could well doubt this, after the Debate in the assembly on the Bill for

———

[1] This letter to Lawrence in London is reprinted from the "Memoir of Abbott Lawrence," p. 87.
[2] United States Minister to France.

enforcing the responsibility of the President & his ministers, after the appearance of the articles in the *Constitutional & Moniteur*, & after the President's Discourse on the twenty fifth of Nov'r, on the occasion of delivering the medals to the artists who had taken part in the Exhibition in London.

Unfortunately, the whole political Government of France, by the late Constitution, was vested in one numerous Assembly, & in the President. There was no third power, no check, no mediator, or moderator, between these, if disagreement should arise, & actual conflict be threatened.

The Assembly and the President were destined to separate forces, both essentially uncontrolled, & if they should come to be opposing forces, & should rush into collision, it was obvious enough that the destruction of one or the other must be the consequence.

This form of constructing a Constitutional Governor was a fatal error, & it is strange that the French People, with their own history before them ever, did not perceive that, which from the first, was sufficiently visible to discerning & reflective minds. It is impossible to unite public Liberty with the safety of society, & the security of persons & property, without guards & balances, & strong barriers, not only against the alleged exercise of the Executive power, but also against the impulsive, sudden & impetuous action of popular bodies.

Despotism may be, & usually is, quite simple in its form of national rule. Where all are subject to the will of one, it is sufficient that the will of that one be expressed; & this, of course, is a short process. But true Republican Liberty cannot subsist without a system of efficient restraints, imposed upon all who exercise political power. Hence the proposition, apparently paradoxical, is strictly true, that Liberty consists in restraint; that is to say, the Liberty of each individual is in proportion to the restraint imposed on other individuals, & public bodies, who might otherwise have the power, as well as the disposition, to do him wrong. Republican Governments, in their fundamental constitutions, in their legislative, & in their judicial administration, must necessarily have something of complexity; and altho' such Governments may sometimes find themselves embarrassed by too much regulation, it is a great mistake to imagine that simplification is a process by which Public Liberty is either secured, or improved. Simplification belongs to Despotisms; regulation belongs to Republics.

It was quite natural that you should be in no haste to appear at the Public reception of the President, after the overthrow of the written Republican Constitution of France. You sympathize, in this respect, with the great body of your countrymen. If that overthrow had become necessary, its necessity is deeply to be deplored; because however imperfect its structure, it was the only great Republican Government existing in Europe, & all Americans wished its success. We feel as if the catastrophe which has befallen it may weaken the faith of mankind in the permanency & solidity of Republican Institutions. Nevertheless, & although our own Government is now the only great Republic on earth, we cling to its principles with increased affection. Long experience has convinced us of its practicability to do good, & its power to maintain Liberty & order. We know that it has conferred the greatest blessings on the country, & raised her to eminence & distinction among the nations; & if we are destined to stand, the only great Republican Nation, so we shall still stand.

Before this reaches you, the election in hand will be over, & if, as is probable, a decided majority of the People should be found to support the President, the course of duty for you will become plain.

From President Washington's time down to the present day, it has been a principle, always acknowledged by the United States that every Nation possesses a right to Govern itself according to its own will, to change its institutions at discretion, & to transact its business thro whatever agents it may think proper to employ. Whatever form of Government may exist in a country, if it be founded on the assent of the People, and appear to be seated & permanent the U. S. considers it as lawfully established. This cardinal point in our policy has been strongly illustrated by recognizing the many forms of political power which have been successively adopted in France in the series of Revolutions with which that Country has been visited. Our first Diplomatic relations with her commenced in the reign of Louis the 16th. After the dethronement and death of that Monarch, in 1793, the political authority of France was vested in a Convention, then in the Council of Ancients & the Council of Five Hundred with an Executive composed of a Directory; next came the Consulate, & next the Empire, & then the Restoration of the Bourbons; then the Revolution of 1831, the elevation of Louis Phillippe, of Orleans, upon the throne; then the Revolution which overthrew the power of Louis Phillippe, & expelled him from the Country; then came the Dictatorship of Gen'l Cavaignac & the Provisional Government; which in its turn, was succeeded by the Late Republic; & the election of Louis Napoleon Bonaparte as President. Throughout the whole of this series of change, the Government of the United States has conducted itself in that conformity to the original principles, adopted by Washington, & made known to our Diplomatic agents abroad, & to the Nations of the world, by Mr. Jefferson's letter to Mr. Gouverneur Morris of the 12th of March 1793. If it has been found somewhat difficult to keep up with these changes the Government of the United States has, nevertheless, kept up with them, & if the French People have now in fact made another, we have no choice but to acknowledge that also; and as the Diplomatic Representative of your Country in France, you will act as your predecessors have acted, & conform to what appears to be settled National Authority. And while we shall most deeply regret, if after so many years of struggle, for liberty and popular institutions, after so many years of war & so much shedding of blood, for the cause, or in the name of Civil liberty it shall be found that France has failed to obtain that great object, & to secure its durability, our ancient ally, has still our good wishes, for her prosperity & happiness & we are bound to leave to her, the choice of means, for the promotion of those ends.[1]

(To Mon. de Sartiges.)

[WASHINGTON Feby 6. 1852]

I am greatly obliged to Mr Sartiges for his unequalled specimen of French Brandy. I do not think I ever tasted any so soft & fine: and I will cordially thank Mr Sartiges to put me in the right way to obtain some of the same quality from France.

D. W.

I am quite obliged to you, My dear Mr. Sartiges, for the present of a most Beautiful Portrait of the French President. It indicates character. I shall give a conspicuous place, in my salon.

We are, My dear Mr Sartiges, Republicans, thoroughly attached to popular, Representative Governments. None else could be possibly established among us. But we admit that one condition is peculiar & what suits us may not, in the opinion of

---

[1] This draft of the letter is in Webster's hand.

others, be suitable to them.   All must admit the admirable ability
with which recent transactions in France[1] have been conducted;
& for my part, seeing the almost unanimous Choice of the whole
people of France, I respect their opinions & wishes & hope, most
earnestly, that all things may result in the prosperity and happiness of France.

Yrs with entire regard

DANL WEBSTER.

(To Joseph B. Varnum, Jr.)

Private.

WASHINGTON Feb 7th. [1852]

Your letter of the 3rd instant was received two days ago; after
I had written an answer to the Committee.   I think it my duty to
state to you exactly how I stand, in regard to the question of
going to New York & making a public address.

One the 9th of May last, a most respectable committee repre-
senting 1000 of the citizens of New York invited me to address
the people of that city, upon public subjects.   I could not at
that time comply with their invitation, but signified that I might
do so at a future day.   Afterwards at various places in your
State I had occasions to express my political sentiments fully and
at large; and it is hardly probable that there will be any considerable wish to hear me further.   Nevertheless this partial obligation is still upon me and I have written to know whether there be
now any wish that it should be fulfilled.   If so I shall present
myself at New York about the 21st or 23rd to fulfil my undertaking[2]—   You will believe me, my dear Sir, when I say, that
in Political discourses, I often refer to the character of Washington, & when so doing never fail to express the highest admiration of his wisdom & patriotism,   Yet a regular discourse
on his "character and services" would be quite too considerable
an undertaking for me under present circumstances to make.

What I think of his character and services has been said very
many times, and others may be found, who, although they may
have said less of his character, may yet have studied it more
deeply and be able to present it in new and more striking lights.
I hope you and the Committee will appreciate the entire sincerity

---

[1] Refers to the Coup d'État of December 2. 1851.

[2] The editor can find no evidence that Webster ever gave the New York
address.

with which I make these remarks. If I should be in New York, I shall attend your celebration with the greatest pleasure and have the opportunity, I hope, of making my profoundly grateful acknowledgements to the committee and all their friends

Yours with entire regard

DANL WEBSTER.

(To Abbott Lawrence.)

WASHINGTON, Jan: 18, 1852

My Dear Sir:

I received this morning Your official Despatches of the 31st. Decr. and 2″ of January, and your very acceptable private Letter of the last mentioned date. I entirely approve of your conduct, in regard to the case of the "Prometheus", and am quite sure the President will approve it with equal cordiality. We are now sure of removing that source of danger, and difficulty between the two countries.

I am happy to be remembered by Lord Granville, whom, on my part, I recollect very well, I had the pleasure of seeing him in Paris, in 1839, and also, for a short time, at Chatsworth. All accounts speak well of him and his appointment to hold the seals of the Foreign office in England is and will be, regarded here, as an omen for the continuance of peace and friendship between the two countries. I will thank you to make a point of calling upon him, and tendering him my best respects, as well as my congratulations on the eminent distinction bestowed upon him by the Queen.

I feel quite unwilling to put Sir Henry Bulwer to the inconvenience of a winter's voyage across the Atlantic.

In my last private letter, I suggested that it would be quite agreeable to me to treat with Mr. Crampton. Sir Henry is very acceptable, and much regarded here. If he can come back to us, a few months hence, we shall be very glad to see him.

I shall probably, tomorrow, send to Congress a copy of my letter to you respecting the "Prometheus", with an extract from your Despatch of the 2. of January. The "note" promised by Lord Granville at 1/2 past 3, on the 2nd not having been received on that day in time for the mail, will of course be forwarded by the next conveyance. Meantime, your statement that Lord Granville has given assurance, "that if the facts are found, on the official reports of the British Officers to be such as stated in your note, the British Government would express their disapproval of the whole matter", will give great satisfaction here.

I write this at my house in the midst of a violent snow storm, and shall send it by a special messenger to Boston, to insure its arrival in season for the steam Packet of the 21st.—

I am yours truly

DANL WEBSTER

Hon. Abbott Lawrence—

P. S.   There are difficulties about the Nicaragua question of several kinds.   Mr. Marcoletta, who is here, says there is no Government in Nicaragua, which he can properly represent, or which can give him instructions.   Mr. Kerr, our Charge' d'Affaires, has never been able as yet, to find any authority to which he could present his credentials.   We wish to have as little to do with these Central American States as possible; our object being, solely or mainly, to give proper protection to the inter-oceanic Canal, contemplated across the Isthmus, in that quarter.

I wish you to suggest to Lord Granville, and converse with him fully on the points, that the English possession of Greytown is almost certain to create occasions for discontent or collision. I have understood that Lord Palmerston was willing it should be ceded to Costa Rica.   If so, why should England be not willing to let Nicaragua have it?

You know that [our] Government, has never been satisfied that Mosquito had a title to the place.   Perhaps Lord Granville would be willing to re-consider, and re-examine that question.

My general idea is, that the U. S. and England should agree, that the police and municipal authority should be in Nicaragua; that Grey-town or St Juan should be a Freeport; that proper regulations, respecting it should be framed; and that Nicaragua should be effectually persuaded to conform to such regulations.

Such is my general notion.

[D. WEBSTER]

(To Franklin Haven.)

Confidential

My dear Sir   WASHINGTON Feby 26, [1852]

I know not whether it be of any importance whether you are here or not yet it may be as well that you should know, that the

decision in the Gaines Case will be made on Monday next at 12.—
Judge Catron delivers the opinion— Judge Wayne dissenting
& delivers a long argumentative opinion addressed to the majority—it goes off on a technicality—this information is strictly
Confidential—being so given to me—as you are my other self—
it is no breach of Confidence to let the soul know that which the
ear heareth—

DANL WEBSTER

(To Millard Fillmore.)

To the President,   NEW YORK Feb 27. [1852]
    My dear Sir,
    I feel greatly concerned at the present state of our affairs with
Mexico.[1] We are making, I fear, no advances toward the accomplishment of the important object which we have in view, and
I think it my duty to suggest some thoughts for your consideration, under the conviction that some new step should be taken
without loss of time.
    First, It is quite evident that Mr. Letcher stands in need of
aid and assistance, although I do not speak this to derogate in
any way from the fidelity or value of his services.   Shall we send
out some competent and energetic person to consult and co-
operate with Mr. Letcher without any official authority & pay
him out of the contingent fund?
    Second, Shall an instruction be sent to Mr. Letcher to be laid
by him, in *totidam verbis* before the Mexican Govt. relating the
history of the transactions connected with the Tehuantepec cause,
repeating our belief of the loyalty and binding force, of the
grant to Garay & his assigns and setting forth in terms, somewhat stronger than we have heretofore used, our expectation that
the treaty will be ratified & an intimation that it is the purpose
of this Govt. to assert the rights of the Company.
    Third. Or would it not be well to instruct Mr. Letcher at once
to withdraw the proposition, heretofore made, to buy off our
obligation, under the 12th article of the Treaty, and to Express
plainly, as the ground of this instruction, an apparent disposition on the part of Mexico, to hold out for unreasonable terms,
& also to delay the settlement of the other question.
    These ideas are stated only for your consideration.   Better

---

[1] See Curtis' "Life of Webster," vol. ii, pp. 542-546.

modes of proceeding may occur to you & the other gentlemen of the Cabinet, fit to decide your course; but I think the time has come for doing something decisive.

Yours always truly,

D. W.

(To Peter Harvey.)

My Dear Sir,   WASHINGTON March 5th 1852
    I reached here in safety, on Wednesday night, the third inst. I saw the President yesterday.   He was very civil and kind, but I had no particular conversation with him.   Gen. Scott, you will perceive, is backing out from his Native Americanism.
    Much of the future will depend on what transpires this Evening in New York—   Say to Mr Haven, I shall write him next mail.   Mr Ashmun left us this morning to return in a week.—
    Yours always, with my best, very best, regards to Mrs Harvey. I think we had a nice time in New York.

DANL. WEBSTER.

(G. J. Abbott [1] (?) to Peter Harvey. (?)

My Dear Sir,   WASHINGTON, April 13th. 1852.
    Political things are becoming very interesting here, and the time is come for decisive action.   The friends of Mr. Webster think that his prospects are decisively brightening, and yield good encouragement.
    The presentation of things is this.—   The Whigs of the South generally have nominated Mr. Fillmore.[2]   This they have done not only from a proper regard for him, but from the fact of his position, which seems to entitle him to notice, but we do not know a man from any Southern State, who would not support Mr. Webster as cheerfully as Mr. Fillmore, and some of them with even more zeal; and, at the same time, it seems to be conceded, on all hands, except by a few of Mr. Fillmore's immediate, personal friends, that he cannot carry New York, while, on the other hand, the Union men are active and zealous for Mr.

---

[1] Apparently the same hand as many of Daniel Webster's letters to Fillmore, which were written by Abbott. Daniel Webster's clerk.
[2] See for a general account of the Convention and nominations, Rhodes "History of United States," vol. i, pp. 253-259.

Webster, as are some of those who have been reckoned as the followers of Mr. Seward. Even the Tribune says, that Mr. Webster can carry New York, although it maintains that it is impossible for Mr. Fillmore to do so. These truths respecting New York will be made manifest in the Convention, and, without the help of New York, there is no chance of electing a Whig President.

The whole South is decidedly against Gen. Scott, and the foreign vote will be against him also, on account of his famous letter to the native Americans; and, what is remarkable,—the native Americans themselves are against him, to a man. It is not supposed that, upon the whole, he has any considerable chance.

Now, my Dear Sir, friends here have assigned one important duty to you, and that is, to take pains to see immediately every delegate, chosen to the Convention from New Hampshire, and from Vermont and arrange matters with them, so that they shall adhere, out and out, for Mr. Webster, not to give him a first vote merely, or to vote for him two or three times, and then go off from some other candidate, or to give out a disposition of—[1]

(From Chas. W. March.)

Dear Sir.   NEW YORK April 8. 1852.

Fairbanks of Charlestown came in last night. He tells me that the Scott-men in Massachusetts, aided by the Custom-House, are working energetically, and boast that they will have their delegates, also in the National Convention. Mr. Fairbanks says that it was through the influence of Greeley, he was left out of the State Central Committee this year, and a Scott-man substituted— and that Greeley with Geo. Morey &c promise the vote of the State ultimately for Scott, in Convention. At the same time, Mr. Fairbanks contends that the removal of Greeley, at this late hour of the administration would be an impolitic proceeding. But if he is not to be removed, it strikes me he should be muzzled, and Mr. Corwin could do it, at least, his machinations should be met and thwarted.

Kellogg, the ejected marshal of the Northern District of New York, has been here, on his return home from Washington. He

---

[1] Here the letter breaks off abruptly, the next sheet being lost.

LETTERS OF DANIEL WEBSTER

tells me that he has none but kind feelings towards you, and that
he only supports Scott as available. If the latter be not nominated in Convention he shall go for you. The Legislature-cau-
cus, you will see has expressed a choice for Scott. This was not
unexpected, and may not be important. It is intended more as a
demonstration against Fillmore— This is intended to operate
elsewhere—no one of course believes it here. The Mirror has
had a series of articles lately in favor of Mr. Fillmore, not injudiciously written upon the whole— Fuller promises, that I
shall insert an equal number for you. The paper has not much
circulation but has its influence nevertheless. I requested Raymond to let me write a series of articles in your favor, for the
"Times"—but he declines, on the ground that he wishes to take
no part in the nomination. He is however for Scott, but ready
to be influenced by Mr. Draper &c

Your friends here meet frequently at their rooms in the Astor,
and report progress. Mr. Grinnell is very busy, enthusiastic and
sanguine. He says that with thirty firm men in Convention, you
can control its vote—and I make it certain that unless we are most
egregiously deceived, you will have more than forty, giving to
Mr Fillmore the unanimous South, *which he will not have.*

I saw Fuller, M. C. from Pennsylvania last night— He says
that he prefers you to any man, but that his State is for Scott.
Still he says there is great dissatisfaction that the State Convention should have appointed the whole delegation to the National
Convention instead of leaving the matter to the Districts, as
heretofore. The consequence will be in his opinion that, as some
delegates had been already appointed by Districts, there will be
contested cases before the National Convention. How would it
do for your friends quietly to elect delegates by Districts and
insist upon the time-sanctioned custom.

Mr. Ashmun writes me that he shall go to Washington early in
the week—

Ever most respy & truly yrs
CHS. W. MARCH

(From Chas. W. March.)

NEW YORK April 12. 52.

Dear Sir

Gov. Jones and Mr. Ewing of Ky. arrived here Saturday
night, on an invitation to be present at the "Clay Festival" this

evening. The invitation was given for more than an ordinary compliment. It means mischief. The most active men of the Clay Club,—Ulman, Nat. Blunt, Nich. Carroll &c. propose to bring forward Gov. Jones as the man to catch Mr. Clay's mantle as that distinguished gentleman departs—and it is not to be supposed that the Governor is ignorant of this intention. Mr. Ewing a representative from Kentucky and a protegé of Mr. Clay told me two months since in Washington—that he looked upon Jones as the most available candidate for the Presidency this coming election. I do not believe however that the movement, unless earnestly responded to at the South, will have any other result than to detach some of Mr. Fillmore's friends from his cause. I have seen a great deal of Gov. Jones since he has been here, and, to do him justice, must say, that he is invariably kind in his language towards you. He says that Mr. Fillmore's nomination, which otherwise could have been received, will not be defeated by the inconsiderate conduct of such friends as Humphrey Marshal, Cabell &c.

Mr. Draper told me last evening that he hoped such an arrangement would be effected between your friends in this city and those of General Scott as to divide the delegation between you & him—that the General's friends will not be hostile to you either in the city or out of it, but would go in with you, and secure your nomination, if the South on leaving Fillmore take you up. This is the consummation to which we would arrive, and perhaps this, is the way in which it is to be easiest accomplished. I do not find among the delegates [up] to this time elected from the State favorable to Gen. Scott, any unkind feeling towards you—

I wrote Mr. Curtis Saturday of my fears about certain districts in Massachusetts, to which I begged him to call your attention. I trust you will hold with me that it is of paramount importance to secure the proper men from Massachusetts. One traitor there could do us more injury than fifty opponents in other States— as was proved by the conduct and insinuations of Lunt in the last convention— I shall write Mr. Harvey on the subject by todays mail. Mr. Ashmun will be here to-night, and I will bring the subject before him, and get him to write.

Great exertions have been made to get up an enthusiastic meeting for the Clay demonstration to-night—which so far as numbers are concerned will doubtless be successful.

Ever most resp'y & truly

CHAS. W. MARCH.

(From G. A. Tavenner.[1])

Hon Daniel Webster   ALEXANDRIA April 8" /52.
    Sir
    The National reputation which you have earned, the position
you occupy, before the Country, as one of its leading statesmen,
And more than all, your fidelity to great National Whig principles, must be my excuse for addressing you upon a subject, now
of peculiar interest to the Whig party of the south—
    It cannot be denied that in all the sectional contests that have
agitated and convulsed the country, the Whigs of the south have
shown a conservative—a national spirit.   They have always been
ready to give a cordial support to northern men however they
might differ from them on abstract questions, provided they were
willing to abide by, and sustain the compromises of the constitution.   After the adoption by Congress of the series of measures
known as the compromise, and after the evidence of acquiescence
both at the North and the South in those measures, and more especially after the decided expression by the Whig caucus at the
commencement of the present session of Congress, we had supposed that, the question of slavery would no longer prevent concert of action among the Whigs in the various sections of the
union, but that an effort would be made to give success to the
principles of the adjustment bill so essential to the best interests
of the country.
    If however the recent vote in the House of Representatives on
the resolutions of Messrs Jackson and Hillyer[2] be a fair indication of public sentiment at the north—if the question of the fugitive slave law is again to be made the subject of agitation—if
this plain provision of the constitution is to be considered of no
binding force and obligation upon the north, then the paths of
the north and the south diverge.
    The constitution guarantees to every section its rights.   It
imposes duties which no section is at liberty to disregard, and so
far as the Whig party of the south is concerned I cannot honestly
act with those who treat as a thing of naught its sacred obligations.   It is to be hoped however that this is not the purpose
of northern Whigs.   It is to be hoped that, the vote on the resolutions to which we have referred does not express the sentiment

---

[1] A Virginia politician.   See Webster's reply.
[2] See "Congressional Globe," vol. xxiv, part 2, p. 983.   The resolution
recognized the binding power of the Compromise of 1850.

of the whig party at the north on the subjects to which they relate. You have the means of knowing the state of public sentiment at the north. You have been identified with no section in sectional controversies. You occupy a position from which you can speak plainly, and I doubt not your advice will be heeded. We are aware that you will differ from many southern whigs on the abstract question of slavery but we also know that you have always stood forth the bold and fearless defender of the constitution and so as that instrument guarantees them to us you have been the advocate of the *rights of the south.* What then in your opinion has the south a right to expect from the north? Upon what platform are the whigs north and south to stand in the coming presidential contest? Is the constitution to be the bond of Union between them? Are the late adjustment measures to be considered a final settlement in principle and substance of all the subjects which they embrace or is the whig party henceforth to be a sectional instead of a great national party. These are questions which address themselves to the friends of the Constitution to the friends of the Union. They are questions upon which the patriotic of all parties should speak out their sentiments. May we not hope that we shall have the benefit of your counsel?

Very Respectfully Your Obt. Svt.

G. A. Tavenner

(To G. A. Tavenner.[1])

Dear Sir,   Washington, April 9. 1852

I have the honor to acknowledge the receipt of your letter of the 8th inst., and thank you for what you are pleased to say, of my fidelity, to great national Whig principles. I trust, there is not a man in the country who doubts my approbation of those measures, which are usually called "Compromise Measures," or my fixed determination to uphold them steadily & firmly. Nothing but a deep sense of duty, led me to take the part which I did take, in bringing about their adoption by Congress, and that same sense of duty, remains with unabated force. I am of opinion that those measures, one and all, were necessary and expedient, and ought to be adhered to, by all friends of the Constitu-

---

[1] See Tavenner's letter to Webster. This letter is copied from the original draft of the letter sent.

tion, and all lovers of their country. That one among them, which appears to have given the greatest dissatisfaction, I mean the Fugitive Slave Law, I hold to be a law, entirely Constitutional, highly proper, and absolutely essential to the peace of the country. Such a law is demanded by the plain written words of the Constitution; and how any man, can wish to abrogate or destroy it, & at the same time say, that he is a supporter of the Constitution, and willing to adhere to those provisions in it, which are clear & positive injunctions and restraints, passes my power of comprehension. My belief is, that when the passions of men subside, and reason and true patriotism, are allowed to have their proper sway, the public mind, north and south, will come to a proper state upon these questions. I do not believe that further agitation, can make any considerable progress at the north. The great mass of the people, I am sure, are sound, and have no wish to interfere with such things, as are, by the Constitution placed under the exclusive control of the separate states. I have noticed, indeed, not without regret, certain proceedings to which you have alluded, and in regard to these, I have to say, that gentlemen may not think it necessary, or proper, that they should be called upon, to affirm, by resolution, that, which is already the existing law of the land. That any positive movement, to repeal or alter, any or all, the Compromise Measures, would meet with any general encouragement, or support, I do not at all believe. But however that may be, my own sentiments remain, and are likely to remain, quite unchanged. I am in favor of upholding the Constitution, in the general, and all its particulars. I am in favor of respecting its authority and obeying its injunctions; and to the end of my life, shall do all in my power, to fulfill, honestly and faithfully, all its provisions. I look upon the Compromise Measures, as a just proper, fair, and final adjustment of the questions to which they relate; and no re-agitation of those questions, no new opening of them, no effort to create dissatisfaction with them, will ever receive from me the least countenance or support, concurrence or approval, at any time, or under any circumstances.[1]

I am, with regard Your obt. servt

---

[1] Charles W. March, in a letter dated New York, April 15, 1852, says: "Your letter to Mr. Tavenner of Va. is well received here. I have heard no one speak against it and the press, with the exception of the Evening Post, always captious and censorious and unjust where your name is mentioned— speak favorably of it."

(Hiram Ketchum to Peter Harvey.[1])

Private

My dear Sir   MONDAY. Apl. 12", 1852.

The young men make a great demonstration on the evening of
Monday 19th. Mr. Stevenson, among other speakers, is I learn
invited to be present. Now I have been at great pains to get up
this meeting hoping, and believing, it would produce a new era
in our proceedings—an era of enthusiasm. This is what we
want, and I desire our friend S. to know that the purpose is to
set the prairie on fire. An excellent address is prepared, and the
young men will get up spirited resolutions. It is not exclusively
a Whig meeting, but a meeting of young men. The address
will be to the young men of the United States. It will cost us a
great deal to get certain portions of our press right—that is to
say we shall have to pay for an immense issue of papers. Not
less than 20000 extras containing the proceedings of the meeting
will be issued. Say this to our friend S. I am now arranging
for this purpose

Bye the bye in respect to money the only safe and efficient way
is to let a number of rich men say to one of their number advance
whatever is necessary and we will see you re-funded—or if any
friend wishes to limit the amount for which he wishes to be held
liable let him say not exceeding $—— No man has paid any
thing but M. H. Grinnell and he has paid more than $3000—he
knows however to whom to look. We must fight the battle to
win, and we can win. I cannot enter into particulars now, but
we feel strong confidence, and are vigorously at work.

                         Yrs truly

                              H. KETCHUM

(To C. J. McCurdy.)

(Private)

                         30TH APRIL, 1852.

We suppose it is not the purpose of Mr. Hülseman the Austrian Charge d'Affaires here, to remain in the Country. His
relations with this Department to which he was accredited, have
not been amicable, for some time; & his conduct, in some respects,
has been so extremely irregular, that I was much inclined some
months ago, to sngnify that his presence here was not longer de-

---

[1] Harvey, of course, represented Webster.

sirable.   But it was thought better, on the whole, that his withdrawal should be his own voluntary act.

I leave Washington today, for my own residence, & shall be absent ten or twenty days, & on my return I shall write you, particularly, on this subject, stating fully what has occurred, and if you think proper you may, on receipt of this, intimate this purpose to the Austrian Secretary of State, for Foreign Affairs; & you may state distinctly, at the same time, that neither the President nor myself have the slightest intention of treating the Austrian Government with disrespect, the complaint is personal, & confined to Mr Hülseman.

[D. WEBSTER]

(To D. Fletcher Webster.)

Dear Fletcher   FRIDAY 1 O clock. [May. 1852]

I have yrs of yesterday, contain'g an acct. of the meet'g &c.— I had intended, before its receipt, to say someth'g on the political contents of your last.

It seems to me, with great deference, that things are not in a good way.   Nobody does any thing, on our side.

Notwithstanding all the "good feel'g," results appear always adverse.   You say, today, that the Atlas Clique have managed to elect their own Deputy,—as you fear; & that Mr Harvey condemns the whole set.   But what does Mr Harvey propose to do?—

Really, I am tired of hear'g any thing upon this subject, unless it is a proposition *to do someth'g*.   If any friends wish to meet to consult *for action*, I will meet with them, at any time, if not confined to my home.   But I have had eno. of cheer'g prospects & sicken'g results.   When is "the meeting" to be called?— & when held.   I wish you, & Mr. Harvey, would go & pass an hour with Mr. Everett—and come to some conclusions, abt. someth'g.

Yrs.   D. W.

(Edward Curtis (?) to Peter Harvey.)

Peter Harvey—   WASHINGTON D. C. 4" May 1852.

My dear Sir—If your Bay State Delegates shall have no

Lunts among them, and, by their example, shall keep firm all the New England delegates that have been chosen as Webster men, our friend stands a good chance to be nominated.   There is *now* no reason to believe that Scott will be nominated, unless the Webster men of the North *desert*, and join the drum & fife party. Those who see Scott, here, every day, say that he swears by the edge of his sword, that he will *not* make any promise or declaration about the Compromise.   He says to Southern Men that he is as much of a Compromise man as Mr. Webster; but he will get no Southern vote in the Convention, unless he *come out*, with a declaration of the Compromise faith.   If he make such a proclamation of his adherence to the Compromise he will lose a *large* share of his Northern supporters, and will get few or no votes from the South.

If Scott can hire the support in the Convention, of so many delegates from the free-states, including deserters in New England of delegates chosen for Mr. Webster, as to get a majority, & be nominated, it is agreed, all around the C——, that the Southern Whigs will go in for the Democratic Candidates (being some man sound on the Compromise) and elect him over Scott. The Southern men who bolted from the Caucus do not declare this, in so many words; but it is what they mean—they will probably attend the Convention, and if our Webster delegates give way, and Scott is thus nominated, they will have another meeting, and turn in to the support of the Democratic Candidate, if he *be*, as he will be sound & firm on the Compromise question.   On the other hand, Peter, if the North, (I mean the Webster force limited as it is) *will not give up, the South will not keep back.* The Fillmore men of the South, seeing the danger of having Scott, and having voted for Fillmore two or three times, will cheerfully join themselves to the supporters of Mr. Webster, and nominate him.   Besides, I know, if you do not, that the Scott men, of the *State of New York*, would not go and hang themselves, if General Scott failing of a southern vote should not get quite enough in other states for a nomination.   So that they could keep Fillmore from having a majority, they would help the South, & and the N. E. States to nominate Mr. Webster.   Peter, take courage & faint not.   Now is the day.   The great superiority of Mr. Webster over all other Statesmen & orators was never so acknowledged by the mass of our people as *at this time*.   His mental efforts are more distinguished for force and variety, this year, than ever. & this is generally acknowledged.   Peter, I am directed to draw upon you. (ask Mr. Horn if I am not,) for the enormous sum of $300. for the support of domestic missions— the missionaries are out, and I am in, for twice that sum since Mr. Horn was here.

Allow me to say that Mr. Warren[1] of Bunker Hill, is one of most sensible, judicious and practical D. W. men that I have ever seen in Washington from the Bay State— He has been here a few days— He has seen & made himself well acquainted with everybody here whom it was profitable to know & confer with.

———

(D. Fletcher Webster to Peter Harvey.)

My dear Harvey   SUNDAY, [May 9. 1852]
    Father is doing very well. He has only strained his *wrists.*[2] Come down & see him. He will be here a week or more. He cannot write himself or he would to you.

                              Yr always
                                      F WEBSTER.

———

(Hiram Ketchum to Peter Harvey.)

My dear Sir   MONDAY May 10—1852—
    I returned from Washington last evg. While I was there, less than two days, I assisted in organizing a club of good fellows at Washington to keep an open room, and to entertain delegates and other important men. Ed Curtis is treasurer, and for their immediate use their club will want $1000—one half of which must come from this place. I desire Curtis to be written to at once by your committee. We must now use our time, and means to the very best advantage.

    It is the universal sentiment—*Let not Mr. Webster make another Speech.* I have received repeated requests to write Mr. Webster to this effect. I want you to say it to him, and it is my earnest request that he speak no more.

                              Very truly
                                      HIRAM KETCHUM.

---

    [1] G. Washington Warren.
    [2] Webster was injured by a fall from his carriage. See account by Lanman in Curtis' "Life of Webster," vol. ii, p. 606.

(From Millard Fillmore.)

My Dear Sir,   WASHINGTON CITY, May, 20th 1852.

Yours of the 12th inst. came duly to hand, but I have delayed answering it, for the purpose of seeing a translation of Mr. Hülsemann's letter, which I did not get until yesterday. I am exceedingly gratified to learn that your injury was not so severe but that we may soon hope to see you with us again. The anecdote, which you relate of your old friend who watched you so intently in the moment of danger, is truly touching, and the graphic manner in which you have described it presents a scene, which would form a beautiful subject for a painting. It must have been some gratification, at least, amid your afflictions to witness the universal sympathy at your misfortune, and the deep interest which everyone took in your recovery. I perceive, by the papers, that you are soon to speak at Faneuil Hall, and I therefore infer, that, with the exception of your hands and arms, you are quite recovered.

In regard to a further reply to Mr. Hülsemann's letter we will consider of that when you return. My own impression is, however, that the most dignified as well as expedient course for us, will be, to limit the reply or communication to Mr. Mc. Curdy to that part of it which complains of the disclosure of his communications by the State Department. Mr. Bodisco expressed a doubt to me whether he is the "Hülsemann," the Author of the Travels in America, which were so justly and severely criticised in the North American Review. But whether he be or not, it seems to me that he is hardly worth, as you say, "a discharge of the lower tier," and it might serve further to irritate the Austrian Government, with which it is our interest, if possible, to be on good terms.

The Mexican Minister has not yet been received, but probably will be on Saturday. I have a copy of his address, which is quite general with warm professions of friendship and a desire to maintain amicable relations between the two governments. I am a little apprehensive, from what President Arista says in his letter to me, that Mr. Letcher went farther than was intended, in *threatening* the Mexican government with an interruption of our peaceful relations in case she did not ratify the treaty. By assuming to treat with her, we certainly conceded, that she had a right either to adopt or reject the treaty. It was our duty, as well to the Tehuantepec Company as to the United States, to make every reasonable effort to secure this right of way and protect whatever rights the Company might have under the Garay grant, but the rights of the Company, like the rights of every other contractor with a foreign nation, or its subjects, are rights growing out of a private contract, and if the Mexican government refuses to fulfil that contract, the proprietors doubtless have a claim for pecuniary indemnity, but that is to be settled, like every other claim of this kind that our citizens may have against a foreign government.   President Arista insists, that they are willing to grant the right of way to our citizens, or others, who will construct the railroad.   But I infer, that the great objection to the Garay grant consists in the fact, that a large territory was granted with it, on each side of the proposed railroad, and a much larger territory was to be open to colonization, and that the Mexicans were justly apprehensive, that if the Americans established so large a colony on the Southern borders of their territory, that it might turn out to be another Texan colony which would involve their nation in war, and might result in another annexation; and, considering what has passed, these apprehensions were not unreasonable— Since you left, Mr. Hargous has submitted a proposition on the subject, which if adopted by the Administration, and sanctioned by Congress, would, I doubt not, finally result in a war between the two countries.   Certainly nothing has been left undone, that could have been done, to secure the rights of the Company and guarantee them by a treaty between Mexico and the United States; but the treaty has failed, and under such circumstances, that I am satisfied, that it can never be ratified, and I shall therefore now wait to see what propositions the new Mexican minister is authorized to make, and I doubt not you will be here before it is necessary to consider them.

I handed your letter to Mr. Hunter that he might copy for you that part of it which you desire.   The weather is yet quite cool, and a fire is not uncomfortable in the morning.   It would be agreeable at all times to have you here, and especially at the Council board, but yet there is nothing particularly pressing, and I beg of you, to make yourself contented and happy, without any unnecessary anxiety about matters here, until you shall feel your self perfectly restored and able to return, when I shall be most happy to welcome you.

I am your obt. servt.

MILLARD FILLMORE.

(Edward Curtis to P. Harvey.) (?)

WASHINGTON D. C. 25 May 1852

My dear Sir.

I recd your letter of April 20th. I concur with the feelings you express, in regard to Mr. Fillmore; but, if the N. E. delegates which, except Maine, have been counted for Mr. Webster would *stand firm*, not going off to Scott, the South will come in for Mr. Webster after a few votes for Fillmore. This is manifest, from the declarations of the leading Southern Whigs who go for Fillmore— They declare this, in the Southern Newspapers, at the meetings held in Alabama, last week, to choose Whig Delegates they resolved to go for Webster after "discharging their duty" to Mr. Fillmore— But if the Webster Whigs at the North, after a vote or two for him, desert and go for Scott, then the *game is up*—no chance is given to the South to turn from Fillmore to Webster.

It is *safe* for the Northern men, who wish to see Mr. Webster President, but who prefer Scott to Fillmore to *hold on for Webster without flinching*, because the figures show that Fillmore, with all his South, & South Western votes, will not have, and *cannot have* votes enough to nominate him. You know that many of the leaders of the Scott party, in New York, w'd prefer *Mr. Webster*, and if Scott be not nominated on the first Ballott, they will show the South that if they redeem their pledges to Mr. Webster they can nominate him. Everything depends upon our friends holding on— I repeat, that they run no risk whatever with Fillmore in holding on to Mr. Webster. With all the noise now made *Fillmore cannot get a majority*, and will be a cruel business in the Webster men of the North to go off for Scott before we give Mr. Webster a chance to get the South— If there were any danger of having Fillmore hoisted on us, by adhering to Mr. Webster, the case w'd be very different.

We have a *certainty* that Fillmore will fall short, though his vote will be large— Under these circumstance, there is no excuse for any body to quit Mr. Webster, who affects to prefer him.

We have a Webster Committee Room in this City, and we are doing our best to get ready for the convention.

Yours truly

EDWARD CURTIS.

530   LETTERS OF DANIEL WEBSTER

(Memorandum.[1])

[JUNE 14, 1852]

Suggestions for the establishment of friendly relations between Austria & the United States.—

An official note from the Secretary of State to the Austrian Chargé d'Affaires in Washington appears to be indispensable, and a preliminary & mutual understanding on the contents of the note is deemed necessary.

Without pretending in the least to dictate the terms of the note—the following points appear to be essential for the purpose.

It would be mentioned that the President had been confidentially informed by the Minister of a friendly power that after his recent arrival from Havana, Mr. Hülsemann had decided to leave Washington & return to Vienna & that he had come to this determination mainly on account of an incident connected with the reception of Kossuth and in consequence of his unpleasant position towards the Secretary of State.

The President has also been informed that his last verbal declaration to Mr. Hülsemann had been found satisfactory by the Austrian government, but that a certain public demonstration and the pending misunderstanding between Mr. Hülsemann & Mr. Webster, rendered it desirable that the verbal declaration of the President should be officially corroborated & in consequence of that desire Mr. Fillmore had authorized Mr. Webster to renew the assurance that the President most sincerely desired to see the former friendly relations completely re-established and to accomplish that object Mr. Webster was authorized to invite Mr. Hülsemann to résume forthwith his suspended intercourse with the American Government.

Mr. Webster could state in his note that he adhered entirely to the contents of the President's last declaration & it would be very courteous if Mr. Webster mentioned in his note his high respect for the Emperor of Austria & express his best wishes for the prosperity and the integrity of the Austrian Empire. Mr. Webster would then state that he was ready to renew the former friendly intercourse with Mr. Hülsemann and in so doing comply as much with the Presidents wishes as well as with his personal feelings.—

---

[1] In Webster's handwriting.

Mr. Webster will probably admit the propriety of sending his card to Mr. Hülsemann.   This courtesy would be highly appreciated.   Mr. Hülsemann would immediately return the visit in person and express the desire that the Secretary of State would enable Mr. Hülsemann to present his respects to the President in the usual way but without any speech.

A short notice to be inserted in the Republic stating that after having received friendly and satisfactory explanations Mr. Hülsemann, the Austrian Chargé d'Affaires, on his return from Havana, had resumed his position and his friendly relations with the American government.—

(To Millard Fillmore.)

(Private)

WASHINGTON June [17] 1852.

My Dear Sir,
   I have sent a communication to Baltimore this morning to have an end put to the pending controversy.[1]   I think it most probable you will be nominated before 1. o'clock.   But this is opinion merely.   Yrs.   D. W.

(Webster's Interview with Chas. A. Stetson.[2])

JUNE 1852

"When he, (Mr. Webster) came down from Washington, after the Baltimore Convention, I thought him feeble and very unwell; several gentlemen called to see him, who noticed it.   After a very serious conversation with him for some time in relation to his personal matter and the condition of politics, I left him.

Late in the day, as I came round the corner of the entry-way near his room, he was standing alone.   I walked up to him, and put my hand upon his breast, and said to him, 'I hope all is right here.'   'Yes, sir,' he replied, 'I am too near God to have a single heart burning against a human creature on the earth, but I have a chagrin as profound as my entire nature, and it is, that after having performed my duty to my southern brethren, *they had*

---

[1] The Whig Convention was then sitting at Baltimore, and General Scott's, Mr. Fillmore's, and Mr. Webster's names were before them.
[2] Account of an interview with Daniel Webster after the Baltimore Convention by his friend, Charles A. Stetson, of the Astor House.

neither the courage or kindness to place me on the record of that convention. I do not say I did not want the nomination, but I would rather have had *their record* than the nomination.' I was struck very forcibly with the manner and feeling with which he uttered these words."[1]

(From Chas. A. Stetson.[2])

ASTOR HOUSE June 29th. 1852.

My Dear Sir,

I have yielded, and you must not blame me, to the request of some old personal friends, to write a letter for Col. Howard of Michigan. I have no word for myself, no heart, had I a word, to write it. I feel like saying to Whig friends

"I hold it, Sir, that we shake hands, and part:
You, as your business, and desire, shall point you.—
For every man hath business, and desire,
Such as it is,—and for my own poor part,
Look you, I will go pray."

I will not trouble you again in these matters

Ever yours faithfully

C. A. STETSON.

(To Fletcher Webster.)

Secret

JULY 4. '52

My Dear Son

I confess I grow inclined to cross the Seas. I meet, here, so many causes of vexation, & humiliation, growing out of the events connected with the convention, that I am pretty much decided & determined, to leave the Department early in August, & either go abroad, or go into obscurity. You may mention this to Mr. Paige, but to no other soul. We leave on Tuesday.

Yrs affectionately

DANL WEBSTER

---

[1] This interview is taken from a newspaper clipping in the possession of Mr. C. E. Bliss, of Bangor, Me. The date and name of the paper cannot be ascertained. There is no one to vouch for the authenticity of the interview. See, however, the volume "Webster Centennial."

[2] Proprietor of the Astor House.

(To Edward Curtis.)

WASHINGTON—July 4" 1852.

My Best of Friends!

I send you a copy of my Speeches; but I write nothing on the blank leaf, but Your Name & my own.

I shall not, now or ever, attempt to thank you, for your affectionate and long continued attachment, and your unbounded Devotion to my character and fortunes.

May Almighty God bless you, and Yours!

DANL. WEBSTER.

(To Charles A. Stetson.)

WASHINGTON July 5th. 1852

My Dear Sir,

The Bar and Bench and others at Detroit have requested that the appointment of a Marshal might be delayed till they can be heard from.

I leave here tomorrow-morning, and hope to be with you tomorrow night.

I agree with you that it is time to shake hands[1] with some folks and part, and there are others I am willing to part with without shaking hands.

Yours truly,

DANL WEBSTER.

(To Millard Fillmore.)

NEW YORK, July 8th. 1852.

To the President,

My Dear Sir.

At Philadelphia a Despatch from Mr. Letcher was put into my hands, which I think of considerable importance, and which I send to the Department to day. When you shall have read it, there are several points to which I ask your attention.

1st. Shall not this Despatch be read to Mr. Crampton, on account of the favorable sentiments expressed by the British minister in Mexico? I know Mr. Doyle. He is a countryman of Mr. Crampton & a good tempered man.

---

[1] See Stetson's letter of June 29, 1852.

2nd. Does not this Despatch enhance the importance of a wise selection of a minister to Mexico?

3d. Would it not be well that I should inform Mr. Hargous, who is now here that the Mexican Government proposes a new contract, & that his Company should consider whether it would not be wise in them to send an agent immediately to Mexico to negotiate for that contract? You will perceive that Mexico is afraid of our reclamations in favor of the Company.

4th. Whether it might not be well that Mr. Hunter should write a note to the Mexican Minister to say, that if he has such instructions from his Government, as make it desirable for him to see me, & if he desire to escape for a few days from the hot weather of Washington, I will meet him in Boston at any time agreeable to himself.

Yours always truly

D. W.

(To John Stimpson.[1])

FRANKLIN July 13. 1852.

My Dear Sir,

I beg you to accept my sincere thanks, for your present of a Cane, made out of the old Ship Constitution, and also for the friendly expressions contained in the accompanying letter. The relic is both interesting and valuable, and I shall ever take pleasure in exhibiting it to my friends.

I remain Dear Sir, with high regard Your obt. Servt.

DAN. WEBSTER.

(From Chas. W. March.)   (?)

N. Y. JULY 14/52.

My dear Sir—

The Scott men are resorting to all kind of expedients to elect Genl. Scott, by attempting to impress upon the country that you had committed yourself to the support of their ticket— A Mr. Talmadge of this city is out in a letter to show you signified your intention to sustain the Whig party & argues that you go for *Scott*— It is too contemptible to treat seriously— I hope you will accept a nomination if tendered to you— No matter what

---

[1] Of Somerville, Mass.

your opponents may say or do?— Had Scott not recd the nomination it was agreed to break up the convention?— This is one of the reasons, why I feel anxious to have you accept in common with thousands of others, to prevent if possible the election of Scott under any contingency— A moments reflection will satisfy you that the suggestion is not ill advised nor impolitic— You have every thing to gain & nothing to lose. Had you not been treacherously dealt with you could not do it, but, what stronger reasons can be assigned to warrant you meeting the wishes of your friends & foiling the ambitious scheming of your opponents.

(To Millard Fillmore.)

Private & Confidential.)

MARSHFIELD Aug. 4. 1852.

My dear Sir;

Enclosed you will find the draught of two Treaties, prepared by Mr Crampton and myself,—one respecting Oregon, and one respecting Copy-right. I forward them in advance of my own arrival; to the end that you may have the longest time for their consideration. I think it very probable that you will be of opinion that, in the embarrassed state of the business before Congress, it will be hardly worth while to submit either of them to the Senate this Session. Indeed, in regard to the Oregon Treaty, the draught differs so far from Mr. Crampton's instructions, that he thinks it will be necessary for him, before he signs it, to consult his Government.

I have been informed of the flare-up in the Senate, yesterday respecting the Fisheries. I have very considerable alarm on this subject. Your enemies, and mine, among the Whigs, and the Young Americans among the Democrats, are very like to join in opposing the Administration and in embarrassing the State of our affairs with England. I have reflected much on the subject of these English orders; as well from the Home Government, as the Canadian Government, respecting interference with our vessels. In my opinion there is solid grounds for remonstrating against both independently of anything which has yet been suggested. Certainly, such seizures are not within the ordinary jurisdiction of a Court of Admiralty. I think the High Court of Admiralty in England could not take cognizance of such a seizure, or condemn the vessel seized, without a special act of the Imperial Parliament; and, as to the Acts of the Provinces, I am prepared to say at once, that we ought not to admit any seizures to be made by Provincial vessels.   It appears to me, that this is a case of an alleged violation of Treaty, by alleged encroachment upon Territory in time of peace.   It is something like the converse of McLeod's case.   Its appropriate remedy is diplomatic complaint, from one Government to the other; and not of redress by the exercise of local jurisdiction.[1]

Have the goodness to think upon this.

Yours always truly

D. W.

(To D. Fletcher Webster.)

WASHINGTON, August 10th 1852

Dear Fletcher,

I arrived last night and am quite well.   Found all well in the household.   I feel much better and stronger, than when I left Marshfield.   I shall stay here for some days.   I know not yet, how long.   The weather is cool, cloudy, a little rainy and quite agreeable.   I have seen the President who appears quite cordial and glad to see me.

Yours affectionately,

DANL WEBSTER.

(To J. L. Petigru.[2])

WASHINGTON. Aug. 15. 1852.

My Dear Sir,

I am very much obliged to you for your friendly letter of the 3d ult, which I have not had time before to acknowledge.   I know your talents and character; I know the truly patriotic sentiments of your breast; I value most highly your good opinion and regard; and the good opinion and regard of other men like you. As to the rest, I have little to say.   The οἱ πολλοι of the Whig party, especially in the north and east, were, in March 1850, fast

---

[1] Before Webster's death, in October, 1852, he partly prepared a long diplomatic letter upon this subject of the fisheries.
[2] Of Charleston.

sinking into the slough of free soilism and abolitionism. I did what I could to rescue the country from the consequences of their abominable politics. I disdain to seek the favor of such persons, and have no sympathy with their opinions. You are of the South, my Dear Sir, and I of the North; but if the degrees of latitude, which divide us, were ten times as many as they are, your thoughts, and my thoughts, your hopes and my hopes for the good of the country would still rush together in a warm, glowing sentiment and a fervent prayer for the preservation of the Union. God help the right.

In regard to your friend, Mr. Charles Warley, let me say that I shall be most happy to be useful to him. Inform me where he now is and I will send him letters which shall make him known in England and France.

I pray you to remember me most kindly to all the members of your Family, and believe me, with entire regard,

Your obedient and humble servant

[DANL WEBSTER]

(To D. Fletcher Webster.)

My Dear Son;   SUNDAY MOR'G, Aug. 22. '52.

I am quite well yet, & feel no symptoms of approaching Catarrh, altho' tomorrow will be the 23d. Sarah says my eyes are clear yet.

I am gett'g thro' my official affairs, & winding them all up. I shall leave a clear field, & there will be little to do, for a month or two, unless there come some new out-break.

I hope the Inspectors will not be fools enough to pay Greeley a cent. The only effect would be that it would be brought agst them, under the next Administration, & Genl Peirce's friend would turn them all out, for that cause. Nobody would interpose for them.

Yrs truly

DANL WEBSTER

(From W. H. Grinnell et al.)

Dear Sir,   NEW YORK, September 24 1852.

After much consideration we have thought it not improper to

address to you a few words on the present aspect of political
affairs with the Whig party.   We venture to do this in the confidence that you will receive this from us, as prompted only by
our sincere interest in whatever affects your position before the
Country, now as ever regarded by us as that of our most eminent
Citizen.

Of the ill success which attended the efforts to promote the
honor and safety of the Country, by presenting you as the Candidate of the great Whig party for the Presidency, we can only
say, that it has occasioned to us, at least; as much sorrow and
chagrin as to any others of your friends political or personal,
and the more that every day adds to the conviction which we expressed always and everywhere before the nomination, that the
triumph of the Whig party would be assured under the auspices
of your great name.

With all these feelings, however, we confess that we have observed with much solicitude the movements made by many of your
friends, in various parts of the Country to connect your name
with the impending Canvas for the Presidency.   We can anticipate no result from them at all suitable to your dignity, or at all
likely to correspond with their wishes.   If the matter should come
to the point of a nomination and the formation of electoral tickets, we can see no prospect of any other issue, than a most false
record of the state of feeling in the Country towards you, an
issue most unfortunate for the Country, and gratifying only to
that faction whom your patriotism and great public services have
made your enemies.

Nor do we think it unworthy of notice that all the best considered and effective efforts in your behalf before the meeting
of the Convention took the shape of presenting your name to the
Ordeal of that body's selection from the Candidates proposed by
the Whig party, a shape suggested, as we then believed, no less
by a wise policy than by a just sense of political fidelity.   In the
disaster which has fallen upon our hopes and plans, we do not
find any warrant to disregard the observance of that good faith
towards the successful competitor, which in a different result we
should rightfully, have claimed from his friends.

The best reflections (which) we have been able to give to this
whole subject, have induced us to think that sound and sober
public opinion, which should never be lightly regarded, deems
a public disclaimer from you of any favor towards movements
further connecting your name with the coming Presidential elec-

tion, as required by your past and present eminent position whether as a Whig or a Statesman; that such is our own feeling we respectfully submit to you; and beg you to consider that whatever may be your decision, we shall never cease to acknowledge the great obligatiors which the Country and the Whig Party have always owed to you, and shall ever remain[1]

Your sincere friends and obedient Servants,

W. H. GRINNELL
WM. M. EVARTS
A. C. KINGSLAND
T. TILESTON
JAMES S. THAYER
J. WATSON WEBB
C. A. STETSON

(To Le Roy Pope et al.)

Gentlemen,   MARSHFIELD, Sept. 28", 1852.

I have the honor to acknowledge the receipt of your communication of the 1st, instant, and thank you, most cordially, for the kind and friendly sentiments which it expresses.

I regret to say, however, that official engagements, of a pressing nature, will prevent me from accepting your invitation to address the citizens of Memphis, [Tennessee] and its vicinity, in the month of October.

I must, therefore, defer, for the present, the pleasure of meeting with you, and the enjoyment of your proffered hospitality.

I am, Gentlemen, with entire regard,

Your obedient servant,

DANL WEBSTER.

(From Richard J. Mapes.)

MARLTON Burlington Co N. J. Oct. 10' /52.

Mr Webster
     Dear Sir

Having been choosen by the American party a candidate for one of the Presidential Electors of New Jersey and they having

---

[1] See Webster's reply on October 13, 1852.

choosen you as their candidate for the highest office in the gift
in the people of this greate Republic and having not yet heard
or seen anything to say definately wether you will alow the
American people to cast their sufferage for you or not wether
you will suffer your name to be used as such I therefor have
taking the boldness (by this method) to ask you the following
question

1st Are you willing to stand the nomination of the American
Party or do you intend to decline it

2nd do you approve of the principles of that party as adopted
by their National convention July 5th 1852 at Trenton (of
which I send you a coppy)

I find in this part of our state a great many of both of the old
parties who will not vote for either Scott or Pierce but have a
greate desire to cast their Votes for the man of their first choice
namely Daniel Webster of Massachusetts for the following reason

1st for the American principles that has always charicterised
your long life of public services to your country.

2nd for your greate Adheisiveness to the Union and the Constitution

3rd As the most capable most worthy and most entitled to it
for the public services rendered the country

The above is no flattery but the true sentiment of the American people of this District which I have given to you in my own
plain contry stile. I shall look anxiously for an answer from
you[1]

(G. J. Abbott to Peter Harvey.)

(*Private & Confidential.*)   MARSHFIELD—Oct. 11/52.
                                    Monday. 3 o'clock

My Dear Sir—

You will doubtless have seen Drs. Jeffries & Jackson, & will
have learned from them precisely what Mr. Webster's position
is.—   Saturday & Sunday—he kept his bed most of the time,
& did not leave his chamber.—   To day he came down for an
hour & then returned to his bed. He is more sick than I have
yet seen him.—

---

[1] This letter is given as an example of many about this date and of like nature
found by the editor among Webster's papers.

Dr. Jeffries will be here to night.

I am afraid that we can look forward but for a short time.——

If you are now in Boston you had better see Dr. Jeffries to-morrow.——

He has not set at the Table since Thursday noon.—— He dictates letters every day—has done so to day—& also attended to his business matters.

Yours always truly

G. J. ABBOTT

(From Moses H. Grinnell.[1])

OCTOBER 9. 1852.

My dear Sir.

I enclose a communication[2] from some of your friends in this City, it breathes the sentiments of your friends here. I send it to you with a heart full of interest and solicitude for your happiness.

Sincerely your friend

M. H. GRINNELL

(To M. H. Grinnell.)

MARSHFIELD Oct. 12' 1852.

My dear Mr. Grinnell,

I received your note of the 9th inst, only yesterday with its enclosure; to which enclosure you will herewith receive an answer.[3]

Your's with constant regard

DANIEL WEBSTER.

(To M. H. Grinnell et al.)

MARSHFIELD, Oct. 13, 1852.

Gentlemen:

I received only yesterday your communication of the 24th of September.

I beg you to believe me sincerely grateful for the assurances

---

[1] Representative from New York (1839-1841) and a member of the famous New York firm of Grinnell, Minturn & Co.

[2] Encloses the letter dated September 24, 1852.

[3] Upon a letter from Joseph Cook *et al.*, asking his support of General Scott, Webster indorsed, "No answer."

of attachment, political and personal contained in your letter.

In respect to the subject of it, I have now to say to you, and to others who have addressed similar letters to me, that I entertain no new opinions, inconsistent with those which I have, heretofore, publicly declared in the strongest manner; and to which I now, and shall always, adhere in their whole length and breadth.

I refer you Gentlemen to my published Works; and, more especially to my speeches in Fanueil Hall, and at Marshfield, on the 20th of September 1842, and the 1st of September, 1848 respectively.

With the highest respect and the warmest attachment

I remain Gentlemen

Most truly Yours

DANIEL WEBSTER.

Messrs
M. H. Grinnell
Wm. M. Evarts
A. C. Kingsland
T. Tileston
James S. Thayer
J. Watson Webb
C. A. Stetson

(Memorandum dictated by Daniel Webster.)

OCT 21, 1852.

My Island farm, so called, contains about 150 acres. With a very fair new built tenants' house &c. I should think with care it might be disposed of for $3000. I do not know how saleable it might be on account of the remoteness of its situation. But it is excellent land, and has this year been the most productive & remunerative of any of my real estate here.

It is under a Mortgage of 1300 dollars, as I think, to the Hingham Saving's Bank. Mr. Thomas knows all about it. This property if a purchaser offers may be sold for the benefit of the Marshfield estate.

I do not know whether the whole or any part of it is within the Marriage Settlement.[1]

---

[1] Mr. Curtis has added: "The above was dictated by Mr. Webster to me on the 21st October 1852, at the time he was preparing his Will.

"He directed me not to incorporate it in the Will, but to leave it a memorandum for the guidance of his Executors.   GEO. T. CURTIS."

(To Mr. Hatch.)

MARSHFIELD [Oct 20, 1852] [1]

Mr. Hatch,[2] I have

A secret to reveal to you.

I want you to light a lamp on on the home squadron—[3]

"My light shall burn & my flag shall fly as long as my life lasts."

Do you see to this Mr. Hatch & let nobody know of it & take them by surprise in the even'g by six o'clock.

There is no one here in my room but you & I & William[4] & if he mentions it I will put a brace of bullets through him.[5]

D. W.

(From Mr. Abbott to Millard Fillmore.)

MARSHFIELD Oct 25, 1852

Sir,

It was my mournful duty * * * to transmit to you yesterday the sad intelligence of the death of Mr Webster, the Secretary of State, at his mansion house on the early morning of the Sabbath [Oct. 24. 1852] * * * His remains will be enterred by the side of those of his family, whose gentle spirits had preceded his own to their destined rest.[6] * * *

---

[1] This note in Daniel Webster's hand, a wretched scrawl, was written, as Mr. Harvey has indorsed, about three days before Webster's death.

[2] Hatch was one of the servants who like Peterson often accompanied Webster upon his fishing expeditions.

[3] The "home squadron" was Webster's name for one of his boats.

[4] Probably William Paige.

[5] The note is evidently a bit of pleasantry on the part of Webster, but see Hatch's own account as given in Curtis' "Life of Webster," vol. ii, p. 684.

[6] Webster's funeral has been beautifully described by his friend Hilliard, who was present. I give here the passage that dwells upon the spiritual effect of the day:

"Who that was there present will ever forget the scene on which fell the rich light of that soft autumnal day? There was the landscape, so stamped with his image and identified with his presence; there were the trees he had planted, the fields over which he had delighted to walk, and the ocean whose waves were music to his ear; there was the house, with its hospitable door; but the stately form of its master did not stand there, with outstretched hand and smile of welcome. That smile had vanished forever from the earth and the hand and form were silent, cold, and motionless. The dignity of life had given place to the dignity of death. There, among the scenes that he loved in life, he sleeps well. He has left his name and memory to dwell forever upon those hills and valleys, to breathe a more spiritual tone into the winds that blow over his grave, to touch with finer light the line of the breaking wave, to throw a more solemn beauty upon the hues of autumn and the shadows of twilight."

Webster's Family Relations

HERE *are set aside the letters that will furnish a thread of family history. The births and deaths and marriages get into such letters. The statesman's interest in his home is illustrated, and also his character in the family life. We may see his interest in the children, his ambition for them, and the means he took to further it. Their opinions, as formed under his strong influence, give us often by reflex suggestion a hint as to his own. The traits of the children excite an interest as to their source. There are suggestions about his method of governing. We may learn whether the family was thoughtful in saving the time and energy of its distinguished head, and whether he turned from the absorbing public life to show a kindly attention to the family.*

We shall learn here the trials of the home-loving wife of the great statesman. The letters of the first wife show the strain of continual sacrifice to the public. She grows apprehensive for him, but still trusts "a life so useful must be the peculiar care of Providence." At times, the eager watch for news of the great actor in human affairs gives way to a despair and the wonder whether it is all worth the anxiety and deprivation. Again she fears that he has no interest in the family, and that her letters weary him with trivial detail of household care. The news she writes is "not quite so important as the news from the Chamber of Deputies," but he must remember that "a woman's life is made up of trifles, so of course must be her letters." She shows a modest jealousy of the claims of the unrequiting public. The letters give ample proof of her own religion and charity, and of her sweet and motherly character.

In the letters to and from the second wife an entirely different relation may be detected. Here is a woman who has had greater social advantages, and who keenly relishes the popularity of her husband, and the social position which his greatness gives her. That is a charming and characteristic picture which we get of her, sitting all New Year's afternoon with her refreshments in readiness, and none coming to enjoy them. She, too, has a warm

[544]

affection for the husband, aside from the admiration for his worldly fame, but it is not the same affection which the first wife had bestowed upon the humble and unknown Webster.

Finally, there are, of course, occasional allusions to the great world outside of the family, and no doubt at times these allusions may give light to the political career of Webster. If so, the arrangement in chronological order will enable the student to find such passages with ease.

(From William Sweatt.[1])

SOUTH STRAFFORD. Vt.
Hon'l. Dan'l. Webster;   Apr. 7th 1851.
    Dear Sir:—
    * * * —You mention the names of some of the schoolmates of your early life, and I have already, some of mine, and I know you will bear with me in patience, while I give you the names of some few of the School Mistresses of my early days— Miss Poor, Miss McGaw Miss Ruth and Miss Judith Elkins, and last, tho by no means the least, in my kind remembrance, was Miss *Grace Fletcher,* afterwards *Mrs. Webster* I think I attended her School, two or three summers— If she, as a wife, exercised that patience, and that sweetness of disposition she did, as a teacher, blessed indeed were you in your selection— * * *
    I am dear Sir, your native townsman
                                        WILLIAM SWEATT

(From Daniel Fletcher Webster.[2])

BOSTON Jany. 1 1822
Dear Papa.
    I wish you a happy new year. I send you with this a lock of dear little Brothers hair.[3] Julia[4] has been a very good girl— Edward[4] is a pretty good boy. Mama wishes to know what our little brothers name is to be.[5]

---

    [1] An old-time friend of Webster. Webster indorsed this, "Answered—send the writer speeches and give the letter to Mr Curtis."
    [2] Webster's first-born son and the only child who survived him. He kept this letter thirty years.
    [3] Indorsed by Daniel Webster, "Eliza and Kippy with Baby's hair."
    [4] Julia was born January 16, 1818; Edward, July 20, 1820.
    [5] The "little brother," born December 31, 1821, was named Charles.

we all send much love to you.

I am dear Pappa

Your affectionate Son

DANIEL.

Little Brother is a New Years present from mama to *papa*

PARLOUR Jan 2ʳᵈ 1822

Mr. Page desires me to fill this *page* & it will prevent the necessity of his writing to day— Mrs. Webster continues remarkably well & the babe looks already as if he could make a good speech before a Jury— * * *

E. B.

(To Mrs. Grace Webster.)

P. S.—[1]

[JAN. 1822]

My dear wife—

I have rec'd your good letter of Saturday— I am glad you had a good ride— I am [expect]ing another letter from Kip & puss. [As to] little Baby's name, I have no choice between two or three. I do dislike double names, unless given for some friend— There seems to be a *show* about it— If you would incline to call him simple *William*, I am perfectly content— It is a good name, & would respond to the name of *my* uncle, and *his* uncle.

Yours always,

D. W.

(From C. W. Greene.[2])

JAM. PLAIN, Decr. 15, 1823.

Dear Sir

* * * Little Charley has had a cold, but Hannah says "he is getting over it nicely." He sends a kiss to every one & says "Pa's gone to Wa'n to make 'peeches." He is a sweet little dog: he insists upon my playing with him when we are together, & I

---

[1] This P. S. was included in a letter addressed to "Mr. James W. Paige, merchant, Boston."

[2] With whom Webster had left Daniel F. and Charles for the winter. Webster preserved this letter twenty-nine years.

was glad to escape from his chamber on Saturday, to avoid his importunity that I would get into the cradle & permit him to rock me. When Mrs. Greene puts on a particular turban he always calls her Mama & seems to love her better for a fancied resemblance. The youngest Appleton has just returned from town & opportunely remarked "Oh Mr. Green I tried to bring you the paper for you to read a short but *sleek*—(I don't know the orthography of this word) speech of Mr. Webster about the Greeks." I do not yet know how "sleek" the speech may have him say "No, *I do*." Julia and Edward are racing about mak- pleased to hear any of the trifles I have mentioned above about your youngest hope. * * *

I am Dear Sir, Very Respy Yr Ob Servs

C. W. GREENE.

* * * I should be sorry that the frequency of my letters should injure the cause of The Greeks by withdrawing your at- tention from it. I have witnessed for months their ʻoppression by the Turks & I ardently long for their liberation.

(Mrs. Grace Webster to Daniel Fletcher Webster.)

My dear Son,   WASHINGTON Jany 3, 1824.

* * * You must write and tell me all about yourself and Charles and how much he has learned to talk, and if he looks just as he did when mama left him. I wish you and he were here, with Hannah, and then I should be very happy, but now I do want to see you so much. You must not let Charles forget "Mama Mama." Sweet boy, how much I would give to hear him say "No, *I do*." Julia and Edward are racing about mak- ing a great noise. Papa is engaged in writing as usual. Re- member much love to Mrs. Greene, regards to Mr. Greene, and a great deal of love to Charley. * * *

Your affectionate Mother

G W

(Mrs. Grace Webster to D. F. Webster.)

My dear Son,   WASHINGTON Jany 16, 1824.

* * * We have all been to Congress to day—we went with the expectation of hearing Mr. John Randolph but he dis-

appointed us completely, he did not even make his appearance in the House.   Poor Neddy went with Janette and John and tho't it a pretty dull way of passing a forenoon and in truth I thought so too, tho' Mr. McDuffie made a long talk, the man who fought a duel so many times over a year ago.   I would rather he had been engaged in the same way, provided it had been as harmless as in the former case.   *   *   *

Papa has bought him a new saddle and bridle and whip and rode out this morning on one of the coach-horses, he went very well but not quite so well as Leicester.   *   *   *

MOTHER.

(Mrs. Grace Webster to D. Fletcher Webster.)

WASHINGTON March 13, 1824.

I am very much obliged to you my dear Son, for a very nice letter, which I received this week from you.   Papa was much pleased to see it so well written.   I am glad to hear that dear little Charley pities the Greeks and intends giving them plum pudding.   I conclude it is his favourite dish.   *   *   *

Your affectionate

MOTHER.

(From Mrs. Grace Webster.)

BORDENTON Sunday Morning
[June 6, 1824] 10 O'clock.

I hope ere this hour, my dear Husband, you are almost at the end of your journey.   You are first, and last, and always in our hearts, and on our minds.   I say *ours* for Julia's bonny hazel eye has often filled with tears since we parted and she could hardly enjoy the luxury of a nice bedroom and delightful bed because dear Papa was in the steamboat and her apprehensions for your safety are very great.   I comforted her and quieted her fears, by our own safety, and by the beauty, and brightness, and stillness, of the night, which on your account was a cause of great joy and thankfulness to me.

The morning tho' warm, is delightful!   A calm tranquility, a sort of sacred stillness, seems to pervade everything around, on a Sabbath morning in the country.

FAMILY RELATIONS 549

Mrs. H.[1] wishes me to tell you that I hear the "church going-bell" tho' I follow the example of the family and stay at home, and she hopes the children hear it also as one of them tho't it a strange village without a church—it must have been one of Puss' remarks. * * *

(From Mrs. Grace Webster.)

SUNDAY EVENING, [June 6, 1824.]

My dear Husband

We have been to Point Breeze to pay our respects to the Count.[2] We found them standing in the door all ready for a little excursion on the water. They very politely urged us to accompany them & stay to supper—but we had taken the children with Mrs. H's woman and Janette and they were walking in the grounds and I feared Julia might be unhappy to see me launched off again in a boat. I therefore told Mrs. Hopkinson if it would be equally agreeable to her we would accompany the party to the barge and then return, which we did. After walking a long way we came to the same covered way which you doubtless remember. There are many relicts of broken statuary of the finest Marble huddled together in the remaining part of one of the wings of the former Palace. It looks more like things we read of than anything I ever saw before. You will see I soon forget that I promised never to write excepting just to say we are well, because you do not take the trouble to read your letters, but this I expect you to read every word, that is if you can—as it is to be conveyed to Philadelphia by hands that once swayed a scepter.[2]

Mrs. H. desires to be especially remembered to you. Good night and pleasant dreams to you my dear love,

Yours—G. W.

(From Mrs. Grace Webster.)

DEC. 4th, (1824) Sat. morning.

My dear Husband,

I have not written to you for several days—indeed, I am sur-

---

[1] Mrs. Joseph Hopkinson. [2] Count Wallenstein.

prised to find how many, I believe not a line since monday.   I have been a good deal occupied, but still not sufficiently so as to have prevented me from writing a line.   William told me he would write you yesterday.   I supposed he told you dear little Charles is sick of a lung fever—he is better this morning the Dr thinks, and I hope he will soon get over it.   *   *   *

Julia's greatest trouble is that she can not go to school.   She is looking on to see me write and says ask Papa what he makes such an x for on his letters, and wishes me likewise to remember that she sends love and kisses. How many hundreds of time I have I written to you love and kisses— I think you must be tired of both.   Charley asked me this morning, "Where is Papa."   I told him.   Why don't he come home, said he, and I confess the truth this has been a very long fortnight since you left.   It seems as you had been gone long enough to return.

from your afft.   G. W.

(From Mrs. Grace Webster.)

MONDAY MORNING, Dec. 6, [1824.]

Our dear little Charley continues much as he has been since the first.   Tho' he has still a very high fever Dr. Warren thinks there is not at present any danger.   I don't know but it would have been better to have kept all my troubles to myself as your knowledge of them can do me no possible good and will give you some anxiety, but you will not I trust be over anxious, but hope, and believe all will yet be well.   Julia and Edward are better.   Julia finds it hard to reconcile herself to staying at home from school, but it is not an affair of great grief to Neddy.   *   *   *

This morning my dear Husband, you will probably resume your duties in the House of Representatives, which I trust you will discharge with fidelity to your country, and honor to yourself.   I feel now as if I could never again be spared from home, and since it seems to be so ordered that you must be away we must be separated.   I hope it will be for our mutual good. Adieu!   Ever yours,

G. W.

(From Mrs. Grace Webster.)

THURSDAY MORNING (Dec. 9, 1824)[1]

My dear Husband,

* * * I have just received your letter of Sat evening from Washington I rejoice you have been once more preserved from the perils of sea and land, and reached your place of destination in safety. I am sorry to hear you have a cold and headache and other things that are not to your mind. You mention but one letter from me, and that seems rather to have given offence than pleasure. I am most unfortunate, not only in my own speeches, but in quieting those of my friends. Mr. B. certainly, I tho't well enough understood by you not to be taken in earnest. It is my prayer that I may never again offend either in word, deed, or thought present, or absent I will set a watch both over my tongue and my pen. * * * Adieu!

Yours as ever

G. W.

(From Mrs. Grace Webster.)

SAT ? MORNING. (Dec. 11, 1824)

My dear Husband,

* * * I hoped I should have another letter to day written in better spirits than your last which was when you had just arrived and things did not go right and you had a headache, and you did not like my letter and I know not how many other things were wrong. In the hope that all things are now right and pleasant and that your cold is well, I am my dear Love,

Truly yours,

G. W.

(From Mrs. Grace Webster.)

MONDAY MORNING, (Dec. 13, 1824)

My dear Husband,

You will probably receive with this a letter from Dr. Warren

---

[1] On December 9th Mr. Webster and a party left Washington to visit Madison and Jefferson. He received one letter during the excursion, which contained the news that his son was ill. He became much depressed and eager to return to Washington. On his arrival he received the news of the death of this favorite child. See Curtis' "Life of Webster," vol. i, p. 222.

which give you a more satisfactory account of our dear little boy than I can give. the Dr thinks there is no alteration in his symptoms since last evening he must of course grow rather more feeble.

I cannot tell you how much I regret that the unpleasant intelligence reached you before you had set out for Monticello, if you had but got away before, you might have enjoyed the excursion, and I now hope my accounts were so favorable as not to destroy your pleasure. I regretted very much not to answer your letter which I received yesterday giving me a little idea how you were situated. *   *   *

I am glad you do not intend to work hard. I hope you will stick to that resolution. I am greatly obliged to all my friends who wish to see me with you, but I cannot be sufficiently thankful that I am with dear little Charles, it would be much more distressing to you as well as me if I were absent. I hope you will not be too anxious about dear little Charles all will be just right.[1] He has been a delightful little creature to me, and I hope he will be spared to us, and if it is best he should be, I know he will—I would therefore say not my *will* but thine O Lord! be done.

Adieu my best earthly friend, may Heaven in mercy preserve you! prays your

Ever afft

G. W.

———

(From James W. Paige.[2])

SUNDAY Dec. 19, 1824.

Dear Sir,

In my letter yesterday I mentioned that Charles Fever had abated & that the pressure on his lungs increased which Doct Warren tho't no unfavourable symptom. *   *   *   His stomach seemed entirely insensible to any medicine. Altho every thing that could be tho't of was resorted too By giving wine and water he revived a little & lingered along until Seven this morning—when sad as it may be I am under the necessity of informing you that a few minutes past *seven this morning he*

---

[1] See among political letters the one addressed to William Plummer by Daniel Webster, dated December 18, 1824: also the letter to Edward Everett, dated December 31, 1824.

[2] Half-brother of Mrs. Webster.

breathed his last & we trust is in a happier world where all pain will cease. You may rest assured that nothing was left undone that could have been of service to him.

Little did any of us think that our next letter to you would be of this character. Mrs Webster is as well & resigned to her lot as could be expected. Cousin Eliza is with her & a no small comfort. Dan'l, Julia & Edward were much affected at the loss of poor Charlie & E. in particular seemed very much grieved & also Dan'l. Julia shows less feeling, but may have felt as bad.

J. W. PAIGE

(From Mrs. Grace Webster.[1])

DEC. 29, (1824)

Till yesterday my dear Husband, I have not for a long time had the satisfaction of writing to you. I should not again attempt it with the difficulty I find in holding the pen but for the hope that it may be some small consolation to you.

Yours of friday I received this morning. I am well aware how different must now be your feelings at the coming in of the mail—now that *hope* is dead. Yes my love, we were too happy, and no doubt needed to be reminded that these treasures which we call *ours* are but lent favors from the moment I receive them I endeavor to consider them as such, but I have need to be reminded—of the frail tenure of this mortal life. * * *

Heaven bless you my love and comfort and sustain you in every trial and bring you at the last to the reward of the righteous

prays your afft.

G. W.

(From Mrs. Grace Webster.[2])

FRIDAY MORNING Dec. 31st (1824)

This my dear Husband, is dear little Charles' birthday! but where is he! in his bed of darkness—every thing looks bright and gay, but cannot bring joy to the heart of a mother who mourns the untimely death of a beloved child. When years since, I sent you a lock of hair with emotions how different from the pres-

---

[1] This letter is printed in Harvey's "Reminiscences of Daniel Webster," p. 322.
[2] This letter is printed in Harvey's "Reminiscences of Daniel Webster," p. 323.

ent—I now send a precious little lock which you have often seen on his beautiful brow. I think it will be some satisfaction to look on it once more. I am sorry not send the pin but it is not quite done. I have often tho't why was the pin you had made for me with the little lock I sent you a mourning one, but it is all right now. * * *

I am very glad that you say you are well. May Heaven long continue the blessing. The children are now all well and all at school.

Yours ever

G. W.

(From Mrs. Grace Webster.)

JAN 1st 1825

I send you a mournful present for New Years—My dear Husband, but you will accept it together with my best wishes. My thoughts often recur to the past—with an aching heart at the break in our little circle—since last New Years. Yet I endeavor not to embitter the present by useless repining. I know that ours is a common calamity and I could not expect to be exempt from an event which happens to all. I desire so to receive this chastisement, that I may be saved one more severe. * * *

I have no letter today. I fear you have grown weary, with writing. Daniel has several times begun to write to you but has not accomplished a letter. He seems to recollect with some degree of pain that you did not write him a single line during your long absence the last year. I fear he has a little of the mother in him. * * *

Yours ever

G. W.

(From Mrs. Grace Webster.)

FRIDAY MORNING, Jany 7th (1825)

My dear Husband,

In my sleep last night you were with us—but I awoke and the delightful vision fled! And long must it be ere I can hope to see you save in the visions of sleep or fancy. It is a long seven weeks since you left us. But here is a letter and from you my dear husband which proves we are not forgotten. It contains

the interesting epitaph on our lamented friend, from Mr. Whitney—it is doubly interesting considering the melancholy fate of
the author. What a dreadful calamity is that to friends but
how much more dreadful to be the parents of such a son—as the
perpetrator of that horrid crime. Such things, my dear love,
ought to reconcile us to our loss. No doubt we ought to rejoice
that

> Ere sin could blight, or sorrow fade,
>   Death timely came with friendly care;
> The opening bud to Heaven conveyed,
>   And bade it bloom forever there.

But it is hard to *resign* objects so dear.[1] * * *
Yours ever,

G. W.

(From Mrs. Grace Webster.)

Boston Jany 12th (1825)

I intended to practice the golden rule my dear Husband, and
tho' I have not received a letter for two or three days to have
written, * * *

The bell rings I hope there is a letter for me. It is—The
letter as I hoped is from yourself. I am sorry to hear you have
the rheumatism. I hope it will soon leave you and that you will
be able to preserve your health. I see you have called up your
bill. It is quite a comfort to see your name in the papers with
now and then a word of your own.

Daniel likes his school very much, but I am thinking you did
not sufficiently appreciate Mr. Green D. says he does not have
half as much study as he had there. I fear there is more play
than anything else. I do not mean in school, but there are so
many boys here I am convinced Boston is not a good place for
Daniel. Boys must have parties & balls, wear white *kid gloves*
and I know not what. But I have endeavored to reconcile Daniel
to the privation of living without these things. There is the
greatest folly at this day—*children are anticipating* all the *pleasures* and *amusements* of *Gentlemen & Ladies*, what then can be
left for those, who shall arrive at that period I am unable to fore-

---

[1] See also the letter printed in Harvey's "Reminiscences of Daniel Webster," p. 323.

see.   Boys even have supper parties and in some instances have drunk so much wine they could hardly be got home and they could not be blamed, how could'any one suppose they could have judgment sufficient to govern them.

I fear you will think this is pretty much like my *scolding* the *servants* You have to hear it.   I hope you will excuse it as it is a long time since I have exercised my *talent.*   *   *   *

Ever yours,

G. W.

(From Mrs. Grace Webster.)

FRIDAY MORNING Jany 14 (1825)

Yours of the 9th my dear Husband, tells me that you are solitary, and that you still have the rheumatism, both of which I regret without the power to cheer or alleviate.   There is a striking, and painful contrast between the present season, and the last, with us my dear Love, but I hope we shall make this as profitable to ourselves as the last was pleasant.

Now is your family agreeable? I have heard much of Mrs. Wool's uncommon powers at conversation—extraordinary information &c &c. and how do you find Mrs. Dwight? And Mrs. Rankin, is she ought like your rib.   You will excuse the vanity which leads me to remember that yours was tho't by Mr. R. to be a model—you need not add he did not know her—I am well aware of that.

Af yours

G. W.

(From Mrs. Grace Webster.)

TUESDAY MORNING Jany 18th 1825.

*   *   *   Yesterday we had Mr. Everetts oration, there are some fine passages in it, indeed, it is all very good and I have no doubt it was very interesting to those, who heard it; but I should rather be the author of one page, of the one that I heard there, than the whole—don't be afraid that I shall make any such remark—

This is as bright and beautiful a morning as that which gave joy to your good mother in the birth of a darling son.   May many as bright and more happy dawn on that son tho' the mother who gave him birth know it not—

Julia desires much love. She has too bad a cold to go to school and poor little Neddy has taken their little green satchel, not with whining face—but a very happy one and gone to school

Yours ever,
GRACE WEBSTER.

(From Mrs. Grace Webster.)

JANY 20th 1825.

I conclude you are much engaged my dear Husband, as I have no letters yesterday nor to day. I somehow depended so much on that pleasure to day as be a little disappointed— You know "indulgence spoils *ladies*" and you are so good in writing I expect *now* a letter at least every other day. * * *

As you once promised to read *all* my letters I ought to be merciful—but perhaps you may have forgot the promise, and if so, I own I ought to excuse you when I prose in this way if you treat mine as you do many of your "esteemed favours." * * *

Adieu—Yours ever

G. W.

(From Mrs. Grace Webster.)

JANY 26th. (1825)

My dear Husband,

I had the pleasure of two letters this morning one from your Brother and one from your goodself. Uncle E.[1] says his business at Concord is adjusted. I hope the good man will get a woman worthy of him[2]—he thinks her all that she ought to be. I hope he never will have occasion to alter his opinion, he knows a little of the sex and therefore probably will not be as sanguine as he might have been once. He tells me he lodged with Mr. Mason and I think he is delighted with him—he says he should be proud of the state with such a man for a senator in congress— I could add with such a senator and such a representative as they

---

[1] Ezekiel Webster.
[2] People in Concord, N. H., who knew Mrs. E. Webster bear witness that 'Uncle E.' did "get a woman worthy of him."

might have I should be proud of N. H.—but they are a degenerate race.

We are all better today.   I have only time to say how much
I am Ever Yours,

G. W.

(From Mrs. Grace Webster.)

FRIDAY Jany 24th (1825)

My dear Husband,
   * * * Do you indeed *believe* Mr. Adams will be President?   The important day is at hand, big with the fate of Caesar and of Rome"   Mr. George Adams is going to be present —it will be a proud day.   I have been expecting Judge Story yesterday and this morning   this was the day fixed for his departure. * * *

Your ever afft

G. W.

(From Mrs. Grace Webster.)

BOSTON Jany 31st 1825.

l had no letter from you yesterday my dear Husband, but hope for one to day, but I do not insist upon it, knowing how much you have to do.   It is a great shame that you have to fight your bill along so.   I am sorry to find Mr. Livingston so much against you.   I don't care about Mr. Wickliffe and such sort of men I like to hear you abuse them.

Judge Story leaves this morning, he has been sick with the prevailing epidemic, which prevented him from going last week with a little party of which Mr. Winthrop not Mr. Bowdoin made one.   I had quite a party for me last evening—Judge Story, Judge Davis, Mr. Willis & Mr. Bliss they are all much engaged in the affairs of Harvard College.   The Judge feels himself much injured by the proceedings.   Mr. Everett I am sorry to find has incurred a good deal odium by the course he has taken.   Next Thursday he is to reply to Judge Story—there will doubtless be a great crowd to hear him. * * *

Adieu!   Yours Ever

G. W.

(From Mrs. Grace Webster.)

My dear Husband,   FEB 3d Thursday morning (1825)
  * * * My poor old thimble! I did not know what had
become of it. I value it only as being a purchase I made when I
lived in Portsmouth; ere the "blight of sorrow had ever come
oe'r me. You were with us here so short a time my Love, I fear
you can hardly see us in your mind's eye—and if you do it is
but a melancholy picture— The little circle broken: one dear
bright link in the chain gone—but yet we hope to be happy
when you return. * * *
  The Coronation is well done, both in paint and likeness. His
Grace looks frighfully like the New Speaker. Who could have
done it? I shall be afraid to show it without your leave. * * *
                Yours ever,
                            G. W.

(From Mrs. Grace Webster.)

                SAT. MORNING Feb'y 5, (1825)
  I somewhat expected a letter from you to day my dear Husband, but from the newspapers I conclude you are very busy,
one of the papers said Congress was like a beehive just before
swarming. Mr. Clay I see is in a fearful passion. It is dreadful to be so abused All the honors this Government can bestow
would be no equivalent to me—but I do not believe if a man acts
always with honor and integrity there is any danger of such
abuse. If I should talk of things too high for me you must just
put it into the fire and forget *it*—not *me*. *T*he children have
come home clamouring for something to eat. They wish they
could go into Aunt Coyles closet and get some of her *good-
ies.*" * * *
                Always Your Affte
                            G. W.

(From Mrs. Grace Webster.)

                FEBY 8th, Tuesday morning. (1825)
  Do you know my dear Husband, that it is a long time since
you have written to me? or are you so much occupied with the
important affairs of the nation as to make you forgetful of such

a trifle as wife. I have not written for a day or two and I recollect I wrote a most stupid uninteresting letter—and I cannot promise to do better today my head does not feel quite right.

You will have seen before this that Gov. Eustis is no more   A new one is already talked of.   I have heard Mr. Blake named as successor.   Now would that suit?   Julia has spoken to two votes for you Mr. Bliss' and Uncle Williams.

The papers have already killed the Hon. speaker[1] in a duel. I hope he will take warning and tho, Mr. Kremer should "cry aloud and spare not" it would be a pity to have bloodshed upon the occasion.   Our friend Mr. Blake thinks there will be much spilt.   *   *   *

Every Yours   G. W.

(From Mrs. Grace Webster.)

My dear Husband,   BOSTON Feb'y 10th, 1825.

Now that the important business of making a President is as I trust over, I hope I shall have letters as usual. I have been wholly neglected for a long week, which being a rare occasion makes it the more worthy of note.   *   *   *

My dear Husband,
Ever Yours,

G. WEBSTER.

(From Mrs. Grace Webster.)

FRIDAY MORNING, Feby 11th [1825]

I am very happy in receiving a short letter from you my beloved Husband. I knew your time must be all filled, and that you can have very little for me. The great question is undoubtedly decided, which has for a long time agitated the Public. Tho' we have very little doubt as to the success of the Northern Candidate, yet we are anxious to *know* how it is. And I am anxious also to know how Mr. Clay and Kremer are coming out.[2] I think you have a great many silly heads as well as wise ones in that honorable body. I cannot tell you how happy I am that

---

[1] Henry Clay. See McMaster's "History of the United States," vol. v, pp. 78, 79.

[2] See McMaster's "History of United States," vol. v, pp. 491–495.

the fourth of March must put an end to those wise deliberations, otherwise I should fear that the whole winter would be taken up in debating how the office should be settled. I fear you think it very foolish in me to meddle with these high matters, but I am so much interested in whatever you are engaged I must prate a little.

Yours ever,

G. WEBSTER.

(From Mrs. Grace Webster.)

MONDAY MORNING (Feb 14. 1825)

My dear Husband,

My letter was forgotten yesterday till it was too late. The news came last night of the election Mr. Adams. I was awakened by the cannon. We had been rather anxiously awaiting the news. I should like to know how the poor old President, Father I mean, bears it. He is very much indisposed Mr. I. P. told me last evening with the prevailing epidemick of this region, I doubt if he will live to see his son clothed with his new honors. * * *

Your letter of the 9th which I received this morning, was an unexpected pleasure I am glad you get so well over the important affair. I do not think the Gentlemen who wasted so much time debating how the thing should be done have raised themselves in the public opinion. Good sense is an invaluable gift. I tho't Mr. McDuffie had had too much to have talked so long and to so little purpose. Excuse the opinions of one who has no right to such a privilege. Ever your afft.

G. W.

Pray tell me how Mr. A.[1] received the intelligence? I have a wish to know if he was moved.

(From Mrs. Grace Webster.)

FEB. 17th Thursday morning. (1825)

I consider it a very fortunate accident my dear Husband, that procured me a letter of nearly three pages I shall, however, be very glad of one an "inch long." * * *

---

[1] Adams.

You have doubtless heard that Mr. Adams heard the news of his son's honors with great composure. His health is better. * * *

Ever affectly Yours,

G. W.

(From Mrs. Grace Webster.)

FRIDAY MORNING Feb. 18th (1825)

Whenever I receive a letter, my dear Husband, I feel as if I must reply. Yours of Sunday was an unexpected favour as I had one yesterday, but tho' unexpected, not the less welcome.

The papers are full of speculations about the offices to be filled and the characters who are to will them, even you do not escape. Mr. Adams situation is not an enviable one. I have felt very much interested in the great affairs at W. and should rather have been there on many accounts than at another session, but I doubt if I ever go there again. Our children, if they live, will require my constant care—more than I could bestow in such a place—and if it must be so, if your duty calls you there, I must submit—it is doubtless best it should be so. * * *

Adieu   Yours Ever

GRACE WEBSTER.

(From Mrs. Grace Webster.)

MONDAY MORNING, Feb. 21st (1825)

I am indebted to you, my dear Husband, for a letter of unusual length and spirits too.

I have not written for several days for I fear if I write oftener my letters will be entirely without value. I, who never stir from my own fireside but to enter a Church, can have nothing to communicate but the health, or sickness of my family, as it please Providence,—the shining of the glorious sun, or the howling of the storm. My life is monotonous indeed, and somewhat dull— but it is doubtless best for me; it gives me time for reflections which the frequent intercourse with the world is too apt [to] banish—from a mind so trifling as I find mine is—and I have many, very many painfully mortifying reflections. It is mortifying to reflect how much I am behind you in everything. I know no one respects, but rather dispises those they consider very much their inferiors. You will perhaps say I am unusually humble, but these are not the feelings of an *hour* or a *day* they are *habitual.* * * *

Mr. and Mrs. Tickner have returned. She made me a very friendly visit the day after her return. I have not yet seen Mr. T. I would not forget that Mrs. Tickner desired me to mention her particularly to you. When you compare her letters with mine, my dear Husband, I am well aware that the difference in length would be the most trifling. You must have the mortification to reflect that Mrs T. is the daughter of a man of *millions,* and has enjoyed, since her infancy, every advantage, which wealth can bestow, while your wife is the daughter of a poor country clergyman—all the early part of her life passed in obscurity, toiling with hands not *"fair"* for subsistence. These are humiliating truths, which I regret more on your account than any other. But, however poor, or however obscure

I am always,

Affectionately,

Yours   G. W.

——————

(From Mrs. Grace Webster.)

FEB. 24th (1825)

My dear husband,   Monday morning.

* * * I shall tell Mrs. Blake how much you wished for her at [illegible], I hope you were as well entertained as upon a former occasion. Mrs B. will never forget the lady in black crescents who amused you both so much.

I wish I had something to interest you but have nothing. According to Dr. Johnson I have the true "epistolic art" which he says is "doubtless to make a letter without affection, without wisdom, without gaiety, without news, and without a secret" affection excepted, have I not? I believe my letters are not wholly without that. * * *

Yours Ever

G. W.

——————

(From Mrs. Grace Webster.)

TUESDAY MORNING March 1st, (1825) 11 o'clock.

My dear Husband,

Mr. Bliss has just been here to inquire if I had any news from you knowing I had a letter this morning. I told him your letter contained none—he then told me there was a report current in town last evening that Mr. Randolph had challenged you for some remarks of yours last year which had just reached him. Mr. B. did not for a moment believe the report, but had manfully contradicted it, still he tho't he should like to know what you had written, which happened to be merely a short notice of your dinner with the President, your enjoyment of our old room, &c., &c. not a word of duels or anything of the sort. I heard the same story at N. Jersey on my return last year—the duel excepted, as Mr. R. was then on the great and mighty deep he could not have heard if you had made the threat. I told Mr. Stockton you were, I believe very angry with Mr. R. but you would not be very likely to threaten any man with a whipping. I have not the least disagreeable apprehension of the truth of the report, my dear Husband, I neither believe Mr. R. would challenge, nor if he did, that you would accept. * * *

G. W.

(From Mrs. Grace Webster.)

SAT. MORNING March 5. (1825)

I have not written you for several days my dear Husband, but among your *numerous* correspondents I can hardly flatter myself that my poor epistles will be missed. I owe you for two letters received yesterday which should have been answered, but I was not in spirits, and as you know that "out of the abundance of the heart the mouth speaketh" I tho't it better for me to be silent.

Mrs. Blake came in and sat an hour and a half in the morning, after having been jambed to a moderate size in attempting to see the dinner tables at old Faneuil where the famous dinner was eaten yesterday in honor of our Yankee President.[1] * * *

That affair of yours and Mr. Randolphs will serve to astonish the people here for some time to come. It is now said that as you would take no notice of Mr. R. Mr. Benton espoused the cause and the quarrel. Can there be any truth in this?[2] * * *

Yours ever

GRACE WEBSTER.

---

[1] John Quincy Adams.
[2] See the correspondence between Daniel Webster and Benton.

(From D. Fletcher Webster.)

BOSTON March 9th, 1825.

My Dear Father

I am very much obliged to you for your letter and am very sorry that I have been so long in answering it. I hope I shall always be a good boy and reallize your wishes and when you are old I shall be a comfort to you in your old age. I have just finished my French which is about the condition of peace which Charles the XII gave to king Augustus. Edward and Julia are writing you letters; Neddy says that he has written you a hundred letters and you have not written him one, and Julia says that she has written you twice. * * *

Your Dutiful and affectionate son

DANIEL F. WEBSTER.

(From Mrs. Grace Webster.)

THURSDAY MORNING March 10th (1825)

I must write this morning my dear Husband, if it be but tell you how much I am disappointed in not having a letter. Your letters are indeed like Angels visits, short and far between. But I have done complaining—as I hope you perceive—I have even become quite stoical. This is the time you fixed on for your return, but I have been silent—I am *patience* personified. * * *

The Inaugural addresses have arrived I have not finished the Presidents but as far as I have read I tho't it sensible. I don't know what sort of an address is expected of a Vice President Mr. Calhoun is a sensible man and I suppose his is right.

I had a letter from your excellent Brother this week he intends to be here about the time of your return. It is before this, decided whether he is to be one of the Representatives to Congress[1] I very much fear he is not If they do not elect him and Mr. Mason New Hampshire ought to be blotted out from the catalogue of States.

We are all well. Edward I think you will find grown considerably. Julia is about the same. I fear you will not find them much improved I believe I have lost the art of managing children—and Julia requires a wiser head than mine, and a bet-

---

[1] Ezekiel Webster was not elected.

ter heart I fear—she is very peculiar in her temper and feelings.
I think it would be for her good to go from her mother but I
doubt if I could be happy without her.

Adieu, remember a little oftener—Your affectionate

GRACE

(From Mrs. Grace Webster.)

BOSTON Jany 16" 1827.

* * * I read with delight Mr Cannings speeches in Parliament he is Jewel in the crown of Great Britain   Such a mind
is one of heavens best gifts every other earthly possession is dross
to it—   You will think I fear, that I am in the heroics this
morning.   I do feel inspired with two letters from *you* and reading Mr Canning speech—but I am

As Ever entirely Yours

GRACE WEBSTER

(From Mrs. Grace Webster.)

JANY 17th [1827]
Wednesday morning

* * * I see a little sparing between you and Mr Forsyth
—but I dont get all the debates—only extracts—it is rather too
late or I would ask to have the Intelligencer sent me—I have
nothing to say today—Julia has been making hearts for you
which are to go in this so you will have our hearts with few words
as they are made up of love

Yours ever

GRACE WEBSTER

(From Mrs. Grace Webster.)

BOSTON, Jany 21st, 1827.

* * * Have you seen Mr Channings discourse at the dedi-
cation of a Church in N. York—   I wish you would read it &
tell me what you think of it; for myself I am sorry he preached
such doctrine.   I should be unwilling to believe him right.   and
I cannot but fear we are wrong to appear to be of that sect—
I am anxious that our children should be taught the right way if
it be possible to ascertain what that is.   I fear my dear Hus-

band that you have not sufficiently considered the subject and I
have been myself too easy—If you have time to give some consideration to the subject I wish you would and write to me—-
With much love

Ever Yours

G WEBSTER.

(From Mrs. Grace Webster.)

BOSTON Jany 29 1827

Full many a Mail has arrived without bringing a line from
you my dear Husband, but I know how you are occupied and that
your whole mind must be engaged in arduous duties and labours.
I hear proud accounts of you by way of Mr Bliss—which recon-
ciles me to the deprivation I mentioned—My Husband is the
centre and the height of my ambition—I fear you will think it
would be better if I were more so for myself—No one could more
ardently wish to be all woman ought to be than I do, but I have
not the courage to pursue a course that would make me what I
would be—The weakness of my sight is too discouraging—I cannot write a short letter without feeling uncomfortable—But no
more of my infirmities. * * *

P. S. (omitted).

G. W.

(From Mrs. Grace Webster.)

BOSTON Feb. 5, 1827

I am very glad to receive a short letter from you to day, my
dear Husband, together with the childrens bon bons they will
be much pleased to see something or anything coming under your
direction—Julia asked me this morning to write for her she
wished me to say she was studying grammar and that she had got
to the head of her class again in geography and goes again to
dancing school— * * *

I am as Ever Yours

G. WEBSTER

(From Mrs. Grace Webster.)

SAT Feb 10th [1827]

* * * You told me in your last that Mr McCready dined

with you   how **do you** find him in private?   he is one of the
few Tragedians that I should feel inclined to know something
of * * *   Mrs J. P. was here Thursday evening   she desired me to ask you the colour of Mrs Lymans dress at the French
Ministers?   Julia said do you suppose Papa can tell black from
white in the night?   for Mr Davis sake I hope you will endeavour
to recollect this important item—   I hope the Court go on
well— * * *

With much love—

Yours Ever—

GW.

(From Mrs. Grace Webster.)

Boston Feb 15th 1827

Amidst your cares, your business, & your pleasures, My dear
Husband, I sometimes fear that if I did not obtrude myself upon
you I should be a thing quite forgotten.   Perhaps you will blame
the thought, but after looking day after day even more than a
week for a letter in vain, I feel a little impatient, but I do not
mean to be unreasonable—   Julia is anxiously waiting for a
letter also   she says "tell Papa I am his correspondent but he
dont correspond." * * *

G. W.

(From Mrs. Grace Webster.)

Boston Feb. 16th 1827

The fear that you will think I wrote rather a complaining letter yesterday my dear Husband, induces me to write again to
day—tho' I have little to say but the often told tale—the repetition of yesterday, our health the weather and our employ-
ments— * * *

I devoted last evening to the reading of the debates in Congress last Saturday—   I don't wonder that you were "right regular tired"   you had many battles to fight.   I cannot be thankful enough that the session is so near the close.

Gov.—Lincoln as you will see most unequivocally declines the
honor of Senator—so that matter I suppose is at rest. * * *

Yours Ever

GW.

(From Mrs. Grace Webster.)

THURSDAY March 8th [1827]

I have got another unexpected pleasure my dear Husband, yours of Saturday. You must indeed feel relieved from a load of care I rejoice with all my heart that you have got over it so well and so soon too for I expected you would have to sit up all night but you anticipated and sat up on Friday night— I hope your good long nap of 24 hours has restored you and that we shall find there is something "left of you yet."   *   *   *

Poor Mrs Bliss expected fully to see her good husband last evening but she has not yet Whether the storm delayed the boat, or whether he waits for the next is uncertain. O! if a husband could *know* the disappointment a woman feels; if he could but *know* the meaning of this most true saying of the wise man hope deferred makes the heart sick it would not be so often felt, but as they do not know—they cannot be so *greatly* to blame so here my reasoning ends—

Yours Ever

G. W.

Julia wishes she had a speaking trumpet that would reach your ear she says she wants to talk with you—

(Mrs. Grace Webster to James W. Paige.)

N YORK Dec 2d (1827)
Sunday 1 'Oclock

My dear Brother,

Mr. W. I believe has kept you informed till yesterday of our state and condition but yesterday, we were neither of us well enough to write conveniently, and did not like to employ anyone for fear of alarming you. I tho't when I found myself confined to the bed with a blister that it would detain as I could not foresee how long that we had reached the climax of our misfortunes but yesterday morning Mr. W. had a sudden and violent attack of rheumatism in his back which has prostrated him completely, he has only sat up long enough to have his bed made—to day— I hope, however, that the worst is over he has much less pain, indeed is quite easy if he keeps entirely still. I think I see mercy in this for if he had been well he tho't he must leave tomorrow, which he was very unwilling to do without me and it would be almost a thing impossible for me to go, for it is with pain & difficulty that I sit at all—   *   *   *

Yours G WEBSTER

———

(To James W. Paige.)

Dear William,   NEW YORK Dec. 3rd. 1827

Mrs Webster wrote you yesterday & I must now continue the melancholy narrative.   I write by the hand of Henry Perkins— I begin with myself—It seems to me that I am a little better to day than yesterday—I am free from pain, & while I lie still am easy & quiet—but I cannot get upon my feet, nor when on them walk across the room without help—   But as I am convalescent & my complaint not dangerous I pay it little regard—the weighty matter is Mrs. Webster's illness, & this I fear has become alarming—last night and to day she has suffered at intervals intense pain from her foot to her hip—to day she has been quite confined to her bed—I am fully convinced that it will not be proper to proceed farther with her until a favourable change shall take place—but how much of her present suffering arises from the disease itself, or from its natural progress, & how much from temporary causes I cannot tell.   If Mrs. Webster should again be as well as when we left home, I think I shall proceed to Washington, leaving her here for a while; & to come to Washington, or return to Boston according to circumstances hereafter.   But until she is much better than she now is, I should not leave her even if I were able to travel myself.   As it is there is little prospect of my getting away before next week.   I shall write you daily, & nothing remains but to hope & pray for the best.

We all send much love to you & Daniel.

Yrs. always truly,

DANIEL WEBSTER

———

(To James W. Paige.)

NEW YORK Decr. 4th, 1827.

Dear William,   Tuesday eveng.

I have the pleasure to say that Mrs. Webster is better than she was yesterday—she slept well last night, & has passed a comfortable day— As for myself, I am much the same, though rather convalescent.

Riley has returned from New Brunswick— As a part of our common luck on his way thither a carriage drove up, furiously, behind him, forced its pole into our coach, & stove the back part of it all to pieces— We shall try to get it mended.

Mrs Webster says that she has nothing to add but that the children are well & all send love

Yrs. truly
DANL. WEBSTER.

(To James W. Paige.)

FRIDAY 1 oclock

Dear William,

I have yours of Wednesday, in which you say something of going to Boston &c.—

I really know not what is best to be done, but will suggest what occurs to me.—

In the first place, I am not now well eno' to set off, on a journey, to N. Y.[1]— My cold, or what remains of it, (which is more than I could wish) is on my chest & lungs.— I have a *cough*, though not hard & obstinate, yet so serious as to admonish me to be *careful*. Taking chances of health & weather, *Tuesday* or *Wednesday* would be the earliest day that I should expect to be able to get away.— That would bring it near the end of the month, before I reached N York— Now, if Judge & Mrs. Story left home at the expected time, they will be *leaving* N York by the time I shall arrive.— So that, after all, I must come back very soon, or come alone afterwards.—

I have looked at all my causes in Court, & am satisfied that I can *very easily* make such arrangements, as that I may be gone a fortnight any time before the 1. of *Feby*.

Now the question is—whether I had not better wait till the Judge & his lady come here, & get settled—& then go & see Grace?

I should prefer, it is true, going while the Boats yet run; but

---

[1] December 13, 1827, Webster left Mrs. Webster and went to Washington, where the pressure of public business demanded his presence. He returned to her on January 3, 1828, and on January 21 she died. See Curtis' "Life of Daniel Webster," vol. i, p. 310.

a land journey, in health, is less hazardous than water passages, while sick—

What occurs to me, as best, on the whole, is that on receipt of this, you go to *Boston*, & give the necessary attention to your own affairs.   If, after being there a few days, you could return, without *any* degree of inconvenience, I should be glad—   But I would not have you derange your own affairs at all.—   In the mean time, I will be governed by my own health, & by what I hear from N. York, as to my going there before your return.— I do most devoutly wish I was able to go tomorrow!

It is obvious to me, that if Mrs W's case should continue, without material alteration for some time, I must vacate my place here.   Personally, I care very little about it, but wish only to fulfill the expectation of my friends, as far as circumstances will allow.—   But on this point, I shall do nothing hastily.—

You will receive this on Monday morning—   I shall get your answer on *Wednesday*.—but, in the mean time, if I hear that Mrs W. is worse, or I should get well myself sooner than I expect, I may probably set off.—

The most I shall fear, after you go, & while you are gone, is, that I shall not get, daily, true accounts.   The Dr. will naturally think that I could do no good, & therefore if Grace should be rather worse might not think it worth while to give me notice. *I must depend on you to make some arrangement by which I shall know, from day to day, & every day precisely how she is*—

P. S.   Mr Sparhawk, one of the reporters of the Senate, thinks of leaving this place for New York tomorrow—if he should, I will try to send a small trunk of children's clothes—if I can get them selected & packed—

Yrs   D. Webster

A certain other situation, ab't which the Papers talk, is equally inconsistent with the present condition of things, even if I had the option.—[1]

———

(From Jeremiah Mason.)

Portsmouth Jany 27, 1828

My dear Friend
Your two letters from N. York prepared us to expect what has

---

[1] Daniel Webster was talked of as Minister to England.

happened. We most sincerely sympathize with you in this event, in all its bearings & aspects, so melancholy & distressing. I know of no occasion, on which I have seen Mrs. Mason more deeply affected.

Without perhaps fully appreciating their extent, I know your sufferings have been, & still are excessive. You have all the consolation that the sympathy of friends, & universal condolence can give. But my knowledge of you, my dear Sir, forbids the hope of much relief or benefit from this source. Your consolation must come from a higher source. Your relief in this great calamity rests with yourself & your God. And there I confidently trust & hope you will find it. This is one of those events which strikingly illustrates the vanity of human expectations, & the imbecility of all human power.

Mr. Ticknor, in a letter of yesterday, says he understands your intention to be to return to Washington in eight or ten days. This as it seems to me ought to depend entirely on your own feelings & the condition of your health. I learn from Mr. Ticknor that your business in the Supreme Court will not be permitted to be pressed on you at this term. This I had anticipated.

We know nothing of the arrangements you have made, or think of making for your children this winter. We understand they are now with you at Mr. Blake's. Mrs. Mason desires me to say to you, that in case you can form no plan for taking care of them more satisfactory, she will most willingly take charge of the two youngest, till your return from Washington next spring. She is aware of the nature of the trust she offers to assume, & will of course execute it with all possible care. If this arrangement appears to you preferable to any other you can make, I request you will assent to it without fear of any apprehended trouble to us. For be assured, my Dr Sir, Mrs. Mason will undertake it most cheerfully.

When I first heard of your being at Boston, I thought of going there to see you. But I fear I shall not be able. A violent snow storm is now raging, & it is impossible to foresee how it will leave the travelling. I am likewise at this time much pressed with engagements for the winter session of Our Supr. Court, which summons at Dover the first of next week. Mrs. Mason desires her most affectionate regards to you.

I am my Dr Sir most faithfully yours

J. Mason.

(From Lafayette.)

PARIS March 13th 1828

My dear Sir

While I Have Been for More than eight Weeks Confined by illness, a Situation much aggravated By the Loss of one of My Beloved grand daughters, and an intimate old female friend and relation, I Have Had also to grieve for the dreadful Blow you are doomed to Bear. My most affectionate Sympathies are with you, My dear friend. George and M. C. Valleur Beg to Be Remembered on the Melancholy occasion. Of that sort of affliction I Have too Cruel an experience not to feel the whole extent of the Calamity that Has befallen you. receive the affectionate Regards of [1]

(From D. Fletcher Webster.)

BOSTON, April 20th, 1828.

My Dear Father,

I received yours of the 13th inst, enclosing my report, I hope Mr Gould will change his opinion. Edward is getting on in school, at a great rate. I agree with you, in your opinion, of Virgil and Cicero; but I do not like Sallust, quite so well. I am now much interested, in Virgil. If when Double Speeder comes down, she "speeds me away from my studies," I shall be content, to have her speed back again.   *   *   *

Your affectionate and dutiful son,

DANIEL. F. WEBSTER.

(To D. Fletcher Webster.)

WASHINGTON May 11. 1828
Sunday morng

My Dear Son

Accustomed, in our happy days, to have my children round me, on Sunday morning, & being now deprived of that pleasure, & indeed, never expecting to enjoy it again, in so great a degree as it has been enjoyed, I devote this morning to the only practicable way of holding intercourse with them. The rest & quiet of the

----

[1] The signature has been cut out of the original, but the letter is in Lafayette's hand.

Sabbath brings you all very freshly to my recollection; & now that the cares & labors of the week have ceased, I have pleasure in devoting my thoughts to my children, altho' accompanied with much melancholy & painful recollections.— My first wish on this occasion, My Dear Son, is to express my satisfaction with your conduct & character, & the good behavior & amiable deportment of Julia & Edward. I am sorry to be absent from you, feeling how especially it has become my duty to redouble my care of you, by the death of your blessed mother. The prospect is, that I shall now soon be with you, & I anticipate the happiness of finding you all in good health, and of hearing good accounts of you from the friends among whom you have passed the winter—

Congress will adjourn the 26—inst— That will bring it to the first of June before I get home, which will be about the close of the Vacation in your School. I was in hopes to spend the vacation with you, but that is now not possible

My wish is you should pass the vacation, under Uncle Williams advice, in the way most agreeable to yourself. Perhaps you may as well go to Boscawen, as any where. Uncle W. will have Speeder down, if you write to him—or you may go up in the Stage Coach, & ride down on Speeder— Whatever arrangement you & uncle William agree to, for passing the holidays, will suit me;—but I think a journey into the Country is probably the best. Your uncle, Aunt, & cousins will be very glad to see you.—

I believe I owe Mr Emerson a letter which I have not time to write. He must take care of you till I come home, & unless he shall already have made you so full of knowledge as that you can hold no more, his further contributions will be desirable—

Give my affectionate love to Julia & Edward—

Your loving father

Dan^L. Webster

Master D. F. Webster

P. S. Since writing this letter, I have recd yrs, with Mr Goulds report, which I enclose. You must try to correct, what he finds amiss, & to add exactness to your other attainments— Tell Mr Emerson I duly recd his letters—& postpone, for a fortnight & to personal communication, a reply thereto—

He does not right to infer assent from silence

Yrs D. W.—

(To Mrs. Ezekiel Webster.[1])

BOSTON, May 16, 1829.

My Dear Sister.

I was glad to hear from you, two days ago.   Julia went to Mrs. Lee's, on Monday, & seems very happy there.   I am to go for her this afternoon, to stay with us till Monday.   We are all quite well, & get along much as usual, except that the House is very sorry, & solitary.

On Thursday next, I go to N. York—to be gone a fortnight— then I have three weeks hard work at home, and what will be next is more than I foresee, but I hope it will be a trip to Boscawen.   Your friends .constantly inquire for you, with great interest, whenever I meet with them.

I believe Mr. P. or Daniel is writing to you today, & will tell you all the news if there be any.   I hear of none, except disasters among the Commercial Gentlemen.   Mr. P. brings "another failure" almost every day.   Judge Story's court is in session ; & this with preparation for my journey, leaves me little leisure.   I shall probably send you another line, before I go, tho' I shall have noth'g interest'g that I know of, to impart.

Yrs. affectionately,

D. WEBSTER.

———————

(From Eliza Buckminster Lee.[2])

R. PLACE Jan 1" 1830

My dear friend,

I am perhaps the *last* to *offer* you my congratulations on the late happy event,[3] but I assure I am not the least interested, nor the most indifferent of your friends—   The date of my letter also reminds me that it is a new-year—and I can add also the wishes of the day ; that this year may be as happy as the happiest of your life, and though I have always believed it, every one who has had the pleasure of an acquaintance with Mrs. Webster tells me, that she will make *every year* a year of happiness to you.

I thank you for your letter giving me notice of your mar-

---

[1] The original of this letter is owned by Edwin W. Sanborn, of New York.
[2] See Curtis' "Life of Webster," vol. i, p. 82.
[3] See Curtis' "Life of Webster," vol. i, p. 345.   Daniel Webster was married in December of 1829 to Miss Caroline LeRoy, the second daughter of Hermann LeRoy, a wealthy merchant of New York.

riage— It was deficient in a few important particulars—as to who were the parties—who were the guests, and by whom it was solemnized— You are in truth not a good narrator of what all ladies like to hear, and my imagination must fill up the great deficiencies your letter. * * *

always truly yrs

ELIZA LEE.

(To Jacob McGaw.[1])

BOSTON, Nov. 18, 1829.

My Dear Sir:—

I have a thousand thanks to give you and Mrs. McGaw for your kind invitation to have Julia with you for the winter. I assure you there are no persons living to whom I would more cheerfully give such a pledge of confidence. I know you would both love her for her own sake, as for her father's and mother's also; but Julia is at present so exceedingly well situated and so attached to her present condition, that it seems it would be wrong to change it. She has passed the summer at Brookline with Mrs. Lee (Eliza Buckminster), and had her instruction from Miss Searle, a young lady of our acquaintance of the best character and qualifications, who lives at Brookline with her mother and sisters. Julia has become quite attached to her, and, now that Mrs. Lee has come into town for the winter, Miss Searle has taken her altogether to herself. In addition to being in an excellent family and having good means of instruction, she is near town, so that her Uncle Paige and other friends can see her frequently in my absence. Under these circumstances, with hearty and repeated thanks for your friendship and kindness, I have concluded to leave her where she is.

And now, my dear sir, I must tell you and Mrs. McGaw (in confidence) a little news—nothing less than my expectation of being again married. The affair is not of long standing, but it looks so much like terminating in a marriage that I may venture to mention it to you—to go no further until you shall hear it from other quarters. The lady is Miss Caroline LeRoy of New York, aged 31 years or thereabouts. She is the daughter of a highly reputable gentleman, now some years retired from mercantile business. Mrs. McGaw will want to know all about her.

---

[1] The original of this letter is owned by Edwin W. Sanborn, of New York.

What I can say is that she is amiable, discreet, prudent, with enough of personal comeliness to satisfy me, and of the most excellent character and principles. With this account of the lady your wife must rest content till she has the means of personal acquaintance, which I sincerely hope may happen soon. Tell her she will be sure to like her. Whether this same lady will go to Washington the first of next month, or whether she will be so cruel as to oblige me to go without her and to return for her to New York, about Christmas, are secrets worth knowing, but which are not known to me. I shall endeavor to set forth strongly the inconvenience of a winter journey from W. to N. Y. and back.

I hope to get away on the 27th inst., and intend taking Julia to New York to make a little visit to Mrs. Perkins and for the purpose of giving her an opportunity of seeing the aforesaid lady.

With grateful and affectionate remembrance to you all, my good old friend, very truly yours,

DANIEL WEBSTER.

(To Mrs. Caroline Webster.[1]*)*

FEB.—15. 1830. Monday morn'g

My Dear Caroline

I suppose we receive just about the same time the melancholy tidings of the death of your dear sister. Altho' it was so fearfully expected, it yet is a great shock to learn the reality & certainty of what was so much dreaded. I have the news in a letter from your father, which I enclose to you, although he has probably written as fully to you as to me.

Her friends have the consolation of knowing that all was done for her, which kindness & affection could do, as well as that her excellent principles & sober & thoughtful character & feelings have prepared her for the change. Her daughter will doubtless feel the loss most deeply, she has been always so much with her mother, & has left her home recently.

I have fully made up my mind to go home, just as soon as the Boats run. Although there is now a great deal of snow & ice, yet we may expect a change soon.— I have never, more than once, known the Boats obstructed by ice after the first of March.

---

[1] See the letter of Mrs. Lee to Webster, January 1, 1830.

If I can get to N. Haven, I shall not mind taking the stage there for Worcester. All arrangements about your coming here may therefore be postponed till I get home.

My cold is nearly gone off— If the ground were in such a condition that I could walk, I think I would soon be quite well, but it is either very icy, & slippery, or quite wet all the time. It has been a severe winter here, as well as everywhere else. I learn that in the Western part of New York the snow was five feet deep, on a level, ten days ago they have had one heavy fall since.

Fletcher wrote me about his matter, but as I am going home so soon, it may be as well to defer any particular answer.

Yrs ever constantly

DANIEL WEBSTER

(From Mrs. Caroline Webster.)

FRIDAY mor'g. 14th May

My dear husband

Your very welcome letter came to hand a few moments since— *dated tuesday* & the *magnolia*—which as you imagined has lost its fragrance—but yet valued as coming from one I sincerely love—

We all envy you the *peas* & *strawberries* I presume we shall very soon have them—we have had a cold storm for a week but to day, getting warm I hope for a pleasant change—Last ev'g drank tea socially with Mrs A. Schmerhorn—Mr & Mrs. A. Ogden & Mr Mrs E K Jones & daughter— R. Rutgers & Genl Jones & Dr Bilby—had a tolerably pleasant evg You were particularly enquired after—I see by the papers to day McKinley has proposed the 31st inst for adjournment & Mr Noble passed a consideration by putting it on the table—I fear & believe now I shall not see you until June—but hope for the last time—I expect to get off all my boxes this afternoon—its a monstrous task for me—as I have to attend to it all— * * *

Julia is quite well—she wrote Mrs Lindsley yesterday & to day is writing her brother Daniel I strive to keep her a little employed—not hard work—where so many temptations surround her—she is going to see Mrs Perkins this morg.

Father seemed gratified with your letter of yesterday—I beg you will continue to write me daily—for I feel greatly disappointed if the day passes without my hearing from you—I expect to see *Noah* in a few days bitter against you—I regretted

Kendalls appointment   Will it not make the Vice President unpopular—that seems the impression here—his vote gives in his
favor—Remember me to all friends—All here unite in love to you
& want very much to see you—

Believe me yours very truly
CAROLINE WEBSTER

* * * *Dont criticise my servants*

(From Samuel B. Wallcot.)

BOSTON Aug 28, 1830.

My dear Sir,
   Daniel was yesterday admitted to the Sophomore Class in
Harvard University after a pretty strict examination, which I
believe he passed creditably to himself.   His character there will
depend very much on his associates & the firmness with which he
may pursue the good resolutions he has formed.   A year of constant & agreeable intercourse with him has made me feel a deep
interest in his welfare, & I believe that your fondest wishes for
him may yet be realised, if he will only use with vigour & constancy the capacities with which he is blest.   * * *

Y'rs very sincerely & respectfully,
SAMUEL B. WALCOTT.

(From D. Fletcher Webster.)

NEW YORK, Jan. 3, 1831.

My Dear Father,
   * * *[1]   I am very sorry indeed, that I have not done more
this term, in reading those authors of whom you approved.   I
know I have not done enough.   I will not attempt to excuse myself any more, for my negligence; but show you that I will amend
for the future, and I hope to meet your approval, at the end of
the second term.   Mr. Quincy told me that I had done very well,
and that the government have nothing to say against me.   Mr.
Farrar had the kindness to pay me a compliment.   I think, I
stand very well with the government,[2] and I know I do with the
students.   If I apply myself as I hope to do; I may perhaps

---

[1] The minor amenities are omitted.   [2] *I. e.*, the faculty at Harvard.

graduate higher than you seem to expect I shall, from the last term. The chief fault is, my dear father, a restlessness; I cannot stick to the same thing long, a fault of which I am as well aware, as yourself. Time and care will I hope correct this. I am a little troubled with my eyes; which are very weak, and it is almost impossible to read in the evening. I have been to Dr Randall and he gave me a wash, which assists them. I shall go home prepared to study and to give you satisfaction.— * * *

Julia joins with me in love to you and Mother

I remain your truly affectionate son,

D. F. WEBSTER.

(From D. Fletcher Webster.)

CAMBRIDGE Febry 6th 1831.

My Dear Father,

I am still pursuing my Greek and Latin with industry, and hope not to give way, any more, to any "besetting sin"; I find pleasure in study, as it brings a reward of satisfaction; which is sufficient to compensate labour. * * * We have been studying Greek for the last week, I have done pretty well in that, and better than ever in Mathematics. We are now on Nautical astronomy, a pretty hard thing, but *practical* and therefore interesting. * * *

Please give my love to Mother and I remain

Your obedient and affectionate son,

D F WEBSTER.

(From D. Fletcher Webster.)

CAMBRIDGE Feb. 25th, 1832.

My Dear Father,

* * * I hope that there is more in me than has yet appeared, for I have done nothing heretofore, and should be very sorry to think that a son of yours was wholly good for nothing; but I fear that people think there is more in me than there really is. I must do all I can to answer their expectations, for it is hard to have expectations raised which can never be fulfilled, yet one ought not to be blamed for not answering them, when they are not just, and founded upon sufficient grounds. * * *

Julia wrote a letter in French to Cousin Eliza a few days ago which was very correct and well written.   I hope she is doing well.   She has improved a great deal in writing.   Edward is studying well, I believe and attends to his books.   He has a great deal of taste for speaking and reading.   I have no doubt he will be a high scholar.

There is a society here which has been lately formed called the Harvard Union the object of which is to encourage debating and speaking.   It is formed by the junction of the Junior and Senior classes.   The first scholars in both founded it.   They wish, as much as possible to do away the distinction of Class and therefore have their officers half from each class.   The sixth or seventh scholar among the Seniors and the best debater has been chosen president and the first scholar secretary; among the Juniors the first scholar also is secretary and I am president.   The officers sit alternately on succeeding evenings.   This was an unexpected honour and I must do something to deserve it.   It will be my turn soon to deliver an essay before them and I am exceedingly anxious to appear well and talk sense.   To this, the choice of a good subject, in which they will all be interested, and upon which I can give some information is mainly necessary.   If you can tell me of some one, of which you may happen to think & which I can understand, it will help me very much.   I was rather averse at first to join, but thinking afterwards that if I could ever be anything, I could be *something* now, and also that considering my connexions I ought not to be behind hand in such things, I signed my name to the constitution.   I hope you will approve of my conduct.

Your very affectionate son
D. Fletcher Webster.

(From D. Fletcher Webster.)

Cambridge March 11th, 1832

My Dear Father,

I am very much obliged to you for your long and kind letter. I hardly see how you found time to write me so long a one.[1]   I assure I will do my best to meet your expectations.   It is, on my word, impossible for me to become first scholar.   I asked my chum about it, and he is a sensible fellow, not telling him anything about your letter, and he said, he had no doubt I was a high

---

[1] This letter has not been preserved.

scholar and might be higher, but knew I could not be first.   The fact is that we have some very capable men in the class, much older than I, and with minds much more matured.

I have no taste for Mathematics and only get them by hard study, while to many of my class, it is a recreation to study mechanics and algebra.

I am perfectly content to stay in Cambridge, and will employ my time, as far as know how, to the best advantage.   You speak, Dear Father, as if I were deficient in something.   Now, I am not conscious of having failed in any thing, this year.   My rank has never been so good, and I have omitted no duties.   I am at a loss to know where you had the idea, that I had neglected anything.   My leisure hours are mostly employed in reading history or some useful book, and I endeavor to waste none of the time I can get from my studies.   *   *   *

I shall deliver that lecture upon Labor, and thank you very sincerely for sending me some ideas on the subject, as well as the subject.   I will try to do myself credit.   *   *   *

Ever your affectionate son
D. FLETCHER WEBSTER.

(From D. Fletcher Webster.)

CAMBRIDGE April 21st, 1832.

Dear Father,

I received your kind letter and also those papers you were so good as to send me— I am very happy to be able to read the debates in Congress which are now very interesting and will I suppose grow more so, as the Session advances to a close.

There has been a good deal of anxiety here to know the result of Mr Houston's affair,[1] People in general wish him punished.

*   *   *   I saw your portraits of the family, and am proud to say, I possess in an equal degree with you, the talent of painting.

E. is doing very well he was last week No. 5 and is now the fourth in his class, with hope of being the third next week. *   *   *

Yours very affectionately
D. FLETCHER WEBSTER.

---

[1] Referring to the trial of Samuel Houston then pending before the House of Representatives.

(From Mrs. Caroline Webster.)

My Dear Husband   BOSTON Monday Evg. Dec. 31st 1832

* * * Mr Davis told me that he intruded himself into your bedroom & disturbed your repose; he told me several anecdotes about you—asked me if I knew you had two young ladies under your care & that application was also made to you, to know if you did not want a boy—I think if I had been you, I should have declined the care of the two ladies. Mr Davis said also that father told him he never had seen you look so well, or appear in such good spirits since he had known you, all of which gratified me exceedingly. * * *

Every one I see looks & talks very blue the *Tariff* seems now to alarm the manufacturers. Mr Crowninshield & Blake last night declared they were prepared for the *worst* & now let it come—Mr Haynes proclamation[1] I have read & think it a bold one—he will soon meet with his deserts I imagine.

I hear Mr Appleton has taken possession of our old parlour & shall not be surprised to hear you have determined to remain with with him. I quite long to hear where you are settled & all your arrangements. I only entreat of you to *keep cool* & not to subject yourself to an attack from those *hot headed* nullifiers. Poor Duff Green is in a sad condition with a broken arm. I trust however that your business will not be delayed on his account & a second *Houston trial ensue.* Do you believe Congress will be convened after the 4th of March. I see some hints of the kind in the papers.

Tomorrow being New Year I shall sit up in due form but question whether I have much company—as it does not seem to be a holiday. The children go to school as usual, but don't like it very well—Daniel's vacation expires day after tomorrow, he has not been to more than two or three parties since you left & has been very regular in his hours—indeed—conducts himself with entire propriety—Julia has recd the promised hat from Papa to day & is much pleased with it. Edward has brought me a monthly report to sign—but I dont think a very good one—23 marks for *misdemeanors* I have given him a long lecture & told him I should enclose the next to you—he says that his marks are for trifles— * * *

[CAROLINE WEBSTER]

---

[1] *I. e.*, as Governor of South Carolina. See "Niles Register," vol. xliii, p. 308.

(From Mrs. Caroline Webster.)

My dear husband   J<small>AN</small> 1st, 1833 Tuesday evg **6** oclock.

A gloomy day this, I have been dressed up all day & the only creature who called was *Allyne Otis* & he sent his card in— I had my table spread with cakes liquor & wine & not a soul to take them. Uncle P. has just gone from here—urged me to go up with him but Miss Kelly has been spending the day with me & I have promised to walk up after tea—he said Harriet had been sitting up also & had no visitors. The fact is I did not expect it, but as I was uncertain & the first New Year I have ever spent here, I would be in readiness to receive calls. I must wish you a happy new year— * * *

                                        Yours ever   C. W.

(From D. Fletcher Webster.)

My Dear Father,   C<small>AMBRIDGE</small> Jan. 22d 1833

I have read your letter several times, and hope to profit by your kind and excellent advice. I have already begun my course and feel myself stronger and stronger every day. The other night I sat up until nearly twelve reading Hume. I am interested in it. I have also read a part of Hawkin's Life of Johnson. A very good biography I should think. We are now studying Latin—Cicero; I am at home in that, as Cicero is a favourite book of mine. I read it with more pleasure than any other of the Classics. I wrote a long theme the other day upon the progress of the arts. * * *

I begin to acquire a little taste for mathematics; we have now come to some practical parts, as navigation and dialling; and such questions as this The angle A being given, and the distance of the foot a tower, from the place where you take the observation, to find the height of tower. This is a great thing in the time of war, to ascertain the height of enemie's camps and forts. It is quite easy and pleasant, and besides to find the latitude and longitude of a place; or your latitude and longitude when at sea. These and other questions of this sort are very interesting, compared with that part of Mathematics which is wholly theoretical. * * *

                    Your ever affectionate son
                                        D. F. W<small>EBSTER</small>.

(To D. Fletcher Webster.)

PITTSBURG, July 5, 1833.

My Dear Son,—

It seems to become doubtful whether I can possibly get home to hear your oration. I regret this, very much indeed, and shall still make every effort in my power to reach Boston in season, but I find so many causes of delay that I cannot say what I may be able to accomplish. I have seldom felt so much concern about anything of the kind as I do upon your success upon that occasion. I pray you spare no pains. Do your best and you will do well enough. It would be a good thing to have printed, if it should be well received. This part of the matter we can see about. I earnestly remind you of the necessity of acting with great caution in regard to all *festivities*. You remember what I said to you on that head and I pray you to forget no part of it. You may ask Mr. —— for any money which you may have just occasion for. Give my best regards to Mr. Paige's and Mr. White's families. I have not heard from mother and Julia since they arrived at Saratoga.[1]

Ever your affectionate father,

D. WEBSTER.

(To Mrs. Ezekiel Webster.[2])

BOSTON, Oct. 26, 1833.

My Dr Sister.

Man is born for disappointments. Events have occurred, in verification of this novel idea, to prevent us from coming to Boscawen. In the first place, the *Courts* have deranged the times of expected sitting, so as to embarrass me not a little. In the next place, Mr. Clay's visit naturally keeps me, for some days, at home. Thirdly, Mrs. W. has been sick, for near a week, & is not yet down stairs; & lastly, she has just learned that some family friends will visit her, early next week, from N. York.

I have written to that good soul, the Revd. C. B. Hadduck that he must come down to see us, about the 7th or 8th of next

---

[1] This letter is taken from a newspaper clipping in the possession of C. E. Bliss, of Bangor, Me. The name and date of the paper are unknown.

[2] The original of this letter is the property of Edwin W. Sanborn, of New York.

month; & have invited him to take you along with him. A little bit of a fall journey seems appropriate to wind up the excursions of the year.

We propose to set forth, on the 13th, for Washington. Both the boys will go with us, & Julia will winter in N. York. Pray give my love to the girls, & Miss Bridge; & do not fail to come & see us. If a ride would not be injurious to Mary-Anne, bring her along. We can learn fashions from her, as she is so recently from the watering places.

Yrs ever truly,

D. WEBSTER.

Just answer this, by a complying line.

(To D. Fletcher Webster.)

WASHINGTON June 5, '34

My Dear Son

I presume you will be in Boston, by the time this letter shall arrive. So soon as you shall have made a short visit to Marsh-field, I wish you to proceed to Exeter with Edward. It is high time he was at School. You will take him to Mr Chadwicks, & see him provided for, as to room &c.— Ask Mr Chadwick to be kind enough to take care of him, in all those respects in which a boy needs looking after. He must, among other things, take the trouble of attending to his personal cleanliness, &c.— In all these particulars enjoin on Edward the importance of exact and steady habits. As to any clothes or books, or other articles, if he shall need them Mr. Chadwick will see him supplied, or tell him where to obtain what he wants.— You must leave him a little pocket money, & a small monthly allowance can be sent him from home— Go with him to Dr. Abbott, & stay in town a day or two, until he has been at school once or twice, & begins to feel a little at home.—

Congress will adjourn, I think, the 30th.—& I shall probably be at home the 10 or 15 July.— I shall be detained here a few days, perhaps by business with the Comm^{rs}, & must stop a day or two on the road.—

Your affectionate father

D WEBSTER

(To Edward Webster.)

BOSTON Aug. 20, 1834

My Dear Son,
Julia told me that you had written to her that you needed some money to pay your expenses home.   I therefore enclose you ten Dollars.   Please bring with you the amount of Col. Chadwick's bill for board, & I will send him a check for the amount. If you owe anything for books or clothes, more than you have means to pay, ask Col Chadwick to pay it, & add the amount to your bill.   Be sure to leave no little debts unpaid.
Your sister says we may expect you toward the end of this week.   You will find some of us, in Summer Street.

Yr affectionate father
[D. WEBSTER]

───────

(From D. Fletcher Webster.)

BOSTON Dec 24th. 1834.

My dear Father,
I received your very kind letter the day we were going to Plymouth & have deferred answering it until our return.   I cannot sufficiently express to you the pleasure I received from it, especially as you were so kind as to tell me of your views & opinions,[1] which, as you may suppose I am most anxious to know, but which you have heretofore seldom spoken to me about.   *   *   *
I see that the House has got fairly embarked on the Money question & if the discussion continues I would not give much for any office under the Federal Government & should think that the successful candidate for the first office might find indeed a very
"Barren sceptre in his grasp" and
"Shorn of half it's fair proportions."
I know you won't approve of the opinion, but I believe that it is a very prevalent idea that there will be a separation very soon, & you will be perhaps sorry to hear, that I am it may be, so ignorant & foolish as to think it would be quite as well for all of us if it should be so, though anyone who has ever read the farewell address of Washington must feel great reluctance & diffidence in saying so.   Don't suppose, Sir, that I talk of this before

─────────────────────────────

[1] Daniel Webster to Fletcher Webster, of which Fletcher speaks, is not to be found.

people, it would hardly become your Son, but in secret I can't help thinking it. * * *

Yr most affectionate Son

FLETCHER WEBSTER.

(From D. Fletcher Webster.)

HOPKINTON Feby 28th. 1835.

My dear Father,

I should have written you much oftener than I have this winter. * * *

I have been "tearing the law to pieces" these last *seven months* that I have been at Hopkinton, and have arrived to such a degree of proficiency as to be able to take care of almost any business that presents itself at our office. * * *

Besides my legal acquirements, I have been making favour with the natives, shall be a voter at our "March Meeting;" next Monday and have some hopes of the responsible office of field-driver or hog-reeve.

I have delivered a long lecture before the Lyceum of the Town and my remarks were so well received by that learned body that I was asked to repeat my lecture and write another in continuation of the subject, which I am now employed upon. * * *

Your ever affectionate Son

F. WEBSTER.

(To Mrs. Caroline Webster.[1]*)*

BANGOR, Friday Eve' Sep. 25, 1835.

My Dear Wife.

I reached Bangor this afternoon at four clock, having left Hallowell a little before 7;—& having travelled the whole distance, 70 miles, in a chaise. The stages were crowded to excess, & one of the agents undertook to bring me along in a chaise, which he accomplished with great speed. The country is somewhat hilly, but the road is smooth, & it is the fashion to drive like Jehu. I am a good deal tired, & I shall go early to bed. Mr. McGaw, & a few other friends have called, & I believe I may expect more at Eve';—but I am quite too much fatigued to see

---

[1] The original of this letter is in the possession of Edwin W. Sanborn, of New York.

much company.   Yesterday I spent at Hallowell, Augusta, & Gardner,—in seeing the people, & the places.   I called on Mr. Vaughan, Dr. Corry, & some other elderly people, & took some pains to go & see Dr. Sewall's mother, and also Mrs. Lindsley's mother.   They both appeared gratified with the attention.   Mr. Evans devoted the day to me & was very kind.   I have two College classmates who are settled in the place, both with families.

Mr. Evans does not go to Washington, till the Spring.

What I shall do tomorrow I do not yet know; but I expect to go up the River, about twelve miles, to see the spot about which the law suit is.   As yet, I have heard nothing from home; it is hardly time.   Adieu, with love to the family,

Yrs ever,
DANL. WEBSTER.

(To Mrs. Caroline Webster.)

NEWYORK, Greenwich St, Saturday, 10 O'clock

[Nov. 28. 1835] (?)

My Dear Wife

I arrived here this mor'g, at 1/2 past 7, just in time for an excellent breakfast.   Our passage was quite fair.   The early part of the night there was some wind & rain, & the sea round Point Judith was a little rough & ragged.   Afterwards we paddled along, over a smooth surface, & with a tolerably clear sky.

All are well here, & all in great good spirits, by reason of excellent tidings from Mrs. Newbold.   They heard of her, for the first time, yesterday.   The letters will be sent to you.   She found herself *entirely well*, on her arrival at Havre—

—I find the Philadelphia invitation here, & shall partake of the dinner about Thursday.—

Mrs. Edgar says the pin-cushion &c is beautiful.   She will write you soon.

Mrs. Perkins has gone to Boston.   Please inquire for her, at Mr. Bryants—the Dr. goes that way in a day or two.

Yrs truly
DANL WEBSTER.

Love to

Miss Ogden, D. F. Webster, Julia Webster, Edward Webster, &c &c &c &c &c &c &c &c.

Miss Wallace desires me to scold Sally Jenkins almost to pieces for not writ'g to her. * * *[1]

(To Mrs. Caroline Webster.)

N. York Decr. 7. '35.

Dear Caroline,

I received your letter yesterday, & all here were very glad to hear from you. This leaving home is a pretty hard matter, to those who go, & to those who stay. It may render a reunion more agreeable & more valued.

I went to Church yesterday morning with Mr. Edgar, & for the rest of the day, except a short call at Mr Curtis', I sat over the fire— Today I have calls to make, & business to attend to, beside a dinner to eat with the Sons of St. Nicholas.

We did wrong in not sending your father some of our apples. He wants two barrels of our *Greenings*. If there comes a moderate turn of weather, you must send them on to him. Mr. Paige will advise Fletcher about the time & mode of shipping them. The Captain must be charged to keep them from frost.

I have paid your butter bill which is enclosed. Also your bonnet bill—$26.25. For both these amounts please give me credit, & charge house-hold expenses. The butter cost 30 cts, here, as you will see. The honor of New England forbids us to send again to N. Y. for butter. Bonnets, you may get where you please.

Father desires his best regards, & will send you the letters from Mr. Newbold as soon as they have been read by friends here.

Adieu, for today

D Webster

Mrs Webster—
I enclose two little bills which do not pass here—

(To Mrs. Caroline Webster.)

Feb. 21. 1836.

Dear Caroline,

I returned the letter, giving so interesting an account of the

---

[1] A list of places where Daniel Webster is invited to dine.

last days & hours of poor Mrs Newbold, presuming that you would naturally wish to preserve it. She departed this life, as her friends would desire she should, full of religious hope, & pious resignation; & it becomes her numerous friends to acquiesce in the dispensation of Providence.

It would give me great pleasure that little Helen should come & live with you. You have my entire approbation in taking any measures, for that end, which you see fit.

I am quite sorry to learn by your letter that you were not in very good health, but hope your indisposition was but slight & temporary. My cold is getting better & I now call myself pretty well. I have had to sit so much at my table, the last month, that I have felt some pain in the chest.— Having omitted all writing for two or three days, it has gone off.— The weather is fine today—warm & bright—& the snow, I hope, will begin to melt away. It is the warmest day we have had since I came to Washington. * * *

Judge Story will leave us in about a week.— I feel very anxious to have the river clear—as I am inclined to go home, so soon as the Boats run.

Yrs ever truly

D. W.

―――――

(To Mrs. Caroline Webster.)

Dear Wife, WASHINGTON Mar. 7th 1836

I recd this morning your letter of the 3d inst. Its important item, is that in respect to Mr Brooks & Sally Ogden. I have expected, for some time, that Mr B. would turn out to be serious, in his attentions to Sally, from the warmth of his expressions to me, before I left home. I like Mr Brooks very much—he has a mild temper, & is always agreeable & sociable in his manners. He will make, I fully believe, a perfectly good husband. There can be no possible objection, but difference of age. If that should be regarded as not insuperable, nothing else could possibly be objected. As to that objection, Sally must judge of it for herself. Such things must be decided by feeling, & fancy. I incline to think, for myself, that she will not refuse Mr B. Looking to all circumstances, I am prepared to hear that a match is to come of it. I should be very, very glad, if we could keep him in Boston—

I write this in the Senate, in the midst of an abolition debate. I hope we shall take the question, & settle the matter today. But there is no knowing— Debate seems endless.

I write today to Mr Birchhead to give me notice of the first movement of the Boats— The weather is mild, but not yet warm.—

Adieu! for today—

I had a pleasant dinner at Mr Agg's—lettuce, asparagus & sea Kail—

[DAN'L. WEBSTER]

(To Edward Webster.)

BOSTON Oct. 8. 1836

Dear Edward,

  * * *[1] It gives me pleasure to learn that you are comfortably settled, & are able to apply yourself to your studies. These are to you, My Dear Son, the golden moments of opportunity, & I ardently hope you will improve them all.

I enclose you a little money, which you must use with careful & exact economy,

With much love to Mr Haddock's family, I am,

Yr affectionate father

DANIEL WEBSTER

(D. Webster's First Will.)

NOVEMBER 1836

I, Daniel Webster, of Boston, in the County of Suffolk, do hereby make & declare this my last will & testament, hereby revoking all wills by me heretofore made—

It is my will that all my just debts be paid, a memorandum of which will be found among my papers. In order to raise money for that purpose, I direct my Executors to collect all the debts which may be due to me at my decease & to sell & dispose of the following described property, viz: the vacant lot in Summer Street in Boston, between the lot on which my house stands, & the house of Mr. White now occupied by Mr Paige; my books; my wine; my furniture & other personal property, except as here-

---

[1] Family plans omitted.

inafter excepted; and also all or any of my property in lands, city lots, Companies, Corporations &c, in Michigan, Ohio, Indiana, Illinois & Wisconsin, or such parts thereof as may be necessary & may be sold to most advantage. And for the like purpose if necessary to sell my land in Derry, New Hampshire, & my farm & lands in Franklin, New Hampshire, &, if further necessary, to sell also such parts of my Marshfield property as may be thought best for the good of my heirs; I intending to leave it in the discretion of my Executors to sell such of the above mentioned property first, as may be in their judgment best—not confining them to the order in which the parcels are here enumerated; first of all, however, applying to the payment of debts, the proceeds of any policy or policies on my own life, which may be running at my death.—

There being a conveyance of my house in Boston in which I now reside, by marriage settlement in trust to my wife for life, & remainder of my heirs, as will appear by the deed, if no other arrangement be agreed on, as better, property must be sold, to pay off a mortgage of nineteen thousand Dollars on the House, so that it may follow the trusts of the settlement unincumbered—

I give to my beloved wife, the coach, pleasure waggons, & coach horses, any hundred volumes of my books which she may prefer, & other furniture which she brought into the house with her, two thousand Dollars worth of plate, & two thousand Dollars a year, during the life time of her father, which is to be in full satisfaction of her right to Dower out of my estate.—

I give & devise the rest & residue of my property real & personal to my children, equally to be divided among them; except as hereinafter excepted; that is to say, that in regard to articles which are valuable as keepsakes or tokens, I dispose of such articles, as follows—viz—

To my wife, I give the picture of myself by Alexander—

To my son Daniel Fletcher, I give the vase presented to me by citizens of Boston, the watch in my pocket, & the picture of myself by Stewart—

To my daughter Julia, I give her mother's picture, by Harding, her mother's watch, and all the little articles which were her mothers, a small picture of myself taken when young; & the little bust, or head of myself, by Ball Hughes—

To my son Edward, I give the plate presented me by Amos Lawrence, the snuff box presented to me by Mr. Bradley, and the large gold watch which I wore in his mother's life-time—and my

Washington medals— And as I have advanced seven thousand Dollars to Fletcher on his marriage, the whole of this is to be reckoned & charged as part of his portion—DANIEL WEBSTER[1]

I hereby nominate and appoint my wife Caroline Le Roy Webster, & my son Daniel Fletcher Webster, and the survivor of them, Executrix & Executor of this my last will & testament— In testimony whereof I have hereunto set my hand & seal this —— day of November in the year Eighteen hundrey & thirty-six—

DANIEL WEBSTER (seal)

Signed, sealed, published, and declared by the said Daniel Webster, as his last will & testament, in the presence of us, who at his request, & in his presence & in the presence of each other, have hereunto subscribed our names, as witnesses—it being on two sheets each of which bears my name—

HENRY W. KINSMAN   D. WEBSTER
CHARLES H. THOMAS
TIMOTHY FLETCHER.

(To Edward Webster.)

WASHINGTON, Feb. 4, 1837.

My Dear Son:

We think it very strange that none of us has had a letter from you, since you arrived at Hanover, tho' your mother & sister have both written you. I requested you, if I remember, to write to some of us once a week; a request, which you will hereafter observe & fulfil, punctually & exactly.

We are quite well. The Session is drawing rapidly to a close, & I expect to be in Boston by the middle of March.

Remember me kindly to Mr. Haddock's family.

Your affectionate father

DANL WEBSTER.

(To Edward Webster.)

WASHINGTON Sep. 16, 1837.

My Dear Son

I will endeavor to send you a little money, in a few days. In

----

[1] "Daniel Webster" signed at the close of the first sheet.

the meantime, I return your letter, in which you will find as many errors, as you see marks.

There are mispellings;

There is no tolerably correct punctuation;

There are instances, in which sentences, after periods, are begun with small letters; and words, which should be begun with large letters, are begun with small ones.

Write me, immediately, a more careful, & a better, letter—

[D. WEBSTER] [1]

———

(To Mrs. Caroline Webster.)

FRIDAY MOR'G
[June 29 1838]

Dear Caroline

I recd last eve. yr. letter of Wednesday, & presume you reached home on Thursday m'n'g.

We are now engaging in a measure respecting Banks which have issued small notes—when that is finished, there will be no other public subjects, of great importance, to be acted on.

My health is getting to be pretty good—though I am not yet entirely well— I am a good deal better, from the prospect of getting away from Washington soon. Mr. Curtis is mending—but he goes seldom to the House.

I cannot say how long before the adjournment I may be able to get away, but I think I shall not stay till the last end. I shall be obliged to stop some days in N. York, on my way home.

The House sat very late last night, and everybody seems at work to get away. Our boxes and trunks have gone to Alexandria—the vessel which takes them will sail on Monday. I have written to Mr Fletcher to take care of them.

The weather continues exceedingly warm—so that I cannot stir out, unless in a carriage, between sun & sun. We have frequent showers, but no heavy rains.

Mr. Curtis desires his regards to you & Julia.

As yet, I have not heard from Fletcher since his departure.

Yrs truly always,

D. W.

We expect a warm Debate today, on Mr. Buchanan's *Special Deposit* Scheme.

---

[1] The signature had been cut out.

(To Edward Webster.)

WASHINGTON July 6, 1838.

My Dear Son

I was glad to receive your letter of the 1st tho' you have been so very negligent & culpable, in the matter of writing. *You must not suffer such neglect to occur again.*

I expect to leave Washington tomorrow, & to be in Boston in a week. I suppose you have a short vacation, after your examination.[1] If so, you will come at once to Marshfield. On the receipt of this, write me immediately, addressed to me at Boston, stating the amount of your Bills, & what money you need, if any before the next term. Your mother & sister, are I presume, now at Marshfield, Mrs. Curtis is at Saratoga. Mr. Curtis has been sick, but is getting well again. Congress adjourns on Monday next. Make my best regards to Mr. Haddock & his family.

Yr affectionate father

DANL WEBSTER

(To Edward Webster.)

MARSHFIELD, Sep. 8, 1838.

My Dear Son.

Your letter, respecting your own private affairs, has caused me very great grief. I am shocked, not only at the folly & guilt of contract'g such a debt, but at the misrepresentations which you must have repeatedly made; as you have always told me that you owed noth'g, which the means I furnished were not competent to discharge. Your letter has remained several days, unanswered, because I had not made up my mind what answer to give. My first feeling was to withdraw you from College, & to let you take care of yourself hereafter. But you letter shows an apparent spirit of repentance, & if I were sure that I could trust that, I might be induced to overlook the enormity of your misconduct. But how can I be sure that *you* have *now* told me the whole truth? How can I trust your present statements? Besides, how was this debt created? Was it by gaming, or other immoral habits, or by mere thoughtlessness, & folly?

I have concluded to go up to Boston, tomorrow or next day; & then, either to go directly to Hanover, or to write you again.

---

[1] Edward was at this time in Dartmouth College.

In the mean time I want to know more about the manner of contract'g this debt; & I expect the whole truth.   I would not expose you to public reproach, nor cast you off, for slight cause; but with all my affection, I will not excuse misconduct, and, especially, I will not put up with any degree or particle of misrepresentation, or concealment of the truth.   On the receipt of this, you will immediately write to me, directed to Boston; & when I receive your letter, I shall determine what course to pursue.[1]

Your affectionate, but distressed father,

DANL. WEBSTER.

(*From Edward Webster.*[2])

HANOVER, Sept. 13, 1838.

My Dear Father.

I received your letter yesterday.   I was aware that it could not but grieve you very much and that was the reason why I never told you before and also made the misrepresentations which you speak of.   And sir I can quiet your fears about my repentance not being real and affected, for I certainly do feel very sorry and penitent and you may rest assured that the like will never occur again.   You wish to know how the debts were contracted.   I will tell you the *truth* now.   You say that you dont know but it was by gaming?   It was not, for I never gambled for a cent in my life, nor do I think I ever shall, for I never could have been led away as far as that if any one had tried me, for I detest the practice and always did.   A good deal is for such things as nuts & raisins, crockery, cigars, candy, pantaloons, chip men, backgammon boards, knife and some *wine* a very little of which I can say with a clear conscience I drank myself, riding on horseback and other ways for pleasure, and I am sorry to say very few of the articles were of any use.   The only immoral thing which I have purchased is wine, the students with whom most of these debts were contracted have graduated so that there would not be the same temptations if I would yield to them, which by the help of a firm resolve I hope I never shall.

---

[1] The stern Puritanism of Webster's character is better illustrated by the letter than any other of which the editor knows.   Edward's reply, which follows, shows that he had been guilty only of the most amusing schoolboy follies, and adds most assuring evidence of his spirit and independence.   This letter is owned by Mr. Edwin W. Sanborn, of New York.

[2] This letter is the property of Edwin W. Sanborn, of New York.

I should be very sorry to be taken away from college, but if you think best I should be willing to go, with the education you have been kind enough to give me and my bodily strength I feel I should be able to take care of myself. If I do not improve upon trial I do not wish nor ask for any further indulgence, and as to the money part of it if by any means by keeping school or in other way I could make that up to you in a measure or in full I should be most happy to do so, and remain my dear Father your most affectionate and deeply penitent son,

EDWARD WEBSTER.

(To Edward Webster.)

BOSTON, Sep. 18, 1838.

My Dear Son

I am very anxious to hear from you, as I am going in a few days, to N. York, & am desirous of reliev'g you, from your difficulties, if I can, before I go. I expected to receive a letter before this time. Lose no time in writing—

Yr affectionate father,

DANL WEBSTER

(To Edward Webster.)

BOSTON Sep. 21, 1838.
My Dear Son

I recd your letter, two days ago, and have made up my mind to put intire trust in your statements—to clear off your embarrassments— & to give you a fair opportunity to retrieve whatever may have been amiss; & to resume your studies.

I now trust, My Dear Son, to hear nothing of you, hereafter, except what may be gratifying.

[D. W.]

(To Mrs. Caroline Webster.)

Private

MONDAY MOR'G [March 2, 1840.]
My Dear Wife,

Amo'g the thi'gs which have worried me for some time, one is the condition of matters at La Salle, & Fletcher's situation. The state of the times, & the rascally & foolish conduct of the Gov't of Illinois has stopped all their public works. The hands

have broke off from the canal,[1] as I understand, leavi'g it unfinished, & probably it may be four five years before it will be
resumed.   In this state of thi'gs, & while it lasts, Peru will be
noth'g—& it will be impossible that there shou'd be any business
there, by which F. could support his family.

Then, again, if there shou'd be a third season, as sickly as
the two last, I should hardly expect him to get through it. Ray's
fever here was noth'g, between ourselves, but a new break'g out
of his old illness.   The Physicians found good reason to think
he had never been well, since his long confinement at Tonawanda.

All these thi'gs give me trouble, but I have not said any thi'g
about them.   I wrote to F. in Peru from N. Y. on the subject of
his health & the climate, &c.   He has not said much, in reply.
Think of these thi'gs, & keep them to yourself—

Yours

D. WEBSTER

(From D. Fletcher Webster.)

My dear Father,   PERU April 16th 1840.

Your kind letter of April 11th has just been received.   There
are two chief reasons why I wish to move East and two chief
favours which I ask of you in order to enable me to do so advantageously.   In the first place, we are very unhealthy here &
though I hope in any event, that we might all live through it,
yet, in the second place, there is no business here worth living
for.

I was unfortunate in coming here—   I came here on the *ebb
tide* and things have been going backward ever since—[2]

The favours I want you to grant are these.   To give me your
countenance and support in forming a connection in New York—
& to let it be understood that the firm will have the benefit of your
advice in all necessary cases.   If these can be granted, I shall
try to leave here—otherwise I dare not venture.   *   *   *[3]

I remain yr. affectionate son

D. F. WEBSTER.

---

[1] The Lake Michigan and Illinois Canal, which was to connect the waters of
the lake with those of the Mississippi River.

[2] Letters from Fletcher Webster to be found among those concerning
Webster's farm interests will fully explain Fletcher's presence in the West and
his life there.

[3] Minor business details omitted.

(To Mrs. Caroline Webster.)

SUNDAY, Aug. 22, 1841.

My Dear wife

I have rec'd y'r letter of the 20th—Friday mor'g—but really know not what to say to that part of it, which regards yourself. You thought you could spend some weeks pleasantly, with your family friends, in & near N. York—& I was very glad that you should; altho' my opinion was that if you left me, you should take somebody with you, & go to Marshfield, to your own home, where you would be independent. But you were resolved against that. What can I do?— I really feel embarrassed, & distressed.— It is impossible for me to leave Washington at present. Congress sits longer than was expected—we are in the midst of most important matters—& my leav'g here for some time to come, is out of all question. I am perplexed. Between your uneasiness where you are, & your indecision where to go, & the critical & harrassing state of th'gs here—I find noth'g to sclace me.

I suppose from Julia's letter, that she will return to Boston by the first of next month. Cannot you stay a few weeks with her? You know, my Dear wife, how much pleasure it would give me to be with you, but you must see how impossible that is, at the present moment, without break'g up here, entirely. Perhaps that will be the end & upshot— I wish only to conduct in such manner as to fulfil my duty to the country, as may best become my own character.[1]

The Senate will probably decide on the Land Bill, & the House on the Bank Bill, tomorrow— After those votes, we shall have a better view of the probably future.

My health is good, although we have had some days of very hot weather. Today I have not been out of the House, except to step into Mr Southard's.

I will endeavor to keep you informed of occurrences here, although I am quite pressed & overwhelm'd with affairs

Yrs affectionately, always,

D WEBSTER

I have corresponded with Mr. K. ab't the well

---

[1] See among the letters under "Webster as a Statesman," Julia Appleton to Daniel Webster, December 11, 1840.

(To D. Fletcher Webster.)

MONDAY MORNING
May 16' 42.
6 o'clock.

Dear F.

If I had received your letter at N. Y. I should have signed B's letters; but it is better as it is. We shall have time to think of matters for a fortnight. I shall get through today with all I can do about Maine, and intend to run down to Me. tomorrow, with Mr. Appleton.

8 o'clock—Since writing so far. I learn that poor Uncle Fletcher is breathing his last. We are all exceedingly shocked, and distressed. He has not been sensible, since yesterday morning.

Mrs. F. is as composed as could be expected. 1 o'clock—I have no time to write your mother today having been up since 5 o'clock and run down with company and business.

Mr. Haven and Mr. William Appleton go to N. Y. this evening, to see what can be done with *the loan.* viz. the 3 1/2 million.

Mr. Jaudon will be this way soon.

Mr. Fletcher's death postponed my visit to Marshfield. Mr. P. and Mr. Appleton—Mrs. P. and Julia are all with the family.

Yours   D. W.

(To Mrs. Caroline Webster.)

SATURDAY EVNG 8 o'clock. [August, 1842]

Dearly beloved,

I believe Fletcher may have written you, today. There is no news, of particular importance. Congress will sit, at least a fortnight, & I hope you will get north, as fast as you can. I really wish you could go to Marshfield, take some friends, & enjoy yourself. Things will necessarily come to a crisis, in ten days or a fortnight.

My annual catarrh begins a little—but I am tolerably well. Mr. J. G. King, & Mr. S. B. Ruggles, & a few members of Congress have dined with me today.

Fletcher is well & very much devoted to business. Mr. Jenifer is here a good deal indeed. Mr. Crittenden has a large & genl. party tonight. It is so far off, & having no carriage, F. & I stay at home. He reads French—& I do nothing.

I really want to see Grace. Give my love to her as well as to Hannah her husband & children.

Mr. Stubbs had not returned when I left the office this P. M. I dare say the carpets are all right & am glad you bought them cheap. *Shall we ever need them?*

Yr's truly always

D. WEBSTER.

(To Mrs. Fletcher Webster.)

WASHINGTON Feb 23, 44.

Dear Caroline

Your letter from Fletcher ought to have gone yesterday, but it was sent here from the Dept. a little too late. I have a very good letter from him, which I shall send to you, in a day or two. A good many people here want to see it, as all are desirous of hearing from him.

I hope, my Dear Daughter, that you and your little one are well. We think much of you. It will be a comfort to get a letter from Fletcher.

I suppose the British minister will take our house, & that we shall all be going north, early next month.

Yrs affectionately

DANL. WEBSTER

(To D. Fletcher Webster.)

WEDNESDAY MORG
Dec. 29—47

My Dear Son

I have yrs of the 29th & am happy to learn you are all well. I will try to find an occasion to write Judge Warren—

I suppose you sent my letter to Mr. *Dorr*— I have not heard from him; have you?

At present, I am quite engaged in those old causes, now on second argument. I am tired of these Constitutional questions. There is no court for them.

Your mother will be along next week. I have only been out once, & that was to Mr Seatons, to a family dinner, Christmas day. My love to Caroline & the children.

Yrs affectionately

DANL WEBSTER

(To D. Fletcher Webster.)

WASHINGTON Jan. 31. 48.

Dear Fletcher;

Your mother has never quite reconciled it to herself that she did not return from New York to visit Julia. She feels concerned about her, & thinks she ought to see her. Not that we suppose Julia is very sick, but she is slender, & ought, as we think the winter may be severe with her, [not to be] in Boston. Mrs. W. wishes to go to N. Y. & indeed it would be agreeable to her to be in Boston, for a day or two, and as the weather is now mild, & she has an escort to N. York, she thinks she will run. So you may look out for her, in the course of the week. I approve her goi'g, on the whole, as she will not be happy until she knows exactly how Julia is.

Yrs affectionately

D. W.

(From Julia Webster Appleton.)

(FEB. 23 1848).

Wednesday P. M.

Oh, my Father.

Sam has just told me that my dear brother is lost to us forever![1] I do not realize it, yet, it seems a troubled dream! & yet when poor Edward left us, for that accursed land, I felt I had looked my last upon him.

Dear little Neddy! I cannot believe you are gone! And how are we to console ourselves. I rejoice in one thing, that he was free from the blood of any man; that he did not die in battle—He went forth to a wicked & cruel war, & there he has died; like many before him; without one friend to smooth his dying pillow. Oh that I had been with him!—

Dear Father, I know it is useless, & wrong for me to write in this way— It was God's will, & "God's will be done—" but now I feel nothing but that my brother in the honor of his youth was a useless sacrifice—to what?—ambition, vain-glory— May God in his mercy, sanctify this great affliction to us all— He has

---

[1] Edward Webster died January 23, 1848, in camp, near the City of Mexico. See the account of Edward Webster in Curtis' "Life of Webster," vol. ii, p. 318; see also "Private Correspondence of Daniel Webster," vol. ii, p. 271.

done what seemed him good, & therefore it is good. We see through a glass darkly, but hereafter we shall understand these hidden things—

God bless & keep you, & comfort you, my beloved Father— I will write to Mother when I feel more composed.

With much love

Your daughter   JULIA.

(To Mrs. D. Fletcher Webster.)

Lady of C   MONDAY MORNG July 25, '52

Green Harbor is not well supplied with Poultry, fit to cook today. Can you afford us a pair of your Boston Chickens? If so, Green Harbor will wait on Careswell this Eve' with a retaliatory Green goose.

D. W.

(To D. Fletcher Webster.)

Dear F.   ELMS FARM. Sunday Eve'.

Col. Webb will be here on Tuesday and have invited Mr. Jno. L. Tucker to come with him. I am in hopes, also, that Messrs. Harvey, Haven, and T. B. Curtis will come up, on that day; and should be glad to have you come with them, if you have no engagement. I asked your Mother to send me up a good leg of mutton We have fine mutton here, but shall have none exactly fit to be used. And I should be glad of one small ham, & of a bit of wild fowl, for Col. Webb and Mr. Blackford, and other distinguished strangers. These articles should come up, either tomorrow afternoon, (—Monday) or by the early train on Tuesday. Your mother will add a loaf or two of bread.

Mr. Blatchford sends his best regards to you and Caroline. I feel quite well under this N. W. wind, as you may suppose, as I am writing here, with good eyes, and a clear head, and without cough, between 9. & 10. O'clock in the evening.

Mr. Appleton's nomination is capital, excellent.—it has taken one great anxiety off my mind.

Goodnight. The wind blows strong— It will make me sleep like a top.—

See Harvey.

Yours affectionately

D. W.

(To D. Fletcher Webster.)

MONDAY MOR'G.
5 O clock.

Dear F

I found all well.   Dan is very happy, hav'g *three* Ladies to attend to, his Grandmother, Cora Fletcher, & Miss Kent—Henry Thos' little neice who has been here, a day or two.   The Major is well.

I shall send up a box of garden things tomorrow—   Look out for Mr. Ashmun, whom I expect tonight.

Yrs   D. W.

(To Mrs. Fletcher Webster.)

SUNDAY MOR'G.

Dear Caroline.

I am sorry to say I have rather a severe influenza today—s'd to be the autumnal edition of the Tyler *grip*—& do not feel quite bright enough to attend the Christen'g of a certain person. Mrs. Webster is also a good deal unwell, from the same cause. We hope, therefore, that it may not be inconvenient for you to postpone the ceremony until next Sunday—

If you wish to send a note to Mr Lothrop, George will br'g it.—

I shall try to creep down to see you, in the afternoon.

Yrs truly

DANL WEBSTER.

(To Mrs. Fletcher Webster.)

Dear Caroline, (Daughter Caroline—not wife Caroline)

I had made up my mind to enjoy the luxury of a dish of *baked beans* today—but am willing to dine with you, & shall do so with great pleasure, if you will *let me br'g my beans with me*—   Therefore, look out for me & the beans, already cooked, at 2 O clock.

D. W.

(To Mrs. Caroline Webster.)

TUESDAY MOR'G

Dear Caroline,

I send you the letters from the Traveller, & the little bills, intended to have been enclosed yesterday.

This mor'g I am goi'g to see my *cheese.* I suppose the owner will wish to show it, with the rest, some days longer; & then I shall ask Mr Le Roy to send it to Boston.

The weather is cold here—& I am sometimes half afraid of bei'g frozen up before I reach Boston. Commodore Chauncey & family are here. Miss C. met with an accident—a fall on the stairs, which caused a very severe lameness, & has detained her here & her mother in the north. the Commodore has now come to take them to W.

Goodbye,—till you hear from me at Philadelphia.

Ever yrs
D WEBSTER

(To D. Fletcher Webster.)

NORWICH, friday Eve' 8 O clock.

Dear F:

You will be glad that we did not venture on the Sound today, after the terrible loss of the Atlantic. We arrived here about 1 O clock; heard the Atlantic was in danger, on or near Fisher's Island, having evidently recd. injury, but as noth'g could get to her, it could not be told whether she was ashore, or at anchor. It now turns out, that night before last, soon after leav'g New London, her steam chest, as they call it, exploded. This of course rendered all her machinery useless, & stopped her motion. It was then blowing hard, & the seas running high. Her anchors were let out, but she dragged them all day yesterday, & last night, drifting away towards Fishers Island. This mor'g, at 1/2 past 4 O'clock her stern parted, & she swung round, & struck her broad side on the rocks, & went all to pieces, in two or three minutes. Noth'g is said to remain visible on the rocks but some frame work, belonging to the engine; or some such part, I did not understand very distinctly what.

She had happened to get inside the principal breakers, & was very near dry land. But the surf was breaking with great violence, so that those who could swim could hardly do better than those who could not.   It is supposed about 50 lives were lost. Twenty two bodies were brought up here this P. M. by the Mohegan, which got to the wreck this mor'g.   There were three Ladies on board, passengers, who were all lost, as were the three chamber-maids.   Capt. Duston was drowned.   Julia will recollect see'g him.   I cannot learn that any of our Boston friends was aboard.   James Stetson was in the Boat, & has given me these particulars.   He did not know any of the persons who are lost, among the passengers.   No blame seems to be imputed to the Captain.   The fault is thought to have been in the machinery.

The wind has gone down, & it is supposed the Sound will be smooth tomorrow.   If it is, we shall proceed on our journey, over L. Island.   If not, we shall wait for settled weather.   After a disaster so appalling, one does not wish to encounter risks.

We find here Mr. Huntintton, Mrs. Rockwell, & other friends.

Yrs affectionately

DANL. WEBSTER.

(To D. Fletcher Webster.)

FRIDAY 1 O clock

Dear F

We were glad to receive yrs, & a long letter from Caroline this mor'g.   Yr mother is down, today, with a headache.   We dined at the Presidents yesterday, & were out the Eve'g before, & I suppose she took some cold.   She will probably get over the headache, by Even'g.——

I really should be glad to see Mr. Harvey.   There are th'gs he could do, better than almost anybody else.   If he can spare the time, pray ask him to come on.

Mr. Calhoun has the floor of the Senate for Monday.   He stands right up for Colgent's (?) resolution & for gett'g a vote of the Senate as soon as may be.

I am quite well, & begin to feel a little rested.—— Pray send on Mr Harvey.——

Yrs   DW

(To Mrs. Caroline Webster.[1])

WASHINGTON June 12 '49
Tuesday Morning
10 O'clock

Dear Caroline

I wrote you yesterday, & to day have the pleasure of receiving yours of Sunday Eve.' & am rejoiced that you & little Cara are well & happy. I think you are delightfully situated, & better off than at home alone.

This is a cold, raw day; & I am sitting before a good fire, & do not intend to stirr abroad at all. The weather is certainly strange. I was at Mr. Seaton's last evening & found him sitting before a blazing grate.

They were all glad to hear from you, & I thanked them duly for the strawberries. Paul left last Eve.' to get ready to go north, on Thursday. Monica stays to day, but takes to morrow for herself, for the same purpose. Sarah & John are our only stay. Sarah has her strawberries for preserves. Mr. Harvey has been here since Saturday, but returns to day. I have not seen any of the Commissioners this morning. Dr. Lyndsley's family are well, though I have not seen the ladies.

Yrs affectionately

DANL WEBSTER

Mrs. Webster

I hear nothing from home. This is not a day for Boston letters.

---

[1] This letter was given to Miss Emma E. Webb, 11 Ohio Street, Bangor, Me., by Mrs. Caroline Le Roy Webster.

Webster's Relations with His Friends and Neighbors.

THE *stern, kingly man that attracted every man's gaze as he walked down State Street in Boston was a very simple country gentleman, among his neighbors at Marshfield. That he could bend and be the daily friend of common men has been told in many places by those who were happy enough to win his friendship. But we feel better convinced of it when we see in his letters the common sense which ignored the difference in mental endowments and said the common thing to common men. True, he had friends who were great—the greatest who lived in the world at the same time—but their bond was not their community of greatness. It was rather a congeniality in common things. He was never fond of parading friendship; but loved rather to be alone with his friends. We never feel sure that we can say certainly that he was selfish. We are very sure that he keenly loved the excellencies of his friends, and that he was generous in the praise of their deserts. He was generous with forgiveness, and he could generously ask a favor. He never minced and said he could just as well get along without it, but, if they chose, they might do him a favor. He threw his whole soul into the asking a kindness, and left himself no retreat.*

The letters given here show him full of sympathy and thoughtfulness for friends in trouble—a common virtue, one may say—yet it was surely something for a great statesman to let the affairs of a nation wait while he wrote a word of comfort to some humble friend of humbler days. He never entered a neighborhood where old friends lived without taking pains to neglect no one. His own hospitality was royal and personal. He did not direct the servants to be entertaining, but he was entertaining himself. As a result, he received such letters as that of William Wirt's, after the latter's visit in 1829. He was ever ready to use his influence for a friend, and his aid was without ostentation. He had a genial humor that saved his dignity from hyper-

sensitiveness. In the correspondence with Sydney Smith that proof of magnanimity is at its best. Much is said of his own efforts as a peacemaker, but the incident in the Appleton correspondence concerning Mr. Lawrence shows that he graced the more difficult position of subjection to the peacemaker.

A matter of considerable interest in the letters to Webster, many of which have necessarily been omitted from this collection, is the way early friends took a life-long interest in him—perfectly natural, of course, but pleasing to see in the concrete. The old friends had such a detailed memory of the slightest incidents in their common past. To have been associated with him in an event seemed to throw a romantic glamour over the things that happened. Another matter of interest is their confidence in the simplicity and candor of his friendship. They expect nothing of him but a simple recognition of the old ties.

In the correspondence with Story we have an unpleasant feeling about the refusal to permit the publication of the letters to and from the father. Webster elsewhere explains that he consistently refused such requests because he did not wish to establish a precedent. The passage of time has removed all the objections that he might have had to such publication, and the letters to which he referred have been published by the Massachusetts Historical Society.

(To Edward Everett.)

WASHINGTON Dec. 31, 1824.

Dear Sir,

I have waited on Mr. Calhoun, with your letter, and said, also, what I thought would be useful.

The world rings with your Plymouth speech; even before the echoes of the P. B. K. oration have entirely subsided.

Yours always,

DAN'L WEBSTER.

P. S. and P. M. I am much obliged to you for your kind letter which has just come to hand. I know that my presence at home could not have altered the course of things, in respect to our little boy.[1] The loss I feel, heavily, but I hope not to be too

---

[1] Referring to the death of his son Charles. See the letters about this date in the division devoted to Webster's family relations.

much depressed by it.   The oftener you call and see Mrs. W. the more she and I shall be obliged to you.

I shall certainly take care to secure snug quarters for your family and mine next year.

(To James W. Paige.)

[MAY 27, 1825, Sandwich, Mass]
Thursday Eve.

D'r Wm.

I am obliged to you for 2 letters.   Dan'l came down very well. We are quite engaged, or I should write more at length.   We shall be home Saturday or Monday, I know not which.   I should have sent you some *trouts* had there been a less number of mouths here.

I do not write Mrs W. as it will probably be too late.   We are well, but too sleepy to write at much length.   Mr. B. is quite well.

Yrs D. W.
10 o'clock—quite asleep.

(To Jacob McGaw.[1])

WASHINGTON Feb. 21, 1827.

My Dear Sir

I have rec'd your letter, and shall lose no time in communicating its contents to the President, and adding my wishes to yours, in favor of Mr. Carr.

It is not my habit to interfere often, in local appointments, out of my own neighborhood; but I shall go out of my usual course, for once, in conformity to your wishes, and to render your friend a service.   I have heard that Mr. Lee, the son in law of Mr. Hook, was a candidate for the office; but know not on what interest, or whose recommendation.

Probably there may be others.   As soon as I shall have learned what the probable result may be, I will give you information.

We felt, My Dear Sir, a very serious disappointment, when,

------

[1] The owner of the original of this letter is Mr. J. B. Foster, of Bangor, Me., who kindly sent the editor this copy.

on our return home in the Summer of 1825 from our journey to the Falls, we learned that you and Mrs. McGaw had just left Boston. I rec'd the note, which you were kind enough to address to me, the day after it was written. Indeed we were actually arrived, *before* you left town, as it turned out; for hoping that you might still be there, I went in search of you, I came on your track when you had been gone but an hour. I need hardly say that there are few of my old friends who keep so green and fresh in my recollections as yourself and wife; but it has so happened that with few have I had the misfortune of such unfrequent interviews and communications. I dare not reckon up how many years it was, last Summer (June) since I escorted *Phebe Poor* to the Banks of Sandy River. *Mrs. McGaw* I have never seen.

Once, when I lived in Portsmouth, you was in my house, for 5 minutes; and with that exception I believe I have not seen *you* since I was a pedagogue, at *Pejwachet*,[1] and we used to play *cribbage, at one o'clock.*

I need not say, and cannot well say, how much interest I feel in the election, pending in your District.

I earnestly hope for a result, which while it will give me great personal gratification will I am sure, promote essentially the public interest.

Pray make my best remembrances to Mrs. McGaw; and be assured of the sincere and hearty regard of

Your old friend

D WEBSTER

(To W. W. Seaton.)

"My dear Sir,—I thank you for the summer ducks, which were found delicious. I thank you for the woodcock, and have yet to thank you for other favorable and friendly kindnesses not forgotten.

"Yours truly,

"DANIEL WEBSTER.

"Mr. Seaton.

"These are black fish, sometimes called *Tautog*. Monica cooks them thus:—

"Put the fish into a pan with a little butter, and let them fry

---

[1] At Fryeburg.

till pretty nearly cooked, then put in a little wine and pepper and salt, and let them stew. She uses no water. A little more wine, pepper, and salt to make a good gravy.

"So says Monica, who stands at my elbow at half past five o'clock. A good way also to make agreeable table companions of these fellows is to barbecue or broil them without splitting.
"D. W.

"Confidential and Diplomatic."

(From Thomas Rich.)

Dear Sir,   CHARLESTON July 16th—1828—
Shortly after you was pleased to favour me with an interview in Boston, I received your friendly communications with $20 enclosed from our good Friend Clarke, to whom I returned my grateful acknowledgement— In the month of January 1827, I was much obliged by the following anonymous letter—
"Rev. & Dear Sir,
Enclosed you receive fifty dollars from your unknown correspondent from the explanation of your suffering condition by the divine interpreter of the heart called Daniel." This day, after such a lapse of time, the enigma is developed.
Be assured, Sir, that my gratitude to the generous *donor* and to *him*, through whose kind intercession I have experienced relief, is warm & unfeigned—

Affectionately—
THOMAS RICH

(From Lafayette.)

My dear Sir   PHILADELPHIA July 24ʰ 1828
Permit me to introduce to you Count Vidua, a very distinguished Piedmontese, who has travelled through a great part of the world, and is now on a tour through the U. S. He brought me most particular introduction from Humboldt, Segur, and other friends. His acquaintance will be pleasing to you and highly useful to him. Most truly
Your affectionate friend
LAFAYETTE

(To Mrs. Cyrus Perkins.)

BOSTON. Decr. 15. 1828.

My dear Mrs Perkins,

I am sorry your good husband should be mortified at not having a house big enough to accommodate travellers on the high road. The same *mortification,* or the same cause for it, would happen to *me,* if he should chance to come this way, at this time, altho' I have lately made a house, & meant to make it big enough.— As it happens, I should hardly feel at liberty to accept your hospitality, on my journey this time, as Mr Blake will go with me, as companion of the voyage, & where he lodges I must lodge. We are thinking of getting away in about a week.

Our children are all well & send a great deal of love. Mrs E. Webster, with her daughters, is now with us, & I hope to keep them for a month or two longer.

I have not met with your sister lately; but I met Miss. Bryant in the street yesterday, & she looked as if she & all the family were quite well.—

Yours ever gratefully & affectionately

DAN^L WEBSTER.

(To Josiah Quincy.[1])

WASHINGTON, January 25, 1829.

My dear Sir,—

I have just closed the perusal of your address, and am not willing to lose a moment in expressing the pleasure, and, allow me to say, the pride with which I have read it. In my opinion it is in the highest degree just, manly, sensible,—full of proof of independence, conscious integrity, and proper self-respect. While you have done your self no more than justice, you have made an exhibition of the measures of the city administration and of their effects which cannot fail to gratify your friends and all good citizens. Heaven punishes folly by granting it its desires; and this penalty I imagine they who are mainly active in producing this change will feel hereafter, if they do not feel it now. Although I deeply regret that change, on public accounts, I yet think it clear that the events which produced it, the feeling which

---

[1] This letter is taken from the "Life of Josiah Quincy," p. 434. Josiah Quincy was at this time Mayor of the city of Boston.

those events have excited, and the use which you have made already, and which I trust you will still further make, of the occasion, will enable you to retire from the government of the city with more solid and brilliant reputation than almost any other state of things which could be reasonably anticipated would have conferred.

I pray you to make my most friendly regards acceptable to Mrs. Quincy and your family, and to believe me, dear sir, with constant esteem, your obedient servant,

DANIEL WEBSTER.

(From Jeremiah Mason.)

PORTSMOUTH April 16. 1829

My dear Sir

I feel distressed and almost overwhelmed by the awfully sudden death of your brother.[1]   The friendship that had subsisted between us, for many years, had afforded me much satisfaction and benefit.   He was embraced in all my plans & hopes of ameliorating the condition of our poor State.   His loss is, in my estimation, nothing less than a public calamity.   A void is made, & I see not how, nor when it is to be filled.

Such has been the havoc of death, for a few years past, among those, whom I most esteemed and best loved, that the world begins to look desolate to me.

To your anguish, my dear friend, I shall not attempt to offer any consolation, other than the assurance of my sincere sympathy.   For such sufferings time may afford alleviation, but no effectual remedy can be found in any considerations confined to this world.[2]

Mrs. Mason unites with me in the kindest regards to you.

I am my Dear sir as ever

Faithfully & affectionately
Yours
J. Mason

---

[1] Ezekiel Webster. He died suddenly, while speaking, standing erect, in the course of an argument in a crowded courtroom.   See "Biography of Ezekiel Webster," in "Private Correspondence of Daniel Webster," vol. i.

[2] For Daniel Webster's reply see "Private Correspondence," vol. i, p. 477, dated April 19, 1829.

(From William Wirt.[1])

BALTIMORE—July 8. 1829.

My dear Sir.

Mrs. W. instructs me to return you her cordial thanks for your attention to her gratification in the letter of *excerpts*—and you must permit me to disburthen myself of the pressure of my feelings so far as to assure you that I shall resent through life (to use an expressions of Boyle's) your unwearied and affecting kindness to me through the whole of my visit to your land of poetic beauty and Arcadian hospitality—that is to say, provided the Arcadians were the people whom the poets describe and not those whom the dim historians represent them to have been— All figures and levity apart, my visit to Boston comes back to me, at times, more like a delightful dream than a reality, so far did it surpass all other comparatively "dull realities of civil life" that I have encountered in the course of my mortal pilgrimage— I have either been supremely fortunate and caught you all in your *mollia*, or rather *mollissima tempera*, or the Southerners who have, heretofore, visited you are ungrateful dogs not to have chanted your character in louder strains— I can tell you, however, that I find here, among the gentlemen of this place, a full response to my strongest notes of admiration. I have not met with a gentleman who has visited your country who is not in perfect union with me—and I know nothing that can compare with it, but the unmixed native stock of Virginia—with a few slight peculiarities, the people of Virginia are identical with those of your people whom I have seen. I make the remark not as Mr. (Gardner?) seemed to suppose in the way of a compliment—for there is no compliment on either side—but as a striking philosophical fact—and I wish to Heaven it were more perfectly known to those most deeply interested to know it— The political elements of dissension are at work among us, and it will require all the attraction of cohesion which mutual knowledge & [illegible] of each other's characters can generate to hold us together—and most happy should I be if I could devise any mode by which I could successfully contribute to such a result— Can you tell me how? "Gentle Shepherd, tell me—how—"

I am glad to hear that our friend Blake is well—and can well

---

[1] This letter is owned by the Hon. George F. Hoar. The writer was author of a life of Patrick Henry. He was one of the most eminent lawyers of his time and was Attorney-General of the United States from 1817 to 1830.

imagine the pleasure of your ride—I w'd have given *an ingot of gold* to have been with you, tho' I might have spoiled your subject—   But I have been even with you both—for I have talked you over, too, again & again—and my listeners seemed well disposed to give me my time—those listeners have generally been "wife, children and friends." and enter keenly into all the sensibilities which my reception in Boston must I think have awakened in a heart even of stone, which mine, however, chances not to be—   By the way of secret and in your ear, I am unaffectedly surprised that such a speech as I made in one cause, sh'd have been thought worthy of so much newspaper notice.   I am not conscious and cannot see at this moment that it was at all beyond an every day speaking in the Supreme court, and yet one who did not know me would suppose from these eulogies that the people of Boston had caught a *hippotamus at the Court*— Be it so, it is a silly bird, they say, that bewrays its own nest— But you and I know a thing or two more upon this subject. Mean time how happy & secure you must feel with the house of your fame on its everlasting rock—like the rocks that form the substratum of your blessed country—I wish I had been as wise all my life as you have been—gone always for substance and not for show, my show through the earlier years of my life, was the eclipse of my substance—and the shadows of that eclipse will haunt me thro' life.   Your Gibraltar front has always been in its sunlight—defying the thunders of the clouds & the ocean— and thus may it ever stand in its proud pre-eminence—It is fit that it should be so—and none but a sacrilege could wish to disturb the aim of nature.

If you should meet with our friend Mr. Justice Story, assure him of my constant and grateful remembrance of his kindness— would to Heaven that I had such a oracle of the law in my neighborhood in the form of a Judge of the Supreme court.   How does he contrive to carry such a load of law with such bouyancy of spirits.   I do not observe that his ability to enjoy sinks the thousandth part of an inch the deeper, with all her load, but makes her way as gaily and sportively as if she were a mere gondoler for pleasure   Such is the effect of a happy constitution, and there is no builder, at last, like nature.

May I beg you, too, to present me, as occasion may offer, respectfully and gratefully to Chief Justice Parker, and the members of the Court of whose indulgence and kindness I shall cherish through this life a religious sense—And to every inquiring friend, if it be not too troublesome, give assurance that their kindness has not been sown on barren ground, but that I have left Massachusetts under a sense of obligation for the delicate and polite hospitalities I received, which neither time nor chance can diminish.

With best regards to Mr. Day,

Yrs truly

WM. WIRT.

(To Jeremiah Mason.)

BOSTON Aug. 11. 1829

My Dear Sir

My stay in Vermont was protracted, so as to run into this month.— I will meet you at Nahant, with pleasure, or at Hampton, at the House near the Beach, if we can fix on any time. This week and next you will be at Court—& I believe I shall go down to the South Shore. The week following is Commencement. Commencement day, & the day after I will give to visiting you, wherever you may choose. Keeping out of places where we shall be obliged to see others.— The Hotel at Lynn, is a very good place—with spare rooms enough— It is far better than Nahant.

Yrs

D. WEBSTER.

(To Dr. Cyrus Perkins.[1])

BOSTON, Nov. 22, 1830.

Dear Sir,

Mrs. W. is in N. York, and I hope you have by this time seen her. She felt, with as much sympathy as I did, your calamity in the death of your son, and will be very glad to see you & Mrs. Perkins. For the last three weeks I have been nearly every day out of town, and have had no opportunity of seeing Mr. Bryant—I shall call today, if the weather permits. On Saturday, I came home from Providence, where I had passed the week. For the next ten days, I propose to sit here, at my office

---

[1] Addressed to Dr. Perkins, Fulton Street, New York. Dr. Perkins attended the first Mrs. Webster in her last illness.

table, to arrange my own personal matters, so as to set my face southward about the first of December.   *   *   * [1]

Remember me affectionately to Mrs. Perkins, and believe me always and truly,

Yrs
(Signed)   D. WEBSTER.

(To ——————.[2])

BOSTON Oct. 7, 1831.

Dear Sir

I have recd your letter of the 3rd.   Its contents surprise me. You say that a person in N.Bedford, *as you understand* quotes me for authority in charging the vice of intemperance on Mr Hodges.   If you will ascertain the *fact* that any person has used my name for any such purpose, & will let me know who he is, I will cheerfully do whatever justice both to Mr. Hodges & myself may appear to require.   In the meantime tho' I do not expect to be quoted, or my name used publicly, to contradict what may never have been asserted.   I can say with the utmost truth that I never heard such a suggestion against Mr. Hodges, in my life, from any quarter.

[DAN'L WEBSTER]

(To Chancellor Kent.[3])

WASHINGTON, June 5, 1832.

My dear Sir,—

I have just opened the newspaper and read the account of Mr. Irving's dinner, and your speech thereat; and I resolved forthwith to write you one line, for the purpose of saying that the speech is a delightful little thing, just, sweet, affectionate. When I read the paragraph in which you prefer what relates to the blue hills and mountain glens of our own country to sketches of foreign scenes and foreign countries, I wanted to

---

[1] The omitted paragraph informs Dr. Perkins that Daniel Webster has drawn for $600 on Mr. Perkins.

[2] This letter is in Daniel Webster's hand, and is evidently the first draft of the letter sent.

[3] Printed in the "Memoirs of Chancellor Kent," p. 235.

seize your hand and give it a hearty shake of sympathy. Heaven bless this goodly land of our fathers! Its rulers and its people may commit a thousand follies, yet Heaven bless it! Next to the friends beloved of my heart, those same hills and glens, and native woods and native streams, will have my last earthly recollections! Dulce et decorum est, etc.

DANIEL WEBSTER.

(To John W. Weeks.[1])

Hon Mr. Weeks.   JUNE 11th. [1832]
    Sir

    I return Mr Clarks letter— I hope means may be found to make out a case for his father, when the Pension Bill comes to be executed.

    Mr Clark, the writer, I have known a great while, & am acquainted with few more worthy men.

    It will, both on his account, & his father's, give me much pleasure to aid in an effort to gratify the Veteran, by obtaini'g a proof of his country's recollection of his services.

With much respect,
Your Ob. Servt
DANL WEBSTER

(To Dr. Cyrus Perkins.[2])

BOSTON. Nov. 9, 34

My Dear Sir

    I arrived this P. M. & now enclose two letters for your use. If you think of any other persons, to whom letters from me would be of the slightest convenience to you, pray write me a line, & they shall be forwarded to Paris, or elsewhere as you may direct, the next Packet.

    Mrs Webster desires me to give her best love to you & Mrs Perkins.— She bids you farewell! with all sincerity of good wishes. Julia prays leave also to tender her affectionate regards; I need not say, My Dear friend, how much of my heart you carry away with you.— May God grant you every blessing; & may we, ere long, welcome you back, with renewed health & augmented happiness.

---

[1] Representative of New Hampshire in Congress from 1829 to 1833.
[2] The original of this letter is in the Dartmouth College Library.

Wherever you go, bear with you the assurance of my constant & cordial attachment.

Adieu!

DANL WEBSTER.

(To Miss Ellen Kelly.[1])

BALTIMORE Decr. 26, 1834.

My Dear Cousin.

I heard yesterday, by a letter from Mr. Paige, of the death of your brother William. It shocked me very much, as I had not heard of his illness, the last letter I recd from Salisbury, left the family as well as usual. If this event shall have taken you to Salisbury, I hope you will write me immediately, as I shall be anxious to know how the rest of the family are.

Mr. Paige wrote me that one of your sisters was sick, tho' he did not mention which. If you are still in Boston, I hope you will write me, & let me know how you are, yourself.— Mrs. W. & Julia are well. We came to Baltimore to spend Christmas and shall go back in a day or two. Do not fail to write me—[2]

Yr affectionate uncle

D. W.

(To I. W. Kelly.[3])

WASHINGTON Jan. 1. 1835.

My Dear Sir:

I recd yours of the 22d, not until yesterday. I wrote you, from Baltimore, about the 26th—which I hope you received.— I trust you are well assured of my sympathy with you, for the loss of your son, & the illness of so many others of your family.— It is a great consolation to know that William died with an untroubled & tranquil mind. I fervently pray that the rest of your children may be soon restored to the enjoyment of perfect health.—*   *   *[4]

DANL. WEBSTER

---

[1] Addressed care of I. W. Kelly, of Salisbury, N. H., to whom the first Mrs. Webster's sister was married.

[2] This letter was kindly loaned by Judge Corning, of Concord, N. H.

[3] This letter is the property of Judge Corning, of Concord, N. H.

[4] Encloses three notes for Mr. Shaw and a check, and asks Kelly to transact some business.

(To Mrs. Caroline Webster.)

HALLOWELL, Wednesday Eve'—Sep. 23. 1835.

Dear Caroline,

You will easily find Hallowell on the map, & here I am, in less than 24 hours from Boston. The weather has been remarkably fine, & the Boats go well, tho', to be sure, for accommodation they bear but a poor comparison with the Southern Boats. I was in Portland this morning from 4 to 8 clock—of course I saw nobody. My friend Mr. Bradley, I learned, was not in town.— The Boat comes no farther than Gardner, half a dozen miles below this place, where Mr. Gardner, and also Mr. Evans lives. Mr. Evans heard of my arrival, & came to me at the Boat. Mr. Gardner met me also, & I called to see the Families of both these Gentlemen. Mr. Gardner's family is in great affliction from the sickness of his daughter, Mrs. Jones— She was married, you know, about the time we saw the family at Washington, & is now thought to be far gone in a decline. They live in a cottage, while they are building a new & most elegant Home.

Mrs. Evans is gay as usual. She inquired much for you, & says you were confidently expected this way. Mr. Evans brought me from the Boat here in his Barouche, & offered me his company tomorrow to call on a few old friends of an elderly class. I mean, among other calls, to go & see Dr. Sewall's mother, & Mr. Lindsley's. I have many friends in the Town, who will of course call to see me. On friday I intend going to Bangor, if the weather should be fair.— Adieu! I have written to Julia, & shall make out a line to Mr. Paige that he may hear of my arrival in safety thus far, if this should not find you in Boston—

Yrs ever truly

DANL WEBSTER

(From N. Ray Thomas.)

DUXBURY. Jan. 20. 1840

* * *[1] In quitting your employment I shall have the satisfaction of knowing that I have discharged the obligation which I was under to you, so far as dollars are concerned. But there are other—& to me *higher* obligations which I feel I never

[1] Minor business details omitted.

can discharge; for through all the changes of my changing life I have had the satisfaction of believing that you were my friend, & of never doubting that this friendship was void of selfishness— *was pure;* and whatever the future may unfold be assured I shall carry with me to the latest hour of my life the purest sentiment of gratitude & esteem.   *   *   *[1]

I remain, most truly yours

N. RAY THOMAS.

(To Mrs. Caroline Webster.)

MONDAY EVE' Mar. 9. [1840] 7 o'clock.

My Dear wife,

I do not recollect that I have told you that Anna Lawrence has been very sick, indeed.   Today she is supposed to be better, but she has had a very dangerous fever.   Dr. S. & Dr. L. have attended her for a fortnight.   It is hoped she is now out of danger.

Mr. Lawrence himself is a good deal unwell, but not alarmingly so.   He has not been out, for several days.

Poor Ray Thomas has been sick again.   He has had a very severe attack of fever, very much such as he has had heretofore. For ten days, he has been confined.   The Dr. says he is recovering.   I have concluded it is not safe to send him to the West. Dr. S. says it may be years before he will cease to have returns of the attack, from which he suffered so much at Buffalo.   He will go back to Duxbury as soon as he is well enough.

Mr. John Reed went to Wisconsin late last Summer—was taken sick at Milwaukee, & just escaped the grave.   He got home—exceedingly feeble—& is now here, but he has frequent relapses, & looks very much exhausted, & altered.   You would hardly know him.   All your other acquaintances I believe are well.

Mr. & Mrs. *Taylor*—Baltimore—were here for a fly'g visit, last week——   She looks very well & happy.

We hear the G. Western is in; & I have hopes we shall hear from Edward.[2]

We expect the mail at 8 Oclock, but I look for no letter from

---

[1] Minor business details omitted.

[2] Upon the return of Mr. and Mrs. Webster, the younger son, Edward Webster, had been left abroad, where he carried on his studies.

you tonight, as you only return today from Westchester— I hope I shall have one tomorrow Eve'—

Adieu! Give my best love to yr father, & Mrs Edgar & family—

Yrs ever truly

D. W.

(To Mrs. Caroline Webster.)

WEDNESDAY EVE' 6 o clock (March 11, 1840)

Dear Caroline,

Poor Ray Thomas is very sick.[1] I have been with him all day, & he will not let me leave his room, hardly long enough to write this. His fever has gone off, in a great measure, but it has left him very much reduced, & desponding, & wander'g. I have written for Henry to come to him immediately— He has a good nurse, Dr. Sewell & D Lyndley both attend him, & every thi'g is done for him that can be done.

I am quite well— I shall write you every day. Mr. Lawrence's family are getting well—

Yrs

D WEBSTER

(To Mrs. Caroline Webster.)

THURSDAY EVE' [March 12, 1840] 11 Oclock

Dear Caroline,

I have only time today, that I have this eve'g recd your letter under cover to Mr. Curtis, & also your other letter—written yesterday mor'g with a postcript at 12 oclock. None of the former letters, written by you, have come to hand—not one—& I now learn, for the first time, that you prefer stay'g in N. Y. till I go to Boston. I have no objection to this, if you prefer it; but it has been very unpleasant not to know what your intentions were—

I have just come from Ray[2]—he has been very wild this Eve'—but is now more composed. Mr. Curtis is with him, & I must go to him in two or three hours—

I will try to write you tomorrow—

Truly yrs   D WEBSTER

---

[1] See Curtis' "Life of Webster," vol. ii, p. 33.

[2] In a previous letter he says, "I have been with him almost all day, as he hates to have me leave him."

(To Mrs. Caroline Webster.)

FRIDAY EVE' 7. Olck. [March 13, 1840]

My Dear Wife,

I have not been in the Senate today, having spent the whole day in looki'g after poor Ray.　He is a very sick man, but I believe he is better, & say Dr S. & Dr. L.　He is so despond'g, & is much out of his mind, that either Mr. Curtis, a Mr. Evans, or myself find it necessary to be with him to keep him from sinking.　He feels as if he should die right off, unless one of us be with him.　We divide the 24 hours between us.　Henry, who has been written for, will probably call on you.　Tell him, that at this hour, he is believed to be decidedly better, but that he is an extremely sick man, & could not have been saved without the closest & most particular attention.　His recovery, now, is not at all certain; but it is hopeful.　I staid with him today, from 4 in the mor'g, till 4 in the P. M.　Mr. Curtis is now with him.　Mr. Evans goes at 10 oclock & I go again at 4 in the mor'g.

Mr. Lawrence's family are all sick.　Anna & Kitty are recovering.　Mr. Lawrence is very sick indeed, & I learn that Mrs. Lawrence & Miss McLeod are taken down today—　Dr. L. thinks Mr. L. better, a little, than he was at 2 o'clock this mor'g, but Dr. Sewall is evidently very much frightened about him.

I trust his life will be preserved.　Mr. Evans has now gone over to see him.　As soon as I close this letter, I am goi'g to bed, as I have had so little sleep lately.　Adieu! my beloved wife—　I hope, among all these troubles, that you preserve your health.

Yours always affectionately

D. WEBSTER

(To Mrs. Caroline Webster.)

SATURDAY EVE 10 clock (March 14, 1840)

My Dear Wife,

I hope Ray is better.　He had a very bad paroxysm this mor'g, at 4 o'clock—　I was sent for, & have been with him all day, except'g time for breakfast and dinner.　He cries so when I propose to come away, that it is impossible to leave him, unless

Mr. C. or Mr. E. can take my place. Mr. C. is now with him, till 4 in the mor'g. I write this the more particularly, as I expect Henry will call on you, as he comes alo'g. Dr. S. & Dr. L. both say he is improving—but he is exceed'gly sick. Two or three times, I thought he wou'd not live an hour. Mr. Lawrence is thought to be better. Miss McLeod is likely to have a settled fever—no letter from you tonight—though I looked for one— Adieu! Yrs l'v'g'y

D. WEBSTER

(To Mrs. Caroline Webster.)

TUESDAY EVE' 8 'clock [March 17, 1840]

My Dear Wife.
    Beyond what I expected this mor'g Ray is yet alive.[1] I do not suppose there is much more—perhaps no more—chance for his recovery—but he is more quiet, & easy—& this is a great consolation. How I do wish he might live till Henry shall arrive here!—
    I am not very well today, from anxiety, & watch'g. I cannot sleep, till his state changes. He is well attended by physicians, friends, & nurses—& every th'g done that promises the best good—
    Mr. Lawrence's family are all recover'g—himself rather slowly.

Yours very truly

DANL WEBSTER

(To Peter Harvey.[2])

(MAY 10 ? 1840 ?)

Dr Sir
    Thank you for your letter. Let the salmon come on, when convenient— Several Whig mouths are watering for it.
    Mrs. W. desires her best regards. All political thi'gs look about right—

Yrs   D. W.

---

[1] Ray Thomas died that evening shortly after eleven o'clock. See Curtis' "Life of Webster," vol. ii, p. 35.
[2] Peter Harvey was the warm friend of Webster during his later years, and wrote "Reminiscences of Daniel Webster."

(To Mr. Connell.¹)

My Dear Sir   BOSTON NOV. 20. 1840

I had a severe illness, though not of long duration, the end of last month in N. Hampshire. I was on my paternal spot, under my own roof, with the graves of all my family near me. I did not feel dangerously sick, at any time, but I was worn out, with fatigue & effort, & had also taken a very heavy cold. After returning to Boston, & staying some days, I went to Marshfield, with my wife. There, the bad weather caught me, & I staid in the House a week, recruiting every day.

———

(From Mrs. Sydney Smith.)

56 GREEN STREET, Grosvenor Sqre.

To have recd. from your hands such a letter of approval *may* justify a little pride as well as much pleasure My dear Sir.— I have cherished the letter as it *was* but natural I should, & I was allow'd to keep it.

Upon principle, dear Sydney destroy'd almost all private letters lest hereafter they should fall into other hands than those they were intended for.

Our old friend ·Mr. Th. Moore is about to prepare a little Memorial of his old friend.— One of the very best of men!— whose great and varied virtues rested not on the surface only!

Most earnestly should I desire to make over to him this little Episode of yourself & Mr. Clay. I subjoin your letter, lest on reperusal you see anything in it to object to.— If you do, your wish for its suppression shall be imperative upon me.

I beg to be warmly remember'd to your companions in travel into these Parts. & I hope you will believe with what truth I subscribe myself your most respectful friend & admirer.

CATHARINE AMELIA SMITH.

P. S. The original is pasted into a book, or I would send it to you but this is a faithful transcript of it.

Perhaps you may have Sydney's letter that *called yours forth.*— If so, it would be *most kind* if some of your family would take the trouble of copying it for me. Sydney's answer to yours I *did* copy before I seal'd it.²

---

¹ This letter is the property of the Pennsylvania Historical Society.
² See "Wit and Wisdom of Sydney Smith."

(To Mrs. Jeremiah Smith.)

Dear Madam: WASHINGTON, January 21, 1843.

On the receipt of your last letter, I wrote to Mr. Ticknor of Boston, whom you know, not only as a scholar, and man of talents, but as a friend of Judge Smith of long standing, desiring his cooperation with me, in preparing an Epitaph.[1] He most readily concurred in my wishes, and very soon sent me a draft. Alterations were suggested, by me, in which he has acquiesced and the result of the whole I now enclose to you. If you shall be satisfied with it, we shall both be quite happy. If alterations occur to you, please suggest them to me with the greatest freedom.

I am Dear Madam,

Yours with true esteem,

DANIEL WEBSTER

(To R. M. Blatchford.[2])

My Dear Sir   MONDAY July 8, '44

I wrote you on Saturday, Yesterday, Sunday, I was at Nahant, & learned from Caroline that you wd. be at Nahant with your daughter, & perhaps your son, on the 10th inst. Your stay, I learn, is to be short; but I must steal you away, for one day, to Marshfield, where we shall be then. Our home will be all in disorder, so that we could not receive your daughter, but *you* like to sleep on a sofa, & care little about eating or drinking, so we can take care of you, for a day or two.

Now, as to the mode of coming.

If you say so, my Boat, the "Comet," shall be at Nahant Monday the 16th & bring you across to us, Wednesday. If the weather be fair, the sail will be beautiful.

Or, to be independent of weather, I will send up a man to meet you, Wednesday at 12 o'clock, at the Tremont House; to show you the way by the Hingham Boat, which leaves at one; & who will take you rapidly from Hingham to Marshfield, with Mrs Webster's horses.

I want much to see you, for a day, at Marshfield, preliminary

[1] See Morison's "Life of Judge Smith," p. 516.
[2] Webster's life-long friend.

to having you there with friends a few weeks later.   Please let me hear from you by Thursday morning next, saying what mode of movement will suit you best.   Any thing, but a balloon, or the "Lightning Express" shall be at your command.

Yrs truly

DANL WEBSTER

(To Nathan Appleton.)

Private.

[AUG 8. 1845]

My dear Sir.

If you deem this a proper letter,[1] (the one enclosed) you may read it to Mr. Lawrence.   If it would be better in any other form, please return it with your suggestions.

My desire is, in effect, to express my readiness to let bye-gones be bye-gones; & to restore the relations between Mr. Lawrence & myself, to the state they were in at the conclusion of the Treaty of Washington.   I always feel that Mr. Lawrence rendered the country eminent service in regard to the negotiation of that Treaty & zealously furthered objects, a good deal important to my own political reputation, in the circumstances, then existing.

I very gladly leave this matter entirely in your friendly direction.

Very cordially, &c.

DANL. WEBSTER.

(To Nathan Appleton.)

MARSHFIELD, Aug. 8. 1845.

My Dear Sir,

I have recd your letter of the 4th instant, & am obliged to you for it, as I regard it as a proof of friendship & kindness.

I assure you, My Dear Sir, that I have no wish to sustain towards Mr. Lawrence any other relations, than those of that cordial regard, which subsisted between us for so many years. I fully appreciate the value of his character, his talents, & the useful part he acts in life, public & private.   We have been politically associated together, & have cooperated, in some emer-

---

[1] See the following letter.

gencies of public affairs, not unimportant, & not terminating, I trust, disadvantageously to the Country. (*If it be Mr Lawrence's desire, it is mine, that our relations,*)[1] hereafter, shall be such, in all respects, as they were formerly, when we were employed, together, in public service.

I am, Dear Sir, with most true regard,

Yours

DANL WEBSTER

(From Nathan Appleton.)

My dear Sir   BOSTON 11 Sept 1845

I duly received yours of the 8th. inst. but owing to my own and Mr. Lawrence's absence from the City, I have not had an opportunity of communicating with him till now.

I avail myself of the permission given me to suggest a slight alteration in the note intended to be transmitted to Mr. Lawrence and which accompanies this.— Instead of the words included in brackets to insert. *It will give me much satisfaction to renew my friendly relations with Mr. Lawrence and that.*— and I would also add at the end—*With regard to what has taken place since, let by-gones be by-gones—but for the future may nothing during our lives mar the good understanding public and private, which it is my wish to cultivate*—or something of that sort.—

I think this change will express more explicitly, what it was your intention to convey—and I am quite sure will receive a cordial response from Mr. Lawrence.— With much esteem very truly,

Yours

N. APPLETON

(To Nathan Appleton.)

Private.

SEPT. 11, 1845.

My dear Sir.

I return the letter, having corrected it, very nearly according to your suggestions.

Yrs. truly

DANL. WEBSTER

---

[1] The lines here italicized are underscored and bracketed in this copy of the letter, and Mr. Appleton's letter, which follows, explains why.

(To Jacob W. McGaw.[1])

WASHINGTON Mar. 13. 49

My Dear Friend,

I lost no time in transmitting your letter to Mr Meredith, accompanying it with some account of the writer

It gives me pleasure to learn, from all that come from your quarter, that you are in good health, and the enjoyment of happiness My own health, also, is good But neither of us is so young, as we were, when Robert Wise ferried us over the River, to shoot pigeons on the Northfield Hills, and when we attended John Wilson's Dancing School, at the South Road.

Yours, mᵒ truly & faithfully,

DANL WEBSTER

———

(To Moore Russell.)

FRANKLIN. Oct. 6th '49

My dear Sir,

I was much interested the other even'ᵍ. by your account of what you remember of early times.

There are few indeed I hardly know any, whose recollection goes so far back, is so clear, and united with faculties so much unimpaired— You alluded to the murder of Mrs Call on this farm. I wish to preserve all that remains known, of that occurrence & the circumstances attending it: and if it will not be giving you too much trouble, shall be quite obliged to you, if you will request one or your sons to commit your recollections to writing.

I think you say the Indian who killed Mrs. Call was called "Old John. Pray tell me all you remember, or have heard of him—who were with him—what were his motives, or what aroused his vengence: what became of him afterwards, & what was his end?

On these points and indeed on all others connected with the case, I should be very glad to be informed of all you know, or have heard: and trust you will excuse me for giving you the trouble of answering the inquiry.

---

[1] Jacob McGaw was a life-long friend of Webster's. The original of this letter is in the possession of C. E. Bliss, of Bangor, Me.

I shall use the occasion, My Dear Sir, to renew the assurances of my great regard and friendship.

I have known you long and esteemed you much: and remember gratefully your kindness and good-will towards me, in the early part of my Professional and Political life.

I fervently pray that Providence may still have you in His Holy Keeping, and that what remains to you of Life may be full of happiness and Christian hope.

DANIEL WEBSTER

(To Henry D. Moore.[1])

LOUISIANA AVENUE Wednesday Morning Aug. 28, '50
My Dear Sir;
I am quite obliged to you for your two bottles of Liniment. It so happened, that at the moment of their reception I was about writing to a Physician for a prescription for such an Article. Once a year, at least, & sometimes oftener, I have a turn of lumbago.

Yrs truly
DANL WEBSTER

(To W. W. Seaton.[2])

"WEDNESDAY MORNING. [1851]
"My dear Sir,—
Your leader to-day is *Capital*. It is exactly the thing needed, and that tone must be continued. The disturbers of the public peace must be made to feel the force of public opinion.
"Yours,

"D. W.

(To W. W. Seaton.[2])

"I am sitting down, all alone at five o'clock, to a nice leg of lamb, etc., and a glass of cool claret—come.

"D. W."

[1] Mr. Moore represented Pennsylvania in Congress, 1849-1853. This letter was kindly lent by Mr. Charles Roberts, of Philadelphia.
[2] Reprinted from the "Life of W. W. Seaton," p. 305.

(To the Duke of Rutland.[1])

DEPARTMENT OF STATE,
Washington, 27 March, 1851.

My Lord Duke.

Among the crowds, who are flocking to England to attend the World's fair, is Mr. John O. Chowles, of our State of Rhode Island. He is an Englishman by birth, and has been a clergyman of the Baptist denomination. He has been very well educated, and is particularly a good classical scholar. Of late years, he has turned his attention, very assiduously, to agricultural topics, and is especially desirous of seeing something of the farming and cultivation of England. He is amiable and trustworthy, and if it should be in your way to show him any kindness, he will receive it with a grateful heart.

I seize the occasion, my dear Duke, to assure you of my faithful memory and recollection of the hospitality of Belvoir Castle, and the most agreeable acquaintances there formed.

Mrs. Webster desires to join me in warm regards to yourself; and we both pray most kind remembrances to your daughter, Lady Emeline and Lady Adeliza. Of your sons, I had only the pleasure of seeing Lord George, to whom please present my respects; but I see them all, daily, now, as they appear in the performance of their parts in the legislation of their country.

I remain, my dear Duke,

With the most faithful regard, yr obt. servt.

[DAN'L. WEBSTER]

(To William Sweatt.[2])

MARSHFIELD, Mass. [April] 12th. 1851.

My Dear Sir,

I can hardly tell you with how much pleasure I have read your letter. I Remember your family very well, and you have stored up in your mind, a great many interesting recollections, respecting our native town. And I am as much astonished as you are, at the ignorance and apparent indifference of the great mass of

---

[1] Directed to Belvoir Castle, Leicestershire. This is taken from the first draft of the letter.

[2] The letter from Sweatt is among the letters concerning the family relations of Webster. See Index.

its present inhabitants, concerning their predecessors, and all that is passed.

I remember all the School masters, whom you mention, tho' I am not clear that I ever attended Master Evans school. Master Quimby is still living, at Portland. He has descendants still living in the neighborhood.

It is pleasant to see, that at an advanced age, you cherish so lively an interest in the past. We belong to the past, and to the future as well as to the present. This our country was ours, before we were born, and will be our country after we are dead. I like to contemplate its history and its probable future fortunes, as well as its present state, and I am thankful my dear Sir; that my lot has been cast in such pleasant places, and without many afflictions. God has given me much to enjoy in this life and holden out hopes of a better life to come.

I tender you, my old townsman, my best wishes for your health and happiness.

Your friend
DANL. WEBSTER.

(From Wm. W. Story.)

BOSTON, Oct 3, 1851.

Dear Sir

I have indulged the hope down to the last moment, that I might be aided by your long friendship with my Father in the preparation of the biography of mine now in the press. I had especially hoped to receive from you more of his important letters. But in this I have been disappointed.[1]

With filial anxiety to place my Father's various services on record, & as far as it can be done without detriment to public interest or to private character, I have found no means accessible to me of exhibiting his intimate relations with yourself, & the Services you invited, which seemed to me so satisfactory as the introduction of some of your letters to him. The occasions to which they relate belong to the history of the Country; they involve no unsettled questions; they do not concern any private character; while they without doubt, help to illustrate my

---

[1] Mr. Story had written a long letter, June 10, 1851, calling attention to the particular letters written by Joseph Story to Daniel Webster which he desired. He also asked for some reminiscences of his father. A still earlier request was made May 20, 1846.

Father's abundance of knowledge, the solidity of his judgment, & the extent to which his counsels were sought on important & public affairs.

Before committing these letters finally to the press I have thought it best to lay them before you hoping for your express sanction to their publication.   As the press now waits, I have entrusted this letter, and the proof therewith to a special messenger by whom I hope to have an answer.

I have the honor to be Your obedt Servant

W. W. STORY

(To William W. Story.)

MARSHFIELD Oct 3d, 1851.
Friday Evening 10 o'clock

Sir,

I have this moment received your communication, with the request for an immediate answer.   All I can say without further reflection is, that my private letters to Judge Story which you propose to publish, are private letters, most of them unimportant, and one or two improper for publication.   I do not therefore consent to the publication of any of them.[1]

Your obedient Servant

DANL WEBSTER

(Mr. Webster's Lines on Foote[2] at Mr. Barney's Dinner at Walker's on Dec. 22, 1851.)

Oh, Thou! whatever name delight thine ear,
Governor, Senator, or Brigadier!
Allow thy friends, who are sincerely thine,
To pledge thy health in bumpers of rich wine,
Although thy name be but thy lower limb,
Thy head and heart are always in good trim.

---

[1] These letters have now been published in the Massachusetts Historical Society Proceedings, in the volume issued in 1901.   There are nineteen written by Daniel Webster to Story, and two written by Story to Daniel Webster.

[2] Henry S. Foote, Senator from Mississippi from 1847 to 1852, and was then elected Governor of Mississippi.   Later he was a member of the Confederate Congress.   The words of this heading are indorsed on the paper containing these lines.

Squadrons of cavalry may be disarmed,
Flying artillery is sometimes harmed,
But Mississippians put all these foes to rout
Whenever they make gallant fight on Foote.

(To J. J. Crittenden.[1])

My dear Sir,—　　　WASHINGTON, [June 11] 1852.

Your note of yesterday has given me relief and pleasure. It is certainly true that your remarks at the President's the day before caused me uneasiness and concern; but my heart is, and has always been, full of kindness for you, and I dismiss from my mind at once all recollection of a painful incident.

Yours, as ever, truly,

DANIEL WEBSTER.

(To A. C. Kingsland.)

My dear Sir.　　　MARSHFIELD July 26. 52.

Enclosed is a very touching letter which Mrs Webster has received today, from Mrs Jones, widow of the late Adjutant General Roger Jones. I do not know the young man, but we have been intimate with the Family, and have respected and loved them much. They are left in a state of great destitution & distress, and we should be infinitely obliged if you could grant what is so earnestly requested.

I am, my dear Sir, Yours mo truly

DANIEL WEBSTER

(From C. C. Felton.[2])

My dear Sir　　　CAMBRIDGE August 2. 1852.

* * *[3] While I have my pen in my hand, I must express to you my grateful thanks for the inestimable gift of a copy of

---

[1] This letter is reprinted from "Life of J. J. Crittenden," vol. ii, p. 37.

[2] This is indorsed by Webster: "Recd. 4th Aug. Ansd. same day." Felton was at this time professor of Greek and later the president of Harvard College.

[3] A few lines containing a promise to come to Marshfield.

your works, with the precious autograph letter accompanying it. I have a son, now an infant, whom, if he lives I shall train up in the study of these volumes, hoping to imbue his mind, from his earliest days, with the noble thoughts, so nobly expressed, in these imperishable discourses; and if he survives me, and is worthy of the gift, though I may leave him nothing else, I shall transmit the legacy of these books, to be a guide of his life, as an American citizen, and a proof that his father was not thought unworthy of your regard.   This will be "enough of heraldry" for him.

 With kindest regards to Mrs. Webster.

  I am, dear Sir,

   Most truly & sincerely yrs

        C. C. FELTON

(To Edward P. Little.)

     MARSHFIELD, Sept. 25. 1852.

My dear Sir,

 I deeply sympathise with you & your children, in the affliction, which you & they suffer, in the loss of a wife & mother, whose life was so invaluable to you & to them and who was so much an object of respect & love, to all who knew her.   I earnestly commend you & yours to patience & trust in God.

 I shall most gladly speak most warmly of yr. estate[1]—to any one whom may think of buying.   I regard it as one of the landmarks in the town, containing good lands & buildings, well cultivated, & fruitful, situated in the bank of the river, a short distance from the sea.

      Your friend

       [D. WEBSTER]

(To Hiram Noyes.)

     MARSHFIELD Sept. 17/52

My Dear Sir—

 I thank you for the box of pears.   They are precious to me, as coming from the Birth place.   The tree which bore them was planted by my maternal Grandfather, who had been a soldier, and lost a leg in the old wars.   He spent the last years of his

---

 [1] Mr. Little had written of the death of his wife and had asked Webster's aid in finding a purchaser for his farm.

life with my Father & Mother. In addition to these pear trees, he planted some apple trees directly South of the present house. They bore delicious fruit, and since my recollection, nobody could compare with the fruit of this orchard, except two clergymen. Rev Jonathan Searle, & Rev. Samuel Wood. I hope John Taylor's family have got over their fright.

Yrs truly

D. W.

(To Rev. Savage.)

Entirely Confidential.

MARSHFIELD Oct. 10th. 1852.

My Dear Sir,

I hear that there is likely to be a controversy between Mr. Horace Noyes and his mother respecting his father's will. This gives me great pain. Mr. Parker Noyes and myself have been fast friends for near half a century. I have known his wife, also, from a time before her marriage, and have always felt warm regard for her, and much respect for her connections in Newburyport. Mr. Horace Noyes and his wife, also, I have long known— Her Grandfather, Major Taylor, was an especial friend of my Father's, and I learned to love every body upon whom he set his stamp. These families, during very many years, have been my most intimate neighbors, whenever I have been in Franklin. It would wound me excessively, if any thing such as a law suit, should now occur between Mother and Son. It would very much destroy my interest in the family; and, whatever might be the result, it could not but cast some degree of reflection upon the memory of Parker Noyes. I know nothing of the circumstances, except what I learn from Mr. John Taylor; and I do not wish to express any judgment of my own as to what ought to be done, at least without more full information, but I do think it a case for Christian intercession. And the particular object of this letter is to invite your attention, and that of the members of the church, to it, in this aspect— Mr. Noyes is understood to have left a very pretty property, but a controversy about the will would absorb, very likely, one half of it. My end is accomplished, my Dear Sir, when I have made these suggestions to you. You will give them such consideration as you think they deserve. It has given me pleasure to hope that I might write half a dozen pages respecting Mr. Parker Noyes and our long friendship; but I could have no heart for this, if a family feud, after his death, were to come in to overwhelm all pleasant recollections.

I dictate this letter to my Clerk, as the state of my eyes precludes me from writing much with my own hand.

Yours with very sincere regard,

DANL WEBSTER

(To D. A. Hall.[1])

AP. 20.

Dear Sir,

Allow me to call your attention to the enclosed, which I have addressed to yourself. My only chance of saving this little sum is for you to go directly to Mr Agg, & make a strong appeal to his sense of *honor*, & his hope of any future respect or regard from me. I ask your attention to the subject, & however it may turn out will see you rewarded.

Yrs truly

D. WEBSTER

I wd give any length of time, if any body, who is trustworthy, would undertake to pay it.

---

[1] Addressed to D. A. Hall, Esq., Washington, D. C. The letter is owned by Mr. Charles Roberts, of Philadelphia, who kindly loaned this and other letters to the editor.

Daniel Webster, the Farmer of Marshfield.

WEBSTER *was, as he often declared, naturally a farmer. To his latest hours he looked back longingly to the boyhood days "when no cock crew so early that I did not hear him." Though he confesses that he never could hang a scythe, yet there is no doubt that he got a pleasure in seeing some one else do it. He knew how everything ought to be done, and no eye was keener for the merits of every farm and every method of farming.*

In the letters and papers here presented, most of them for the first time, one may see the intimate knowledge that he had of every tree and shrub, every variety of fruit, of grains and of vegetables. He lists the cattle, measures them, watches their growth and health, and studies the question of profit in handling them. To satisfy him the steers must be as well "trained and drilled as a couple of dining-room waiters at the Astor House." He takes an honest pride in his Ayrshires, his Alderneys and his Durhams. Old St. Stephen, the Hungarian bull, does not lose favor even after he has nearly killed Webster's favorite farmer, John Taylor—not even after Fletcher Webster has denounced all Hungarian quadrupeds and bipeds—classing St. Stephen with Kossuth. He took a quiet pleasure in having steers so terrible that, where they were, "people must tremble for their skins." When he was sick at Franklin he took a real joy in lying on the sofa and seeing the droves of cattle pass. There are thoughtful cautions in his letters that the oxen are not to be over-loaded, and, on the other hand, the thrifty solicitude that there be no idle teams. Even the "piggery" was an object of his care, which did not cease until their hams were properly cured and hung up for future consumption.

Wherever Webster traveled, his mind was alert for every detail of the country's agriculture. In England he took notes upon the method of ditching and tilling. He studied the methods of irrigation and the nature of the soils. Shrewd observations are noted on the way to make farming profitable. He returned from the South delighted that he could talk, like an eye-witness, of cotton fields, rice plantations, turpentine, and cypress swamps. The information gained in these journeys he sought to apply to farming at Marshfield and Franklin.

He loved personally to superintend every detail of the farm work. Memoranda were made to distinguish between the different varieties of fowl and cattle and trees. He directed the construction of the buildings, even giving measurements and size of timbers. The letters contain kindly cautions for the future and gentle reminders of failures in the past. The farmers are told to be ever on the watch for kelp when the sea threw it on the shore. Nothing, he constantly urged, could more enrich the land. He showed the necessity of working the ground well. "We want no pennyroyal crops," he adds facetiously. Minute directions are given for the trial of new implements. He sends newspaper clippings about the use of guano and bones and sulphuric acid. There are suggestions for little economies and detailed plans for laying away the provisions for the winter, with observations on the best methods of preserving. He lays out the farm work for a season, mapping the ground and planning for the most successful rotation of crops. Then come the genial, hearty letters in the spring, warning the farmers that he will soon "be among them and put the plows going." Everybody must be stirring. The boat must be painted, the boathouse mended; brush piles are to be burned and rubbish cleared away. All look forward to his coming and loved to hear him say, "After all, this is the very sweetest spot in the world."

At Marshfield or Franklin he was a farmer among farmers. We find his neighbors sending him gifts of their most choice stock or their rare seeds and shrubs. He in turn was always sympathetic and thoughtful and neighborly. To the farmers of his own lands he said, as in his letter to John Taylor, "You and I are farmers; we never talk of politics—our talk is of oxen." When he came home to "the old elms and the sea," he delighted in the sight of Seth Peterson "in his red shirt sleeves." He is willing to share their simple fare; they are to make no extra preparations; but, as he writes, just "have a fire to hang a pot over to boil a piece of pork." On the farm he is up with or before the dawn, and many of his letters are dated half-past four or five in the morning. He KNEW *the morning, he said; he was acquainted with and loved it, "fresh and sweet as it is, a daily new creation breaking forth and calling all that have life, and breath, and being to new adoration, new enjoyments, and new*

THE FARMER OF MARSHFIELD

gratitude." His enjoyment of the farm was real, direct and intensive. He was as proud of John Taylor's fine carrots as of the reply to Hayne. "Oh, Marshfield, Marshfield!" he cried in his letters from Washington, and he watched eagerly, amid the affairs of state, for Porter Wright's "Gazette," as he calls the letters about the farm.

In reply he rarely mentioned public affairs, and never but once did he write politics to his farmers, and then he said he never would again. He closed that letter with an exhortation to John Taylor to thank God, morning and evening, that he was born in such a country—"which does not oppress you, which does not bear you down by excessive taxation; but which holds out to you and to yours the hope of all the blessings which liberty, industry and security may give." Usually his communications were plain farmer's letters, but there were exceptions, as is that cheery, poetic letter to John Taylor, where he pictures the spring thaw and "the little streams running down the southern slopes of the Punch Brook pasture, and the new grass starting and growing in the trickling water all green and bright and beautiful." He even quoted a charming passage from "Mr. Virgil," and asked honest John Taylor whether the verses did not call to his mind his own "Durham oxen, smoking from heat and perspiration." After all, he concluded, Mr. Virgil only said things which John Taylor "up at Franklin" understood as well as ever the sensible author did. With this exception, the letters were sternly practical and departed from the themes of cattle, grain and produce only when they, perchance, discussed the bargains to be made with the renters of his land, or were filled with indignation because they had not treated him fairly.

He loved to talk of "a little farm well tilled," but he evidently was ambitious for a great estate. He had Washington and his great plantation in mind. Among the letters here presented we shall find him sending Fletcher into the West to care for the lands in which he had already invested, and to buy others. Then, with an even more elaborate scheme, he sends Ray Thomas upon another commission, which, with the earlier, failed and left the great statesman struggling in the toils of debt until his dying day. The plans failed not so much from lack of judicious management on the part of Webster as from the fact that he bought his lands just at the beginning of great business depression, when all land value in the West began to decline.

It will be of interest to notice the dates of these letters devoted

*to the vocation he loved, and see from what great national con-
cerns he turned to write them; for, as he said, his mind rested
when he thought of Marshfield. "I shall take to myself the
wings of the morning," he wrote to his son when his health had
been endangered by overwork, and the phrase well described the
eagerness of his flight to Marshfield. There, as he said, he
grew stronger every hour. "The giants grew strong again by
touching the earth; the same effect is produced on me by touching
the salt seashore."*

(Mr. Webster on Farming.[1])

[1852]

"General Wilder and gentlemen of the United States Agricultural Society, I am happy to see you, one and all. Brother
farmers, you do me no more than justice when you call me the
'Farmer of Marshfield.' My father was a farmer, and I am a
farmer. When a boy among my native hills of New Hampshire,
no cock crew so early that I did not hear him, and no boy ran
with more avidity to do errands at the bidding of the workmen
than I did.

"You are engaged in a noble enterprise. The prosperity and
glory of the Union are based on the achievements of agriculture.
Gentlemen, I will say to you what I have never before said, that
when, forty-five years ago, I was called to Dartmouth College
to pass my second graduation, I attempted, in my humble manner, to speak of the agricultural resources of the country, and
to recommend, for their fuller development, organized action and
the formation of agricultural societies; and, if memory does not
betray me, it was at about this period of time that the first agricultural societies of this country were formed in old Berkshire
and Philadelphia; (loud cheers by the delegates from Pennsylvania and Massachusetts;) and though I have never seen that
unimportant production since that day, the partiality of any of
my curious friends (bowing and laughing) may be gratified by
exploring amongst the slumbering archives of Marshfield. When,
some thirty years ago, I went to Marshfield, some of my kind

---

[1] During the meeting of the United States Agricultural Society in Washington several of the delegates called on Mr. Webster. He received them very
cordially in his dining-hall, and, after shaking hands with the company,
addressed them as above.

neighbors would call to inquire the state of politics in the South, and others to know a bit of law from 'the squire.' I told them, 'I have come to reside among you as a farmer, and here I talk neither politics nor law.' Gentlemen, I am naturally a farmer; I am most ardently attached to agricultural pursuits; and though I cultivate my lands with some little care, yet, from the sterility of the soil, or from neglected husbandry on my part, in consequence of my public engagements, they afford no subsistence to myself and family. To you, farmers of the West and South, the soil of Marshfield may look barren and unfruitful. Sometimes the breezes of the broad Atlantic fan it; sometimes, indeed, unkindly suns smite it. But I love its quiet shades, and there I love to commune with you upon the ennobling pursuits in which we are so happily engaged. Gentlemen, I thank you for this visit with which you have honored me. My interests and my sympathies are identified with yours. I shall remember you and this occasion which has called you together. I invoke for you a safe return to your homes. I invoke for you an abundant harvest; and if we meet not again in time, I trust that hereafter we shall meet in a more genial clime and under a kindlier sun. Brothers farmers, I bid you good-morning." [1]

(Seeds, Plants and Trees from Mr. Peirce's.[2])

[1832]

Seeds.

Willow Oak. Chestnut oak. Spanish oak. Pin oak. Box Oak. Black Jack Oak. Grey Oak.

—as many of the above varieties, as may be convenient.— Black Walnut.

Not a great many nuts will be needed, of any one kind— say, from a pint to half a gallon.—

Plants.—

Sassafras	20	American lime or White	
Sweet gum	10 or 15	Bass	20
Red mulberry	10	Fringe tree	10
Judas tree	10	Spice wood	5

[1] This is taken from a newspaper clipping the source of which is not noted. Internal evidence seems to vouch for its authenticity.

[2] This memorandum in Webster's hand is indorsed by him in the words of this heading. The trees seem to have been meant for Marshfield.

Dogwood	20	Willow oaks	30
Iron wood	1 or 2	Chestnut oaks	30
Black gum	5	Norway fir, Cypress—	
Spikenard	5	Yew—Juniper 2 or 3	
Tulip popular	20 or 30	each. Clematis—Ivy—	
(some large)		Sarsaparilla. Tennes-	
Chincapin	10	see Rose.	
Papaw or custard apple		European Larch	10 or 5
5 or	10	Black walnuts	20
(or less)			

Several sorts, besides the Tennessee, of Reeving (?) Roses.—
put them in pots, & the pots put in a large box.—say, 20 planted,
in all—or 25—(at 25 cts if duplicate) otherwise, 37 1/2—
20 Hollys, in pots.—

My man, Charles Brown, will call on Mr. Peirce the 15th of
October. He will give any aid he can, in collecting the seeds,
& getting up the plants; &, when all are ready, will take the
charge of them to Alexandria.— Mr. Peirce will please write
me, when the whole is shipped off, directed to Boston—with the
bill—c—

D. WEBSTER.

I will thank Mr. Peirce to give, on the paper, such directions,
as he may think useful, abt. the management of these plants, &
seeds, the sort of soil for sowing & setting them, &c.—to be
minuted agt. the article.—

This is the substance of the order left with Mr. Peirce—not
exact, in all things.—

(Provisions.)

[1833]

For beef, fresh or corned, & for tongues, sent to Mr Saunder-
son, in the Quincy market—

Mr. S. will have ready for you, & perhaps will send, every other
Monday morning, a piece of corned beef— If you do not like
the piece, you can give direction for one different.

For poultry, of all sorts, send to Mr *Baldwin*—

For fresh pork, hams, sausages, or anything of that kind, send
to *Boyd & Dinsmoor*

For apples, nuts, & things of that kind, send to Mr Tombs—
and for all sorts of vegetables—
For mutton, apply to Mr Knight—
For Butter, send to Mr Hovey; & let him know who sends—
For Mutton, to Denison, Moses & Co.
Broomfield Street—[1]

(Memoranda Upon Farming in England.[2])

OSSINGTON, NOV. 8. 1839.

Tile draining began in this part of England.   Probably the
Duke of Portland was the first to commence the practice to any
great extent.   Hitherto, the practice has spread more in Scotland, than in England; but now it is adopted with much spirit,
in this part of the latter country.   Thro. all this region, the
substratum is a stiff, tenacious clay; & for such lands dra'g is
useful.   Of course, it cannot be required, in sandy, or porous
soils.   In this part of England, where the lands are clayey, &
where there is often not natural descent enough to take off the
water rapidly from the surface, it is said that dra'g will add a
fifth, or a fourth, to the Wheat crop.   It costs six pounds per
acre, of which cost the tiles constitute one half.   The drains are
made seven yards apart, & the tiles laid 20 inches deep.   A sort
of plough, made for the purpose, is first used, which cuts up the
sod, 8 inches wide, & 6 deep, & turns it handsomely over on one
side.   The rest of the digging is by the spade—the tiles are
then laid, & covered & the turf turned back.   The tiles are abt.
14 inches long—and may be said to be the section of half a
cylinder, of about 4 inches diameter inside—the shell about 1/3
or 1/2 an inch thick—   In general, they are not quite a semi-
circle—but a half cylinder, a little flattened ⊐ —this mark
may represent the part view of the end, or outfall, of a tile drain,
& so give the shape of the tile.—
I have been today over fields drained, & others by their side,
not drained.   The difference is obvious & remarkable.   The first,
notwithstanding the extreme wetness of the weather, are capable
of rec'g. seed wheat—some are sown—the others are altogether
too wet.   Water is running very fast out of the outfalls, or ends

---

[1] In Daniel Webster's hand.
[2] These notes in Daniel Webster's hand.

of the drain—and none seen stand'g on the top. What is remarkable, is, that drained lands suffer less from the scortch'g heats of summer, than the lands without drains. The reason is thought to be, that b'g kept generally drier, they do not bake in the sun, when hot weather comes, as lands do that have been wet on the top.

When there are cold Spgs in the land, the drains are made much deeper—sometimes 5 or 6 feet.

On the whole, it seems reasonable to believe that much of the strong clayey lands of England will shortly be improved, in its productiveness, by the process of dra'g, 20 per cent—

Tenants are so sensible of draining, that tho' tenants at will, yet, hav'g an expectation to remain, they will be at the expense of mak'g the drains, the Landlord furnishing the tile. The recommendation of tile, is the comparative cheapness of carriage. The D. of P. supposes also, that the tile drains are less likely to get out of repair—& it is certain that the labor of lay'g them is much less than that of stone.

The land here is not *stoney*—few stones are to be found. It is rather a rich soil, & all underneath a rigid, dark colored clay.

Sheep. Mr. D. hires this year 3 rams, at 12 £ each— A Gentleman in Williston (?) gives 80 £ for the use of one— A ram should not have more than 80 ewes.

A good Leicester will clip 8 lbs.

Memo fence

6 stands of wire, running thro Posts—abt. 6 inches apart— & 1/3—or toward 1/2 inch—in diameter—1/3 is large end— A great deal of hurdle fence and for temporary purposes.

OSSINGTON Nov. 11.

I have this day been to see the stock of Mr. Parkinson, a distinguished cattle breeder in this country, who occupies a farm belong'g to Lord Scarborough. His breed is the short horn. He showed us, I should think, from fifty to a hundred animals. They are fine, but prices enormously high. For his best cows, he asks 80 to 100 guineas. For 2 yr old heifers in calf 50 £ for a bull calf 30 or 40 £ and for one bull calf, not more than six weeks old, of a very favorite mother & by a distinguished bull, he said he should refuse 100 guineas. I think I have seen as good animals, tho' these are very fine. I find the red—& red &

white color—not liked—the grizzled or fawn & blueish—the *speckled*, rather than the black & white—&c. are preferred.

[Diagram was inserted here.]

Memo. Mr. Doncaster.[1]—

to preserve Swedes Turnips, throw them into heaps, no matter how large, & throw over them loose straw, or litter— If bound close, they are apt to rot.

Mr. D. has the greatest opinion of tares—winter tares—sown in August,—2 bushels to the acre—& 3 pecks rye—to hold it up. —mows it for cattle—just before ripe—use it green—or dry it—

(Duke of Portland's Water Meadows.[2]*)*

MEADOWS.

The Duke told me his *carrier* was 5 miles long—the river is the *Mason* (?)—

At present, he waters about 300 acres. His manager gave me the following statement—

—1. The water is kept at work the whole year, flow'g over some part of the land. It is watered, part at a time—& as well in winter as summer.—

—2. Ab't. Christmas, South down ewes, bei'g then lambs, are put to feed on this land. It will then be as green as land in June. In March, the lambs are sold, & will be worth at 8 weeks old 2 1/2 to 3 £ each—

—the sheep are then taken off—& the land watered. The water is kept on 3. 4. 5. or even 6 days—till it is seen that the grass has got a good start—

It is mowed in May, & will yield 2 tons—

—It is watered again, & mowed in July—2 tons more— And again in the fall—two tons more.—

The third mow'g is now goi'g on— I saw the grass & should think the quantity not too high stated. The cattle are now eat'g it, green but it may be dried, if weather suits.

These fields have never been manured—though some of them have been mowed ten to 15 years. Their product is as great now as ever. The water leaves a little sediment, on the grass, as

---

[1] This is a memorandum made by Webster while in England.
[2] A memorandum in Webster's handwriting, made while in England.

thick as a knife. 400 hundred cattle are kept on part of this produce. I saw abt. 150—very fat & fine—many of them worth 30 to 40 £ a head. This land, 20 years ago, was a barren part of Sherwood forest— It was sold for a shilling an acre. It is now worth from 3 to 4£. Just along on the edges you still see, gorse, viz, (heath) fern &c growing on the sandy rough lawns —the whole region is thin, sandy soil—red sand stone ly'g below the surface— Some of these fields are so sandy, as that the sand was blown by the wind. The River runs thro the town of Mansfield, & is supposed to b'g some nutritious aliment for plants along with it.— Sort of grass—this grass is generally *hay seed*—by which is meant seed of natural grasses, generally found in Derbyshire—where it is to be bought—it seems a good grass— tho' some thot it [illegible]—sometimes whole clover is sown— sometimes rye grass. Mr Tibbels does not like——.

——————

(Memorandum for Farming for 1848.[1])

[FRANKLIN]
1st. All land, planted or sowed, except up on the hill, must be ploughed with the subsoil plough, as well as the common plough. To this, there must be no exception, not even of a single rod.—
2. On the North side of the Road, plant & sow

8 acres of corn	8
3 Do. of turnips	3
3 Do. of potatoes	3
1 Do. of white beans	1
	15

The corn to be at the upper end of the field; then turnips, then potatos, then beans.
The turnip land to be dressed with ashes, if to be had, at about 100 bushels to the acre.
All the land should be ploughed this fall.
Plant the potatos early; for the kind, consult Govr. Hill.
II. Great field.
1. Sow oats, where the corn is now standing.

---

[1] Indorsed "Northfield, or 15 acre piece—and the Great Field."

2.   Sow oats & peas where the potatos grew, this year, at the rate of 1/2 bushel, of each, to the acre.

Be sure to get good seed peas.—

(Memorandum for Mr. Taylor.[1])

NOVE. 3, 1850—

Things in and about the House,—appels—scend two barrels to Mr Blackford

" one to S. A. Appleton one in cellar for my Self.

Hams to be put into ashes, boiled up & placed in the T. Chamber—

2. Dun fish. to be left in the Same room,—   Bottels of sperits & wine to be Counted & Locked up in the wine Closet—

;With tea Sugar candles coffee &c 1 pare Pistols fishing rod Spyglass, &c.

(Farming for 1851.[1])

1 Continue the plowing on the Hills.

Have the piece measuered immeditly, & the account scent to me, I will in Season direct about the manure & the Crops to be put in,   Probaly potaters turnips & Beets & a small patch of beans & a nother of peas,—

2 Break up in the Spring 12 acers at the lower part of the field plant 10 acers with corn, land well manured 2 acers on the highest part with potaters with out manure,—

3,— Sow oats & Grass Sceed on the following peeces viz—

In the 15 acer lot, 4 1/2 acers—

Where the corn is know standing 6 3/4 acers,

Where the potaters ware this year in 2 peices 4 acers, in all, 15 1/4 acers—

4. one rye field on the Hill probaly say 8 1/2 acers—

5. Take care of my Mothers Garding, & the Land adgoining & put it in good order.   do not plow up her Garding, plant the rest with Punkins,

6. plow the orchard & sow it with oats,   Take away the ded & Useless treas, & set out a few nice young ones—

---

[1] This is in John Taylor's hand, but is evidently from Webster's dictation.

In the Spring, be sure to dig Round all the apple trees in the South parster,

—Fill my shed ac ful as nessecery with Sound wood—

—make 6, or 8, Gates, 3 of them Like Mr Noyes— Repare my Boat, make oars &—Co—

—Let Charles Keep one 4, or 5, or 6, Turkes— Take 2, for Thanksgiving & Crismas, Git the rest fat, & scend them to Revere House— Rais 100 Chickens next year,—

(Memorandum of Cattle.[1])

MARSHFIELD Nov. 8. '50.

Working oxen, & Steers trained & *to be* trained
1 pair white faced oxen, 6 or 7 years old—
    when in flesh 7 feet
4. 5 yr old oxen, viz
    Durhams 7 feet
    Black & red 7 feet in flesh
1 pair 4 yr olds jumpers. 6 feet 7 inches
4 pr 3 yr olds viz
    twins, 6 ft. 3.
    Black Steers same
    Red & lined back—6 ft. 4 inches
    Yellow steers, 6 ft. 3 inches
2 yr olds
    3 pairs viz.
    1 pr raised at home, lap horn—
    2 pair had last year of Mr Ames—
Yearli'gs
    1 pair—raised at home likely
    1 pr Devon Steer calves
Miscellaneous Steers, &c—
    1 pr big greys.
    1 odd Ayrshire Steer.
    3 Bulls Devon—
    Ayrshire
    Alderney.
9 beef cattle

---

[1] In Daniel Webster's hand.

Cows
At the large Barn
   3 Full blooded Ayrshires—
   1. Raised here—
   1. Seth Weston
   1 imported
5 Alderneys—one old mouse color—
   1 from Mr Calls, several years ago
   2. imported this year—
   note 1 imported this yr for Mr Haven, black, red & white—
1 red 3 yr Ayrshire cow
1 Noyes cow 1/2 Ayrshire—
2. 3 yr old heifers
———
11 in all
Cottage—
   1 Devon
   2 twins
———
   3

[etc. etc.]

Canvass back, & red heads.—

The most obvious differences between these varieties are three.
1. The length of the bill; the red head has a bill nearly half an inch shorter, & rather stouter, & more blunt.—
2. The size of the foot; the canvass back has a very broad web;— the Red head, a much narrower web, & more slender foot.—
3. Generally, the Canvass back is the whitest back.—
Of both sorts, the Drake has a blacker, & the duck a redder head: & the Drake also is most usually of the whitest back.—

Memo.
Abt. a mile from the Capitol, north, by the side of a row, or branch, & near the house of Mr. Moore, there may be found, within a very small place, the following different species of oak, viz.
White oak
Red oak
Black oak
Willow oak

Gray oak
Spanish oak
Pin oak
Box oak
Black Jack oak
Chestnut oak

June 20. 1832.

Sheep Marks.

We have now Three Breeds of full blooded imported Sheep; viz: Leicester, Cheviot, & South Down Every sheep & lamb, known to be full blooded, of these Breeds, must be carefully marked, with a Separate mark for each Breed—

1. Leicester; a hole punched through the right or left ear.

2. Cheviot a hole punched through the ear opposite to that on which the Leicester is marked. The Cheviots, or some of them, are already thus marked. See that, in due season, all are.

3. South Down. A proper crop, or mark in one ear. There should be no *slits*. Those look bad, & sometimes tear. But take out a small triangle, with a little chissel, or an iron made for the purpose, thus — or, if you have an iron made for the purpose, cut may be in the shape of a half moon, thus ⌒ —

In like manner, we have two distinct breeds of cattle, viz. Ayrshire, & Herefordshire. Let them, at least all the young ones, be marked in the same manner—& let the mixed breds run, unmarked.

A regular account must be kept, of the birth of every full blooded calf.

Our stock of cattle & sheep, (all paid for except what you owe Mr Ames) is worth at least 3000 Dollars— We must take care of them, & begin a course of regular sales next Spr'g. It is time, now to *sell* someth'g. We have been *buying* a good while.

Yrs. D. W.

Plan of Farming

The general plan of farming for the year, laid down last Fall, must be pursued; subject to such alterations as circumstances may require—

An important item is the New Orchard. I wish this to be *particularly well done*—

Mr Breck will furnish the Trees, apple & peach—or tell us where they can best be had. I wish them to be handsome, & thrifty, as near of a size as may be, & *taken up with the greatest care.* This is a main point. I have lost hundreds of dollars, by lay'g & plant'g trees, taken up without roots. I am afraid to trust any nursery man's workmen with this. Mr Thomas, or Mr Gardner, or some other competent person must see to the whole of it. Let no Tree be brought away from the Nursery, till it has been examined, & found to have a fair & good root. This is all important. The sett'g out will be done under Mr Morison's directions, & eye; & will of course be well done.

I hope the corn field on the Island, which was one of the last additions to our plan of the years work, will come to someth'g. We have learned, by this time, not to plant corn, unless on ground thoroughly manured.—

It is a great object to plough the land, on the side hill, in front of the House, as proposed— I like the plan of furnishing a team, & having the plough'g done by the acre.—

As to cattle—

I have not much to say, until I hear from you. I suppose 4 or 6 of the oxen should be turned out to be fatted—and about 20 head sent, in May, to Franklin.

—The "mismatched" oxen—the "Harlow" oxen & the "Kelley Oxen," may stay at home, & fatted—& the odd ox. This will leave for work the 4 large red oxen, & the Brown 5 yrs olds. Or one pair of these last may be turned out, if there will be teams enough, without. For Franklin, there may go up the large John Taylor steers—the 4 yr old steers, if not thought good to keep for work, & some of the likeliest three year olds—& two year olds— Or if pastur'g be wanted by the neighbors, some of the oxen may be sent up—

I suppose the oxen at the Island, might as well be fatted, this year.

The large 3 yr olds (now soon to be 4) I hope will be found good to work, & fit to be kept at home— I think 6 old oxen, & 6 4 yr olds, & 3 yr olds will be team enough— If not, add another pair of 3 yr olds— There will soon be 4.— Keep a good team, & enough at it, but noth'g useless—

Ox Barn.

1st. hovel.   2nd.
The mountaineers—   The Durham Steers—
The white faces—   The Ames Steers—
The Black & Red—   The Hazeltine Steers—
On the other side—
The Jumpers—
The Twins—
The 2 yr old Steers,
The yearl'g Steers, &c.—

For Fletcher's Barn
Some of the Steers which have now in our pasture, & perhaps the 4. 3 yrs. olds, which we turned down below the other day.

As to the 5 yr. old oxen, if they are not sold, they may stand in Fletcher's Barn, & eat turnips, till somebody wants them, for beef or work—

I have no objection to keep the white faced 3 yr. olds, if there is room, & nobody wants them for work'g cattle.

(Keeping of the Cattle.)

1. Put the 20 steers, now in the pasture, into Mr. Osgood's barn, in one or more hovels, as may be convenient, & let them be regularly tied up, every night, & properly taken care of.   Put no other cattle in this barn.—

2. Let the Hereford Bull & cow stand in the West end of the great Barn, & also the black 2yr. old, now in milk, unless she be sent to Marshfield.

3. Keep the calves wholly by themselves.

4. Tie up the rest, in the three hovels, & let them have the large yard.

(Cattle—Franklin.)

10 fat 4 yr. old steers—for the market 6 full grown working oxen—3 Mr. Taylor & Mr. White The Nesmith oxen, & the two off oxen.—6. 4 yr. old steers, for work, viz. the Triest steers, the Mountaineers, & the steers raised here.

2 cows—6 3yr. old steers; viz. the black steers—& the two pair of Sawyer steers.

The Sawyer Steers may be sold for beef, if thought best. The Triest Steers, & the mountain steers not for sale.

The off oxen, one or both may be sold, for good prices— The two pairs of Sawyer steers may be sold, or sent to Marshfield if you & Porter think best.— I incline rather to see them; but you & Porter Wright [best] may judge.

If the two off oxen will bring high prices, they may be sold; altho. I think they would make fine Marshfield Beef.

Cattle.

1. Beef cattle. There are 4.— The Barrett oxen, the cow & the 3yr. old steer—all to be fed.

When Capt. Sawyer next comes along let him take the off Barrett ox, & the cow.

Feed the 3yr. old steer while the pumpkins hold out;—then sell them to the butcher, & give me credit for them.

Feed the near Barrett ox, till Christmas; then kill him, & give me credit for him, at current price for the best beef—not less than 6.50 per 100.

Cows—

There are six cows, now on the farm, & will be a seventh next Spring. Mr. Taylor may have the use of 4. to be kept on the farm, being the Ayrshire cow, black—white face cow, & the two cows bought of Mr. Kendrich at $20 a yr for each—he to have the calves, & without—charge for the Bull—

The black two yr. old heifer, now in milk, to be sent to Marshfield, if convenient— The Hereford cow, & the other black heifer to be left, to rear calves. I may put on the farm a cow or two more, to raise calves.—

Mr Taylor will come down, on Friday next the 3rd—bringing the cow —& the two sheep—nicely dressed.

Swine.—

Fatten the great hog; when killed, take 200 lbs as the part belonging to Mrs. Taylor's dairy— give me credit for the residue, as agreed.

Fatten the small farrow hog; when killed, put it up for me, in a nice barrel, by itself, & put it in my cellar. Cure the hams and shoulders. Cure & smoke the hams & shoulders, of this hog, & smoke them, & put them up nicely, in cotton cloth, & ashes.

Keep the two sows, & raise pigs as fast as you can; & sell none till further orders.

Sheep.

There are now 51 half-blood Leicesters—13 half-blood South Downs—12 half-blood Merinos— 1 full blooded Leicester Buck   4 half blooded, do.   Oo—1 Full blooded South Down.

1 Sell all the half-blood Merinos at once.—

2. Sell the two smartest half-blood Leicesters.

3. Put half the Leicester Ewes to the full blooded Leicester Buck; & half to the large half-blooded Do.

4. Put all the South Down Ewes to the South Down Buck. Keep the breeds entirely distinct.   All the sheep must be kept, better than common.

In September, some of the oldest Ewes, & weathers, must be brought down to the barn, & fed—

To be sent to Mr. Webster at Marshfield.

1. The handsome 3 yr old Hazeltine Steers—dark red—

2. The red steers, with brown faces—3 yr. old of my first purchase, of Mr. Pike—   Mr. Pike gets a handsome pair to be sent in their room—

3. 1   dark chestnut 2 yr old—Hazeltines

4. one pair 2yr old—bought here of Mr. Bates.

5. one pair large limbed—red 2 yr old steers.

6. one pair 2 yr. old—large bodied—Plymouth

7. one pair Do. one yellow and large; the other speckled, & not quite so big—

8.   One pair Do.—red—very much alike—horns turning in—

In all, 4, 3 yr. old steers—& 12 2yr old. and 4 yearlings' steers, to be bought by Mr. Pike.   Mr. Pike is also to but 12 more steers, say 2—3 yr olds, & ten—2 two yr old—or 4 3yr olds, & 8, 8 yr olds, if better opportunity, & one handsome beef oxen—also 2 or three milch cows, if they can be had, large & handsome, & *not milch calfs*—all them to be left with Mr. Taylor.

D. W.

Agriculture.

Bone manure

A good article on this subject, is 7 vol. of Highland Society— page 75. by Mr. Lincoln's—Experiments prove it an excellent manure, wherever *lime* is deficient.

On calcareous earths it produces little effect—
The quantity, 36 bushels to the acre.

Top Dressiing for pastures.

Same vol. 159.—very good essay.

Materials for top dressing—lime—soil—stable manure. *good earth, having lain in the cow yard & become saturated* is better than any th'g else.—

manure, like lime, is a certain cure for mess, (?) & fogy— will br'g white clover.

Sea weed is also highly recommended. & *shelly sand—a por- iion, musceles*

—*All fields should be sheltered, by a belt of wood*—

Same subject page 82.

Old pastures should never be broke up—it takes a life, to re-establish them—for all soils, conta'g acid salts, lime is necessary.

A Field Gate p. 210.—

bars, taper'g—from 4 to 3 in breadth from 1 1/4 to 3/4″ thick   not hung between the posts, but on the face of the hang'g post—

By this means it falls quite back, so that carts do not strike it—

—the upper hinge shortens, by means of a screw & nut.—

[Diagram was inserted here.]

Vol. 8. p. 113.

Lucerne.

sowed 3 acres—in April.   18 lbs. to the acre.   light, sandy, but deep soil.   sown in hills—*it must be hand weeded*—hills 9 or 12 inches or 15 apart—a tolerable crop in the fall—

—cleared again in Sp'g—*5 feet high by June.*   4. abundant crops.

—*stands 17 years without manure*

It must be mowed with great care, the first year—

The best way is, to sow it as much as 15 inches apart, so as to clean between the rows, with a hoe—

Put the seed into a bottle, with a hole, or quill, in the cork— 25 lb to an acre is not extravagant—& I think not too much, for our land—

There is, in the same vol, an account of sundry very successful experiments of manuring land, by sowing buck wheat, & plough'g it in—

(Observations upon Mr. LeRoy's Farm.[1])

TUESDAY, May 28. [1851] (?)

Arrived at Avon, eve' of 27. On 28th A. M. visited Mr E. LeRoy's farm. It lies on the Genessee River, north of the road, lead'g from Avon Bridge, & consists of 1800 acres.

—The land is of three characters. 1. Flats. This is purely alluvial, low, & level. It is subject to be overflowed. When the county was settled, much of it was prairie. It has great depth of loose soil, vegetable mould, & other deposits. On the banks of the river, where the roots of trees are exposed, they are seen six, eight, or ten feet from the surface. The trees still remain'g are fine, especially elm and white oak, some of them very large. This land is adapted to grazing, but uncertain for wheat. In very dry seasons, wheat has succeeded on it. 2. The *hazel* flat. This is a table of land, rather higher than the last mentioned. It is flat, well covered with wood, undoubtedly, I think alluvial, but an earlier formation. It is not usually overflowed, & is, perhaps, more valuable than the lower flats; as adapted to wheat, as well as grazing. 3. Upland. This seems a peculiar soil. It is full of small stones, & the ground covered with a growth of oaks, of no great size. To the eve, it does not seem to be extraordinary land, but its fertility is very great, especially for wheat & clover. When ploughed little pebbles, stones or clay as they would seem, are turned up, in great plenty; but these crumble, or dissolve, by exposure to the air, & seem to be marl, or a mixture of lime & clay, or some such th'g, which I do not exactly know about. This land grows better by cultivation. It will yield two crops of wheat—then one of clover.—then one yr pasturage; & then wheat again; all without manure.— The only rotation seems to be, from wheat to pasturage, sometimes cutting with the scythe, the first year after wheat.

The lands up & down the River seem much like Mr LeRoy's.— I saw no difference between his flats, & those at Genesee.— The highland, or upland, near Genesee, was higher, & seemed to have a heavier original growth.

Mr. LeRoy cuts, on his lower flats, 200. or 250 tons of hay. This is housed in small barns, or barracks, stand'g round on the flats, & is fed out, thence, to the cattle. The cattle live on the meadows, thro' the winter, except work'g oxen, milch cows &c.

---

[1] The memorandum is in Webster's handwriting. The date is probably 1851.

And so do the sheep. Mr. Le R. winters 100 or 150 head of cattle, & feeds out to them 2 tons of hay a day— This is carried & spread over the field, by a sled, or waggon; so that the growth of the flats is consumed on them. These flats are sometimes plowed, but some of them have not been ploughed for 40 yrs, & yet bear good grass.— The feed is now abundant.—

(To Mrs. Caroline Webster.)

JAN. 11. 1836 Monday 2. clock in Senate

Dear Wife

In writing to you yesterday, I forgot to say a word about the big *cheese.*—Mr. *Meacham*[1] the Donor, has gone to Boston—& you will probably have seen him, before this reaches you.— He wants to exhibit the *Cheese,* I suppose, to get a little something to pay expense of transportation &c.— I have given him a letter to Mr. I. P. Davis— I think it is unwise in him to have *an exhibition*— I think he is better without it—on that point, however, he must consult Mr. I. P. D.

—No message from the President today—

Yrs

D. W.

(To Ray Thomas.?)

SENATE, friday April 29 (1836)

Dear Sir

I have recd copy of your log book up to April 24. P. M. *Seatime*—all well & right. I hope you will secure the avenue ag't. these overflowings of land— Please continue your esteemed favors— I hear there is another young lady in Milk Street.—

I notice that Mr Winthrop advertises the silver "Abele"—or silver leaved poplar—or whatever you call it—such as is in the centre of the circle , in front of the House.

He says he has them, by hundred & thousands & that they grow remarkably well on the Beacon st. In this last particular, I incline to think he is right. If you think so, please ascertain

---

[1] See "Private Correspondence," vol. ii, p. 14, Meacham to Webster, December 8, 1835.

how cheap they are—& if they are cheap, quite cheap, you might get a parcel & set out—a good many on Cherry Hill, & others elsewhere— They are very pretty, & if hardy, will soon cover the ground, & I incline to think they are rather hardy.

Yrs always

D. W.

What has become of Charles Henry Thomas Esq ? ? ?

(To D. Fletcher Webster.)

WASHINGTON, May 13. 1836—

My Dear Son,

This letter came today.—

I have not heard from you, beyond Hagerstown. If I get no letter by tomorrow, I shall have considered you will have reached Wheeling—will be fast passing on, & I shall therefore next address you at *Toledo.*— We have nothing of much interest here.   The H. of R. are still debating to *what Comee* they shall refer the land Bill.

The City has been full of Boston people—   Col. Perkins, Mr Wm Sullivan & daughter, Mr R. G. Shaw & family, Mr Bradbury & daughters, &c.—

—No news from N. York.

[D. WEBSTER] [1]

(To Mr. Murphy.[2])

WASHINGTON May 23, 1836.

My Dear Sir

I have rec'd y'r letter of the 16, & am glad to hear from you. My Londonderry land rises every day, at least in my own estimation.   I might be persuaded, possibly, to take 40 Dollars an acre for it, now, (tho' I do not engage to do so) because I want money, but if not disposed of by the first day of July its price will be 50 Dollars pr acre, & from that day nobody need look at it with an expectation of buying it for less.

We have very hot & very dry weather here.   Mrs. Webster &

---

[1] This letter is in Daniel Webster's hand, but unsigned. Fletcher Webster was on his way west to look after his father's land interests there.

[2] This letter is in the possession of Judge Corning, of Concord, N. H.

Julia are still N. York, but I expect them here this week. I fear Congress will sit to the end of June.

Yrs

D. WEBSTER

(To I. W. Kelly.[1])

WASHINGTON June 9. 1836.

Dr Sir

The difficulty with Josiah White is, that there is neither gratitude, honesty, or truth about him. I have written to Dr. Prescott to take possession of all the wood which is cut, & not drawn off.

By your account he expects to get his living—to buy his flour, hay &c—by cutting & selling wood, on my land. Let me know if the writ of possession is yet in force, or can be revived. As he has planted, I may leave him through this season, if he behaves well—but my patience is exhausted—& I will have no more to do with him.

Yrs

D. W.

(To D. Fletcher Webster.)

WASHINGTON June 12, 1836

My Dear Son

Your letters to Mr Davis & Mr Cramer, (not Kremer) were recd about a week ago, & were very satisfactory to those Gentlemen. They praised them highly, as evincing intelligence, on your part, & attention to the important business in which you are engaged. Mr Edward Curtis happened to be here, & praised them, & still more regretted that he was not with you.

I have no letter from you since you left Toledo; but I learn by a letter from Mr. Davis that you left Detroit, on horseback, about the 27th of May, I suppose for Jackson, White Pigeon, & so on to Michigan City & Chicago.— At the latter place, you will have found various letters from us. It is still uncertain when Congress will rise; but various things call me to the North, & it is my purpose to depart between the 24th June & 1st of

[1] I am indebted to the kindness of Judge Corning, of Concord, N. H., for this letter.

July. We have nothing very interesting. It has been, on the whole, a dull & barren session, with this exception, that it will have ended with the creation of two new States. The Toledo boundary, I believe, goes around to the Ohio claim entirely.

We hear little from Boston. At last date, Mr White's family not left home, five days ago. I believe he is detained by Mr Delands illness. The East Boston lots, it is said, sold very well.

Under another cover, you will find a communication, upon a particular, & new undertaking. As Mr Upton has brought this about, partly for the reason of giving you business, I doubt not you will do your very best to accomplish the expectations of the parties. You will continue to address me after the receipt of this, supposing this does not reach you till after the 24th, as I presume it will not, as at Boston.— Indeed I may be already leaving Washington when this reaches Chicago.

About coming home—when may we look for you? I think, there is sometimes fever & ague in the lake Country, & as you are not yet well (*acclimated*) if that is the word, you would do well not to stay too long, especially if it should be probable that the affairs which you will have on hand will call you back in the fall. It is expected very important sales will take place in Wisconsin, in October, as you will have learned, & a great many people will be present. There is no doubt, that if you come home in August, having done tolerably well so far, you can take back a good deal of money in the fall. What I would suggest, is, that, with the advice of Harding, & other friends in Chicago, as of Mr Whitney at Green Bay, you employ one or two good men—say two, & send them in different directions to explore for you, in Wisconsin, in the lands which are expected to be for sale. If you then return some weeks before the sale, you will then receive their report, & act accordingly. I understand, where one has the requisite previous knowledge, a favorable opportunity of entering lands exists, just at the close of the public sales, while others are gone into the woods to examine, &c— All these things, however, you will know more about, than I could tell you. Mr Haight leaves this place for Wisconsin this week,— He will probably find you at Chicago. He thinks you ought, by all means, to attend the sale, as he thinks the Company, assembled on that occasion, will be willing to give *you* one or two prime chances. There is something in this, worthy of being considered.

In all your operations you should appear to be acting for yourself; or, at least, for yourself & me; and as it is very probable that this business may induce you to make your home in that region, at least for some time, you should, on all occasions, act as much [as] possible as if you were already a Western man.

Mr Davis intends going to Detroit, immediately on the rising of Congress. Very possibly, you may fall in with him, some-where. I think it likely you will not receive this letter, until you have seen the waters of the Missippi.

Adieu! My Dear Son— I shall expect to receive a letter, in 5 or 6 days, announcing your arrival in Chicago.—

Your affectionate father

DANL WEBSTER

D. F. Webster Esq

With other members of Congress, I have taken a small inter-est in *Winnebago City*—this is *fancy* stock. I expect little or nothing from it. * * *[1]

(From D. Fletcher Webster.)

PERU [Illinois] Dec. 28, 1837.

My dear Father

Since I wrote you last I have made a long visit to St. Louis, on business for the Col. I had a very tedious time coming home on account of delays from the interruptions of navigation by the ice. * * *

I shall be very glad to see Lowrie; though I am somewhat afraid that he will be spoilt by the Col's. rascally Irishmen who are the laziest set of good for nothing rogues that I ever saw. We have had a good deal of trouble with them; I shall hail Ray's arrival with great pleasure as a signal for their dispersion. We are surrounded by Irish—more than half the Col's tenants & all his workmen & women are from Green Erin. They steal from us by the wholesale. I hope a few years will make a great change in the population of Peru & Salisbury. * * *[2]

I saw the President's message in St. Louis— I thought there was not much in it. How contemptible his allusions to the elec-tions were— What would Gen. Washington or John Adams have thought of such paragraphs in a President's message.

The Col. says that Illinois will go about right. * * *

FLETCHER WEBSTER

[1] Address omitted.
[2] The omitted paragraph concerns Fletcher's private business.

(To N. Ray Thomas.[1])

WASHINGTON March 5, 1838.

Mr. N. Ray Thomas
   Sir,

You are now about to proceed to Illinois and other North-western states as my agent, Your principal duties will be of two kinds.

1st. In the first place you will have the care & disposal of the lands lots and parcels of real Estate belonging to me in Ohio, Indiana, Illinois, Michigan & Wisconsin with power to sell excepting the estate or farm called Salisbury near La Salle. You take with you an account of these pieces & parcels of property of which account I also retain a duplicate. You take also the patents, land office receipts & deeds & agreements of individuals showing my title— There are shares also in incorporations and Joint Stock Companys of which you have the regular evidences. My design is that you should sell this property or any part of it if opportunity should offer which you think favourable. In the course of the ensuing season I hope you will be able to visit most parts of the country where this property lies so as to ascertain its value, and be able to act understandingly in the sale of it. You are also authorized to exchange any of it for other property if a favorable opportunity arises, and in case of sale of any part you may re-invest in other purchases in your discretion. It is not my wish to extend my interest in that country, but rather to contract it, and to dispose of a great part of what I own as soon as the time shall be favourable; still you may reinvest in cases that seem to be advantageous— You will take care not to interfere with my agreements with Geo. W. Jones & Levi C. Turner or other persons who have purchased for me with which agreements you are acquainted. In case of sale you will see the proper commissions paid to those who made the purchases, according to their respective agreements.

2nd. Your other main duty will be to carry on my farm called Salisbury. You will look at the Deeds which are said to be sent to Ottawa—see what land they contain, and see what land they comprise— My wish is to have a very large farm, as large as

---

[1] A younger son of the family from whom Daniel Webster purchased his estate at Marshfield, Mass. In the summer of 1837 Webster had made a journey through the West. He now proposed to establish a large estate in that country. See Curtis' "Life of Daniel Webster," vol. i, p. 571.

one active man can well superintend the management of— If
this estate be not large enough at present, find out what adjoining lands may be bought and at what prices— Fletcher and his
family live in the house, and I presume you will live with them—
You will keep an account of whatever produce of any kind he
receives and of whatever he contributes towards the pay of any
labourers or for other purposes— My object is to realize an income from this farm— You will therefore manage it with
economy and to the best possible advantage— The farm must
be well stocked—you will employ your own labourers and will
have no master over you in whatsoever respects the farm, but will
of course consult freely with Fletcher on all important matters,
not only in relation to the farm, but in other concerns of mine—
You will keep accurate & exact accounts of expenses & income
from the farm, as also proper accounts of all sums received &
paid on my account in the sale or purchase of property, or otherwise.   You will please write me regularly on the *first, fifteenth*
and *last* days of every month and oftener if occasion requires.

As to compensation it is understood between us that you shall
receive *Two thousand dollars* for one year, commencing on the
first day of January last— You are to be allowed travelling
expenses from Boston to La Salle, and also travelling expenses,
on all journeys undertaken from La Salle on my business—
Your personal expenses Clothing board &c you will defray yourself— You will be entitled to keep a horse on the farm for your
own use—

Yours truly
DANL WEBSTER

(From D. Fletcher Webster.)

PERU. [Illinois] Sept. 26th. 1838.

My dear Father,
   Things occur every day to delay me and every day I rejoice
that I am still here to attend to them, although I am indeed most
anxious to see you all & my wife & child again. * * * If
Ray Thomas were here I should be more able to leave, but there
is no one to take proper charge of the *farm;* the men are becoming clamorous for pay and I have been obliged to give them
all I could raise in any manner & indeed to furnish some supplies
besides.   Your farm is not carried on well nor can it be on the

present plan.   It is too expensive.   I have very much to say to
you on this subject when we meet.   Ray has done all he can &
everything has been made the best of—but I will keep all my
remarks until we meet.   *   *   *

DANIEL F. WEBSTER.

(From E. Phinney.)

My dear Sir   LEXINGTON [Mass.] 25th March 1839.
    I send you three of my pigs, of which I beg you will do me
the favor to accept.   ....
.... ; it will give me pleasure to renew your stock, and
as I hold, that, to one who has done so much to *save our bacon,*
every farmer should feel himself bound to furnish him with the
best materials for the making of his own.
    With proper treatment I have no doubt you will find them to
be an ornament to any swinish community.—   Please direct
your farmer not to feed to high least they wax fat & become idle
and useless—
    With my sincere respect
              I am Dr Sir yr
                  Obt Servt.

E. PHINNEY.

(To D. Fletcher Webster.)

My Dear Son,   WASHINGTON Jan. 5. '40.
    This Mr. Hancock, whom I believe you have seen, lives near
Fremont, close by Mr. James.—   He says he has a very good
estate, with nurseries &c, which he is in danger of losing, for the
want of one or two thousand Dollars, & that if he must sacrifice
it, he prefers it should fall into my hands, as an old acquaintance.
I do not know that any thing can be done for him, as I have
no money, but he was so urgent that I promised to write to you.
If he could be bought out, cheap, or any arrangements made, that
should compensate for a great sacrifice,—& if the creditor would
wait till next autumn, perhaps something might be done.   But
there must be a strong inducement—   At any rate, I cannot
come under obligation to pay any money, short of the next autumn.   Perhaps you can make an agreement with the creditors,
to suffer his debt to remain, until, having seen what Hancock
proposes, you shall see me here.—

I pray you, ascertain what has been done with the Bank Mortgage on Mr. Hubbard. Has suit been brought upon it?— And what has been done with Mr. Hubbard's Bill in Equity?—

As you were at Chicago, you probably learned something of these things.

There is nothing particular new here. Genl Harrison will hardly be here before February. His Cabinet is not yet understood to be made up, & nothing known beyond what is generally said to be settled, as to two seats in it.

All were well at home, when I last heard. We have had a series of very cold days, which are continuing—

Yrs affectionately

DANL WEBSTER

(To John Taylor.[1])

Dear Sir   WASHINGTON May 23. 1840.

Mr Samuel Lawrence of Lowell has presented to you & me a bull calf, now at Lowell, one month old. It is from a full blooded imported Devonshire bull, & a fine cow, 7/8" Devonshire, and one eighth Durham. It is bright red, except the tip of the tail, which is white, and a little white about the fore feet. I wish you to send for him, as soon as you receive this. I expect he will make something more than common. The blood is excellent for steers & also for milk. He now drinks milk— He must be taken up carefully in a cart well fed with milk by the way & have as much milk as he wants till I see you. Do not put him to any cow—but give him milk in a pail. Send for him as soon as you can.

I wish I could say when Congress will adjourn. One of my first visits when I get to Boston will to Franklin. Remember the turnips—I will write to Henry W send you directions & to Mr Fletcher to send you up some seed. Sow about June 20th— I sow in drills 28 inches apart—that admits the plough. Has Seth Weston sent you your plough?— The land should be ploughed just before sowing, the seeds soaked, so as to start quick, and then the turnips will get ahead of the weeds. I hope you will make the fields shine this year.

We shall write you in season about the horses.

Yrs truly

DANL WEBSTER.

---

[1] Webster's farmer on the estate in Franklin, N. H.

(To Mrs. Caroline Webster.)

TUESDAY 3 o'clock [Sept. 29, 1840]

Dear Wife

I could not get away this eve'g, on acct of the necessity of correct'g the report of my speech. I go tomorrow—right thro to Wilmington—& stop at Phila. on my return.— I feel better today than I have done for two months—but I am run down & run over with calls. Give my love to Julia & S. I shall expect to find a letter at Washington.

Yrs always l'v'ly

D. W.

What a lovely night you had— I got up once or twice to look out—today is lovely Oh, Marshfield!—Marshfield!

———

(To Mrs. Caroline Webster.)

FRANKLIN [N. H.] Oct. 26, [1840] Monday morg.

Dear Wife,

You will perceive, that this letter is in the hand writing of Mr. Haddock; and it is well, that he is with me, for I have been quite unwell for the last three or four days. They carried me from Nashua to Francestown & from Francestown to Oxford, in these miserable go-carts, called barouches—all open at front, and, as the wind was from the North-West, with much rain, I had to bear the beating of both. I took up Mr Haddock at Hanover, and, when I arrived at Oxford, on Thursday evening, I felt down sick, and went immediately to bed; and kept it till noon, on Friday, when I went out, and made my speech, returned & went to bed again, & sent for a Physician. This Physician gave me quantities of Calomel, and, on Saturday morning I felt somewhat better. I was received into the home of Col. Bissell, a gentleman, whom you saw on the 10th of Sept. at our rooms, with Mr. Britton. He and his wife are the kindest people in the world, and gave me every attention. I don't know, that I shou'd have escaped a fever, if I had been obliged to take the room of the tavern. Feeling better on Saturday morning, and the gentlemen furnishing a close carriage for Mr Haddock & myself, we set out for this place, but only reached Andover that day; for when I got there I was very much fatigued. We arrived yesterday at ten Oclock; but, still, I did not feel well. Common medicine, such as magnesia &c. seemed to have no effect. My skin was very dry and hard. I, therefore, sent for a Physician, & told him to give me a powerful emetic, which he did. I have heard of Thompson's Medicine, some called "screw auger," some called "wild-cat," but I never took any thing which made such thorough work with me; I feel much relieved this morning, and mean to get up by & by. But I dictate this, from my bed. By way of variety & amusement we had a fall of six inches of snow last night! I shall not be able of course, to attend the meeting at Salisbury today. I lament this very much; but it cannot be helped.

I have written to Mrs. Heeley to inform all inquirers, that I shall make no more speeches any where, or under any circumstances. I shall keep still, here, today, and amuse myself by looking out upon the snow. And as soon as I feel able, I shall take the stage coach to Nashua, & so home.

Mrs. Ezekiel is about visiting Boston. I think I shall meet her at Concord, and bring her along. John [Taylor's] Family are well. He'd a severe fit of illness in the summer, arising I suspect, from overwork; but he is now quite restored. When we saw him, he was fearful, that the drought would much diminish his crops, but they came in better than he expected. He beats all N. H. for turnips & carrots, which important things I thus mention to you because, when you have all read this letter, in Boston, I wish you to send it to Henry Thomas; and for the particular benefit of Henry, I wish to add, that John will send down the oxen by the first opportunity, and, perhaps, two or three young cattle with them.

And so no more at present.

> Yours truly
> DANL WEBSTER
> in bed

(To Mrs. Caroline Webster.)

FRANKLIN Oct. 27, 1840.

My Dear Wife,

I am much relieved since my letter of yesterday, by the severe operation of medicine, the night before. I am, however, exceedingly weak, & find it most comfortable to be on the sofa &

dictate a letter to you. I had thought of going homeward to-morrow, but the dampness of the air, occasioned by the fall of snow, may render it imprudent, unless I should recover my strength very fast.

Mr. Kelley & Mrs. Pierce have been down this morning and made me a call. They are quite well; Mrs. Kelley seemed not be in good health; she is more feeble than usual.

The meeting at Salisbury, which I was not able to attend, went off very well. Mr. Bartlett & Mr. Joel Eastman addressed the people.

I have just been out of doors to see John Taylor's beeves and turnips. I pass the time lying on the sofa, & looking out of the window, to see the droves of cattle pass, & hearing John Taylor and our cousin talk. Several friends have called, but have kindly made their visits short. Mr. Noyes inquires kindly after you; so does Mr. Pierce. Mr. Haddock sends much love to his dear good Aunt, & more especially to his cousin Julia and her little girl.

I am charged with burning the—Convent at Charles-town.[1] Do you recollect how I did it! Will you promise not to betray me, if I deny it!

I see there is a great row in N. York.

> Yrs &c
> DANL WEBSTER
> by C. B. H.

(To Mrs. Caroline Webster.)

> FRANKLIN Wednesday mor'g
> [Oct. 28, 1840]

Dear Caroline,

I write you today, with my own hand, that you may be assured of my convalescence. I staid at home yesterday, very much, and lolled on the sofa. Mrs. Mr. Kelley & Ellen, Mr. Noyes & others called in. I talked of every th'g but politics, & speeches, but not a word of that. What doings in N. Y! I do

---

[1] In the *North American Review* of January, 1841, vol. liii, p. 268, there is quoted from "Grattan," an anonymous writer in the Washington *Globe:* "Daniel Webster was reposing on a couch in his marble palace at Boston, and enjoying from his windows the conflagration of the Charlestown Convent in 1836, while a word from him might have put a stop to the devastation." There were three miles of buildings between his house and Charlestown.

believe that B. F. Butler is one of the greatest rascals living.[1] I hope he will come to his deserts.

I am sorry today the weather remains damp, & the snow does not go off, though it is not very cold. Unless tomorrow should be a decided bad day, I shall go to Concord in the P. M. & home the next day. I wish you had come here as I proposed. I would staid a week longer, for the pleasure of rest & quiet. Mr. Haddock will probably quit this Eve'g. He has been of great service to me; & I leave him room here for a post script, to give you an account of what he proposes for the winter.

Yrs truly
DANL WEBSTER.

My dear Aunt.

You see that uncle writes a little like an old man. His hand trembles a grain. I think this is more owing to politics than sickness; though he looks rather wan, I must confess; and I have all the labor of disposing of John Taylor's turkies & squash pies. Mr. Webster is very prudent in this particular, indulging himself with a little gruel & a cup of tea now & then. The symptoms of disease are clearly much abated; and I doubt not he will be able to ride tomorrow, if the skies smile.

I hope to see you in the winter, at Washington, where I propose to spend a month. Possibly I may meet you at New York before you go on.

With true regard
Yours &c
C. B. HADDUCK.

(To Seth Weston.[2])

Nov. 1, 1842

Dear Sir;

As to the fatting sheep, please send one, well dressed, to Mr. Appleton, the middle of this month, & one to Mr. Paige, the first of Decr.— If either of them write for it, of course send another.

You may as well continue to feed them on oats & corn, instead of turnips, as they are so soon to be killed. You can kill one for your own use that of the neighbors whenever you like.—

---

[1] Benjamin F. Butler, of New York.
[2] Mr. Webster's farmer on the Marshfield farm.

As to the beef cattle, get the red ox & the cow along pretty fast, but do not kill either, till further directions—

As to kelp, should it come on, I am more & more in doubt what to do with it.

I think,

1st. that we shall not get along to our minds, with either the Peach orchard, or the piece enclosed on the Hill without another coat of manure, either plowed in or spread on the land.

2. That it is not best to break up any land in the pasture, till those two pieces are put in proper condition.

Therefore, let us, either,

1st. Spread the ashes on the Peach Orchard, & run the chance of grass coming up; & top dress the lower piece with kelp, if we get any, or plough up both, and manure them as well as we can. These two pieces are as much exposed to view, as any two on the farm.   They look ugly, & will, till properly manured.   Think of these matters.

D. W.

(To Seth Weston.)

WASHINGTON Mar: 31, 1843.

Dear Sir:

We have had warm weather lately, with much rain; and as it looks as if the winter was at last breaking up, I have come to a sudden conclusion, that I must be among you, & put the ploughs going.

Look out for me, at Green Harbour, on Friday next, the 7th day of April, at 1 o'clock.—(dinner abt. 2)— Probably Edward, or Mr. Appleton, or both, will be with me.   We shall want nothing to eat, but pork and potatoes, & a fish, which I intend to take.   Lydia & Aunt Browne, or somebody else to help Lydia, must be put in requisition, as soon as you receive this; that the House may be opened, & aired.

The large Boat must be launched, & in order.   The admiral must bestir himself.   The black mare must be in readiness, &c.

Nothing but bad weather, or accident, will prevent me from arriving, as above.   If anything occurs, I will give you notice.

Yrs truly

DANL WEBSTER

(To Seth Weston.)

Dear Sir,   FEB. 25. 46

I have written for a "Biddell's Scarifier", & a Garrett's Horse Hoe"—

See what is said in pages 9 & 10, of the book I now send you, on the subject of White Mustard— I have written for some seed—

—I am expecting to hear from you every day, about Franklin.

Yrs   D. W.

(To Seth Weston.)

Dear Sir   NEW YORK Tuesday Novr. 3 (1846).

A rain commenced here on Friday, Eve, & continued, moderately, & with wind, till Saturday afternoon.   A strong blow then sprung up at N. E. & the rain increased.   All day on Sunday wind & rain continued; & so through yesterday— Last night the wind hauled to the S. E. where it is now; & it has been raining quite hard, in successive showers, this morning.   At the present moment, (10 O clock) light appears in the west & it looks as if it would clear.   You have heard of the accident to the Oregon, & the disaster of the Rhode Island.   Notwithstanding this violent eastern wind, the weather has been warm as summer, & is so now.   This is remarkable.   I hope the rain has reached southward, so that our parched lands may be refreshed, & the springs filled.   I am thinking of kelp.   The S. E. wind may br'g it along.

We shall leave here tomorrow, if the weather is fair; but in all probability shall not reach Marshfield till Saturday mor'g; by the early train— If we do not send other word, let the waggons there be ready for us, at Kingston— I suppose two must be sent, on account of trunks.

Yrs truly
DANL WEBSTER.

(To Seth Weston.)

Dear Sir,   WASHINGTON Jan. 14. 47.

We arrived here on Saturday, the 9th, & it was fortunate we

did so, as a very heavy snow fell, on Sunday, & Sunday night. The weather is uncommonly cold, for this place.

I rec'd you first number soon after arriv'g, & was glad to hear from you, & to know that are well.   It is far more agreeable to think of Marshfield, than it is to think of the Mexican War. News this morn'g from New Orleans is rather alarming.   There is reason to fear that Genl. Santa Anna may have fallen, with a Superior force, on one of the detachments of our Army.— We shall know, in a day or two.

Before leav'g Boston, I spoke to Mr. Howe to send down some lumber by Capt. Sherman.   This will save the necessity of buy'g at Quincy.

If all signs do not fail, I shall be able to send some money next week.

Yrs truly
DANL WEBSTER

I shall soon look for No. 2 of the Gazette.   You will find writ'g paper, quills &c, in my Library, or in my office.

———

(To Seth Weston.)

WASHINGTON Feb. 12, 1847.

My Dear Sir

I recd your letter yesterday.   The arrangements made or proposed, respecting the Cottage, &c are entirely approved, & may be carried into effect, as soon as convenient.

The little addition to be made to the Cottage must be neat, & well put on, so as not to look bad.   I should like to know a little more about the plan, & probably shall have time & opportunity; since I have concluded to go home, before we undertake any long journey.   Congress rises on the third, & I shall probably see you by the 10th of March.

I am glad the hands find a little kelp, now & then.   Whatever leisure time they have, I hope they will employ on the stones, & in the new field.

I expect to find Mr. Whit'g with a handsome, well trained, young team of four or five yokes.

I enclose a check for $250.   Danl Wright must have someth'g tho' I hoped he w'd have picked up enough in Boston.   Some little press'g things you can pay off. Mr. Cushman, probably, can wait without inconvenience, till I get home.

The weather here has been remarkably changeable, rain'g one day, & freez'g the next. We are quite well. If I remain of the opinion to make a journey to the South, Mrs. W. will be likely to stay here, while I am gone home.

Yrs truly
DANL WEBSTER

Keep up the Gazette.

(To Porter Wright. ?)

Dear Sir MAR. 29. 47.

I wrote you yesterday, but by accident the letter failed to get to the P. Office— It goes with this—

I send now some memoranda, to which I wish to draw your attention, with that of Henry Thomas & Porter—

Any thing you send off, on *Friday mor'g*, will find me *here,* or be sent on, & overtake me at Richmond— Address me, *as here.*

You must all take a day, to make out a despatch. Tell me the present state of things, as fully as you can, in all respects— farming, cattle, oxen, cows, calves, sheep, lambs, goats & kids— horses, mares & colts, & swine & pigs.

—Is the business arranged, between Porter & Mr Morrison, about exchange of Houses &c—?—

—Tell me all, that all of you can think of— Mr Baker will *report* on geese, turkies, chickens &c.—

Is the new hen house ready?— When will the hens move?

We must lay out, once more, coops for turkeys, at home, & on the island.

I shall continue to write to you, as things may happen to come to my mind—

As far as I can now see, I shall smell the ocean at Marshfield, just about the first of June. It may be 5 or 10 days earlier.

Porter will get a little mon'y for his beef, & I must know what else will be wanted, to preserve life till I come.—

—I hope some stones have been hauled for the wall, in front of the House. We ought to make a good long stretch, this Spring— It should be built immediately after planting.

Yrs. D. W.

(To W. W. Seaton.[1])

BOSTON, June 21, 1847.

My dear Sir,

—We came up from the place of places,[2] three days ago, and have inflicted on ourselves a residence of that length in Boston; to-day we hasten back to the Old Elms and the Sea. Mrs. Webster has received J——'s letter from New York, and bids me say that she has obeyed all its injunctions, requests, and intimations.

Our journey was shortened, to our disappointment. Still it was pleasant. We saw many new things and many good people. I can now talk, like an eyewitness, of cotton-fields and rice plantations, turpentine, cypress swamps, and alligators.

—Think of us at Marshfield,—on our piazza, with now and then a grandchild with us, a pond near, where 'cows may drink and geese may swim,' and Seth Peterson, in his red shirt-sleeves, in the distance. Then there is green grass, more than we saw in all the South,[3] and then there is such a chance for rest, and for a good long visit from 'tired Nature's sweet restorer'.—

Yours,

D. W.

(To Porter Wright.)

BOSTON Nov. 15—47. Monday Morn'g.

Dear Porter Wright;

A Devonshire Bull, & heifer, will probably be sent to the farm, this week—about Wednesday or Thursday— Let them both be kept at the ox barn, so as not to mix with our old stock— The Bull must be kept up. Perhaps a good place would be the little hovel in the Piggery. They are Devonshires; the heifers is 2 yrs old, & *very* large. Perhaps she is likely to be better for calves than for milk. She is of the same family as the bull; but it is in calf by another Devonshire bull, imported by the Society—

If the weather should continue open, & there should be no

---

[1] Reprinted from the "Life of W. W. Seaton," p. 305.
[2] Marshfield.
[3] In a previous letter he asserted: "There is more greenwood now in Marshfield than in South Carolina and Georgia."

kelp, & you should get time to plough any, I wish you would plough the orchard, near the house. Those apple trees need help from ploughing & manure.

There is ploughing enough, also, to be done in the Cushman field.

Yrs   D. W.

The Bull & Heifer are from Mr. Samuel Lawrence, at Lowell. Mr. Barker must take good care of the man, while he chooses to stay—

———

(To Seth Weston.)

WASHINGTON Decr. 24. '47.

My Dear Sir

I thank you for your letter, & shall be quite obliged to you to write me, once a week, as heretofore—

Tell our good friend that money was very scarce, when I left Boston, but that I have the promise of some, shortly—, I send a little today to Porter, for Mr. Hathaway & Sylvester, who are quite in want.

—I hope you keep ice, & the ice house, in memory. What little ice we were obliged to br'g last summer from Boston cost us money enough to build a good ice house.

I am anxious to hear about kelp.— If the *fish* will keep off, & *kelp* will not come on, they [will] very much break up our farming projects.

We have an expensive team, eat'g hay & turnips, & doi'g little—

How is Porter?

Yrs   D. WEBSTER.

———

(To Seth Weston.)

WASHINGTON Jan. 23. 48.

My Dear Sir;

I was glad to hear, by your letter, that Porter Wright's wife was better. We had begun to be concerned about her.

The winter, so far, has been unsteady, but I presume the last four or five nights have made ice, with you. Here the weather has been very fine, for near a week. The days are warm, & the nights clear.

I should be very sorry to lose Mr. Hatch, but I really do not see how I can agree to raise his wages.   Our labor already costs so much, I cannot make it cost more.   I like him very well, especially as a hand to go with me in the Boat, & to take care of our navigation.   But on the farm, you know, there are some sorts of hard work which he cannot well do.   Though quite sorry to part with him, I shall have no hard thoughts, if he finds he can do better, elsewhere.   If he should not stay, the Boats will probably all remain, till July.

As soon as the Supreme Court adjourns, I shall take a run home, say about 10. or 15. March.   By that time, I hope we shall have some good beef to sell.

Do the turnips hold out?   Are there any sound potatos remaining?—   Does kelp make its appearance?   How do the sheep look?   Do they get some good English hay?—

But I must not ask too many questions.

Yrs.   D. Webster.

(To Seth Weston.)

Dr Sir;   April 22. [1848]

Sow your two sorts of oats quite distant from one another. & from all other fields of oats—so as to keep the seed distinct—one is Scotch Oats—the other Orchard oats—   The weather is now fine—let the work go ahead—employ what hands are necessary —remember to mow down the little corner of bushes—in the lower pasture—just this side the Boat House.—left hand—   Let Boat House & Bath House be whitewashed—& the Summer house painted—

I shall be with you before June.—   The cottage ought to be opened the first day of June, & the work on the House begun, Monday, the 5th—   See that all things are ready—write for money, if you need it—

Do not let the men *overload* the steers.   You have cattle & horses enough—always use strong teams—

I send a check for $50.—lest you should want it for *corn.* It seems we stand well for Leicester lambs—full bloods—that is good.

Keep the best of the heifer calves.—kill, or alter the males,— no half blood bulls—or half blood rams—

Yrs   D. W.

(To Porter Wright.)

WASHINGTON Feb. 9. '49.

Dear Porter

Mr. Thomas has written me about the sheep.   You must sell what you can, & get rid of them as well as you can.   At any rate, purify the flock.

You may sell some of the poorer sort of cows, if buyers offer, at a fair price.   I wish all to be done, that can be done, to get forward the Gardner's house.   I have supposed, that Charles Peterson could be at work on doors, window frames, planing boards &c, unless he is engaged on the cellar kitchen.

Yrs   DANL WEBSTER

(To Porter Wright.)

BOSTON Friday, noon Nov 9. [1849]

Porter.

We shall go down Monday, by the morning Train to Cohasset, and shall be there, I suppose, by 11 oclock.

We shall want you to send up a double waggon, and my Chaise—Monica may cook for us a dish of beans, and a turkey—one of the four from the Island.

As to cattle, which Daniel Wright could not sell, we must do as well as we can with them.   I shall not send them back to Brighton.   Some of the best we must feed a little, with salt-hay, turnips, &c—sell to anybody, that will buy.

Look out for Kelp.   You have teams enough.

Yours

D. W.

(To Porter Wright.)

BOSTON Monday Morn'g. 8 oclock—Dec. 49

Porter

It is rainy, & has been snowing, and the wind, so far as I can see, is East.   I suppose you will not think it a proper day for killing the cattle, & I shall not go down till it clears, & the sun gets out again.   If tomorrow morning be fair look for me by the early Kingston train.

My notion is;

That the poor-house man will take (one) of the Phillips oxen— Then, fill my *two* small high tubs, with the best pieces of the other Phillips ox, & with some pieces from one of the other oxen. This I want put up in the very best manner, with salt, saltpetre, & sugar.

If it turns out (to) be right, three months hence we may be able to sell, at that time, one pair of the fat oxen—

Then, there must be some beef, salted, for Mr. Baker's use, & a piece to hang up fresh.

The same for Fletcher's people, to use this winter. Of course this need not be of the best pieces.

Then put up what you want for the Cottage, & be sure to put up enough, & put it up well. Remember, that for the two last years, our beef has not turned out first rate. You must all do your best this year—

Then after the Cottage is supplied, let the rest go to the workmen, or neighbors, giving the workmen the first offer.

As to salt. There are sent down 30 bushels of Turk's Island Salt, which looks well. And 20 Bushels of *Trapney*, which is said to be good for beef. Trapney is an Island, I believe within the Straits— The Salt is said to be better than that of St. Uber— And I learn in the market that many people now prefer Turk's Island, for beef as well as pork— But I think it will be well to try the Trapney. You might, if you choose, put a little Turk's Island with it—

I have written this, lest you should need directions, before I get down-— But it is most probable that I shall go down to-morrow, if not this Eve'. Send for me, as soon as it is fair

Yrs   D. W.

I shall want to see Mr. Ames very much—

(To John Taylor.)

April 8. (1850?)—

Dear Sir

I should be glad to carry out our whole plan of farming, but if labor is too high, we must cut short. I cannot think of giving 16 or 17 Dollars a month. Crops will not pay for labor at this rate. I am willing to give as much as we have given hereto-fore ; &, on the whole, must leave the matter pretty much to your discretion.

As to potatoes, if you conclude to go on, & make a field, you must look up the seed. You know I told you to get some of Gov. Hill. He calls them York reds. There is nothing quite so good as the Mercers; & perhaps you will be obliged to go to Boston to get them. We have none to spare at Marshfield.

I enclose you $80—in Bank notes. If you need more money before I get home you may sell 50 bushels of corn— Keep all the rest, & all the oats. If you don't find good grass seed at hand, you may send an order to "Joseph Breck Esq, Agricultural Warehouse, Boston—" I will write to him to answer all your calls.

I send you several parcels of garden seeds. Keep what you want, & give some to the neighbors— You might leave some of the parcels with Mr. Nesmith, or Mr. Ladd, or Mr. Colburn, &c. at the village for general distribution. I do not know how good they are.

D. W.

(To Porter Wright.)

WASHINTON, Nov. 28. '50.
Thanksgiv'g morn'g, 1/2 past 5 O clock.

Porter Wright

I am glad you have got some kelp, & hope more may come ashore.

I suppose it is as well to kill the hogs, or most of them now; but I have some mind to keep two of the largest till January, & see what they will come to. We have never kept any of this stock till they had fairly got their growth. They might be kept in the Piggery. If you see no objection to this, let it be so. Pork may be worth more in January than it is now.

I wish a half barrel of nice pork to be sent to Mrs. Blatchford, some of it in thick pieces, & some in thinner. You will of course fill my tub, & may also save a few butt ends, in case they should be needed. I suppose it will be best to let the hands have what they want; but six Dollars, seems very low, for pork so well fatted on sound corn. If you keep two till January, it will probably be best to send them to Boston. I must leave these things very-much to your judgment.—

It is time, also, I presume to slaughter the Beef cattle, or dispose of them. Be sure to keep beef enough for cottage use.

The Stevens oxen must be fed longer, & until they get quite fat. What will be wanted for my tub & Fletcher's will come out of them. And I think I will have a 1/2 barrell lightly salted, & sent on here. I can write about that, hereafter.—

All the things have arrived, and in uncommon good order. We are all well here. Mrs. W. will be here next week.

Yrs
DANL WEBSTER

You have done very well, as to ploughing. But the weather is still so mild, that I should not be surprised to hear the ploughs were going again.

(From John Taylor.)

SUNDAY EAV. Franklin May the 2d, 1852.—

Mr. Webster
    Dear Sir
    * * * Last Friday—the last day of April—I drove 50, hed of Cattle up, and Turned them into the Punch Brook Paster.

When we let them out of there Several yards, whear thay had Bin shet *up for six months,* it was a great site to behold, runing &, bellering, I never saw creatures appear to be so happy. they Run nearly all the way up *The sand* hill, and cept runing til they reached the parster gait—yesterday I drawd up 6, hundred of hay to them, but they would not Eat it. they ware all ful &, bright. I shal not carry them any more hay, unless, we have another cold storm.

    I am, Sir, Your most obedient servant.

JOHN TAYLOR

(To David Tomlinson.)

MARSHFIELD 11 May 1852.

Dr Sir,
    It is very kind of you to send me a few sprouted chestnuts. I value the gift & thank you for it. I have on my farm most sorts of trees which the climate will bear, but as it happens, I have not one good chestnut tree. Your present, therefore, has come in good time. If any tree should be produced from these nuts, I shall call them the Tomlinson chestnuts.

Owing to an accident which has much affected the use of my hands & arms, for the present, I do not write without much difficulty, but I make an effort to sign this letter with my own hand.

Your obliged brother farmer & fellow citizen.

DANL WEBSTER.

(To Porter Wright.[1])

Porter Wright,   WASHINGTON, June 1, 1852.

I received your letter at New York, and was glad to hear, that Mr. Weston was getting better.   Tell him not to work too hard; if he should be laid up we should be half ruined.   Remind him of the new sills to the cow-barn.   Summer is coming on at a full gallop.   You will very soon need a place for your hay.   I wish Mr. Weston to employ all the help he needs, and to be in time with every thing.   I think more of his head than of his hands.

You appear to have got along wonderfully well in planting, and all must now be left to Providence; you will of course write me weekly, or oftner, and ask further directions if such be needed.   Take care not to work too hard yourself.   It is quite as much as you ought to do, to superintend others.

If the season is good, I wish to do our very best for turnips. Remember the two acres near the Mason gate [grew] great turnips with the help of Ezra Wright's manure heap.

We all arrived here safe last Saturday evening, being the 29th inst. and found the household all well.

I am quite well except my hands and I use them as little as possible.

Yours truly
DANL WEBSTER

June 2, Yrs of 29, rec'd this morning.

(To Porter Wright.)

Porter Wright.   WASHINGTON June, 9" 1852.

I expect a letter from you to day, but having a word to say I say it this morning, before people are stirring.

I expect to be in Marshfield before the month is out, and

---

[1] Dictated to G. J. Abbott.

among other things necessary to be done, one is, to put all the boats in order, Mr. Hatch must go up and bring down the Lapwing, and the small boats must be repaired and painted, and all that is necessary done, with sails, oars, cables, and anchors. The boat-house must be whitewashed and useless rubbish cleared out of it. The road leading down to it must be a little repaired. Gates put in order &c.— Do not forget to cut up the little cedar bushes, in the lower part of the Baker field.

Are you well supplied with Turnip seed. If not you must go to Mr. Breck. Be sure to get the best sorts. For Swedes I suppose Skirving's purple top, such as we have used is the best. Of the White Turnips, I suppose the Pomeranian Globe may be the best, although there are other good sorts of Globe Turnips.

You must consult Mr. Breck about this, and perhaps Mr. Morrison can have something useful to say. I hope to see something rather *extra* on the two acres by the Mason gates—

We are all well, & trust you are well at Marshfield. If, before I get home, you see any appearance of the return of *hard heads* upon the shore, let me know.

Yr friend
Danl Webster

(From John Taylor.)

Mr Webster.
Dear Sir   Franklin Sept 16th. 1852.

I arrived Home last Eavning, at 4. O'clock. my wife was fritend to See me come home a Live, she thought I must of bin kild,— *She* scent Two teligraphs after me, I got home before she had Received an anser from eather, Tenn years ago my Wife Opened one of my Letters Which she received, I was at Brighton at the time, When I got home—I told her That She must not, never Open my Letters in my Absence, in openening the Letter which you wrote me the 13th my Wife thought that I must be—Ded.

Last Saturday & Sunday ware Two verry rany days here. I think the Cattle will do Well here til Mr Webster comes Up, the Poltery yarrd will Be finished this week,
as well,
I am, Sir, Your most obedient Servant,

John Taylor

I Bought me a Larrg Box of fish In, Boston,

(To D. Fletcher Webster.)

Dear Fletcher,
FRIDAY 28 'Feby.

I recd your letter, about the Illinois land—quite well written—
Those farms are valuable—& I shall not sacrifice them.   I
hope to get along, *without disturbing their condition, at all, at
present.*—   I hope we shall all live out all our days! yet.
          Yrs D. W.

———

(To John Taylor.)

(M. SEP. 5.)

Dr Sir

We had up our 5 yoke of 4 yr old steers, today, & measured
them.—   The smallest girted 6 ft. 7 inches, the largest 6 ft. 11
inches.   The black steer and his mate went 6 ft. 9 inches.

If you get in the rye, this week & all necessary things done,
you may come down the early part of next week, leaving Henry
to take the lead & go ahead with the men.

Let me hear from you.

D. W.

———

(To John Taylor.)

Dr Sir
(JAN. 6).

I am glad to learn that you are all well, & doing well.

I cannot buy Mr Farewell's oxen.   Money is too scarce.   Besides, it is not good management to exchange young cattle for
old.   The growth is loss, when that is done—   We can get you
something to do the work in the spring.   I hope to hear from
you, regularly.

D. W.

———

(To John Taylor. ?)

Dear Sir

We must have a *larder*, which you may as well be mak'g, when
you cannot get out doors.

—It may be an Octogon—about 10 or 12 feet in diameter—&
as many high—& then a roof to turn the rain—   It should be
paved, a little higher than the earth, so that water will drain off.—

There must be windows, with Shutters of coarse wire—as well
as with glass.—   The object will be to admit the air when neces-

sary—but to be able to shut out the sun, & the flies & mosquitos—
Plan a little someth'g, & knock out the stuff—   I shall see
you before March is out.

Yrs   D. W.

Any lambs or calves yet?

(To John Taylor.)

Dear Mr Taylor,   Boston Sep. 30 Tuesday—
I have a subsoil plough, to be sent to you, by the cars to Con-
cord.—   Let it follow the other plough 6 or 8 inches deep—
Mr. Calef understood the idea—   Push it through all the potatoe
ground in the meadow—& next year you will not want for po-
tatoes—   Let this be done exactly & *no mistake*
I got home well.   Henry went to Marshfield this forenoon.
I follow this afternoon.

Your friend
D WEBSTER

(To Porter Wright.)

SATURDAY MOR'G.

Dear Sir,
It will be some days before I can come down to Marshfield.   If
other business will allow, I want you to try the *muscles*.   I should
like to have some spread, pretty thick, on the east side of the
fence, proposed to be ploughed, over by the great rocks, &
ploughed in—   Let the piece run the whole length, from fence,
& be as wide as you can get muscles—   If this weather holds, I
hope you will be able to do someth'g.

Yrs
D. WEBSTER

(To Porter Wright.)

BOSTON, Thursday Morning.

Porter:—
Mr Bartlett, the double Ploughman, wishes us to try the
plough, last sent, on some land already broken up, with a pair
of horses.

If the weather is good, and the land in order, I wish you to try this, next Saturday: either on the corn field, near Fletcher's, or on the Potato field.

Let the horses be in good condition, and work 8 hours.

If it cannot be done on Saturday, it must be put off till Tuesday.

The bouts will be rather short, in the field near Fletcher's.

If you take a piece in the Potato field, it might be well to clear off the tops.

Yours,

D. W.

(To Porter Wright.)

AUGUST 27

Porter Wright

I wish Mr Ames to buy me 30 yearlings, or two year old steers, or part of each age; and rather prefer some of each. When purchased, I wish him to mark them, with a W— If he wants money he may draw on me, at 5 days sight, and send the Bill to me, wherever I may be. His draft, or Commission, or compensation in any way, will be promptly paid. You know what kind of cattle we want; not very expensive, or fancy animals, but fair, tolerably large, and growthy steers. I care little about pairs, or matches; but do not want any mean things.

I am quite willing you should employ the man, with the machine to thrash grain, if you think best.

We shall lose something in the straw, but you have so much work to do, I think the grain may as well be thrashed by the machine.

I hope this cool and dry weather will help save the potatos.

Yours

D. W.

Webster's Intellectual Interests.

THE ready interest that Webster always manifested in all manner of intellectual pursuits is shown in his public speeches and published letters. There was nothing narrow in his whole mental make-up. Only two subjects would occur to one trying to think of the deficiencies in Webster's general culture. One looks in vain for any evidence that he cared for music or art. He had the keenest appreciation for the beauty in natural objects, and a love for the pleasing out-of-door sounds, but the themes of art and music never were touched by the pen that ventured upon almost every other phase of human interest. He loved poetry, even dabbled in it himself, in his early days, as we have seen in the "Fragments Concerning His Early Life." We can find plenty of evidence of his love of Shakespeare and of Milton. There have been preserved among his papers many notes on matters of pure literature. Nevertheless his mind was essentially practical; more likely to expend its energy upon utilitarian things.

The letters and papers here presented show his interest in popular education, industrial, technical and mechanical education, and in scientific contributions of the more practical nature. He regarded political economy as "solemn commonplace" in a great part, and thought their rules "fail in their application." In his talk about college life he advances interesting ideas upon the object of education and his theory of attaining it.

Probably nothing is so characteristic of the man on his literary side as the letter by Abbott, his amanuensis, which tells of the vast literary plans of his master. The great mind wandering over the fields of thought found alluring themes on every side. The plans floated easily in the massive head, but the physical energy, the tireless patience, and the sacrifice of the world that would have been necessary to carry out the details were wanting. He loved too well to feel his power over men, and to get the immediate returns for efforts made. He could put forth a giant's strength for an hour or a day, but he had not the tough endur-

ance of the writer of literary monuments. In his plan of a history we have a proposed work as pretentious as that of Gibbon, but he never would have carried it out, had he been granted the longevity of Methuseleh. True, his collected speeches make an impressive monument, but, if we examine it, we shall find it an aggregation of smaller productions rather than a massive unity —a pyramid rather than an obelisk.

He always took a great interest in historical literature, and seemed especially impressed with the political value of a broad dissemination of our national history, and of monuments to commemorate great historical events.

Little is given here of his interesting descriptions of travel.[1] I have, however, listed the letters of the Private Correspondence, which contain these essays. He was an alert traveler and thereby gained much both of knowledge and of culture.

(To James W. Page.)

Saratoga, Sunday morning
[July 10, 1825]

Dr Wm.

We came here yesterday, from Albany. As at present arranged the rout is pleasant. A coach brought us nine mile— We then entered a canal packet boat—ascended three or four locks, & came along through a country of very good scenery nine or ten miles, where we left the canal, & were brought here in a carriage. We had an opportunity of seeing the junction of the Western & Northern canals, & the passage of the former over the Mohawk river, in what they call an acqueduct. The river here is about 400 yrds wide—stone piers are erected & on them a plank canal is made, large enough for the usual boats &c We saw also the falls called the Cohoes. At Ballston we stopped but a few minutes, our Ladies think that the Saratoga waters would suit their complaints better. This morning they have drank not a little from the Congress Spring— There is said to be more company here than is usual for the season. We shall probably stay till Tuesday— At Utica we expect letters from you. I hope to get a copy of my speech,[2] somewhere along. I do not

---

[1] The letter to McGaw, October 11, 1828, found among the religious letters, contains some interesting comments.

[2] The First Bunker Hill Address.

know what is the nearest Postoffice to Niagara Falls, on the American side— Some of the Gentlemen who have been there can tell you. I shall inquire for letters at Lewiston, & at Black rock, unless I hear from you at Canandaigua that you write to some other place. I shall also inquire at the nearest P. Office.

Mrs W. has told you, I suppose, all about Catskill Mountains. We professed to wish that you & Mr. Mrs. Blake had been there with us. She says she has today no particular commission to charge you with.

I pray you remember me to Mr. & Mrs. Blake. I trust the lady has recovered her voice, & wish they were setting out with us for Niagara.

Love to the children

Yrs   D. W.

(To Jared Sparks.[1])

February 4, 1826.

* * * It will give me true pleasure to aid you in your intended collection of General Washington's works, in any and all ways in my power. Judge Story has not yet arrived, but we expect him this eve. I will have an early conversation with him on the subject. I think your proposed work one of great importance, and which you could so execute as to do yourself great credit. * * *

DANIEL WEBSTER.

(To Mr. Hope.[2])

My Dear Sir   BOSTON Jan. 12. '49

The bearer of this, Revd. John Miller, of New Jersey, is a Gentleman of character, & science, who proposes to spend some months, in Edenburgh, in the prosecution of his studies.

He is interested in the Department, which is distinguished by Sir Wm Hamilton's labors; and is desirous, also, of witnessing the order & arrangement of the Scotch Universities.— The shortest line from you to Sir Wm, or to some Gentleman in the University, will be a great favor to him, & will quite oblige me.

---

[1] Taken from Sparks' "Life and Writings," vol. i, p. 402. Daniel Webster was then a member of the House of Representatives for Massachusetts.

[2] Addressed to Hon. Mr. Hope, Lord of Sessions. This letter is owned by Mr. Charles Roberts, of Philadelphia.

Fondly cherishing the recollection of a former short acquaintance, & with sentiments of the most sincere regard,

I am, Dear Sir,

Yours cordially

DANL WEBSTER

(To Samuel N. Sweet.[1])

Dear Sir, WASHINGTON, December 31st, 1849.

I have had very frequent occasions to answer the same inquiry as that which you propose to me in your letter of the 26th of this month.[2] The speech to which you refer is my composition. The Congress of the Revolution sat with closed doors, and there is no report of the speeches of members on adopting the Declaration of Independence. We only know that John Adams spoke in favor of the measure with his usual power and fervor. In a letter, written from Philadelphia soon after the Declaration was made he said it was an event which would be celebrated in time to come by bonfires, illuminations, and other modes of public rejoicing. And on the day of his death, hearing the ringing of bells, he asked the occasion, and being told that it was the 4th of July, and that the bells were ringing for Independence, he exclaimed, "Independence forever!" These expressions were used, in composing the speech, as being characteristic of the man, his sentiments, and his manner of speech and elocution. All the rest is mine.

With respect, your obedient servant,

DANL. WEBSTER.

(To Rev. A. Potter.[3])

My Dear Sir WEDNESDAY MORNING

I send you Mr Turner's book. There is much in it, which a mere general scholar will be disposed to pass over hastily; but the latter part of the first, & the whole of the second volume, I think interesting.

So is the account of the population of Europe, in the com-

---

[1] This letter is printed in Lanman's " Life of Webster," p. 154.

[2] Asking if John Adams really made the speech which Webster put in his mouth in the oration on Adams and Jefferson.

[3] Addressed to Rev. A. Potter, Chestnut Street (probably Philadelphia). This letter belongs to Mr. Charles Roberts, of Philadelphia.

mencement of the work.   This seems to me the best thing I have
seen, on that difficult subject—the dispersion of mankind over
the earth—

Yrs very truly

D. WEBSTER

———

(To Dr. Warren.[1] ?)

I am about to state to you a fact, for the cause of which you
may inquire of the learned.   Three or four hours yesterday, I
stood on my feet, shaking hands incessantly with visitors, and of
course, always shaking with the right hand, my left hand having
nothing to do, all the while, but hang down quietly.   At the close
of this labor, my right arm and hand, felt no fatigue or pain,
but severe pain affected my left arm, from the shoulder to the
ends of the fingers.   I do not quite understand this.   I am aware
that nerves go off in pairs, from the spine to the limbs, and that
such is the sympathy of the system, that what affects one pair, is
apt to affect the corresponding pair on the other side.   But how
the right arm & hand, which went through the heat of the engagement, should suffer little or nothing, while the left arm &
hand, which were non comb'ants should suffer so much, a good
deal puzzles me.   I have experienced the same thing frequently
before, but on those occasions, have supposed the cause to be the
holding of my hat in my left hand for a long time, for such holding, you know, will fatigue the arm.   But yesterday my left arm
and hand, had no such hat to hold.   They seem to think that
their fellows on the other side, were worse off than they really
were, & this apprehension, seems to have produced great uneasiness, & sympathetic pain.

———

(Memorandum.[2])

This is a coin of Wm & Mary—   Sometimes, or on some coins,
both both faces were on one side, *cheek by Jole*—   Hence Green,
in his poem on Spleen, says

> —"of Kitty, aunt left in the lurch,
>   On grave pretence to go to church,
>   Espied in hack, with lover fine,
>   *Like Will. & Mary on the coin.*"

---

[1] This is a dictated unfinished letter of Daniel Webster.
[2] In Daniel Webster's hand.

(From Timothy Pickering.[1])

BOSTON, July 19, 1826.

Dear Sir,

Yesterday I received from my son Octavius a letter informing me that you wished to see the original letter from Mr. John Adams,[2] referred to in my prefatory remarks to reading the Declaration of Independence, three years ago, and the remarks also: both are inclosed. And for the more precise understanding of Mr. Adams' letter, I also inclose the copy of mine, to which it is an answer, and of my reply, making my acknowledgments for that answer. Of all these papers I pray you to take particular care, and to return them to me by my son, or other safe hand, when you shall have done with them.

All unpleasant feelings towards Mr. Adams, had ceased long before the occurrence of the above mentioned correspondence. A subsequent event obliged me, in my own vindication, to expose publicly his faults. Still I view, as I have always viewed him, as a man of eminent talents, zealously, courageously & faithfully exerted in effecting the Independence of the Thirteen United Colonies: and I believe that he, more than any other individual, roused and prepared the minds of his fellow citizens to decide positively and timely that greatest revolutionary question.

Very respectfully, I am, dear Sir,
Your obedt. Servt,
T. PICKERING.

(To Jared Sparks.[3])

OCTOBER. 12, 1826

* * * "I have read Mr. Cardozo's book, and looked into McCulloch; but the field spread out so wide before me that I gave up the idea of entering upon it with any view of writing. A great part of Mr. Cardozo's notes are taken up in commenting on Smith and Ricardo. The very statement of the questions in

---

[1] The services of T. Pickering as a patriot in the Revolution are well known. He was Adjutant-General, a member of the Continental Board of War, and finally Quartermaster-General during the Revolution. He was Postmaster-General and Secretary of War under Washington and finally Secretary of State. Later he was Senator from Massachusetts.

[2] About this time Webster was preparing for his Adams and Jefferson oration, delivered August 2, 1826.

[3] Taken from Sparks' "Life and Writings," vol. i, p. 272.

difference between him and them, so as to be intelligible to general readers, would occupy the space of a short article. I must confess, morover, that there is a great deal of solemn commonplace, and a great deal also of a kind of metaphysics, in all or most of the writers on these subjects.[1] There is no science that needs more to be cleared from mists than that of political economy. If we turn our eyes from books to things, from speculation to fact, we often, I think, perceive that the definitions and the rules of these writers fail in their application. If I live long enough, I intend to print my own thoughts (not, however, in any more bulky form than a speech, or an article in the 'North American') on one or two of the topics discussed by Mr. Cardozo. But when that leisure day, necessary even to so small an affort, may come, is more than I can say. * * *

D. WEBSTER.

_____

(To Albert Picket et al.[2])

Gentlemen,
WASHINGTON Jany. 3d. 1835

I have received your letter of the 13th of December.

Entertaining the deepest conviction of the utility and necessity of popular Education, and feeling the most sincere and grateful respect for those, who, in the capacity of teachers, devote their labors and lives to that great object, it would give me true pleasure to comply with your request, if existing duties and engagements would allow. But I cannot flatter myself with the hope of being able to visit the West, in the Autumn of this year.

If I should again have the gratification of being in Ohio, which I very much desire, it must be in the spring, in consequence of the nature of my private and professional engagements at home.

I proffer to you Gentlemen, my most cordial good wishes; my most zealous cooperation and service, in whatever I may be useful to your association; and pray you to believe that it is with no common degree of regret, that I find myself obliged to decline the honor which you have tendered to me.[3]

With much personal regard

[D. WEBSTER]

_____

[1] See "Private Correspondence of Daniel Webster," vol. i, p. 500.
[2] Committee of a Teachers' Association of Cincinnati, Ohio.
[3] This letter is from a draft in Daniel Webster's hand.

(To Daniel P. King.[1])

BOSTON May 30 1835.

My Dear Sir,

I received a good while ago your address at the Celebration of the Lexington Battle in Danvers which you were so good as to send me, together with the very kind letter which accompanied it, and I must not omit, even at this late hour, to express my thanks for the great pleasure I have received from its perusal.

The scenes described in your Address are always full of interest to the mind of an American, but they receive an additional charm, when presented to our view along with so many most exciting reminiscences of former times, as you have given us. One feels transported back to the period when these occurrences were not History but present realities. It is well that the events and characters of the Revolution should often be brought to the minds of this generation. It will help to keep alive those sacred principles, which, as you truly remark, lay at the foundation of the Revolutionary struggle. But, My Dear Sir, your Address needs no aid from the nature of the subject to give it interest. Its own merits, apart from anything extrinsic, will sufficiently commend it to the favorable attention of the reader. For one, I can assure you I have received very great satisfaction from its pages. I cannot express a stronger wish than that it may conduce as much to make its author favorably known to the public, as I am sure it will, to the pleasure of others.

Allow me, Sir, to express my grateful sense of the compliment you have been so partial as to pay me in the selection of your son's name, and to proffer my best wishes for the health and happiness of my namesake. May he be an honor to himself, to his parents and his country.[2]

I, am, My Dear Sir, Most Truly.—

[DANIEL WEBSTER]

---

[1] Who had sent him an address, printed at Salem, 1835, commemorative of seven young men of Danvers, who were slain in the Battle of Lexington. He complimented Webster and said he had named his son after "the statesman whose motto is 'Our country, our whole country and nothing but our country.'"

[2] This is taken from Daniel Webster's draft of the letter sent.

(To J. Q. Adams.¹)

BOSTON, Oct. 31st, 1836
Sir:

All the manuscript dissertations received from your hands, on the subject of the Congress of Nations, for the amicable settlement of National differences, and the abolition of War, are herewith returned.   My engagements have allowed me not as much time for examining them as I would have desired.   The attention which I have been able to give to the subject, has however convinced me, that the writers generally, have not come up to the probable expectation, of the donors of the prize, the magnitude of which, might reasonably have been expected to bring into the field, a strong array of competitors.   In many of their productions, there is more of declamation than of argument, and in very few, if in any of them, is that profound and philosophical investigation of the subject which it was undoubtedly the object of the prize donors, to encourage and furnish.

There is moreover, in too many instances, an obvious want of chasteness and good taste, and even of grammatical accuracy, in the composition.   In making these general criticisms, let me not be understood as applying them indiscriminately, and with equal rigor, to each of the Essays, nor of suggesting that I find nothing in them to approve.   While I note their faults I acknowledge that they have their merits also.   The writer of the Essay marked "I", has in my judgment rather distanced his rivals, and to him, so far as it depends upon me, I should be willing to award the prize.

Your obedient servant,

DAN'L WEBSTER.

(To James J. Mapes.²)

WASHINGTON, February 20, 1840.
Sir,

I have had an opportunity of looking over the first number of the American Repertory, published by you, and highly approve of its general object.

It is a time when great good may be done to the arts, to the

---
¹ This letter is owned by Charles Francis Adams.
² Printed in the "American Repertory," vol. i, p. 175.

cause of industry, and to the prosperity of labor, by a wide diffusion and extension of the more important and practical
branches of knowledge.

I happen to have an account of "Oram's Compressed Fuel",
for Steam Engines, which I do not remember to have seen published in the United States. I send it to you for publication in
your periodical, if you think proper.

With respect, your obedient servant,

DANIEL WEBSTER.

(Remarks on Education.[1])

[1845]

He alluded first to the universal interest felt in all ages in the
subject of education. He glanced at its importance to every
individual as involving that culture both of intellect and the
heart, and essentially connected with his present and eternal happiness.[2]

And the youth of this age and country, he said, should be
sensible of the peculiarly propitious circumstances in which they
are placed, and appreciate the privileges by which they are distinguished from those of every past generation, and every other
land. To see the truth and force of this, we need only cast our
eye up and down this beautiful Valley of the Connecticut,
adorned not more by its natural scenery and fertile soil, than by
the numerous, and flourishing seminaries of learning scattered
over its bosom. The spot where he stood, seemed peculiarly
favored; presenting on the one hand, an Academy, annually
furnishing the colleges from twenty five to fifty young men, to
be liberally educated; on the other a high school delightfully
located and in efficient and prosperous operation; and here a
College, young indeed, but a most honourable monument to the
patriotism & piety which laid its foundations. The very infancy of the Institution he would remark, had its peculiar advantages, and the circumstances, which to many young men,
might seem disadvantages, were far less so than is often sup-

---

[1] A newspaper report of an address by Webster.
[2] This printed report of a speech was found among the newspaper clippings
which Webster had evidently collected, for many of them bear his handwriting. This is indorsed by him simply "Amherst—Andover." On
September 8, 1836, Webster delivered an address at Harvard's bicentennial
celebration, of which we have only a meager report. See "History of Harvard
University," by Josiah Quincy, vol. ii, p. 685.

posed. Costly apparatus, and splendid Cabinets, have no magical power to make Scholars. In all circumstances as a man is under God, the master of his own fortune, so he is the maker of his own human intellect, that it can grow only by its own action, and by its own action it will most certainly and necessarily grow. Every man therefore must in an important sense educate himself. His book and teacher are but *helps;* the *work* is his. A man is not *educated* until he has the ability to summon, in any emergency, all his mental powers to vigorous exercise and controul them in that exercise till he effect his purposed object. It is not the man who has seen most, or read most, or heard most, who can do this; such an one is in danger of being borne down like a beast of burden by an overloaded mass of other men's thoughts. Nor is the man who can boast merely of native vigor and capacity; the greatest of all the warriors that went to the siege of Troy had not the preeminence because nature had given him strength and he carried the largest bow, but because *self-discipline* had taught him how to bend it.

He said it was his opinion that among the improved modes of teaching, which characterize the present state of the science and the art, those would be found most useful that should have the greatest tendency to bring the mind of the student near to the mind of the teacher. Mind is excited by close intercourse, by contact as it were, with mind. The attention of both parties must be drawn by a constant attraction to some common point. Let the powers of the student be examined, tried, exercised, strengthened, guided by this kind of intercourse. Let it extend to every study, and be applied to every little thing in the whole course of instruction, and be felt daily and hourly. Of such communion of mind with mind, of such action of mind upon mind, the effects will be at once displayed. It is like what is often seen around the beautiful mountain which adorns this horizon, when, drawn mutually together, cloud approaches cloud; then, and then only, is there a transmission and reception and interchange of the electric fluid.

He closed his remarks (to which this abstract by no means does justice) by painting the anguish of heart which, in the just retribution of heaven, must torture the man who, when his country and his religion call for his services, too late finds that he has abased the privileges resulting from a free government and from Christianity, and has wasted the short but precious portion of his immortal existence which was allotted for his self-education.

(*To Edward Curtis.?*)

RALEIGH. North Carolina. May 1, 1847 (?)
—buildings,[1] & there are sundry handsome residences, belongi'g to Judges, Lawyers, Physicians, &c, & to some rich planters, who live here, but whose estates are elsewhere. On the whole, it is a pleasant, green look'g, respectable little City. But it was a mistake to br'g the Govt. here. It should have been fixed at Fayetteville, on Cape Fear River, quite a favored spot for commerce, & now the great town for distribution of traffic, inland. Here, is no navigation, & no facilities for manufacturers. The abstract idea of a local centre brought the Govt. [here.]? Like many other abstract ideas, its application to practical life & business has not been found satisfactory. We arrived here on Saturday, at 12 O'clock; found the Govr's. coach at the cars, & were recd by him & his wife, at the Govt. house, with great kindness. We are of course well lodged. Gov. Graham, late Senator in Congress, is a highly respectable person, of an old North Carolina Family, & a true & sound Whig. Here lives Mr Badger, now about in the Circuits, Mr. Haywood, late Senator in Congress, Mr. Iredell, formerly also a Senator, & many other respectable families. The Govr. makes a dinner on Monday, Mrs. Haywood gives a party the same Eve'g, & Tuesday mor'g we depart, for Charleston by way of Wilmington.[2]

[D. W.]

(*Correction of a Translation.*[3])

JUNE 12. 1851
Lawfully—"legitemately," as used here, is not English, It

---

[1] This fragment is in Daniel Webster s hand and written on part of a sheet containing a letter of Mrs. Webster to Mr. Curtis.

[2] The letters that especially show Webster's keen interest in travel are: Daniel Webster to Mrs. Paige, Charleston, May 9, 1847; Daniel Webster to Seth Weston, Charleston, May 10, 1847; Daniel Webster to Mrs. Paige, Columbia, S. C., May 13, 1847; Daniel Webster to Mrs. Paige, Columbia, S. C., May 15, 1847; Daniel Webster to R. M. Blatchford, Marshfield, December 7, 1847; Daniel Webster to Mrs. Paige, April, 1849; Daniel Webster to Mrs. Paige, April 23, 1849; Daniel Webster to R. M. Blatchford, August 8, ——: Daniel Webster to R. M. Blatchford, August 10, ——: Daniel Webster to Fletcher Webster, Capon Springs, June 27, 1851. All of the above letters are to be found in "Private Correspondence." vol. ii, pp. 244, 246, 249, 252, 315, 318, 332, 335, 446.

[3] This was written by Daniel Webster at the end of a translation made for him at the State Department. It is but a fragment, but too good to lose.

is ambitious Americanism.   "Legitimate" means of *lawful origin*
We are most sure of writing good English, when we use the
plainest words.—

(To Mrs. Harriette Story Paige.)

BOSTON May 2d 1848

My Dear Sister
   This Book is said to be the best existing Index to Shakespeare;
It is by a Lady,[1] & I ask leave, most affectionately, to present
this Copy, to another Lady, who knows Shakespeare, who can
appreciate all facilities of reference, to his immortal passages,
& who, I hope, will not be displeased, to receive this from me.—
                                        DANL WEBSTER

(G. J. Abbott to Edward Everett.)

WASHINGTON, April 12, [1854]

Dear Sir,
   You may perhaps remember that I informed you, a short time
after Mr. Webster's death, in reply to your inquiry as to the
progress which Mr. Webster had made in the "History of Washington's Administration,"—that only the general plan of the
work had been sketched.   This was prepared under the following circumstances.
   During the last year of Mr. Webster's life he not unfrequently
spoke of the manner in which he proposed to employ his time
after his retirement from office and public life.
   The first time he mentioned this subject to me was at Marshfield in October 1851.   He had just written the dedications of
the several volumes of his works, & read such parts of the Memoir
as you had then submitted to him.   It appeared to strike him
more forcibly than ever before how long his life had been protracted; for, he remarked, he found that he had been personally
engaged in the discussion of almost every great question which
had, at any time, occupied public attention during the last half
century, while his memory reached back to the period of the
adoption of the Constitution itself.
   He told me that his work on the Constitution had long occupied his mind and was so well matured that he could dictate it as

---

[1] Mary Cowden Clarke.

fast as I could take it down, and he even thought that he could prepare a volume in a month. He proposed that I should leave Washington with him, go down to Marshfield & render such assistance, as his amanuensis, in the preparation of this latter work, as I was able.

We were interrupted in the conversation, and it was not again resumed at Marshfield.

You are well acquainted with the reasons growing out of the state of public affairs which induced him to defer his resignation.

After his return to Washington he would occasionally revert to the subject, thus showing his interest in it, & that he still looked forward to its accomplishment as the crowning effort of his life. Especially was this the case during the time he was engaged in the preparation of his Historical Discourse.

At this time, also, he was making those arrangements in regard to his cemetery, of which he speaks in one of his letters to Mr. Fillmore. There was evidently a strong impression upon his mind, perhaps I might say presentiment, that the remaining intellectual labor which he designed to accomplish must speedily be commenced and finished. The severity of his autumnal catarrh in 1851, & the serious tone in which he would sometimes speak of its recurrence in 1852, showed that it gave him much anxiety.

He remarked one day, when we were alone, that he should complete his seventieth year in the following January, & that he had been for some time thinking of resigning his seat in the cabinet, & he proposed to do it when he should reach that age: something he added respecting the seeming impropriety of holding a subordinate position after reaching that period of life, and of receiving instructions from a younger man. He said he should not again enter into active practice at the bar, as he more & more disliked the contests, often exciting and wrangling, in which he must sometimes engage with young men. He spoke of the more congenial pursuits with which he intended to occupy himself,—his little book—which he designed as a relaxation from his more serious studies—on the birds & fishes of Marshfield; of this he repeated to me a chapter on the cod-fish,—an imaginary conversation between Seth Peterson and an intelligent boy. As you may readily conceive with Mr. Webster's interest in the subject, his acquaintance with it, his great fund of anecdotes, & the great simplicity & clearness with which it would have been treated, the work would have been one of the most popular & fascinating books of the day.

He subsequently referred to his proposed work on the evidences of Christianity. This was a favorite idea with him, & he often spoke of it in Washington, & when he left there in 1852, he directed me to bring the copies of Cicero de Natura, which he proposed to translate & illustrate with notes. And when near the termination of his life, finding that even this could not be accomplished in the very presence of death, he condensed into an epitaph the expression of his belief in Christianity in the place of an irresistible argument which he hoped to have made.

[*A sheet of Mr. Abbott's letter has been lost.*]

in which he was greatly interested. In the summer of 1852 I collected, at his suggestion, and sent to Marshfield, such public documents and books as would be useful for consultation & reference in the preparation of the Work.

While in the cars on our return from Trenton, where he had argued the great India rubber case, I called his attention to some proposed alterations & corrections of the proof sheets of the Historical Discourse which had been sent to him for his inspection. I noticed, afterwards, as he sat alone in his seat, that his mind was occupied, & I forebore to interrupt him.   He soon called me to his side, and,—in that earnest & impressive manner, which he so frequently assumed in the last months of his life, and which made us feel that whatever he said, it was intended we should remember,—stated at considerable length the outlines of his proposed Work on the Constitution.

Some days, subsequently, in the little office in his house, [at Washington] he dictated the heads of this conversation, or rather the general plan of the Work as it then lay in his mind.

He directed me carefully to place this memorandum among his private papers in my case.

He did not again revert to this paper.

After Mr. Webster's death, on my return to Washington, I looked for this paper but was unable to find it.   Frequent & careful searches were made both in the Department and among my own papers.

I felt quite certain that I had taken it to Marshfield in September 1852, though I was confident it had not been called for by Mr Webster.   At last, I became satisfied that it had been left at Marshfield, & would be found among Mr. Webster's papers, or that, by some mischance, it had been destroyed: This I feared as the original was taken down so rapidly that it is almost illegible, & might easily have been mistaken for useless memoranda. Fortunately, I found last night, in a very safe place, the long missing paper, which I hasten to transcribe & place in your hands.

With great regard
Very truly Yours,

G. J. ABBOTT.

(History of Washington's Administration.)

Mr. Webster thinks of writing a History of the Constitution and of the Administration of the First President,—the Work to be comprised in about fifty chapters of fifty pages each, to commence with the First Congress,

As showing the sense of the country upon the importance of a United Government.

Not to relate the military events of the War of the Revolution, but to record the proceedings which led to the adoption of the Articles of the Confederation.

To state things as they existed at the peace of 1783.

Their insufficiency to answer the purposes which a Union of the States was designed to accomplish,

The growing necessity in the minds of men, of a Government, which, instead of acting through the authority of the States, should act directly on individuals.

The state of the country at the conclusion of peace.

A geographical description of the settled parts of it.

The population of the respective states.

Their Agriculture, Commerce and Manufactures.

A good Map.

The continental debt then existing.

The debts of the several States.

The inability of Congress and the States to pay their debts.

Proceedings of Legislative and other public bodies in the States, showing the unsatisfactory state of things, and the necessity of a new form of Government.

The proceedings which led to the meeting of delegates at Annapolis.

The proceedings of the Congress of the Confederation, and especially the Reports of the Committees.

Mr. Hamilton, Madison and others.

The meeting of the Convention in Philadelphia in May 1787.

Full Biographical notices of its members.

Its proceedings and discussions.

The Constitution as the result of the deliberations of this Convention.

Its publication and the proceedings of Congress thereupon,
Its discussions before the people
The Federalist.

The debates in the several State Conventions.

The general principles of the Constitution as a popular representative Government.

Montesquieu.

The difficulty of framing a provision for an Executive head.

The happy contrivance for the Constitution of the Senate.

The Constitution.

Its compactness, its brevity, and its comprehensiveness.

Its felicity in declaring what powers Congress should possess, and what powers the several States should cease to exercise.

An examination of the powers of Congress, with the reason for each, and so of the Judiciary power and the Executive power.

The great idea that such a Government must have an ultimate construction and power of decision respecting the extent of its own authority,

The necessity that a legislative power should be accompanied with a commensurate Judicial and Executive authority.

The influence of commercial necessity as producing a disposition to adopt this constitution.

The Public Lands,

The National Debt, and the certainty that it could not be paid under the existing provisions.

The interest with which the World looked upon this great experiment of Republican liberty.

Dr. Paley,

The adoption of the Constitution by nine States,

The election of the first President,

The difficulty of assembling the first Congress.

The Inauguration of Genl. Washington at New York,

The early Laws,

The organization of his Cabinet,

Acts of Congress authorizing the appointment of Executive officers, or Heads of Administration,

A general view of the country at that time, in regard to its domestic situation, its industry, trade, &c. and in regard to its foreign policy.

General Washington's first Inaugural speech.
These topics to form the first volume.

(Volume Second.)

Gen. Washington's domestic policy.
The payment of the public debt.
The establishment of a Commercial system.
The Revenue system.
The Currency,
The Bank,
The Mint,
The Naturalization laws,
The policy of the Government in regard to the industrial Arts.
The sale of public lands.
Copy right, and Patent Inventions,
The Census.
The Judiciary. (a most important chapter).
The men who formed the act,
Richard Henry Lee.
Simeon Strong &c.

The character of the men who composed the first Administration, and the leading members of Congress, of whom, biographical notices shall not have been made under a previous head.

The establishment of a seat of Government in the District of Columbia, and the laying out of the City of Washington.

Rebellions in Pennsylvania, and other domestic occurrences.

Rapidly growing prosperity of the country under this new Government.

Popularity of the Administration at home, and the rapidly growing respect for the country abroad.

The beginning of settlements in the North West Territory &c, &c,

(Volume Third.)

General Washington's second election.
The French Revolution,
Our connection with France, and the commencement of this revolution to be stated and discussed at large,
Washington's proclamation of neutrality,
Policy of this measure, and its Justice towards France. under the Treaty of alliance of 1778 to be fully considered.

The general principles of Washington's Administration in regard to our foreign relations,

Neutrality.

Non Intercourse.

The equality of Nations,

The exactness with which Washington demanded all proper respect from other Nations.

His Justice united with high bearing,

The British Treaty of 1794,

The mobs in Philadelphia and Boston,

Washingtons dignified conduct, and rebuke of the disturbers,

His letter to Boston.

The virtuous *Ten*

Mr Jay,

Lord Grenville,

The unconsciousness at that time of the probable growth of American Commerce, and especially of the production of Cotton in the United States.

The consequence of this production, and its influence upon Slavery in the United States,

The difficulties with France,

The state of the country at the close of Washington's Administration in March 1797.

Its resources, Commerce and manufactures,

The rise of the Federal and Republican parties,

John Adams,

Thomas Jefferson,

The close of Washingtons Administration, and his farewell address,

A comparison of the Character of Washington with those of the most distinguished public men of Ancient and Modern times.

For comments of Webster on oratory and rhetoric see Webster's "Private Correspondence," vol. i, p. 463, and vol. ii, p, 111.

Webster, the Sportsman

WEBSTER *would have been a warm personal friend of Izaak Walton or of Nimrod, if either had been so fortunate as to be his contemporary. His fame went far and wide, and gun clubs and angling clubs all over the land made him an honorary member. The attention evidently pleased him, for he kept their certificates and letters; some of them many years.*

Many times in his letters we hear of his "John Trout" rod, and, as he playfully threatened, "the halibut and bluefish might tremble," when he went forth with his "Old Kill-all." Some one had made him a gift of two silver-mounted rods and reels, a book of flies and hooks, and he promptly gave the outfit that distinguishing title. Armed with this and rowed by "Commodore" Hatch and Peterson, he fairly warned the perch and pickerel to "look out for themselves." He not only caught, but he studied fish and knew their history, as we may see in the letter to Mr. Clark. He even enjoyed "the subordinate pleasure of listening to the recital of the capture of fish and the battles with the mosquitoes."

He was quite as enthusiastic with the gun as with the rod. His farms were regular preserves; he didn't "want a man with a gun around his place." He was insatiable. Ticknor writes of his being out thirteen hours with no regular meals, and never tired nor hungry while there was a bird to be seen. If he was in Boston, he suddenly had business at Marshfield, if there was "a flight of coots." Mrs. Webster gives us a pleasant picture of the man whose imposing dignity had so often won the "applause of listening senates." He comes in from the day's hunt with forty-six birds, "beetle-heads, red-breasts and humilities." He had "burned all his powder, fired all his shot, broke his ramrod—got no dinner," and walked for hours in the tide-covered marshes. He says that if he "had only known where they were he might have gone to them in a chaise."

This last phase completes the picture of Webster in his everyday life as we can get it from his correspondence. If he was, as his greatest enemy, Theodore Parker, conceded, "the greatest figure that has appeared upon this earth since the time of Charlemagne," it was due in part to the fact that he was an out-of-doors man.   He took from the vital air and the genial sun, as much as from his books, the undying eloquence that still moves us from the silent pages, though the voice of the living speaker is no more.

(To Porter Wright.)

Porter Wright   APRIL 16.

I thought it was *Asa* Delano, the Carpenter, not *Nathl*, who wanted to go into the John Taylor House.   Mr. Nat Delano is an excellent man, & I like him much—& is very handy with a Boat; but he has always a gun in his hand, & if he lives in that house, he will kill every quail, for 6 miles all around,—& not leave one for me.   I do not wish to say this to him, exactly; but I do not incline to let him in.   You may say, that I prefer letting it to those who work altogether on the Farm.

Yrs D. W.

(To D. Fletcher Webster.)

                                            THURSDAY MOR'G 8 O clock.
Dear F.

I suppose we shall need a considerable rally of cavalry this mor'g; & would be obliged to you to be here, between 9 & 10 with Fanny—   Please ascertain what Ladies at your House propose to take the field.   Mrs. W. cannot go out, on acct of the expected visit from Plymouth friends.   I suppose your wife must keep her state for the same reason—   If she be well eno., & circumstances allow, I should like to give her a short drive in my "Ferrinton"?—

Pray let Mr. Alwell go this mor'g & shoot some brown backs, peeps, or someth'g else.   We must have a dish of birds.   If he gets any, let him br'g them up, by 2 or 3—& *pick* them, or have them picked.   Some of our people are tired & some sick.   We shall look for you, at dinner, if agreeable to you.

Yrs D. W.

Do you want a bit of Halibut?

(To Mrs. W. W. Seaton.[1])

"FRIDAY MORNING.

"Dear Mrs. Seaton,—As I could not accompany Mr. Seaton on his expedition to Piney Point, I hope for the subordinate pleasure of listening to his recital of its incidents, his capture of fishes, his battles with the mosquitoes, etc., etc.

"I wish, therefore, to engage him to dine to-morrow at five o'clock here, at the Burdine Mansion, with one or two friends only; and I write this to insure your influence on the occasion.

"Mr. Curtis took an abrupt departure last evening, leaving messages of love for your household with me.

"I sent over a letter to Fletcher's, yesterday, and had a kind reply from M——. But she did not 'catch the idea.'

"I shall be obliged to come round this evening, and go into explanations.

"Yours, with the truest regard,
"DAN'L WEBSTER."

"Dear W. W. S.,—Fish all right for to-morrow. Let them *bask* in Monica's ice-chest till the day comes.

"D. W.

"5 o'clock."

(Mrs. Grace Webster to James W. Paige.)

SANDWICH August 22d 1825.

My dear Brother,

The day you left us we were all rather sad, and something stupid. The next you recollect was fixed on for our excursion to Naushon.[2] We set out accordingly about ten o'clock Mr. Blake and William Fessenden in a chaise, Mrs. Blake & son & Master Daniel in Barouche, Mr. Webster & myself bringing up the rear. Our ride was pleasant, the day just warm enough. We passed through the town of Falmouth—a very pleasant place indeed—from thence to Woods' Hall where we dined, and then took shipping in a nice little boat, sometimes rowing, sometimes sailing. The company all, excepting myself, amused themselves with fishing for [illegible] tho' not very successfully—there were enough taken, however, for supper. * * *

[1] Reprinted from the "Life of W. W. Seaton," p. 304.
[2] One of the Elizabeth Islands, off Buzzards Bay.

We reached the cove about six in afternoon.   The next was the important day on which a "stag was to die.   Our huntsmen one, and all, excepting, George, whose charge was within doors, began the chase immediately after breakfast.   Before twelve they returned, Mr. Webster having killed a fine Doe and one of the party a Stag.   We all regretted you could not have been one of the party.   They went again after dinner, started three deer and they tho't wounded one, but killed none.   *   *   *

The Gentlemen have come bringing their spoils with them, so adieu for the present.   Fine luck which always gives good spirits. I thot I would run up and finish my letter while while the guns were burnished for the afternoon's heat.   *   *   * [1]

(Mrs. Grace Webster to James W. Paige.)

My dear Brother,   SANDWICH [Mass.] Sept. 6, 1826.
*   *   *   Mr. W. has just returned from the field [to day] with more than one feather to day.   He went out with Mr. Child and usual attendants to the great marshes and brought home 70 large birds—Mr. W. shot 46 with his own hand, consisting as I hear the catalogue of ring-tailed curlews, Beetle-heads, red breasts, Humilitys and greybeaks—much the greatest part being red breasts.   He is very tired or he would write to Mr. Blake. he says he burnt all his powder—fired away all his shot, broke his ram-rod—got no dinner, and walked a long way on the Marshes after they were covered with the tide—he wishes you to tell Mr B. that he never saw better shooting in the great marshes—and that if he had known where the birds were to be found—he might have gone directly to them with a chaise.   So no more of birds.   Tomorrow we intend to show Eliza Cotuit and Mashpee lake   *   *   *

Your afft
Sister
G. W.

(Mrs. Grace Webster to James W. Paige.)

My dear Brother,   SANDWICH, Sep 5, 1826
Mr Webster arrived yesterday at a much earlier hour than I

---

[1] Unsigned, but written by Mrs. Grace Webster. It is on this outing at Sandwich that Webster first saw and was attracted by Marshfield.

expected and brought an unexpected guest, tho' I wrote to Eliza to come I nevertheless, did not expect her. Mr. W. has taken her & Julia down to the beach notwithstanding the wind which has blown a *gale* here ever since yesterday morning—it is very unpleasant to me.   *   *   *

Your affectionate Sister

G. W.

I forgot to say that Mr. W. has had fine sport today 17 large birds—before dinner

(George Ticknor to Prescott.[1])

SUMMER. 1828

*   *   *   But Mr. Webster is a true sportsman. He was out 13 hours today, without any regular meal, and is now as busy as a locksmith, with his guns. He seems to feel as if it were the one thing needful to kill birds and neither to tire or grow hungry while one can be seen. It has already made him look bright and strong again, for he came from Nantucket in but a poor condition.   *   *   *

(To Stephen White.)

BOSTON, Sep. 10 [1832]
Monday 4, P. M.

My Dear Sir

I came from Green Harbour this morning, I am sorry to say left Mrs W. a little unwell. She wrote you a letter last Eve; & left it for a finishing P. S. this morning; but when morning came, she was not well enough to attend to it. The amount of her epistle, she desired me to communicate to you; it is, that Mr Jones still is at M. & of course her visits to C. H. must be p-poned, some days. Mr Jones likes to stay with his son, as long as he can, & likes *fishing* also,—in which occupation he is engaged today, with Commodore Peterson & Hatch.[2] He will probably set forth tomorrow, direct for Providence. A thousand thanks & apologies were written, or to be written, & sent, for

---

[1] Taken from "Life of George Ticknor," vol. i, p. 387.
[2] Daniel Webster always called his boatman Hatch, Commodore.

him, by my wife to you & your damsels—but Cheney Hill lay so remote from his line of March, that he was obliged to give up the idea of visiting it.

I must remain here in Court Street for a day or two; after that, (my wife being well) we can come to C. H. at any time, that may suit you.   I can send for Mrs W.; but perhaps it will be as well, & so she seemed to think, that the whole matter should be put off till next week, & that we should come up on Monday, & go to C. H. on Tuesday.   I must be back again toward the end of next week, as Com'd. Peterson expect a flight of *coots*, positively, by the 24th Inst.—

Possibly you may be this way, tomorrow, or Wednesday morning, in which case I shall have the happiness of seeing you;— I intend going to M. Wednesday 1 o'clock, if I do not conclude to send for Mrs. W

Yrs truly ever
DANL. WEBSTER

(To Seth Weston.)

N. Y. THURSDAY
MOR'G

My Dear Sir,   13th of Aug. (1846).
I go East this Eve'g; & shall probably be in Marshfield as soon as you receive it, within one day.   Mrs. W. I presume is in Boston—   We shall make our appearance, probably, Saturday forenoon.   If not done already, I wish you to put the *curlew* all right—& make that *dog* point better.   I shall want to know what way the wind is.

If Saturday be a good day, Mr Hatch must lay in stores of Halibut, Cod & Hadduck—lest it should be rain'g the first of next week—

I think we shall be down by Saturday's mid day train.   Tell Monica.   Probably Mrs. W. may write to her—if not, she may expect us to a good chowder on Saturday.

D. W.

(To D. Fletcher Webster.)

Dear Fletcher,   MARSHFIELD May 3 1849.
Pray bring down a reel for my old "Kill-all," John Trout's

making. It must have a ring, or clasp, for the rod to run through; diameter of ring about an inch. Reel not too heavy.

Yrs,

DANL WEBSTER.

(From R. B. Forbes.)

BOSTON May 30, 1849

My dear Sir,

I have the pleasure to send under charge of Capt Morris of the Tow Boat or of Nicholas Berry, a small Schooner to be known as the "Lapwing," which vessel I beg you to accept as a small token of the respect I entertain for your character, as well as in acknowledgment of your kindness to me & to my cousin Mr T S Forbes, now in China—

Perhaps Mr Sam Hall, late ship carpenter now *alderman,* may go with the craft

I have been unable to procure from him any Bill for work done on the boat since he learned she was for yourself— * * *

Very respectfully

Yr Obed Servant

R. B. FORBES

(To Mr. Blatchford.)

WASHINGTON, June 15. '49.

Friday 2 O clock.

My Dear Sir,

I am sorry you have lost your cause, but am delighted to hear of you back again to New York. I have been so engaged here, for 8 or 10 days that I have hardly been able to raise my eyes from my table. I will write you again tomorrow, and tell you when I think I can get to N. York—and take you to Marshfield. And then, let the halibut and blue fish tremble!

I am in extraordinary good health. This is the first really warm day—and I keep in—

Yours

D. W.

I should like to be engaged to argue your cause before the Queen in Council.

(To D. Fletcher Webster.)

JUNE 28, 50

My Dear Son;   friday mor'g

I have recd., gladly, your letters, by sundry successive mails, but have not been diligent to answer them. This week I have also been rather busy— We passed two days at Piney Point— The weather was very warm— I tried the Sheep's heads, two mor'gs, with some success.

Yesterday I made a little speech, in answer to Mr. Soulè. To-day, I am trying to bring up my correspondence.

I have written Porter Wright that you would let him have $100— I have not *one cent*, I am, besides, overdrawn at Merchts Bank $200— Could you & our ever kind Mr Harvey raise me $500—on my acceptance, payable here, at 60 or 90 ds. Pray lose no time in letting me know, as I fear I shall fall into a bog.

Yrs D. W.

I am glad you are going to celebrate the 4th. make something of it.

———

(To John Taylor.)

CAPON SPRINGS Hampshire County
Virginia—among high mountains.

John Taylor   (June 29, 1851)

I expect to leave this place tomorrow, & reach Washington Tuesday, the first day of July. As soon as possible, after the 4th I hope to get off to the North.

I do not intend to spend a great deal more time in Washington till October. I hope to make you several visits—long & good. Probably I shall now go to Marshfield first. I shall want the Boat to be ready for Lake Como. You will not have time to attend to it yourself, but I wish you to get Mr. George, or some other carpenter, to put it into first rate repair. See that there are good oars, cable, & anchor. Have it well painted, & all ready to be launched on my arrival. We will keep it near Mr. Hancock's where it will be safe. Perch, Pickerel, as well as Sheldrakes must look out for themselves. It is very hot weather in these parts. I hope you are all well, & going ahead.

Yr friend
DANL WEBSTER.

(To Benjamin C. Clark.)

Mr. Paige's, Nahant,
Friday Morning, July 23rd., 1852.

My young Friend:

I propose joining you this morning, to pay our respects to the Tautog, but fear we shall hardly be able to tempt them from their lurking-holes, under this bright sun. They are naturally shy of light. "Tautog" means simply the "black fishes," "og" being a common termination of plural nouns in the language of our Eastern Indians. I believe the fish is not known in Europe. Its pricipal *habitat* originally seems to have been Long Island Sound, Buzzard's Bay, and the Elizabeth Islands. Seventy years ago the Hon'ble Stephen Gorham, father of the Hon'ble Benjamin Gorham, now of Boston, brought some of these fish alive from New Bedford and put them into the sea at Boston. They are now found as far East as the mouth of the Merrimac. They abound, as you know, on the south side, as well as on the north side of our Bay. Indeed, it is thought that by their own progress north they doubled Cape Cod, not long after Mr. Gorham's deposit, at Boston.

Thirty years ago, Mrs. Perkins, the wife of the late Samuel G. Perkins, a lady whose health led her to pass her summers on the sea-coast and who had a true love for fishing, caught a Tautog, with a hand-line, off these rocks, which weighed 20 lbs.

It will suit me quite as well to go off again, in the beautiful "Raven," if we can obtain plenty of bait, and especially if your Father will accompany us.

Yours truiy,
Dan'l Webster.

To Mr. Clark, my Companion of Yesterday, Nahant.

---

[1] This letter appeared in the New York *Independent*, August 4th, 1881.

Webster's Personal Finances

THE task of presenting Webster's PUBLIC finances would be far pleasanter, for in his long public career he rarely made a mistake upon which all competent critics would agree. His policy would be questioned by one partizan or another to-day, but, on the other hand, he would have good financiers who would defend him honestly. But his personal finance causes a pitying smile whenever mentioned. Even his own letters show that he was careless in keeping accounts and careless in handling money. They show that he neglected his business engagements. But that was not serious enough in itself to account for his being harassed and hounded during the whole of the latter part of his life by creditors. Had he never gone into public service, he would have been rich in spite of carelessness. He earned fees that were enormous for that day. But, as he said, and plainly showed by his accounts, NULLIFICATION cost him many thousands of dollars. The time that he was compelled to spend in the Senate lost him time in the Supreme Court...From about 1830 his finances began to trouble him, and then his heavy speculations in western lands, about 1835, got him more deeply engaged, and by 1840 the period of real financial embarrassment begins. Then his purse became "like a keg, soon emptied, if tapped at both ends, and then turned over, and the bung knocked out," as he wrote Seth Weston. The letters here given show him shrewd enough in bargaining, and, in his letter to Griswold, ready enough to demand his pound of flesh.—Nor was he wholly regardless of expense, as his comment on the cost of living at the Tremont indicates. Is it not possible to believe that Webster sacrificed financial success to public weal—or, if we choose to be more cynical, to his political ambitions?

(To ————————.)

NEW YORK, Dec. 21, 1829.
I have your letter respecting the 1000 Doll. note of Mr.

——s. I cannot say whether the debt is mine or Mr. ——s, not having, however, any recollection of any debt of mine for which security was given in that form. I inclose a paper in note form, to be made up into a note of a thousand dollars, or any less sum, to be signed by Mr. ——, in order to get a discount to pay this note, and we will ascertain, hereafter, whose debt it is. I am confident it is not mine, but may be mistaken. I have written to him on this matter, saying I should forward an indorsement to you, and saying, also, that if he found it difficult to get a discount, you would help him to some part of the money, as I shall pick up some little fees, and see them to my credit in bank at Boston before 5 Jan.[1]

D. WEBSTER.

(To Mr. Kinsman.?)

Dear Sir   WASHINGTON Decr. 21, 1831

I have recd your letter, respecting the Antelope.[2] It is quite certain, I think, that the Commissioners *will require* the regular proofs of condemnation, in England. In other cases, I have never known such proofs to be dispensed with, unless on the ground that they had been lost, by time or accident.

I notice your payment of Dr Sewalls draft, in which you did righ.

I owe a bill of 130 or 140 Dlls to Hilliard Gray & Co, booksellers, & they seem to be quite persevering *dunners*— Will you please go & pay it, & take a receipt in full—

I go next week to Annapolis, to argue a cause in the Maryland court. Let your letters come *here* as usual—& they will be forwarded—   Yours truly,

D. WEBSTER

(To John R. Thomson.[3])

My Dear Sir,   BOSTON, Aug. 6. 1833

On my arrival in Boston, a few days after I had the pleasure

---

[1] This letter is taken from a newspaper clipping in the possession of C. E. Bliss, of Bangor, Me. The original is, however, in the possession of C. P. Greenough, of Boston.
[2] The *Antelope*, captured July 13, 1812. This claim was one which was settled by the treaty with Denmark.
[3] Secretary Delaware and Raritan Co.

of exchanging a word with you on the RailRoad. I found your letter of the 12th of July, indorsing a bank note of 100 Dollars, as a retainer from the "Delaware & Raritan Canal, and Camden & Amboy RailRoad." My family being at Marshfield I proceded immediately to that place, I have there been staying ten or twelve days, to recruit from the fatigue of a long journey.

On coming to town and recurring to your letter, it occurs to me that there may be some difficulty in accepting this Retainer, especially as it is a *general* one, & for all causes. I have understood that some other RailRoad was in contemplation, thro' N. Jersey, which may possibly come in competition with this. So I was informed while in N. York, on my [way] home, & so I have since learned also. And it so happens, that in this new projected road, family friends and connections of mine are interested, I believe, to some considerable extent. I have not been retained, by those concerned in this new road, but on account of the connection of Mr. LeRoy, & other members of his family in it, I feel unwilling to be retained for any opposing interest. If I am in any error, as to the controversies which your company anticipates, or there be any question respecting which they would desire my professional advice or aid, I shall very gladly tender both.

Under all the circumstances, it has seemed to me to be the proper course to return the The Retainer, I leave the matter for the further consideration of your company, in this view.

I pray the most respectful remembrance to Mrs. Thomson, & the members of her family, I am, with rgard,

Your Obt. Servant.

[D. Webster. MSS]

(To H. W. Kinsman.)

Private & Confidential.

Washington Jan. 11. 1834

My Dear Sir.

I wish to write you a letter, in confidence, for your own eyes & Mr Brook's.—

The subject, is the French claims, before 1800. I moved on that subject, early in the session—had a committee appointed—myself at the head of it, & we have reported a Bill. By proper pains, the Bill *will assuredly pass the Senate.* Two members of the Com^{ee.} (Mr Grundy & Mr. Preston) told me they sh'd be glad to vote against it, if they could, but they could not answer the argument in its favor. I have proposed Wednesday, the 5th of Feb., for taking it up.—

It is time, therefore, I think, to move in the matter of the agency. If the Gentlemen in interest, in our quarter, desire my aid, I wish them to settle that point, before a host of other persons apply. Will you, therefore, shew this letter to Mr Brooks, &, if necessary, to Mr. Edward Brooks;—it need go no farther— If Mr Brooks thinks proper, let him draw up an agreement, substantially like that in the case of the Spanish treaty; let him sign it himself, and ask others to sign it, If this can be done, to such an extent as to make it an object, you may say to Mr Brooks that it is my intention very much to relinquish other profefsional employment, & give my strictest personal attention to this business. It will [be] an object to do so, provided I can obtain the agency of the greater part of the interest, in our region.

If such an agreement shall be signed by Mr. Brooks & others, Mr S. White would take pains to get signers. Indeed if Mr Brooks enters into the object, you may afterwards shew this letter to Mr. White. I do not wish to be connected with any other person, in the agency, whatever, For what assistance you render, I shall of course compensate you, as we may agree; but I wish to take the whole responsibility on myself, with nothing to do with any other agents.—

It would oblige me if you could attend to this soon, & let me know the result. Tell Mr Brooks, there is nobody here, out of doors, that can do any good.

Yrs   D. WEBSTER

(To H. W. Kinsman.)

WASHINGTON Jan—13—1834
Dear Sir

I have received the enclosed, this morning. It w'd be a good thing, I think, for Mr Brooks to write to Mr Bartlett, or Mr Nelson, on the subject of my letter of yesterday. It may be very probable that all the Newburyport Gentlemen are already engaged to Mr Cushing; if so, it is well. But if unengaged, very probably they w'd sign my paper.— Of course, Mr Brooks will not mention anything of this letter.—

Mr Charles Russell, of New Bedford, has a claim, I believe a large one. *You* might write to him, saying you are connected with me, & that we should be willing to take the agency of his claim on the same terms as that of others—

Yrs   D. WEBSTER

Mr Russell has written me, like many others, to press this indemnity.

———

(To I. W. Kelly.[1])

WASHINGTON Jan. 29. 1835.

Dear Sir,

Your two missing letters, were brought to me yesterday. One, a letter about Family affairs, the other a letter about the land, ending, (or enclosed) with, a mortgage deed; three notes, a rough sketch of the land &c.— From circumstances, I incline to think these letters were mislaid in the Post office here. As you will have recd the other mortgage deed, & notes, I need not execute this, as I presume—

By the description in this deed, & the plan, I see how the land lies. I am quite satisfied with the bargain— I think I have been fortunate in getting a good pasture—

I am inclined to buy Mr. Quimby's, if he should be disposed to sell, as I should think he would be, rather than to make so much fence. You may manage with him, as you see fit, & get the land, if you can, at a fair rate. Give him to understand at once, that we must fence, if he does not sell— I would give him something more, per acre, than we gave Mr. Shaw, rather than not get it—but would not give an extravagant price. If you find him disposed to make a bargain, which you think it for my interest to comply with, you may conclude it, at once, without further reference to me—name a day, when the money shall be paid, & the deed executed; & put it just so far ahead that you can write to me—& I will send a check for the cash.— Put the bargain at once into writing, & sign it, as my agent.—or, what will be shorter—go to Mr. Nesmith, have the deed made out & executed, & left with him, till you bring the money.—

I should think he would rather sell, for a little something more per acre than was given to Mr Shaw, rather than make 300 rods of fence, to enclose only 28 acres of land—

Manage the matter, as well as you can.

———

[1] This letter is in the possession of Judge Corning, of Concord, N. H.

I do not know whether the Widow—Tandy's dower land, is for sale or not—
It is an awkward little piece, to lie in the middle of our pasture, but as it is a wood lot, I suppose it will not create any necessity of fencing.   I suppose she has but a life estate in the land; who owns the reversion?
Since writing you the other day, I have heard from Capt. Stevens, respecting the House, &c—& shall write him, this mail or the next.—

Yrs with regard
Danl Webster

(To Mrs. Caroline Webster. ?)

Private   *(1836)*

I cut the enclosed out of a N. O. paper.[1]
Mr Livingston has set a good example.   I had just as much to do with the cause as he had.   As yet, I have not said anything about my fee.   If they pay Mr Livingston 25.000, they can hardly fail to give me also a pretty handsome sum.   But probably they will cut him down, not a little.   I imagine he may get a good fee, however.
—*Keep all this entirely to yourself-*

D. W.

(To Samuel Jaudon.[2])

My Dear Sir   *(1839)*
Although we have had little direct communication, since you went abroad to put matters of finance right in Europe, yet you have been too conspicuous to be lost sight of, & I seem to know as much about your daily movements, as when you were in Phila.— The last I heard of your wife, was, that she appeared in the brilliant circle in the Abbey, on day of the Coronation.   She got out, without suffocation, & no doubt will regard it as a spectacle to be remembered.   Without waiting, according to fashion, for the end of this epistle, I wish, in this early stage of it, to pray you to make my affectionate regards, & remember me to all the cis-Atlantic children.

---

[1] The newspaper clipping stated that Edw. Livingston had drawn on the city for $25,000.
[2] A banker in London, formerly a cashier in the Bank of the United States. See Curtis' "Life of Daniel Webster," vol. ii, p. 18.

My main object, My Dear Sir, in writing you at this time, is to communicate a plan, which I have formed, or wish to form, for the purpose of crossing the water. I have a very great desire to see England, once; & if this desire is ever gratified, it must be done soon. But my circumstances require, that I should connect some business arrangements with the purpose of my voyage; indeed, that I should make such arrangements its leading object.

Tired of the sacrifices, which I had been making by remaining in Congress, I endeavored, in 1836 to resign my seat, & with intention of ret'g to the Law. But I could not resign. My papers were sent back, as friends wd. not hearken to any suggestion of leaving my place.

Seei'g, then, that I must do something, with a view to future means of liv'g, I entered on *Western investments*, partly in company with Col. Perkins, partly in a company of which Govr. Cass was Chief, & partly on my own separate account. These investments were made by faithful & careful agents, principally in agricultural lands of excellent quality, in Ohio, Illinois, Michigan & Wisconsin. Prospects of profit seemed fair, at the time, & I purchased as far as my means & credit would go.

The events of 1837, although they have not effected the ultimate value of this property, have retarded its sale. It is still all on hand, and the general progress of settlement, in these states; & the immense emigration into them, greater the last fall than ever before, so far as respects North Illinois & Wisconsin, have no doubt greatly enhanced its value. Now, if I can dispose of this, or a large part, by a trip to England, I should both gratify my curiosity, & improve my circumstances.

I know, that English Capitalists, proposing to invest in this Country, prefer stocks, or public Securities, in some form. But I have supposed it possible, that upon a proper representation of values, it might be possible to dispose of this private *p'p'y*.

I could take with me

1. Regular Government titles to 15. or 20. thousand acres of excellent Farming & timber lands, in various parts of the States & Territory above mentioned.

2. Certificates of the best men in that County, Gov. Duncan, Mr. May, &c &c &c—that the lands would not be rated light at 5 Dollars an acre, cash, now; & that in all probability that they would double in value, in 5 yrs.

3. Proof that the title is perfect, & that there is no danger of disturbances, from taxes.

4. Good title to sundry parcels of City property, in La Salle, hitherto called Peru, & to a large & very elegant tract of land adjoining. You know where La Salle is. It is at the entrance of the Illinois Canal, into the Illinois River, at the head of Navigation. It is a point of great centrality, many lines of communication meet at it, & it must inevitably become a most important place. Even under all the disadvantages of recent times, it has increased rapidly. The Canal will probably be finished in 3 Seasons more; & when that shall be accomplished, it must be at once a point of great traffic & exchange of merchandise. I own, (with D. F. W.) a good deal of land, in the City, necessary for building as the place would grow, & a most splendid tract near it, divided from the lines of the town only by a *quarter section* (to speak in the language of the land laws) owned by Col. Perkins.

This tract contains 12 or 13 wooded acres. It is the most beautiful land I ever saw, lying high near the River, & interspersed with timber & meadow land, most delightfully. It is not at all extravagant or excessive, to put this tract at 50 Dollars an acre. I think that fair and competent judges would estimate my property in & about Peru, at 100,000 Dollars I am sure, at least, they wd be of opinion it would be worth that sum, & fast risi'g in value, on the completion of the Canal.

I possess various other things, such as interests in City lots, in mineral lands, & sundry corporations, & also in the Clanogen Grant, which b'g of a more uncertain nature, I do not b'g forward, for sale, as clearly valuable & certain ppty.

Now, the question is, can this property be sold in England? If it can, I will cross the water. If it cannot, I can hardly afford to lose the time from my profession, & to bear the expenses of the trip.

Within ten days, the Legislature of Mass are to make choice of a Senator, for the next six years. After much hesitation, as to what I ought to do, I have concluded to say nothing. I presume, therefore, that I shall be reelected. If I should be encouraged to go to England, I should leave America the first of May, & ret'n in the autumn. If determined on go'g, it is likely Mr. Le Roy would give his daughter a few thousand dollars, to enable her to accompany her husband; & we should take Julia with us. A sale of this property would enable me to replace what friends, (known to you) have advanced to me, & to remain in public life. If it cannot be accomplished, on either side of the water, I must change the Senate for the Bar of the Boston Courts.

I know, My Dear Sir, from long experience of y'r kindness, that you will give this matter some consideration. If you think any th'g can be done, I shall go forth. If otherwise, I shall then feel that you w'd have obliged & assisted me, if you could. It is a matter of importance, as it is likely to settle the question whether I am ever to see England.

You will best know what form to put these thi'gs in, if I go over with them. As to titles, I shall see them all clear, & properly certified by public official personages.

I have not mentioned this subject to my wife, nor to more than two persons livi'g, besides this communication to yourself. In two or three days I shall be in Phila. & may perhaps suggest it to Mr B. I hope for answer from you, to be rec'd here as early as the middle of March; till which time I shall not make my purposes and projects public.

I am, Dr Sir, all[1]

[D. W.]

(To Charles H. Upton.[2])

WASHINGTON Mar: 26, 1842.
Sir

I have no answer to make to your letter, of yesterday beyond what I stated when you called on me. Any person may threaten to appeal to the public, when he presents a claim, which cannot be sustained, & is not admitted. No doubt, he may in this way inflict some degree of pain; & if you should see fit to resort to such a proceeding, in this case, the pain would be measured by the consideration that that treatment was received at the hands of the son of a Gentleman with whom I have been on friendly terms for twenty five years, & who recently went to his grave, without supposing, so far as I know, that he had any claim, legal or equitable agt. me, although he is known to have been, for many years, living in this city in circumstances far from affluent; I will only make one remark on the subject, more. The acceptance for $350, so far as I remember, was made at your father's

---

[1] Taken from first draft of the letter probably sent. It is in Daniel Webster's hand.

[2] This copy is taken from Daniel Webster's draft of the letter. The letter is in reply to one written by Upton, dated March 25, 1842, in which a threat is made of an appeal to the public if Webster does not pay the acceptance which Webster here explains.

request, on security of a claim assigned to me. Afterwards the claim was rec'd, but it did not amount to the sum. I was therefore a loser, as I mentioned to you, & as I have more than once mentioned to your father. I cannot correspond with you further on the subject; but repeat, that your father died very considerably in my debt.

If under these circumstances, you think it just to seek to annoy me by useless Newspaper publications, it is a matter which I must leave you to reconcile to your conscience & character.

Yrs respectfully

(To Seth Weston.?)

My Dear Sir   NEW YORK Jan. 27 1845.

My money in Boston did not hold out quite so well as I expected. I thought there was something of it, for me—but a keg is soon emptied, if it be tapped at both ends, & then turned over, & the bung knocked out.

I enclose herein a check for $500 on the *New York* Merchants Bank. Mr. Haven, at the *Boston* Merchants Bank will readily give Boston money. Instead of sending up my check for $700. please send up this. I will endeavor to send you the other $200. as soon as I reach Washington.

Remember that you must put your name on this check.

I think it very likely that Mr. G. B. Weston would give you Bills for this check. But certainly Mr. Sprague, or Mr. Jones, can get cash for it, at the Boston Merchants Bank.

I go on south, tomorrow morning

Yrs always

DANL WEBSTER

Write me, to Washington, & tell me among other things, how the ice comes on. To hear from Marshfield is almost the only pleasure I expect to enjoy at Washington.

(To D. Fletcher Webster.)

Private

N. YORK Feb. 24, 1845.

Dear Fletcher

The illness of some of the judges, & other causes, render it improbable that any case of mine will be reached at this session of the Court. I do not incline, therefore, to hasten back to Washington as nothing is likely to take place then, between this & the 4th of March, which I have a particular fancy to see.

I think of occupying my time here till Saturday morning, talking over my own matters, & especially looking after my western lands, or some of them. What do you think the Peru farms, all four of them, are worth? I wish you would write me a letter describing this property, speaking of it as it ought to be spoken of, & saying that the title is clear, &c. Let it be a letter which can be shown. If you have an opportunity, by a safe hand, send me the title deeds, which I suppose are in the trunk which you brought home from Washington, though I am not quite certain. If I can make any arrangement to get any money on these farms, you would have some part of it.

I have also some chance of getting a little advance on the Mexican scrip, Please regard this as private, & answer it by return of mail.

Yrs   D. WEBSTER

(To D. Fletcher Webster.)

Dear Fletcher   JAN. 30. 1846
I have recd your of the 28 this morng. I am really perplexed, & distressed, beyond description, & half inclined to give up every thing in despair. You say that the Gentlemen call for a *list*—why certainly I have given the list three or four times, *& I have no copy here.* Besides the debts now immediately pressing, are known by everybody to be on the list; viz the Bank debts here, the debts in N. York &c.— Mr Jaudon, who has been here, knows all about these debts, & will see to the payment of them, if he can be put in possession of the means.

—Seems to me, it is mere formality to call for new lists— At any rate, I can give none without going home—

I can do no more—& do not wish to be written to again on the subject. I rather let it all go, & go home, as I must do. You may show this to whom you see fit.—

I infinitely regret the thing was ever begun. It has given me a whole year of anxiety, & yet comes to nothing. I cannot write any more about it, nor say any more about it. If there is anything to be put into Mr Jaudons hands, for purposes which all know were the original purposes, & *which cannot be put off longer*, I shall be glad. If not, I can do nor say anything more about it, but must go home.

Yrs affectionately

DANL WEBSTER

(To D. Fletcher Webster.)

FEB. 17. 1846

Dear Fletcher

I intimated to you that Mr Haven would not get here. So it turns out. He got to N. Y. & then wrote me, that not finding that he had power over the funds collected, by which *he could apply them to their well known original purpose*, he halted; & I have heard nothing since. He has probably gone back. I knew it would be so; & I now know that I must go home. I do not suppose there was ever so unfortunate & vexatious a business.— I can stand it no longer.

Yrs   D. W.

(To D. Fletcher Webster.)

JAN. 10 (1847)

Dear F.

I send you a letter from Mr. Dorr, with copy of my answer. It is better to let him run. I shall not take his $100— You may, if you choose. Perhaps he misunderstood you; & there is someth'g in the fact, that he has distributed the money. If he comes to you, it will be better for you not to have any quarrel with him. He is a respectable & honest man, but he hates to part with his money. He may, perhaps, be useful to you, hereafter.

Yrs.   D. W.

(To Peter Harvey.)

WEDNESDAY MOR'G NOV. 24. '47

My Dear Sir;

I do not see how I can get along, without anticipating, in some way, my Jan. Installment, at the Hospital Life Insr. Office. In these emergencies, I have usually gone to Mr. Haven; but he has so often taken pains to oblige me, that I quite dislike to trouble him again. I think too, I have heard he is not well, & is, doubtless, just now very much engaged.

I have made out a power of attorney to you, to receive the money, which will be payable Jan. 1.

I want $500. today, & the residue by the 10th Decr. Do you see how what I desire can be accomplished?

Yrs

D. W.

———

(To D. Fletcher Webster.)

WASHINGTON Decr. 20. '47

My Dear Son

I have recd your letter of the 17. of this month.

In all former cases of recovery of claims agt foreign Governments, I have rec'd a commission of 5 per cent. I have known no smaller charge, in general, either in the English, Spanish, Danish or Mexican cases—

But as Mr Dorr paid a good deal of personal attention to his case, I should be content to charge only 1/2 the customary commission. It is proper, too, I think to deduct the $100. advanced to you.

Stati'g the amount on these principles, he may remit the balance, in a check on Boston, to me.

I shall immediately inquire for the names of the steamer, according to his wish. Leaving your mother in N. Y. I arrived here, quite well, yesterday morn'g.

Yours affectionately

DANL WEBSTER

———

(To Samuel Jaudon.)

WASHINGTON, Decr. 26. '47

My Dear Sir

I am glad Mr. Cape has written to you, & that you are willing to look into the accounts.

As to the large claims, I have the sincerest conviction,—indeed I know—I do not owe a dollar. On the contrary, there is a balance due me; but how much that balance ought to be considered to be, might be a question.

I acknowledge the account sent me some time ago, for taxes; I am disposed to make arrangements for payi'g it.

As to titles. I believe there will be found few or no defects, except that in regard to several parcels, a deed may be wanted from Mr. Henry Hubbard, which I have his written promise to make. I must, of course, stand to my warranties.

It is hardly possible, I think, to get along with this business, till I can go North. I could not so describe the papers needed, so that they could be selected from a very great mass. Besides, I should have occasion to see Mr Hubbard, as well as Mr. Fletcher Webster, who knows more of the titles than I do, & who was acquainted with the case, fully, at the time the conveyances were made.

As soon as the Supreme Court rises, I will go home & get the papers, & pay immediate attention to the subject.

I will thank you to communicate this to Mr. Cape, who has always treated me in a very kind & friendly manner. * * *

Yours. DAN'L WEBSTER.

(*To D. Fletcher Webster.*)

DECR. 30. [1847] Thursday mor'g.

Dear F.

I was glad to get a short note from you this mor'g. You need not fear my going into St. Croix or other project. I have neither money nor credit for such things.

Today I have a bad cold, & feel unwell; but must go into court.

Yrs affectionately

D. W.

I do not get my English papers.

(*To Porter Wright.*)

WASHINGTON, Feb. 2, '50.

Porter Wright;

Mr. Weston will hand you $100—& I will try to send you some more soon—

I have no objection to parting with the Ames steers, or the Haseltine, or both, for money to pay debts, at a fair price; but

I do not care about exchanging with Mr. Delano. The offer you have made ($15) is enough— I would not give any more. Mr. Ames may take the Brown oxen—indeed I would sell almost anything, to pay debts— But everything seems low—

If you do not trade with Mr. Delano, we will fat the mountaineers, & look up something else for beef, next month, when I come home. If we keep the white faced oxen, the black and red steers, the large Durham steers, & the jumpers, we shall do pretty well for teams, though another pair for Fletcher's barn might be useful— The Locke oxen, perhaps, might go there—

I have written Mr. Stevens of the Revere House about the Potatoes. He will write for what he wants. I will take Mr. Sampson's. How is it about ice?—[1]

Please write me once a week—

Yrs   DANL WEBSTER

(To Worcester Webster.)

Dr Sir,   BOSTON May 8, 1850.

That old note, which I was sued upon, has got into Execution, & must be immediately paid. I must depend on your gett'g discounted the note, which I now enclose, & plac'g the amt. to my credit in the Merchants Bank, Boston, on or before the 15TH inst—this *must* be done.

I leave on the 10th for Washington.—

Give my love to your wife. I hope you are well. You see I am in hot water. Lend a helping hand—

Be sure to comply with what is written on the other page.

Pray for the Peace of Jerusalem.

Yr cousin
DANL WEBSTER

(To George Griswold.)

Confidential.

My Dear Sir,   MARSHFIELD. Oct. 8th. 1852.

I trust you have been satisfied, as well as the rest of us, with

---

[1] This letter is copied from a newspaper clipping—newspaper unknown—contained in a collection of Websteriana owned by C. E. Bliss, of Bangor, Me.

the Decree, which has been entered up by the Court in the India Rubber cause at Trenton; & I hope, my Dear Sir, that you will not think me obtrusive, if, in connection with this subject, I call your attention to your very kind and confidential letter to me of the 18th of March last.[1]

Always most truly
& cordially yours—
D. W.

(To D. Fletcher Webster.)

Mar. 2.

Dear F.

I do not know that any th'g can be done for Haddock.—certainly noth'g this way.— If he was to come to Boston, in the Spr'g, with good proofs of the value of property, proposed to be mortgaged, we w'd make an effort for him.

I beg you, write him, & insist upon his mak'g out my title to the land, I bought, thro. him.— Have that attended to.—

We have had a most severe snow storm, for 3 days. I have not seen the like in Washington.

The mails are all behind.— Halibuts tails & all.

I intend to pass this day in my room, answering letters, clearing the table, &c. &c.

Yrs. D. W.

(To D. Fletcher Webster.)

Sunday mor'g Decr. 6.

Dear Fletcher

I arrived last eve'g, & found the House open, & warm. Yrs, enclosing a line to Mr. Carlisle, was brought me this mor'g. I will send it to him, & ask him to come & see me; & shall be glad to press this Spanish claim to some result.

At N. York Genl. C. gave me 100 hundred Dollars, which I sent you, from Phila.— He rather complained of the amount of the Bill, & said he must consult other parties; & added that he

---

[1] The letter referred to is not published, but it contains a promise on the part of Mr. Griswold to pay Webster $1,000 if the India Rubber Case is won. Webster's argument in this case was published in pamphlet form, but is not contained in the "Works."

would attend to it, when he got to N. York; which he wished me to say to you.

I was sorry, & am sorry, you did not come to Philad, because you had excited expectations in me, & I had excited them in others. I think you ought to have come, at any inconvenience or cost. You will, beside, have no such good opportunity to arrange for a profitable lecture, or two, in that City.

I do not hear from Mr. Harvey, who rather disappointed me also, in not appearing at Phila. I am anxious to know whether things make progress.

I have as yet seen nobody.

Yrs. D. W.

(To D. Fletcher Webster.)

SATURDAY Mar: 24,

Dear Fletcher

I have written a short letter to Mr. Harvey, today, of such a character that he may *show it.*

I may soon write him privately— Things go on here, I think well enough, at least, they look about right, so far. I must stay here till I get your matter thro'; & perhaps shall hardly get away much under a week— The difficulty is to know where to go, when I get to Boston. It is too expensive to stay at the Tremont—& the East winds will be cold at Marshfield.

We are quite well.

D. W.

Webster's Religious and Moral Character

THE *comparatively little that Webster had to say upon moral issues during his long public life contains what subjective evidence we have as to his moral and religious character. The editor has placed here such letters of Webster as illustrate these matters and have little or no relation to his political career. Among his formal productions his speech in the Girard College case is most prominent in elucidating his religious views. Among the few papers on this subject, we have mentioned a confession of faith written at the age of 25, and given a short address made at a Sunday school meeting some twenty-four years later. In the McGaw letter there is a brief sentiment upon natural religion— his "conviction of the existence and perfection of the Deity."*

There is in the letter to Rev. Goddard a conventional statement of his belief in immortality. The inscription for his tomb which he personally dictated, gives further testimony of this belief. The inscription may be found in the closing pages of Curtis' "Life of Webster." In the Private Correspondence (Vol. i, p. 453), the letter to Mr. Haddock throws additional light upon his religious views.

That he wished his name identified with religious activities is testified by various certificates and papers among his literary remains. His certificate of life membership in the American Bible Society, and his appointment as an honorary member of the American Board of Commissioners for Foreign Missions, are among the Greenough papers.

Of his charity and philanthropy there is abundance of evidence among his letters. There is in this collection a letter showing his indignation at misplaced charity, and another showing his compassion and willingness to aid an unfortunate who had been guilty of a crime. There are preserved here very definite statements of his reverence for the Sabbath and his thorough approval of the cause of temperance.

As concerns his own moral habits, we have the entry in James Kent's diary, and the somewhat conflicting testimony of Web-

ster's physician. I wish to add here that, after reading the testimony of many men who knew him, and after reading through many years of his correspondence, the unimportant letters of which are not published, I am convinced that, though Webster drank wine at his table, as did most men of his social standing at that time, and though he used liquors for medicinal purposes, I do not believe, as is often reported, that he ever appeared before a public assembly in an intoxicated condition, or, indeed, that he ever on account of liquor lost perfect control of his mental faculties.   James Kent's testimony that Webster lived too well, must be accepted in the sense that he was a lover of rich and highly seasoned foods, and of good wines in moderation.   In the letter to Anderson, he has expressed his sentiments upon the temperance movement, and I think no one will accuse Webster of hypocrisy, whatever other charge has been made against him. That he suffered in his later years because of early ignorance of some of the laws of health, we cannot doubt.   But, it was the result of ignorance and carelessness and not willful immorality. Webster had inherited too much of the Puritan for that.

Many dark hints have been made, in conversation, concerning Webster's relations with women, and one reputable historian, Mr. Rhodes, has suggested in his characterization of Webster that "he was not scrupulous in observing the Seventh commandment."   That his personality was most attractive to women there is every testimony, but there is absolutely nothing but idle gossip, that I can find, which substantiates the charge that he took advantage of this power to charm.   His friends rejected with horror the insinuation of such an immorality, and his enemies gladly accepted the "trifles light as air" which gave such calumny its slightest weight.   The truth seems to be that Webster suffered the penalty which invidious cynicism always visits upon the man whose nobility of person and grace of manner give him favor in the eyes of womankind.

(To Jacob McGaw.[1])

My Dear Friend,   Boston Oct. 11. '28
     I thank you for your letter of Sep. 25, detailing the incidents

---

[1] This letter was published in the New York *Sun* of January 16, 1894.   The editor takes it from a clipping in the possession of Mr. C. E. Bliss, of Bangor, Me.

of your tour. It has enabled me to go, pretty accurately, over your track. I have followed you, by the means of it, repeatedly from Boston round by the West, & home to Bangor. I well understand how you should feel excited by visiting such places as Kingsbridge, White Plains, Benn. Heights etc. I never knew a man yet, nor a woman neither, with a sound head & a good heart, that was not more or less under the power, which these local associations exercise.

It is true, that *place*, in these things, is originally accidental. Battles *might have been* fought elsewhere, as well as at Saratoga, or Bennington. Nevertheless here they *were fought;* & nature does not allow us to pass over the scenes of such events with indifference, unless we have a good share of bluntness & stupidity, or unless the scenes themselves have become familiar by frequent visits to them. For my part I love them all, and all such as they. An old *drum* hangs up in the Senate Chamber of Mass. taken from the Hessians at Bennington, & I do not think I ever went into the room without turning to look at it. And that reminds me to say, that I have a pair of silver *sleeve buttons*, the material of which my father picked up on, & brought away from, that same field of Bennington. If I thought either of my boys would not value them, fifty years hence, if he should live so long, I believe I should begin to flog him, now.—

The day we parted here was, in truth, very hot. I reached Falmouth, at evening, very much exhausted by heat & fatigue. The next morning we embarked for Nantucket, & had a good passage. There I staid a week, exceedingly busy, all the time, & hurrying thro' business, in order to shorten our stay. Work & heat, (a good deal too much of it both) made me sick; & after I returned from the Island, it was a month before I felt quite well. Cooler weather & repose have, at length, accomplished my restoration. My health is now good, & I shall have occasion for all of it, for the next month or two, during which professional engagements are usually most pressing.

Julia and Edward are still at Boscawen. At the end of this month they will come home, and both their little cousins with them. Mrs. E. Webster is to come down, & to keep all the children here, for a month or two, while her husband is engaged with the Courts, & the legislature— My present purpose is not to be in great haste to depart for Washington, unless some urgent public duty should require it. In the present condition of my household, it is a great object to shorten my absence as far as I well can. I rejoice that you found your little daughter, & your other connexions well; & that the journey proved so favorable to Mrs. McGaw's health. Nothing is better, I think, than a tour of that sort, once in a while, to places not before visited, & to the midst of society a little different from that in our own circle. It is not only gratifying, at the moment, but furnishes many things to think about, & talk over, for a long time. The mind requires occasionally a supply of new ideas, or else it is likely to get out of stock. New books (or books never read before) will sometimes enable the inner man to gratify himself with a change of ideas, which are his diet), & a visit to new scenes & new circles, often does the same thing more effectually. For my part, I journey a good deal, but it is all on the beaten track from Boston to Washington. Once we made an exception, & went, as you know, to Niagara— It was a high gratification. I advise you to keep your eye on such a tour, at some time, hereafter. Why is it not a sort of duty, before we leave this world "thus wondrous fair", to see all the wonders, which it is fairly in our power to see, &, by beholding them to derive a new excitement to our veneration & adoration of the Deity?

I confess that natural Religion—that conviction of the existence & perfection of the Deity, which the contemplation of natural objects produces,—grows daily more & more impressive on my mind. But I must stop—or I shall write a sermon—Adieu— I have not written so tediously long a letter, in a twelve month.

Give every good wish of my heart to your wife—and, as we Yorkers say, "the same to yourself"—[1]

Yrs always truly
DANL. WEBSTER.

(From Ralph Randolph Gurley.[2])

My Dear Sir,   WASHINGTON May 15th 1830

Having knowledge of your disposition to relieve the unfortunate, may I solicit your charitable attention to the Bearer a very respectable man of colour, who is seeking some aid to redeem

---

[1] The editor not wishing to divide this letter, has chosen to place it here, although some of the matters treated would place it in another division.

[2] From 1822 to 1872 R. R. Gurley was agent and secretary of the American Colonization Society and was one of the founders of Liberia. He edited the *African Repository* and wrote several books.

his family. You will be glad to know that the family of *Philip Lee*, in behalf of which I once sought your friendly assistance, are now free & happy.

with the highest respect
& esteem, ever
Your friend &
servant
R R GURLEY

(Speech at a Sunday School Meeting.[1]*)*

CITY OF WASHINGTON, Feb. 16, 1831.

Francis S. Key, Esq. of Georgetown D. C. proposed the following resolution:

Resolved, "That the Directors of the American Sunday Union have justly estimated the piety and patriotism of their countrymen, in relying upon them for the accomplishment of the great object they have resolved to execute—and that Committees be appointed to solicit donations throughout the District in their behalf."

This resolution was seconded by the Hon. DANIEL WEBSTER, member of the Senate of the U. States from the state of Massachusetts, who expressed in a few words his approbation of the objects of the meeting.

Notwithstanding the very general provision made for education, in the part of the country to which he belonged, yet Sunday Schools were there extensively established; and their usefulness universally acknowledged.

Most great conceptions were simple. The present age had struck out two or three ideas, on the important subject of education, and the diffusion of religious knowledge, partaking, in a very high degree, of this character. They were simple; but their application was extensive, direct, and efficacious. Of these, the leading one, perhaps, was the distribution of the Holy Scriptures, without note or comment; an idea, not only full of piety, and duty, and of candour also, but strictly just and philosophical; since the knowledge of the general truth must, of necessity, be communicated, before there can exist a capacity to examine and decide on those different views and inferences, em-

[1] This is taken from a newspaper clipping contained in Webster's collection now in the library of the New Hampshire Historical Society. The name of the paper has not been noted on the clipping.

braced by Christians of various denominations and various opinions.

The object of Sunday Schools, and of the particular resolution now before the meeting, was, as he understood it, of similar large and liberal character. It was to diffuse the elements of knowledge, and to teach the great truths of Revelation. It was to improve, to the highest of all purposes, the leisure of the Sabbath; to render its rest sacred, by thoughts turned towards the Deity, and aspiring to a knowledge of his word and will.

There were other plans of benevolence, about which men might differ. But it seemed to him, there could be no danger of error here. If we were sure of any thing, we were sure of this, that the knowledge of their Creator, their duty and their destiny, is good to men; and that, whatever, therefore, draws the attention of the young to the consideration of these objects, and enables them to feel their importance, must be advantageous to human happiness, in the highest degree, and in all worlds. In the great wants of their moral nature, all men are alike. All were born in want of culture, in want of knowledge, in want of something to explain to them, not only what they may see around them, but their own nature, condition and destiny. In civilized times, and in a Christian land, the means of this knowledge were to be supplied to the young, by parental care, by public provision, or by Christian benevolence. They were not assembled in pursuance of a call, made by this last means of operation. It was to afford to some what all needed. It was to administer to the indispensable moral necessities of mankind. It was to supply, or aid in supplying, the elements of knowledge, religious, moral and literary, to the children throughout a most interesting and important portion of the country. He was most happy to concur in this object, and to be present at this meeting, to give it his aid and encouragement.[2]

(To Rev. Kingston Goddard.[1])

My Dear Sir:—

In thanking you for a beautiful and excellent sermon, with

---

[1] A confession of faith written by Webster at the age of twenty-five years, may be found in "History of Salisbury," collated by J. L. Dearborn, p. 839, also in New Hampshire Gen. Association Minutes, 1848, pp. 77, 78.

[2] This letter is taken from a newspaper clipping in the possession of C. E. Bliss, of Bangor, Me. Neither date nor name of paper is known.

which I was much impressed, it occurred to me to suggest to you, perhaps presumptiously, that motives of a strong and peculiar character might be addressed to the third and last class of persons described by your text.

"Domestic happiness, that only bliss
Of Paradise that has escaped our fall,"

is yet, like all things earthly, transitory.— The circle of family love must one day be broken up by death; but if its members are led to become Christians, it will be joined again, and united to the great family of the redeemed and blessed in another world.— The idea is common, but judging from my own feelings, and what we see of its effects on others, it is persuasive and touching.

Undoubtedly, an amiable man, with tender sentiments and affections, is liable to think of no greater felicity than is afforded by the domestic circle. Do you remember Dr. Watts' stanza—

"The fondness of a creature's love
How strong it strikes the sense!
Thither our warm affections move,
Nor can we call them thence."

I pray you my dear sir, to excuse this apparent abruptness from a stranger, but a very sincere and most respectful good wisher.

DANL. WEBSTER.

(To Joshua C. Oliver, Philadelphia.)

Sir   WASHINGTON Jan. 3, [1833]

I have rec'd your letter. Mr. Fuller, to whom you refer, was teller in the B. U. S. at Boston. He was tempted, by his necessities I suppose, to appropriate to his *own use*, certain monies of the Bank. I have no doubt, that when he began the peculation, he intended to replace the money, but he was not able to do so; & his defalcation being found out, he was prosecuted, & severely punished. I know little of him, except that his character was good, among the gentlemen in the Bank, till his misconduct was discovered. He is an uncommonly good writer, a correct accountant, & I have no doubt has capacity enough to earn a support for himself & family, if he could get into some proper employment.   As for his diligence & fidelity, he must himself make them manifest.   I cannot vouch farther than for his competency & ability.

If he can get some employment, such as that of a writer, or accountant, by which he support himself & family, by hard work, until he can acquire confidence, it is the best thing for him.

Yrs   [D. WEBSTER][1]

(To John Fuller.[2])

Sir   WASHINGTON Jan. 3 (1833)

I have rec'd y'r letter   I am very sorry I was not able to speak to Dr. Perkins, in your behalf; but so many things pressed on my attention, that I could not find an opportunity—

I have written to him, by this Post, & also to Mr Oliver

I hope you may get into some business such as shall enable you to maintain your family; but things depend on yourself, & on your own strict conformity to every dictate of duty & prudence. You cannot restore yourself to confidence without exemplary good conduct & strict diligence; & such you must make it your purpose to exhibit.—

With good wishes for yourself & family I remain

Yrs

D. WEBSTER.

(To Horatio G. Cilley.[3])

WASHINGTON Sunday Evening Feby. 25, 1838.

My Dear Sir,

Before this reaches you, you will probably have heard of the death of your Nephew, the Honble Mr Cilley, member of the House of Representatives from the State of Maine.

This melancholy event was the result of a Duel, fought yesterday afternoon, between him & the Honble Mr Graves, a member of the same House of Congress, from the State of Kentucky.

I have no authentic information of the circumstances which led

---

[1] This is the draft of the letter sent and is in Daniel Webster's hand.   There is among the Webster papers a like letter to Dr. Perkins.

[2] A young man who had embezzled from his employers and for whom Daniel Webster had been asked to intercede.

[3] Horatio G. Cilley, of Deerfield, N. H.

to the contest, nor of those which accompanied it. The friends of the Parties will no doubt immediately lay before the public statements of such particulars as they may suppose friends may desire naturally to be informed of. The main object of this letter, is to express my commiseration with the numerous branches of your family, with whom I have been more or less acquainted, at this afflicting occurrence. Mr Cilley himself I had not known much. He had so recently become a member of Congress, that our acquaintance was slight. I had heard him speak in his place, once or twice, however, & I thought he spoke with ability. But having known his father, & most of his uncles, either in public or private life, & having had some little acquaintance with his relatives, of his own generation, I have felt it a kind of duty to express toward them condolence, & commiseration; & I ask you to communicate these sentiments, as you may meet with the members of the family, whom I know.

The members of the Delegation from Maine, in both Houses, all of whom are deeply affected by the event, will do all that remains to be done. The funeral will probably be attended tomorrow. How melancholy it is, My Dear Sir, that neither law, nor religion, nor both, can check the prevalence, in society, of the practice of private combat![1]

With friendly regard,
Yours
DANL WEBSTER.

(To Mrs. Caroline Webster.)

My Dear Wife   WEDNESDAY EVE' Feb. 12 (1840)

I recd yr letter, night before last, giving the awful account of poor Mrs. M's conduct. It has made my heart bleed. I have regarded her as an excellent religious woman. She was with our family, in times of affliction, & I had the most grateful & respectful feelings towards her. And her husband—poor Mr. March— what will he do. He & I were young men together— Our fathers were friends. We were fellow lodgers, at the commencement of life, & have been friends ever since. Many, many years ago, he introduced me to the first circle of N. Y. friends, which I ever had;—Mr. Gracie, Mr. Lenox, D. B. Ogden, John Welles, Saml

[1] A copy of this letter was kindly sent me by Horatio Gates Cilley, of Manchester, N. H.

Boyd, &c &c.   I declare I have had no happiness since I rec'd y'r letter.   The only consolation is, the woman must be crazy. She cannot be so wicked as to do such things in her right mind. Poor Mr. M, I fear, will go crazy himself.

I have been very busy all day, in preparing some written arguments for the Court—& in passing two or three hours in the Senate.   Nothing of importance in the political world has occurred since I wrote you last.   Mr. Hoffman is said to have made a very good speech today, on some subject, in H of R. His reputation is fast rising, in Congress.   You know he has a son.   I have not seen Mrs. H.

Night before last, Mr. & Mrs. Curtis went to a party at Mrs. O. Taylor's.   Tonight, there is an assembly, which they also attend. Tomorrow Eve, a party at Mr. Forsythe's, & very soon another at Mrs. Clement Hills.   I attend none of them.

I have sent Mr. Jones a P. office Book.   My news from Boston is not very fresh, but I had a letter from Julia some days ago. She says Mr. Davis was rather better.

It is now the middle of Feby, & in six weeks I shall be making a visit to Boston—   Pray remember that, & come along as soon as you can.   I hope this milder weather is favorable to your father. Pray give my love to him.   I do not expect him to take the trouble of answering my letters; but if any thing important occurs, I will write him again soon.

If our friends, the Messrs. Whites, have at last reaped the fruits of their conduct, in supporting the outrageous policy of Genl Jackson, in regard to money matters, I shall not be so unchristian as to rejoice in their misfortunes, but I shall pray that this discipline may tend to their improvements, & edification.

Adieu!   Yrs always, (with a rascally steel pen)

DANL WEBSTER

(Extract from the Diary of James Kent.[1])

AUG 22 1840

"August 22.   Daniel Webster dined with me on his own invitation.   He was on his way to Morristown and to Sussex County to meet a gathering of the Whigs.   Dr. Condit, of Morristown, dined with me.   Mr. Collins dined here.   It was a very interesting party, and Mr. Webster charmed the party.   He is 57 years

---

[1] Printed in the "Memoirs of Chancellor Kent," 261.

old, and looks worn and furrowed; his belly becomes protuberant, and his eyes deep in his head. I sympathize with his condition. He has been too free a liver. He ate but little, and drank wine freely."

(To Thomas Fessenden et al.[1])

WASHINGTON, December 19, 1842.

Gentlemen:

It will not be in my power to be among you on the 22nd, but my heart is always with those who, on that occasion, render honor to the virtues of our Pilgrim Fathers.

The simple language of the venerable Historian of Connecticut is, that our ancestors came hither "to settle on bare creation."— But they acted on principles, and set an example, which converted this bare creation into as fair an inheritance, as has ever fallen to the lot of man. Providence disciplines men for the tasks which they are called on to perform; and the difficulties which these emigrants encountered, were hardly more than were requisite to give them the fearlessness of purpose, and hardihood of character, which were demanded by their situation.

For all their toils, they were rewarded, by their success, by the sense of duty well performed, and by the happy consciousness, that they had been made instruments, by which God had introduced civilization and Christianity, into a new world.

Happy founders of a new Society! Fortunate benefactors of succeeding times! May all who enjoy the blessings secured by their efforts, cherish their memories, and imitate their virtues.

I am Gentlemen, with regard, vours

DANIEL WEBSTER.

(To Charles W. Ridgely.)

WASHINGTON March 3, 1845.

Dear Sir,—

I feel greatly honored by your communication; which I received on my return to this city from the North, on Saturday; and am sincerely obliged to my friend Mr. Williams, for causing me to be made a member of the Baltimore Sabbath Association.

---

[1] This letter is owned by the Hon. George F. Hoar.

The longer I live, the more highly do I estimate the importance of a proper observance of the Christian Sabbath, and the more grateful do I feel towards those who take pains to impress a sense of this importance on the community.   The Lord's day, is the day on which the Gospel is preached! it is the day of public worship throughout the world.   And although we live in a reading age, and in a reading community, yet the preaching of the Gospel, is the form in which human agency has been, and still is, most efficaciously employed for the spiritual improvement of men.   That the poor had the gospel preached to them, was an evidence of his mission, which the Author of Christianity himself proclaimed.   And to the public worship of the Deity, and the preaching of the Gospel, the observance of the Sabbath, is obviously essential.

I am, dear Sir, with much regard,

Your obedient Servant

DANIEL WEBSTER.

(To —————.¹)

MAY 28. '46

D'r Sir

If you know the writer of this letter, & he is both poor & deserving, you may say to him, when you see him that I am just about as poor as he is—that I have worked more than twelve hours a day for fifty years, on an average.   That I do not know, experimentally, what wealth is, nor how the bread of idleness tastes— But that I have been generally blessed with good health, in my person, & in my family, for which I give thanks to Providence.   And that I have compassion for such cases of sickness & affliction as appear to have visited him & his family.   And if you think five or six dollars would be well bestowed, please hand it to him on my account.—

Now, another subject.   I was foolish eno to buy of W. W. the home in which Mrs Sargent lives.—   I have no use for it, & should be glad to sell it—and, for a fair price, would sell with it, the land in Northfield, near it—   I suppose this land is, or will be, soon, valuable, if factories are to be built near it—

What is the House, & the Land worth?

Yr   D. W.

---

¹ There seems to be no way of ascertaining to whom the letter was written.

(To Rev. Ichabod S. Spencer.[1])

My Dear Sir—   WASHINGTON, Dec. 7, 1850.

I am greatly obliged to you for sending me a copy of your sermon delivered on the 24th of November. It is refreshing to read a production which, founding itself upon the express injunction of the holy scriptures, goes back from theory to commandment, from human hypotheses and speculation to the declared will of God.

Obedience to established government is something more, and much more, than a mere idea of expediency; it is a Christian duty. You say, very truly, that "law is a friend to the human race." Without law the human race must have remained forever in a state of barbarism. Law pervades the physical universe, and pervades equally the social system of mankind.

You are, of course, familiar with Hooker's celebrated, most truthful and most sublime description of law. If you have not recurred to it lately, allow me to ask you to turn to it. I never read it without the strongest emotions. "Of Law nothing more can be said than that her seat is the bosom of God, her voice the harmony of the universe," etc. To the same effect is the beautiful ode of Alcaeus, translated by Sir William Jones. But, pardon me, my dear sir, I am making suggestions to one who is more fit to make them to me. I am appearing to lead, where I am quite content to follow.

Yours, with the sincerest regard,

DANIEL WEBSTER.

(To Porter Wright.)

Mr Porter Wright   WASHINGTON, M 7'' '51.
    Dear Sir.

Almost all John Taylors family are sick with two diseases,— hooping cough and measles; it would an act of charity for Mrs Baker to go up and see them for a couple of days.

Yours truly

DANL WEBSTER.

---

[1] On Sunday, November 24, 1850, Rev. Dr. Ichabod S. Spencer, of Brooklyn, N. Y., preached a sermon on the Fugitive Slave Law. The sermon was published in pamphlet form, and Dr. Spencer sent a copy to Daniel Webster. In acknowledgment of the receipt of the sermon, Mr. Webster wrote Dr. Spencer this letter. The editor takes this from a newspaper clipping belonging to C. E. Bliss, of Bangor, Me.

(To F. D. Anderson et al.)

MARSHFIELD, October 8, 1851.

Gentlemen:

It is a matter of deep regret to me, that I did not receive your kind letter of the 9th of August till a very late day. I was in the mountains of New Hampshire, taking a breath of my native air, and it was the last of August before I returned. I know not whether, if I had received your communication sooner, it would have been in my power to attend the meeting to which I was invited, but I should have been able to have given a more timely answer.

There can be no question that the Temperance movement, in the United States, has done infinite good. The moral influences of the Temperance associations has been everywhere felt, and always with beneficial results. In some cases, it is true, the Temperance measures have been carried to excess, where they have invoked legislative penalties, and sought to enforce the virtue of Temperance by the power of the Law. To a certain extent, this, no doubt, is justifiable and useful; but it is the moral principle of Temperance, it is the conscientious duty which it teaches, to abstain from intoxicating draughts, such as are hurtful both to mind and body, which are the great agents for the reformation of manners in this respect.

Your order is quite right in connecting benevolence and charity with Temperance. They may well go hand-in-hand. He whose faculties are never debauched or stupefied, whose mind is always active and alert, and who practices self-denial, is naturally drawn to consider the deserving objects which are about him, that may be poor, or sick, or diseased.

Love, Purity, and Fidelity are considered Christian virtues; and I hope that those "banners" which bear these words for their motto may rise higher and higher, and float more and more widely through this and all other countries.

You have invited me, gentlemen, if I could attend the meeting, to address the members of your order on the great subject of Union. I should have done so with pleasure, although I do not propose to continue the practice of addressing great multitudes of men; yet I could not have refused to have expressed my opinions on the great topics of the day, in the State of Maryland. Out of the abundance of the heart the mouth speaketh.

I pray you to be assured, gentlemen, that I value highly the opinion you have expressed for my public character and conduct; and I indulge the hope that I may ere long meet some of you in the city where my public duties are discharged; and most of all, I fervently trust that you and I, and your children and my children will remain fellow-citizens of one great united Republic, so long as society shall exist among us. While I live, every effort in my power, whether made in public or in private life, will be devoted to the promotion of that great end.

I am, gentlemen, very respectfully, your obliged friend and fellow citizen.[1]

DANIEL WEBSTER.

(To Porter Wright.)

Dear Porter Wright
    JAN. 11, 1852.
I have rec'd your letter of the 7th. We are quite anxious about your wife, & hope you will write us a short line often. You have the sick all round you. If there be any thing in our House that can do them good, be sure to let them have it. Mrs. Webster & I are quite well.

Yrs   DANL WEBSTER

(To D. Fletcher Webster.)

N. Y. Sunday, Nov. 7. 2 o'clock
Dear Fletcher
We left Boston yesterday at 4, for this City by way of Norwich, but having got aground in the Thames, at low water, were delayed, & arrived here only at 1/2 past 12 today. I shall stay here but a day or two, tho' Mrs. W. may stay longer, & come on with Edward, whom we left behind.

Caroline wrote us of the folly of Chas Mettinger, which is confirmed here. Ann is greatly distressed, & crying her eyes out.

I gave the undutiful boy a place, mainly, that he might be of help to his poor mother, who was worked so hard for him; & since he behaved so improperly and ungratefully, I choose to have

---

[1] This letter was written in answer to an invitation from Mr. F. D. Anderson and others to attend a celebration of the temperance cause in Harford County, Maryland. This copy is taken from a volume in the possession of Mr. C. E. Bliss, of Bangor, Me., entitled "John Randolph of Roanoke," by F. W. Thomas, p. 373.

no more to do with him; and unless you know good reason to the contrary, I wish you to pay him off, & dismiss him, before I reach Washington. I presume Ann will remain here. I have not yet seen Mr. Curtis, nor anbody else. Mrs. W. & Uncle G. quite well.

Yrs truly
DANL WEBSTER

(John Jeffries to Mr. Sleeper.[1])

BOSTON, Nov. 20, 1852.
Mr. Sleeper; Sir,— I send you for publication the remarks made by me at a late medical dinner. I am not confident that it is in the precise terms which I then used, but it is a correct account of the incidents to which I referred on that occasion.

Your obedient servant,
JOHN JEFFRIES.

On Wednesday, the 10th inst., I had the pleasure of dining with the "Southern District Medical Society," at New Bedford, and in answer to a call to give some information regarding the sickness of the late Hon. Daniel Webster, I took occasion after a brief statement of his case, to make some remarks calculated to remove aspersion upon his moral character; and particularly to show that the assertion was false that he was under the influence of intoxicating liquor on the occasion of his public address in Faneuil Hall on May 22d, 1852. A declaration to this effect I had heard several times emanating from persons of intelligence and influence. I did not intend to vindicate the character of Mr. Webster—it needed no defence. I did it to disabuse the minds of those who had heard it, from the influence of a direct assertion which I knew to be without any foundation. I meant by a simple relation of circumstances under my own observation to show that the charge was entirely untrue.

I stated that after the injury Mr. Webster received from a fall from his carriage in Duxbury in May, he came to this city, and was under my professional care for some days previous to the delivery of his speech; that I had visited him two or three times daily, and had reduced his diet below his usual mode of living, in consequence of inflammation in his arm.

---

[1] This letter is taken from a newspaper clipping made by Peter Harvey.

That on the day of his address, I visited him twice in the morning, and dressed his arm particularly for the occasion. After dressing him I said "I have kept you very low, sir, for some time, and as you have an arduous duty to perform to-day, I think I shall advise you to take a glass of wine at dinner, and to eat a little meat."

He was walking across the room at this time, when he stopped, and turning towards me, replied in a familiar but decided manner—

"I don't know, Doctor; I think I shall not. I have found the benefit of temperance. I shall take a cup of soup, retire to my chamber and lie down for two hours, then I shall dress and be ready for his Honor the Mayor when he calls to attend me to Faneuil Hall."

At his request I went with him to the Hall, and am fully convinced that he had not on that day, or for some days preceeding, taken even the smallest amount of stimulating drinks. I admitted that Mr. Webster was in the occasional use of wine, and sometimes of other alcoholic drinks, and gave as a probable reason that it was much more the custom in Washington than in this City; But I confidently expressed the opinion that no man could be produced, who could show that he knew—although many might erroneously presume, as in the instance above referred to—that his great intellect was ever clouded by stimulants; or that he was unfitted at any time, even for the production of State papers.

I avail myself of this opportunity to add a few words more in confirmation of what I have stated above.

At the time of his reception by the City, Mr. Webster appeared to possess his full intellectual strength. In reply to an apprehension expressed by me that morning, he said:

"I feel as able to make a speech of two hours' duration, as ever I did in my life."

But he was laboring under great physical debility, requiring the constant assistance of an attendant about his person. This was dispensed with, by a great effort on his part, as was also a sling for his arm, because he did not wish to appear before his fellow-citizens as a sick man.

I have always found Mr. Webster perfectly obedient as a patient, especially in following strictly the diet and regimen prescribed for him.

The nature of the complaints for which I have attended him, has required that these restrictions should be sometimes severe, and on one important occasion, were directly opposed to his own view of his case; but he nevertheless yielded implicitly to my instructions.

In his last sickness he required the most exact admeasurement of such stimulants as were thought advisable, and would take none without my express directions.

I am also assured that he always practiced the greatest self-denial whenever especially called upon for the exertion of his intellectual powers.   The mighty productions of his pen exhibit the clearness of his intellect as much as the profoundness of his thought.   The most rigid casuist may be defied to point to one line in his voluminous works which indicates the weakness of the inebriate.

I fear that I have trespassed too much upon your indulgence, Mr. Editor, and will only express, in conclusion, my regret that I do not feel at liberty to give you, for publication, some observations upon the religious character of Mr. Webster; a subject which I entered upon in my late remarks, but had not time to continue.

Some unintentional inaccuracies have entered into the memoriter report of the gentlemen at New Bedford, which do not, however, affect the general truth of his statements.

THE END.

CHRONOLOGICAL INDEX

LETTERS FROM DANIEL WEBSTER

LETTERS FROM DANIEL WEBSTER 757

762   CHRONOLOGICAL INDEX

LETTERS TO DANIEL WEBSTER

MISCELLANEOUS

768　　CHRONOLOGICAL INDEX

MISCELLANEOUS 769